Fodor's

South Africa

by Andrew Barbour

"When it comes to information on regional history, what to see and do, and shopping, these guides are exhaustive."

—*USAir Magazine*

"Usable, sophisticated restaurant coverage, with an emphasis on good value."

—Andy Birsh, *Gourmet Magazine* columnist

"Valuable because of their comprehensiveness."

—*Minneapolis Star-Tribune*

"Fodor's always delivers high quality...thoughtfully presented...thorough."

—*Houston Post*

"An excellent choice for those who want everything under one cover."

—*Washington Post*

Fodor's Travel Publications, Inc.
New York • Toronto • London • Sydney • Auckland
http://www.fodors.com/

Fodor's South Africa

Editor: Stephen Wolf

Contributors: Rob Andrews, Robert Blake, Karen Cure, Robert Fisher, Janet Foley, Sylvia Gill, Phyllis Hands, Laura M. Kidder, Pat Kossuth, Peter Noel-Barham, Louise Orlando, Tracy Patruno, Myrna Robins, Linda K. Schmidt, Mary Ellen Schultz, Professor Basil Schulze, M. T. Schwartzman (Gold Guide editor), Dinah Spritzer

Creative Director: Fabrizio La Rocca

Cartographer: David Lindroth

Cover Photograph: Peter Guttman

Design: Between the Covers

Copyright

First Edition

ISBN 0–679–03090–5

Special Sales

PRINTED IN THE UNITED STATES OF AMERICA

10 9 8 7 6 5 4 3 2 1

CONTENTS

ON THE ROAD WITH FODORS

A GOOD TRAVEL GUIDE is like a wonderful traveling companion. It's charming, it's brimming with sound recommendations and solid ideas, it pulls no punches in describing lodging and dining establishments, and it's consistently full of fascinating facts that make you view what you've traveled to see in a rich new light. In the creation of this brand-new guide to *South Africa*, we at Fodor's have gone to great lengths to provide you with the very best of all possible traveling companions—and to make your trip the best of all possible vacations.

About Our Writers

What you'll read in these pages is the Herculean effort of one extraordinary writer, with local contributions from a few others who lent their pens.

Andrew Barbour took the scenic route back to his native South Africa, driving a battered 1960 Land Rover from London to Cape Town with his wife. On their one-year trek, they braved malaria, amoebic dysentery, and a bizarre cow disease, while stopping frequently to retrieve parts of their car that had fallen off. The trip was a sabbatical for Andrew after three years as founding editor of the *Berkeley Guides,* a budget travel series written by students at the University of California at Berkeley. Andrew's association with Fodor's goes back to 1989, when he joined the company as an editor, tackling books on Australia, Thailand, Bermuda, and cruise ships. Upon his return from South Africa, he rejoined Fodor's in the exciting role of editorial director of new media.

Phyllis Hands, recently retired principal of the Cape Wine Academy, is one of South Africa's foremost wine experts. A delightful raconteur and much loved figure in the Winelands, she is the author of *South African Wine,* an encyclopedic study of wine making in South Africa. Phyllis recently launched her own wine consulting business.

Pat Kossuth, who spent her youth in some of Britain's far-flung African dominions, is the wine and food critic for the *Pretoria News.* Author of six cookbooks, Pat has written for some of South Africa's most prestigious magazines, as well as the respected *Perrier Restaurant Guide.* She now divides her time between her home in Pretoria and a lovely cottage in Hermanus, in the Western Cape's Overberg.

Peter Noel-Barham, one of South Africa's most colorful and ebullient gourmets, has cut a swath through the South African restaurant scene both as critic and successful restaurateur. His work has appeared in such magazines as *Wine, House and Leisure, Signature,* and *Style,* and for several years he wrote a weekly food column for *Star Tonight!,* a leading entertainment daily. In addition to his duties as president and founder of the Champagne and Oyster Society, Peter is currently writing a series of books on food.

Myrna Robins, who writes for the *Cape Argus* newspaper, has repeatedly been voted South Africa's best food writer. Author of several cookbooks on the Cape's vibrant cuisine, including *Cape Flavour— A Guide to Historic Restaurants of the Cape,* she lives in the shadow of Table Mountain and spends her weekends in the exquisite hamlet of MacGregor, in the Riviersonderend Mountains.

We would also like to thank **Louise Orlando,** a freelance writer and author and Andrew Barbour's wife, who wrote the book's shopping sections; **Professor Basil Schulze,** one of Durban's leading citizens and an expert on that city's dining scene; and **Sylvia Gill,** a freelance writer and public relations expert who is a font of knowledge about South Africa's rapidly changing tourism scene.

What's New

A New Design

If this is not the first Fodor's guide you've purchased, you'll immediately notice our new look. More readable and easier to use than ever? We think so—and we hope you do, too.

And in South Africa

Foreign visitors, particularly those from Britain and Germany, have been pouring into South Africa since the 1994 elections. After years of vainly pushing the beauties of the country, the South African tourist industry is now scrambling to meet demand, and new hotels and companies are popping up everywhere.

The huge international **Hyatt** chain is building at least two new hotels, one in the tony Johannesburg suburb of Rosebank, the other on the site of a new convention center in Durban. Meanwhile, the **Edward,** one of Durban's most historic hotels, has closed for a major facelift intended to transform it into a five-star international hotel. Major renovations are underway at a score of other hotels.

In Zululand and Maputaland, in the wild northern reaches of KwaZulu-Natal, the groundwork is being laid for a series of game lodges that may someday rival those of the Eastern Transvaal. The **Conservation Corporation,** which already operates the exclusive Phinda Resource Reserve in Zululand, is planning a new lodge on a deserted stretch of dunes, and **Zululand Safaris,** a major tour operator in the region, is constructing a luxury lodge on the edge of Lake St. Lucia, a glorious wetland teeming with birds, crocodiles, and hippos.

In **Cape Town,** the city that has benefited most from the recent tourism boom, plans are afoot to build a major new resort at the waterfront, and rumor has it that it may be a floating hotel. Even more grandiose are the city's hopes to host the **2004 Olympic Games.** The Olympics have never been held in Africa, and Cape Town hopes to capitalize on this, although the city's infrastructure can barely cope with the current visitor flow.

Rumors are also rampant that a **new international airport** will be constructed at Hazyview, a small town near Kruger National Park. From it, visitors could be funneled directly into the game-rich Eastern Transvaal, bypassing Johannesburg altogether.

In light of these events, it's disappointing to see yet another international airline serving South Africa go belly-up. **USAfrica,** flying between Washington and Johannesburg, declared bankruptcy in 1995, leaving South African Airways as the only airline offering direct service to the United States. Consequently, the high cost of airline tickets to South Africa seems likely to endure.

Airfares aside, South Africa is now one of the most affordable destinations in the world—if you have foreign currency. Just four years ago, the U.S. dollar bought only 2.76 South African rands; today, it buys 3.64 and there's no sign of the rand strengthening soon.

On a sour note, crime continues to escalate in major cities, and visitors must take basic precautions to ensure their safety: Do not walk alone at night, and keep all valuables and jewelry well hidden (*see* the Gold Guide for further precautions).

How to Use this Guide

Organization

Up front is the **Gold Guide,** comprising two sections on gold paper that are chockfull of information about traveling within your destination and traveling in general. Both are in alphabetical order by topic. **Important Contacts A to Z** gives addresses and telephone numbers of organizations and companies that offer destination-related services and detailed information or publications. Here's where you'll find information about how to get to South Africa from wherever you are. **Smart Travel Tips,** the Gold Guide's second section, gives specific tips on how to get the most out of your travels, as well as information on how to accomplish whatever you plan to do in South Africa.

Chapters in this guide are arranged in the way that most travelers move through South Africa. Each chapter covers exploring, shopping, sports, dining, lodging, and arts and nightlife, and ends with a section called Essentials, which tells you how to get there and get around and gives you important local addresses and telephone numbers.

Stars

Stars in the margin are used to denote highly recommended sights, attractions, hotels, and restaurants.

Restaurant and Hotel Criteria and Price Categories

Restaurants and lodging places are chosen with a view to giving you the cream of the crop in each location and in each price range. Price categories are as follows:

For restaurants:

CHART 1

CATEGORY	COST*
$$$$	over R80
$$$	R60–R80
$$	R40–R60
$	under R40

Rates are per person, excluding drinks and service.

For lodgings:

CHART 2

CATEGORY	(A) COST* CHAPTERS 2, 4, 5, & 7	(B) COST* CHAPTERS 3 & 6
$$$$	over R600	over R750
$$$	R400–R600	R500–R750
$$	R250–R400	R250–R500
$	under R250	under R250

Rates are for a double room, including VAT and Tourism Promotion Levies. The cost may also include breakfast and dinner.

Hotel Facilities

Note that in general you incur charges when you use many hotel facilities. We let you know what facilities a hotel has to offer, but we don't always specify whether or not there's a charge, so when planning a vacation that entails a stay of several days, it's wise to ask what's included in the rate.

Dress Code in Restaurants

Look for an overview in the Dining section of Smart Travel Tips in the Gold Guide pages at the front of this book. We typically note a dress code only when men are required to wear a jacket or a jacket and tie.

Credit Cards

The following abbreviations are used: **AE**, American Express; **DC**, Diners Club; **MC**,

MasterCard; and **V**, Visa. Discover is not accepted outside the United States.

Please Write to Us

Everyone who has contributed to *South Africa* has worked hard to make the text accurate. All prices and opening times are based on information supplied to us at press time, and Fodor's cannot accept responsibility for any errors that may have occurred. The passage of time will bring changes, so it's always a good idea to call ahead and confirm information when it matters—particularly if you're making a detour to visit specific sights or attractions. When making reservations at a hotel or inn, be sure to speak up if you have a disability or are traveling with children, if you prefer a private bath or a certain type of bed, or if you have specific dietary needs or any other concerns.

Were the restaurants we recommended as described? Did our hotel picks exceed your expectations? Did you find a museum we recommended a waste of time? We would love your feedback, positive and negative. If you have complaints, we'll look into them and revise our entries when the facts warrant it. If you've happened upon a special place that we haven't included, we'll pass the information along to the writers so they can check it out. So please send us a letter or postcard (we're at 201 East 50th Street, New York, NY 10022.) We'll look forward to hearing from you. And in the meantime, have a wonderful trip!

Karen Cure

Karen Cure
Editorial Director

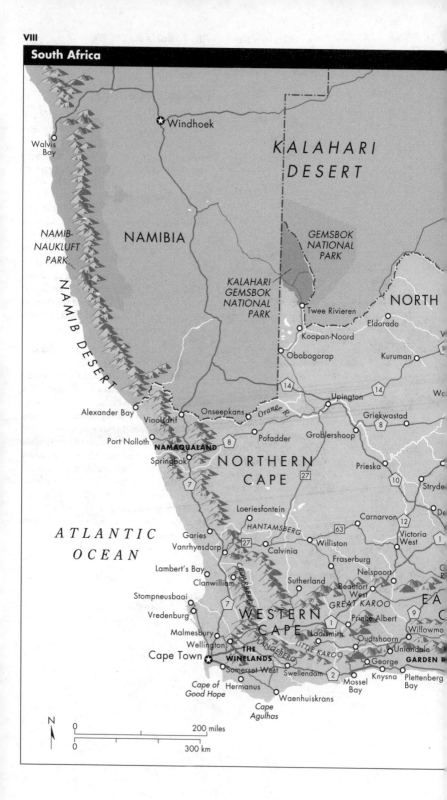

Walvis
Bay

Windhoek

KALAHARI
DESERT

NAMIB-
NAUKLUFT
PARK

NAMIBIA

GEMSBOK
NATIONAL
PARK

KALAHARI
GEMSBOK
NATIONAL
PARK

NORTH

NAMIB DESERT

Twee Rivieren

Eldorado

Koopan-Noord

Kuruman

Obobogorap

14

Upington

14

Wc

Alexander Bay

Onseepkans

Orange R.

Griekwastad

8

Vioolsdrif

Port Nolloth

NAMAQUALAND

8

Pofadder

Groblershoop

Springbok

NORTHERN
CAPE

Prieska

27

10

7

Loeriesfontein

Carnarvon

12

Stryde

ATLANTIC
OCEAN

HANTAMSBERG

63

De

Garies

27

Williston

Victoria
West

1

Vanrhynsdorp

Calvinia

Fraserburg

Lambert's Bay

Nelspoort

GR
R

Clanwilliam

Sutherland

Beaufort
West

EA
C

Stompneusbaai

GREAT KAROO

Vredenburg

WESTERN
CAPE

Prince Albert

9

Malmesbury

Ladismith

Oudtshoorn

Willowmo

Wellington

THE

LITTLE KAROO

Uniondale

GARDEN R

Cape Town

WINELANDS

Somerset West

Swellendam

George

Knysna

Plettenberg
Bay

Cape of
Good Hope

Hermanus

2

Mossel
Bay

Waenhuiskrans

Cape
Agulhas

N

0   200 miles

0   300 km

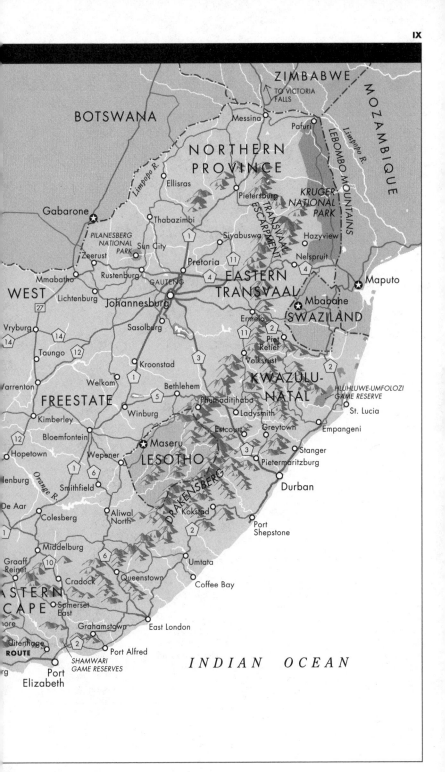

World Time Zones

Numbers below vertical bands relate each zone to Greenwich Mean Time (0 hrs.).
Local times frequently differ from these general indications,
as indicated by light-face numbers on map.

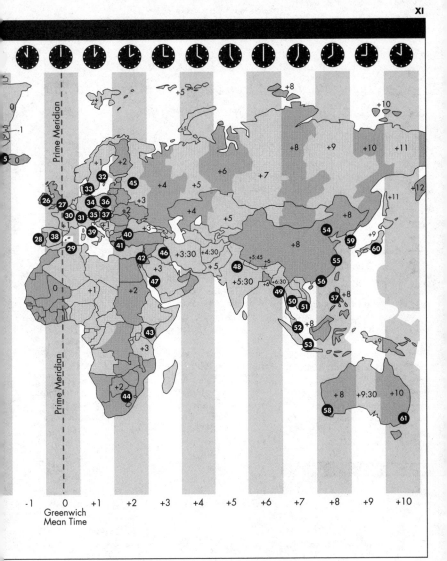

THE GOLD GUIDE / IMPORTANT CONTACTS

IMPORTANT CONTACTS A TO Z

An Alphabetical Listing of Publications, Organizations, and Companies That Will Help You Before, During, and After Your Trip

No single travel resource can give you every detail about every topic that might interest or concern you at the various stages of your journey—when you're planning your trip, while you're on the road, and after you get back home. The organizations, books, and brochures listed in Important Contacts A to Z will supplement the information in *Fodor's South Africa*. For related tips on visiting South Africa and background information on many of the topics below, study Smart Travel Tips A to Z, the second half of the Gold Guide.

A

AIR TRAVEL

The major gateways to South Africa are Johannesburg, Cape Town, and, to a lesser extent, Durban. South African Airways and American Airlines offer joint nonstop service from New York (JFK) to Johannesburg on Monday, Wednesday, and Friday; a Saturday flight stops to refuel at Isla do Sal, a tiny island off the coast of West Africa. Nonstop service is also available on South African Airways from Miami to Cape Town. Flying time from Miami to Cape Town is 14 hours; from New York, the flight takes

15–17 hours, depending on whether it stops at Isla do Sal or not. The London–Johannesburg flight lasts about 12 hours.

CARRIERS

Carriers serving South Africa direct from the United States include **South African Airways** (☎ 800/722–9675) and **American Airlines** (☎ 800/433–7300), but you can often get much cheaper fares aboard such foreign carriers as **Alitalia** (☎ 800/223–5730) and **Egypt Air** (☎ 212/315–0900), with connections in Rome or Cairo. From the United Kingdom, **British Airways** (☎ 0181/897–4000) and South African Airways operate regular service to Johannesburg, Cape Town, and Durban.

One advantage of flying South African Airways is the **African Explorer** ticket, issued outside of South Africa; for more information, *see* Air Travel *in* Smart Travel Tips, *below.*

COMPLAINTS

To register complaints about charter and scheduled airlines, contact the U.S. Department of Transportation's **Aviation Consumer Protection Division** (C–75, Washington, DC 20590, ☎ 202/366–2220). Complaints about lost baggage,

ticketing problems, and safety violations may also be logged with the **Federal Aviation Administration (FAA) Consumer Hotline** (☎ 800/322–7873).

CONSOLIDATORS

Established consolidators selling to the public include **BET World Travel** (841 Blossom Hill Rd., Suite 212-C, San Jose, CA 95123, ☎ 408/229–7880 or 800/747–1476); **Council Charter** (205 E. 42nd St., New York, NY 10017, ☎ 212/661–0311 or 800/800–8222); **Euram Tours** (1522 K St. NW, Suite 430, Washington DC, 20005, ☎ 800/848–6789); **TFI Tours International** (34 W. 32nd St., New York, NY 10001, ☎ 212/736–1140 or 800/745–8000); **Travac Tours and Charter** (989 6th Ave., 16th Floor, New York, NY 10018, ☎ 212/563–3303 or 800/872–8800; 2601 E. Jefferson, Orlando, FL 32803, ☎ 407/896–0014 or 800/872–8800); and **UniTravel** (Box 12485, St. Louis, MO 63132, ☎ 314/569–0900 or 800/325–2222).

PUBLICATIONS

For general information about charter carriers, ask for the U.S. Department of Transportation's free brochure **"Plane Talk: Public Charter Flights"** (Aviation Consumer Protection Division, C–75, Washington, DC 20590, ☎ 202/366–2220). The Department of Transportation also publishes a 58-page booklet, **"Fly Rights,"** available from the Consumer Information Center (Dept. 133B, Pueblo, CO 81009; $1.75, make checks payable to Supt. of Documents).

For other tips and hints, consult the Consumers Union's monthly **"Consumer Reports Travel Letter"** (Box 53629, Boulder, CO 80322, ☎ 800/234–1970; $39 annually); the newsletter **"Travel Smart"** (40 Beechdale Rd., Dobbs Ferry, NY 10522, ☎ 800/327–3633; $37 annually); *The Official Frequent Flyer Guidebook,* by Randy Petersen (4715-C Town Center Dr., Colorado Springs, CO 80916, ☎ 719/597–8899 or 800/487–8893; $14.99 plus $3 shipping); *Airfare Secrets Exposed,* by Sharon Tyler and Matthew Wonder (Universal Information Publishing; $16.95 plus $3.75 shipping from Sandcastle Publishing, Box 3070-A, South Pasadena, CA 91031, ☎ 213/255–3616 or 800/655–0053); and *202 Tips Even the Best Business Travelers May Not Know,* by Christopher McGinnis (Irwin Professional Publishing, 1333 Burr Ridge Pkwy., Burr Ridge, IL 60521, ☎ 800/634–3966; $10 plus $3 shipping).

WITHIN SOUTH AFRICA

Five major domestic airlines serve the coun-

try's nine principal airports (numbers listed are for Johannesburg offices): **South African Airways** (☎ 011/356–1111) and its commuter airline, **SA Airlink** (☎ 011/394–2430); **Phoenix** (☎ 011/803–9773); **Comair** (☎ 011/921–0222); and **Sun Air** (☎ 011/397–2244).

B
BETTER BUSINESS BUREAU

For local contacts in the hometown of a tour operator you may be considering, consult the **Council of Better Business Bureaus** (4200 Wilson Blvd., Arlington, VA 22203, ☎ 703/276–0100).

BUS TRAVEL

Greyhound (Johannesburg office, ☎ 011/333–2130) and **Translux Express** (Johannesburg office, ☎ 011/774–3333) operate extensive bus networks that serve all major cities in the country. In the Cape provinces, **Intercape Mainliner** (Cape Town office, ☎ 021/386–4400) offers the most comprehensive service.

PASSES

Translux Express (*see above*) sells a variety of **Lux Passes** that allow pass holders to travel anywhere on the Translux route network within a predetermined number of days.

C
CAR RENTAL

Major car-rental companies represented in

South Africa include **Avis** (☎ 800/331–1084, 800/879–2847 in Canada); **Budget** (☎ 800/527–0700, 0800/181–181 in the United Kingdom); and **Hertz** (☎ 800/654–3001, 800/263–0600 in Canada, 0181/679–1799 in the United Kingdom), known as Imperial in South Africa. Rates in South Africa begin at $20 per day and 20¢ per kilometer (about 30¢ per mile) for an economy car. You must rent for a minimum of three days to qualify for a free 200-kilometer daily allowance. Rates for rentals of three to seven days range from $40 to $60 a day, including 14% Value Added Tax (VAT).

CHILDREN AND TRAVEL

FLYING

Look into **"Flying with Baby"** (Third Street Press, Box 261250, Littleton, CO 80126, ☎ 303/595–5959; $5.95 plus $1 shipping), cowritten by a flight attendant. **"Kids and Teens in Flight,"** free from the U.S. Department of Transportation's Aviation Consumer Protection Division (C–75, Washington, DC 20590, ☎ 202/366–2220), offers tips for children flying alone. Every two years the February issue of *Family Travel Times* (*see* Know-How, *below*) details children's services on three dozen airlines.

LODGING

Many of South Africa's luxury lodges and

private game reserves do not accept children under 10 or 12 without prior arrangement, and many other hotels require children to eat dinner at a separate, earlier seating. **Southern Sun** (☎ 011/482–3500), the giant hotel group that operates Southern Sun and Holiday Inn properties throughout the country, and **Karos Hotels** (☎ 011/643–8052), allow children under 18 to stay free when accompanied by a parent.

CUSTOMS

U.S. CITIZENS

The **U.S. Customs Service** (Box 7407, Washington, DC 20044, ☎ 202/927–6724) can answer questions on duty-free limits and publishes a helpful brochure, **"Know Before You Go."** For information on registering foreign-made articles, call 202/927–0540.

CANADIANS

Contact **Revenue Canada** (2265 St. Laurent Blvd. S, Ottawa, Ontario K1G 4K3, ☎ 613/993–0534) for a copy of the free brochure **"I Declare/Je Déclare"** and for details on duties that exceed the standard duty-free limit.

U.K. CITIZENS

HM Customs and Excise (Dorset House, Stamford St., London SE1 9NG, ☎ 0171/202–4227) can answer questions about U.K. customs regulations and publishes **"A Guide for Travellers,"** detailing standard procedures and import rules.

D
FOR TRAVELERS
WITH DISABILITIES

COMPLAINTS

To register complaints under the provisions of the Americans with Disabilities Act, contact the U.S. Department of Justice's **Disability Rights Section** (Box 66738, Washington, DC 20035, ☎ 202/514–0301, FAX 202/307–1198, TTY 202/514–0383).

ORGANIZATIONS

FOR TRAVELERS WITH HEARING IMPAIRMENTS➤ Contact the **American Academy of Otolaryngology** (1 Prince St., Alexandria, VA 22314, ☎ 703/836–4444, FAX 703/683–5100, TTY 703/519–1585).

FOR TRAVELERS WITH MOBILITY PROBLEMS➤ Contact the **Information Center for Individuals with Disabilities** (Ft. Point Pl., 27–43 Wormwood St., Boston, MA 02210, ☎ 617/727–5540, 800/462–5015 in MA, TTY 617/345–9743); **Mobility International USA** (Box 10767, Eugene, OR 97440, ☎ and TTY 503/343–1284, FAX 503/343–6812), the U.S. branch of an international organization based in Belgium (*see below*) that has affiliates in 30 countries; **MossRehab Hospital Travel Information Service** (1200 W. Tabor Rd., Philadelphia, PA 19141, ☎ 215/456–9603, TTY 215/456–9602); the **Society for the Advancement of Travel for the Handicapped** (347 5th Ave., Suite 610, New York, NY 10016, ☎ 212/447–7284, FAX 212/725–8253); the **Travel Industry and Disabled Exchange** (TIDE, 5435 Donna Ave., Tarzana, CA 91356, ☎ 818/344–3640, FAX 818/344–0078); and **Travelin' Talk** (Box 3534, Clarksville, TN 37043, ☎ 615/552–6670, FAX 615/552–1182).

FOR TRAVELERS WITH VISION IMPAIRMENTS➤ Contact the **American Council of the Blind** (1155 15th St. NW, Suite 720, Washington, DC 20005, ☎ 202/467–5081, FAX 202/467–5085) or the **American Foundation for the Blind** (15 W. 16th St., New York, NY 10011, ☎ 212/620–2000, TTY 212/620–2158).

IN THE U.K.

Contact the **Royal Association for Disability and Rehabilitation** (RADAR, 12 City Forum, 250 City Rd., London EC1V 8AF, ☎ 0171/250–3222) or **Mobility International** (Rue de Manchester 25, B-1070 Brussels, Belgium, ☎ 00–322–410–6297), an international clearinghouse of travel information for people with disabilities.

PUBLICATIONS

Several publications for travelers with disabilities are available from the U.S. government's Consumer Information Center (Box 100, Pueblo, CO 81009, ☎ 719/948–3334). Call or write for a free catalog of current titles.

The 500-page *Travelin' Talk Directory* (Box

3534, Clarksville, TN 37043, ☎ 615/552–6670; $35) lists people and organizations who help travelers with disabilities. For specialist travel agents worldwide, consult the *Directory of Travel Agencies for the Disabled* (Twin Peaks Press, Box 129, Vancouver, WA 98666, ☎ 206/694–2462 or 800/637–2256; $19.95 plus $2 shipping).

TRAVEL AGENCIES AND TOUR OPERATORS

The Americans with Disabilities Act requires that travel firms serve the needs of all travelers. However, some agencies and operators specialize in making group and individual arrangements for travelers with disabilities, among them **Access Adventures** (206 Chestnut Ridge Rd., Rochester, NY 14624, ☎ 716/889–9096), run by a former physical-rehab counselor. In addition, many general-interest operators and agencies (*see* Tour Operators, *below*) can also arrange vacations for travelers with disabilities.

FOR TRAVELERS WITH MOBILITY PROBLEMS➤ A number of operators specialize in working with travelers who have such impairments: **Accessible Journeys** (35 W. Sellers Ave., Ridley Park, PA 19078, ☎ 610/521–0339 or 800/846–4537, FAX 610/521–6959) is a registered nursing service that arranges vacations; and **Flying Wheels Travel** (143 W. Bridge St., Box 382, Owa-

tonna, MN 55060, ☎ 507/451–5005 or 800/535–6790) is an agency that has expertise in wheelchair travel in South Africa.

DISCOUNTS

Options include **Entertainment Travel Editions** (Box 1068, Trumbull, CT 06611, ☎ 800/445–4137; $28–$53, depending on destination); **Great American Traveler** (Box 27965, Salt Lake City, UT 84127, ☎ 800/548–2812; $49.95 annually); **Moment's Notice Discount Travel Club** (163 Amsterdam Ave., Suite 137, New York, NY 10023, ☎ 212/486–0500; $25 annually, single or family); **Privilege Card** (3391 Peachtree Rd. NE, Suite 110, Atlanta, GA 30326, ☎ 404/262–0222 or 800/236–9732; $74.95 annually); **Travelers Advantage** (CUC Travel Service, 49 Music Sq. W, Nashville, TN 37203, ☎ 800/548–1116 or 800/648–4037; $49 annually, single or family); or **Worldwide Discount Travel Club** (1674 Meridian Ave., Miami Beach, FL 33139, ☎ 305/534–2082; $50 annually for family, $40 single).

DRIVING

AUTO CLUBS

The **Automobile Association of South Africa** (A.A. House, De Korte St., Braamfontein, Johannesburg 2017, ☎ 011/407–1000) extends privileges to members of the American Automobile Association (AAA, ☎ 800/564–6222 to join) in the United States and the

Automobile Association (AA, ☎ 01256/20123) in Britain. Contact a local office in your home country for more information.

E

ELECTRICITY

Send a self-addressed, stamped envelope to the **Franzus Company** (Customer Service, Dept. B50, Murtha Industrial Park, Box 142, Beacon Falls, CT 06403, ☎ 203/723–6664) for a copy of the free brochure "Foreign Electricity Is No Deep Dark Secret." *See also* Packing for South Africa *in* Smart Travel Tips A to Z, *below*.

EMERGENCIES

South Africa's national emergency number for the **police** is 10111; and for an **ambulance** it is 10177.

G

GAY AND LESBIAN TRAVEL

ORGANIZATIONS

The **International Gay Travel Association** (Box 4974, Key West, FL 33041, ☎ 800/448–8550), a consortium of 800 businesses, can supply names of travel agents and tour operators.

PUBLICATIONS

The premier international travel magazine for gays and lesbians is *Our World* (1104 N. Nova Rd., Suite 251, Daytona Beach, FL 32117, ☎ 904/441–5367; $35 for 10 issues). The 16-page monthly *"Out & About"* (☎ 212/645–6922 or

THE GOLD GUIDE / IMPORTANT CONTACTS

800/929–2268; $49 for 10 issues) covers gay-friendly resorts, hotels, cruise lines, and airlines.

TRAVEL AGENCIES

The largest agencies serving gay travelers are **Advance Travel** (10700 Northwest Fwy., Suite 160, Houston, TX 77092, ☏ 713/682–2002 or 800/695–0880); **Islanders/Kennedy Travel** (183 W. 10th St., New York, NY 10014, ☏ 212/242–3222 or 800/988–1181); **Now Voyager** (4406 18th St., San Francisco, CA 94114, ☏ 415/626–1169 or 800/255–6951); and **Yellowbrick Road** (1500 W. Balmoral Ave., Chicago, IL 60640, ☏ 312/561–1800 or 800/642–2488). **Skylink Women's Travel** (746 Ashland Ave., Santa Monica, CA 90405, ☏ 310/452–0506 or 800/225-5759) works with lesbians.

H
HEALTH ISSUES

FINDING A DOCTOR

For members, the **International Association for Medical Assistance to Travellers** (IAMAT, 417 Center St., Lewiston, NY 14092, ☏ 716/754–4883; 40 Regal Rd., Guelph, Ontario, Canada N1K 1B5, ☏ 519/836–0102; 1287 St. Clair Ave., Toronto, Ontario, Canada M6E 1B8, ☏ 416/652–0137; 57 Voirets, 1212 Grand-Lancy, Geneva, Switzerland; membership free) publishes a worldwide directory of English-speaking physi-

cians meeting IAMAT standards.

MEDICAL-ASSISTANCE COMPANIES

Contact **International SOS Assistance** (Box 11568, Philadelphia, PA 19116, ☏ 215/244–1500 or 800/523–8930; Box 466, Pl. Bonaventure, Montréal, Québec, Canada, H5A 1C1, ☏ 514/874–7674 or 800/363–0263); **Medex Assistance Corporation** (Box 10623, Baltimore, MD 21285, ☏ 410/296–2530 or 800/573–2029); or **Travel Assistance International** (1133 15th St. NW, Suite 400, Washington, DC 20005, ☏ 202/331–1609 or 800/821–2828). Because these companies also sell death-and-dismemberment, trip-cancellation, and other insurance coverage, there is some overlap with the travel-insurance policies sold by the companies listed under Insurance, *below*.

WARNINGS

The **National Centers for Disease Control** (Center for Preventive Services, Division of Quarantine, Traveler's Health Section, 1600 Clifton Rd., MSE03, Atlanta, GA 30333, automated hot line 404/332–4559) provides information on health risks abroad and vaccination requirements and recommendations. *See also* Health Concerns *in* Smart Travel Tips A to Z, *below*.

I
INSURANCE

Travel insurance covering baggage, health,

and trip cancellation or interruptions is available from **Access America** (Box 90315, Richmond, VA 23286, ☏ 804/285–3300 or 800/284–8300); **Carefree Travel Insurance** (Box 9366, 100 Garden City Plaza, Garden City, NY 11530, ☏ 516/294–0220 or 800/323–3149); **Tele-Trip** (Mutual of Omaha Plaza, Box 31716, Omaha, NE 68131, ☏ 800/228–9792); **Travel Guard International** (1145 Clark St., Stevens Point, WI 54481, ☏ 715/345–0505 or 800/826–1300); **Travel Insured International** (Box 280568, East Hartford, CT 06128-0568, ☏ 203/528–7663 or 800/243–3174); and **Wallach & Company** (107 W. Federal St., Box 480, Middleburg, VA 22117, ☏ 703/687–3166 or 800/237–6615).

IN THE U.K.

The **Association of British Insurers** (51 Gresham St., London EC2V 7HQ, ☏ 0171/600–3333; 30 Gordon St., Glasgow G1 3PU, ☏ 0141/226–3905; Scottish Provident Bldg., Donegall Sq. W, Belfast BT1 6JE, ☏ 01232/249176; and other locations) gives advice by phone and publishes the free *"Holiday Insurance,"* which sets out typical policy provisions and costs.

L
LODGING

APARTMENT AND VILLA RENTAL

Contact **Property Rentals International** (1008 Mansfield Crossing Rd., Richmond, VA

23236, ☎ 804/378–6054 or 800/220–3332).

FARM STAYS

Contact **Farm and Country Holiday** (8 Erin Rd., Rondebosch, Cape Town 7700 [mailing address: Box 266, Newlands 7725], ☎ 021/689–8400, FAX 021/685–1974.

GAME LODGES

Safariplan/Wild African Ventures (673 E. California Blvd., Pasadena, CA 91106, ☎ 800/358–8530) and **Sites of Africa** (Box 781329, Sandton 2146, South Africa, ☎ 011/883–4345), also known as Game Lodge Reservations, act as central reservations and information clearinghouses for a large number of game lodges throughout southern Africa.

HOME EXCHANGE

Principal clearinghouses include **HomeLink International/Vacation Exchange Club** (Box 650, Key West, FL 33041, ☎ 305/294–1448 or 800/638–3841; $60 annually), which gives members four annual directories, with a listing in one, plus updates; and **Intervac International** (Box 590504, San Francisco, CA 94159, ☎ 415/435–3497; $65 annually), which has three annual directories.

HOTELS

Since the 1994 elections, such major international chains as **Hyatt International** (☎ 800/228–9000) have begun constructing hotels around the country. At press time, however, the

hotel scene was still dominated by South African conglomerates, most notably the **Southern Sun Group** (Johannesburg office, ☎ 011/482–3500), which operates Southern Sun Hotels, Southern Sun Resorts, and Holiday Inn Hotels. Southern Sun also manages the budget French hotel chain, **Formule 1** (Johannesburg office, ☎ 011/440–1001). Other major South African chains are **Karos Hotels** (Johannesburg office, ☎ 011/643–4343) and **Protea Hotels** (Johannesburg office, ☎ 011/484–1717).

The **Leading Hotels of South Africa** (Johannesburg office, ☎ 011/884–3583) is a loose association of the country's most exclusive hotels and lodges.

Portfolio of Places (Johannesburg office, ☎ 011/880–3414, FAX 011/788–4802) publishes *The Country Places Collection,* a widely respected list of South Africa's best small country hotels and lodges, as well as select city hotels. Portfolio also publishes a similar guide to bed-and-breakfasts.

M
MAIL

American Express cardholders or traveler's check holders can have mail sent to them at the local American Express office. For a list of offices worldwide, write for the *Traveler's Companion* from **American Express** (Box 678, Canal St. Station, New York, NY 10013).

MONEY MATTERS
ATMS

Cirrus has more than 1,000 ATMs in South Africa at Standard Bank branches; for foreign **Plus** locations, consult the Plus directory at your local bank.

CURRENCY EXCHANGE

If your bank doesn't exchange currency, contact **Thomas Cook Currency Services** (41 E. 42nd St., New York, NY 10017 or 511 Madison Ave., New York, NY 10022, ☎ 212/757–6915 or 800/223–7373 for locations) or **Ruesch International** (☎ 800/424–2923 for locations).

WIRING FUNDS

Funds can be wired via **American Express MoneyGram℠** (☎ 800/926–9400 from the United States and Canada for locations and information) or **Western Union** (☎ 800/325–6000 for agent locations or to send using MasterCard or Visa, 800/321–2923 in Canada).

P
PASSPORTS AND VISAS

U.S. CITIZENS

For fees, documentation requirements, and other information, call the **Office of Passport Services** information line (☎ 202/647–0518).

CANADIANS

For fees, documentation requirements, and other information, call the

THE GOLD GUIDE / IMPORTANT CONTACTS

Ministry of Foreign Affairs and International Trade's **Passport Office** (☎ 819/994–3500 or 800/567–6868).

U.K. CITIZENS

For fees, documentation requirements, and to get an emergency passport, call the **London Passport Office** (☎ 0171/271–3000).

PHOTO HELP

The **Kodak Information Center** (☎ 800/242–2424) answers consumer questions about film and photography. An informative book on taking expert-quality travel photographs is *Kodak Guide to Shooting Great Travel Pictures* (Fodor's Travel Publications, 800/533–6478 or from bookstores; $16.50).

R
RAIL TRAVEL

A trip aboard the famous **Blue Train** (Box 2671, Joubert Park 2044, ☎ 011/773–7631, FAX 011/773–7643) has long been one of the highlights of any trip to South Africa. Since its inception in 1923, the *Blue Train*'s 24-hour passage between Cape Town and Johannesburg through the Karoo Desert has served as a standard for luxury and shameless pampering. Unfortunately, standards have slipped in recent years while the prices of tickets have reached stratospheric levels ($725 per person for the least expensive compartment). It's still a glorious ride, but for that price it should be flaw-

less. The quality of the food (French preparations of South African produce) can be heavenly or downright ordinary. The service of some stewards lacks polish, too. Accommodations range from standard compartments with shared toilet facilities to magnificent suites with private lounges and en suite bathrooms. Decor looks dated, however, and standard cabins have little to differentiate them from ordinary train compartments. In addition to its regular run between Cape Town and Johannesburg, the *Blue Train* occasionally goes to the game-rich Eastern Transvaal and journeys farther to view the splendors of Victoria Falls in Zimbabwe. All meals and alcohol are included in the ticket price, and the train serves superlative South African wine.

A new competitor that is earning rave reviews at the expense of the *Blue Train* is romantic **Rovos Rail** (Box 2837, Pretoria 0001, ☎ 012/323–6052, FAX 012/323–0843), 12 beautifully restored Edwardian-era carriages drawn by a steam engine. The luxury train carries a maximum of 46 passengers, attended by 16 staff members, including two gourmet chefs. In addition to two-day Cape Town—Johannesburg runs ($1,080 per person), Rovos Rail offers a variety of trips ranging from a four-day jaunt to the Eastern Transvaal to a 12-day rail safari to Dar es Salaam in Tanza-

nia, stopping at Victoria Falls on the way. Trips are coupled with excursions, such as a game drive in a private reserve in the lowveld (low-lying subtropical area in the Eastern Transvaal). The ticket covers everything, including alcohol and meals.

Mainline Passenger Services (Box 2671, Joubert Park 2044, ☎ 011/773–2944), part of the South African rail network known as Spoornet, operates an extensive system of passenger trains connecting most major cities. Departures are usually limited to one per day, although trains covering minor routes leave less frequently. Distances are vast, so many journeys require overnight travel. Traveling first class is your best bet, and it doesn't cost significantly more than second class. You must reserve tickets in advance for first- and second-class accommodation, whereas third-class tickets require no advance booking. You can book up to three months in advance with travel agents, reservations offices in major cities, and at railway stations.

Accompanied children under age 7 travel free; children 7–12 pay half fare (*Blue Train* excluded).

S
SENIOR CITIZENS

ORGANIZATIONS

Contact the **American Association of Retired Persons** (AARP, 601 E St. NW, Washington,

DC 20049, ☎ 202/434-2277; membership $8 per person or couple annually). Its Purchase Privilege Program gets members discounts on lodging, car rentals, and sightseeing.

For other discounts on lodgings, car rentals, and other travel products, along with magazines and newsletters, contact the **National Council of Senior Citizens** (1331 F St. NW, Washington, DC 20004, ☎ 202/347-8800; membership $12 annually) and *Mature Outlook* (6001 N. Clark St., Chicago, IL 60660, ☎ 312/465-6466 or 800/336-6330; subscription $9.95 annually).

PUBLICATIONS

The 50+ Traveler's Guidebook: Where to Go, Where to Stay, What to Do, by Anita Williams and Merrimac Dillon (St. Martin's Press, 175 5th Ave., New York, NY 10010, ☎ 212/674-5151 or 800/288-2131; $12.95), offers many useful tips. *"The Mature Traveler"* (Box 50400, Reno, NV 89513, ☎ 702/786-7419; $29.95), a monthly newsletter, covers travel deals.

STUDENTS

GROUPS

A major tour operator running trips to South Africa is **Contiki Holidays** (300 Plaza Alicante, Suite 900, Garden Grove, CA 92640, ☎ 714/740-0808 or 800/466-0610).

HOSTELING

Contact **Hostelling International–American**

Youth Hostels (733 15th St. NW, Suite 840, Washington, DC 20005, ☎ 202/783-6161) in the United States; **Hostelling International–Canada** (205 Catherine St., Suite 400, Ottawa, Ontario K2P 1C3, ☎ 613/237-7884) in Canada; and the **Youth Hostel Association of England and Wales** (Trevelyan House, 8 St. Stephen's Hill, St. Albans, Hertfordshire AL1 2DY, ☎ 01727/85-215 or 01727/845-047) in the United Kingdom. Membership ($25 in the United States, C$26.75 in Canada, and £9 in the United Kingdom) gets you access to 5,000 hostels worldwide that charge $7-$20 nightly per person.

ID CARDS

To be eligible for discounts on transportation and admissions, get the **International Student Identity Card** (ISIC) if you're a bona fide student or the **Go 25 Card** if you're under 26. In the United States, the ISIC and Go 25 Card cost $18 each and include basic travel-accident and illness coverage, plus a toll-free travel hot line. Apply through the Council on International Educational Exchange (*see* Organizations, *below*). Cards are available for $15 each in Canada from **Travel Cuts** (187 College St., Toronto, Ontario M5T 1P7, ☎ 416/979-2406 or 800/667-2887) and in the United Kingdom for £5 each at student unions and student travel companies.

ORGANIZATIONS

A major contact is the **Council on International Educational Exchange** (CIEE, 205 E. 42nd St., 16th Floor, New York, NY 10017, ☎ 212/661-1450) with locations in Boston (729 Boylston St., 02116, ☎ 617/266-1926); Miami (9100 S. Dadeland Blvd., 33156, ☎ 305/670-9261); Los Angeles (10904 Lindbrook Dr., 90024, ☎ 310/208-3551); 43 other college towns nationwide; and the United Kingdom (28A Poland St., London W1V 3DB, ☎ 0171/437-7767). Twice a year, it publishes *Student Travels* magazine. The CIEE's Council Travel Service is the exclusive U.S. agent for several student-discount cards.

AESU Travel (2 Hamill Rd., Suite 248, Baltimore, MD 21210, ☎ 410/323-4416 or 800/638-7640) sells budget airfares to South Africa. **Campus Connections** (325 Chestnut St., Suite 1101, Philadelphia, PA 19106, ☎ 215/625-8585 or 800/428-3235) specializes in discounted accommodations and airfares for students. The **Educational Travel Centre** (438 N. Frances St., Madison, WI 53703, ☎ 608/256-5551) offers rail passes and low-cost airline tickets, mostly for flights departing from Chicago. For air travel only, contact **TMI Student Travel** (100 W. 33rd St., Suite 813, New York, NY 10001, ☎ 800/245-3672).

In Canada, also contact **Travel Cuts** (*see* above).

THE GOLD GUIDE / IMPORTANT CONTACTS

T
TELEPHONES

The country code for South Africa is 27. When dialing a South African number from abroad, drop the initial 0 from the local area code.

LOCAL CALLS

A three-minute local call costs 20¢. South Africa has two types of pay phones: coin-operated phones that accept a variety of denominations and card-operated phones. Available in R10, R20, R50, and R100 denominations, phone cards are incredibly useful, saving you the hassle of juggling handfuls of coins. In addition, a digital meter tells you how much credit remains while you're talking. Telephone cards are available in news shops and tobacconists, but you can buy them for slightly less at offices of Telkom, the national telephone company.

South African phone numbers are not standardized, so don't be surprised to find some telephone numbers with fewer digits than others. Some remote farms and lodges still use a central exchange. This is slowly changing; some of the numbers in this book may already be out of date, in which case call directory assistance at 1023 (local) or 1025 (national). You do not need to dial the area code when making a local call.

LONG DISTANCE

You can make international calls with a Telkom phone card, but it's just as easy to use calling cards issued by major phone companies such as **AT&T** (local access number, ☎ 0800–990–123), **MCI** (local access number, ☎ 0800–990–011), and **Sprint** (local access number, ☎ 0800–990–001), all of which can be accessed via a local number. These cards are especially useful when you're staying in hotels, which tend to tack a hefty surcharge onto international calls.

TOUR OPERATORS

Among the companies selling tours and packages to South Africa, the following have a proven reputation, are nationally known, and offer plenty of options.

GROUP TOURS

For escorted tours to South Africa, contact **Abercrombie & Kent International** (1520 Kensington Rd., Oakbrook, IL 60521, ☎ 800/323–7308, FAX 708/954–3324); **Esplanade Tours** (581 Boylston St., Boston, MA 02116, ☎ 800/628–4893, FAX 617/262–9829); or **Wildlife Safari** (346 Rheem Blvd., Moraga, CA 94556, ☎ 800/221–8118, FAX 510/376–5059). **Discover Tours** (6776 Magnolia Ave., Riverside, CA 92506, ☎ 800/545–8653, FAX 909/684–7281), offering trips of 4–17 days, specializes in coach tours for first-time visitors, particularly senior citizens.

PACKAGES

Most of the companies that specialize in group tours to South Africa also offer independent or customized vacation packages. For more choices, try **African Travel** (1100 E. Broadway, Glendale, CA 91205, ☎ 800/421–8907 or 800/252–0493 in CA, FAX 818/507–5802); **Africa Tours** (875 Ave. of the Americas, Suite 2108, New York, NY 10001, ☎ 800/235–3692, FAX 212/563–4459); **Big Five Tours & Expeditions** (819 S. Federal Hwy., Suite 103, Stewart, FL 34994, ☎ 800/244–3483, FAX 407/287–5990); **Born Free Safaris** (12504 Riverside Dr., North Hollywood, CA 91607, ☎ 800/372–3274, FAX 818/981–8312); **Design Travel & Tours** (340 W. Butterfield, Suite 2A, Elmhurst, IL 60126, ☎ 800/543–7164, FAX 708/530–0059); **Luxury Adventure Safaris** (4635 Via Vistosa, Santa Barbara, CA 93110, ☎ 800/733–1789, FAX 805/964–8285); **Safaricenter** (3201 N. Sepulveda Blvd., Manhattan Beach, CA 90266, ☎ 800/223–6046, FAX 310/546–3188); **Safari Consulants** (4N211 Locust Ave., West Chicago, IL 60185, ☎ 800/762–4027, FAX 708/513–0209); **Safariplan/Wild African Ventures** (673 E. California Blvd. Pasadena, CA 91106, ☎ 800/358–8530, FAX 818/796–6365); **SITA World Travel** (8127 San Fernando Rd., Sun Valley, CA 91352, ☎ 800/421–5643, FAX 818/767–4346); **South African Adventures** (6075 Roswell Rd., Suite 304, Atlanta, GA 30328, ☎ 800/999–

7180, FAX 404/851–9816); **Sue's Safaris** (Box 2171, Rancho Palos Verdes, CA 90274, ☎ 800/541–2011, FAX 310/544–1502); or **United Touring International** (400 Market St., Suite 260, Philadelphia, PA 19106, ☎ 800/223–6486, FAX 215/985–1008).

FROM THE U.K.

Contact **British Airways Holidays** (Astral Towers, Betts Way, London Rd., Crawley, West Sussex RH10 2XA, ☎ 01293/72–2727, FAX 01293/72–2607); **Kuoni Travel** (Kuoni House, Dorking, Surrey RH5 4AZ, ☎ 01306/74–0888, FAX 01306/74–0328); or **Thomas Cook** (Box 5, 12 Coningsby Rd., Peterborough, Cambridgeshire PE3 8XP, ☎ 01733/33–0399, FAX 01733/50–5784).

THEME TRIPS

If you're outdoorsy, look into the **American Museum of Natural History**'s "Discovery Tours" (79th St. and Central Park W, New York, NY 10024, ☎ 212/769–5700 or 800/462–8687), and the offerings of **Wildland Adventures** (3516 N.E. 155th St., Seattle, WA 98155, ☎ 206/365–0686 or 800/345–4453).

BIRD-WATCHING➤ **Lawson's Tours** (Box 507, Nelspruit 1200, ☎ 01311/55–2147, FAX 01311/55–1793), led by famed ornithologist Peter Lawson, is the premier bird-watching tour company in South Africa. Lawson is

incredibly knowledgeable and passionate about birds, a passion that he communicates to his guests. Lawson also conducts photographic and general wildlife tours.

GAME VIEWING➤ **Mountain Travel/Sobek** (6420 Fairmount Ave., El Cerrito, CA 94530, ☎ 800/227–2384, FAX 510/525–7710) leads tours into the game parks of the Eastern Transvaal, with overnight accommodation at bush camps and private lodges.

GOLF➤ **International Travel Co.** (4134 Atlantic Ave., Suite 205, Long Beach, CA 90807, ☎ 800/257–4981, FAX 310/424–6683) offers a range of golf trips to South Africa, as well as more general tours.

PHOTOGRAPHY➤ **Bushtracks** (Box 4163, Menlo Park, CA 94026, ☎ 415/326–8689, FAX 415/321–4456) leads group tours and creates customized independent itineraries with an emphasis on wildlife photography.

SENIOR TRAVEL➤ **Grand Circle Travel** (347 Congress St., Boston, MA 02210, ☎ 800/221–2610, FAX 617/346–6120) conducts escorted 16-day tours to South Africa for senior citizens, touching on the country's major highlights, including Kruger National Park.

PUBLICATIONS

Consult the brochure **"On Tour"** and ask for a current list of member operators from the NTA (*see* Organizations, *above*). Also get a

copy of the **"Worldwide Tour & Vacation Package Finder"** from the USTOA (*see* Organizations, *above*) and the Better Business Bureau's **"Tips on Travel Packages"** (Publication No. 24-195, 4200 Wilson Blvd., Arlington, VA 22203; $2).

TRAVEL AGENCIES

For names of reputable agencies in your area, contact the **American Society of Travel Agents** (ASTA, 1101 King St., Suite 200, Alexandria, VA 22314, ☎ 703/739–2782).

U
U.S.
GOVERNMENT
TRAVEL BRIEFINGS

The U.S. Department of State's Overseas Citizens Emergency Center (Room 4811, Washington, DC 20520; enclose SASE) issues **Consular Information Sheets,** which cover crime, security, political climate, and health risks as well as embassy locations, entry requirements, currency regulations, and other routine matters. (Travel Warnings, which counsel travelers to avoid a country entirely, are issued in extreme cases.) For the latest information, stop in at any U.S. Passport Agency office, consulate, or embassy; call the interactive hot line (☎ 202/647–5225 or fax 202/647-3000); or, with your PC's modem, tap into the Bureau of Consular Affairs' computer bulletin board (☎ 202/647–9225).

THE GOLD GUIDE / IMPORTANT CONTACTS

V

VISITOR INFORMATION

SOUTH AFRICAN GOVERNMENT TOURIST OFFICES

For information about traveling to and within South Africa, contact the nearest office of the **South African Tourism Board** (Satour).

In the U.S.: 500 5th Ave., 20th Floor, New York, NY 10110, ☎ 800/822–5368, FAX 212/764–1980; 9841 Airport Blvd., Suite 1524, Los Angeles, CA 90045, ☎ 800/782–9772, FAX 310/641–5812.

In Canada: 4117 Lawrence Ave. E, Suite 205, Scarborough, Ontario, M1E 2S2, ☎ 416/283–0563, FAX 416/283–5465.

In the U.K.: No. 5 & 6 Alt Grove, Wimbledon SW19 4DZ, ☎ 0181/944–8080, FAX 0181/944–6705.

W

WEATHER

For current conditions and forecasts, plus the local time and helpful travel tips, call the **Weather Channel Connection** (☎ 900/932–8437; 95¢ per minute) from a Touch-Tone phone. On the Internet, you can access the four-day forecast for 688 cities worldwide through **Fodor's** own website (http://www.fodors.com/).

WINE

SHIPPING WINE HOME

Many wineries will mail your wine purchases to your home. Wine dispatched to the United States and Canada is usually sent as an "unsolicited gift" at the buyer's risk. It's not strictly legal, and if customs stops the shipment they will either make you pay customs duties or confiscate it outright. Some wine shippers in South Africa report no problems mailing wines to the United States and Canada; others report a high failure rate. The most reliable shipper is **Steven Rom** (Checkers Galleria Centre, 76 Regent Rd., Sea Point, South Africa, ☎ 021/439–6043, FAX 021/434–0401). If you don't want to take the risk, contact one of the companies in the United States and Canada that import a wide range of Cape wines: **Cape Venture Co.** (☎ 203/329–6663), **South African Wine Club** (☎ 800/504–9463), or **Maisons Marques & Domaines U.S.A.** (☎ 510/286–2010); and in Canada, **Remy Canada Inc.** (☎ 416/485–3633) or **Peter Mielzynski Agencies Ltd.** (☎ 905/820–8180).

SMART TRAVEL TIPS A TO Z

Basic Information on Traveling in South Africa and Savvy Tips to Make Your Trip a Breeze

The more you travel, the more you know about how to make trips run like clockwork. To help make your travels hassle-free, Fodor's editors have rounded up dozens of tips from our contributors and travel experts all over the world, as well as basic information on visiting South Africa. For names of organizations to contact and publications that can give you more information, see Important Contacts A to Z, *above.*

A
AIR TRAVEL

If time is an issue, **always look for nonstop flights,** which require no change of plane. If possible, **avoid connecting flights,** which stop at least once and can involve a change of plane, although the flight number remains the same; if the first leg is late, the second waits.

ALOFT

AIRLINE FOOD➤ If you hate airline food, **ask for special meals when booking.** These can be vegetarian, low-cholesterol, or kosher, for example; commonly prepared to order in smaller quantities than standard catered fare, they can be tastier.

SMOKING➤ On U.S. carriers flying to South Africa and other destinations abroad, a seat in a no-smoking section must be provided for every passenger who requests one, as long as they have complied with the airline's deadline for check-in and seat assignment. If smoking bothers you, request a seat far from the smoking section.

Foreign airlines are exempt from these rules but do provide no-smoking sections. British Airways has banned smoking, and South African Airways prohibits smoking on all domestic flights.

CUTTING COSTS

The Sunday travel section of most newspapers is a good source of deals.

CONSOLIDATORS➤ Consolidators, who buy tickets at reduced rates from scheduled airlines and sell them at prices below the lowest available directly from airlines—usually without advance restrictions. Sometimes you can even get your money back if you need to return the ticket. Carefully read the fine print detailing penalties for changes and cancellations. If you doubt the reliability of a consolidator, **confirm your reservation with the airline.**

MAJOR AIRLINES➤ The least-expensive airfares from the major airlines are priced for round-trip travel and are subject to restrictions. You must usually **book in advance and buy the ticket within 24 hours** to get cheaper fares. **When you are quoted a good price, reserve it on the spot**—the same fare on the same flight may not be available the next day. Airlines generally allow you to change your return date for a $25 to $50 fee, but most low-fare tickets are nonrefundable. However, if you don't use it, you can apply the cost toward the purchase price of a new ticket, again for a small charge.

TRAVEL PASSES➤ South African Airways' **African Explorer** pass allows you to travel within the country, between 4 and 8 legs, at a discount. Itineraries must be specified in advance, and the pass must be purchased in conjunction with an international ticket. You can however change the travel days on your itinerary without penalty, provided seats are available. The pass is valid for one month's travel.

C
CAMERAS, CAMCORDERS, AND COMPUTERS

LAPTOPS

Before you depart, **check your portable computer's battery,** because you may be asked at security to turn on the computer to prove that it's what it appears to be. At the airport, you may prefer to **request a manual inspection,** although security X-rays do not harm hard-disk or floppy-disk storage. Also, **register your foreign-made laptop with U.S. Customs.** If your laptop is U.S.-made, call the consulate of the country you'll be visiting to find out whether or not it should be registered with local customs upon arrival. You may want to **find out about repair facilities at your destination** in case you need them.

PHOTOGRAPHY

Always **store film in a cool, dry place**—never in the car's glove compartment or on the shelf under the rear window.

Every pass of film through an X-ray machine increases the chance of clouding. To protect it, carry it in a clear plastic bag and **ask for hand inspection at security.** Such requests are virtually always honored at U.S. airports, and are usually accommodated abroad. Don't depend on a lead-lined bag to protect film in checked luggage—the airline may increase the radiation to see what's inside.

VIDEO

Before your trip, **test your camcorder, invest in a skylight filter to protect the lens, and charge the batteries.** (Airport security personnel may ask you to turn on the camcorder to prove that it's what it

appears to be.) The batteries of most newer camcorders can be recharged with a universal or worldwide AC adapter–charger (or multivoltage converter), usable whether the voltage is 110 or 220. All that's needed is the appropriate plug.

Videotape is not damaged by X-rays, but it may be harmed by the magnetic field of a walk-through metal detector, so **ask that videotapes be hand-checked.** Videotape sold in South Africa is based on the PAL standard, which is different from the one used in the United States. You will not be able to view your tapes through the local TV set or view movies bought there in your home VCR. Blank tapes bought in South Africa can be used for camcorder taping, but they are pricey. Some U.S. audiovisual shops convert foreign tapes to U.S. standards; contact an electronics dealer to find the nearest.

CUTTING COSTS

To get the best deal, **book through a travel agent and shop around.** When pricing cars, **ask where the rental lot is located.** Some off-airport locations offer lower rates—even though their lots are only minutes from the terminal via complimentary shuttle. You may also want to **price local car-rental companies,** whose rates may be lower still, although service and maintenance standards may not be up to those of a na-

tional firm. Also **ask your travel agent about a company's customer-service record.** How has it responded to late plane arrivals and vehicle mishaps? Are there often lines at the rental counter, and, if you're traveling during a holiday period, does a confirmed reservation guarantee you a car?

Always **find out what equipment is standard** at your destination before specifying what you want; **do without automatic transmission or air-conditioning** if they're optional.

INSURANCE

When you drive a rented car, you are generally responsible for any damage or personal injury that you cause as well as damage to the vehicle. Before you rent, **see what coverage you already have** under the terms of your personal auto-insurance policy and credit cards. For about $14 a day, rental companies sell insurance, known as a collision damage waiver (CDW), that eliminates your liability for damage to the car; it's always optional and should never be automatically added to your bill.

REQUIREMENTS

In South Africa a foreign driver's license is acceptable, as long as it's valid. To rent a car, you must be over 25 years old and have a minimum of five years' driving experience.

SURCHARGES

Before picking up the car in one city and

leaving it in another, **ask about drop-off charges or one-way service fees,** which can be substantial. Note, too, that some rental agencies charge extra if you return the car before the time specified on your contract. To avoid a hefty refueling fee, **fill the tank just before you turn in the car.**

CHILDREN AND TRAVEL

BABY-SITTING

For recommended local sitters, **check with your hotel desk.**

DRIVING

If you are renting a car, **arrange for a car seat when you reserve.** Sometimes they're free.

FLYING

Always **ask about discounted children's fares.** On international flights, the fare for infants under age 2 not occupying a seat is generally either free or 10% of the accompanying adult's fare; children ages 2 through 11 usually pay half to two-thirds of the adult fare. On flights within South Africa, children under 2 not occupying a seat pay 10%, while children 2–11 pay 67% of the adult fare.

BAGGAGE➤ In general, the adult baggage allowance applies for children paying half or more of the adult fare. Before departure, **ask about carry-on allowances** if you are traveling with an infant. In general, those paying 10% of the adult fare are allowed one carry-on bag, not to exceed

70 pounds (32 kilograms) or 45 inches or 115 centimeters (length + width + height) and a collapsible stroller; you may be allowed less if the flight is full.

SAFETY SEATS➤ According to the FAA, it's a good idea to **use safety seats aloft.** Airline policy varies. U.S. carriers allow FAA-approved models, but airlines usually require that you buy a ticket, even if your child would otherwise ride free, because the seats must be strapped into regular passenger seats. Foreign carriers may not allow infant seats, may charge the child rather than the infant fare for their use, or may require you to hold your baby during takeoff and landing, thus defeating the seat's purpose.

GAMES

To keep kids from getting fidgety while riding in planes, trains, and automobiles, **consider packing compact, specially designed games:** Travel Battleship ($7); Travel Connect Four, a vertical strategy game ($8); the Travel Yahtzee dice game ($6); the Travel Trouble dice and board game ($7); and the Travel Guess Who mystery game ($8).

LODGING

Most hotels allow children under a certain age to stay in their parents' room at no extra charge, whereas others charge them as extra adults. Some resorts and lodges don't allow children at all, so

be sure to **ask about the cutoff age.**

CUSTOMS AND DUTIES

IN SOUTH AFRICA

Visitors over 18 years of age may bring in duty-free gifts and souvenirs to the total value of R500 (about $140), plus 400 cigarettes, 50 cigars, 250 grams of tobacco, 2 liters of wine, 1 liter of other alcoholic beverages, 50 milliliters of perfume, and 250 milliliters of toilet water.

BACK HOME

IN THE U.S.➤ You may bring home $400 worth of foreign goods duty-free if you've been out of the country for at least 48 hours and haven't already used the $400 exemption, or any part of it, in the past 30 days.

Travelers 21 or older may bring back 1 liter of alcohol duty-free, provided the beverage laws of the state through which they reenter the United States allow it. In addition, 100 non-Cuban cigars and 200 cigarettes are allowed, regardless of your age. Antiques and works of art more than 100 years old are duty-free.

Duty-free, travelers may mail packages valued at up to $200 to themselves and up to $100 to others, with a limit of one parcel per addressee per day (and no alcohol or tobacco products or perfume valued at more than $5); on the outside, identify the package as being for personal use or an unsolicited gift, specifying the contents and their retail value. Mailed items do not count as part of your exemption.

IN CANADA➤ Once per calendar year, when you've been out of Canada for at least seven days, you may bring in C$300 worth of goods duty-free. If you've been away less than seven days but more than 48 hours, the duty-free exemption drops to C$100 but can be claimed any number of times (as can a C$20 duty-free exemption for absences of 24 hours or more). You cannot combine the yearly and 48-hour exemptions, use the C$300 exemption only partially (to save the balance for a later trip), or pool exemptions with family members. Goods claimed under the C$300 exemption may follow you by mail; those claimed under the lesser exemptions must accompany you.

Alcohol and tobacco products may be included in the yearly and 48-hour exemptions but not in the 24-hour exemption. If you meet the age requirements of the province through which you reenter Canada, you may bring in, duty-free, 1.14 liters of wine or liquor *or* 24 12-ounce cans or bottles of beer or ale. If you are 16 or older, you may bring in, duty-free, 200 cigarettes, 50 cigars or cigarillos, and 400 tobacco sticks or 400 grams of manufactured tobacco. Alcohol and

tobacco must accompany you on your return.

An unlimited number of gifts valued up to C$60 each may be mailed to Canada duty-free. These do not count as part of your exemption. Label the package "Unsolicited Gift—Value under $60." Alcohol and tobacco are excluded.

IN THE U.K.➤ From countries outside the European Union (EU), including South Africa, you may import duty-free 200 cigarettes, 100 cigarillos, 50 cigars or 250 grams of tobacco; 1 liter of spirits or 2 liters of fortified or sparkling wine; 2 liters of still table wine; 60 milliliters of perfume; 250 milliliters of toilet water; plus £136 worth of other goods, including gifts and souvenirs.

D
DINING

Dress in most restaurants tends to be casual, but draw the line at wearing shorts and a halter top to dinner at any restaurant away from the beach. Very expensive restaurants and old-fashioned hotel restaurants (where colonial traditions die hard) may require a jacket and tie. *See also* Pleasures & Pastimes *in* Chapter 1.

FOR TRAVELERS
WITH DISABILITIES

South Africa is slowly adding facilities for travelers with disabilities, but standards vary widely from place to place. Many of the large

chains now offer one or more rooms in their hotels specially adapted for travelers with disabilities.

When discussing accessibility with an operator or reservationist, **ask hard questions.** Are there any stairs, inside *or* out? Are there grab bars next to the toilet *and* in the shower/tub? How wide is the doorway to the room? To the bathroom? For the most extensive facilities, meeting the latest legal specifications, **opt for newer accommodations,** which more often have been designed with access in mind. Older properties or ships must usually be retrofitted and may offer more limited facilities as a result. Be sure to **discuss your needs before booking.**

DISCOUNT CLUBS

Travel clubs offer members unsold space on airplanes, cruise ships, and package tours at as much as 50% below regular prices. Membership may include a regular bulletin or access to a toll-free hot line giving details of available trips departing from three or four days to several months in the future. Most also offer 50% discounts off hotel rack rates. Before booking with a club, **make sure the hotel or other supplier isn't offering a better deal.**

DRIVING

South Africans drive on the left. For pedestrians, that means that you should look right before crossing the street. The country has a superb network of multilane roads and highways, some of which charge a toll. **The speed limit on major highways is 120 kph (75 mph), but many drivers far exceed that.** In fact, South Africans tend to be aggressive and reckless, thinking nothing of tailgating at high speeds and passing on blind rises. During national holidays, the body count from highway collisions is staggering. The problem is compounded by widespread drunk driving, even though the legal blood-alcohol limit is 0.08. Local minibus taxis pose another threat, swerving in and out of traffic without warning to pick up customers. For obvious reasons, the wearing of seat belts is required by law.

South African roads have wide shoulders, separated from the main lanes by a yellow line. Slow traffic is expected to pull onto this shoulder to allow faster traffic to pass, but be sure that the shoulder ahead is not obstructed by cyclists, pedestrians, or a stopped vehicle. If a slower vehicle pulls onto the shoulder to allow you past, it's common courtesy to flash your hazard lights a couple of times in thanks.

In very remote areas, only the main road might be paved, while most secondary roads are of high-quality gravel. Traffic is often light in these areas, so be sure to carry a spare, a jack, a tire iron, and extra water.

Huge **24-hour service stations** are positioned at regular intervals along all major highways. Self-service stations do not exist, so an attendant will pump the gas, check the oil and water, and wash the windows. In return, tip him or her R2–R3. South Africa still uses leaded gasoline, and many vehicles operate on diesel—be sure you get the right fuel. Petrol is measured in liters, and expect to pay the equivalent of US$2–US$2.50 a gallon, about twice what you would pay in the States.

Many cities, most notably Johannesburg, now use **mini traffic circles** in lieu of four-way stops. These are extremely dangerous, since many drivers don't bother to stop. Theoretically, the first vehicle to the circle has right-of-way; otherwise, yield to the right. In practice, keep your wits about you *at all times*.

Two final notes: In South African parlance, **traffic lights are known as "robots."** And for Americans and Canadians, don't forget: **Drive left, and look right.**

H
HEALTH
CONCERNS

Unless signs indicate otherwise, **you can drink the water and eat all fresh produce in South Africa.** The major problem facing travelers is malaria, which occurs in the prime game-viewing areas of the Eastern and Northern Transvaal and in northern KwaZulu-Natal. **All travelers heading into these regions should take antimalarial drugs.** Chloroquine and paludrine are widely prescribed together, but there is evidence of resistance to these drugs. A more effective measure is Lariam (mefloquine), although this can cause side effects. See your doctor at least one month before your departure.

The best way to prevent malaria is to avoid being bitten by mosquitos in the first place. After sunset, wear long-sleeve pants and shirts, apply repellent (100% DEET is good), and use mosquito nets if they're provided. Upon returning home, if you experience flulike systems, including fever, painful eyes, backache, and severe headache, be sure to tell your doctor that you have been in a malarial zone.

Many lakes and streams, particularly in the eastern half of the country, are infected with *bilharzia* (schistosomiasis), a parasite carried by a small freshwater snail. The fluke enters through the skin of swimmers or waders, attaches itself to the intestines or bladder, and lays eggs. Symptoms of this treatable condition include blood-tinged urine, general malaise, and abdominal pain. **Avoid wading in still waters or in areas close to reeds.** Fast-moving water is considered safe.

South Africa has no national health system, so check your existing health plan to see whether you're covered while abroad and supplement it if necessary. South African doctors are generally excellent. The equipment and training in private clinics rival the best in the world, but public hospitals tend to suffer from overcrowding and underfunding.

SHOTS AND MEDICATIONS

Aside from malaria tablets (*see above*), travelers entering South Africa within six days of leaving a country infected with yellow fever require a yellow fever vaccination certificate.

I

INSURANCE

Travel insurance can protect your ticket investment, replace your luggage and its contents, or provide for medical coverage should you fall ill during your trip. Most tour operators, travel agents, and insurance agents sell specialized health-and-accident, flight, trip-cancellation, and luggage insurance as well as comprehensive policies with some or all of these features. Before you make any purchase, **review your existing health and homeowner's policies** to find out whether they cover expenses incurred while traveling.

BAGGAGE

Airline liability for your baggage is limited to $1,250 per person on domestic flights. On international flights, the airlines' liability is $9.07 per pound or $20 per kilogram for checked baggage (roughly $640 per 70-pound bag) and $400 per passenger for unchecked baggage. Insurance for losses exceeding the terms of your airline ticket can be bought directly from the airline at check-in for about $10 per $1,000 of coverage; note that it excludes a rather extensive list of items, shown on your airline ticket.

FLIGHT

You should **think twice before buying flight insurance.** Often purchased as a last-minute impulse at the airport, it pays a lump sum when a plane crashes, either to a beneficiary if the insured dies or sometimes to a surviving passenger who loses eyesight or a limb. Supplementing the airlines' coverage described in the limits-of-liability paragraphs on your ticket, it's expensive and basically unnecessary. Charging an airline ticket to a major credit card often automatically entitles you to coverage and may also embrace travel by bus, train, and ship.

HEALTH

If your health-insurance policy does not cover you outside the United States, **consider buying supplemental medical coverage.** It can pay for $1,000 to $150,000 worth of medical and/or dental expenses incurred as a result of an accident or illness during a trip. These policies also may include a personal-accident, or death-and-dismemberment, provision, which pays a lump sum ranging from $15,000 to $500,000 to your beneficiaries if you die or to you if you lose one or more limbs or your eyesight, and a medical-assistance provision, which may either reimburse you for the cost of referrals, evacuation, or repatriation and other services, or may automatically enroll you as a member of a particular medical-assistance company. (*See* Health Issues *in* Important Contacts A to Z, *above.*)

FOR U.K. TRAVELERS

You can buy an annual travel-insurance policy valid for most vacations during the year in which it's purchased. If you go this route, make sure it covers you if you have a preexisting medical condition or are pregnant.

TRIP

Without insurance, you will lose all or most of your money if you must cancel your trip due to illness or any other reason. Especially if your airline ticket, cruise, or package tour is nonrefundable and cannot be changed, it's essential that you **buy trip-cancellation-and-interruption insurance.** When considering how much coverage you need, look for a policy that will cover the cost of your trip plus the nondiscounted price of a one-way airline ticket should you need to return home early. Read the fine print carefully, especially sections defining "family member" and "preexisting medical conditions." Also **consider default or bankruptcy insurance,** which protects you against a supplier's failure to deliver. However, such policies often do not cover default by a travel agency, tour operator, airline, or cruise line if you bought your tour and the coverage directly from the firm in question.

L
LANGUAGE

South Africa has a mind-numbing 11 official languages: English, Afrikaans, Ndebele, Northern Sotho, Southern Sotho, Swati, Tsonga, Tswana, Venda, Xhosa, and Zulu. Happily for visitors, English is the widely spoken, unofficial lingua franca, although road signs and other important markers often alternate between English and Afrikaans (South-African Dutch).

South African English is heavily influenced by Afrikaans and, to a lesser extent, by some of the African languages. First-time visitors may have trouble understanding the South African accent, which lengthens certain vowels, clips others short, and swallows still others. Listed below are some of the words, both English and Afrikaans, that you should know. For a list of culinary terms, *see* Dining *in* Pleasures & Pastimes *in* Chapter 1.

Bakkie: pickup truck
Bottle store: liquor store

Dagga: marijuana
Jol: a party
Howzit?: how are you?
Izit?: really?
Just now: soon
Lekker: nice
Oke: fellow, chap
Robot: traffic light
Shame: how cute *or* what a pity
Shebeen: township bar
Sis: gross, disgusting
Takkie: sneaker
Toyi-toyi: to dance in protest
Voetsak!: go away, get lost

LODGING

The South African Tourism Board (Satour) operates a grading system rating the quality of a hotel. A one-star rating suggests the bare essentials, while a hotel with a five-star rating (the highest) can be assumed to meet high international standards. Bear in mind, though, that stars relate to the level of facilities provided (e.g., TV, heated towel rack, room service, etc.), *not the quality of the hotel.* In a second, more subjective rating system, Satour awards silver plaques to those few hotels that offer an extraordinary level of service.

Most hotel rooms come with en suite bathrooms, and you can usually choose between rooms with twin or double beds. A full English breakfast is often included in the rate, particularly in more traditional hotels. In the luxury lodges of the Transvaal Escarpment, the rate usually covers the cost of dinner, bed, and breakfast, while in game lodges the rate includes everything but alcohol.

APARTMENT AND VILLA RENTALS

If you want a home base that's roomy enough for a family and comes with cooking facilities, **consider a furnished rental.** It's generally cost-wise, too, although not always—some rentals are luxury properties (economical only when your party is large). Some send an illustrated catalogue and others send photographs of specific properties, sometimes at a charge; up-front registration fees may apply.

HOME EXCHANGE

If you would like to find a house, an apartment, or other vacation property to exchange for your own while on vacation, **become a member of a home-exchange organization,** which will send you its annual directories listing available exchanges and will include your own listing in at least one of them.

M
MAIL

The South African mail service is increasingly unreliable. Mail can take weeks to arrive, and money and other valuables are frequently stolen from letters and packages. You can buy stamps only at post offices, open weekdays 8:30–4:30 and Saturdays 8–12. Federal Express and several other express-mail companies offer more reliable service.

RECEIVING MAIL

The central post office in each city has a poste restante desk that will hold mail for you. Be sure the post office's mail code and your name are prominently displayed on all letters. A better place to receive mail is American Express offices (*see* Mail *in* Important Contacts A to Z, *above*). Most hotels also accept faxes and express-mail deliveries addressed to their guests.

MEDICAL ASSISTANCE

No one plans to get sick while traveling, but it happens, so **consider signing up with a medical assistance company.** These outfits provide referrals, emergency evacuation or repatriation, 24-hour telephone hot lines for medical consultation, dispatch of medical personnel, relay of medical records, cash for emergencies, and other personal and legal assistance.

MONEY AND EXPENSES

The unit of currency in South Africa is the rand (R), with 100 cents (¢) equaling R1. Bills come in R10, R20, R50, R100, and R200 denominations, which are differentiated by color. Coins are minted in R5, R2, R1, 50¢, 20¢, 10¢, 5¢, 2¢, and 1¢ denominations. Prices quoted throughout the book are in rand, except in Chapter 8, Victoria Falls, where prices are given in American dollars.

ATMS

Cirrus, Plus, and many other networks connect-ing ATMs operate internationally. Chances are that you can **use your bank card at ATMs** to withdraw money from an account and get cash advances on a credit-card account if your card has been programmed with a personal identification number, or PIN. You may, however, need to obtain a special card and should check a month in advance in case you need to order one. Also **check on frequency limits** for withdrawals and cash advances, and **ask whether your card's PIN must be reprogrammed** for use in South Africa. Four digits are commonly used overseas. Note that Discover is accepted only in the United States.

On cash advances you are charged interest from the day you receive the money, whether from a teller or an ATM. Although transaction fees for ATM withdrawals abroad may be higher than fees for withdrawals at home, Cirrus and Plus exchange rates are excellent because they are based on wholesale rates offered only by major banks.

COSTS

Because of inflation in South Africa, it's difficult to give exact prices. It's safe to say, though, that the country is an extremely cheap destination for foreign visitors. With the weakness of the rand against major foreign currencies, visitors will find the cost of meals, hotels, and entertainment considerably lower than at home.

A fabulous bottle of South African wine costs about $10, and a meal at a prestigious restaurant won't set you back more than $30 per person. Double rooms in the country's finest hotels may cost $250 a night but $100 is more than enough to secure high-quality lodging in most cities. Hotel rates are at their highest during peak season, November through March, when you can expect to pay anywhere from 50% to 90% more than in the off-season.

Not everything in South Africa is cheap. Expect to pay international rates and more to stay in one of the exclusive private game lodges in the Eastern Transvaal. Mala Mala, the most glamorous lodge in the country, charges $1,000 per couple per night. Flights to South Africa and within the country itself are also extremely expensive.

The following are sample costs (in American dollars) in South Africa at press time: Cup of coffee 50¢–75¢; bottle of beer in a bar 75¢–$1; ¼ roasted chicken with salad and drink at a fast-food restaurant $3–$4; room-service sandwich in a hotel $4–$7; a 2-kilometer (1¼-mile) taxi ride $3.

EXCHANGING CURRENCY

For the most favorable rates, **change money at banks.** You won't do as well at exchange booths anywhere else, although you may find their hours more convenient. To avoid lines at airport exchange booths, **get a small amount of currency before you leave home.**

For safety's sake, keep all foreign-exchange receipts until you leave South Africa. South Africa has restrictions on how much money its citizens can take out of the country, so you may need the receipts as proof when changing any unspent rand back into your own currency. You must also have a permit from the South African Reserve Bank (Box 427, Pretoria 0001, ☎ 012/313–3911) to take more than R500 out of the country.

TAXES

HOTEL➤ Hotels that participate in Satour's grading system add a Tourism Promotion Levy of R1.70–R5.70 per room to the bill, depending on the establishment's star rating.

VAT➤ The VAT, currently a whopping 14%, is included in the price of most goods and services, including hotel accommodations and food. To get a VAT refund, foreign visitors must present their receipts (minimum of R250) at the airport, and be carrying any purchased items with them or in their luggage. You must fill out Form VAT 255, available at the airport VAT refund office, and each receipt must be an original tax invoice, containing the vendor's name and address, VAT registration number,

and the words "tax invoice." Refunds are given in the form of a check, which can be cashed immediately at an airport bank. If you have packed your purchases in luggage that you intend to check, be sure you visit the VAT refund desk **before you go through check-in procedures.** For items in your carry-on baggage, visit the refund desk in the departures hall.

TRAVELER'S CHECKS

Whether or not to buy traveler's checks depends on where you're headed; **take cash to rural areas and small towns, traveler's checks to cities.** The most widely recognized are American Express, Citicorp, Thomas Cook, and Visa, which are sold by major commercial banks for 1% to 3% of the checks' face value— it pays to **shop around.** Both American Express and Thomas Cook issue checks that can be countersigned and used by you or your traveling companion, and they both provide checks, at no extra charge, denominated in various non-U.S. currencies. So you won't be left with excess foreign currency, **buy a few checks in small denominations** to cash toward the end of your trip. Record the numbers of the checks, cross them off as you spend them, and keep this information separate from your checks.

WIRING MONEY

You don't have to be a cardholder to send or receive funds through

MoneyGram[SM] from American Express. Just go to a MoneyGram[SM] agent, located in retail and convenience stores and in American Express Travel Offices. Pay up to $1,000 with cash or a credit card, anything over that in cash. The money can be picked up within 10 minutes in the form of U.S. dollar traveler's checks or local currency at the nearest MoneyGram[SM] agent, or, abroad, the nearest American Express Travel Office. There's no limit, and the recipient need only present photo ID. The cost runs from 3% to 10%, depending on the amount sent, the destination, and how you pay.

You can also send money using Western Union. Money sent from the United States or Canada will be available for pickup at agent locations in 100 countries within 15 minutes. Once the money is in the system, it can be picked up at any one of 25,000 locations. Fees range from 4% to 10%, depending on the amount you send.

P
PACKAGES
AND TOURS

A package or tour to South Africa can make your vacation less expensive and more convenient. Firms that sell tours and packages purchase airline seats, hotel rooms, and rental cars in bulk and pass some of the savings on to you. In addition, the best operators have local representatives to help you out at your destination.

A GOOD DEAL?

The more your package or tour includes, the better you can predict the ultimate cost of your vacation. Make sure you know exactly what is included, and **beware of hidden costs.** Are taxes, tips, and service charges included? Transfers and baggage handling? Entertainment and excursions? These can add up.

Most packages and tours are rated either deluxe, first-class superior, first class, tourist, or budget. The key difference is usually accommodations. If the package or tour you are considering is priced lower than in your wildest dreams, **be skeptical.** Also, **make sure your travel agent knows the hotels** and other services. Ask about location, room size, beds, and whether the facility has a pool, room service, or programs for children, if you care about these. Has your agent been there or sent others you can contact?

BUYER BEWARE

Each year consumers are stranded or lose their money when operators go out of business—even very large ones with excellent reputations. If you can't afford a loss, take the time to **check out the operator**—find out how long the company has been in business, and ask several agents about its reputation. Next, **don't book**

unless the firm has a consumer-protection program. Members of the USTOA and the NTA are required to set aside funds exclusively to cover your payments and travel arrangements in case of default. Nonmember operators may instead carry insurance; look for the details in the operator's brochure—and the name of an underwriter with a solid reputation. Note: When it comes to tour operators, **don't trust escrow accounts.** Although there are laws governing those of charter-flight operators, no governmental body prevents tour operators from raiding the till.

Next, **contact your local Better Business Bureau and the attorney general's office** in both your own state and the operator's; have any complaints been filed? Last, **pay with a major credit card.** Then you can cancel payment, provided that you can document your complaint. Always **consider trip-cancellation insurance** (see Insurance, above).

BIG VS. SMALL➤ An operator that handles several hundred thousand travelers annually can use its purchasing power to give you a good price. Its high volume may also indicate financial stability. But some small companies provide more personalized service; because they tend to specialize, they may also be experts on an area.

USING AN AGENT

Travel agents are an excellent resource. In

fact, large operators accept bookings only through travel agents. But it's good to **collect brochures from several agencies,** because some agents' suggestions may be skewed by promotional relationships with tour and package firms that reward them for volume sales. If you have a special interest, **find an agent with expertise in that area;** the ASTA (see Travel Agencies in Important contacts A to Z, above) can give you leads in the United States. (Don't rely solely on your agent, though; agents may be unaware of small-niche operators, and some special-interest travel companies only sell direct.)

SINGLE TRAVELERS

Prices are usually quoted per person, based on two sharing a room. If traveling solo, you may be required to pay the full double-occupancy rate. Some operators eliminate this surcharge if you agree to be matched up with a roommate of the same sex, even if one is not found by departure time.

PACKING FOR SOUTH AFRICA

In South Africa, it's possible to experience muggy heat, bone-chilling cold, torrential thunderstorms, and scorching African sun all within a couple days. The secret is to pack lightweight clothes that you can wear in layers, and at least one sweater. If you're coming in winter or going game viewing at a private lodge, take along a warm jacket, too. It can get mighty cold sitting in an open Land Rover at night.

South Africans tend to dress casually, donning shorts and T-shirts as soon as the weather turns pleasant. People dress much as they do in the United States: Businessmen still wear suits, and if a couple is going out to a fancy restaurant, they tend to get dolled up.

In summer, lightweight cottons are ideal, but highveld (South Africa's high interior plateau) evenings can be cool. Highveld winters are famous for frosty early mornings and nights, but afternoon temperatures often top 60°F or 70°F.

It's easy to get fried in the strong African sun, especially in mile-high Johannesburg where the temperature can be deceptively cool. Pack plenty of sunscreen, sunglasses, and a hat. An umbrella comes in handy during those late-afternoon thunderstorms.

If you're heading into the bush, consider packing binoculars, a strong insect repellent like 100% DEET, and sturdy pants that can stand up to the wicked thorns that protect much of the foliage. Avoid garish clothing that will detract from the bush experience of others, and leave behind perfumes, which mask the smell of the bush and also attract insects. Lightweight

hiking books are a good idea if you plan to follow any of South Africa's great trails; otherwise, a sturdy pair of walking shoes should suffice.

Bring an extra pair of eyeglasses or contact lenses in your carry-on luggage, and if you **use medication,** pack enough to last the trip or have your doctor write a prescription using the drug's generic name, because brand names vary from country to country (and you'd need a prescription from a doctor in the country you're visiting). **Don't put prescription drugs or valuables in luggage to be checked,** for it could go astray. To avoid problems with customs officials, carry medications in original packaging. Also don't forget the addresses of offices that handle refunds of lost traveler's checks.

ELECTRICITY

To use your U.S.-purchased electric-powered equipment, **bring a converter and an adapter.** The electrical current in South Africa is 220 volts, 50 cycles alternating current (AC); wall outlets take plugs with three round prongs.

If your appliances are dual-voltage, you'll need only an adapter. Hotels sometimes have 110-volt outlets for low-wattage appliances marked FOR SHAVERS ONLY near the sink; don't use them for high-wattage appliances like blow-dryers. If your

laptop computer is on the old side, carry a converter; new laptops operate equally well on 110 and 220 volts, so you need only an adapter.

LUGGAGE

Free airline baggage allowances depend on the airline, the route, and the class of your ticket; ask in advance. In general, on flights between the United States and foreign destinations, you are entitled to check two bags—neither exceeding 62 inches, or 158 centimeters (length + width + height), or weighing more than 70 pounds (32 kilograms). A third piece may be brought aboard; its total dimensions are generally limited to less than 45 inches (114 centimeters), so it will fit easily under the seat in front of you or in the overhead compartment. In the United States, the FAA gives airlines broad latitude to limit carry-on allowances and tailor them to different aircraft and operational conditions. Charges for excess, oversize, or overweight pieces vary.

If you are flying between two foreign destinations, note that baggage allowances may be determined not by piece but by weight—generally 88 pounds (40 kilograms) in first class, 66 pounds (30 kilograms) in business class, and 44 pounds (20 kilograms) in economy. If your flight between two cities abroad *connects* with

THE GOLD GUIDE / SMART TRAVEL TIPS

your transatlantic or transpacific flight, the piece method still applies.

SAFEGUARDING YOUR LUGGAGE➤ Before leaving home, **itemize your bags' contents** and their worth, and label them with your name, address, and phone number. (If you use your home address, cover it so that potential thieves can't see it.) Inside your bag, **pack a copy of your itinerary.** At check-in, **make sure that your bag is correctly tagged** with the airport's three-letter destination code. If your bags arrive damaged or not at all, file a written report with the airline before leaving the airport.

PASSPORTS AND VISAS

If you don't already have one, **get a passport.** While traveling, **keep one photocopy of the data page** separate from your wallet and leave another copy with someone at home. If you lose your passport, promptly call the nearest embassy or consulate, and the local police; having the data page can speed replacement.

U.S. CITIZENS

All U.S. citizens, even infants, need a valid passport (but no visa) to enter South Africa for stays of up to 90 days. New and renewal application forms are available at any of the 13 U.S. Passport Agency offices and at some post offices and courthouses. Passports are usually mailed within four weeks; allow five weeks or more in spring and

summer. U.S. passports are valid for 10 years.

CANADIANS

You need a valid passport (but no visa) to enter South Africa for stays of up to 90 days. Application forms are available at 28 regional passport offices as well as post offices and travel agencies. Whether for a first or a subsequent passport, you must apply in person. Children under 16 may be included on a parent's passport but must have their own to travel alone. Passports are valid for five years and are usually mailed within two to three weeks of application.

U.K. CITIZENS

Citizens of the United Kingdom need a valid passport (but no visa) to enter South Africa for stays of up to 90 days. Applications for new and renewal passports are available from main post offices as well as at Passport Offices in Belfast, Glasgow, Liverpool, London, Newport, and Peterborough. You may apply in person at all passport offices, or by mail to all except the London office. Children under 16 may travel on an accompanying parent's passport. All passports are valid for 10 years. Allow a month for processing.

PERSONAL SAFETY

Crime is a major problem in South Africa, particularly in large cities, and all visitors should take precautions to protect themselves. Do not walk alone at

night, and exercise caution even during the day. Avoid wearing flashy jewelry, and don't invite attention by wearing an expensive camera around your neck. If you are toting a handbag, wear the strap across your body; even better, wear a money belt.

Carjacking is another problem, with armed bandits often forcing drivers out of their vehicles at traffic lights, in driveways, or by faking an accident. Keep your car doors locked at all times, and leave enough space between you and the vehicle in front so you can pull into another lane if necessary. If you are confronted by an armed assailant, **do not resist.** The countryside is much safer, but bandits do pose a problem in certain areas, most notably along the Wild Coast and in the Transkei, previously a quasi-independent homeland.

S

SENIOR-CITIZEN DISCOUNTS

Senior citizens, known as "pensioners" in South Africa, often receive substantial discounts on admission prices and tickets. Many establishments, however, require a South African pensioner's card, not available to foreign travelers. It doesn't hurt to ask for a discount, though. **Mention your senior-citizen status up front** when booking hotel reservations, not when checking out, and before you're seated in restaurants, not when paying your bill. Note that discounts may be limited to certain menus, days, or hours. When renting a car, **ask about promotional car-rental discounts**—they can net lower costs than your senior-citizen discount.

SHOPPING

Be very picky about what you buy in South Africa. Imported clothes are expensive, and the local versions tend to be shoddily made. Traditional arts and crafts—whether they're made in South Africa or other African countries—are better buys. Keep an eye out for Zulu baskets, Ndebele beaded aprons, Kuba cloth from Zaire, fetishes and masks from West Africa, and Mali mud cloth and wedding blankets. Be wary of cheap imitations, though. "Ebony" carvings often achieve their black luster through the use of shoe polish. Real ebony is heavy, and you can't scratch the black off.

STUDENTS ON THE ROAD

To save money, **look into deals available through student-oriented travel agencies.** To qualify, you'll need to have a bona fide student ID card. Members of international student groups also are eligible. *See* Students *in* Important Contacts A to Z, *above*.

T

TIPPING

Tipping is an integral part of South African

life, and tips are expected for services that you might take for granted at home. Most notable among these is when you fill up with gas; there are no self-service stations, and you should tip the attendant R2–R3. In restaurants, the size of the tip should depend on the quality of service, but 10% is standard, unless, of course, a service charge has already been added to the bill. Give the same percentage to bartenders, taxi drivers, and hairdressers. Hotel porters should receive R1.50–R2 per bag. *See* Chapter 9, Big Game Adventures, for advice on tipping trackers and game rangers.

W

WHEN TO GO

South Africa being in the Southern Hemisphere, its **seasons are reversed**—it's summer in South Africa during the American and European winter.

Peak tourist season is November through March, when hotel prices rise dramatically and making a reservation can be difficult. The situation is exacerbated during major school holidays—especially December 1–January 15, the South African equivalent of summer vacation—when South African families take to the roads in droves. Schools also have two weeks' vacation around Easter and a month in July.

In terms of weather, **the best time to visit Cape Town is from November**

through March. Keep in mind, however, that the shoulder months of October and April can be fabulous and uncrowded. Cape winters (May–August) are cold, windy, and rainy.

Much of the rest of the country receives its rain in the hot summer months. As a result, **summer game viewing in the Eastern Transvaal can be difficult,** with the animals hidden in dense foliage. The best time for seeing animals is during the dry winter season (June–August), when trees have no leaves and the game gathers around the few remaining water sources; prices are lower at this time of year, too, but it can be very cold. **A happy compromise may be spring and autumn** (October and April), the shoulder seasons.

Johannesburg and the highveld enjoy glorious summers, with hot, sunny days broken by afternoon thunderstorms. Winter nights are frosty; days are generally mild and sunny.

KwaZulu-Natal is warm year-round, but summers are steamy and hot, and August sees high winds buffet the coastline. The water along the KwaZulu-Natal coast is warmest in February, but it seldom dips below 65°F at any time of year.

The following are average daily maximum and minimum temperatures for some major cities in South Africa.

THE GOLD GUIDE / SMART TRAVEL TIPS

Climate in South Africa

CAPE TOWN

Jan.	79F	26C	May	68F	20C	Sept.	66F	19C
	61	16		48	9		48	9
Feb.	81F	27C	June	64F	18C	Oct.	70F	21C
	61	16		46	8		52	11
Mar.	77F	25C	July	64F	18C	Nov.	75F	24C
	57	14		45	7		55	13
Apr.	73F	23C	Aug.	64F	18C	Dec.	77F	25C
	54	12		46	8		59	15

DURBAN

Jan.	82F	28C	May	77F	25C	Sept.	73F	23C
	70	21		57	14		59	15
Feb.	82F	28C	June	73F	23C	Oct.	75F	24C
	70	21		52	11		63	17
Mar.	82F	28C	July	73F	23C	Nov.	77F	25C
	68	20		52	11		64	18
Apr.	79F	26C	Aug.	73F	23C	Dec.	81F	27C
	63	17		55	13		68	20

JOHANNESBURG

Jan.	79F	26C	May	66F	19C	Sept.	73F	23C
	59	15		45	7		50	10
Feb.	77F	25C	June	61	16C	Oct.	75F	24C
	57	14		39	4		52	11
Mar.	75F	24C	July	63F	17C	Nov.	75F	24C
	55	13		39	4		55	13
Apr.	70F	21C	Aug.	66F	19C	Dec.	77F	25C
	50	10		43	6		57	14

SKUKUZA (KRUGER NATIONAL PARK)

Jan.	91F	33C	May	82F	28C	Sept.	84F	29C
	70	21		50	10		55	13
Feb.	90F	32C	June	79F	26C	Oct.	86F	30C
	68	20		43	6		61	16
Mar.	88F	31C	July	79F	26C	Nov.	88F	31C
	66	19		43	6		64	18
Apr.	84F	29C	Aug.	81F	27C	Dec.	90F	32C
	59	15		48	9		68	20

1 Destination: South Africa

THE LONG ROAD HOME

I TOOK THE LONG WAY HOME, stealing a year with my wife to drive from Britain to South Africa in an old Land Rover. It was a lifelong dream, a chance to see what lay between Kipling's "great grey-green, greasy Limpopo" and the shifting sands of the Sahara.

When we finally crossed Beit Bridge, the border post between Zimbabwe and South Africa, we felt like we had driven out of Africa into the United States. A smartly dressed immigration official used a computer and bar code to register our entry, and a Kentucky Fried Chicken—the first in a strip of fast-food franchises and gas stations—greeted our arrival in the town of Messina.

As a South African, I shouldn't have been surprised, but months of traveling had altered my perceptions and expectations. This was not the Africa I had recently come to know—of drunk soldiers, officials on the take, and a decaying colonial infrastructure. Yet it *was* undeniably Africa, the stubby tail of a continent linked by history, geography, and blood. And therein lies the great riddle of this country. South Africa occupies a bizarre middle ground, caught between the First World modernity of the West and Africa—poor, addled Africa. And no one's quite sure which way it will go.

At first glance, South Africa seems to be a developed country. Its cities are forests of glass towers, the roads are all immaculately paved; you'll see more cellular phones in Johannesburg than in New York, and its number of BMWs and Mercedeses is probably second only to Germany's.

Yet just a few kilometers from where chlorinated, fluoridated water sparkles out of hotel faucets, black women and children queue for hours at a community's sole tap, waiting their turn to fill large buckets, hoist them onto their heads, and begin the long trek home. The juxtaposition of wealth and poverty is mind-blowing. The majority of South Africa's 31 million blacks live in pockets of poverty where electricity and basic sanitation are luxuries, and entire communities are constructed from corrugated iron, cardboard, and old tires.

Unless you actively seek it, you might not see this side of South Africa, hidden from view by the old Nationalist government. Occasionally, from the windows of a speeding car, you may glimpse a blur of blowing trash, mangy dogs, and ramshackle hovels. You can even take a tour to see black townships like Soweto and Crossroads, once-familiar names from the nightly news. But for the most part, your experience in South Africa will be a white one. Despite a black majority of nearly six to one, the people you meet, the food you eat, and the hotels where you sleep are likely to be products of European culture. Most blacks you encounter will be waiters, porters, game trackers, and bus drivers.

The April 1994 elections were supposed to change all that and to usher in a new era of democracy in South Africa, of black political power and freedom. And as far as the foreign press and most outside observers were concerned, it did. For them, the election was the climax—and the resolution—of the South African problem. They patted themselves on the back for a job well done, packed their bags, and left. Chalk one up for the good guys. The truth is that the election represented only the end of the beginning. While the rest of the world celebrated its good deed, the citizens of South Africa were left grappling with a whole new set of political realities.

For me, nothing captured the nuances of the new political landscape better than a small plate I bought while traveling in the Drakensberg mountains. Crafted by a semiliterate black artist, the plate depicts a group of whites and blacks standing together, but in the corner a large dog is shown attacking an approaching black. The painted caption reads: "Yes, we know that the apartheid is gone between whites and black people, but white people's dogs are still on, because when they see a black man, they want to bite him. I don't know why."

In five heady years, decades of apartheid legislation were scrapped: Gone are the hated pass laws that regulated the movement of blacks; gone is the Group Areas Act that governed where everyone could live; and, with the victory of the African National Congress (ANC) in the 1994 elections, gone is a political system that denied a voice to the country's majority. But no amount of legislation can change the savage bite of three centuries of cultural, social, and economic apartheid—a visceral reaction made up of equal parts habit and fear. You cannot change attitudes overnight.

FOR NELSON MANDELA, president of the new South Africa, the task ahead is Herculean: Bring that dog to heel, and try to dissuade aggrieved blacks from lashing out in retaliation. Whites control the lion's share of the economy, yet they make up only 12% of the population. They own the nicest homes and most of the land, drive the finest cars, and pull down the biggest salaries. Ironically, considering his 27 years of incarceration at their hands, Mandela needs the whites as much as they need him: They look to him to safeguard their interests, while he looks to them to keep Africa's most sophisticated economy humming, creating jobs and attracting foreign investment.

The pressure from blacks, who have had their noses pressed to the shop window for so long, may prove irresistible, however. Before the election, interviews showed that many blacks expected to receive a large house, a car, and good job after an ANC victory. The Reconstruction and Development Program (RDP), the government's project for rebuilding the infrastructure in black communities, did promise to build a million homes in five years, but the program is already far behind schedule. Black unemployment is at a staggering 45%–50%, and millions more make only a minimum wage. In a country where 50% of blacks are illiterate and men and women are routinely burned as witches as part of traditional beliefs, holding up pie charts of foreign investment doesn't do much good. How long before the country must face the ticklish issues of land allocation, of resources, and jobs on a mass scale?

However, the challenges facing the new South Africa cannot be boiled down to a simple issue of rich and poor, black and white. If we learned anything from the country's long years of anguish, it's that *nothing* in South Africa is ever black and white. South Africa is a mosaic of over a dozen black tribes, dominated by the Zulu, Xhosa, and Sotho peoples, each with their own proud, sometimes militaristic, traditions and culture. Throw in 3 million Afrikaners (Dutch descendants also known as Boers), 2 million English-speaking South Africans, 3 million coloreds (people of mixed descent), and a million Indians, and the former Yugoslavia begins to look positively homogeneous.

In KwaZulu–Natal Province, the competing Zulu-dominated Inkatha Freedom Party (IFP) and the ANC have already eschewed the ballot box in favor of spears, knives, and automatic weapons, and hundreds of people have died since the election. You don't have to look far to see the results of such freelance politicking. Africa is littered with the failed examples of countries that started out on the road to democracy, only to end up blindsided by tribalism, ignorance, and greed.

Only a rapid rise in the standard of living can head off an increase in such strife and curb a spiraling crime rate. For better or worse, the government is looking to America for examples of how to integrate blacks into the upper strata of the work force. And, as in America, the solutions have opened a can of worms that seethes with issues of injustice, entitlement, and merit. Affirmative action is the program du jour, and the English-language newspapers are filled with familiar stories of underqualified blacks taking jobs from whites, and of lowering admission standards at elite universities. Among young whites, many of whom voted for democracy, there is a growing sense of despair that no jobs are open to them, and renewed talk of emigration.

Where South Africa differs from America, however, is in its willingness to confront these issues head-on. Race is not the minefield that it is in the United States. There are no sacred cows or sugar-coated code words. South Africans—white, black, Indian, and colored—have lived with issues of race for so long that they speak of it with a candor that makes Americans squirm. This is, after all, a country that has made a cottage industry out of racial discord. South Africa's entire world of arts and letters has drawn its inspiration from the cauldron of conflict. Writers like Mark Mathabane, Alan Paton, Nadine Gordimer, André Brink, and Athol Fugard all won international recognition with their stories of South Africa's racially warped society.

Ironically, the ANC victory in 1994 punctured this high-flying balloon, and South Africa's politically charged culture has lost much of its air. South Africans, so long denied a window on the outside world, have increasingly turned abroad for their cultural fix. Today, the worst exports of American and Australian TV clutter the screens, and you're as likely to see NBA basketball highlights as cricket, the national summer sport. In the townships, blacks espouse black American styles of dress, and one of the largest gangs in the townships around Cape Town is known as the Americans. Chicago Bulls caps are hot items, and American accents flood the airwaves, even when they're pushing South African products. The influx of imports threatens to smother post-apartheid culture in its infancy.

Although its present scale is unprecedented, American cultural influence is nothing new in South Africa. In the '40s and '50s, my mother would religiously head to the cinema each week to see the latest Hollywood offering. The English-speaking population, in particular, has long looked to America and Britain for its cultural connections, never quite prepared to sever its ties in favor of an identity rooted in Africa alone. The Afrikaners, descendants of the first Dutch settlers who arrived in South Africa in 1652, called us *soutpiels,* literally "salt dicks," an obscene pejorative referring to settlers with one foot in Africa and the other in Britain, straddling the sea.

M Y FAMILY GOES BACK eight generations in South Africa. I am African as much as any white in the United States is American. Yet there is no denying that Afrikaners have a stronger tie to the country than

most English South Africans. They have shed more blood for it, and their history is tied to the land. Theirs is the stuff of pioneer legend—of guiding ox-drawn wagons over treacherous mountain passes, of forging a place for themselves out of the hot sands. The Afrikaners are often called the White Tribe of Africa, a hard, resilient people who give no quarter and expect none in return. On an African scale, they are modern-day Zulu who vanquished all the tribes around them, just as Shaka's warriors had done a century before.

The English, by contrast, were traditionally traders and businessmen, out of touch—like any urban dweller—with the rhythms of the land. Perhaps that is why so many English-speaking South Africans emigrated when the heat was on, when South Africa seemed to melt before our very eyes. Our departure stemmed not from some failed sense of belonging but a lack of connectedness. The Boers were tied to the land—they could not, would not leave. We were tied only to our trades.

My family left South Africa—twice. The first time, the ache of homesickness brought us back only to have the country's political woes drive us out again. For thousands of South Africans, the decision to leave was one of the most gut-wrenching of their lives. Even today, we return from visits to South Africa laden with specialties like fish paste and biltong (jerky), not just for the taste but its sheer familiarity, its link to a past that we sloughed off only reluctantly. The former head of the South African Tourism Office in New York confided that she used to run for cover whenever an expatriate wandered in seeking a familiar accent and shared memories.

It *is* hard for South African expatriates to close the door on the past. A few times each year, a day will dawn in New York or London that possesses the clarity of crystal, as if the day had been struck on a tuning fork. In that clarion perfection, the trucks and cars sound different, even the bark of a dog is amplified, and we're pulled back to Johannesburg, a mile high and a million miles away, and the memory of it is almost painful.

During my latest trip back, everyone asked the same question: "Are you going to move back?" I wanted to say yes, that I would return tomorrow. But I am now an American citizen, have an American wife, and have forged too many ties in the United States. If I were to go back, I would find myself toting jars of salsa and brownie mixes with the same religious fervor with which I now carry fish paste. Like so many South Africans, I'm caught in limbo, the *soutpiel* of the '90s, one leg in the New World and the other in the new South Africa.

OR BLACK SOUTH AFRICAN emigrés, the circumstances of their departure were far more dire: Face prison or death, or flee. In Lusaka and Gaborone, thousands of black exiles—members of the ANC—found temporary refuge from the long arm of the South African government. Theirs was not an emigration, but a strategic retreat—a fallback from where they all vowed to return. And return they did, pouring back in the early '90s, their exultant faces telling the story as they emerged blinking from the hold of the aircraft.

I have often wondered what brings us all—white and black—back to this troubled land. It's a beautiful country for sure, "lovely beyond any singing of it," as Alan Paton wrote. But it wasn't for the scenery in the townships that the black exiles returned. What it was, and continues to be, is home, a collective experience we all share. It's strange how so much of what we remember has to do with smells: pap (maize meal) cooking in cast-iron pots, grass fires on the highveld, even the distinctive tang of the dust.

We are all bound up in these memories, and our futures are intertwined whether we like it or not. That is why the radical political fringes seem so frightening: the Pan African Congress with its motto of "One settler, one bullet," and the neo-Nazi AWB (Afrikaner Weerstandsbeweging) with its call for a separate white state.

The 1994 elections in South Africa were nothing less than a miracle, a second chance at redemption. And the architect of that redemption has been Nelson Mandela. Twenty-seven years of prison have left Mandela with the same burning idealism that he displayed at his trial in 1964.

"I have fought against black domination and I have fought against white domination," he told the courtroom. "I have cherished the ideal of a democratic and free society in which all persons live together in harmony and with equal opportunities. It is an ideal which I hope to live for and achieve. But if needs be it is an ideal for which I am prepared to die."

He is a true statesman, perhaps the most imposing leader on the planet. And, ominously, the future of the country rides on shoulders visibly weakened by advancing years and a life of deprivation. No one in South Africa commands the respect and affection of South Africans like Mandela, and what will happen when he is gone is anyone's guess.

Nothing illustrated Mandela's power better than the 1995 Rugby World Cup final between South Africa and New Zealand in Johannesburg. Rugby is a religion among South Africa's whites, and the new government had hinted that the Springbok, the symbol of white rugby, would be replaced after the tournament. So when President Mandela appeared at the final in the green and gold jersey of the Springboks, the crowd went berserk. His was a simple gesture, yet it spoke volumes to the predominantly white fans that packed the stadium. In turn, they responded by singing a Zulu work song and furiously waving the new South African flag. The words of the song welled up from 62,000 voices, the rich, deep sounds resounding through the stadium. It was a particularly African sound, sung by Africans who happened to be white, in appreciation of an African leader who happened to be black. Listening and watching, you could feel the nation shiver at the possibilities.

—by Andrew Barbour

WHAT'S WHERE

Johannesburg
A mile high, South Africa's largest city sprawls across the highveld plateau, its soaring skyscrapers giving way to endless suburbs. Johannesburg is built—literally and figuratively—on gold, and the relentless pursuit of wealth has imbued it with a pulsing

energy. Much of the anti-apartheid struggle was played out in the dusty black townships ringing the city, and a tour of Soweto and the city center will give you a feel for the new South Africa. Johannesburg itself is an unlovely city, with few attractions to hold you long. Arrange a trip down a gold mine, and then take yourself north to Pretoria, the genteel capital of South Africa, or to Sun City, a glittering fantasyland of casinos, golf, water rides, and big-game adventure.

Eastern Transvaal

Classic Africa—the Africa of heat, thorn trees, and big game—unfolds before you in the Eastern Transvaal, a wild and beautiful province abutting Mozambique. The great allure here is game-watching, either in famed Kruger National Park or in an exclusive private reserve. But the province has much more to offer than animals. The Drakensberg mountains split the province in two, dividing the subtropical lowveld from the high interior plateau. Tucked away in these mountains of mists, forests, waterfalls, and panoramic views lie some of South Africa's most luxurious hotels and lodges, as well as beautiful hikes and historic gold-rush towns.

Cape Town and the Peninsula

Capetonians tend to look with pity upon those who don't have the good fortune to live in their Eden. Their attitude is understandable—Cape Town is indeed one of the world's fairest cities. Backed by the familiar shape of Table Mountain, the city presides over a coastline of unsurpassed beauty: of mountains cascading into the sea, miles of beaches, and 17th-century wineries snoozing under giant oaks. Modern South Africa was born here, and the city is filled with historic reminders of its three centuries as the sea link between Europe and the East. Today, Cape Town is home to the country's best museums, restaurants, and hotels.

The Western Cape

This diverse region serves as the weekend playground for Capetonians. The jewel of the province is the Winelands, a stunning collection of jagged mountains, vine-covered slopes, and centuries-old Cape Dutch estates that produce some of the world's finest wine. Farther afield, the Overberg

is a quiet region of farms and beach resorts that ends at Cape Agulhas, the southernmost tip of Africa. The long, lonely coastline is a marvel of nature—rocky mountains dropping sheer to the sea, pristine beaches, and towering dunes. The west coast and Namaqualand is a desolate landscape dotted with tiny fishing villages and isolated diamond mines. For much of the year, it's barren and blisteringly hot, but every spring the region stages one of the most spectacular wildflower shows in the world. Inland, the pretty towns of the Cedarberg mountains and Hantam Plateau make great bases for long hikes and drives.

The Garden Route and Little Karoo

The Garden Route is a beautiful 208-kilometer (130-mile) stretch of coast that takes its name from the region's year-round riot of vegetation. Here, you'll find some of South Africa's most inspiring scenery: forest-cloaked mountains, myriad rivers and streams, and golden beaches backed by thick, indigenous bush. You'll also find Plettenberg Bay, South Africa's glitziest beach resort, and Knysna, a charming town built around an oyster-rich lagoon. The Little Karoo, separated from the coast by a range of mountains, is a semi-arid region famous for its ostrich farms, turn-of-the-century "feather palaces," and the Cango Caves, one of the world's most impressive networks of underground caverns.

Durban and KwaZulu-Natal

Steamy heat, the heady aroma of spices, and a polyglot of English, Indian, and Zulu give the bustling port city of Durban a tropical feel. Some of the country's most popular bathing beaches extend north and south of the city; inland you can tour the battlefields where Boer, Briton, and Zulu struggled for control of the country. The Drakensberg mountains are a breathtaking sanctuary of soaring beauty, crisp air, and some of the country's best hiking. In the far north, Hluhluwe-Umfolozi and several private reserves offer visitors a big-game experience rivaling that of the Eastern Transvaal.

Victoria Falls

Straddling the border between Zimbabwe and Zambia, Victoria Falls deserve their reputation as one of the natural wonders of the world. Dwarfing Niagara, the falls silence visitors with their sheer power and majesty. Equally impressive is the setting, a living reminder of Livingstone's wild Africa: Elephants browse on islands upstream, lions pose as golf-course hazards, and monkeys frolic on hotel lawns. The small settlement of Victoria Falls has become a full-fledged adventure center, where you can experience world-class white-water rafting one day and extraordinary bungee-jumping the next, as well as canoeing on the Zambezi and taking game drives into some of the continent's best game parks.

Big Game Adventures

Nowhere on the continent do wild animals enjoy better protection than in South Africa, and nowhere do you have a better chance of seeing Africa's big game—elephant, black and white rhino, lion, buffalo, cheetah, and leopard. The experience of tracking game in a Land Rover or of taking a wilderness trail with an armed ranger will fill you with awe for the elemental magic of the African bush.

PLEASURES & PASTIMES

Beaches

South Africa has some of the finest beaches on earth—literally hundreds of miles of golden sands, often without a soul on them. The surf is big, though, and dangerous undertows and side washes are common. Beaches in major cities have lifeguards, and helicopters periodically patrol the coastline. Cape Town and the entire Western Cape have glorious beaches, but the water is extremely cold year-round, and wind can be a problem. The water is warmer along the Garden Route, with the best swimming beaches found at Plettenberg Bay. Around Durban and the resorts of KwaZulu–Natal, the water is ideal for swimming, but keep an eye out for the stinging Portuguese man-of-war (bluebottle), particularly when the wind is coming from the east. All major resort beaches in KwaZulu–Natal are protected by shark nets. For truly deserted beaches and warm water, head to Rocktail Bay Lodge in the far north of KwaZulu–Natal.

Bird-Watching

Bring your binoculars if you like birds, because South Africa ranks as one of the finest bird-watching destinations on the planet. Kruger National Park alone has recorded more than 500 different bird species, many of breathtaking beauty. The best time for bird-watching is October–April, when migrants are in residence.

Canoeing and White-Water Rafting

The world's most incredible one-day white-water rafting trip is on the Zambezi River, through the gorges below Victoria Falls. It's an adventure you won't soon forget, and no prior experience is necessary. Another great trip is canoeing on the Zambezi above the Falls, where the river is wide and sluggish, dotted with islands on which hippos and elephants feed.

Cricket

White South Africans are crazy about it—during international matches, you'll often find crowds gathered in front of the windows of electronics stores watching the action. These international competitions, known as test matches, are played against teams from England and former colonies like India, West Indies, and Australia, and a one-day test match is as riveting as anything baseball can produce. The longer five-day test matches involve subtle nuances of strategy that will confound—and probably bore—anyone not born to the game. South Africa's various provinces also compete against each other in the annual Castle Cup competition. A major push is under way to introduce cricket into black communities, but it remains an essentially white sport.

Dining

South Africa won't unseat France anytime soon from its culinary throne. But there are three bright spots that you should keep in mind. The first is the abundance of fresh seafood, from plump Knysna oysters to enormous Mozambiquean prawns to the Cape's own magnificent clawless lobsters, known as crayfish. The second is the country's love affair with Indian cuisine, first brought to South Africa by Indian laborers in the 19th century. Samoosas and curries appear on almost every menu, and the fast food of choice in Durban is bunny chow, a curry-filled loaf of bread. Cape Malay represents South Africa's own cuisine, a centuries-old blend of recipes brought by early Dutch settlers and slaves transported from the Dutch East Indies. Most evident in the Cape, Cape Malay cuisine is characterized by mild, slightly sweet curries and the use of aromatic spices.

Here is a brief glossary of South African cooking terms:

Biltong. An integral part of South African life, biltong is air-dried meat, made of everything from beef to ostrich, kudu, and impala. Unlike jerky, it's not smoked. Strips of meat are dipped in vinegar, rolled in salt and spices, and hung up to dry. You can buy it in strips or ready-cut into bite-size chunks.

Bobotie. A classic Cape Malay dish consisting of delicately spiced ground beef or lamb topped with a savory custard.

Boerewors. Afrikaans for farmer's sausage (say "*boor*-ah-vorse"), this is a coarse, flavorful sausage with a distinctive spiciness. It's a standard feature at *braais* (*see below*).

Braai. Short for *braaivleis* (grill meat), braais are the South African equivalent of a barbecue—and a way of life. South Africans consume enormous amounts of meat, and a braai invariably consists of more than a hamburger thrown on the grill. Expect lamb chops, boerewors (*see above*), chicken, steak, and beer, beer, beer. Sports stadiums even have special beer-and-braai areas where fans can cook up a storm, and some national parks offer visitors the use of free gas grills.

Bredie. Bredie is a slow-cooked stew, made with everything from meat to water lilies.

Sosaties. In this South African version of a kebab, chunks of meat are marinated in Cape Malay spices and grilled.

Pap. Also known as *putu,* pap (pronounced "puhp") is a maize-meal porridge that is a staple for many black South Africans. At braais, you may find it served as an accompaniment to boerewors, topped with stewed tomato and onion.

Peri-Peri. Based on the searing hot piri-piri chile, peri-peri sauce was introduced by Portuguese immigrants from neighboring Mozambique. There are as many recipes as there are uses for this tasty condiment and marinade. Some recipes are tomato-based while others use garlic, olive oil, and brandy. Either way, peri-peri brings out the best in grilled prawns and chicken.

Potjiekos. Another type of stew (pronounced "*poy*-key-koss"), simmered in a three-legged wrought-iron cooking pot. Visitors to private game lodges are likely to sample impala potjiekos at least once during their stay.

Fauna

No trip to South Africa would be complete without animal-watching in one of the country's game parks, public or private. South Africa is one of the few places left in Africa where you have a good chance of seeing the Big Five: lion, leopard, buffalo, black or white rhino, and elephant, as well as a host of other animals including cheetah and wild dog. South Africa may not have the vast herds of East Africa, but it has far more species of animals, and its big-game experience rivals the best on the continent.

Fishing

South Africans are among the most avid anglers in the world. During peak holidays, the long coastline is lined with surf-casters trying for everything from cob to stumpnose, rock cod, shad, blacktail, and moonfish. Trout-fishing in the Natal Midlands and Transvaal Drakensberg is also a major draw. Around Victoria Falls, you have a chance to experience a thrill of a lifetime—tiger fishing. Aptly named, the tiger fish is an incredibly strong fighter, with jaws like a bear trap. They make bass look like wimps.

Flora

The country's floral wealth is astounding. Many small parks in South Africa support more plant species than the entire British Isles. Nowhere is this blessing of nature more evident than in the Cape, home to the smallest and richest of the world's six floral kingdoms. More than 8,500 species of plants grow in the province, of which 5,000 are endemic. Much of the Cape vegetation consists of *fynbos* (pronounced "*feign*-boss"), hardy, thin-leaved plants ideally suited to the Cape environment. Proteas, including the magnificent king protea, are examples of fynbos.

Golf

The success of local heroes like Gary Player, David Frost, and Ernie Els confirms that golf in South Africa has a fervid following. The country has dozens of championship-quality courses, many designed by Gary Player himself. The stretch of coastline extending south from Durban has gone as far as to christen itself "The Golf Coast." Visitors can arrange to play on almost any course in the country, and greens fees are low compared with those in the United States. Don't expect golf carts—a caddy carries your clubs—and the pace of play tends to be faster than it is stateside.

Hiking

Hiking is a major activity in South Africa, and you'll find trails almost everywhere you go. Perhaps the most exciting hikes are the wilderness trails conducted by rangers in Kruger National Park and Hluhluwe–Umfolozi, where hikers sleep out in the bush and spend the day tracking animals, learning about the ecology, and becoming familiar with the ways of the wild. The country's most famous route is the Otter Trail, a five-day hike that runs through pristine wilderness along the coast of the Garden Route. More traditional hikes, ranging in length from a couple of hours to a week, wend through the scenic splendors of the Drakensberg mountains, the Cedarberg mountains in the Cape, or Blyde River Canyon in the Eastern Transvaal.

Reading for Your Trip

History and Politics. For 45 years, South Africa's political and historical writing focused on the issues of apartheid. With the democratic elections of 1994, much of that writing lost its relevance or, at the very least, became badly dated. Since then, a stream of hastily compiled histories has appeared, as have some long-awaited autobiographies and personal accounts. Foremost among these is *Long Walk to Freedom,* by Nelson Mandela. An inspiring account of the triumph of idealism, the book looks back over Mandela's life and also takes a pragmatic view of the difficult political road ahead—it should be required reading for South Africans and visitors alike. *Rainbow People of God* tells the story of another of the heroes of the anti-apartheid movement, Archbishop Desmond Tutu, through his speeches, sermons, and letters from 1976 to 1994.

One pre-apartheid book that survived the transition to democracy is *My Traitor's Heart,* by Rian Malan, an Afrikaner journalist who worked as a crime reporter for a South African newspaper. Notable for its searing honesty, the book apportions blame for South Africa's problems on everyone. Disgusted with the simplistic portrayal of South Africa's agony in black and white terms, Malan reveals the infinite shades of gray that color almost every issue—shades that the election has not washed away.

A classic and very readable study of the San (Bushmen), Elizabeth Marshall Thomas's *The Harmless People* describes the traditional ways of this culture endangered by the intrusion of industrial civilization. *Frontiers: The Epic of South Africa's Creation and the Tragedy of the Xhosa People,* by Noël Mostert, is an immense book covering an immense range of time. It tells of an important, little known chapter in the transition from the old world to modernity hinging as so often it did on a clash of races.

Fiction. South African writers have drawn steadily from the well of racial injustice to produce some of the finest literature of the 20th century. One of the first such novels may also be the best: Alan Paton's *Cry the Beloved Country* (1948). The story of a black father who heads to the city to save his son from execution for murder, the book contains writing of such breathtaking beauty and emotion that you find yourself reading passages again and again. In *Kaffir Boy,* Mark Mathabane paints a stark picture of life under apartheid from a black perspective. The title of the book itself is intended to shock—in South African vernacular, "kaffir" is the stinging equivalent of "nigger." Nadine Gordimer, who won the Nobel Prize for Literature in 1991, is known both for her short stories and her novels, including *July's People,* an account of a black servant who shelters his white employers when South Africa is consumed by civil war. Other major writers include J.M. Coetzee (*The Life and Times of Michael K, Waiting for the Barbarians,* and other books), winner of the Booker Prize; Athol Fugard (*Master Harold . . . and the boys, Boesman and Lena*), South Africa's most famous playwright and, for many years, a voice of sanity in the wilderness of apartheid; and André Brink (*An Act of Terror*).

South African writing has far more to offer than the carcass of apartheid, however. Until the turn of the century, South Africa was a wild frontier of marauding animals, gold rushes, and exotic diseases. No book captures this pioneer excitement better than *Jock of the Bushveld,* by Sir Percy Fitzpatrick. Set in the late 19th century, this classic of South African literature follows the exploits of Jock, a fearless Staffordshire terrier, in the untamed bush of the Eastern Transvaal.

A short-story writer who captured the slow, measured life of Afrikaner farmers and early settlers is Herman Charles Bosman. Laced with humor and irony, Bosman's stories recapture a time in South Africa's history when survival was a triumph and religion a necessary crutch. Bosman's stories are now available in a variety of anthologies.

Lost World of the Kalahari, by Laurens van der Post, mentor to Britain's Prince Charles, is a fascinating mix of fact and fantasy, recalling the author's expedition into the Kalahari Desert after World War II to study the Bushmen (San). The book has a mystical, religious quality befitting a people who live in complete harmony with nature.

Rugby

Although long associated with white Afrikaners, rugby became a unifying force in South Africa during the 1995 Rugby World Cup, when South Africa's "Springboks" beat the New Zealand "All Blacks" in the final, sparking a nationwide celebration among all races. Except for standouts like Chester Williams, rugby is still a largely white sport, and inspires a devotion bordering on religion. In addition to a series of international matches staged each year, the rugby calendar is notable for the Currie Cup, played to decide the best provincial team in the country. In 1995, the "Banana Boys" of KwaZulu–Natal took the trophy.

Surfing

In the cult movie *Endless Summer,* globetrotting surfers discovered the perfect wave at Cape St. Francis, near Port Elizabeth. South Africa *is* one of the major surfing countries in the world, with South Africans figuring prominently on the professional circuit. Durban is probably the center of wave mania, hosting a series of international competitions each year; other great surfing spots include Port Elizabeth and Plettenberg Bay. The beaches around Cape Town and up the West Coast (Elands Bay, particularly) are famous, too, although you need a wetsuit to survive the cold water.

Videos

Most movies about South Africa focus on the tragedy of apartheid. In the latest offering, James Earl Jones follows in the footsteps of Sidney Poitier in a remake of Alan Paton's classic *Cry the Beloved Country* (*see* Reading for Your Trip, *above*). *Cry Freedom,* starring Denzel Washington and Kevin Kline, follows the story of journalist Donald Woods and Steve Biko, a prominent black activist who was murdered in police custody in Port Elizabeth. *A Dry White Season,* with a cameo appearance by Marlon Brando, is another heavy-hitting apartheid drama. *Breaker Morant,* a superbly crafted Australian movie about the Boer War (1899–1902), looks at British military hypocrisy through the eyes of three Australian soldiers on trial for shooting Boer prisoners. *Zulu,* starring Michael Caine, is a jingoistic but gripping retelling of the Battle of Rorke's Drift, during the Zulu War of 1879. The movie spawned several other Zulu movies, among them *Zulu Dawn* and *Shaka Zulu.* The South African movie industry, although in its infancy, has produced one major hit, *The Gods Must be Crazy,* the enchanting story of a San (Bushman) clan in the Kalahari Desert.

Wine and Beer

Forgotten during the years of international sanctions, South African wines are only now getting the recognition they deserve. Visitors to South Africa will be delighted by the quality and range of wines available, including Pinotage, a uniquely South African blend of pinot noir and cinsault grapes (cinsault is known in South Africa as hermitage). Equally appealing are the low, low prices: Expect to pay no more than $10 for a superior bottle of wine. South Africans are big beer drinkers, too—almost in the same league as Australians. South African Breweries (SAB) has a virtual monopoly on beer, and you're likely to drink a fair share of either Castle or Lion lager, pleasant, slightly hoppy beers. Just remember that South African beer has a high, 5% alcohol content.

FODOR'S CHOICE

Special Moments

★ **A sunset picnic atop Table Mountain, Cape Town.** Pack a bottle of chilled Cape wine, some good bread, and cheese, and take the cable car to the summit, where the views stretch forever and sunset never quits. Warning: This is *extremely* romantic.

★ **Walking in wildflowers in spring, Namaqualand.** "The Garden of the Gods" is an apt epithet for the annual wildflower spectacular, when the drab desert hillside explode in a rainbow of colors.

★ **Driving over the Swartberg Pass, Little Karoo.** A precipitous, gravel track wends through the Swartberg mountains dividing the Little Karoo from the vast expanse of the Great Karoo desert. The scale of the landscape is numbing and the views intense, with a barren, clean beauty typical of this part of Africa.

★ **Watching whales at Hermanus.** From July to November, whales make their annual procession up the coast of South Africa. From the cliff-top walkways of Hermanus, you look straight down on these graceful behemoths.

★ **Hiking at Cathedral Peak, Drakensberg mountains.** The awe-inspiring beauty of the mountains around Cathedral Peak makes it a hiker's dream, with dozens of walks and trails that tackle the surrounding peaks or disappear into hidden gorges and valleys. Take a cooling dip in a mountain stream, search for ancient Bushman paintings, or just drink in the unbelievable views.

★ **Wine-tasting and lunch at Vergelegen, Somerset West.** After 300 years, this lovely wine estate is more gracious than ever, encouraging visitors to dally in the formal gardens, relax under the ancient camphor trees, savor the estate wines, and lunch on a veranda overlooking manicured lawns and rose gardens.

★ **A game drive in Sabi Sand Game Reserve.** Few things in life are more thrilling than trailing a pride of lions through the bush in an open Land Rover. And nowhere are you more likely to see this spectacle than in Sabi Sands, the country's foremost private game reserve.

★ **White-water rafting on the Zambezi River, below Victoria Falls.** A white-water trip down one of Africa's great rivers is a nonstop roller-coaster ride of thrills and spills, with the added grandeur and drama of the surrounding landscape.

★ **Sundowners amid the towering dunes at Waenhuiskrans.** Hop on board a Land Rover for a memorable trip through a giant dune field, stopping on the crest of a powdery dune for sundowners overlooking the Indian Ocean.

Dining

★ **Bosman's, Paarl.** Superb Continental cuisine and peerless service make dinner at this elegant Winelands restaurant in the famous Grand Roche Hotel an affair to remember. $$$$

★ **Buitenverwachting, Cape Town.** A gorgeous, historic winery provides the backdrop for the best food in the Cape, a mouthwatering blend of Continental savoir faire and the freshest Cape ingredients. Simply not to be missed. $$$$

★ **Cybele Forest Lodge, Kiepersol.** Traditional five-course dinners, prepared with flair and skill, make a trip to this cozy sanctuary in the hills well worthwhile. $$$$

★ **Linger Longer, Johannesburg.** When goose-liver pâté sets you on cloud nine before you even reach main courses of crisped duckling or boned loin of lamb with garlic and mustard, this is, without a doubt, Johannesburg's finest. $$$$

★ **Royal Grill, Durban.** This lovely restaurant is a standard-bearer of culture in Durban, a reminder of a grander, more gracious age. Delicate Continental cuisine complements its turn-of-the-century elegance. $$$$

★ **Artists' Café, Sabie.** Eccentric, uneven, but ever delightful, this Italian spot hides in an old railway station in the mountain mists of the Eastern Transvaal. $$

★ **Muisbosskerm, Lambert's Bay.** Traditional Afrikaner food and alfresco dining on the beach are the draws of this West Coast favorite, where guests watch seafood being cooked on open fires and in huge black pots. It's rustic, beautiful, and a lot of fun. $$

Lodging

★ **Cellars Hohenort, Cape Town.** Backed by vineyards and beautiful mountains, this tranquil hotel occupies a historic Cape manor and an adjoining wine cellar. The sense of peace and stillness really is magical, and the hotel itself exudes class. $$$$

★ **Hunter's Country House, Plettenberg Bay.** Check into this peaceful lodge and you may never want to check out. Surrounded by thick indigenous forest, it is an oasis of taste and elegance, and a wonderful place to unwind. $$$$

★ **Mount Nelson, Cape Town.** The grande old dame of Cape Town, this historic hotel has been the place to see and be seen in Cape Town for nearly a century. $$$$

★ **Palace of the Lost City, Sun City.** For sheer, unadulterated extravagance, you can't beat this fantastic and fantastical hotel, built to resemble an ancient African palace. No expense has been spared, and the results are breathtaking. $$$$

★ **The Plettenberg, Plettenberg Bay.** Jaw-dropping views of the sea and the sweep of the bay are the main draws of this tasteful hotel in the heart of South Africa's premier beach resort. It's a great place to drop anchor a while. $$$$

★ **Arniston Hotel, Waenhuiskrans.** In a remote Cape Malay fishing village on a coastline of towering dunes and crystal water, this is one of South Africa's great beach retreats. $$$

★ **Simunye Pioneer Settlement, Melmoth.** Nowhere do you come closer to traditional Zulu culture than at this remote luxury lodge. Horses carry you in, and there's no electricity, but it's an unforgettable, magical experience—a rare opportunity to meet South African blacks one-on-one. $$$

Private Game Lodges

★ **Londolozi Tree Camp, Sabi Sands.** This small lodge does almost everything right, from rooms of unmatched elegance to superb cuisine and game-viewing. A class act all the way. $$$$

★ **Singita, Sabi Sands.** Like something from *Out of Africa*, this lodge raises bush luxury to new heights, while delivering one of the best game-viewing experiences on the continent. $$$

★ **Phinda Forest Lodge, Zululand.** Hidden in the green world of a sand forest, this elegant lodge uses glass instead of walls to make you feel like you're living outside. The effect is startling and magnificent, as is the animal-watching and range of activities. $$

★ **Tanda Tula, Timbavati.** You sleep under canvas, but luxury is the name of the game at this super bush camp. Enjoy en suite bathrooms, comfy beds, and tasteful furnishings while listening to lions roar outside your tent. $$

★ **Nottens Bush Camp, Sabi Sands.** Hurricane lanterns, rustic cabins, and down-home hospitality give you a real taste of life in the bush. Don't come for the game, but the sheer thrill of being in Africa. $

★ **Rocktail Bay Lodge, Maputaland.** With miles of empty beaches, giant turtles, dune forests—nothing but nature as far as the eye can see—this tiny lodge is one of the most special places in the country. $

GREAT ITINERARIES

As with any vacation, you have to decide whether to try to see everything or to get to know some areas well at the price of foregoing others. If you want to spend more time with your feet on the ground in any one place, just add or subtract from what's listed below. These itineraries provide guidelines at a glance for how to make your way through South Africa's incredible countryside.

Highlights of South Africa

This itinerary takes you on a whirlwind tour of the very best that South Africa has to offer. You may want to allow for more time to stop and smell the roses, to savor some attractions more than others.

Length: 22 days

Day 1: Arrive in Johannesburg. Take a half-day tour of the city or of Soweto, or just relax after the long flight.

Day 2: Drive four hours to the Eastern Transvaal, via Dullstroom and Long Tom Pass. Spend the night in one of the region's luxury lodges.

Day 3: Explore the escarpment, stopping at Pilgrim's Rest and following the scenic route along the edge of the escarpment past the viewpoints of God's Window, Bourke's Luck Potholes, and Three Rondawels. Descend through Abel Erasmus Pass to the lowveld. Spend the night in one of the lodges near Hazyview or White River.

Day 4: Enter Kruger National Park. Spend the rest of the day searching for game, and overnight in a rest camp.

Day 5: Spend another whole day and night in the park.

Day 6: Leave the park mid-morning and head for one of the private game lodges bordering Kruger. Take an afternoon/evening game drive, followed by dinner around a blazing fire in a traditional reed enclosure.

Day 7: Spend another entire day and night at the private lodge.

Day 8: Leave the lodge mid-morning and return to Johannesburg for the night.

Day 9: Board the luxury Blue Train or the steam-driven Edwardian carriages of Rovos Rail for an overnight ride to Cape Town, passing through the vast Karoo Desert.

Day 10: Arrive in Cape Town mid-morning. Explore the city on foot and take the cable car to the top of Table Mountain.

Day 11: Tour the Cape Peninsula by car, leaving plenty of time to explore Constantia, Cape Point, and Chapman's Peak. Return to the city for the night.

Day 12: Drive to the Winelands, an hour outside Cape Town. Explore the historic town of Stellenbosch, lunch in one of the region's famous restaurants, and sample the wines at several estates. Spend the night in Stellenbosch or Paarl.

Day 13: Leave the Winelands via Somerset West and follow the dramatic coastline through the Overberg to Hermanus. Spend the night here or continue to Cape Agulhas, the southernmost tip of Africa, and overnight at Waenhuiskrans.

Day 14: Drive to Swellendam, and then turn east to Mossel Bay at the start of the Garden Route. Drive through the mountains to Oudtshoorn in the Little Karoo. Visit the Cango Caves and an ostrich farm. Spend the night in Oudtshoorn.

Day 15: Drive over the Swartberg Pass to Prince Albert and return to Oudtshoorn via Meiringspoort.

Day 16: Descend to the coast through the Outeniqua Pass, and head east through George and Wilderness to Knysna. Continue east along the Garden Route to the beach resort of Plettenberg Bay.

Day 17: Drive to Port Elizabeth, stopping at Nature's Valley and the mouth of the Storms River.

Day 18: Fly to Durban. Drive west to the Drakensberg Mountains and spend the night at a mountain lodge.

Day 19: Spend another day and night in the Drakensberg Mountains.

Day 20: Drive six hours back to Johannesburg. Continue to Sun City for the night.

Day 21: Explore Pilanesberg National Park, overnighting either in the park or at Sun City.

Day 22: Return to Johannesburg for your flight home.

Out of Africa

This itinerary emphasizes the wild side of Africa, with plenty of game-viewing, unpopulated wilderness, and wide-open African spaces.

Length: 15 days

Day 1: Arrive in Johannesburg. Catch a connecting flight to Skukuza in Kruger National Park. Overnight at Skukuza.

Day 2: Rent a car to explore Kruger National Park. Overnight at a rest camp.

Day 3: Explore Kruger for another day and night.

Day 4: Leave the park at midday and check in at one of the private lodges bordering Kruger. Go for an afternoon/evening game drive, followed by dinner around a blazing fire in a traditional reed enclosure.

Day 5: Spend another day and night at the private lodge.

Day 6: Drive through Swaziland to Maputaland, in northern KwaZulu–Natal. Spend the night at Rocktail Bay Lodge, an unspoiled paradise for beach walking, swimming, and fishing.

Day 7: Spend another day and night at Rocktail Bay.

Day 8: Drive to the private Phinda Resource Reserve or Hluhluwe-Umfolozi Game Reserve. Arrive before noon to participate in the rest of the day's activities.

Day 9: After the morning game drive, take your car to Durban and catch a flight to Cape Town. Spend the night in Cape Town.

Day 10: Drive north up the West Coast, stopping at West Coast National Park, Langebaan, Eland's Bay, and Lambert's Bay, home of a colony of gannets.

Day 11: Head east to Calvinia on the Hantam Plateau, and then south to Clanwilliam, passing through wild mountain country that hides ancient Bushman paintings and giant cedars. Spend the night in Clanwilliam.

Day 12: Return to Cape Town via the Winelands. Explore the city or tour the peninsula. Overnight in the city.

Day 13: Fly to Victoria Falls in Zimbabwe. Visit the Falls.

Day 14: Go white-water rafting or canoeing on the Zambezi, or take a game drive to Zambezi National Park or Hwange National Park. Overnight in Victoria Falls.

Day 15: Fly to Johannesburg in time for your flight home.

Cape Classic

Length: 16 days

This itinerary concentrates on the Western Cape, the most cultured region of South Africa, where you'll find gracious estates, fine wine, and the country's best restaurants. It also has some of the most dramatic landscape in the country.

Day 1: Fly into Cape Town. Spend the rest of the day recovering from your flight.

Day 2: Tour the city center on foot. Take a ride up Table Mountain.

Day 3: Explore the peninsula, including Kirstenbosch Botanic Gardens, the wineries of Constantia, Cape Point, and Chapman's Peak.

Day 4: Drive up the West Coast, visiting West Coast National Park and Langebaan.

Day 5: Continue up the West Coast to Eland's Bay and Lambert's Bay, before heading inland to Calvinia and Clanwilliam to overnight.

Day 6: Drive south to the Winelands. Tour Stellenbosch, Paarl, and Franschhoek, and taste wine at some of the historic estates. Overnight in the Winelands.

Day 7: Continue your exploration of the Winelands, perhaps venturing over some of the high passes separating the valleys.

Day 8: Leave the Winelands via Somerset West and follow the dramatic coastline through the Overberg to Hermanus. Spend the night here.

Day 9: Continue to Cape Agulhas, the southernmost tip of Africa, perhaps making a detour to visit the historic village of Elim. Overnight at Waenhuiskrans.

Day 10: Drive to Swellendam, and then turn east to Mossel Bay at the start of the Garden Route. Drive through the mountains to Oudtshoorn in the Little Karoo. Spend the night in Oudtshoorn.

Day 11: Visit the Cango Caves and an ostrich farm. Drive over the Swartberg Pass to Prince Albert and return to Oudtshoorn via Meiringspoort.

Day 12: Descend to the coast through the Outeniqua Pass, and head east through George and Wilderness to Knysna. Spend the night at Knysna.

Day 13: Continue east along the Garden Route to the beach resort of Plettenberg Bay.

Day 14: Stop at Nature's Valley and the mouth of the Storms River on your way to Port Elizabeth. From there, continue straight to Shamwari Game Reserve for the night.

Day 15: Spend another day and night at Shamwari.

Day 16: Return to Port Elizabeth, and fly out in time to catch your connecting flight home.

FESTIVALS AND SEASONAL EVENTS

South Africa's top seasonal events are listed below. Contact the South African Tourism Board (Satour) or provincial tourist organizations for exact dates and further information.

SUMMER

EARLY JAN.➤ The 17-day **Cape Coon Carnival** celebrates the New Year in grand style, as thousands of coloreds dressed in bright costumes take to the streets of Cape Town to sing and dance.

AUTUMN

APRIL➤ The **Two Oceans Marathon** draws 8,000 runners for perhaps the most scenic race in the world, a grueling 56-kilometer (35-mile) course that circumnavigates part of the Cape Peninsula, including the dizzying heights of Chapman's Peak Drive.

WINTER

JUNE➤ The **Comrades Marathon** is an agonizing, 80-kilometer (50-mile) double marathon and South Africa's most famous sporting event. The race, run between Pietermaritzburg and Durban, wends through the glorious scenery of the Valley of a Thousand Hills.

JUNE–JULY➤ The **sardine run** occurs every year, when huge shoals of these small fish migrate up the south coast of KwaZulu-Natal. Men, women, and children race into the water, using whatever's at hand—buckets, nets, even clothing—to capture the slippery fish.

JULY➤ The **Durban July** is the country's biggest horse race and fashion love-fest, where women race-goers compete to wear the most outrageous, glamorous attire.

JULY➤ The **Durban Tattoo,** a 17-year tradition, is a military pageant filled with music, color, pomp, and ceremony.

JULY➤ The **Gunston 500 Surfing Championships** in Durban draw the world's best to compete in the South African leg of the international surfing circuit.

JULY➤ The **National Arts Festival** in Grahamstown is the country's most famous celebration of the arts, a wild and wacky 10-day extravaganza showcasing the best of South African theater, film, dance, music, and art.

SPRING

AUG.–SEPT.➤ The **wildflowers of Namaqualand and the West Coast** are one of nature's great spectacles, with bright spring blooms emerging in their millions from the seemingly barren semidesert. Several of the region's towns hold major flower festivals.

AUG.–NOV.➤ The annual **whale migration** along the Western Cape coast of the Overberg brings southern right whales, humpback whales, and Bryde's whales close to shore, giving even landlubbers a great view of these graceful leviathans.

OCTOBER➤ Purple **jacaranda blossoms** blanket the pleasant captial city of Pretoria, whose quiet streets are lined with these elegant trees.

2 Johannesburg

Vast in size and in human ambition, Johannesburg is built on gold, and the relentless pursuit of wealth has imbued it with a pulsing energy. Much of the country's anti-apartheid struggle was played out in the dusty black townships ringing the city, and a tour of Soweto and the city center will give you a feel for the new South Africa. Arrange a trip down a gold mine, then take yourself north to Pretoria, the genteel capital of South Africa, or to Sun City, a glittering fantasyland of casinos, golf, water rides, and big-game adventure.

JOHANNESBURG IS THE LARGEST CITY in sub-Saharan Africa—a modern, bustling metropolis that powers the country's economy. Home to more than 6 million people, it sprawls across the featureless plains of the mile-high highveld, spawning endless suburbs that threaten even Pretoria, more than 30 miles distant. It feels like Los Angeles in the veld, and most visitors leave almost as quickly as they arrive.

Jo'burg, as it is known, owes its existence to vast underground riches. Gold was discovered here in 1886 by an Australian, George Harrison, who stumbled upon a surface deposit while prospecting on the Witwatersrand (White Water Ridge). Unknown to him, he was standing atop the world's richest gold reef, and his discovery sparked a gold rush unrivaled in history. Gold remains the lifeblood of Johannesburg, and the mines that ring the city now delve more than 2 miles into the earth to extract the precious yellow metal.

It's difficult to overstate the impact of these goldfields on the development of Johannesburg and modern South Africa. In 1899, Britain engineered a war with the Boer Republics just to get its hands on them, and the entire cultural and political fabric of black South Africa has been colored by gold. Over the course of the last century, millions of blacks from South Africa, Mozambique, Zimbabwe, and Botswana have made the long journey to I'Goli (a Zulu name meaning "the place of gold") to work in the mines. Forced to live in all-male hostels far from their families, they developed a distinct mine culture that they took with them when they returned to their villages. Go to a wedding in a remote corner of Zululand, and you'll notice that traditional dancers keep their arms and legs close to their bodies, a dance style that developed from necessity in mining hostels' narrow, overcrowded corridors.

More than anything else, gold has brought about the urbanization—and politicization—of the black population. People follow money, and Johannesburg became a magnet for hundreds of thousands of unemployed rural blacks. By the start of World War II, huge squatter camps—the precursors of townships like Soweto (an abbreviation for "southwestern townships")—had sprouted on the periphery of the city. By the 1960s, township poverty and overcrowding had become the kindling on which South Africa's hated apartheid legislation poured petrol. All that was needed was a match. In June 1976, police fired on Soweto students protesting the use of Afrikaans in schools, and the townships burst into flame. More than 1,000 people lost their lives in the year of rioting that followed. Ten years later the townships were ungovernable, and the country began its slow burn toward civil war.

Now, under South Africa's first democratic government, blacks continue to pour into the city. And like the first miners who rushed to stake their claims here, they have gold fever. Everyone, it seems, is out to make a buck. The city pumps with an invisible energy, an explosive combination of need, greed, and ambition. It's no surprise that Johannesburg moves faster than any city on the continent.

Very little of the city's past—white or black—has survived this single-minded pursuit of money. Johannesburg builds constantly, paving over the unsightly cracks of history. Even the old mine tailings, the very symbols of the city's raison d'être, are rapidly disappearing. New methods for extracting gold have made it profitable to reprocess these familiar yellow mountains. From a traditional traveler's perspective,

Johannesburg is a bust, which is why most visitors spend a night here after their flight then head straight to more scenic locales.

It would be a mistake to pass through Johannesburg, though, and not tour Soweto or see the city center, for both provide a glimpse of the country's future. Downtown, amid the concrete canyons of the country's financial heart, a new South Africa is emerging, one previously hidden in the townships: The sidewalks are suddenly alive with vendors hawking vegetables, young women ladling out *pap* (maize meal) and sauce, and herbalists dispensing *muti* (traditional medicine). It's black, it's different, and it's here to stay.

While sidewalk markets are bustling, "white flight" has knocked the city center into an economic tailspin. More and more businesses are relocating to the affluent northern suburbs, most notably Sandton. The trend bears an uncanny resemblance to the collapse of America's inner cities. The major rap against the city center is violent crime, and there *is* a good chance of being mugged, or worse. Do what you have to—travel in a group, hire a bodyguard, or just don't carry any valuables—but at least take a look downtown. If you restrict yourself to the affluent northern suburbs, you might as well have booked a flight to New Jersey.

Indeed, the northern suburbs look as if they belong anywhere *but* Africa. Most of the blacks you're likely to see are gardeners or uniformed maids. Shopping malls go out of their way to make customers feel like they're in Florence or Paris. Most disturbing of all, however, is the pervasive sense of fear. Appalled by the surge in black crime, whites live behind great walls, protected by 24-hour security services and the most sophisticated defense systems outside the Pentagon.

If the city beyond the gates seems fraught with danger, life within the suburban *laager* is good. Johannesburg's glorious climate seldom disappoints, and many whites structure their days around the pool and the *braai* (barbecue). It's a typically suburban lifestyle, forgettable in its ordinariness and enviable for its sense of contentment. To someone passing through, however, it's a closed world of limited interest. If you do decide to spend time in the city, you're better off focusing on the events and revolutions that have kept South Africa on the front page of newspapers for decades: Take a tour through Soweto, cruise the city center, and descend into a gold mine. Once you've done that, go be a tourist somewhere beautiful.

Less than an hour north of Johannesburg lies Pretoria, the country's pleasant capital. Once a bastion of hard-line Afrikanerdom, the city is now home to President Mandela, and a refreshing cosmopolitan breeze blows through the streets. In addition to several historic buildings, Pretoria is most famous for its jacaranda trees, whose purple blossoms blanket the city in September and October. Like Johannesburg, Pretoria lies in the tiny province of Gauteng ("how-teng"), a conurbation on the highveld, 6,000 feet above sea level. You have to travel 90 minutes beyond the borders of Gauteng to reach Sun City, an entertainment and gambling resort set amid the arid beauty of North West Province. Here you'll find Las Vegas–style hotels, championship golf courses, water rides, as well as the Pilanesberg National Park, the third-largest national park in South Africa.

Caution: For information on personal safety, *see* the Gold Guide.

EXPLORING

Numbers in the margin correspond to points of interest on the Johannesburg map.

Johannesburg is not a city you explore in the same way that you might explore Rome or London—it sprawls for miles and miles. Sites are too few and far between to justify a connect-the-dots walking or driving tour.

❶ A great place to get a feel for the city's layout is the **Top of Africa** observation deck atop the downtown Carlton Centre. It may not be the World Trade Center—the building is only 50 stories high—but it does offer a 360-degree view of the city, including its trademark mine dumps. Notice the absence of high-rise buildings to the south: The warren of mining tunnels has made the ground too unstable to support skyscrapers. A tacky bar and restaurant serves drinks and light meals. *Carlton Centre, Main St.,* ☎ *011/331–6608.* ☛ *R6.50 adults, R3 children.* ☉ *Daily 9 AM–11:30 PM.*

Very few buildings of historical value have survived Johannesburg's headlong rush for profit. Even so, you can see a number of its landmark structures if you walk or drive from the Carlton Centre down Commissioner Street to Sauer Street, then return via Market Street. This route takes you past the 1896 **Victory House,** the Edwardian-style **Standard** and **First National** banks, the Florentine palace–inspired **City Library,** and the grandiose 1913 **City Hall.**

★ ❷ The **Johannesburg Art Gallery** stands north of the Carlton Centre in a superb site on Joubert Park. The museum is a must on any itinerary, if only for its extensive South African collection. Such distinguished South African artists as Pierneef, Gerard Sekoto, and Willie Bester are well represented, and there are stupendous examples of African beadwork and wood sculpture. The gallery also houses a fine collection of 19th- and 20th-century English and French painting, modern sculpture, and 17th-century Dutch works. *Joubert Park,* ☎ *011/725–3130.* ☛ *Free.* ☉ *Tues.–Sun. 10–5.*

Diagonal Street, which angles across the city grid between Market and Jeppe streets, is the most interesting avenue in central Johannesburg. Old tin-roofed shops with rickety wood balconies house Indian merchants touting everything from spices to colorful sari silks.

★ ❸ While you're on Diagonal Street, be sure to stop in at the **KwaZulu Muti Shop,** also known grandly as the Museum of Man and Science. Muti is the Zulu word for medicine, the various natural cures and potions used by *sangomas* (traditional healers) to treat disease. Baboon skulls, ostrich feet, and animal skins hang from the ceiling, which is so low you have to crouch. Dried monkeys, their faces frozen in a death scream, stare fixedly from the walls; behind the counter stand bottles of colorful elixirs and baskets brimming with herbs, bark, and seed pods. In the semidarkness at the rear of the shop, a wizened old man pounds out a slow beat with a wood mortar and pestle. It's a fascinating place—an African place—that is simultaneously entrancing and repulsive. *Corner of Diagonal and President Sts.,* ☎ *011/836–4470.* ☉ *Weekdays 7:30–5, Sat. 7:30–1.*

It's a major culture shock to duck outside the muti shop and look straight into the flawless glitter of an all-glass skyscraper. This high-rise (11 Diagonal St.) was designed by Chicago architect Helmut Jahn and is shaped like a beautifully faceted diamond. The juxtaposition is mind-blow-

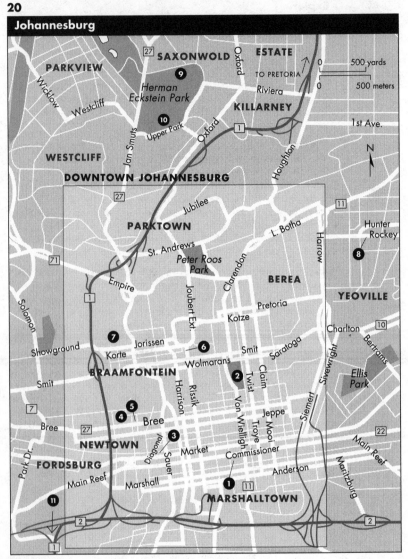

Gertrude Posel
Gallery, **7**

Gold-Mining
Statue, **6**

Gold Reef City, **11**

Johannesburg Art
Gallery, **2**

Johannesburg
Zoo, **10**

KwaZulu Muti
Shop, **3**

Market Theatre
Complex, **5**

Museum Africa, **4**

Rockey Street, **8**

South African
National Museum of
Military History, **9**

Top of Africa, **1**

ing, symbolic of the challenges facing a country with one foot in the first world and the other in the third.

 ④ A few blocks west, in the downtown's semi-industrial section of Newtown, stands **Museum Africa.** This is the first major museum to attempt to give credit to the blacks' contributions to the development of the city. An excellent exhibit traces the impact of gold on the lives of the black population, from the miners forced to live in male-only hostels to the burgeoning townships with their squatter camps, *shebeens* (bars), and vibrant township jazz. Another exhibit retraces the fight for democracy and the run-up to the elections that gave Nelson Mandela the presidency. The museum is also home to a first-rate display of ancient San (Bushmen) rock art. Upstairs, the Bensusan Museum examines the art and technology of cameras with fun hands-on exhibits. *121 Bree St., Newtown,* ☎ *011/833–5636.* ☞ *R2 adults, R1 children.* ☼ *Tues.–Sun. 9–5.*

⑤ Adjacent to Museum Africa is the **Market Theatre complex** (corner of Bree and Wolhuter Sts., Newtown), an interesting collection of alternative shops, theaters, galleries, bars, and coffee houses.

⑥ For a tasteful reminder of Johannesburg's history, head north to Braamfontein, on the ridge overlooking the city center. The **Gold-Mining Statue** (corner of Rissik and De Korte Sts., Braamfontein) is one of the most famous symbols of the city. It depicts three men—two black and one white—drilling a rock face. It's a beautifully balanced sculpture that captures the physical effort of mining for gold deep underground. The bronze, by sculptor David McGregor, was a gift from the Transvaal and Orange Free State Chambers of Mines.

⑦ Also in Braamfontein is the **Gertrude Posel Gallery,** hidden away in an institutional building at the University of Witwatersrand. It houses the first-rate Standard Bank Collection of African Art. Much of the work, particularly the beadwork, comes from southern Africa, but the collection also includes masks, headrests, pots, drums, and initiation statues from West Africa, as well as Kuba cloth from Zaire. *Campus level, Senate House, University of Witwatersrand, Jorissen St.,* ☎ *011/716– 3891.* ☞ *Free.* ☼ *Tues.–Fri. 10–4.*

Northern Suburbs

⑧ The northern suburbs are by and large forgettable—like suburbs anywhere in the world. A noteworthy exception is **Rockey Street** in Yeoville, on the northern fringe of the city center. Rockey Street is a slice of New York's East Village in Africa. Hard-rock clubs and ethnic eateries rub shoulders with tattoo parlors, secondhand bookshops, lingerie and leather stores, and boutiques selling African beads. Out on the street, white youths with pink mohawks and nose rings hang out with blacks dressed in the latest fashions. Say what you will, but it's one of the few places where black and white mix easily in the city.

⑨ Farther into the northern suburbs, in Saxonwold, the excellent **South African National Museum of Military History** examines South Africa's role in the major wars of the 20th century, with an emphasis on World War II. On display are Hurricane and Messerschmidt fighters, various tanks of English and American manufacture, and a wide array of artillery. Among the most interesting exhibits are the modern armaments South Africa used in its war against the Cuban-backed Angolan army during the 1980s, including highly advanced artillery, French-built Mirage fighters, and Russian tanks stolen by the South Africans from a ship en route to Angola. *20 Erlswold Way,* ☎ *011/646–5513.* ☞ *R4 adults, R1 children.* ☼ *Daily 9–4:30.*

⑩ The war museum stands in the northeast corner of the **Johannesburg Zoo,** a pleasant but unremarkable place that can be swamped with schoolchildren during the week. *Upper Park Rd., Forest Town,* ☎ *011/682–3418.* ☛ *R8 adults, R5 children.* ⊙ *Daily 8:30–5:30.*

South of Town

⑪ **Gold Reef City,** 15 kilometers (9 miles) south of downtown, is the most popular tourist attraction in the city. Go figure. The place is a rinky-dink theme park that transforms a bona fide part of Johannesburg's gold-mining history into banal kiddie rides and trite entertainments. Tucked away amid all the dross are some original 19th-century mining cottages and a couple of interesting museums, but it's all difficult to take seriously. The only redeeming aspects of a visit are going down an old gold mine, seeing molten gold being poured, and watching a gum-boot dance, a riveting hostel dance developed by black miners. *Northern Pkwy., off N1, Ormonde,* ☎ *011/496–1600.* ☛ *R20 including all rides and shows; mine tour R14 extra.* ⊙ *Tues.–Sun. 9:30–5. Dancing at 11:30 and 3; mine tours every 30 mins 10–5.*

Off the Beaten Path

Cullinan Diamond Mine, 48 kilometers (30 miles) east of Pretoria, is a fully operational mine that is three times the size of the famous hole at Kimberley. The 3,106-carat Cullinan diamond was unearthed here in 1905, a giant crystal that was later cut into several smaller stones including the Star of Africa. Machinery extracts 12 tons of kimberlite and 6,000 carats of diamonds each day. About 80% of these are for industrial use, but the rest are high-grade gems. On the mine's one daily tour you'll see the big hole, watch a 12-minute video, pass through a typical mine security check, view replicas of the most famous diamonds, and travel through a mock-up of an underground tunnel. *Premier Diamond Tours, 95 Oak Ave., Cullinan,* ☎ *01213/4–0081. No children under 10.* ☛ *R18. Tours daily at 10:30.*

Lion Park may be worth a visit if you've been to the game reserves and failed to see a big cat, or if you simply don't have time to view lions in their natural element. Otherwise, it's a bit of a bust. The park, which consists of a series of enclosures of a few acres each, contains dozens of lions who lie around all day waiting for feeding time. You drive yourself through the park, and the only excitement comes when the lions decide to chew on your tires. The highlight of a visit is the petting area, where you can pick up lion cubs—and pay R2 for each snapshot you take. A game farm stocked with herd animals like zebra and wildebeest surrounds the lion enclosure. *Rietvallei Rd., Honeydew,* ☎ *011/460–1814.* ☛ *R20 per person.* ⊙ *Daily 8–4:30.*

The **Lippizaner Centre,** midway between Johannesburg and Pretoria, is home to white Lippizaner stallions, a distinguished breed of horses with a centuries-old lineage. The horses are trained in the classical Spanish riding style, and during their weekly shows perform a complex ballet of exercises to the strains of Verdi, Mozart, and Handel. *Dahlia Rd., Kyalami,* ☎ *011/702–2103.* ☛ *R20 adults, R10 children. Performances Sun. at 11. Closed mid-Oct.–mid-Nov.*

SHOPPING

Johannesburg is the best place in the country to buy quality African art, whether it's tribal fetishes from Central Africa or oil paintings by early white settlers. Dozens of galleries and curio shops are scattered throughout the city, often selling the same goods at widely different prices. Newtown Market Africa, which you should consider seeing before making purchases elsewhere, has the best prices (*see* Markets, *below*).

And if you thought America had a thing for malls, wait until you see Jo'burg's northern suburbs. Blink and another mall has gone up. Even more astonishing is how exclusive they are, lined with chi chi shops selling the latest from Italy, France, and the States—at twice the price you would pay at home. In addition to these boutiques, most malls feature department stores like Edgars and Woolworth's, as well as cinemas and restaurants.

Malls

The major mall in Johannesburg is **Sandton City** (corner of Sandton Dr. and Rivonia Rd.), with hundreds of stores and a confusing layout that guarantees you'll get lost for days. The wing of shops leading from the mall to the Sandton Sun Hotel has some worthwhile African art galleries. Adjoining Sandton City is **Sandton Square** (5th St.), built to resemble an Italian palazzo, complete with expensive Italian shops, bakeries, and restaurants. Closer to the city, **Hyde Park Mall** (Jan Smuts Ave., Hyde Park, ☎ 011/788–4750) is the city's most upscale shopping center, where fashion victims come to sip cappuccino and browse in Exclusive Books, a branch of the country's best chain of book stores. Rosebank is a happening suburb focused on a conglomeration of five shopping centers (Cradock St., between Biermann Ave. and Baker St.). The great plus about **Rosebank Mall** is that you can actually walk and sit outside—something of a novelty in security-conscious Johannesburg. This is the place to come for casual al fresco lunches at one of the area's many cafés and restaurants. Downtown, adjoining the Carlton Hotel, the **Carlton Centre** (corner of Commissioner and von Weilligh Sts.) is home to 200 stores. It has little to offer the foreign visitor, though, except a wonderful West African clothing boutique, Badia Clothing (*below*).

Markets

Newtown Market Africa, a flea market held every Saturday in front of the Market Theatre, is the best place in town for African art and curios at low, low prices. Vendors from Cameroon, Nigeria, and Zaire come here to sell masks, fetishes, traditional wood pillows, Kuba raffia cloth, and Mali blankets. Bargain hard and you should be able to get vendors to knock a third off the price. *Wolhuter St., between Bree and Jeppe Sts., no ☎. ⊙ Sat. 9–4.*

Rosebank's Rooftop Fleamarket features a lot of locally made crafts, kitsch, bread, cheese, biltong (jerky), and mass-produced African curios. *Rosebank Mall, 50 Bath Ave., Rosebank, ☎ 011/788–5530. ⊙ Sun. 9–5.*

Specialty Stores

AFRICAN ART

Abyssinia Art Gallery, in the Market Theatre complex, has an excellent collection of masks, glass beads, Ethiopian silver crosses, carvings, and spears from various African tribes. Prices are decent. *Shop 8, Market Theatre complex, corner of Wolhuter and Bree Sts., Newtown, ☎ 011/834–2301. ⊙ Mon.–Sat. 9–5.*

Everard Read Gallery is one of the largest privately owned galleries in the world. It acts as agent for several important South African artists, as well as a number of international contemporary artists. The gallery specializes in wildlife paintings and sculpture. *6 Jellicoe Ave., Rosebank, ☎ 011/788–4805. ⊙ Mon.–Sat. 9–6.*

Kim Sacks Gallery, in a lovely old home, has one of the finest collections of authentic African art in Johannesburg. Displayed throughout its sunny rooms are Zairian raffia cloth, Mali mud cloth, Zulu telephone-wire baskets, and an excellent collection of original masks and carvings from across the continent. Unusual wood sculptures, ceramics, and prints by outstanding South African artists are also for sale. Pieces are labeled by country and tribe of origin; when possible, they are also dated. Prices are high. *Corner of Frances St. and Cavendish Rd., Bellevue,* ☎ *011/648–6107.* ⊙ *Mon., Tues., Thurs. 9–5 and 5:30–8:30; Wed. and Fri. 9–5; Sat. 10–3.*

Master Weavers sells locally woven rugs and tapestries, most done in muted colors and depicting people or scenes from nature. Prices are high. *Sandton City, Sandton,* ☎ *011/884–2517.* ⊙ *Mon.–Sat. 9–5.*

Rural Craft has a good collection of Xhosa and Ndebele beadwork, including wedding aprons and jewelry. The shop also sells fabrics made by rural women in Lesotho and Swaziland. *Tyrwhitt Mall, 31 Tyrwhitt Ave., Rosebank,* ☎ *011/880–9651.* ⊙ *Weekdays 8:30–4:30, Sat. 8:30–2:30.*

Soweto Art Gallery, tucked away in three small rooms in a shabby downtown office block, is a no-nonsense shop where the paintings are mostly unframed or stacked against the wall. Elegant it's not, but the gallery features the works of some very talented African artists from townships all over the Johannesburg area. Oils, lino cuts, and sculpture are all represented. *34 Harrison St., Suite 34, 2nd Floor, Johannesburg,* ☎ *011/836–0252.* ⊙ *Weekdays 8–6, Sat. 8–1.*

Totem Gallery specializes in artifacts from West and Central Africa, including Kuba cloth from Zaire, Dogon doors from Mali, glass beads, masks from Burkina Faso, and hand-painted barbershop signs. Some pieces come with detailed descriptions of their history. Prices are high. *Sandton City,* ☎ *011/884–6300.* ⊙ *Mon.–Sat. 9–5:30; Hyde Park,* ☎ *011/447–5005.* ⊙ *Weekdays 9–5, Sat. 9–4.*

AFRICAN CLOTHING

Badia Clothing is the shop to visit for high-quality, traditional West African clothing at reasonable prices. These colorful garments are imported from countries like Cameroon, Nigeria, and Senegal. In addition, the store has a small collection of hats, fabrics, and leather slippers from Morocco. *Carlton Centre, Commissioner St., Johannesburg Central,* ☎ *011/331–3813.* ⊙ *Weekdays 9–5:30, Sat. 9–3.*

BOOKS

Exclusive Books (Sandton City, ☎ 011/883–1070; Hyde Park Mall, ☎ 011/788–0724) is the best chain of bookstores in the country, with a great selection of African literature, history, travel, and culture.

GOLD

Krugerrands are among the most famous gold coins minted today. Bearing the image of President Kruger on one side and a springbok on the other, they lost some of their luster during the apartheid years, when they were banned internationally. Krugerrands are sold individually or in sets containing coins of one ounce, ½ ounce, ¼ ounce, and ¹⁄₁₀ ounce of pure gold. You can buy Krugerrands through most banks in the city, but several branches of First National Bank sell them over the counter. The most convenient branches are in Sandton City, Carlton Centre, and Rosebank.

SPORTS AND THE OUTDOORS

Participant Sports

Golf

Johannesburg's finest golf courses are open to foreign visitors, although weekend play tends to be restricted to members only. Expect to pay R70–R100 for a round. The century-old **Royal Johannesburg Golf Club** (Fairway Ave., Linksfield North, ☎ 011/640–3021) has two courses: The East Course is the more famous of the two, and has hosted the South African Open seven times. The **Wanderers Golf Club** (Rudd Rd., Illovo, ☎ 011/447–3311), permanent host of the South African P.G.A. Championship, is a tough course, well bunkered and with plenty of water on the early holes; it demands exacting iron shots to its small greens. **Glendower Club** (Marais Rd., Bedfordview, ☎ 011/453–1013) lies in a nature reserve. The recent addition of more water hazards and extra length makes this one of the most challenging courses in the country. You can rent clubs at Royal Johannesburg and at **Roger Manning Golf Shop** (Huddle Park Golf Course, adjoining Royal Johannesburg, Linksfield North, ☎ 011/640–3065).

Spectator Sports

Cricket

The **Wanderers' Club** (21 North St., Illovo, ☎ 011/788–5010) is the country's premier cricket ground, and the site of many of the international contests between South Africa and touring sides from England and its former colonies.

Rugby

South Africa's showcase rugby stadium is **Ellis Park** (Staib St., Doornfontein, ☎ 011/42–8644), where the Springboks beat New Zealand's All Blacks to win the 1995 World Cup. It's a magnificent stadium, capable of seating nearly 65,000 people. It's home to the Transvaal rugby team, which competes against other provincial sides in the annual Bankfin Currie Cup competition.

DINING

By Peter Noel-Barham

Unlike Cape Town, Johannesburg has no cuisine of its own. What it does have is an array of first-class restaurants, including some of the country's finest French and Italian eateries. Surprisingly, seafood in Jo'burg restaurants is often better than what you find down at the coast. Most restaurants lie in the northern suburbs and are accessible only by car.

For a description of South African culinary terms, *see* Pleasures & Pastimes *in* Chapter 1. For price ranges, *see* Chart 1 *in* On the Road with Fodor's.

Downtown

$$$ **Gramadoelas at the Market Theatre.** A cosmopolitan clientele of diplo-
★ mats, playwrights, and actors frequents this attractive restaurant that specializes in traditional South African cuisine. The decor is a fascinating jumble of Africana, including huge Cape Dutch canvases and rustic oil lamps. Initially focused on Cape Malay dishes, the restaurant has widened its scope to include traditional African dishes like mopani worms, stewed dried caterpillars served with *peri-peri* (Por-

tuguese chili sauce). If a starter of worms makes you wriggle, opt for *snoek sambal* with *moskonfyt,* a smoked fish pâté served with a syrup made from the residue of wine-pressed grapes. Main courses include traditional *bobotie* (spiced minced lamb with a custard topping), *sosaties* (curried kebabs), and *tomato bredie* (tomato-based stew). For dessert, don't miss Cape *melktert* (spiced custard tart) or delicious malva pudding, made with apricot jam and vinegar topped with cream and sugar. ✕ *Market Theatre, Wolhuter St., Newtown,* ☎ *011/838–6960. Reservations advised. AE, DC, MC, V. Closed Sun.*

$$ Leipoldt's. Named after the writer who first celebrated the national cuisine, this restaurant focuses on traditional South African fare, much of which traces its origins to the Cape Malay community. More than 60 dishes are served buffet-style, and you can try as many as you'd like. Typical offerings are tomato bredie (tomato-based stew), sosaties (marinated meat brochettes), bobotie (spicy minced mutton with a custard topping), and *boerewors* (a coarse farmer's sausage). For dessert, try syrupy *koeksisters* (a super-sweet doughnut) or melktert (custard tart). Faded historic photographs and animal heads on the walls provide South African ambience. ✕ *94 Juta St., Braamfontein,* ☎ *011/339–2765. Reservations advised. AE, DC, MC, V. Closed Sun. No lunch Sat.*

$ Chon Hing. Tucked away in a side street and looking a little world-weary, this Chinese restaurant is still one of the best kept secrets of the cognoscenti. No cloths mask the Formica tabletops, and the chairs are upholstered in red plastic, but in a place like this it's the food that keeps people coming back again and again. You can order one of the set menus, but you're better off selecting dishes from the two pages at the back of the menu. Good choices are beef flank served with noodles or rice, prawns stuffed with minced chicken, and calamari in black bean sauce. For a real treat, order steamed rock cod. ✕ *26 Alexander St., at John Vorster Sq., Ferreirastown,* ☎ *011/83–3206. BYOB. Reservations advised. AE, DC, MC, V.*

Northern Suburbs

$$$$ Daruma. Long regarded as *the* Japanese restaurant in town, Daruma continues to draw crowds despite its high prices. You can sit at the sushi bar or opt for the small Shogun-Noma room, divided into private dining areas by wood-and-paper screens. The menu covers the full range of Japanese cuisine, from sashimi to soba noodles. You can also order various set menus. The ingredients are absolutely fresh and the presentation superb. ✕ *Corner of Corlett Dr. and Atholl Oaklands Rd., Melrose North,* ☎ *011/880–2548. Reservations required. AE, DC, MC, V. No lunch Sun. Closed Mon.*

$$$$ Linger Longer. Ever since the annual "Top Ten" restaurant awards were
★ initiated a decade ago, this restaurant has stood among the top three. Set in the spacious grounds of a former home in Wierda Valley, it has an air of gracious elegance. Some rooms have a Wedgwood-like quality—deep green walls with pale trim and striped curtains—while others glow in salmon pink. A goose-liver pâté appetizer is one of the dishes that made Linger Longer famous. Excellent main courses include crisped duckling in ginger and lemon-grass sauce, and boned loin of lamb with garlic, parsley, and coarse-grain mustard. Among the imaginative desserts, crepes filled with warm cream cheese, vanilla, and brandied raisins are particularly good. ✕ *58 Wierda Rd., Wierda Valley,* ☎ *011/884–0465. Reservations advised. AE, DC, MC, V. Closed Sun. No lunch Sat.*

$$$$ Ma Cuisine. In this French restaurant, since chef-patron Jorn Pless shapes a *table d'hôte* around what he buys fresh at the market each

day, you don't know what you're going to eat until you sit down—
and even then you have no choices. If that smacks of culinary roulette,
rest assured that almost everyone comes out a winner. Most diners find
that they haven't tasted anything as exquisite as Pless's well-balanced
meals in years, and he is never short of people willing to place their
gastronomic enjoyment in his hands—among them Queen Elizabeth
II. Lunch is a three-course affair, dinner a full-blown five courses, including a starter, fish, sorbet, main course, and dessert. You can watch
the chefs at work in the glassed-in kitchen. ✕ *40 7th Ave., Parktown
North,* ☏ *011/880–1946. Jacket and tie. Reservations required. AE,
DC, MC, V. Closed Sun. and Mon.*

$$$$ **Pescador Restaurant.** Tucked away in a suburban shopping center, this
Portuguese restaurant serves some of the best seafood in Gauteng. Diners come from far and wide for butterflied queen prawns marinated
in a beer, garlic, and chili sauce, then grilled. The combination platter
of succulent, tender calamari and juicy prawns is another favorite. Don't
forget to ask about the line fish specials, especially if it's the season for
musselcracker or "74," two of South Africa's tastiest fish. The atmosphere is relaxed and friendly, and the decor has a distinctly Portuguese flavor, with murals of villages and fishing bric-a-brac on the
walls and old sails on the ceiling. ✕ *Grayston Centre, Grayston Dr.,
Sandown,* ☏ *011/884–4429. Reservations advised. AE, DC, MC, V.
No lunch Sat.*

$$$ **Ciro at the Ritz.** This elegant restaurant occupies a quaint, old house
in Parktown North. Sit inside under the lovely pressed-tin ceiling or
opt for the adjoining conservatory, with hanging plants and a large sky-
light. Ciro's forte is imaginative dishes based on French-Italian provin-
cial cuisine, including such appetizers as duck livers with mango on a
potato galette served with an orange-port sauce. For a main course,
veal scallops are pan fried either with fresh porcini mushrooms grat-
inéed with brie or with a nut crust topped with sliced avocado and served
with a mint-cucumber yogurt sauce. A worthwhile dessert is cherry
cheesecake mille-feuille, made with layers of phyllo pastry, ricotta
cheese, and mascarpone, served with a fruit coulis. ✕ *17 3rd St., Park-
town North,* ☏ *011/880–2470. Reservations advised. AE, DC, MC,
V. Closed Sun. No lunch Sat.*

$$$ **Ile de France.** Chef-owner Marc Guebert is the only member in Africa
★ of the *Maîtres Cuisiniers de France,* that illustrious group of chefs that
includes the likes of Roger Vergé, Pierre Troisgros, and Paul Bocuse.
Each member specializes in a particular culinary realm, and Guebert
champions soufflés. In fact, to visit his restaurant and not eat his soufflé Grand Marnier is considered something of a gastronomic gaffe. For
starters, try grilled goose liver served with a Madeira sauce, or fried
calves' brains in black butter and capers. His quenelles, flavored with
smoked salmon and coated with chardonnay sauce, are light as clouds.
More down to earth is a superb rack of lamb. For a gastronomic treat,
try the *menu dégustation,* a six-course tasting menu that costs about
R110. ✕ *26 Cramerview Centre, 227 Main Rd., Bryanston,* ☏ *011/706–
2837. Reservations advised. AE, DC, MC, V. No lunch Sat.*

$$$ **O Fado.** Floor-length check tablecloths and hand-painted crockery el-
evate this Mozambique-Portuguese restaurant above the level of a
neighborhood *tasca.* Solid choices include *caldo verde,* a potato-based
kale soup with a slice of *chourico* sausage; grilled sardines with roasted
peppers, sliced onions, and boiled potato; and *bacalhau a bras,* shred-
ded salt cod mixed with fried potatoes, egg, and onions, garnished with
tomato and olives. The restaurant is also renowned for its prawns (the
seafood platter is enough for two), and grilled chicken peri-peri is al-
ways a safe bet. For a dessert with a difference, try the avocado-and-

Downtown Johannesburg Dining & Lodging

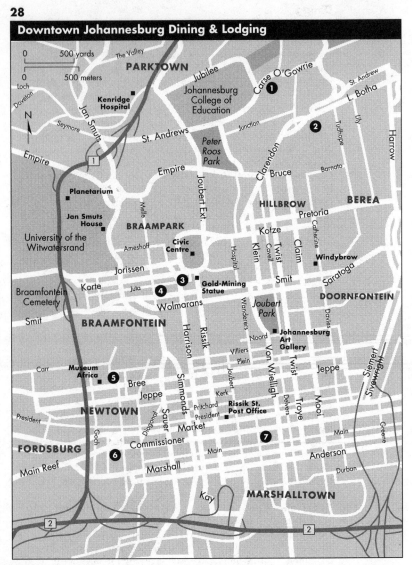

Dining

Chon Hing, **6**

Gramadoelas at the
Market Theatre, **5**

Leipoldt's, **4**

Lodging

The Carlton, **7**

Hotel Formule 1, **2**

The Parktonian, **3**

Sunnyside Park
Hotel, **1**

Northern Suburbs Dining & Lodging

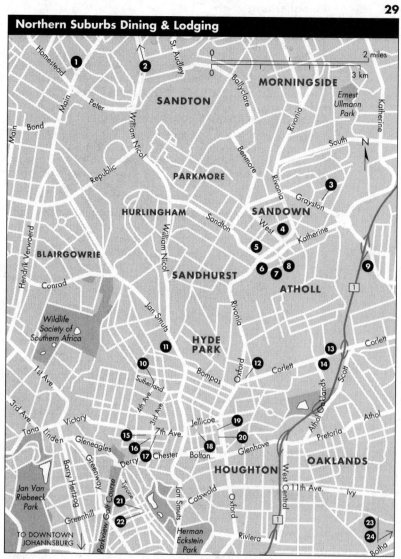

Dining

Armadillo, **15**

Ciro at the Ritz, **16**

Daruma, **14**

Franco's Pizzeria &
Trattoria, **22**

Ile de France, **1**

Linger Longer, **7**

Ma Cuisine, **17**

O Fado, **11**

Osteria Tre
Nonni, **10**

Paros Taverna, **19**

Pescador
Restaurant, **3**

Plaka Taverna, **12**

Red Chamber
Mandarin
Restaurant, **20**

Shamiyana, **13**

Turtle Creek
Winery, **8**

Widgeons Bistro, **21**

Lodging

Balalaika Hotel &
Crown Court, **4**

Holiday Inn Garden
Court–Sandton, **6**

Holiday Inn
Johannesburg
International, **24**

Hotel
Formule 1, **9, 23**

Karos Indaba, **2**

Rosebank Hotel, **18**

Sandton Sun &
Towers, **5**

gin ice-cream cake. ✘ *Hutton Ct., 291 Jan Smuts Ave., Hyde Park,* ☎ *011/880–4410. Reservations advised. AE, DC, MC, V. Closed Sun. No lunch Sat.*

$$$ Osteria Tre Nonni. Paintings and yellowed photographs of aged grandfathers peer down from the whitewashed walls of this North Italian restaurant in Craighall. Prices are high, but the place is always abuzz with elegant Italian families tucking into *paglia e fieno alle noci* (green and white homemade spaghetti with nuts, onions, brandy and cream), sole baked in foil with porcini and truffles, and delicious *filetto al pepe verde* (beef fillet with whiskey, cream, and green Madagascar peppercorns). Carpaccio—paper-thin slices of raw veal with mushrooms, olive oil, celery, parmesan, and lemon—makes a magnificent starter. ✘ *9 Grafton Ave., Craighall,* ☎ *011/327–0095. Reservations required. DC, MC, V. Closed Sun. and Mon.*

$$$ Paros Taverna. This Greek restaurant is hidden at the top of a flight of stairs in the Rosebank Mall, where, on warm summer nights, you can sit outside on the sheltered terrace and sip a bottle of retsina while dipping into bowls of *tzadziki* (yogurt and garlic), *taramousalata* (fishroe dip), and puréed eggplant with onions and garlic. By far the best dish on the menu is *kalamarakia,* incredibly tender squid grilled in olive oil, garlic, and lemon. A couple of orders of kalamarakia and a mixed platter of nine *mezede* (appetizers or side dishes) can easily feed four. For dessert don't miss homemade halvah ice cream. ✘ *Rosebank Blvd., Oxford Rd., Rosebank,* ☎ *011/788–6211. Reservations advised on weekends. AE, DC, MC, V. Closed Mon.*

$$ Armadillo. Tables spill out onto the sidewalk at this trendy restaurant in Parktown North, which serves a small but tasty menu of Mediterranean fare. It's a great place to graze, since the size of the dishes falls somewhere between that of an hors d'oeuvre and a main course. Seven pizzas are on offer—the best comes topped with tangy Italian sausage. Other recommendations are *prego* salad, spicy strips of fillet sautéed and served atop mixed greens and grilled eggplant slices; and tender, succulent calamari, served in a skillet in its own juices. For dessert, brownbread ice cream makes for a tasty change. ✘ *Corner of 3rd and 7th Aves., Parktown North,* ☎ *011/447–5462. Reservations for lunch only. AE, DC, MC, V.*

$$ Shamiyana. This Punjabi restaurant has a strong reputation among local curry aficionados and visiting North Indians. Soft Indian music, red walls, and a tented ceiling create an authentic Indian feeling. Select from a wide array of tandoori, kebab, biryani, and vegetarian dishes. One favorite is chicken *makhanwala,* a mildly spicy dish of boneless chicken cubes cooked with cashew nuts and cream in tomato sauce. To cool down afterward, try one of the many flavors of ice cream. Prices appear reasonable, but remember that you pay extra for side dishes, bread, and rice. ✘ *71 Corlett Dr., Birnham,* ☎ *011/786–8810. Reservations advised. AE, DC, MC, V.*

$$ Turtle Creek Winery. Scion of the illustrious Linger Longer, this brash young progeny has inherited some of the wit and wisdom of its parent, if not its elegance and high prices. Here, young sophisticates hang out sipping South Africa's best wines (available by the glass), helping themselves to tapas, and dining on focaccia topped with roast lamb, tomato, olives, basil, and garlic. Tables spill out of the high-ceilinged bar onto an oak-shaded patio, which quickly fills with an after-work crowd. Try fresh baked trout wrapped in vine leaves and stuffed with anchovies, tomato, and garlic, or cassoulet of lamb with white beans, smoked sausage, baby onions, and feta. Their steak-and-kidney and chicken-thyme-and-mushroom pies are famous, too. Pass up dessert in favor of a platter of cheeses and a glass of port. ✗ *58 Wierda Rd. W, Wierda Valley, Sandton,* ☎ *011/884–0466. Reservations advised. AE, DC, MC, V. No dinner Sun.*

$$ Widgeons Bistro. Dark green walls and plaid tablecloths lend old-world charm to this intimate Parkview restaurant. The menu is eclectic, with flavors of Italy, colonial Africa, and the Far East. Spaghetti *con aglio e oglio,* with a smattering of chilis, is the tastiest in town. Penne *ai Communisti,* made with onions, smoked salmon, and a splash of vodka is also very good. Otherwise, try the seafood platter, cooked with coconut milk, peri-peri, brandy, wine, and lots of coriander. The restaurant is licensed, but feel free to bring your own bottle. ✗ *60 Tyrone Ave., Parkview,* ☎ *011/486–2053. Reservations advised. AE, DC, MC, V. Closed Sun. No lunch Mon.*

$ Franco's Pizzeria & Trattoria. Dark wood paneling, red-check tablecloths, and soft Italian music give this spot a welcoming appeal. Chef-owner Franco Forleo comes from Brindisi and specializes in southern Italian cuisine. The menu includes 14 variations of pizza and a range of pasta dishes, but habitués usually choose one of the specials, such as *capelli al salmone e caviale* (angel-hair pasta with smoked salmon and caviar), or seasonal *frutti di mare* like butterfish, yellowtail, and kabeljou. Remember to bring your own wine—and that this is one of the few restaurants open for lunch on Saturday. ✗ *Parkview Centre, 54 Tyrone Ave.,* ☎ *011/646–5449. BYOB. Reservations advised. AE, DC, MC, V. Closed Mon.*

$ Plaka Taverna. Greek music floats above the buzz of conversation, a gyro spit turns slowly near the door, and a refrigerated case displays an array of mezede. Most people sit on the roofed terrace or at the few street-side tables. Start with a couple of ouzos and share a platter of gyro meat, feta, olives, cucumber, and tomato. Follow that with a platter of meze, a Greek salad, and a carafe of wine, and your bill will still be under R40 per person. If you're really hungry, choose the spit-roasted lamb or grilled chicken marinated in olive oil, garlic, and lemon juice. ✗ *3a Corlett Dr., Illovo,* ☎ *011/788–8777. Reservations advised on weekends. AE, DC, MC, V. Closed Mon.*

$ Red Chamber Mandarin Restaurant. This is where the Chinese community gathers on Sunday morning for its traditional dim sum or *yum char* (tea and snacks). During the rest of the week, chefs from Taiwan, Hong Kong, Beijing, and Guangzhou turn out some of the best Chinese food in the city, drawing a loyal following of wealthy Chinese locals. There are more than 100 dishes on the menu, but feel free to make special requests—some of the best dishes aren't listed. Highlights include cubes of eggplant and chili cooked and served in a sizzling wok, and steamed shrimp dumplings. ✗ *Rosebank Mews, Rosebank,* ☎ *011/ 788–5536. Reservations advised. AE, DC, MC, V. Closed Tues.*

LODGING

When choosing a hotel in Jo'burg, your most important consideration should be location. The city center remains the financial and business heart of the city, and its streets give visitors a taste of the emerging new South Africa. It's also the most dangerous part of the city, so you should exercise caution during the day and *never* walk the streets after dark, when everything closes. Hotels in the northern suburbs tend to be safer, with easy access to shopping malls, cinemas, and restaurants. Sandton is rapidly developing into a major new commercial center, although it still feels like a suburb. For price ranges, *see* Chart 2 (A) *in* On the Road with Fodor's.

Downtown

$$$$ **Carlton.** Since 1972 this hotel has set the standard for luxury accom-
★ modation and service in Johannesburg. It also charges hundreds of
rand less than the Sandton Sun. The hotel occupies a skyscraper in the
heart of the city center, making it an ideal choice for businesspeople—
Hillary Clinton is but one of the U.S. dignitaries who have stayed here.
The lobby sets the tone for the hotel with its rich burgundy tones, mar-
bled floors, wood paneling, and beautiful Asian art. Standard rooms
are currently being refurbished, but differ little from equivalent rooms
in other hotels. Individually decorated suites, on the other hand, are magnificent: huge and incredibly opulent. If you want extra comfort without the expense of a suite, stay in the Carlton Court, a 62-room annex
that has exceptional service. Rooms here are small but elegant, with subtle lighting, subdued rust-toned furniture, and a battery of push-but-
tons controlling everything from the TV to the curtains. Carlton Court
guests have access to the exclusive Club Room Restaurant, open 24 hours.
⌖ *Main St. (mailing address: Box 7709, Johannesburg 2000),* ☎ *011/
331–8911,* ℻ *011/331–3555. 452 rooms with bath. 3 restaurants, 2
bars, room service, pool, health center. AE, DC, MC, V.*

$$$ **Parktonian.** Close to the Rotunda transport center, the major theaters,
and just a three-minute drive from the central business district, this
Braamfontein property offers the best value in the city—even if its neigh-
borhood isn't safe to walk in at night. The guest rooms are all suites,
by far the largest of any city hotel. All have a separate living room and
bedroom, minibar, cable TV, and veranda. Brown shag carpet makes
the rooms unnecessarily dull. You can enter the hotel directly from a
secure parking garage. ⌖ *120 De Korte St., Braamfontein (mailing ad-
dress: Box 32278, Braamfontein 2017),* ☎ *011/403–5740,* ℻ *011/403–
2401. 308 rooms with bath. 2 restaurants, bar, room service, pool, health
center. AE, DC, MC, V.*

$$$ **Sunnyside Park Hotel.** Just minutes by car from the city center, this
Parktown hotel is one of the few in the city with a history. Built in 1895
as a mansion for a mining engineer, it later served as the residence of
Lord Milner, eventual governor of the Transvaal. New sections have
been added to the original mansion, but wood paneling and old prints
help to recapture something of the hotel's illustrious past. Rooms are
pleasant, done in autumnal tones with bird prints and wicker furniture. Request a front-facing room overlooking the gardens. Service is
not one of the hotel's strong points: Rooms may not be ready by mid-
afternoon and the front-desk staff could be more helpful. Unfortunately,
recent years have seen an alarming increase in crime in the area around
the hotel. ⌖ *2 York Rd., Parktown (mailing address: Box 31256, Braamfontein 2017),* ☎ *011/643–7226,* ℻ *011/642–0019. 96 rooms with
bath. Restaurant, 2 bars, room service, pool. AE, DC, MC, V.*

$ **Hotel Formule 1.** This budget French chain has five identical hotels around
Johannesburg and near the airport, each built from prefabricated parts
and assembled as though from a giant Lego set. The hotels are designed
to overcome the worst failings in human nature, with wall-mounted
TVs and beds, self-flushing toilets, and communal, self-cleaning showers (none of the rooms has a bathroom). You're not quite sure whether
you're in prison or the 21st century. That said, you won't find clean
accommodations any cheaper. ⌖ *1 Maree St., Bramley Park, Sandton,*
☎ *011/887–5555,* ℻ *011/887–5632; 1 Mitchell St., Berea,* ☎ *011/484–
5551,* ℻ *011/484–5705; corner of Herman and Kruis Sts., Isando,*
☎ *011/392–1453,* ℻ *011/392–3087. AE, DC, MC, V.*

Northern Suburbs

$$$$ **Sandton Sun & Towers.** This five-star hotel in Sandton adjoins one of
★ the largest and most exclusive malls in the country, and it's close to
the burgeoning collection of businesses that have fled to the northern
suburbs. The Sun and Sun Towers are two nominally separate hotels,
linked by a walkway and sharing facilities. Both occupy high-rises with
commanding views of the northern suburbs and the highveld. The focal
point of each hotel is a central atrium soaring the height of the building. Guest rooms are small but superbly laid out, with understated lighting and elegant decorative touches. There is little to recommend one
hotel over the other, although the Towers is smaller and farther removed
from the bustle of Sandton Mall. The Towers also has two floors of
executive suites, with their own bar, breakfast room, and full-time staff.
⌖ *Corner of 5th and Alice Sts. (mailing address: Box 784902, Sandton 2146), Sandhurst 2196,* ☎ *011/780–5000,* FAX *011/780–5002. 565
rooms with bath. 4 restaurants, 2 bars, room service, 2 pools, health
center.*

$$$ **Balalaika Hotel & Crown Court.** Part of the Protea chain, the Balalaika
enjoys a good location in Sandton. A walkway leads to the pleasant
Village Walk shopping center, with its cinemas, restaurants, and bars.
Built around two inviting garden courtyards, the hotel is divided into
two parts: the original Balalaika, whose rooms are cheaper and slated
for renovation, and the far more attractive Crown Court, with rooms
furnished with all the amenities you would expect in a major interna-
tional hotel (separate bath and shower, minibars, cable TV, and air-
conditioning). Numerous hunting prints on the walls and bars with names
like Lords and the Village Tavern establish an ersatz English identity.
Still, comfortable and clean, it offers much better value than the nearby
Holiday Inn Crowne Plaza. ⌖ *Maude St., Sandown, Sandton 2199,*
☎ *011/322–5000,* FAX *011/322–5021. 325 rooms with bath. 2 restau-
rants, 2 bars, room service, 2 pools. AE, DC, MC, V.*

$$$ **Holiday Inn Johannesburg International.** A few hundred yards from
the airport, this Holiday Inn stands head and shoulders above the other
airport hotels. Most guests spend one night here either at the beginning or end of their trip, even though there's precious little to do outside the hotel. Rooms are attractively furnished, with bright bedspreads
and avant-garde wall prints. Shuttle buses run to the airport every 15
minutes. If you're coming by car, the easiest way to reach the hotel is
to drive through the airport and follow the signs marked AIR FREIGHT.
⌖ *Off R24, Kempton Park (mailing address: Box 388, Kempton Park
1620),* ☎ *011/975–1121,* FAX *011/975–5846. 365 rooms with bath.
Restaurant, bar, room service, pool. AE, DC, MC, V.*

$$$ **Karos Indaba.** Indaba is an African word for meeting place, and an
apt name for one of the major conference venues in Johannesburg, ca-
pable of hosting several major functions simultaneously in a wide va-
riety of board rooms, auditoriums, and ballrooms. The property is huge,
covering more than 30 acres on the outskirts of Johannesburg, about
30 minutes by car from both the airport and the city center. The hotel
itself is very attractive, with a thatched roof lending rustic African charm
to an otherwise business-oriented establishment. Rooms in the older
thatched section are comfortable but a bit dark. Rooms in the newer
Ninth Block are lighter, done in attractive greens and rusts, and fea-
ture their own verandas and minibars, as well as separate bath and
shower. Sunday brunch under the jacarandas on the hotel's terrace is
a local favorite. ⌖ *Hartebeespoort Dam Rd., Witkoppen (mailing ad-
dress: Box 67129, Bryanston 2021),* ☎ *011/643–8052,* FAX *011/643–*

4343. *220 rooms with bath. Restaurant, bar, room service, pool, health center, tennis, squash.*

$$$ **Rosebank Hotel.** Ideally situated 15 minutes by car from the city center and just minutes on foot from the shops, cinemas, and restaurants of Rosebank's malls, the Rosebank is another favorite among businesspeople who appreciate low-key atmosphere and efficient service. Guest rooms are attractively decorated with prints and dark wood furniture and paneling. If you like being able to walk out of your hotel, this is a much better choice than the Sunnyside or the Parktonian: The streets of Rosebank are among the safest and most interesting in Johannesburg. ☎ *Corner of Tyrwhitt and Sturdee Aves., Rosebank (mailing address: Box 52025, Saxonwold 2132),* ☎ *011/447–2700,* FAX *011/447–3276. 318 rooms with bath. 3 restaurants, 2 bars, room service, pool, hair salon. AE, DC, MC, V.*

$$ **Holiday Inn Garden Court–Sandton.** This no-frills hotel was knocked together in record time for the 1995 Rugby World Cup. If it has a prefabricated feel, it's also ideally located, catercorner from the Sandton City mall. Rooms are small and functional, but clean, each with two double beds, air-conditioning, TV, and tea- and coffeemakers. ☎ *Corner of Katherine St. and Rivonia Rd. (mailing address: Box 783394, Sandton 2196),* ☎ *011/884–5660,* FAX *011/783–2004. 157 rooms with bath. Restaurant, bar, pool. AE, DC, MC, V.*

THE ARTS AND NIGHTLIFE

The best place to find out what's going on in Johannesburg is in the Tonight section of the *Star,* Johannesburg's major daily. Another great source of information is the weekly *Mail & Guardian.* Make your bookings through **Computicket** (☎ 011/445–8445), which has outlets throughout the city, including most major malls.

The Arts

Classical Music

The **National Symphony Orchestra** (☎ 011/714–4501) stages concerts in Linder Auditorium (Johannesburg College of Education, St. Andrews Rd., Parktown) and occasionally at City Hall (corner of President and Simmonds Sts., Johannesburg Central).

Theater

The beautiful **Alhambra Theatre** complex (corner of Sivewright Ave. and Beit St., Doornfontein, ☎ 011/402–6174) is made up of three theaters: the Alhambra, the Rex Garner, and the Richard Haines. The complex presents primarily mainstream productions, including a lot of West End and Broadway material. Recent productions have included such works as *The Sisters Rosensweig* and Terrence Rattigan's *In Praise of Love.*

The **Civic Theatre** (Loveday St., Braamfontein, ☎ 011/403–3408) is Johannesburg's principal cultural venue. Housed in a slick, modern complex, the Civic features one enormous theater and three smaller stages. Many productions have a South African focus, showcasing works by such famous local talents as Pieter-Dirk Uys and Paul Slabolepszy.

The **Market Theatre** (corner of Bree and Wolhuter Sts., ☎ 011/832–1641) occupies an old Indian produce market that dates back to the early 1900s. Now completely refurbished, the three-theater complex has a wealth of character and includes a great bar and restaurant and an art gallery with changing exhibits. Theater productions include

everything from plays by Athol Fugard to imported West End come-
dies. Experimental plays get the litmus test of audience approval at the
Market Theatre Laboratory, across Bree Street.

Nightlife

Multiracial Hillbrow used to be the city's nightlife center, but the
neighborhood has become a crime-ridden, no-go zone full of hookers,
massage parlors, and porno houses. In its place, **Rosebank** has emerged
as the hot new spot, and you'll find clubs, bars, and coffee shops scattered through the neighborhood, particularly along Oxford Road.
Rockey Street in Yeoville also has a happening nightlife scene, with clubs
and bars offering everything from jazz to grunge. Unfortunately, the
street is also a popular hangout for drug dealers and addicts. Many
white residents of the northern suburbs, concerned about personal safety,
head to the new **Randburg Waterfront** (Republic Rd., Randburg), a gim-
micky, mall-like development of almost a hundred restaurants, bars,
and clubs clustered around an artificial lake.

Bars and Pubs

The **Guildhall Executive Bar and Restaurant** (Meischkes Bldg., Market St., ☎ 011/836–5560), in the city center, is the oldest bar in Johannesburg. Walk through swinging doors into a paneled room rich
with wood and smoke.

Hooters (corner of Bolton Rd. and Bath Ave., Rosebank, ☎ 011/442–
7320), a cavernous bar, may be the biggest meat market in the city,
particularly on Friday in summer when an after-work crowd jams its
outdoor veranda.

The Yard of Ale (Market Theatre complex, Bree St., ☎ 011/836–
6611), in the city center, is a great, no-nonsense bar with an outdoor
veranda. It's a good place to quaff a few brews before heading to Kippies (*below*) or after working up a sweat at the Saturday flea market.

Live Music

District Six Jazz Café (Shop 169, Waterfront, Republic Rd., Randburg, ☎ 011/789–9809) is a fully licensed restaurant serving Cajun
and Cape Malay food. It features live jazz on Wednesday, Friday, and
Saturday nights.

Shebeen of Rosebank (Oxford Rd., Rosebank Mall, ☎ 011/788–9247)
started out as a place where whites went to get a taste of the townships
without ever leaving the comfort of a mall. Since then, it's taken on a
life of its own and is now popular for drinking and dancing.

Kippies (Market Theatre complex, off Bree St., Newtown, ☎ 011/834–
3743) is the city's premier jazz venue, featuring the best of South
African jazz, both traditional and township. It also serves light meals.

The **Fairway Cafe** (76 Op Den Bergen St., Fairview, ☎ 011/624–
1894), known by regulars as Bob's Bar, is famous among Johannesburg's literati. It's the place to go if you want alternative culture
without grunge.

At the **House of Tandoor** (26 Rockey St., Yeoville, ☎ 011/487–1569)
you'll find some of the best live jazz and blues in town, either in the
Back Bar or the Blues Kitchen.

Rattlesnake Roadside Diner (Mutual Village, Rivonia Blvd., Rivonia,
☎ 011/803–9406) bills itself as a '60s dining experience, but when
the partyers start singing and dancing on the tables, no one really cares.

Picasso Bistro (Old Mutual Sq., 169 Oxford Rd., Rosebank, ☎ 011/788–1213) is a sophisticated wine bar and coffee house. Open late, it's *the* place to see and be seen in Rosebank.

Nightclubs

Jagger's (Mutual Sq., Rosebank, ☎ 011/788–1718), underneath the Tivoli Pizza Restaurant, is a popular techno-pop dance club.

Krypton (Constantia Centre, Tyrwhitt Ave., Rosebank, ☎ 011/442–7372) is a gay techno club, with dancers grooving wall-to-wall to an urgent, unending beat.

EXCURSIONS

Pretoria

Exploring

Numbers in the margin correspond to points of interest on the Pretoria map.

Pretoria is often overshadowed by Johannesburg, 48 kilometers (30 miles) to the south, and few people outside South Africa know it as the country's capital. It's a pleasant city, with a number of historic buildings and a city center that is easily explored on foot. Pretoria is famous for its jacaranda trees, and the best time to visit is in the spring (September and October), when the city is blanketed with their purple blossoms. Founded in 1855, the city was named after Andries Pretorius, the hero of the Battle of Blood River (*see below and* Chapter 7), and it has remained a bastion of Afrikaner culture. With the triumph of the Nationalist Party in 1948, it also became the seat of Afrikaner power, and the city developed a reputation for hard-line Afrikaner insularity. Much of that has changed in recent years, and President Nelson Mandela now occupies the lovely Union Buildings overlooking the city. International acceptance of the new South Africa has also seen an influx of foreign embassies and personnel, bringing a refreshing cosmopolitan feel to the city. As a result, many of the country's finest restaurants have gathered in Pretoria.

If you're coming from Johannesburg, your first stop should be the ❶ **Voortrekker Monument and Museum,** an unabashed tribute to the ideals at the heart of apartheid. Indeed, it's difficult to overstate the religious and political importance of this monument to the Afrikaner population. Completed in 1949, the monument honors the Voortrekkers, Boer families who rejected British rule in the Cape and in 1835–38 trekked into the hinterland to found their own nation. The Hall of Heroes traces in its frieze the momentous events of their Great Trek, culminating in the Battle of Blood River (December 16, 1838), when a small force of Boers defeated the Zulu army without losing a single life (*see* Chapter 7). The Voortrekkers considered this victory a confirmation of their special relationship with God, and the monument is heavy with symbolic reminders of the event. Each year, at precisely noon on the anniversary of the battle, a ray of sunlight strikes the cenotaph engraved with the words "We for thee, South Africa." An adjoining museum displays scenes and artifacts of daily Voortrekker life, as well as the Voortrekker Tapestries, 15 pictorial weavings that trace the historical high points of the Great Trek. *Off M7. Follow brown signs off M1,* ☎ *012/323–0682.* ☛ *Monument: R4 adults, R2.50 children; museum: R5 adults, R3 children.* ⊙ *Daily 9–4:45.*

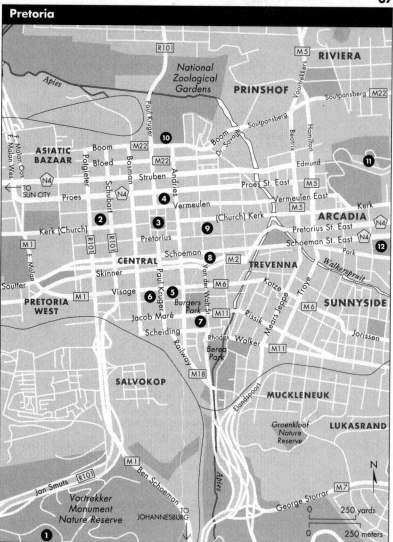

Pretoria

Church Square, **3**

City Hall, **6**

J.G. Strijdom
Square, **9**

Kruger House
Museum, **2**

Melrose House, **7**

National Zoological
Gardens, **10**

Pierneef Museum, **4**

Pretoria Art
Museum, **12**

Staats Model
School, **8**

Transvaal Museum, **5**

Union Buildings, **11**

Voortrekker
Monument and
Museum, **1**

② Return to the highway and drive into the city. Turn right on Kerk (Church) Street and park. The **Kruger House Museum** was the home of Paul Kruger, who served as president of the South African Republic between 1883 and 1902 and is one of the most revered figures in South African history. The home, still fully furnished, is humble and somber, befitting this deeply religious leader. Exhibits in the adjoining museum trace Kruger's career, culminating in his exile by the British and eventual death in Switzerland in 1904. Of particular interest are the expressions of support that Kruger received from all over the world, including the United States, when Britain instigated the Boer War (1899–1902). *Kerk St. at Potgieter St.,* ☎ *012/326–9172.* ☛ *R5 adults, R3 children.* ⊙ *Mon.–Sat. 8:30–4, Sun. 11–4.*

③ Head down Kerk to **Church Square.** A statue of President Kruger by Anton van Wouw dominates the pleasant square, which is flanked by some of Pretoria's most historic buildings: The Old Raadsaal (Town Hall), built in early Italian Renaissance style; the Palace of Justice, which was used as a military hospital during the Boer War; and the modern Provincial Administration Building.

④ Walk a block north on Paul Kruger Street and turn right on Vermeulen Street to reach the **Pierneef Museum.** In a turn-of-the-century house, the museum displays works by Jacob Pierneef (1886–1957), one of South Africa's finest painters. Remarkable for his great range of styles, he is most famous for his unique, almost abstract renderings of South African landscape. *Vermeulen St., between Andries and Paul Kruger Sts.,* ☎ *012/323–1419.* ☛ *Free.* ⊙ *Weekdays 8:30–4.*

⑤ Head back to Church Square and continue down Paul Kruger Street another four blocks to the **Transvaal Museum,** the best natural science museum in the country. It houses an extensive collection of land and marine animals from around the world, with an emphasis on African wildlife. The museum also features the Austin Roberts Bird Collection, a comprehensive display of southern African birds. Much of the museum is laid out with students in mind, and exhibit descriptions are exceptionally informative. Of particular interest are the Genesis exhibits, tracing the evolution of life on earth, and the geology section, with displays of weird and wonderful rocks and minerals. This is a great place to bring kids. *Paul Kruger St., across from City Hall,* ☎ *012/322–7632.* ☛ *R4 adults, R2 children.* ⊙ *Mon.–Sat. 9–5, Sun. 11–5.*

⑥ Across Paul Kruger Street from the museum stands **City Hall,** an imposing structure that borrows freely from classical architecture. The tympanum on the front of the building is by Coert Steynberg, one of South Africa's most famous sculptors. It symbolizes the growth and development of Pretoria. Statues of Andries Pretorius, the hero of the Battle of Blood River, and his son Marthinus, the city's founder, stand in the square fronting City Hall.

⑦ Continue down Paul Kruger Street for one block and turn left on Jacob Maré Street to reach **Melrose House.** Built in 1886, this opulent structure is one of the most beautiful Victorian homes in the country, with marble columns, mosaic floors, and lovely stained-glass windows. The house is furnished in period style. Its huge dining room is where the 1902 Treaty of Vereeniging was signed, ending the Boer War. *275 Jacob Maré St.,* ☎ *012/322–2805.* ☛ *R2.* ⊙ *Tues.–Wed. and Fri.–Sat. 10–5, Thurs. 10–8, Sun. noon–5.*

⑧ Return to the center of the city by way of Van der Walt Street. At the corner of Skinner Street, you'll pass the brick **Staats Model School,** a fine example of a school from Transvaal Republic days. During the Boer

War it served as a prison for British officers. It was from here that Winston Churchill made his famous escape after being captured by the Boers near Ladysmith. Appropriately, the school now houses an education department.

⑨ Continue up Van der Walt Street until you reach **J. G. Strijdom Square,** named for one of South Africa's prime ministers. The square is dominated by a huge bust of Strijdom. Despite the fervid anti-communist stance of the old Nationalist government, its monumental architecture bears a striking resemblance to that of old Soviet states—J. G. Strijdom's head could just as easily be Lenin's.

⑩ To reach the remaining points on this tour, you will need transportation of some sort. The **National Zoological Gardens** lie on the northern fringe of the city center. Pretoria's zoo is considered one of the world's best, with an enormous collection of animals from almost every continent. The animal enclosures here are much larger than those of most zoos, but a cage is still a cage. A cable car (R6.50, 3.50 children) transports visitors high above the zoo to a hilltop lookout. *Boom St.,* ☎ *012/328–3265.* ☛ *R12 adults, R6 children.* ☉ *Daily 8–5:30.*

⑪ The **Union Buildings** rise east of the city center, atop a rocky ridge known as Meintjies Kop. Designed by Sir Herbert Baker, this impressive red sandstone complex is home to the administrative branch of government, and now serves as the headquarters of President Nelson Mandela. The complex incorporates a hodgepodge of styles—a Spanish-tile roof, wood shutters inspired by Cape Dutch architecture, and Greek columns—that somehow works beautifully. Formal gardens step down the hillside in terraces, dotted with war memorials and statues of former prime ministers. The view of the city from here is superb. *Access off Kerk St. Not open to the public.*

⑫ In the valley directly below the Union Buildings lies the **Pretoria Art Museum,** an unimpressive gallery space with a very impressive collection of South African art. Much of the collection consists of works by famous white artists, including Pierneef, van Wouw, Irma Stern, and Hugo Naudé, but more and more black artists are now receiving recognition—look for works by Ephraim Ngatane (1938–71), an early exponent of township art. The museum also stages changing exhibitions. *Corner of Schoeman and Wessels Sts.,* ☎ *012/344–1807.* ☛ *R2.* ☉ *Tues. and Thurs.–Sat. 10–5, Wed. 10–8, Sun. 10–6.*

Dining
For price ranges, *see* Chart 1 *in* On the Road with Fodor's.

$$$$ **Chagalls at Toulouse.** At the end of their meal, a contingent of visiting French chefs gave this restaurant a standing ovation. The food is *that* good. Chef Eric Springer has worked in the kitchens of some of Paris's most famous restaurants, and his haute cuisine *Française* is considered the finest in South Africa. The menu changes twice a year and invariably creates a stir. Start with such appetizers as creamed cauliflower with crumbed Irish salmon, or lobster and potato Charlotte in caviar and salmon-egg butter. Main courses include lightly roasted breast of wild duck served with warm potato salad and confit of duckling leg, and marinated fillet of kudu antelope dressed with apple and nuts. The restaurant's setting, in a country lodge on the outskirts of Pretoria, is lovely. ✗ *Fountains Valley, Pretoria,* ☎ *012/341–7511. Jacket and tie. Reservations advised. AE, DC, MC, V. Closed Sun. No lunch Sat.*

$$$ **La Madeleine.** Noted for its classical and creative French cuisine, this
★ restaurant ranks among the country's top ten. The wine list, too, has

won a slew of awards. The menu changes daily, depending on what's available at the market. Expect as a starter a salad with langoustine in a parcel of phyllo pastry served on a swirl of gazpacho. A typical main course might be two quails, boned and cooked in puff pastry and served with marsala sauce. Desserts include such heavenly treats as honey ice cream with chocolate mousse cake and crème brûlée. ✗ *258 Esselen St., Sunnyside, Pretoria,* ☎ *012/44–6076. Reservations required. AE, DC, MC, V. Closed Sun. and Mon. No lunch Sat.*

$$$ La Perla. This grand Continental restaurant is a favorite haunt of ambassadors and ministers. The interior, with wood-paneled walls and tables separated by etched-glass panels, is ideal for private, power lunches. The menu includes a selection of standard European dishes like pan-fried quail with fresh herbs, piccata Milanese, and saddle of game. Starters include a half-dozen snails and prawns on a skewer. Meticulous preparation and service make up for any lack of innovation in the menu. The wine list is also outstanding. ✗ *211 Skinner St., Pretoria,* ☎ *012/322–2759. Reservations required. AE, DC, MC, V. Closed Sun. No lunch Sat.*

$$ Brasserie de Paris. This delightful French oasis occupies an unassuming building in suburban Hatfield. In typical Parisian style, café tables adorn the outside veranda; inside, simple table settings recall the restaurant's Gallic roots. Appetizers include frogs' legs Provençal and delicious pâté *en croute*. For a main course, choose between ox tongue in white wine sauce with gherkins and mustard and duck leg cooked slowly with veal stock and red wine, served with a shallot sauce. Fish is also on offer, including skate wings. ✗ *525 Duncan St., Hatfield,* ☎ *012/342–5057. Reservations advised. AE, DC, MC, V. Closed Sun. No lunch Sat.*

The Arts

CLASSICAL MUSIC

The **Transvaal Philharmonic** plays in the State Theatre (Church St., Pretoria, ☎ 012/322–1665).

THEATER

The **State Theatre Pretoria** (Church St., Pretoria, ☎ 012/322–1665) is home to the Performing Arts Council Transvaal (PACT), a state-funded group that supports a wide range of theater, as well as ballet and opera companies.

Pretoria Essentials

ARRIVING AND DEPARTING

By Bus. Translux (☎ 012/315–2333) and **Greyhound** (☎ 012/315–2515) buses run regularly between Pretoria (Pretoria Station, corner of Paul Kruger and Scheiding Sts.) and Johannesburg's Rotunda on their way to destinations around the country.

By Car. The quickest way to reach Pretoria from Johannesburg is via the N1 Highway, which turns into the R28 as it nears the city. Outside rush hour, the 30-mile drive takes no more than half an hour.

CONSULATES AND EMBASSIES

Australian High Commission. *292 Orient St., Arcadia, Pretoria,* ☎ *012/342–3740.*

Canadian Embassy. *1103 Arcadia St., Hatfield, Pretoria,* ☎ *012/342–6923.*

U.K. Embassy. *255 Hill St., Arcadia, Pretoria,* ☎ *012/43–3121.*

U.S. Embassy. *877 Pretorius St., Arcadia, Pretoria,* ☎ *012/342–1048.*

VISITOR INFORMATION
Pretoria Tourist Rendezvous Centre. *Corner of Prinsloo and Vermeulen Sts.,* ☎ *012/313–7980,* ⬛ *012/313–8460.*

The **National Parks Board** handles accommodation reservations for all national parks and can furnish information. *643 Leyds St., Muckleneuk (mailing address: Box 787, Pretoria 0001),* ☎ *012/343–1991,* ⬛ *012/ 343–0905.*

Sun City

Sun City is a huge entertainment and resort complex in the middle of dry bushveld, 177 kilometers (110 miles) northwest of Johannesburg. It's the dream child of Sol Kerzner, the South African entrepreneur who first saw the possibilities of a casino in the rocky wilds of the Pilanesberg mountains. Now, nearly two decades later, Sun City comprises four hotels, two casinos, major amphitheaters, and a host of outdoor attractions. The complex is split into two parts: the original Sun City and the Lost City, a new project anchored by the magnificent Palace Hotel—worth a visit in itself.

Comparisons with Las Vegas are inappropriate. Sun City is a resort, not a city, although it does rely on the same entertainments: gambling, slot machines, topless revues, and big-time extravaganzas. Sun City stages the country's largest rock concerts, major boxing bouts, and the occasional Miss World Pageant. It also displays that familiar Vegas sense (or lack) of taste—the Palace being a notable exception—doling out the kind of ersatz glitter and glare that appeals to a shiny polyester crowd.

The resort burst onto the international scene in the apartheid era, when a few American and British music stars broke the cultural boycott to play Sun City. Back then, it was part of Bophuthatswana, one of the nominally independent homelands designed to rob blacks of their South African citizenship by giving them a semblance of self-government. Today, Bophuthatswana has been reabsorbed into South Africa as part of the new North West Province.

Sun City's genuine appeal lies not in the slots but in the remarkable Palace Hotel and the nearby Pilanesberg National Park (*see* Chapter 9). The national park, the third largest in the country, offers a chance to see the Big Five (lion, leopard, elephant, rhino, and buffalo)—and is malaria-free to boot. You can either drive yourself through the park or join guided tours in open-air Land Rovers; all of the safari companies will pick you up at your hotel.

Sun City also offers a full round of outdoor sports and activities, including two Gary Player–designed golf courses and a man-made lake where visitors can waterski, parasail, and sailboard. The latest addition is Valley of the Waves, a giant pool that creates perfect waves for body-surfing onto a man-made beach.

Lodging

Accommodation in Sun City is very expensive, and only the Palace can justify its rates. You may opt to stay instead in the nearby rest camps and private lodges of the Pilanesberg National Park (*see* Chapter 9).

CATEGORY	COST*
$$$$	over R900
$$$	R700–R900
$$	R500–R700
$	under R500

All prices are for a standard double room, including VAT and any Tourism Promotion Levies.

$$$$ **Palace of the Lost City.** Even if you never go near Sun City, consider
★   staying at this soaring, magnificent complex. It's the most spectacular hotel in the country, and has become an attraction in its own right. Given the tackiness of Sun City, you would think any hotel based on the concept of a lost African palace would suffer from theme-park syndrome. Nothing could be further from the truth. Sculpted cranes and leaping kudu appear to take flight from the hotel towers, elephants guard triumphal stairways and bridges, and graceful reminders of Africa strike you at every turn. No expense has been spared—the hotel cost R800 million—and the attention to detail is mind-boggling. All rooms have hand-carved doors and furnishings; the jungle paintings on the ceiling of the lobby's rotunda took 5,000 hours to complete; and the hand-laid mosaic floor is made up of 300,000 separate tiles. Guest rooms, done in rich earth tones, blend African motifs with delicate Eastern touches. Carved wooden screens open into an elegant bathroom with separate bath and shower, and a huge wood armoire hides a safe, TV, and minibar. If you really want to splurge, choose one of the grand suites (at over R12,000 per night). The hotel's two restaurants serve some of the finest cuisine in the country. ☎ *Box 308, Sun City 0316,* ☎ *01465/7–3121,* 📠 *01465/7–3101. 338 rooms with bath. 2 restaurants, 2 bars, room service, pool. AE, DC, MC, V.*

$$$ **The Cascades.** The lavish use of mirrors, brass, and black marble in the lobby sets the tone for this sophisticated high-rise hotel, only yards from the Lost City's massive entertainment center. Rooms have an understated African elegance, decorated in soothing rust colors highlighted with bold blues and yellows. All overlook the Gary Player golf course, the gardens, and an artificial waterfall. For the best views, request a room on an upper floor. ☎ *Box 2, Sun City,* ☎ *01465/2–1000,* 📠 *01465/7–4210. 242 rooms with bath. 3 restaurants, 2 bars, room service, pool. AE, DC, MC, V.*

$$ **Sun City Hotel.** This is the original Sun City property, and it still houses the gaming casino, banks of slot machines, and the topless extravaganza. If gambling and nonstop action are your scene, this will appeal to you, but most people find its tackiness overwhelming. The main room is decked out like a Tarzan jungle, with palms and man-made waterfalls, rope walkways, and rain forest and bamboo murals. The sound of rushing water drowns out the jangle of the slots somewhat, but nothing can conceal the glitter of this lurid spectacle. Thankfully, the rooms are a big improvement. Muted rusts and browns predominate, and the furniture is inspired by elegant, old Cape designs. ☎ *Box 2, Sun City,* ☎ *01465/2–1000,* 📠 *01465/7–4210. 340 rooms with bath. 4 restaurants, 2 bars, room service, pool, casino. AE, DC, MC, V.*

$ **The Cabanas.** After the bells and whistles of the Sun City Hotel, this budget option comes as a peaceful surprise. Paths thread through pleasant gardens to the rooms, in small apartment blocks overlooking a man-made lake. They are clean and cheerful, with tile floors, bright bedspreads, and sliding glass doors that open onto the lawns. All have TV, tea- and coffeemakers, and air-conditioning. The hotel's proximity to Waterworld, a playground, and a petting zoo makes it a popular choice for families. ☎ *Box 2, Sun City,* ☎ *01465/2–1000,* 📠

01465/7–4210. 300 rooms with bath. 2 restaurants, 2 bars, pool. AE, DC, MC, V.

Sun City Essentials
ARRIVING AND DEPARTING

By Bus. Impala Tours (☏ 011/974–6561) operates a daily bus service to Sun City from Johannesburg's Rotunda (corner of Leyds and Loveday Sts., Braamfontein). The bus leaves at 9 and returns at 5. A same-day return ticket costs R55, and a one-way fare costs R45.

By Car. Plan about 1½–2 hours to drive the 177 kilometers (110 miles) to Sun City from Johannesburg. The best route is up the N1 to Pretoria, then west by way of the N4.

By Plane. Sun Air (☏ 011/397–2244 in Jo'burg, 01465/2–1359 in Sun City) offers daily service (except Sat.) to Sun City from Johannesburg, and thrice-weekly flights from Durban and Cape Town.

JOHANNESBURG ESSENTIALS

Arriving and Departing

By Bus
All inter-city buses depart from the Rotunda (corner of Leyds and Loveday Sts., Braamfontein), the city's principal transport hub. **Greyhound** (☏ 011/333–2134) and **Translux** (☏ 011/774–3333) operate extensive routes around the country. **Intercape Mainliner** (☏ 011/333–5231) runs to Cape Town; both **Golden Wheels** (☏ 011/773–4552) and **Roadshow Intercity** (☏ 082/449–9037) offer economy fares to Durban.

By Car
Major rental agencies with offices in either the city or in Sandton include **Avis** (Carlton Hotel, Main St., Johannesburg Central, ☏ 011/331–6050), **Budget** (Holiday Inn Crowne Plaza, corner of Rivonia Rd. and Grayston Dr., Sandton, ☏ 011/883–5730), **Dolphin** (196 Oxford Manor, Illovo, ☏ 011/447–6573), and **Imperial** (Sandton Sun, corner of 5th and Alice Sts., Sandhurst, ☏ 011/883–4352; Juta St., behind the Parktonian, Braamfontein, ☏ 011/339–3762).

By Plane
Johannesburg International Airport, formerly known as Jan Smuts, lies 19 kilometers (12 miles) from the city. Most international flights depart from this airport. For flight arrival and departure information, call 011/975–9963. Major airlines serving Johannesburg include **Air Namibia** (☏ 011/442–4461), **Air Zimbabwe** (☏ 011/331–1541), **Alitalia** (☏ 011/880–9259), **British Airways** (☏ 011/441–8600), **KLM Royal Dutch Airlines** (☏ 011/881–9696), **Lufthansa** (☏ 011/484–4711), **Qantas** (☏ 011/884–5300), **South African Airways** (☏ 011/333–6504), and **Swissair** (☏ 011/484–1980).

In addition to South African Airways, the major domestic carriers serving Johannesburg are **Comair** (☏ 011/921–0222), **Phoenix Airways** (☏ 011/803–9773), **S.A. Airlink** (☏ 011/394–2430), and **Sun Air** (☏ 011/397–2244).

The airport has a tourist information desk, a VAT refund office, and a computerized accommodation service.

BETWEEN THE AIRPORT AND JOHANNESBURG

Impala Tours (☏ 011/974–6561) runs buses between the airport and the Rotunda (corner of Leyds and Loveday Sts., Braamfontein), near the city center. Buses make the 30-minute trip every half hour, and charge R25. **Magic Bus** (☎ 011/884–3957) operates a minibus airport service every half hour that calls at the Holiday Inn Crowne Plaza (Sandton), the Balalaika, and the Sandton Sun & Towers. The trip costs R40 and takes 35–50 minutes. Magic Bus also offers door-to-door pickup anywhere in the city for R120; two or more passengers pay R65 each.

Rental-car companies with offices at the airport include **Avis** (☎ 011/394–5433), **Budget Rent-a-Car** (☎ 011/394–2905), **Dolphin Car Hire** (☎ 011/394–8832), **Imperial** (☎ 011/394–4020), and **Tempest Car Hire** (☎ 011/394–8626).

Taxis are available from the ranks outside the terminals. Licensed taxis must have a working meter. Expect to pay about R90 for a trip to the city center or to Sandton.

By Train
Johannesburg's **train station** is opposite the Rotunda (Leyds St. at Loveday St.) in Braamfontein. The famous, luxurious *Blue Train*, which makes regular runs to Cape Town as well as the Lowveld and Victoria Falls (*see* Rail Travel *in* the Gold Guide), departs from here, as do **Mainline Passenger Services** (☎ 011/773–2944) trains to cities around the country. Trains to other major cities include the *Trans-Karoo* to Cape Town, the *Komati* to Nelspruit in the Eastern Transvaal, and the *Trans-Natal* to Durban.

Getting Around

Most visitors need concern themselves only with the city center and the northern suburbs. The city center is laid out in a grid, making it easy to get around, but it's not advisable to tour the area on foot except in groups. Jan Smuts Avenue runs north from the city center right through the major suburbs of Parktown, Rosebank, Dunkeld, Hyde Park, Craighall, and Randburg. The William Nicol Highway splits off this avenue and runs toward Sandton, the emerging new city center. An easier way to get from the city center to Sandton is up the N1.

Taxis
Don't expect to rush out into the street and hail a taxi. There are taxi ranks at the airport, the train station, and the Rotunda, but as a rule you must phone for a cab. Taxis should be licensed and have a working meter. Two of the most reliable companies are **Maxi Taxi** (☎ 011/648–1212) and **Rose Taxis** (☎ 011/725–3333 or 011/725–1111). The meter starts at R2 and clicks over at a rate of R3 per kilometer. Expect to pay about R90 to the airport from town and about R55 to the city center from Sandton.

Guided Tours

Diamond Tours
Mynhardts conducts 45-minute tours of its diamond-cutting operation, beginning with a 10-minute video on the history of diamonds. You are then taken to the cutting and polishing factory, where you'll learn how to evaluate a stone. You can also purchase diamonds if you wish. For information on a tour of a working diamond mine, *see* General-Interest Tours, *below, and* Off the Beaten Path, *above. 240 Commissioner St., Johannesburg Central,* ☎ *011/334–8897. Tours are free, by appointment only.* ☉ *Weekdays 8:30–4:30.*

General-Interest Tours

Springbok Atlas (☎ 011/493–3780) and **Jimmy's Face to Face Tours** (☎ 011/331–6109) offer two- to three-hour tours of the city that may include visits to the Johannesburg Stock Exchange, the observation deck of the Carlton Centre, the diamond-cutting works, and some of the city's more interesting parks and suburbs. Other tours explore Pretoria; Cullinan, a working diamond mine; and Sun City and the Pilanesberg National Park.

Gold-Mine Tours

The **Chamber of Mines** (5 Hollard St., Johannesburg Central, ☎ 011/838–8211) conducts weekly tours of a working gold mine that include a visit to a workers' hostel, a trip down a mine shaft, and a demonstration of molten gold being poured. The tours, which take place on Tuesday, Wednesday, and Thursday, leave Johannesburg around 6 AM and return only about 5 PM. Lunch is included; reservations are essential (cash only).

Township Tours

Jimmy's Face to Face Tours (☎ 011/331–6109) offers the best tours of the townships. The three-hour Soweto tour takes you in minibuses through the largest black city in Africa. The tour looks past the headlines to show visitors how urban blacks live from day to day. Jimmy's Johannesburg Night Tour features an authentic local meal, a theater production, and some township jazz.

Important Addresses and Numbers

Consulates and Embassies

Pretoria is the capital of South Africa, and most embassies are located there (*see* Pretoria Essentials, *above*). Some countries also maintain consulates in Johannesburg.

U.K. Consulate. *19th Floor, Sanlam Centre, corner of Jeppe and Von Wielligh Sts., Johannesburg,* ☎ *011/333–2624.*

U.S. Consulate. *11th Floor, Kine Centre, corner of Market and Kruis Sts., Johannesburg,* ☎ *011/331–1681.*

Emergencies

Dial 999 for an **ambulance** and 10111 for the **police.**

HOSPITAL EMERGENCY ROOMS

In the event of a medical emergency, you're advised to seek help at one of the city's private hospitals. Among the most reputable are **Milpark Hospital** (Guild Rd., Parktown, ☎ 011/726–3124), **Rosebank Clinic** (14 Sturdee Ave., Rosebank, ☎ 011/788–1980), and **Sandton Clinic Private Hospital** (corner of Main St. and Peter Pl., Lyme Park, ☎ 011/709–2000).

Travel Agencies

American Express. *Kine Centre, 141 Commissioner St., Johannesburg,* ☎ *011/331–7291; Upper Mall, Hyde Park,* ☎ *011/788–1630,* FAX *011/880–1936.* ☉ *Weekdays 8:30–5, Sat. 9–12:30.*

Rennies Travel is the representative of Thomas Cook in South Africa. *95 Kerk St., Johannesburg,* ☎ *011/333–0460; Surrey House, 35 Rissik St., Johannesburg,* ☎ *011/492–1990.* ☉ *Weekdays 8:30–4, Sat. 8:30–11.*

Visitor Information

Johannesburg Publicity Association sells a useful brochure, "The Gateway to Africa," which details most of the city's sights and attractions. *North State Bldg., corner of Kruis and Market Sts.,* ☎ *011/336–4961.*

3 The Eastern Transvaal

Archetypal Africa—land of big game and primal wilderness—unfolds before you in the Eastern Transvaal. The great allure here is game-watching, either in famed Kruger National Park or in an exclusive private reserve. All of this lies beneath the majestic Transvaal Escarpment, among whose mountains of mists, forests, waterfalls, and panoramic views you'll find some of South Africa's most luxurious hotels and lodges, as well as beautiful hikes and historic gold-rush towns.

THE EASTERN TRANSVAAL SPREADS EAST from Johannesburg to the border of Mozambique. In many ways, it's South Africa's wildest and most exciting province. The Transvaal Escarpment cuts the province in two, dividing the high, interior plateau from a low-lying subtropical belt that stretches to the Indian Ocean. The lowveld, as it is known, is classic Africa, a land of heat, dust, thorn trees—and big game. Here you will find the famous Kruger National Park and the country's premier game lodges. Information about these and South Africa's other big-game parks can be found in Chapter 9. This chapter focuses on the Escarpment itself, a continuation of the 1,120-kilometer (700-mile) Drakensberg Range, which stretches all the way from southwestern KwaZulu-Natal.

The Escarpment offers a stark contrast to the lowveld: It's a mountainous area of trout streams and waterfalls, endless views, and giant plantations of pine and eucalyptus. Lower down, the forests give way to banana, mango, and papaya groves. People come to the Escarpment to hike, unwind, and soak up its beauty. Touring the area by car is easy and rewarding—here, unlike in the Natal Drakensberg, you can reach many of the best viewpoints without stepping far from your car.

In addition, the Escarpment provides a reprise of some of South Africa's most interesting and historic events. A major gold strike in Pilgrim's Rest in 1873 sparked a gold rush every bit as raucous and wild as those in California and the Klondike. Miners from all over the world descended on these mountains to try their luck in the many rivers and streams. The safest route to the gold fields was the 800-kilometer (500-mile) road from Port Natal (now Durban), but many opted for a 270-kilometer (170-mile) shortcut from Lourenço Marques (now Maputo), in Mozambique. This route passed through the wilds of the lowveld, where malaria, yellow fever, lions, and crocodiles exacted a dreadful toll.

Those early gold-mining days have been immortalized in *Jock of the Bushveld,* a classic of South African literature. Jock was a Staffordshire dog whose master, Sir Percy Fitzpatrick, worked as a transport rider during the gold rush. Later, Sir Percy entertained his children with tales of Jock's exploits as they traveled the Eastern Transvaal, braving leopards, baboons, and all manner of dangers. Rudyard Kipling encouraged Fitzpatrick to write down the stories, and 100 years later Jock is still a household name in South Africa. You'll see dozens of Jock-of-the-Bushveld markers all over the Eastern Transvaal—seemingly wherever he cocked a leg.

Although some of the gold-rush atmosphere persists, particularly in the historic town of Pilgrim's Rest, the hardships endured by those early pioneers are now difficult to imagine. The Transvaal Escarpment today is very much the land of the guest lodge, chichi country retreats intended to help Johannesburg executives unwind after a week of chasing their secretaries. The emphasis at these lodges is on pure, luxurious self-indulgence, including elegant five-course dinners and massive English breakfasts. Many come to the Eastern Transvaal simply for this.

Their quality of service and accommodation is very high by South African standards. Even when you're paying premium rates, though, don't be surprised to have dogs and cats bounding through the dining room. Almost every lodge has its contingent of free-roaming pets, so if you're allergic or dislike animals, be sure to do some research before you reserve. While a lodge may be considered perfectly okay for cats and dogs, it's a no-go zone for children, whom most lodges consider little more than two-legged rodents. Most of them won't admit children under the age of 12 or 14. Indeed, some lodges display an almost monastic respect for peace and quiet, even eliminating televisions and radios from the rooms. So if you find yourself whispering in the bar, order another round of martinis.

These lodges are not for everyone, and you can choose from several other options, including regular hotels. If you're watching your pennies, consider staying in a self-catering cottage and driving to one of the lodges for their five-course dinners, which are usually a good value.

One benefit of staying on the Escarpment is that it allows you to sleep in the cool, malaria-free uplands and descend into the sweltering lowveld only for game-viewing drives. Most of the lodges in this chapter are no more than an hour by car from Kruger National Park and the exclusive game lodges of the Sabi Sands. Organized tours can take you for day or night drives and bring you back in time for bed.

Where you stay on the Escarpment may well dictate the kind of weather you get. In low areas like White River and Hazyview, summer is hot and there is a small malaria risk. Higher up, around Pilgrim's Rest, Graskop, and Sabie, the weather can be chilly, even in summer. At these elevations fog and mist can also be a hazard during the summer.

Warning: The lowveld and parts of the Transvaal Escarpment are malarial zones, and all visitors are advised to take anti-malarial drugs.

EXPLORING

Numbers in the margin correspond to points of interest on the Eastern Transvaal map.

This tour assumes that you are driving from Johannesburg. If you fly into the state capital of Nelspruit instead, it's easy to pick up the tour by driving north along the R37 to Sabie. Either way, you could complete the whole tour in two days, but you're better off budgeting three or more if you plan to linger anywhere. And to jump off from the eastern end of this tour into Kruger National Park or one of the private game lodges, add another three days or more.

About 2½ hours east of Johannesburg on the N4, take the turnoff to **Belfast** and follow the R540 out of town for 35 kilometers (22 miles)
❶ to **Dullstroom.** This tiny hamlet sits amid rolling, grass-covered mountains and sparkling streams. At 6,600 feet, it's one of the coldest towns in South Africa, and sweaters and roaring fires are common comforts even in mid-summer. Dullstroom is the trout-fishing capital of the Eastern Transvaal. The fish were introduced into the streams of the Transvaal Drakensberg at the turn of the century, and trout-fishing is now the third-largest moneymaker in the region, after timber and tourism. There is very good dining and lodging in town (*below*).

From Dullstroom, follow the R540 another 58 kilometers (36 miles)
❷ to **Lydenburg,** in an open plain between the Drakensberg and Steenkampsberg mountains. The town was founded in 1849 after the early Boer settlers (Voortrekkers) were forced to abandon their original settlement at Andries-Ohrigstad, where many of them died from malaria. Shaken by those years of death and misery, the survivors gave the new town the name Lydenburg, which means "town of suffering." Ironically, Lydenburg prospered so well that in 1857 its citizens seceded from the Transvaal during the incessant bickering that marked rela-

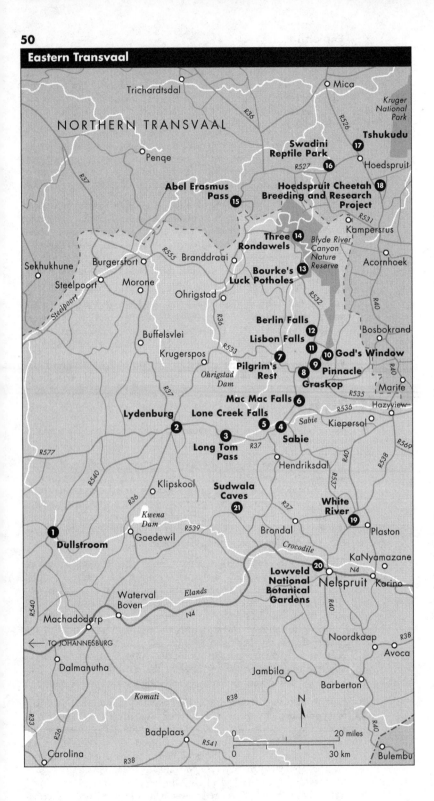

NORTHERN TRANSVAAL

Trichardtsdal

Mica

Kruger National Park

Penqe

Swadini Reptile Park

Tshukudu ⑰

Hoedspruit

R527 ⑯

⑱ **Hoedspruit Cheetah Breeding and Research Project**

Abel Erasmus Pass ⑮

R531

Kampersrus

Three Rondawels ⑭

Blyde River Canyon Nature Reserve

Acornhoek

Bourke's Luck Potholes ⑬

Sekhukhune

Burgersfort

R555

Branddraai

Steelpoort

Morone

Ohrigstad

Bosbokrand

Buffelsvlei

Berlin Falls ⑫

Krugerspos

R533

Lisbon Falls ⑪

⑩ **God's Window**

Pilgrim's Rest ⑦

⑨

Ohrigstad Dam

⑧

Pinnacle

Graskop

Marite

Mac Mac Falls ⑥

R535

Hazyview

Lydenburg ②

Lone Creek Falls

⑤ ④

Sabie

Kiepersol

③

Sabie

R569

Long Tom Pass

R37

Hendriksdal

Klipskool

Sudwala Caves

R37

White River ⑲

㉑

Plaston

Kwena Dam

R539

Brondal

KaNyamazane

① **Dullstroom**

Goedewil

Crocodile

㉚

Lowveld National Botanical Gardens

N4

Karino

Nelspruit

Waterval Boven

Elands

N4

R40

Machadodorp

Noordkaap

R38

← TO JOHANNESBURG

Avoca

Dalmanutha

Jambila

Barberton

Komati

R38

N

Badplaas

R541

0   20 miles

0   30 km

Carolina

R38

Bulembu

tions among Voortrekker factions. "De Republiek Lydenburg en Zuid-Afrika," as the new country was known, remained independent for three years before rejoining the Transvaal.

The excellent Lydenburg Museum lies within the **Gustav Klingbiel Nature Reserve,** about 3 kilometers (1½ miles) east of town along the R37. The museum traces human development in the region from the Early Stone Age (1.5 million–150,000 years ago) to the present. Exhibits display tools and artifacts from each period. The most important archaeological find in the area has been the Lydenburg Heads, seven clay heads dating back to AD 490, during the Early Iron Age. The heads are thought to have been used in initiation ceremonies, either as masks or icons. The pieces on display are reproductions of the originals, now in the South African Museum in Cape Town. *R37, 2½ km (1 mi) east of Lydenburg,* ☎ *01323/2121.* ☛ *R7 per vehicle.* ⊘ *Daily 8–4.*

❸ From the Klingbiel Nature Reserve, follow the R37 as it begins its winding ascent toward the spectacular **Long Tom Pass.** Beautiful as it is, this mountain pass is more famous for its historical associations. For it was here, from September 8 to 11, 1900, that one of the last pitched battles of the Boer War (1899–1902) was fought. Lydenburg had fallen easily to the British on September 7, but the retreating Boers reformed on the heights above the town and began shelling the British with their two remaining Creusot siege guns. Known as Long Toms because of their long barrels and range, these guns could hurl a 90-pound shell a distance of nearly 9½ kilometers (6 miles). The guns were a tremendous headache for the British, who could not match their range. The Boers, struggling to get these monsters up the pass, can hardly have felt any more kindly toward them—a minimum of 16 oxen were required to pull each gun. It took the British two days to winkle the Boers out of their positions on the pass and drive them over the steep wall of the Escarpment. Even then, the Boers managed to set up a gun position on the other side of the valley to shell the British as they maneuvred down the **Staircase,** a series of switchbacks zigzagging down the pass. You can still see the shell holes in the Staircase.

❹ As you descend from Long Tom Pass, the town of **Sabie** comes into view far below, in a bowl formed by the surrounding mountains. It is by far the most pleasant and enjoyable town in the region, with plenty of restaurants, shops, and bars. It makes a great base for exploring.

Gold was first discovered in appreciable amounts in the Eastern Transvaal around present-day Sabie. On November 6, 1872, a prospector named Tom McLachlan located rewarding deposits of gold in a creek on the farm known as Hendriksdal, now a small hamlet about 16 kilometers (10 miles) from Sabie. Sabie itself owes its origins to an altogether luckier strike. In 1895, Henry Glynn, a local farmer, hosted a picnic at the Klein Sabie Falls. Loosened up by a few drinks, his guests started taking potshots at empty bottles arrayed on a rock ledge. The flying bullets chipped shards of rock off the cliff face, revealing traces of gold beneath. Fifty-five years later, when mining operations closed down, more than 1 million ounces of gold had been taken from the Klein Sabie Falls.

Today, timber has replaced gold as the community's livelihood. The town sits in the heart of the world's largest man-made forest: More than 1,154,000 acres of exotic pine and eucalyptus. The first forests were planted in 1876 to provide the area's mines with posts and supports. Today, much of the timber is still used to prop up shafts in the Witwatersrand mines.

Back in your car, drive down Main Road to the bottom of town and turn left onto Old Lydenburg Road. This 6½-kilometer (4-mile) dead-end road leads to three of the region's principal waterfalls—Bridal Veil Falls, Horseshoe Falls, and Lone Creek Falls. **Lone Creek Falls,** the last stop along the road, is the prettiest and most peaceful of the three, and the most accessible to the elderly and those with disabilities. An easy, paved walkway leads to the falls, which plunge 225 feet from the center of a high, broad rock face framed by vines and creepers. The path crosses the river via a wooden bridge and loops through the forest back to the parking lot. If you're feeling energetic, follow the steep steps leading up to the top of the falls.

Return to Sabie along the same road and turn left toward Graskop and Pilgrim's Rest. The road climbs gradually up the Escarpment through plantation forests to **Mac Mac Falls,** the most famous and impressive of the falls in the Eastern Transvaal. Set in an amphitheater of towering cliffs, the falls plunge 215 feet into a pool, and rainbows play in the billowing spray. Unfortunately, you can view the falls only from an observation point surrounded by thick wire fencing, which destroys much of the atmosphere. The falls owe their interesting name to President Thomas Burger, who, while visiting the nearby gold diggings at Geelhoutboom in 1873, noticed that many of the miners' names began with "Mac," revealing their Scottish background. He promptly dubbed the area Mac Mac.

The road ends at a T-junction. Turn left onto R533 to climb the Bonnet Pass up to **Pilgrim's Rest.** The town is a delightful, albeit touristy, reminder of gold-rush days. It was the first proper gold-mining town in South Africa, centered around the richest gold strike in the Eastern Transvaal. Alec "Wheelbarrow" Patterson, a taciturn Scot who had struck out on his own to escape the hordes of new miners at Mac Mac, discovered gold in September of 1873. Mining operations ceased only in 1972, and since then the entire town has been declared a national monument. Many of the old corrugated-iron houses have been beautifully restored and now serve as museums, hotels, gift shops, and restaurants. It's definitely worth a visit, even for just a few hours.

The corrugated-iron houses that you see today date from the more staid years after 1900 when Pilgrim's Rest had become a company town. During the mad years of 1873–1875, when most of the alluvial gold was panned by individual prospectors, Pilgrim's Rest consisted of nothing more than a collection of tents and mud huts. Rumors about the richness of the strike quickly carried around the world, and miners drifted in from California, Australia, and Europe. By January 1874, more than 1,500 diggers were working Pilgrim's Creek. Only a few struck it rich; the rest spent their earnings in the numerous canteens until their claims played out and they drifted off.

Your first stop should be the **Information Centre** (*see* Visitor Information, *below*), in the center of town, where you buy tickets to the various museums. Start your walking tour at the top end of town at **St. Mary's Anglican Church.** Built in 1884, the iron-roofed stone building replaced the original makeshift wattle-and-daub structure. It really must have been an uphill battle for the early ministers to lure miners from the town's 18 canteens. After a backbreaking week spent on the sluices, Holy Communion just didn't pack the punch of a belt of Cape brandy or Squareface gin.

Continuing down Main Street, you come to the tiny **Pilgrim's and Sabie News Printing Museum,** with displays of antique printing presses and old photos. The building, constructed in the late 19th century as a residence, later served as the offices of the weekly *Pilgrim's and Sabie News.* The first newspaper in Pilgrim's Rest was the *Gold News,* published in 1874 and notable for its libelous gossip. The editor, an Irishman by the name of Phelan, felt obliged to keep a pair of loaded pistols on his desk. *Main St., uptown, no ☎.* ☞ *R1.50 adults, 50¢ children. Tickets available from information center.* ⊙ *Daily 9–1, 1:30–4.*

TIME OUT If you do nothing else in Pilgrim's Rest, stop for a drink at the **Royal Hotel bar** (Main St., uptown, ☎ 01315/8–1100). The building first served as a chapel at a girls' school in Cape Town. It was dismantled in 1870, shipped to Lourenço Marques (now Maputo), then carried by ox wagon to Pilgrim's Rest, where it ministered a different kind of spirit to thirsty miners. The bar retains much of its gold-rush atmosphere, with wood-panel walls, an antique cash register, and a wonderful old bar counter. If you're hungry, you can order fish and chips or steak and eggs.

Across the street and to the left is the **House Museum,** which re-creates the way of life of a middle-class family in the early part of this century. Constructed in 1913 of corrugated iron and wood, the house is typical of buildings erected at the time throughout the area. *Main St., uptown, no ☎.* ☞ *R1.50 adults, 50¢ children. Tickets available at information center.* ⊙ *Daily 9–1, 1:30–4:30.*

The **Pilgrim's Rest Cemetery** sits high on the hill above Main Street. To get here, follow the steep path that starts next to the picnic area, near the post office. The fascinating inscriptions on the tombstones evoke the dangers and hardship of life in the Eastern Transvaal a century ago. The tombstone of Fred Sanders, for example, tells how he was "shot in a skirmish with kafirs [sic] on the 27th August, 1878, aged 24." Tellingly, most of the dead were in their 20s and 30s, and it's amazing how many hailed from Wales, Scotland, and England. The cemetery owes its improbable setting to the **Robber's Grave,** the only grave that lies in a north–south direction. It contains the body of a thief who was banished from Pilgrim's Rest for stealing gold from a tent; the man foolishly returned and was shot dead. He was buried where he fell and the area around his grave became the town's unofficial cemetery.

Return down the hill and walk left on Main Street to the **Dredzen Shop and House Museum.** In 1930, 16 general dealers lined the streets of Pilgrim's Rest. By 1950 mine production had taken a nose-dive and most of the businesses had shut down. This museum re-creates the look of a general dealer during those lean years. The attached residence focuses on life in Pilgrim's Rest in the years immediately following World War II. *Main St., uptown, no ☎.* ☞ *R1.50 adults, 50¢ children. Tickets available at information center.* ⊙ *Daily 9–1, 1:30–4:30.*

You can also tour **Alanglade,** the beautiful home of TGME's mine manager, set in a forested grove a mile north of town. The huge house was built in 1916 for Richard Barry and his family and is furnished with pieces dating from 1900 to 1930. Look carefully at the largest pieces, and you will see that they are actually segmented, so they could be taken apart and carried on ox wagons. *Vaalhoek Rd., off R533, no ☎.* ☞ *R2 adults, R1 children. Tickets available at information center.* ⊙ *Tours Mon.–Sat. at 10:30 and 2.*

Drive back through Pilgrim's Rest and continue for about a mile until you reach the **Diggings Museum,** in the creek where the alluvial gold was originally panned. On display are a water-driven, three-stamp battery as well as some of the tents and wattle-and-daub huts typical of the early gold-rush years. The tour lasts about an hour, and is more enjoyable than actually informative. The retired prospector who conducts the tours enlivens the proceedings with yarns about the old days. Visitors see a display of gold-panning and poke around in some of the old diggings. *R533, no ☎. ☞ R1.50 adults, 50¢ children. Tickets available at information center. ⊙ Tours daily at 10, 11, noon, 2, and 3.*

From Pilgrim's Rest, return down the Bonnet Pass on the R533 to
⑧ Graskop, 20 kilometers (13 miles) away. Graskop means Grassy Head in Afrikaans, and it's easy to see how the town got its name—it sits on a lovely grassy plateau, high up in the mountains. Graskop bills itself as the "Window on the Lowveld," and several nearby lookouts do have stunning views over the edge of the Escarpment. Unfortunately, the town itself is largely forgettable, although it makes a good base for exploring the region.

Follow the R532 out of Graskop. After 3 kilometers (1½ miles), turn right onto R534, a loop road that runs right along the edge of the Escarpment. The road snakes through coniferous forest until it reaches
⑨ the turnoff to the **Pinnacle** (Rotstoring). Flanked by sheer cliffs, this towering needle of rock rises out of a deep gorge and looks out over the lowveld. A small stream fed by a waterfall rushes through the bottom of the gorge, almost hidden by dense bush.

⑩ Continue another 4½ kilometers (3 miles) to **God's Window,** the most famous of the lowveld viewpoints. Part of the Blyde River Canyon Nature Reserve, it's geared for tourists, with toilet facilities, paved parking areas, curio vendors, and marked walking trails. The altitude here is 5,700 feet, just a little lower than Johannesburg. But you still feel as though you're standing on top of the world, because the Escarpment drops away almost vertically to the lowveld. Paved walking trails lead to various lookouts. The God's Window lookout has a view back along the Escarpment framed between towering cliffs. For a broader panorama, follow the paved track up through the rainforest to a small, unfenced area that offers sweeping views of the entire lowveld. On sunny days, carry water—it's a tiring 10-minute climb.

The R534 ends at a T-junction. From here you can take a left and return to Graskop, 10 kilometers (6 miles) away, or you can turn right (a sign indicates Ohrigstad) and follow R532 to Blyde River Canyon.

Even if you're continuing on to the Blyde River Canyon, it's worth head-
⑪ ing left for a half mile to **Lisbon Falls.** Set in a bowl between hills, the falls cascade 120 feet onto rocks below, hurling a lovely spray over a deep pool.

Heading back in the other direction, follow R532 toward Ohrigstad.
⑫ The turnoff to **Berlin Falls** lies a mile farther on. A small stream, Waterfall Spruit, runs through a broad expanse of grassland to the falls. The falls themselves are a thin stream that drops 150 feet into a deep-green pool surrounded by tall pines.

Continue north on R532. The dense plantations of gum and pine fall behind, and the road runs through magnificent grass-covered peaks.
⑬ Some 32 kilometers (20 miles) north of Berlin Falls lie **Bourke's Luck Potholes.** Named after a gold prospector, the potholes are a series of bizarre holes carved into the rock in the gorge where the Treur and Blyde Rivers converge. The holes have been dug by the abrasion of pebbles suspended in the swirling water. Here, as well, is the headquarters for the **Blyde River Canyon Nature Reserve,** one of South Africa's scenic highlights. The canyon begins here and winds northward for nearly

32 kilometers (20 miles). Several long canyon trails start from here (*see* Sports and the Outdoors, *below*), and an interesting nature center explains the geology and ecology of the canyon. *R532,* ☎ *01315/81215.* ☛ *R2.50 adults, children under 6 free.* ⊙ *Reserve: daily 7–5. Visitor center: daily 7:30–4.*

Continuing north from Bourke's Luck Potholes, you get occasional glimpses of the magnificent canyon and the distant cliffs of the Escarpment. Nowhere, however, is the view better than from **Three Rondawels** (Drie Rondawels), 14 kilometers (9 miles) from the potholes. This is one of the most spectacular viewpoints in South Africa—you'll find it in almost every travel brochure. The Blyde River, hemmed in by towering buttresses of red rock, snakes through the bottom of the canyon. The Three Rondawels are rock formations that rise up from the canyon floor and bear a vague similarity to the round, thatched African dwellings known as rondawels.

⑭

The R532 also ends at a T-junction. Turn right onto R36 to begin the beautiful descent down the Escarpment through **Abel Erasmus Pass.** The **J.G. Strijdom Tunnel,** burrowing through the mountainside, serves as the gateway to the lowveld. As you emerge from the dark mouth of the tunnel, the lowveld spreads out below you, and the views of both it and the mountains are stunning.

⑮

Once on the flat plains of the lowveld, the road cuts east through plantations of mango and citrus. Keep an eye out for a lovely example of a baobab tree, on the right-hand side next to a fruit stand. These weird and wonderful trees don't grow much farther south than this.

Just outside Hoedspruit, **Swadini Reptile Park** has a large collection of snakes, lizards, and other creepy-crawlies. The rangers are extremely friendly and knowledgeable, and will take non-poisonous snakes out of their pens for your inspection. This is a great place to bring children. *R527, 6 mi from Hoedspruit,* ☎ *01528/3–5203.* ☛ *R8.50 adults, R6.50 children.* ⊙ *Daily 8–5.*

⑯

Hoedspruit itself is a nondescript place, little more than a supply depot for the surrounding farms. This is diehard Afrikaner country, and it's not unusual to see men packing pistols on their hips.

From Hoedspruit, turn left onto R40 and drive 4 kilometers (2½ miles) to **Tshukudu.** This 12,350-acre game farm bills itself as a safari lodge, but it's more like an animal park. Go somewhere else for a two- or three-night big-game adventure, but stop here for a day visit, which includes lunch, a game drive (including a stop at a lion pen), and a bush walk. The highlight of the day is the chance to meet some of the farm's orphaned animals, many of them completely tame. Don't be surprised if you're ambushed by a tame lion, nudged by a wildebeest, or accompanied by two baby elephants on your bush walk. Advance reservations are essential. *R40, north of Hoedspruit,* ☎ *01528/3–2476.* ☛ *R50 (includes lunch, game drive, and walk). By appointment only.*

⑰

From Tshukudu, head back down R40 past Hoedspruit to the **Hoedspruit Cheetah Breeding and Research Project.** This is ostensibly a breeding station for cheetahs, but it doesn't feel any different than a zoo, and many locals doubt whether any of these animals will ever be successfully placed in the wild. After viewing a video, you can tour the animal pens in a minibus. During the 60- to 90-minute journey, you'll see the very rare king cheetah, notable for its exaggerated black spots, as well as wild dogs and orphaned animals such as rhinos and servals (medium-sized cats). *R40, south of Hoedspruit,* ☎

⑱

01528/3–1633. ☛ *R17 adults, R7 children.* ☉ *Hourly tours Mon.–Sat. 8:45–3:45.*

 The R40 runs south through lowveld thornscrub, with the distant barrier of the Escarpment visible on the right. It passes through the service town of Hazyview before continuing on to **White River,** a pleasant farming town with several interesting arts and crafts shops.

From White River it's just 19 kilometers (12 miles) to Nelspruit. Although it serves as the capital of the Eastern Transvaal, Nelspruit has little to offer other than the **Lowveld National Botanical Gardens.** Set on the banks of the Crocodile River, these gardens display over 500 plant species indigenous to the valley, including a spectacular collection of cycads and ferns. Several trails wind through the gardens, one leading to a pleasant waterfall. *2 mi outside Nelspruit on White River Rd.,* ☏ *01311/55–1988.* ☛ *R3.50 adults, R1 children.* ☉ *Daily Oct.–Apr. 8–6, May–Sept. 8–5:15.*

From Nelspruit, follow N4 back toward Johannesburg. After 25 kilometers (16 miles), exit for **Sudwala Caves,** some of the oldest known caves in the world. In the 19th century, they were used by the Swazi king as a shelter from attack. Unfortunately, the 45-minute tour of the caverns is ruined by corny guides who insist on finding shapes like E.T. and doves in the weird contortions of the rock. (Lose the guide, and the caves would be amazing.) Next door is Dinosaur Park, an open-air museum with life-size re-creations of nearly 100 dinosaurs. The entrance fee for both attractions is steep by South African standards. *6 mi off N4,* ☏ *01311/6–4152.* ☛ *Cave: R18 adults, R9 children; park: R10 adults, R5 children.* ☉ *Cave: daily 8:30–4:30; park 8:30–5.*

SPORTS AND THE OUTDOORS

Hiking

The Transvaal Escarpment is laced with hiking trails, some as short as 10 minutes, others taking several days. Local tourist information centers have descriptions and maps of trails in their areas.

Blyde River Canyon Nature Reserve
The **Blyde River Canyon Trail** is a 56-kilometer (35-mile) hike that runs from God's Window right along the edge of the Escarpment to the Sybrand van Niekerk resort. The mountain scenery is spectacular, making it one of the most popular trails in the country. Several shorter trails explore the canyon from trailheads at Bourke's Luck Potholes. The number of hikers on these trails is controlled, so it's essential to reserve far in advance. To make a booking, contact the Blyde River Canyon Nature Reserve office (☏ 01315/8–1215).

Lydenburg
The 5,400-acre **Gustav Klingbiel Nature Reserve** (R37, ☏ 01323/2121) is made up of mountain grassland populated by eland, kudu, blue wildebeest, leopard, and other animals. Four hiking trails meander through the park, ranging from the 5-kilometer (3-mile) Pedi Route to the two-day, 19-kilometer (12-mile) Ribbok Route.

Pilgrim's Rest
The 1,225-acre **Mount Sheba Nature Reserve** contains one of the last stands of indigenous forest in the Transvaal Drakensberg. Fourteen trails of varying difficulty run through the reserve, each taking from 1½ to

2½ hours. Some walks lead to waterfalls hidden in the bush or to pools where you can swim. A map is available from the reception desk at the Mount Sheba Hotel (*see* Dining and Lodging, *below*).

Horseback Riding

Sabie Horse Trails (Box 571, Sabie 1260, ☎ 01315/4–1011 ext. 205) leads horse rides of 1–5 hours through the forested Sabie Valley. Longer rides feature brunch or a braai.

DINING AND LODGING

By Andrew Barbour and Pat Kossuth

At most of the guest lodges on the Escarpment, the price includes a five-course dinner and a full English breakfast. Vegetarians should call ahead to make special arrangements. Some of the lodges and hotels offer special rates, particularly mid-week. For price ranges, *see* Charts 1 and 2(B) *in* On the Road with Fodor's.

For a description of South African culinary terms, *see* Pleasures & Pastimes *in* Chapter 1.

Dullstroom

DINING

$$ Die Tonteldoos. Recently awarded the blazon of the Chaine de Rotisseurs, this small bistro is a popular stop for travelers on the way to or from the lowveld. Owner Brian Whitehorn's menu is heavily influenced by French cuisine, with many sauces based on rich reduction. Highly recommended are the steak fillet topped with camembert and red wine sauce, and any of the game pies. For something lighter, consider spinach and feta cheese in phyllo pastry or a silky trout terrine accompanied by sage and olive bread. Garden salads and open sandwiches on chunky wholewheat bread are popular snacks. ✗ *R540, Dullstroom,* ☎ *01325/4–0115. Reservations required weekends. AE, DC, MC, V.* ⊗ *Daily 8 AM–8:30 PM.*

DINING AND LODGING

$$$$ Walkersons. No other Eastern Transvaal lodges offer such genuine luxury—like the wealth of antiques and works of art found in the public areas—and few can match this setting on a 1,500-acre farm of grass-covered hills laced with trout streams. The main lodge, built of stone and thatch, overlooks a small dam. Inside, such disparate items as Persian rugs, French tapestries, and 19th-century English oils come together beautifully. All rooms face the lake and have sponge-painted walls, mosquito nets, and fireplaces. Two-thirds of the farm has been made into a nature reserve stocked with general game like wildebeest, springbok, blesbok, and zebra. Guests can follow several walking trails through the reserve or take a two-hour game drive in an open Land Rover. The lodge's five-course dinner is flawlessly presented. A meal might begin with Roquefort mousse with figs or smoked trout in phyllo baskets. Following a soup of brandied butternut squash and nutmeg, expect as a main course something like beef fillet with green pepper sauce and rosemary potatoes. 🏠 *Off R540, 13 kms (8 mi) north of Dullstroom (mailing address: Box 185, Dullstroom 1110),* ☎ *01325/4–0246,* 𝖥𝖠𝖷 *01325/4–0260. 15 rooms with bath. Restaurant, bar, pool, hot tub, trout fishing, game drives. Breakfast and dinner included. No children under 12. AE, DC, MC, V.*

$$$ Critchley Hackle Lodge. Foreign travelers often use this country lodge midway between Johannesburg and Kruger Park as a one-night stopover on their way to the lowveld, but for South Africans it's more of a weekend getaway, promising a relaxed country atmosphere and lovely antiques and roaring fires. Rooms in stone and brick cottages arranged around a trout pond all have their own fireplaces. Wooden chests, floral curtains, and rough brick walls contribute to their warm, rustic feel. An unfortunate drawback is traffic noise from the nearby R540. The dining room exudes a formality that works well for dinner but can seem heavy at other meals. The five-course dinner is standard lodge fare, not altogether memorable, with an emphasis on roasts. Light lunches are served on the patio. ⌖ *Off R540 (mailing address: Box 141, Dullstroom 1110),* ☏ *01325/40145,* FAX *01325/40262. 19 rooms with bath. Restaurant, bar, indoor pool, sauna, tennis, trout fishing. Breakfast and dinner included. No children under 12. AE, DC, MC, V.*

$$ **Dullstroom Inn.** In an old trading store that dates from 1910, the inn is more famous for its pub than its accommodations. That may change under the new ownership of the Briggs family, who have refurbished the rooms and priced them competitively. Rooms are small but attractively done in colonial style, with floral patterns and old-fashioned iron bedsteads. No rooms have a phone or TV. If you're not staying at the inn, it's still worth stopping at the wood-paneled pub, with its roaring fire and excellent selection of draft lagers and bitters. The extensive pub menu features such staples as steak-and-kidney pie, ploughman's lunch, and oxtail. Try the guinea fowl casserole and sticky toffee pudding. ⌖ *Corner of Teding van Berkhout and Oranje Nassau Sts. (mailing address: Box 44, Dullstroom 1110),* ☏ *01325/4–0071,* FAX *01325/4–0278. 11 rooms with bath. Restaurant, pub. Breakfast included. AE, DC, MC, V.*

Graskop

DINING

$ **Harrie's Pancake Bar.** Harrie's was the original pancake bar in the area, and it's still the best. (Tour groups know this, too, so you might have to stand in line on weekends.) If the weather's fine, take a seat on the veranda overlooking the street. Otherwise, warm yourself by the fire inside and listen to classical music while mulling over the selection of pancakes and infusion coffees. Pancakes in South Africa are a thicker version of crepes, stuffed with either dessert fillings or savories like ground beef, Dutch bacon, ratatouille, or spinach and feta. ✗ *Corner of Louis Trichardt Ave. and Kerk St.,* ☏ *01315/2281. Wine and beer only. AE, MC, V.* ☉ *Dec.–Apr., daily 10–6; May–Nov., daily 9–4:30.*

LODGING

$$ **Graskop Hotel.** Aside from self-catering establishments, this is the only decent option in Graskop. And in fact it's rather attractive. The public areas are elegant showrooms for an interesting collection of African art. Zulu baskets brighten long corridors, avant-garde metal ostriches flank the foyer, and Swazi pots and sculpture dot the lounge. Rooms are light and airy, with white walls, green wicker furniture, and lots of blond wood. Unfortunately, the walls are too thin to keep out noise from neighboring rooms. ⌖ *Main St. (mailing address: Box 568, Graskop 1270),* ☏ *and* FAX *01315/7–1244. 24 rooms, 18 with bath, and 15 family cottages. 2 restaurants, bar, pool. Breakfast included. AE, DC, MC, V.*

$$ **Lisbon Hideaway.** In a peaceful meadow overlooking a small stream,
★ this self-catering establishment makes a great base from which to explore the Escarpment. Graskop, several waterfalls, and the magnificent viewpoints of God's Window are minutes away. Accommodation is either in wood cabins or an old, stone miner's cottage that sleeps four. The wood cabins are modern and comfortable, done in wicker and floral patterns. Each cabin sleeps a maximum of six, with two bedrooms, a living/dining room, and a fully equipped kitchen. Don't let

the self-catering set-up put you off. Talkative owner Phillip Flischman runs the Spar supermarket in Sabie and will stock the kitchen for you on request. ⊠ *Lisbon Falls Rd., off R532, 10 km (6 mi) from Graskop (mailing address: Box 43, Graskop 1270),* ☎ *01315/7–1851. 3 chalets and 1 cottage, all with bath. No phones. MC.*

Kiepersol
DINING AND LODGING

$$$$ Blue Mountain Lodge. A member of Small Luxury Hotels of the World, this exclusive retreat elicits either fervent support or scorn—there is little room in between. The emphasis here is on creating a fantasy get-away for jaded city-dwellers. The owners, Valma and Kobus Botha, both worked in the film industry, and their lodge has a setlike quality. Artificial moss adds instant age to stone work, and sponge-painting creates an illusion of fading murals on palace walls (it looks terrific if you're in a romantic mood, fake if you're a cynical old bugger). Compared with similarly priced rooms at Cybele (*below*), the eight Victorian suites are huge, impeccably maintained, and better value. Each of them follows a theme, ranging from English country to American Colonial, and all have fireplaces, verandas, and minibars, but no TV. The best is the Out of Africa Suite, done all in white, with billowing mosquito netting, white bedspreads, lots of wood, and a claw-foot bathtub in the center of the room. Avoid the less expensive Quadrant suites, however. Set in a cobbled courtyard reminiscent of old Europe, they feel too sharp and angular, a flaw not helped by gaudy stripes painted on the walls. Meals are a refreshing departure from the traditional offerings of other lodges. The cuisine is lighter, with a nouvelle California style that pairs sweet and savory, Western and Asian tastes. Look for dishes like a quenelle of lobster and mussels on a bed of roasted peppers, papaya salad with peanut sauce, or cabeljou (a local sea fish) with litchi sauce. Presentation and service are superb. ⊠ *Off R514, 10 km (6 mi) from Kiepersol (mailing address: Box 101, Kiepersol 1241),* ☎ *and* FAX *01317/6–8446. 13 rooms with bath. Restaurant, bar, pool, bass-fishing. Breakfast and dinner included. No children under 12. AE, DC, MC, V.*

$$$$ Cybele Forest Lodge. Cybele started the whole concept of the country
★ lodge in the Eastern Transvaal, and to a large extent it still sets the pace, as its awards suggest. It is Cybele's service that separates it from its competitors, and that's essentially what you pay for. The staff has achieved a fine mix of professionalism and friendliness, and they go out of their way to make visitors feel special. The English-country decor of the main lodge complements the service. The two living rooms, warmed by fires and cluttered with attractive bric-a-brac and books, have a reassuring, lived-in feel. Once you leave the warmth of the public rooms, though, much of Cybele's magic is lost, and if you were to judge the lodge solely on its guest rooms you would likely be disappointed. The cottage and studio rooms are small and undistinguished. The larger Garden and Courtyard suites, decorated in English-country style, are comfortable but show signs of wear. The magnificent Paddock Suites, however, with thatched roofs and spectacular views over the forested hills, have their own garden and swimming pool and a private outdoor shower hidden in the foliage—sort of a *Blue Lagoon* scene for the over-40 crowd. Cybele built much of its reputation on the quality of its food, and it certainly keeps customers coming back. The traditional five-course dinner melds classic French and traditional English country cooking. A light mushroom broth might be followed by risotto with ratatouille, then a choice of rack of lamb or trout fillets with a light lemon-cream sauce. For dessert, a rich gâteau with choco-

late sauce would be typical. 🖭 *Off R40 between Hazyview and White River (mailing address: Box 346, White River 1240),* ☏ *01311/5–0511,* FAX *01311/3–2839. 12 rooms with bath. Restaurant, bar, pool, horseriding, trout-fishing. No children under 10. Breakfast and dinner included. AE, DC, MC, V.*

LODGING

$$ Carrigans Country Estate. Modeled after old gold-rush homes in Barberton and Pilgrim's Rest, the cottages at this lovely bed-and-breakfast have wraparound verandas that overlook the distant hills of the Drakensberg. Each two-bedroom cottage is decorated in period style, complete with a fireplace, mosquito netting, and a claw-foot bathtub. All cottages have fully equipped kitchens and their own living and dining rooms, but no TV. The nearest grocery store is 5 kilometers (3 miles) away, but if you don't care to cook, the owner's wife will prepare a supper hamper (R50 per person) of gazpacho, smoked trout, roast chicken, and dessert. Even better, Cybele's wonderful food is just a five-minute drive away. 🖭 *Off R40, between Hazyview and White River (mailing address: Box 19, Kiepersol 1241),* ☏ *01315/4–3451,* FAX *01315/5–1390. 4 cottages, each with 2 en suite bedrooms. Pool. No children under 12. Breakfast included. AE, DC, MC, V.*

Pilgrim's Rest

DINING

$ The Vine Restaurant and Pub. In a former trading store dating from 1910, this restaurant uses antique sideboards, sepia photos, and country-style wood furniture to capture a gold rush–era feeling. The food is straightforward and hearty. Try traditional South African *bobotie* (a curried ground-mutton pie), *potjiekos* (stew), or oxtail and samp (corn porridge). Or order a meat pie or toasted sandwich. The pub in the back is charmless—you're better off drinking at the Church Bar at the Royal Hotel (*see below*). ✕ *Main St., downtown Pilgrim's Rest,* ☏ *01315/8–1080. AE, DC, V.*

DINING AND LODGING

$$$ Mount Sheba Hotel. High above Pilgrim's Rest and surrounded by indigenous forest and grass-covered peaks, this resort enjoys one of the most spectacular settings in the Eastern Transvaal. Come here to relax and to walk (*see* Participant Sports, *above*), but think twice about making the hotel a base for exploring. The 8-kilometer (5-mile) dirt road leading to it is so badly rutted that many guests won't want to brave it more than once. The best rooms are the duplexes, in a long curving wing of thatched, whitewashed brick. Duplexes feature an upstairs bedroom and a downstairs sitting area and veranda. Some of the rooms look a little tired, and the bathroom carpets are often damp and smelly. Dinner is a traditional five-course set menu. Unfortunately, the food lacks flair, and the service is well meaning but untrained. Expect a starter like feta cheese in phyllo pastry, followed by a traditional main course like roast beef with Yorkshire pudding. On weekdays, lunch is a simple buffet (R12.50) served by the pool overlooking the mountains. 🖭 *Off R533, 19 km (12 mi) from Pilgrim's Rest (mailing address: Box 100, Pilgrim's Rest 1290),* ☏ *and* FAX *01315/8–1241. 25 rooms with bath. 2 restaurants, 2 bars, room service, pool, health center, squash, tennis. Breakfast and dinner included. AE, DC, MC, V.*

LODGING

$$ Royal Hotel. Established in 1873, this hotel dates back to the very beginning of the gold rush in Pilgrim's Rest—you'll see its corrugated-iron facade in many sepia photos displayed around town. Rooms are small and tucked away behind the street, but it's worth staying here to get into the spirit of the town. Reproduction four-poster beds, wood ceiling fans, and marble-and-oak washstands in the rooms help recapture their original Victorian look. None has a TV or phone. The Royal also owns several other Victorian buildings around town, including the 14-room Pilgrims and a variety of smaller cottages. But unless you want to take an entire cottage for yourself, opt for the main hotel. ☎ *Main St., in upper town (mailing address: Box 59, Pilgrim's Rest 1290),* ☎ *01315/8–1100,* FAX *01315/8–1188. 42 rooms with bath. Restaurant, bar. Breakfast included. AE, DC, MC, V.*

$ **District 6 Miners' Cottages.** On a hill above Pilgrim's Rest, these self-catering cottages are the best value in town. The cottages are all miners' homes dating back to 1920, and they're delightful. From their verandas there are spectacular views of the town and surrounding mountains. The interiors are furnished with period reproductions, complete with wood floors, brass bedsteads, and claw-footed tubs. Each cottage consists of a small living room, two double bedrooms, a fully equipped kitchen and pantry, and a bathroom. You can walk to the two restaurants in town in five minutes. ☎ *District 6, Pilgrim's Rest (contact Pilgrim's Rest Information (see below), ☎ 01315/8–1211; after hrs, collect keys from Royal Hotel. 7 cottages with bath and kitchen. No phones or TV. No credit cards.*

Sabie

DINING

$$ **Artists' Café.** Run by the cosmopolitan duo of Frans Mulder and Julius
★ Bramley, this delightful Italian restaurant is unlike anything else in the Eastern Transvaal. It is housed in a former railway station in Hendriksdal and doubles, as you'd expect, as an art gallery. Rough whitewashed walls and corrugated-tin roofing provide the simple backdrop for Coptic crosses, African masks, and colorful tapestries. A self-taught chef, Frans freely adapts recipes from a host of cookbooks. His freshly prepared dishes are frequently excellent but occasionally miss the mark. A starter of *bruschetta ai funghi* (toasted Italian bread drizzled with olive oil and garlic and topped with mushrooms) may work wonderfully, while *tagliatelle arrabbiata* (pasta with a spicy tomato sauce) might be spoiled by the addition of crushed ginger snaps. However, the setting is perfect. ✕ *Hendriksdal, off R37, 16 km (10 mi) from Sabie,* ☎ *01315/4–2309. Reservations required. MC, V. Closed Mon. No dinner Sun.–Wed.*

$$ **Hill Watering.** Tucked away in a suburban home in Sabie, this guest lodge cum restaurant is the domain of the artistic Jonathan Montague-Fitt. His presentation of pecan-encrusted chicken supreme or fillet Teriyaki with angel hair noodles and Japanese crudités is inspired. Starters include such delights as trout and scallion roulade with horseradish mousseline, or Stilton soup with sesame croutons. Soufflés, both sweet and savory, rise to astonishing heights, while the chocolate and hazelnut mille feuille never fails to please. ✕ *50 Marula St., Mount Anderson, Sabie,* ☎ *01315/4–1421. Reservations required. AE, DC, MC, V. No lunch.*

LODGING

$ **Percy's Place.** This tiny hotel in the center of Sabie is the best value in
★ the entire Eastern Transvaal. Rooms are individually decorated in bright country style, and have tea- and coffeemakers and overhead fans. There are no phones or air-conditioning, and only one of the suites has a TV. Breakfast is not included, but several cafés are within easy walking distance. Guests check in next door at the Zeederberg Coach-

house. ☎ *Corner of Ford and 10th Sts., Sabie 1260,* ☎ *01315/4–3302. 5 rooms with bath. MC. V.*

Schoemanskloof

DINING AND LODGING

$$ Old Joe's Kaia. Many visitors hurtling down the N4 from Johannesburg to the lowveld break their journey at this lovely lodge. Originally a country store, the main part of the hotel burned down in 1993 but has been beautifully rebuilt. It is another of the best values in the region. Don't expect luxury or pampering, but you can expect comfortable rooms, a warm welcome, and good food—at half the price of luxury lodges. Opt for one of the small Kaia rooms with timber ceilings, white crocheted bedspreads, and wicker furniture, or settle into a timber cabin built on stilts overlooking the Crocodile River valley. None of the rooms has a phone, air-conditioning, or TV. The emphasis in the kitchen is on fresh ingredients and home-style cooking. Look for dishes such as spicy cheese balls with pears, chili chicken, and gooseberry and passion fruit brûlée. Because of its setting on a steep, wooded hillside, Old Joe's is a problem for guests with mobility problems. ☎ *R539, 23 km (14 mi) from Montrose Falls (mailing address: Box 108, Schagen 1207),* ☎ *and* ⓕⒶⓍ *01311/6–3045. 13 rooms with bath. Restaurant, bar, pool. No children under 12. Breakfast and dinner included. AE, DC, MC, V.*

White River

DINING AND LODGING

$$$$ Highgrove House. On a hillside overlooking avocado and banana orchards, this former farmhouse is considered one of the very best lodges in the country. Rooms are in white cottages scattered about the lovely gardens, and each has a veranda, sitting area, and fireplace. The decor, both in the main lodge and the cottages, has colonial overtones, with plenty of gathered curtains and floral upholstery. The lodge bears distinct similarities to Cybele (*see above*), but lacks that lodge's easy-going atmosphere. Here, you don't feel quite at liberty to lie on the couches or throw your leg over the side of an armchair. For that very reason, perhaps, the lodge is immaculate. Highgrove serves an excellent five-course Anglo-French dinner. A typical meal might be a melange of Knysna oysters, quail eggs, and caviar with a sour cream dressing followed by slivers of guinea fowl and foie gras with a port and cranberry sauce. One heavenly dessert is tartelettes of fresh figs and almonds. Weather-permitting, lunch and breakfast are served in the gazebo by the pool. Non-guests must reserve ahead for meals. ☎ *R40, between Hazyview and White River (mailing address: Box 46, Kiepersol 1241),* ☎ *01311/5–0242,* ⓕⒶⓍ *01311/5–0244. 8 suites. Restaurant, bar, pool. No children under 12. Breakfast and dinner included. AE, DC, MC, V.*

$$$ Hulala Lakeside Lodge. This attractive lodge sits on a forested promontory, surrounded on three sides by a large dam. All rooms have water views, and the majority of activities involve swimming or boating on the lake. Guest rooms, in sandy yellow cottages, have a warm, comfortable feel, thanks to overhead beams, ivory stucco walls, and matching floral bedspreads and curtains. If you can, book the Malachite Suite, in a lovely cottage set apart from the main buildings, with a four-poster bed and its own swimming pool. The lodge's five-course dinner, served in an elegant, candlelit room, is ambitious but inconsistent. Lamb with figs might stand out, whereas trout in cream sauce proves bland and uninspired. Breakfast and light lunches are served on the veranda under large umbrellas, overlooking the pool and lake. ☎ *Off R40, be-*

tween Hazyview and White River (mailing address: Box 1382, White River 1240), ☎ *and* FAX *01311/51–710. 21 rooms with bath. Restaurant, bar, room service, pool, water sports. No children under 10. Breakfast and dinner included. AE, DC, MC, V.*

$$$ **Kirby Country Lodge.** This is one of those relaxed places where guests can kick back and not worry about appearances. If the rooms aren't as fancy as those at some of the lodges, they're not as expensive either. The fact that 70% of its guests are repeat or referral visitors is an indication that the lodge is doing something right. Owners Geoff and Debbie March personally welcome you to their thatched, white-brick farmhouse set in pleasant gardens shaded by enormous trees. Much of the furniture in the guest rooms is antique, either hand-me-downs from the March family or unearthed in attics. Rooms have phones, but no air-conditioning or fans. Debbie prepares most of the food, with an emphasis on Continental cuisine. Look for chilled soups and smoked trout in summer, as well as roasts and fillets. Debbie's winter specialty of oxtail falls gently off the bone. For dessert, expect crème brûlée, chocolate mousse, or a traditional bread-and-butter pudding. Lunch is for residents only, and non-guests must book for dinner. ⌘ *Off R538, between White River and Plaston (mailing address: Box 138, Plaston 1244),* ☎ *01311/3–2645. 8 rooms with bath. Restaurant, bar, pool. No children under 12. Breakfast and dinner included. AE, DC, MC, V.*

EASTERN TRANSVAAL ESSENTIALS

Arriving and Departing

By Bus

Greyhound (☎ 01311/2–5134) offers daily service between Johannesburg and Nelspruit (Joshua Doore Centre). The trip takes five hours.

By Car

It takes less than four hours to drive the 350 kilometers (220 miles) from Johannesburg to Nelspruit, capital of the Eastern Transvaal and a major gateway to the region. The easiest way to get there is to drive north on the N1 to Pretoria and then cut east on the N4.

By Plane

Nelspruit Airport (☎ 01311/43192), less than an hour from most sights in the Eastern Transvaal, is served by **Inter Air** (☎ 01311/4–1175), **Metavia** (☎ 01311/4–3141), and **S.A. Airlink** (☎ 01311/2–5257).

Comair (☎ 01311/6–5644) flies twice daily between Johannesburg and **Skukuza Airport,** just inside Kruger National Park. Passengers must pay an R50 Parks Board tax for landing in a national park.

By Train

Spoornet's *Komati* train (☎ 011/773–2944) travels between Johannesburg and Nelspruit via Pretoria daily. The trip takes about 12 hours. The luxury **Blue Train** (*see* Rail Travel *in* the Gold Guide) also makes occasional runs from Pretoria to Nelspruit; **Rovos Rail** (*see* the Gold Guide, *above*), the Edwardian-era competitor of the *Blue Train*, travels from Pretoria to Komatipoort, just outside Kruger National Park. Most passengers combine a journey on Rovos Rail with a package trip to a game reserve or one of the exclusive lodges on the Escarpment.

Getting Around

By Car

Renting a car is the only option if you really want to explore the Eastern Transvaal. **Avis** (☎ 01311/4–1087), **Budget** (☎ 01311/4–3871), and **Imperial** (☎ 01311/4–3210) all have offices at Nelspruit Airport. **Avis** (☎ 01311/6–5651) also has a desk at Skukuza Airport, in Kruger National Park. If you're planning to drive from Johannesburg, *see* car rental information *in* Chapter 2.

By Minibus

Public bus service is limited or nonexistent in the Eastern Transvaal. If you don't have your own car, you're dependent on one of the tour companies to get around the Escarpment and into the game reserves (*see* Guided Tours, *below*). Many of these companies also operate shuttle services that transfer guests between the various lodges and to the airport. It's usually possible to hire these chauffeured minibuses on an hourly or daily rate.

Guided Tours

Orientation

All tour operators offer a package of trips that cover the major sights of the Escarpment, as well as game-viewing trips into Kruger National Park and private reserves. The most reputable operators in the area are **Dragonfly Safaris** (Box 1042, White River 1240, ☎ 01311/5–1060, FAX 01311/5–1061), **Green Rhino** (Box 1441, White River 1240, ☎ 01311/3–1952, FAX 01311/5–1638), **Mfafa** (Box 3334, Nelspruit 1200, ☎ and FAX 01317/6–8398), and **Welcome Tours** (Box 997, Johannesburg 2000, ☎ 011/442–8905, FAX 011/442–8865).

Flight Seeing

Lodge Hopper Tours (Box 2801, Nelspruit 1200, ☎ 01311/58–1103, FAX 01311/58–1440) and **Dragonfly Helicopter Adventures** (Box 1042, White River 1240, ☎ 01311/5–0160, FAX 01311/5–1061) offer short flips over the mountains in Bell Jet Ranger helicopters, as well as more exotic trips including champagne breakfasts in the mountains and moonlight picnics.

Important Addresses and Numbers

Emergencies

In case of an emergency, contact the **police** at 10111. In the event of a serious medical emergency, contact **MRI** (☎ 01311/5–3331) or **Criticare Helivac** (☎ 01311/4–7150) helicopter emergency services.

The best-equipped hospitals in the lowveld are in Nelspruit: **Nelspruit Private Hospital** (☎ 01311/4–7150) and **Rob Ferreira Hospital** (☎ 01311/4–3031).

Visitor Information

Nelspruit Publicity Association. *Shop 5, Promenade Centre, corner of Paul Kruger and Louis Trichardt Sts.,* ☎ *01311/55–1988,* FAX *01311/55–1350.* ☉ *Weekdays 8–5, Sat. 9–1.*

Pilgrim's Rest Information Centre. *Main St.,* ☎ *01315/8–1211.* ☉ *Daily 9–12:45, 1:15–4:30.*

Sondela, the SATOUR office in Sabie, provides information on the area and also hires out mountain bikes. *Main St., Sabie,* ☎ *01315/4–3492.* ☉ *Mon–Sat. 8–5, Sun. 9–1.*

4 Cape Town and the Peninsula

Backed by the familiar shape of Table Mountain, Cape Town presides over a coastline of unsurpassed beauty: of mountains edging the sea, miles of beaches, and 18th-century wineries snoozing under giant oaks. Modern South Africa was born here, and the city is filled with reminders of its historic role in overseas trade between Europe and the East. Today, Cape Town is home to the country's best museums, restaurants, and hotels.

IF YOU VISIT ONLY ONE PLACE in South Africa, make it Cape Town. Sheltered beneath the familiar shape of Table Mountain, this historic city is instantly recognizable, and few cities in the world possess its beauty and style.

A stroll through the lovely city center constantly reveals the city's three centuries as the sealink between Europe and the East. Elegant Cape Dutch buildings, with their whitewashed gables, abut imposing monuments to Britain's imperial legacy. In the Moslem quarter, the call to prayer echoes from minarets while the sweet tang of Malay curry wafts through its cobbled streets. And everywhere, whether you're eating outdoors at one of the country's best restaurants or sipping wine atop Table Mountain, you sense—correctly—that this is South Africa's most urbane, civilized city.

As impressive as all this is, though, what you will ultimately recall about Cape Town is the sheer grandeur of its setting—Table Mountain rising above the city bowl, the sweep of the bay, and mountains cascading into the sea. You will likely spend more time marveling at the views than anything else.

The city lies at the northern end of the Cape Peninsula, a 25-mile tail of mountains that hangs down from the tip of Africa, ending at the Cape of Good Hope. Drive 15 minutes in any direction and you will lose yourself in a stunning landscape of 18th-century Cape Dutch manors, historic wineries, and white-sand beaches backed by sheer mountains. Francis Drake wasn't exaggerating when he called the peninsula "the fairest Cape we saw in the whole circumference of the earth," and he would have little cause to change his opinion today. You could spend a week just exploring the city and peninsula, and a lifetime discovering the nearby wonders of the Western Cape (*see* Chapter 5), including the Winelands, one of the great highlights of a trip to South Africa.

Capetonians know they have it good and look with condescending sympathy on those with the misfortune to live elsewhere. On weekends, you'll find them out hiking, sailing, and biking in their African Eden. At night, they congregate at the city's fine restaurants, fortified with the Cape wine that plays such an integral role in the city's life. Laid-back Cape Town has none of the frenetic energy of hard-nosed Johannesburg. Maybe it has something to do with the fact that Cape Town doesn't need to unearth its treasures—the beauty of the place smacks you in the face as soon as you roll out of bed.

In this respect, the city is often likened to San Francisco, but Cape Town has what San Francisco can never have—history and the mountain. Table Mountain is key to Cape Town's identity. It dominates the city in a way that's difficult to comprehend until you visit. In the afternoon, when creeping fingers of cloud spill over the mountain and reach toward the city, the whole town seems to shiver and hold its breath. Depending on which side of the mountain you live, it even dictates when the sun will rise and set.

Indeed, the city owes its very existence to the mountain. The freshwater streams running off its slopes were what first prompted early explorers to anchor here. In 1652 Jan van Riebeeck and 90 Dutch settlers established a revictualling station for ships of the Dutch East India Company (VOC) on the long voyage east. The settlement represented the first European toehold in southern Africa, and Cape Town is still sometimes called the Mother City.

Those first Dutch settlers soon ventured into the interior to establish their own farms, and 140 years later the settlement supported a population of 20,000 whites as well as 25,000 slaves brought from distant lands like Java, Madagascar, and Guinea. Its position on the strategic cusp of Africa, however, meant that the colony never enjoyed any real stability. The British, entangled in a global dogfight with Napoléon, occupied the Cape twice, first in 1795 and then permanently in 1806. With them they brought additional slaves from Ceylon, India, and the Philippines. Destroyed or assimilated in this colonial expansion were the indigenous Khoikhoi (Hottentots), who once herded their cattle here and foraged along the coast.

For visitors used to hearing about South Africa's problems in black and white, Cape Town will come as a surprise—the city is black, white, and *colored*. Today, more than 1 million coloreds—the term used to describe people of mixed race, of Khoikhoi or slave descent—live in the city and give it a distinct spice.

Perhaps the greatest celebration of this colored culture is the annual Coon Carnival, when thousands of wild celebrants take to the streets in vibrant costumes to sing *moppies* (vaudeville-style songs), accompanied by banjos, drums, and whistles. The carnival is the most visible reminder of a way of life that saw its finest flowering in District Six, a predominantly colored neighborhood on the fringes of the city center whose destruction is probably the most tragic result of apartheid in Cape Town. By all accounts District Six was a living festival of music and soul, a vibrant community bound by poverty, hope, and sheer joie de vivre. In 1966 the Nationalist government invoked the Group Areas Act, rezoned District Six a whites-only area, and razed it. The scars of that event still run deep. A new museum seeks to recapture the mood of the lost community, and moves are afoot to rebuild the area with low-cost housing.

Other legacies of apartheid remain festering wounds. Each year for decades, thousands of blacks have streamed down to the Cape in search of work, food, and a better life. They end up in the squatter camps of Crossroads and Khayelitsha, names that once flickered across TV screens around the globe. Many visitors never see this side of South Africa, but if you make the one-hour trip to the Winelands along the N2, you can't miss the pitiful shacks built on shifting dunes as far as the eye can see. After the First-World luxury of the city center, the sight is a sobering kick in the stomach. A tour of these areas offers a glimpse of the old South Africa—and the enormous challenges facing the new one.

EXPLORING

Cape Town is surprisingly small. The center of the city is known as the City Bowl, cradled between the sea and a semicircle of mountains, including Table Mountain. An orderly street grid and the constant view of Table Mountain make it almost impossible to get lost. Major arteries running toward the mountain from the sea are Adderley, Loop, and Long streets; among the major cross streets are Strand, Longmarket, and Wale. The heart of the historic city—where you'll find many of the museums and major buildings—is Government Avenue, a pedestrian mall at the top of Adderley Street. St. George's Mall, another major pedestrian thoroughfare, runs the length of commercial Cape Town.

Once you leave the City Bowl, orienting yourself becomes trickier. As you face Table Mountain from the city, the distinctive mountain on your left is Devil's Peak; on the right are Signal Hill and Lion's Head. Signal Hill takes its name from a gun fired there every day at noon. If you look carefully you will see that Signal Hill forms the body of a reclining lion, while the maned Lion's Head looks south past Table Mountain. On the other side of Signal Hill and Lion's Head lie the Atlantic communities of Sea Point, Clifton, and Camps Bay. Heading the other way, around Devil's Peak, you come to Cape Town's exclusive southern suburbs—Rondebosch, Newlands, Claremont, and Constantia. The happening Waterfront lies north of the City Bowl on the other side of the horrendous freeways that separate the docks from downtown.

The Cape Peninsula extends 40 kilometers (25 miles) below the city, culminating at Cape Point in the Cape of Good Hope Nature Reserve. A spine of mountains runs down the center of the peninsula, crowding most of the towns and roads onto a narrow shelf next to the sea. The east side of the peninsula is washed by the waters of False Bay. Here, connected by a coastal road, lie the resort towns of Muizenberg, St. James, Kalk Bay, and Fish Hoek, as well as the naval base at historic Simon's Town. The western shores of the peninsula are wilder and emptier, pounded by huge Atlantic swells. In addition to the tiny hamlets of Scarborough, Kommetjie, and Noordhoek, you'll find the fishing port of Hout Bay and the dizzying heights of Chapman's Peak, one of the most awe-inspiring drives in the region.

Tour 1: Table Mountain

Along with Victoria Falls (*see* Chapter 8), Table Mountain is one of southern Africa's most beautiful and impressive natural wonders. The views from its summit can reduce you to speechless awe. The mountain rises over 3,500 feet above the city, its flat top visible to sailors 64 kilometers (40 miles) out to sea. In summer, when the southeaster blows, moist air from False Bay funnels over the mountain, condensing in the colder, higher air to form the tablecloth of cloud. Legend attributes this low-lying cloud to a pipe-smoking contest between the Devil and Jan van Hunks, a pirate who settled on Devil's Peak. The Devil lost, and the cloud serves to remind him of his defeat.

The first recorded ascent of Table Mountain was made in 1503 by the Portuguese admiral Antonio de Saldanha, who wanted to get a better sense of the topography of the Cape Peninsula. He couldn't have asked for a better view. In one direction you look down on today's city, cradled between Lion's Head and Devil's Peak. In another, you see the crescent of sand at Camps Bay, sandwiched between the sea and the granite faces of the Twelve Apostles. Farther south, the peninsula tails off toward the Cape of Good Hope, its mountains forming a ragged spine between False Bay and the empty vastness of the Atlantic. No matter where you look, you just can't get over how *high* you feel.

Despite being virtually surrounded by the city, Table Mountain is a remarkably unspoiled wilderness. Most of the Cape Peninsula's 2,200 species of flora are found on the mountain, including magnificent examples of fynbos, silver trees, and red and blue disas. The best time to see the mountain in flower is between September and March, although you can be sure to find some flowers whatever the time of year. Long gone are the days when Cape lions, zebras, and hyenas roamed the mountain, but you can still sometimes glimpse grysboks (small antelopes), baboons, and rock dassies (hyrax).

Atop the mountain, well-marked trails offering 10- to 40-minute jaunts crisscross the Western Table near the cableway. Numerous other trails continue on to the other side of Platteklip Gorge and into the mountain's catchment area, where you will find several reservoirs, hidden streams, and more incredible views. Be aware, though, that the weather can turn quickly. Even if you're making only a short visit, be sure to take along a sweater. If you're planning an extended hike, carry water and plenty of warm clothing.

During the warm summer months Capetonians are fond of taking picnic hampers up the mountain. The best time to do this is after 5: Sipping a glass of chilled Cape wine while watching the sun set from Table Mountain is one of life's great joys. Otherwise, you can choose between two restaurants: The Table Mountain Tuck Inn dishes up snacks and drinks on an outdoor terrace, and the Table Mountain Restaurant serves burgers, fish, lasagna, and sandwiches, as well as breakfast. Both are open between 8:30 AM and 9 PM.

You have only two ways of reaching the top of the mountain: Walk, or take the cableway.

Riding the Cableway

Cable cars take five minutes to reach the summit. The problem is getting on one in the first place. In peak season, between mid-November and mid-March, lines from one to nine hours are not uncommon for those who haven't booked ahead. Even with a reservation, be prepared to wait up to 30 minutes. To make a booking, you must appear in person at the Lower Cableway (☎ 021/24–5148), the Tourist Rendezvous Travel Centre (Adderley St., ☎ 021/418–5222), or at the information center at the Waterfront (☎ 021/418–2369). Bookings (R2 per person) are nonrefundable, and in peak season you're advised to make them a week in advance. Unfortunately, there's no guarantee that the mountain won't be covered in cloud or closed entirely due to high wind or rain. If you can't obtain a reservation, your best chance of riding up may be with a tour company (*see* Guided Tours *in* Cape Town Essentials, *below*). Otherwise, arrive early in the morning before the first car departs or after 5 in the evening. *Tafelberg Rd., ☎ 021/24–5148. Round-trip fares, R21 adults, R10 children; one-way fares, R12 adults, R5 children. MC, V. ☉ Nov. and mid-Jan.–Apr. 8 AM–9:30 PM, Dec.–mid-Jan. 7 AM–10:30 PM, May–Oct. 8:30–5:30.*

The Lower Cableway lies on the slopes of Table Mountain near its western end. It's a long way from the city on foot, and you're better off traveling by car, taxi, or bus. To get there from the City Bowl, take Buitengracht Street toward the mountain. Once you cross Camp Street, Buitengracht becomes Kloof Nek Road. Follow Kloof Nek Road up through the residential neighborhood of Gardens to a traffic circle; turn left on Tafelberg Road and follow the signs to the Lower Cableway.

A **Golden Arrow bus** (the destination placard reads KLOOF NEK) leaves every 30 minutes from OK Bazaars on Adderley Street and stops at the traffic circle on Kloof Nek, about 2 kilometers (1.2 miles) from the Cableway. Transfer there to the **Cableway Shuttle,** which meets the bus. The whole trip takes 30 minutes and costs R3.

A **taxi** from the City Bowl to the Lower Cableway costs about R25.

Walking up the Mountain

More than 300 walking trails—some easy, some insanely difficult— wend their way up the mountain. The two most popular set out from the Kirstenbosch National Botanic Gardens (*see* Tour 4, *below*) and from Tafelberg Road (via Platteklip Gorge), the road that leads past the Lower Cableway. Both are strenuous hikes rather than climbs, and the ascent takes 2–3 hours. If you don't feel comfortable tackling the mountain alone, contact one of the many services offering guided walks to the top, including **Leading Edge** (☎ 021/61–9673), **Ideal Tours** (☎ 021/468–5415 or 083/653–9744), and **John McDonnell** (☎ 021/45–2503). Guided tours take from two to seven hours; expect to pay R50–R100 per person, which includes descent by cable car.

Tour 2: The City Bowl

Numbers in the margin correspond to points of interest on the Cape Town map.

① This walking tour begins at **Captour's Tourist Rendezvous Travel Centre** (*see* Important Addresses and Numbers *in* Cape Town Essentials, *below*) and covers most of the major monuments and buildings associated with the settlement of Cape Town. At no time during the tour will you be more than a 15-minute walk from your starting point.

② Head up Adderley Street toward the **Golden Acre** shopping center. Until earlier in the century, this part of the city was all at sea—literally. The land was reclaimed as part of a program to expand the docks. If you look at old paintings of the city, you will see that originally waves lapped at the very walls of the Castle (*see below*), now more than half a mile from the ocean. At the bottom of the escalator leading from the railway station into the Golden Acre is a solid black line that marks the approximate position of the shoreline in 1693.

Adderley Street, originally named Heerengracht after a canal that ran the length of the avenue, has always been Cape Town's principal thoroughfare. It was once the favored address of Cape Town's leading families, and its oak-shaded sidewalks served as a promenade for those who wanted to see and be seen. By the mid-19th century the oaks had all been chopped down and the canal covered over, as Adderley Street became the city's main commercial street. By 1908 it had become such a busy thoroughfare that the city fathers paved it with wooden blocks in an attempt to dampen the noise of the countless wagons, carts, and horses' hooves.

③ Turn left on Darling Street and head toward the castle. The **Grand Parade,** once a military parade ground, is now nothing but a bleak parking lot. A statue of Edward VII watches over the cars like a parking attendant. It was here, upon his release on February 11, 1990, after 27 years in prison, that Nelson Mandela addressed an adoring crowd of more than 100,000 supporters. A dull flea market is held here on Wednesday and Saturday mornings. Just across the way is the beautiful former **City Hall,** now home to the Cape Town Symphony Orchestra and the City Library. Much of the interior is badly run-down, alas.

★ ⑤ Despite its name, the **Castle of Good Hope** isn't one of those fairy-tale fantasies you find perched on a cliff above the Rhine. It is a squat fortress that hunkers into the ground as if to avoid shell fire. Built between 1665 and 1676 by the Dutch East India Company (VOC) to replace an earthen fort constructed by Jan van Riebeeck in 1652, it is the oldest building in the country. Its pentagonal plan, with a diamond-shaped bastion at each corner, is typical of the Old Netherlands defense system adopted in the early 17th century. The design was intended to provide covering fire for every portion of the castle. As added protection, the whole fortification was surrounded by a moat, with the sea nearly washing up against its walls. The castle served as both the VOC headquarters

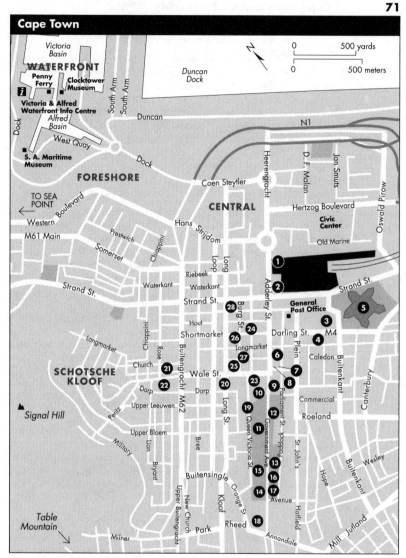

Cape Town

Bertram House, **18**
Bo-Kaap, **21**
Bo-Kaap Museum, **22**
Captour's Tourist
Rendezvous Travel
Centre, **1**
Castle of Good
Hope, **5**
City Hall, **4**
Church Street, **25**
Company's
Gardens, **11**
Delville Wood
Monument, **15**
Golden Acre, **2**
Grand Parade, **3**
Great Synagogue, **17**
Greenmarket
Square, **26**

Groote Kerk, **6**
Houses of
Parliament, **9**
Jewish Museum, **16**
Koopmans-De Wet
House, **28**
Long Street, **20**
Old Town House, **27**
Queen Victoria
Street, **19**
St. George's
Cathedral, **23**
St. George's Mall, **24**
Slave Tree, **7**
South African
Cultural Museum, **8**
South African
Library, **10**

South African
Museum, **14**
South African
National Gallery, **13**
Tuynhuys, **12**

and the official governor's residence, and it still houses the regional headquarters of the National Defence Force.

Tours of the castle—they are the only way to get inside—cover the ramparts, magazine, dungeons, and torture chamber. It can be torture just listening to the tour guides, some of whom will bore you to tears. Fortunately, you can explore the excellent William Fehr Collection on your own. Housed in the governor's residence, the collection consists of antiques, artifacts, and paintings of early Cape Town and South African history. Conservationists should go upstairs to see John Thomas Baine's *The Greatest Hunt in Africa,* celebrating a "hunt" in honor of Prince Alfred when nearly 30,000 animals were driven together and slaughtered. *Buitenkant St.,* ☎ *021/408–7911.* ☛ *R5 adults, R2 children, R10 families.* ☼ *Daily; tours at 10, 11, noon, 2, and 3.*

❻ Retrace your steps toward Adderley Street, turning left a block before you get there onto Parliament Street, to reach the spare, sober **Groote Kerk** (Great Church), one of the most famous churches in South Africa. It was built in 1841 on the site of an earlier Dutch Reformed church dating from 1704. The adjoining clock tower is all that remains of that earlier building. Among the building's interesting features are the enclosed pews, each with its own door. Prominent families would buy their own pews—and lock the doors—so they wouldn't have to pray with the great unwashed. The enormous pulpit, which dates from 1789, is the work of the famous sculptor Anton Anreith and carpenter Jan Jacob Graaff. The lions supporting it are carved from local stinkwood; the upper portion is Burmese teak. The organ, with nearly 6,000 pipes, is the largest in the Southern Hemisphere. Approximately 200 people are buried beneath the Batavian soapstone floor, including eight governors. *43 Adderley St., but enter on Church Sq.,* ☎ *021/461–7044.* ☛ *Free. Free guided tours on request.* ☼ *Weekdays 10–2.*

❼ The Groote Kerk faces Church Square, now a parking lot, where churchgoers used to unharness their oxen. On the skinny traffic island in the middle of Spin Street rests a concrete plaque marking the location of the **Slave Tree,** an enormous Canadian pine under which slaves were auctioned. Slavery began in the Cape Colony in 1658, when free burghers petitioned the government for farmhands. The first group of 400 slaves arrived from Guinea, Angola, Batavia (modern Java), and Madagascar. During the first British occupation of the Cape (1795–1803), 17,000 slaves were brought from India, Ceylon, and the Philippines, swelling the total slave population to 30,000. Slavery was abolished by the British in 1834, an act that fueled one of South Africa's great historical events, the Great Trek, when thousands of outraged Afrikaners set off in their covered wagons to establish a new state in the hinterland.

★ ❽ A brass plaque commemorating the slave tree and a cross-section of the tree itself are on display in the **South African Cultural Museum,** next door on Adderley Street. Ironically, the museum started out as a slave lodge, built in 1679 by the Dutch East India Company. Today, the museum is a great place to come for an overview of South Africa's early settler history. Displays detailing the settlement and colonization of the Cape are superb; letters, coins, paintings, clothes, and furniture bring the period almost palpably to life. The museum also has minor collections of Roman, Greek, Egyptian, and Asian antiquities, as well as displays of antique silver, musical instruments, glass, ceramics, weapons, and coins. From 1815 to 1914, the building served as the Supreme Court. *Corner of Adderley and Wale Sts.,* ☎ *021/461–8280.* ☛ *R2 adults, R1 children. Guided tours on request.* ☼ *Mon.–Sat. 9:30–4:30.*

❾ Next door stand the **Houses of Parliament,** which you can tour during the Easter and winter recesses, or attend debates when Parliament is in session. Foreigners wishing to watch a debate must bring passports and reserve a space in the gallery, either by visiting Room 12 or calling ahead. The current buildings were constructed in 1885 by Charles Freeman, but they have been expanded many times. Paintings of former Speakers of the House adorn the chambers. *Parliament St.,* ☎ *021/403–2460.* ☛ *Free. Tours at 11 and 2 during Easter and winter recess. Gallery seating by arrangement.* ☉ *Weekdays 9–4.*

Go around the back of the Parliament buildings and head up Government Avenue, a pleasant, oak-shaded walkway that leads past many of the country's most important institutions and museums. The huge white **❿** building on your right is the **South African Library,** the oldest in the country. The National Reference Library, as it is also known, owes its origin to Lord Charles Somerset, governor of the Cape Colony, who in 1818 imposed a wine tax to fund the creation of a library that would "place the means of knowledge within the reach of the youth of this remote corner of the Globe." In 1860 the library moved into its current home, a neo-Classical building modeled after the Fitzwilliam Museum in Cambridge, England. The library has an extensive collection of Africana, including the works of many 18th- and 19th-century explorers. *Botanical Gardens,* ☎ *021/24–6320.* ☛ *Free.* ☉ *Weekdays 9–6, Sat. 9–1.*

Continue up Government Avenue into the loveliest part of the city, a broad swath of greenery crisscrossed by pedestrian promenades. It's a great place to sit on a bench and watch the world go by. At the center ★ **⓫** of this green lung lie the **Company's Gardens,** all that remains of a 21-morgen (43-acre) garden laid out by Jan van Riebeeck in April 1652 to supply fresh vegetables to ships on their way to the Dutch East Indies. By 1700, free burghers were cultivating plenty of crops on their own land, and in time the VOC vegetable patch was transformed into a botanic garden. It remains a delightful haven in the city center, graced by fountains, exotic trees, rose gardens, aviaries, and a pleasant outdoor café. At the bottom of the gardens, close to Government Avenue, look for an **old well** that used to provide water for the town's residents and the garden. The old water pump, engraved with the maker's name and the date 1842, has been overtaken by an oak tree and now juts out of the tree's trunk some 6 feet above the ground. A huge **statue of Cecil Rhodes** looms over the path that runs through the center of the gardens. He points to the north, and an inscription reads: "Your hinterland is there," a reference to Rhodes's dream of extending the British Empire from the Cape to Cairo.

Again continue along Government Avenue. Walk past Parliament to **⓬** the **Tuynhuys** (Town House), the offices of the State President. Parts of the Tuynhuys date back to the late-17th and early 18th centuries. Unfortunately, the building is not open to the public.

★ **⓭** The **South African National Gallery** stands farther up Government Avenue. The museum houses a decent collection of 19th- and 20th-century European and British artists, but it's most interesting for its South African works, many of which reflect the country's traumatic history. Look for Willie Bester's *Challenges Facing the New South Africa,* done in wood and mixed media. A recent exhibition highlighted the art and culture of the Ndebele people. The museum café serves salads, sandwiches, pastas, and cakes. *Government Ave., Gardens,* ☎ *021/45–1628.* ☛ *Free.* ☉ *Mon. 1–5, Tues.–Sun. 10–5; closed Good Fri., Dec. 25.*

⑭ The **South African Museum** is a natural history museum that may well disappoint nature lovers. Its exhibits are mediocre and concentrate primarily on sea mammals. Far more interesting is the section on African peoples and cultures. A Bushmen diorama traces the history and way of life of the San (Bushmen), and includes wonderful examples of their rock paintings and tools. Similar exhibits examine the Khoikhoi (called Hottentots by the Dutch), Nguni, and Sotho peoples. As South Africa struggles to come to grips with its apartheid past, there is some debate about why these San and black cultural exhibits are included in a museum devoted to the study of animals, whereas white and Asian cultures are celebrated at the South African Cultural Museum. It's a very good question. The adjoining planetarium stages a variety of shows throughout the week. *25 Victoria St.,* ☏ *021/24–3330,* FAX *021/24– 6716.* ☛ *Museum: R2 adults, children free; planetarium: R5 adults, R3 children.* ◔ *Museum: daily 10–5. Planetarium shows Tues.–Fri. at 1; Sat. at noon, 1, and 2:30; Sun. 2 and 3:30.*

⑮ The temple in front of the South African Museum is the **Delville Wood Monument,** which honors South Africans who died in the fight for Delville Wood during the great Somme offensive of 1916. Of the 121 officers and 3,032 men who participated in the three-day engagement, only five officers and 750 men survived unhurt. Facing the memorial is a **statue of Brigadier-General Lukin,** who commanded the South African Infantry Brigade in World War I.

⑯ Directly across Government Avenue from the South African Museum is the **Jewish Museum.** Housed in the first synagogue in South Africa (1863), the museum profiles Jewish communities around the Cape as well as Jewish history in South Africa. Many of South Africa's Jews came here from Lithuania. Today, some 20,000 Jews live in Cape Town. In the apartheid years, when South Africa's future hung in the balance, their numbers declined noticeably. Many emigrated to the United States, Canada, and Australia. Jews have experienced little discrimination in South Africa, either under the apartheid Nationalist regime or the new ANC government. *84 Hatfield St.,* ☏ *021/45–1546.* ☛ *Free.* ◔ *Tues., Thurs. 2–5; Sun. 9–12:30.*

⑰ Next door is the **Great Synagogue,** built in 1903 in the baroque style. Take particular note of its twin towers and dome. The building is kept locked for security purposes, but ask in the offices (84 Hatfield St, ☏ 021/45–1405) at the back of the building to be let in. Services are held twice daily.

⑱ Continue up Government Avenue to **Bertram House.** Built around 1840, this is the only surviving Georgian brick town house in Cape Town. Once a common sight in the city, these boxlike, double-story houses were a response by the English community to Cape Dutch architecture. The projecting front porch was intended to shield the house from the worst effects of the frequent southeasters. The collection of furniture, silver, jewelry, and Chinese porcelain recaptures the look and feel of an early 19th-century family home. A guidebook available at the entrance describes the entire collection. *Corner of Government Ave. and Orange St.,* ☏ *021/24–9381.* ☛ *R1 adults, 50¢ children.* ◔ *Tues.– Sat. 9:30–4:30.*

TIME OUT Government Avenue ends opposite the famous gateway to the **Mount Nelson Hotel** (76 Orange St., ☏ 021/23-1000), erected in 1924 to welcome the Prince of Wales on his visit to the Cape. The "Nellie" remains Cape Town's most fashionable and genteel social venue. More importantly, it serves the city's best high tea. You can have yours in the lounge or on the garden terrace, and diners can select from a host of savories and sweets, including a traditional English cream tea.

⑲ Head back down Government Avenue and cut across the front of the South African Museum to **Queen Victoria Street,** lined with some of the city's most stately buildings, including the National Archives, the Land Bank, the State Attorney's office, the Supreme Court, and the City and Civil Service Club.

⑳ For something completely different, head down Bloem to **Long Street.** The section of Long between Orange and Wale streets features some magnificently restored Georgian and Victorian buildings. With their wrought-iron balconies and fancy curlicues, these colorful houses are reminiscent of the French Quarter in New Orleans. During the '60s, Long Street did a good imitation of the Big Easy, with a host of bars, prostitutes, and no-tell hotels. It's still great fun browsing among the many specialist shops on Long Street, including antiques dealers, secondhand bookstores, pawn shops, and vintage-clothing outlets.

★ ㉑ Turn left on Wale Street and walk four blocks to the **Bo-Kaap,** historic home of the city's Muslim population brought from the East as slaves in the late-17th and early 18th centuries. Today, the area remains strongly Muslim, and it's fascinating to wander the narrow cobbled lanes past mosques and colorful, flat-roofed houses. Many of the homes combine elements of Cape Dutch and British architecture, and altogether they represent the largest collection of pre-1840 architecture in South Africa. The Bo-Kaap is also known as the Malay quarter, despite the fact that its inhabitants originated from all over the East, including the Indonesian archipelago, India, and Madagascar.

㉒ Near the corner of Wale and Rose stands the **Bo-Kaap Museum.** Built in the 18th century, this museum was originally the home of Abu Bakr Effendi, a well-known member of the Muslim community. The house has been furnished to re-create the lifestyle of a typical Malay family in the 19th century. Since the exhibits aren't labeled, you might do better to visit the museum as part of a guided tour of the Malay quarter (*see* Guided Tours *in* Cape Town Essentials, *below*). *71 Wale St.,* ☎ *021/24–3846.* ☛ *R1 adults, children free.* ◔ *Tues.–Sat. 9:30–4:30.*

㉓ Retrace your steps down Wale Street to **St. George's Cathedral,** the religious seat of one of the most recognizable faces—and voices—in the fight against apartheid. Archbishop Desmond Tutu used his position as the first black archbishop of Cape Town to denounce apartheid and press for a democratic government. Today, Tutu continues to be a voice of moderation and tolerance in a society whose radical fringes threaten to rip it apart. The present Anglican cathedral was designed by Sir Herbert Baker in the Gothic Revival style; construction began in 1901, using sandstone from Table Mountain. The structure contains the largest stained-glass window in the country, some beautiful examples of late-Victorian stained glass, and a 1,000-year-old Coptic cross. *Wale St., no* ☎. ☛ *Free.* ◔ *Daily 8–5. Services weekdays 7:15 and 1:15; Sat. 8; Sun. 7, 8, 9:15, and 11.*

㉔ Across Wale Street is the entrance to **St. George's Mall,** a pedestrian promenade that stretches almost all the way to the Foreshore. Shops and cafés line the mall, and street vendors hawk everything from T-shirts to African arts and crafts. The mall is particularly interesting on Saturday mornings when buskers and dancers gather to entertain the crowds.

㉕ From St. George's Mall, turn left onto **Church Street,** the center of Cape Town's art and antiques business. The section between Burg and Long streets is now a pedestrian mall as well, filled with art galleries, antiques dealers, and small cafés. On Friday, the street is used for an antiques and flea market.

★ ㉖ Head down Burg Street to reach **Greenmarket Square,** the center of the city since 1710. For more than a century, this cobbled square served as a forum for public announcements, including the 1834 declaration abolishing slavery. In the 19th century, the square became a vegetable market as well as a popular watering hole—the city's hardest boozers used to drink themselves comatose at the nearby Old Thatched Tavern and London Hotel. Today, the square is a fun open-air market, with vendors selling a wide selection of clothing and sandals, as well as African jewelry, art, and fabrics.

㉗ The **Old Town House** faces onto the square. For 150 years this was the most important civic building in Cape Town. Built in 1755 as a guard house, it also saw duty as a meeting place for the Burgher Senate, a police station, and from 1840 to 1905 as Cape Town's city hall. The building is a beautiful example of urban Cape Dutch architecture, with thick whitewashed walls, green-and-white shutters, and small-paned windows. Today, the former city hall is home to the Michaelis Collection, an extensive selection of brooding Dutch landscape paintings, as well as changing exhibits. *Greenmarket Sq.,* ☎ *021/24–6367.* ☛ *Free.* ☉ *Daily 10–5; closed Jan. 1, Good Fri., Dec. 25.*

Work your way back to Long Street and walk toward the sea. When ㉘ you reach Strand Street, turn right to reach the **Koopmans-De Wet House.** Now a museum, this lovely 18th-century home is a haven of peace in the city center. The structure you see today dates largely from the period 1771–93. It is notable for its neoclassical facade, which has been variously attributed to Anton Anreith and Louis Thibault. The house enjoyed its heyday under Maria de Wet (1834–1906), a Cape Town socialite who entertained most of the major figures in Cape society, including Boer presidents and British governors. The furnishings date back to the early 19th century, when the house belonged to Maria's grandmother. The collection includes a stunning selection of antiques, carpets, paintings, and porcelain. Buy or borrow the excellent guide to the museum, which describes every item in the collection. *35 Strand St.,* ☎ *021/24–2473.* ☛ *R1 adults, 50¢ children.* ☉ *Tues.–Sat. 9:30–4:30.*

TIME OUT The **Martin Melck House** (96 Strand St., ☎ 021/419–6533), three blocks from Koopmans-De Wet House, is a beautiful 18th-century building that served as the parsonage for an adjoining Lutheran church. It's home to **A Table at Colin's,** a delightful spot to pause over an elegant lunch under white fabric umbrellas in the brick courtyard shaded by trees and pink bougainvillea. An exhibition space upstairs displays modern works by South African artists; all are for sale.

Tour 3: The Victoria & Alfred Waterfront

Capetonians are almost unanimous in their praise of the Victoria & Alfred Waterfront, a six-year project undertaken to breathe new life into a historical part of the city docks. Today, the Waterfront is Cape Town's most vibrant and exciting attraction, the focus of the city's nightlife and entertainment scene. Hundreds of shops, cinemas, restaurants, and bars share quarters in restored warehouses and dock buildings, all connected by pedestrian plazas, promenades, and canals. It's clean, it's safe, and it's car-free. In the next few years, the Waterfront will expand even further to incorporate new marinas and residential areas, and there's even talk of a floating resort. This walking tour visits the Waterfront's historic buildings, as well as some of its modern attractions.

Victoria & Alfred Waterfront Information Centre has the lowdown on everything happening in the area, including upcoming events and shows. Here you can arrange walking tours of the Waterfront and book reservations for the Table Mountain cableway. A scale model shows what the Waterfront will look like when it's finished. *Opposite V&A Hotel,* ☎ *021/418–2369,* FAX *021/21–2565.* ☉ *Weekdays 9:30–5, weekends and holidays 9:30–6.*

From the Information Centre, walk down Dock Road to the long, narrow stone shed that once housed the **Rocket Life-Saving Apparatus.** In the days before helicopters and rescue craft, this gear was used to rescue seamen from the many ships that foundered in Table Bay. The procedure was very basic: A rocket attached to a long rope was fired out to a sinking ship and seamen were winched ashore along the rope. The apparatus was last used—unsuccessfully—just 30 years ago.

Next door is **Mitchell's Waterfront Brewery** (Dock Rd., ☎ 021/419–5074), one of a handful of microbreweries in South Africa. The brewery produces four beers: Foresters Draught lager, Bosuns Bitter, Ravenstout, and Ferryman's Ale. Weekdays at noon the brewery offers tours (R4), which include a beer-tasting and a look at the fermentation tanks.

The heady smell of malt emanating from Mitchell's Brewery will be enough to send anyone with a thirst into the adjoining **Ferryman's Tavern** (Market Plaza, ☎ 021/419–7748). Constructed in 1877 of bluestone and Table Mountain sandstone, this is one of the oldest surviving buildings in the harbor. Before 1912, the temperance movement in Cape Town had managed to force a ban on the sale of alcohol within the docks. As a result, a host of pubs sprang up just outside the dock gates, particularly along Dock Road.

Facing Ferryman's Tavern is the **AGFA Amphitheatre,** a popular outdoor performance space that offers shows almost daily, ranging from concerts by the Cape Town Symphony Orchestra to gigs by jazz and rock bands. Check with the Information Centre for the schedule of events. The amphitheater stands on the site where, in 1860, the teenage Prince Alfred inaugurated the construction of a breakwater to protect shipping in the harbor. Table Bay was never an ideal natural harbor. In winter, devastating northwesterly winds would pound any ships caught in the exposed waters. Between 1647 and 1870, more than 190 ships went down in Table Bay. Since the breakwater was built, only 40 ships have foundered in Table Bay.

From the amphitheater, walk over to **Quay 5** (in front of Tequila Cantina) and the **Victoria Basin,** embarkation point for many of the boat tours of the harbor and Robben Island. Victoria Basin was constructed between 1870 and 1905 to accommodate the huge increase in shipping following the discovery of diamonds at Kimberley and gold on the Witwatersrand. Across the basin is the South Arm, used as a debarkation point for British troops, horses, and material during the Boer War (1899–1902). Much of the fodder for the British horses was shipped in from Argentina and catastrophically infested with rats and fleas. As a result, bubonic plague broke out in Cape Town in February 1901, creating wholesale panic in the city. African dockworkers, suspected of harboring the disease, were forbidden to leave the city and ultimately confined to specific quarters. During the epidemic, 766 people contracted the plague. Three hundred seventy-one of them died.

The unremarkable brick building at the end of Quay 5 belongs to the Department of Correctional Services. It is from here that prisoners are ferried out to **Robben Island,** the notorious prison in Table Bay that held apartheid South Africa's most famous opponents, including Nelson Mandela, Robert Sobukwe, and Walter Sisulu. The island, whose name means seal in Dutch, has served as a prison since the 17th century, first for lepers, paupers, and mental patients, and later for political prisoners of the British, including the Xhosa chief Nxele in 1820. In 1982, Nelson Mandela was transferred from Robben Island to a prison on the mainland; he was released on February 11, 1990. Tours of the island can be arranged (*see* Guided Tours *in* Cape Town Essentials, *below*).

Walk back past the red Fisherman's Choice restaurant to Market Square and the mustard-colored **Union-Castle House,** designed in 1919 by Sir Herbert Baker as the headquarters for the famous Union-Castle shipping line. Before World War II, many English-speaking South Africans looked upon England as "home," even if they had never been there. The emotional link between the two countries was symbolized most strongly by the mail steamers, carrying both mail and passengers, that sailed weekly between South Africa and England. In 1977, amid much pomp and ceremony, the last Union-Castle mail ship, the *Windsor Castle,* made its final passage to England. Even today, older South Africans like to wax lyrical about the joys of a voyage on one of those steamers. Union-Castle House is now home to several banks and small businesses. Inside Standard Bank, you can still see the iron rings in the ceiling from which mail bags were hung.

Walk past the NSRI shed and round the bottom of Alfred Mall to the end of the pierhead. The **Victoria Museum Ship** is a replica of an 18th-century Royal Navy frigate, complete with cannons and creaking spars. The ship contains an interesting collection of treasures salvaged from the many wrecks that litter South Africa's coastline and elsewhere. Among the retrieved artifacts are George IV sovereigns, pieces of eight from Mexico, rusted cannons, and portholes from the *Lusitania.* Most of the exhibits come from 18th- and 19th-century wrecks. *Pierhead,* ☎ *021/25–4127.* ☛ *R6 adults, R3 children.* ☉ *Daily 9–6.*

Next to the Victoria is the **Penny Ferry,** a rowboat service that carries passengers across the cut, the narrow entrance to the Albert Basin. The Penny Ferry was started in 1871 to row harbor employees across the cut to the South Quay, where Bertie's Landing, a popular bar and restaurant, now stands. The service was extended to the public in 1880, the fare set at a penny. It now costs R1. Keep an eye out for **Cape fur seals,** which like to hang out in the water and on the wooden docks surrounding Bertie's Landing.

Back on North Quay, follow the cut past the Alfred Mall to the **S.A.S. Somerset,** the only surviving boom-defense vessel in the world. During World War II, harbors were protected against enemy submarines and divers by booms, essentially metal mesh curtains drawn across the harbor entrance. The *Somerset* (then named the H.M.S. *Barcross*) controlled the boom across Saldanha Bay, north of Cape Town. You can explore the entire ship, including the bridge and the engine room (*see below*).

The ship is part of the **South African Maritime Museum.** Although the museum is unfinished, it provides a fascinating look at ships and the history of Table Bay, including an excellent model of Cape Town harbor as it appeared in 1886. In the model workshop you can watch modelers build scale replicas of famous ships. *Dock Rd.,* ☎ *021/419–2505.* ☛ *R2 adults, R1 children 7–13 (includes* ☛ *to S.A.S. Somerset).* ☉ *Daily 10–5.*

Head back to the Information Centre. From there, cross Dock Road and climb the stairs to **Portswood Ridge,** where there are several late-19th-century buildings originally used by the harbor administration. Today, many of these have been converted into office space. At the top of the stairs stands the brick **Time Ball Tower,** built in 1894. Before the advent of modern navigational equipment, ships needed to know the exact time to help them calculate their longitude. Ship navigators would set their clocks by the time ball, which would fall every day at noon, much like the ball that marks the stroke of midnight in Times Square on New Year's Eve.

Next to the tower is the original **Harbour Master's Residence,** built in 1860. In front there is a beautiful, century-old dragon tree, a native of the Canary Islands. The resin of this tree species, known as "dragon's blood," was used in Europe to treat dysentery.

Take the stairs back down to Dock Road and turn right to reach the new **aquarium.** At press time, the aquarium was still under construction, so consult the Information Centre (*see above*) for details about shows and prices.

Tour 4: The Peninsula

Numbers in the margin correspond to points of interest on the Cape Peninsula map.

This driving tour takes you south from Cape Town on a loop of the peninsula, heading through the scenic southern suburbs before running down the False Bay coast to Cape Point. It's a magnificent drive back to the city along the wild Atlantic coast. Plan a full day to travel the entire loop, more if you like to dally along the way.

Take the N2 or De Waal Drive (M3) out of the city center. The two highways merge near **Groote Schuur Hospital,** where Dr. Christian Barnard performed the world's first heart transplant in 1967. They split again soon after—follow the M3 toward Muizenberg and the southern suburbs.

❶ After 1 kilometer (½ mile) you pass **Mostert's Mill,** one of only two remaining windmills in the Cape. Built in 1796, the thatched wheat mill consists of a tower with a rotating cap to which sails were attached. Mills like this were once common all over the area. Inside you can see the original mechanism, but it's not necessarily worth pulling off the highway to see. *Rhodes Dr., Mowbray, no* ☎. ☉ *Daily 9–5.*

★ ❷ Continue on the M3 for another kilometer (½ mile) to the exit marked with a sign to the **Rhodes Memorial.** Cecil John Rhodes (1853–1902), one of Britain's great empire-builders, served as prime minister of the Cape from 1890 to 1896. He made his fortune in the diamond rush at Kimberley, but his greatest dream was to forge a Cape–Cairo railway, a tangible symbol of British dominion in Africa. The classical-style granite memorial sits high on the slopes of Devil's Peak, in a part of Rhodes's old estate, Groote Schuur. A mounted rider symbolizing "Energy" faces north toward the continent for which Rhodes felt such

burning passion. A bust of Rhodes dominates the temple itself—ironically, he's leaning on one hand as if he's about to nod off. *Off Rhodes
Dr., Rondebosch,* ☏ *021/689–9151.* ☛ *Free.*

TIME OUT The **Rhodes Memorial Tea Garden,** tucked away under towering pines
behind the memorial, is a pleasant spot for tea or a light lunch. Tables
on the outdoor terrace have lovely views out over the Cape Flats.
Closed Mon.

Return to the M3 and head south toward Muizenberg. After 1½ kilometers (1 mile), exit right onto Rhodes Avenue (M63). This road winds
★ ❸ through huge groves of pine and eucalyptus to the **Kirstenbosch National Botanic Gardens,** one of the most beautiful spots in the entire
Cape. The gardens extend up the eastern slopes of Table Mountain,
overlooking the Cape Flats and distant mountains. Walking trails meander through the gardens, and grassy banks are ideal for a picnic or
afternoon nap. The plantings are limited to species native to southern
Africa. Much of the focus is on fynbos, hardy, thin-leaved plants that
proliferate in the Cape. Among these are proteas, including silver trees
and king proteas, ericas, and restios (reeds). Another extraordinary feature of the park is a large cycad garden. Sunday concerts are held here
in summer. The outdoor restaurant is popular among Capetonians on
weekends. *Rhodes Ave., Constantia,* ☏ *021/762–1166.* ☛ *R4 adults,
R1 children.* ☉ *Apr.–Aug., daily 8–6, Sept.–Mar., daily 8–7.*

Turn right as you leave the Botanic Gardens. When you reach a T junction, turn right again and begin the winding climb up to the pass at
Constantia Nek. From the traffic circle at the top you can either cut
over the mountains and down into Hout Bay (*see below*), or turn left
onto the M41 (the sign reads WYNBERG AND GROOT CONSTANTIA) and
begin the snaking descent into Constantia.

Backed by the rugged mountains of the Constantiaberg and overlooking the Cape Flats and False Bay, **Constantia** is an idyllic spot to
while away a day—or a week. Vineyards carpet the lower slopes, while
plantations of pine predominate higher up. This is very much the do-
main of the suburban gentry—until recently, they rode to hounds in
Constantia—and horses and BMWs are frequent sights on the roads.
If you don't have time to visit the Winelands (*see* Chapter 5), Constantia
is a more-than-adequate substitute. Three major wineries have tasting
rooms.

Constantia takes its name from the wine estate founded here in 1685
by Simon van der Stel, one of the first Dutch governors of the Cape.
After his death in 1712, the land was subdivided, with the heart of the
★ ❹ estate preserved at **Groot Constantia.** The enormous complex enjoys
the status of a national monument and is by far the most commercial
and touristy of the wineries. Van der Stel's magnificent homestead, the
oldest in the Cape, lies at the center of Groot Constantia. It's built in
traditional Cape Dutch style with thick whitewashed walls, thatched
roof, small-pane windows, and ornate gables. The house itself is a museum, furnished with exquisite period pieces. The old wine cellar sits
behind the manor house. Built in 1791, it is most famous for its own
ornate gable designed by sculptor Anton Anreith. The cellar houses a
wine museum, with displays of wine-drinking and storage vessels dating back to antiquity.

In the 19th century, the sweet wines of Groot Constantia were highly
regarded in Europe and especially favored by King Louis Philippe and
Bismarck. Today, Groot Constantia is known for its splendid red

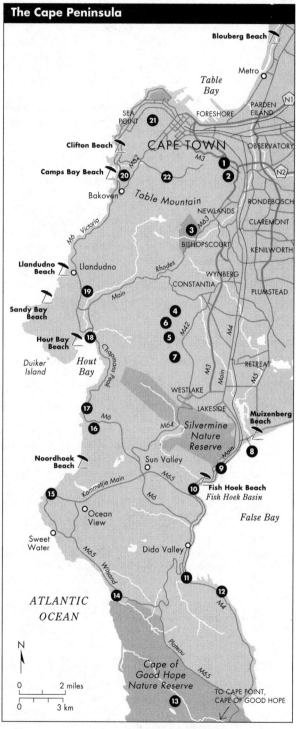

The Cape Peninsula

wines. The best is the excellent Gouverneurs Reserve, made from mostly cabernet sauvignon grapes with smaller amounts of merlot and cabernet franc. Full of tannin and fruit, this big, robust wine will be at its best in eight to ten years. The Pinotage is consistently good, too, reaching its velvety prime in about five years. The estate operates two restaurants: the elegant Jonkershuis (*see* Dining, *below*) and the Tavern, which serves light meals at picnic tables on the lawn. You can also bring your own picnic and relax on the lawns behind the wine cellar. *Off Main Rd.,* ☎ *021/794–5128.* ☛ *Museum: R2, wine-tasting: R6, cellar tours: R6.* ☉ *Daily 10–4:30. Cellar tours hourly 10–4.*

Leaving Groot Constantia, turn right on Main Road then right again onto Ladies Mile Extension (a sign points you to Muizenberg and Bergvliet). Another right at the first traffic light puts you onto Spaanschemat River Road, and a final right turn funnels you onto Klein Constantia Road. Follow this to **Buitenverwachting,** a gorgeous winery that was also once part of van der Stel's original Constantia farm. *Buitenverwachting* means "beyond expectation," and its setting certainly surpasses anything you might have imagined: An oak-lined avenue leads past the Cape Dutch homestead to the thatched modern cellar. Acres of vines spread up hillsides flanked by more towering oaks and the rocky crags of the Constantiaberg.

Buitenverwachting's wine is just as superb as its setting. The largest seller is the off-dry Buiten Blanc, an easy-drinking blend of a few varieties. The best red is Christine, which until the 1991 vintage was known as Grand Vin; it's a blend of mostly cabernet sauvignon and 30% merlot. The winery's restaurant (*see* Dining, *below*) is probably the finest in the Cape. *Off Klein Constantia Rd.,* ☎ *021/794–5190,* FAX *021/794–1351. Tastings free.* ☉ *Weekdays 9–5, Sat. 9–1.*

TIME OUT   Buitenverwachting serves great picnic lunches under the oaks on the estate's lawns. It's an idyllic setting and a most civilized way to cap off a morning of wine-tasting. Each picnic hamper is packed with a selection of breads, meat, chicken, pâtés, and cheeses. You can buy a bottle of estate wine as an accompaniment to the meal. The picnic costs R25 per person and reservations are essential (☎ 021/794–1012). *Closed Sun.*

Turn left out of Buitenverwachting and continue for ½ kilometer (¼ mile) to **Klein Constantia.** *Klein* (rhymes with "stain") means "small" in Afrikaans, and indicates the relative size of this portion of van der Stel's original Constantia estate. The winery has an impressive modern cellar, deliberately unobtrusive so as not to detract from the vine-covered mountain slopes. Its Cape Dutch homestead, visible as you drive in, was built in the late 18th century. This estate also produces wines of superb quality, as awards displayed in the tasting area attest. The excellent Sauvignon Blanc is used as a point of reference by many South African connoisseurs and vintners. Whereas early vintages were particularly opulent, more recent ones have been a little racey upon first release. The closest you'll come to the famous Constantia wine of the 18th century is the Vin de Constance, a sweet wine made from predominantly muscat de Frontignan grapes. The Cabernet Sauvignon is one of the best produced in the Cape—a collector's wine that will develop wonderfully over time. *Klein Constantia Rd.,* ☎ *021/794–5788,* FAX *021/794–2464. Tastings free.* ☉ *Weekdays 9–5, Sat. 9–1. Cellar tours by appointment.*

Head back down Klein Constantia Road. Just past the turnoff to Buitenverwachting, turn down Nova Constantia Road, which leads to Spaanschemat River Road. Go right and continue about 2 kilometers (1 mile) to the junction with Tokai Road. Turn right again at the **❼** PORTER SCHOOL sign and drive 1 kilometer (½ mile) to **Tokai Manor.** Built in 1795 it's one of the finest Cape Dutch homes in the country. The famed architect Louis Michel Thibault designed its facade. The homestead is reputedly haunted by a horseman who died when he tried to ride his horse down the curving front steps during a drunken revel. Stop for a look even though the house isn't open to the public.

Return to the junction and continue straight on Tokai Road, which meets up with the M3. Follow the signs to Muizenberg through various twists and turns until you end up on the M4. After ½ kilometer (¼ mile), **Boyes Drive** leads off the M4. If you prefer scenic views to historical sites, Boyes Drive is probably a better option than the main highway. The drive runs high along the mountains, offering panoramic views of False Bay and the Hottentots Holland mountains, before rejoining the M4 at Kalk Bay (*see below*).

The M4, or Main Road, on the other hand, takes you into the center **❽** of **Muizenberg.** At the turn of the century this was the premier bathing resort in South Africa, attracting many of the country's wealthy mining magnates. The mansions along Main Road date back to this period. Today, Muizenberg remains popular among locals, particularly surfers, who prefer the comparatively warm waters of False Bay and its white-sand beach. Long gone, though, are the days when anyone thought of Muizenberg as chic. A drab complex of shops and fast-food outlets, complete with kiddie pools, blights the beachfront, and even the views of mountains and sea cannot fully make up for it.

Emerging from the town center, Main Road runs parallel to the sea. Watch on your right for a small thatched building with rough, whitewashed walls. This is **De Post Huys** (Main Rd., ☎ 021/788–7035), one of the oldest surviving buildings in the country. It was constructed in 1673 as a look-out post and signal station. At press time the building was closed to the public, but it may reopen soon.

Continue down the street to **Rhodes Cottage Museum.** Considering the great power wielded by Cecil Rhodes, his seaside cottage was surprisingly humble and spare. Yet this is where the man who was instrumental in the development of present-day South Africa chose to spend his last days in 1902, preferring the cool sea air of Muizenberg to the stifling opulence of his home at Groote Schuur. The cottage has been completely restored, including the bedroom where he died. Other rooms display photos documenting Rhodes's life. His remains are buried in the Matopos Hills in Zimbabwe. *246 Main Rd., Muizenberg,* ☎ *021/788–1816.* ☛ *Free.* ☺ *Tues.–Sun. 10–1 and 2–5.*

From Muizenberg, Main Road heads down the peninsula, hugging the shore of False Bay. Strung out along this coastline are a collection of small towns that long ago merged to form a thin suburban belt between **❾** the ocean and the mountains. The name of **Kalk Bay** recalls that seashells were once baked in large kilns near the shore to produce lime (*kalk*). Today, a small harbor shelters the town's weathered fishing fleet. Across the bay lies Seal Island, home to large populations of seals and sea birds. The waters surrounding the island are a breeding area for the great white shark.

⑩ Fish Hoek is one of the most popular resorts on the False Bay coast, with a smooth, sandy beach that is protected from the frequent summer southeasters by Elsies Peak. It's also one of the best places to see whales during calving season. Fish Hoek is the only teetotaling town in the country. In 1810, Lord Charles Somerset issued the first grant of Crown land in Fish Hoek on condition that no wine house should ever exist on the property. Somerset was evidently alarmed by the excesses associated with a wine house near Kommetjie, where wagon drivers would become too drunk to deliver their supplies to the Royal Navy at Simon's Town.

★ **⑪ Simon's Town,** by far the most interesting of the False Bay communities, serves as a base for the South African Navy. Men in uniform brush shoulders with anglers and tourists, and residents of the town have preserved and nurtured its proud naval history stretching back two centuries. More than 20 buildings on the main street alone date back to the mid-19th century. Though it is named after Simon van der Stel, one of the first Dutch governors of the Cape, most of the town's history is British. It was here in 1795 that British troops landed before defeating the Dutch at the Battle of Muizenberg, and the town served as a base for the Royal Navy from 1814 to 1957, when it was handed over to South Africa. The batteries of naval and antiaircraft guns along St. George's Road leading into town are reminders that this is still an active naval station.

Exhibits in the **Simon's Town Museum** trace the town's early history, its development, and its relationship to the British and South African navies. Other displays focus on the Khoikhoi and San, the earliest inhabitants in the area. The museum is housed in the Old Residency, built in 1777 for the governor of the Dutch East India Company. *Court Rd., Simon's Town,* ☎ *021/786–3046.* ☛ *R2 adults, R1 students.* ☉ *Weekdays 9–4, Sat. 10–1; closed public holidays.*

The **S.A. Naval Museum** stands next door. Here you come to appreciate the role of South Africans in the two world wars. Perhaps the most interesting display is a life-size reconstruction of the operations room and control center in a modern submarine. The museum occupies the Mast House and Sail Loft, an 1815 building originally designed to store ships' masts, some as long as 117 feet. *St. George's Rd., Simon's Town,* ☎ *021/787–4686.* ☛ *Free.* ☉ *Daily 10–4.*

St. George's Road leads to Jubilee Square, a dockside plaza that serves as the *de facto* town center. Next to the dock wall stands a sculpture of **Just Nuisance,** a Great Dane adopted as a mascot by the Royal Navy during World War II. Just Nuisance apparently liked his pint of beer and would accompany sailors on the train into Cape Town. He had the endearing habit of leading drunk sailors—and only sailors—that he found in the city back to the Union Jack Club, where they could sleep it off. The Navy went so far as to induct him into the service as an able seaman attached to H.M.S. *Afrikander.* He died at the age of seven in April 1944.

At the southern end of town, just off St. George's Road, stands the **Martello Tower.** Built in 1795, it is the oldest surviving British building in South Africa. This circular tower was modeled after a fort at Cape Mortella in Corsica that caused enormous problems for a British fleet during the Napoleonic Wars. It is not open to the public, but you can get into the base to view the exterior on weekdays from 10 to 3:45.

⑫ On the outskirts of town lies **Boulders Beach,** a series of small coves tucked away among giant boulders. The swimming here is fine—no heavy surf or currents—but the beach is most interesting for its resident colony of jackass penguins. This is one of only two mainland colonies of these birds in southern Africa. The other colony is at Betty's Bay in the Overberg (*see* Chapter 5).

Simon's Town is the last community of any size before you reach Cape Point. From here, the road traverses a wild and windswept landscape as beautiful as it is desolate. The mountains, covered with rugged fynbos, descend almost straight into the sea. Don't be surprised to see troops of baboons lounging beside the road.

★ ⑬ The **Cape of Good Hope Nature Reserve** covers some 19,100 acres, including Cape Point and the Cape of Good Hope. Much of the park consists of rolling hills covered with fynbos and laced with miles of walking trails, for which maps are available at the park entrance. It also has beautiful deserted beaches. Eland, baboons, ostrich, and bontebok are among the animals that roam the park. A tarred road runs 14 kilometers (8 miles) to the tip of the peninsula. A turnoff leads to the Cape of Good Hope, a rocky beach at the southwesternmost point on the continent. A plaque marks the spot—otherwise you would never know you're standing on a site of such significance. The opposite is true of Cape Point, a dramatic knife edge of rock that slices into the Atlantic. Looking out to sea from the viewing platform, you *feel* you're at the tip of Africa, even though that honor officially belongs to Cape Agulhas, about 160 kilometers (100 miles) to the southeast (*see* Chapter 5). From Cape Point the views of False Bay and the Hottentots Holland mountains are breathtaking. The walk up to the viewing platform and the old lighthouse is very steep, but a shuttle bus (R2) makes the run every 10 minutes or so. Take along an anorak or sweater—the wind can snatch you bald-headed. A small shop sells snacks and curios. *Off the M65 and M4,* ☎ *021/780–1100.* ☛ *R5 per person (R10 minimum).* ۞ *Daily 7–5.*

TIME OUT The **Homestead Restaurant,** midway through the Cape of Good Hope Nature Reserve, is a great place to warm up over coffee on a windy day or to drain a beer on the terrace when the weather's fine. The food can be dreadful, so have lunch in Simon's Town or Hout Bay or bring your own food.

Head left out of the nature reserve onto the M65, drive 8 kilometers (5 miles), then turn left again to continue on the M65 to Scarborough **⑭** and Kommetjie. **Scarborough** is a tiny holiday community with one of the best beaches on the peninsula (*see* Beaches, *below*). From Scarborough the road hugs the shoreline, snaking between the mountains and the crashing surf. Another beach, which makes Scarborough's pale in comparison, lies about 5 kilometers (3 miles) farther on and is visible from the road. To reach it, turn left at the turnoff to Soetwater, and then left again at the bottom of the hill.

⑮ **Kommetjie** is a quiet fishing village known for its crayfish (clawless lobsters). It's also a popular spot for birders, since this is the roosting area for four species of cormorant, as well as the Arctic tern in winter. A 45-minute walk down Long Beach leads to the wreck of the *Kakapo,* a steamship that went aground on her maiden voyage in 1900.

From Kommetjie the M65 leads to a major intersection. Turn left onto the M6 (Hout Bay), go through one set of lights, and then turn left again, following the signs to Hout Bay. The road passes through the

⑯ small community of **Noordhoek** (*see* Beaches, *below*) before beginning its treacherous climb around Chapman's Peak.

A trip around the peninsula exhausts anyone's supply of superlatives, but it's hard to beat the dramatic beauty of the 10-kilometer (6-mile)

★ ⑰ stretch of road between Noordhoek and Hout Bay known as **Chapman's Peak Drive**, designed by Robert Glenday and built over seven years, ending in 1992. The road literally clings to the mountainside, with a narrow retaining wall separating you from a sheer drop into the sea below—528-feet down at its highest. It's dizzyingly beautiful, made more so by the fact that the road constantly ducks and weaves.

⑱ From Chapman's Peak you descend into the fishing village of **Hout Bay,** cradled in a lovely bay and guarded by a 1,000-foot peak known as the Sentinel. Hout Bay is the center of Cape Town's crayfishing industry, and the town operates several fish-processing plants. Mariner's Wharf is Hout Bay's salty answer to the Waterfront in Cape Town, a collection of bars and restaurants situated on the fishing dock. You can also buy fresh fish at a seafood market and take it outside to be grilled. Cruise boats depart from Hout Bay's harbor to view the **seal colony** on Duiker Island (*see* Cape Town Essentials, *below*).

Stay on the M6 (a sign reads CITY AND LLANDUDNO) when it splits off the M63. After less than a kilometer (½ mile), turn right on Valley Road

⑲ to the **World of Birds,** where you can walk through aviaries housing 450 species of indigenous and exotic birds, including eagles, vultures, penguins, and flamingos. No cage separates you from the birds, allowing you to photograph even giant raptors from impossibly close quarters. *Valley Rd., Hout Bay,* ☎ *021/790–2730,* 🖷 *021/790–4839.* ☛ *R13 adults, R6.50 children.* ☉ *Daily 9–6.*

From Hout Bay the M6 climbs past the exclusive community of **Llan-**

⑳ **dudno** and then runs along the coast to **Camps Bay,** a popular holiday resort with a long beach and plenty of restaurants and bars. The craggy faces of the Twelve Apostles, huge granite buttresses reaching down to the sea from the mountains behind, loom over the town.

Follow Victoria Road (M6) out of Camps Bay and turn right at the sign reading KLOOF NEK ROUND HOUSE. This road snakes up the mountain until it reaches a five-way intersection at Kloof Nek. Make a

★ ㉑ sharp left onto the road leading to **Signal Hill.** This road swings around the shoulder of Lion's Head and then runs along the flank of Signal Hill. The views of the city below and Table Mountain are superb. The road dead-ends at a parking lot overlooking Sea Point and all of Table Bay. For more great views of the city, return to the Kloof Nek inter-

㉒ section and take **Tafelberg Road** past the Lower Cableway (*see* Tour 1, *above*). The road traverses the northern side of Table Mountain before ending at Devil's Peak. From the Kloof Nek intersection, you can descend into the city directly or return to Camps Bay and follow the coastal road back to the city. This route takes you through the beautiful seaside communities of **Clifton** (*see* Beaches, *below*) and **Bantry Bay,** and then along the seaside promenade in **Sea Point.**

Off the Beaten Path

District Six Museum. Housed in the Buitenkant Methodist Church, this new museum preserves the memory of one of Cape Town's most vibrant multicultural neighborhoods, and the district's destruction in one of the cruelest acts of the apartheid Nationalist government. At press time, this museum was still assembling its collection, but you can still get a feel for life in District Six through photographs and articles donated by ex-residents and their children. One ex-resident has donated District Six's street signs, which he had taken as a memento, keeping them hidden for years out of fear. *25a Buitenkant St., ☎ 021/461–8745. ☛ R3 donation requested. ⊙ Mon.–Sat. 10–4:30.*

The **Irma Stern Museum** is dedicated to the works and art collection of Irma Stern (1894–1966), one of South Africa's greatest painters. The museum, administered by the University of Cape Town, occupies "the Firs," Stern's home for 38 years. She is best known for her African studies, particularly her paintings of indigenous people inspired by trips to the Congo and Zanzibar. Her collection of African artifacts, including priceless Congolese stools and carvings, is superb. *Cecil Rd., Rosebank, ☎ 021/685–5686. ☛ R2 adults, R1 students, children under 3 free. ⊙ Tues.–Sun. 10–1 and 2–5.*

SHOPPING

A number of surprisingly good stores in Cape Town sell African art and crafts. None of the work is local—much of it comes from Zululand or neighboring countries—so prices tend to be slightly higher than at their point of origin. Street vendors, particularly on St. George's Mall and Greenmarket Square, often sell the same curios for half the price.

The Captour desk at the Tourist Rendezvous Travel Centre (*see* Important Addresses and Numbers *in* Cape Town Essentials, *below*) has helpful brochures describing an Antique Route and an Arts and Crafts Route that cover the city and the peninsula.

Markets

Greenmarket Square is an open-air market where artisans and hawkers sell their wares. You can get good buys on clothing, T-shirts, handcrafted silver jewelry, and locally made leather shoes and sandals. It's lively and fun whether or not you buy anything. ⊙ *Mon.–Sat. 9–4:30.*

Red Shed Craft Workshop is a genuine workshop where you can watch artisans blowing glass, knitting sweaters, or weaving rugs. All of their work is for sale. *Victoria Wharf, Waterfront. ⊙ Mon.-Sat. 9–7, Sun. 10–6.*

Waterfront Art and Craft Market features the works of over 140 artisans and artists. This indoor market offers an assortment of hand-crafted jewelry, rugs, glass, pottery, and leather shoes and sandals. *Waterfront, ☎ 021/418–2850. ⊙ Weekends and public holidays only, 8:30–6.*

Specialty Stores

AFRICAN ART

African Heritage is an upscale shop specializing in jewelry from all over Africa, including Tuareg bangles and Ethiopian silver crosses strung on beaded necklaces. The store also carries works by local artists. *Shop 102, Victoria Wharf, Waterfront, ☎ 021/21–6610, FAX 021/21–7413. ⊙ Weekdays 9–7, weekends 9–5.*

African Image sells traditional and contemporary African art and curios. Look for colorful cloth from Nigeria and Ghana, plus West African masks, Malian blankets, and beaded designs from southern African tribes. A variety of Zulu baskets is also available at moderate prices. *52 Burg St., ☎ and* FAX *021/23–8385. ⊘ Weekdays 8:45–5, Sat. 9–1:30.*

The Collector is for serious buyers with unlimited spending power. This museumlike shop offers a small, select assortment of works ranging from West African ornamental beads to hand-painted Tuareg leather pillows and Zairian Kuba knives. Tags describe the place of origin and uses of all pieces. It's an interesting place in which to learn about African artifacts. *59 Church St., ☎ 021/23–1483. ⊘ Weekdays 10–1 and 2:15– 4, Sat. 10–1.*

Third World Spectator carries a large selection of traditional southern African artifacts ranging from Zulu beer pots to wooden meat trays, Tonga stools, and wooden earplugs (used to stretch earlobes). The shop also features an assortment of musical instruments. *Shop 8, Protea Assurance Bldg., Greenmarket Sq., ☎ and* FAX *021/24–2957. ⊘ Weekdays 9–5, Sat. 9–1.*

AFRICAN CLOTHING AND FABRICS

N.C.M. African Styles is the place to go for traditional West African clothing. One of the most striking outfits is the brightly colored *bubu*, a loose-fitting garment with a matching head wrap. If you have a few days to spare, you can order a custom outfit from a wide selection of fabrics. *150 Main Rd., Claremont, ☎ 021/683–1022. ⊘ Weekdays 9–5:30, Sat. 9–1:30.*

Mnandi carries a range of African fabrics, including traditional West African prints and Dutch wax prints. They sell ready-made African clothing for adults and children. You can also have clothing made to order. *90 Station Rd., Observatory, ☎ 021/47–6814,* FAX *021/47–7937. ⊘ Weekdays 9–5:30, Sat. 9–1.*

BOOKS

Exclusive Books is one of the best all-round bookshops in the country. This chain also carries a wide selection of local and international periodicals, and a beautiful collection of coffee-table books on Africa. However, be prepared to pay at least twice as much for paperback and hardcover books as you would in the United States or Britain. *Victoria Wharf, Waterfront, ☎ 021/419–0905. ⊘ Weekdays 9–7, Sat. 9 AM–11 PM, Sun. 10–9.*

CRAFTS

The Cape Heritage Shop sells a variety of hand-crafted goods made only in Cape Town. You'll find hand-painted pillowcases, tablecloths, wall hangings, T-shirts, cards, wire sculptures, pottery, glassware, toys, and jewelry. *Corner of Burg and Church Sts., ☎ 021/24–9590,* FAX *021/24– 3159. ⊘ Weekdays 9–5, Sat. 9–1.*

SPORTS AND THE OUTDOORS

Participant Sports

Diving

Divers can explore several of the hundreds of wrecks that litter the waters around the Cape Peninsula, as well as several marine reserves. Far more exciting is the chance to descend in a diving cage among great white sharks, which breed in the waters around the Cape. All the major diving companies offer PADI or NAUI scuba-diving courses for around R600. Contact **Aquasport** (Strand St., across from Cape Sun Hotel, ☎ 021/419–1835), **Blue Print Diving** (Quay 5, Waterfront, ☎

021/418–5806), or **Waterfront Scuba** (Hout Bay harbor, behind NSRI, ☎ 021/790–1106).

Fishing

Charlie Day at **Bluefin Charters** (☎ 021/783–1756 or 082/892–4966) takes up to six people deep-sea fishing in his 38-foot boat. The trip, which departs from Hout Bay at 6:30 and returns at 5, costs R2,500, and customers must provide their own food and booze. Among the likely catches are dolphin, long-fin and yellow-fin tuna, yellowtail, and mako shark. **Neptune Deep Sea Angling** (☎ 021/782–3889) offers two types of fishing in its 24-foot ski-boat: bottom fishing in Simon's Town Bay for kabeljou, snoek, yellowtail, and crayfish (in season); and deep-sea fishing for marlin and other big game fish. Think twice about going far out to sea in such a small boat if you suffer from motion sickness. A whole day's fishing costs about R1,000.

Golf

Most golf clubs in the Cape accept visitors, but prior booking is essential. Expect to pay R40–R80 for 18 holes. Most clubs offer equipment rental. The Winelands in particular has some spectacular courses (*see* Chapter 5).

Clovelley Country Club (☎ 021/782–6410) in Fish Hoek is a tight course that requires masterful shot placement from tee to green. **Durbanville Golf Club** (☎ 021/96–8121) may not be the most challenging course in the Cape but it compensates with tremendous views and bird life. **King David Country Club** (☎ 021/934–0365) is famous for its layout, with undulating fairways and elevated tees; the 12th hole plays into the wind and is probably the toughest par-3 in the Cape. **Milnerton Golf Club** (☎ 021/52–1047), sandwiched between the sea and a lagoon, is the Cape's only links course and can be very difficult when the wind blows. **Mowbray Golf Club** (☎ 021/685–3018), with its great views of Devil's Peak, is a magnificent parkland course that has hosted several major tournaments over the years; there are a number of interesting water holes. Unfortunately, noise from the highway can spoil the atmosphere. **Rondebosch Golf Club** (☎ 021/689–4176), also in the shadow of Devil's Peak, is a gently undulating course that crisscrosses the Black River several times. Founded in 1885, **Royal Cape Golf Club** (☎ 021/761–6551) in Wynberg is the oldest course in the country and has hosted the South African Open numerous times. Its beautiful setting and immaculate fairways and greens make a round here a must for visitors. The club does not rent equipment, however. **Westlake Golf Club** (☎ 021/788–2020) is laid out around a large lake in the shadow of rocky mountains; holes 7 and 14 are extremely difficult.

Horseback Riding

Sleepy Hollow Horse Riding (Sleepy Hollow La., Noordhoek, ☎ 021/789–2341) offers 1½- and two-hour rides down Noordhoek Beach, a gorgeous, 6-kilometer (4-mile) expanse of sand that stretches from Noordhoek all the way to Kommetjie. Experienced guides lead the rides, which are limited to six people. Moonlight, champagne, and sunset rides are also offered.

Swimming Pools and Baths

Even on the hottest days, you have to be a seal to swim in the Cape's frigid waters (*see* Beaches, *below*), and many Capetonians opt to cool off in the city's municipal swimming pools instead. **Long Street Swimming Pool** (Long St., Cape Town, ☎ 021/400–3302), in the center of town, features a heated swimming pool and Turkish steam baths. In the southern suburbs, head for **Newlands Swimming Pool** (corner of Main and Sans Souci Rds., Newlands, ☎ 021/64–4197). If you want to go to the beach *and* swim, head for the **Muizenberg Seawater Swimming Pool** (Muizenberg Beach Front, ☎ 021/788–7881) or **Sea Point Seawater Swimming Pool** (Beach Rd., Sea Point, ☎ 021/434–3341).

Spectator Sports

Cricket

The huge sporting complex off Boundary Road in Newlands is known country-wide simply as Newlands. It's the home of the **Western Province Cricket Union** (☎ 021/64–4146), which competes in the annual Castle Cup against provincial sides from all over South Africa. Newlands is also one of the major venues in the country for one- and five-day test matches, when the South African team takes on international touring sides.

Rugby

Western Province Rugby Football Union (Boundary Rd., Newlands, ☎ 021/689–4921) also calls the huge Newlands sports complex home, playing in a brand-new stadium built for the Rugby World Cup in 1995. During the winter, Newlands is the site of annual Currie Cup matches against other South African provincial teams, as well as test matches between the Springboks and international touring sides.

BEACHES

With panoramic views of mountains tumbling down to the ocean, the sandy beaches of the Cape Peninsula are stunning, and a major draw for Capetonians. Beautiful as they may be, don't expect a traditional beach holiday of sun, sand, and splashing in the surf. The water around Cape Town is very, very cold. Beaches on the Atlantic are washed by the Benguela Current flowing up from the Antarctic, and in mid-summer the water hovers around 12°–15°C (55°–60°F). The water on the False Bay side is usually 5°C (9°F) warmer. If you *are* looking for a classic beach holiday, head for the warm Indian Ocean waters of KwaZulu-Natal (*see* Chapter 7) or the Garden Route (*see* Chapter 6).

The major factor that affects any day at a Cape beach is wind. In summer, howling southeasters, known as the Doctor, are all too common and will ruin any trip to the exposed beaches of False Bay; during these gales you're better off on Atlantic beaches. The easiest way to tell if the southeaster is blowing is to look at Table Mountain—if it is wearing its shroud of cloud, it means that the Doctor is in.

Every False Bay community has its own beach, but most are not reviewed here. In comparison with Atlantic beaches, most of them are built-up and unappealing, sandwiched between the sea and the commuter rail line. Once you travel south on the peninsula past Simon's Bay, beaches become wild and undeveloped, especially in the Cape of Good Hope Nature Reserve. Wherever you go, remember that the surf is dangerous, with powerful waves, strong undertow, and dangerous rip tides. Lifeguards work many of the main beaches, although some have rescue service only on weekends and during school holidays.

Atlantic Coast

The beaches below are listed from north to south and are marked on the Cape Peninsula map.

Blouberg. On the other side of Table Bay, 25 kilometers (16 miles) from the city, this beach commands the most famous view of Cape Town and Table Mountain. It is divided into two parts: Big Bay, which hosts a lot of surfing and sailboarding contests; and Little Bay, better suited to sunbathers and families. It's frequently windy, which is fine if you want to fly a kite but a nuisance otherwise. Swim in front of the lifeguard club. *Follow N1 north toward Paarl, and then R27 to Milnerton and Bloubergstrand.*

Clifton. This is where the in-crowd comes to see and be seen. Some of the Cape's most desirable houses cling to the slopes above the beach, and tall schooners often anchor in the calm water beyond the breakers. Granite outcroppings divide the beach into four segments, imaginatively known as First, Second, Third, and Fourth beaches. Fourth Beach is popular with families, while the others support a strong social and singles scene. Swimming is reasonably safe here, although the undertow is strong and the water, again, freezing. Lifeguards are on duty. On weekends and in peak season, Clifton can be a madhouse and your chances of finding parking are nil. *Off Victoria Rd., Clifton. Hout Bay bus from OK Bazaars on Adderley St.*

Camps Bay. Table Mountain and the granite faces of the Twelve Apostles provide the backdrop for this long, sandy beach that slopes gently down to the water from a grassy verge. The surf is powerful and there are no lifeguards, but sunbathers can cool off in a tidal pool or under showers. The popular bars and restaurants of Camps Bay lie only yards away across Victoria Road. One drawback is the wind, which can blow hard here. *Victoria Rd. Hout Bay bus from OK Bazaars on Adderley St.*

Lladudno. Die-hard fans return to this beach again and again, and who can blame them? Its setting, among giant boulders at the base of a mountain, is glorious, and sunsets here attract their own aficionados. Unfortunately, the surf is very dangerous, as the wreck of the tanker *Romelia* offshore attests. Lifeguards are on duty. If you come by bus, brace yourself for a long walk down (and back up) the mountain from the bus stop on the M6. *Take Lladudno exit off M6 and follow signs. Hout Bay bus from OK Bazaars on Adderley St.*

Sandy Bay. Backed by wild dunes and fynbos, Cape Town's unofficial nudist beach is also one of its prettiest. Sunbathers can hide among rocky coves or frolic on a long stretch of sandy beach. Shy nudists will appreciate its isolation, 20 minutes on foot from the nearest parking area in Llandudno. Wind, however, can be a problem: If you're caught in the buff when the southeaster starts to blow, you're in for a painful sandblasting. Getting here by bus poses the same problem as the trip to Lladudno (*see above*). *Take Lladudno exit off M6 and follow signs to Sandy Bay. Hout Bay bus from OK Bazaars on Adderley St.*

Hout Bay. This beach appears to have it all: a knockout view of the mountains, gentle surf, and easy access to the restaurants and bars of Mariner's Wharf. The reality is not quite so stunning, with the town's industrial fishing harbor and its mini-oil slicks and other waste products nearby. *Off the M6, Hout Bay. Take Hout Bay bus from OK Bazaars on Adderley St.*

Noordhoek Beach. This may be the most impressive beach on the peninsula, a vast expanse of white sand stretching 6½ kilometers (4 miles) from the base of Chapman's Peak to Kommetjie. It's also one of the wildest and least populated, backed by a lagoon and nature reserve.

Because of the wind it attracts horseback riders and walkers rather than sunbathers. Lifeguards are on duty during peak season, however. *Off the M6, Noordhoek. No bus service.*

False Bay

Muizenberg. Once the fashionable resort of South African high society, this long, sandy beach has lost much of its glamour and now appeals to families and beginner surfers. A tacky pavilion houses a swimming pool, water slides, toilets, changing rooms, and snack shops. The beach itself is lined with colorful bathing boxes of the type once popular at British resorts. Lifeguards are on duty, and the sea is shallow and reasonably safe. *Catch Cape Metro train on Simon's Town line.*

Fish Hoek. Protected by Elsies Peak, this sandy beach attracts a lot of retirees, who appreciate the calm, clear water—it may be the safest bathing beach in the Cape. Fish Hoek is also popular with catamaran sailors and boardsailors, who often stage regattas offshore. Jager Walk, a pathway that runs along the rocky coastline, begins at the beach's southern end. *Catch Cape Metro train on Simon's Town line.*

DINING

By Myrna Robins

Cape Town is the culinary capital of South Africa. Nowhere else in the country is the populace so discerning about food, and nowhere else is there such a wide selection of restaurants from which to choose. Western culinary history here dates back more than 300 years—Cape Town was founded specifically to grow food—and that heritage is reflected in its own style of cuisine as well as a number of restaurants operating in historic town houses and 18th-century wine estates.

Dutch settlers, French Huguenots, and the English have all placed their stamp on the region's cuisine, but none more so than the Malay slaves brought here in the late 17th century. It is their influence that gives Cape cuisine its distinctive use of spices. Cape curries tend to be mild compared to their Indian counterparts, and they are generally quite sweet. A good example of classic Cape cuisine is *bobotie,* a semisweet curried mince topped with savory custard.

It can be surprisingly difficult to find truly first-class seafood in Cape Town, but don't leave without trying crayfish, the clawless rock lobster with succulent tail meat. You'll also find linefish—any of the numerous game fish hooked in Cape waters by line fishermen, as opposed to school fish netted by trawlers—on menus all over town. Among the best from Cape waters are kingklip, kabeljou, snoek, and yellowtail.

Don't expect to see too many non-South African wines on restaurant wine lists. The close proximity of Winelands vineyards inspires fierce loyalty in Capetonians (as well as penny-pinching common sense), and they tend to fuss a great deal over which wines to drink with their meal. One great boon of the Cape's wine heritage is that you can bring your own wine into even the most exclusive restaurants, often with no corkage fee. If fees are charged, they tend to be small (R3–R5).

For a description of South African culinary terms, *see* Pleasures & Pastimes *in* Chapter 1. For price ranges, *see* Chart 1 *in* On the Road with Fodor's.

City Center

$$$$ **Mount Nelson Grill Room.** Befitting its setting in the city's most historic and unashamedly colonial hotel, this restaurant has a formal, clubby feel, enlivened by the sparkle of silver and cut glass. A singer croons the old familiars as gentlemen sway with their wives on the dance floor. Luxurious ingredients predominate in first courses of smoked duck and quail, oysters, foie gras, and Norwegian salmon. For a main course, consider such traditional dishes as chateaubriand and rack of lamb, or flambéed specialties like prawns, spiced calamari, or liver and kidneys. For dessert, order the Cape's own Malva pudding, flamed with ginger brandy. Alas, the quality of the food can fluctuate wildly. An authoritative wine list offers the best South African vintages, supplemented by labels from every major wine-growing country. ✗ *Orange St., Gardens,* ☎ *021/23–1000. Reservations required. Jacket required. AE, DC, MC, V. No lunch.*

$$$$ Tastevin. Stunning chandeliers, dark paneling, and beautifully set tables create an ambience both formal and elegant in this favorite of the expense-account crowd, hidden away in the upscale Cape Sun Hotel. Classic French technique and a dash of style characterize preparations that nevertheless make good use of southern African fish, shellfish, and meat. For a taste of local ingredients, try smoked ostrich or springbok (venison) carpaccio as a starter. The chef specializes in poultry and red meat, perfecting dishes like roast loin of lamb under a thyme crust and venison medallions in red wine sauce with *rösti* potatoes. Desserts display artistic flair: Mousses and soufflés float on sauces streaked with fruity purées and garnished with berries. The wine list features Nederburg auction wines and a few classic French vintages. ✗ *Cape Sun Hotel, Strand St., Cape Town,* ☎ *021/23–8844. Reservations advised. Jacket and tie. AE, DC, MC, V. Closed Sun., Mon. No lunch.*

$$$ The Edge. You can soak in the atmosphere of busy harbor life whether
★ you sit inside or out at this excellent Waterfront restaurant. The exciting menu successfully unites Pacific rim cuisine, Cape flavors, and Mediterranean and Floridian concepts. Cape rock lobster (crayfish) makes an affordable and unusual first course, served as sesame-crusted croquettes with a mustard sauce and coriander cream. Smoked Karoo venison, teamed with a tangerine liqueur sauce and sweet-corn chili salsa, offers palate-tingling contrasts of flavor. No fish is more typically Cape than snoek; here it comes as fish cakes with a fresh tomato sauce and Haitian slaw. Even the catch of the day is treated imaginatively, crusted with pecans and pumpkin seeds and served with a crayfish relish. Desserts include delectable roasted bananas, phyllo-wrapped and drizzled with rum syrup. ✗ *1 Pierhead, Waterfront,* ☎ *021/21– 2583. Reservations required in season; no reservations for outdoor tables. AE, DC, MC, V.*

$$$ Floris Smit Huijs. This appealing restaurant occupies a restored 18th-
★ century town house in the city center, and draws a devoted lunch crowd of office workers and gourmets. The menus reflect Asian, European, and African influences gathered during partners Steve Moncrieff and Piero Romero's extensive travels. Tastes of the Cape are offered in first courses like Malay chicken salad with garlic, ginger, and coriander, or marinated salmon trout. Seafood and vegetarian pastas are inventive. More substantial dishes include Tunisian-style lamb with honeyed aubergine on a tomato and chili salsa, and medallions of venison on a juniper berry and game sauce. A small dessert list stars a good chocolate mille-feuille. The wine list is small but carefully chosen. Street parking is a nightmare at lunch, but there is a garage a block up the hill. ✗ *55 Church St.,* ☎ *021/23–3414. Reservations advised, required for lunch in season. AE, DC, MC, V. Closed July and Sun. No lunch Sat.*

$$$ Panama Jack's. In this raw-timber structure in the heart of the docks, the music is loud, tables are crowded, and decor is nonexistent, but nowhere else in town will you find bigger crayfish. Choose one from the large, open tanks or stick to less expensive fare like mussels, oysters, calamari, and local fish. The seafood platter for two is huge, but much of it tastes like it was fried earlier. It can be tough to find this place at night, so you may want to come here for lunch your first time. ✗ *Royal Yacht Club basin, off Goliath Rd., Docks,* ☎ *021/47–3992. Reservations advised. AE, DC, MC, V. No lunch Sat., Mon.*

$$$ Rozenhof. Within easy walking distance of the hotels in Gardens, this
★ late-18th-century town house offers stylish fare and one of the best wine collections in town. Yellowwood ceilings and brass chandeliers provide historical Cape touches, and works by local artists adorn the walls. The menu is inspired by both Asia and the Mediterranean, with occasional offerings of time-honored local dishes. Summer salads make delectable first courses, and the cheese soufflé with herbed mustard cream has become a classic. Cape salmon trout is complemented by an asparagus flan and a chunky tomato and basil vinaigrette, and the duck comes with a glaze of ginger and Cape citrus liqueur. Layers of local Gorgonzola and *mascarpone* (Italian cream cheese) paired with preserved figs and a glass of port make a savory-sweet alternative to Provençal and Italian desserts. ✗ *18 Kloof St., Cape Town,* ☎ *021/24–1968. Reservations advised. AE, DC, MC, V. Closed Sun. No lunch Sat.*

$$ Tokyo. Run by a Japanese father-and-son team, this city-center restaurant is the most affordable of the few Japanese eateries in town. Black trelliswork, lacquered trays, and colorful kimonos create a suitable atmosphere. The sushi bar features fish bought fresh each morning from Cape harbors. Diners can also order *teppanyaki* (meat, seafood, and vegetables grilled on hibachi tables) and *tempura* (shrimp or vegetables fried in a feather-light batter). The *bentou* fish box makes a perfect lunchtime sampler. ✗ *31a Long St., Cape Town,* ☎ *021/23–6055. No reservations. AE, DC, MC, V. Closed July and Sun. No lunch Sat.*

$$ Wangthai. Thai restaurants are only now catching on in South Africa, and this is one of the best. *Satays,* grilled meat with a spicy peanut dip, make a good starter, as do spring-roll-wrapped prawns. *Tom Seab* is an outstanding aromatic beef broth scented with galangal, a type of ginger. Colorful stir-fries combine chicken, pork, or beef with the fresh tastes of coriander leaves and sweet basil or the fire of roasted chilies. Pungent red and green curries are tempered by coconut milk and mounds of sticky rice. Wangthai's setting in an office block on the Foreshore won't win any awards, but it's convenient to city-center hotels and the Tourist Rendezvous Travel Centre. ✗ *31 Heerengracht St.,* ☎ *021/418–1858. Reservations advised. AE, DC, MC, V. No lunch weekends.*

$ Biesmiellah. In the heart of the Malay Quarter, this long-established restaurant is one of the best places to sample Cape Malay cuisine. Starters include *samoosas,* deep-fried pastry triangles with a spicy meat or vegetable filling; chili bites, crisp-fried dumplings with a kick; and *churas,* battered potato balls spiked with chili and fresh coriander. Curries come in varying strengths: Shrimp and beef are usually fiery, the mutton milder. Essential accompaniments are rice or *rotis,* Indian flatbreads that have become an integral part of Cape Malay cooking. Other specials include *denningvleis,* a fragrant sweet-sour mutton dish, and *bredie,* slow-cooked mutton and vegetable stew. For dessert try the spiced vermicelli pudding popular with Muslims during Ramadan. No liquor is allowed on the premises. ✗ *2 Upper Wale St.,* ☎ *021/23–0850. Reservations advised in season. AE, DC, MC, V. Closed Sun.*

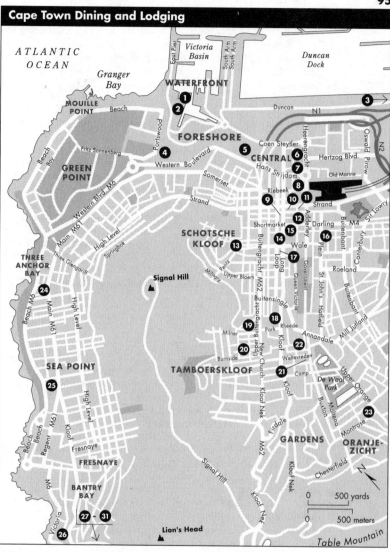

Cape Town Dining and Lodging

Dining
Biesmiellah, **13**
Blues, **27**
The Edge, **1**
Floris Smit Huijs, **14**
Jackson's, **25**
Mount Nelson Grill Room, **23**
Panama Jack's, **3**
Rozenhof, **18**
San Marco, **24**
Squares, **12**
Tastevin, **11**
Tokyo, **10**
Wangthai, **7**
Yellow Pepper Deli and Eaterie, **17**

Lodging
Bay Hotel, **28**
Breakwater Lodge, **4**
Cape Sun, **11**
The Capetonian, **6**
City Lodge, **5**
Ellerman House, **26**
Holiday Inn Garden Court–Greenmarket Square, **15**
Holiday Inn Garden Court–St. George's Mall, **8**
Hout Bay Manor Hotel, **29**
Lady Hamilton Hotel, **21**
Metropole Hotel, **9**
Mijlof Manor Hotel, **13**

Monkey Valley, **30**
Mount Nelson, **22**
Peninsula Hotel, **25**
Place on the Bay, **31**
Townhouse Hotel, **16**
Underberg Guest House, **20**
Victoria & Alfred Hotel, **2**
Villa Belmonte, **23**

$ Squares. Overhanging St. George's Mall, this California-style restaurant is a great place for breakfast, lunch, or snacks. Unusual dishes like pasta with egg, bacon, and sun-dried tomatoes add variety to the usual Continental and English breakfasts. At lunch, along with sandwiches and salads, seafood choices include grilled linefish and fried calamari with rice and lemon thyme mayonnaise. Pizza and pasta continue to be hot favorites, too. For an indulgent finale, order the dense chocolate brownie with ice cream and hot chocolate sauce. ✗ *Stuttafords Town Sq., St. George's Mall,* ☎ *021/24–0224. Lunch reservations advised. AE, DC, MC, V. Closed Sun. No dinner.*

$ Yellow Pepper Deli and Eaterie. For good, home-cooked food at bargain prices this trendy outlet has few rivals. Diners can order from a chalkboard menu or select what they fancy from dishes displayed behind a glass counter. Sophisticated Greek *mezes* (appetizers) and frogs' legs precede hearty dishes like vegetarian lasagna, moussaka, Cape-style chicken pie, and peasant sausage casserole. Arrive early to claim a portion of Malva pudding, an outstanding version of this traditional Cape baked dessert—fluffy, syrupy, and topped with cream. Try to sit in the high-ceilinged, arty interior, since tables on the pavement suffer from the noise and fumes of traffic. ✗ *138 Long St.,* ☎ *021/24–9250. No lunch reservations. AE, DC, MC, V. Closed Sun. No dinner Mon.–Thurs.*

Atlantic Coast

$$$ Blues. Doors open to frame an inviting vista of palms, sand, and azure sea from the balcony of this very popular restaurant in Camps Bay. The mood and menu are Californian, the clientele young and sophisticated. Appetizers inspired by Thailand and the Mediterranean are juxtaposed with local smoked salmon trout and West Coast mussels. Pizza and pasta are deservedly popular, and the quality of the fresh line- and shellfish is virtually guaranteed. Crisp stir-fried vegetables add color to generous portions that are attractively presented. For dessert, try chocolate brownies, sticky toffee pudding with butterscotch sauce, or one of the great American ice-cream concoctions. ✗ *The Promenade, Victoria Rd., Camps Bay,* ☎ *021/438–2040. Reservations required in season. AE, MC, V.*

$$$ San Marco. ★ Restaurants open and close in Cape Town with alarming speed. This Italian institution in Sea Point is a happy exception, a meeting place for generations of diners since it first opened its doors as a gelateria. As the interior suggests, you don't come here for the decor but for consistency and authenticity and for dishes that are cooked only after you order them. Start with superb grilled calamari, then move to homemade pasta or one of the veal dishes—escalopes cooked with sage and white wine are especially good. If one of the less common Cape linefish such as elf (shad) is offered, don't miss it. Finish with a selection of the house's renowned ice creams and sorbets, dressed with a splash of liqueur. ✗ *92 Main Rd., Sea Point,* ☎ *021/439–2758. Reservations required in season. AE, DC, MC, V. Closed Tues. and 1 month in mid-winter. No lunch Mon.–Sat.*

$$ Jackson's. ★ Award-winning chef John Jackson uses Cape ingredients to create the vibrant flavors of Provence, Italy, and the Middle East, drawing inspiration for soups and elegant stir-fries from the Far East. A meal could begin with fresh Namibian oysters or Moroccan lamb *kefta* (patties) and *harissa* (chili sauce), then move on to kingklip, a favorite Cape fish baked with rosemary, tomato, and feta cheese. Thai chicken and litchis are teamed with cashew nuts and lemongrass, while baked duck is marinated in Singaporean spices and topped with a tropical-fruit sweet-and-sour sauce. A refreshing dessert is Provençal fen-

Dining
The Africa Cafe, **4**
Au Jardin, **6**
Blues, **2**
Buitenverwachting, **15**
The Cellars, **9**
Constantia Uitsig, **14**
Emily's Bistro, **3**
The Fisherman's
Cottage, **12**
Gaylords, **19**
Jonkershuis, **13**
Mr. B, **7**
Parks, **11**
Shrimptons, **18**

Lodging
Alphen Hotel, **10**
Auberge Penrose, **5**
The Bay Hotel, **2**
British Hotel, **21**
The Cellars–Hohenort
Country House
Hotel, **9**
Constantia Uitsig, **14**
Hout Bay Manor
Hotel, **16**
Lord Nelson Inn, **20**
Monkey Valley, **17**
Palm House, **8**
The Place on the Bay, **1**
The Vineyard, **6**

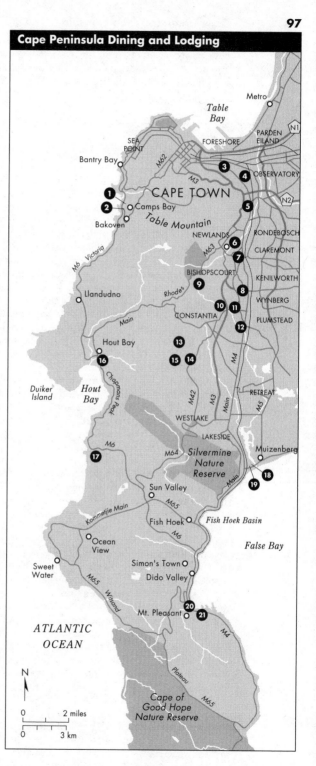

nel sorbet. Standards occasionally slip when Jackson is off duty; otherwise the restaurant offers mostly five-star dining at two-star prices. He also presides over the adjoining Café Bijou (open daily), with a lighter but equally sophisticated menu. ✗ *313 Beach Rd., Sea Point,* ☎ *021/439–8888. Reservations advised. AE, DC, MC, V. Closed Sun. No lunch.*

Southern Suburbs

$$$$ **Buitenverwachting.** Situated on a historic wine estate in Constantia,
★ this superb restaurant is consistently rated among the country's top ten. Window-side tables provide superb views of the vineyards sloping up toward the mountains. Master chef Thomas Sinn has presided over the kitchen since the restaurant's beginning, and his talent never falters as he daily conjures up new items, including an imaginative *amuse-bouche*. Meticulously prepared dishes are presented with artistic flair— and often a surprise element. Sinn's Continental background is revealed in dishes like calf's tongue with horseradish and potatoes, and rabbit rösti with mustard sauce. Otherwise, look for dishes based on local seafood and Karoo lamb and game. Kudu antelope is smoked and layered into a sort of lasagna with cabbage; ostrich comes plain or smoked with shallot confit. Many dessert masterpieces use local fruit, among them mango and plum sorbet with fresh berries and an amaretto parfait with mangoes and litchis. ✗ *Klein Constantia Rd., Constantia,* ☎ *021/794–3522. Reservations required. AE, DC, MC, V. Closed July, most public holidays, Sun., Mon. No lunch Sat.*

$$$$ **The Cellars.** Classic table settings and highly professional service complement artfully presented fare in this restaurant in the historic Cellars-Hohenhort Hotel in Constantia. Chef Christaan Campbell's seasonal menus draw their inspiration from French contemporary and English country-house cuisines, while making full use of the Cape's bounty of seafood, meat, and fresh produce. Summer starters include chilled marinated West Coast mussels and a paupiette of salmon and lobster on zucchini. For a main course, consider tender ostrich fillet or sautéed game fish with olive oil and basil. An excellent dessert is the caramelized apple tart and ice cream sparked with a classic Constantia tangerine liqueur. The luncheon menu is lighter and less expensive. ✗ *15 Hohenort Ave., Constantia,* ☎ *021/794–2137. Reservations required. AE, DC, MC, V.*

$$$ **Au Jardin.** In this corner of the historic Vineyard Hotel in Newlands,
★ complete with fountain and views of Table Mountain, talented French chef Christophe Dehosse and his team imbue classic French cuisine with subtle Cape and Mediterranean accents. *Amuse-bouches* preface appetizers of baked chèvre, smoked salmon trout on warm potatoes, and roasted aubergine timbale on tomato and zucchini salad. Bouillabaisse and poached linefish are well prepared by Dehosse's kitchen. Duck breast comes with a confit of stewed onions, roasted garlic, and diced peppers. For dessert, try roast fig with wildflower-honey ice cream. A three-course set menu at lunch makes a less expensive alternative to the à la carte menu. ✗ *Vineyard Hotel, Colinton Rd., Claremont,* ☎ *021/683–1520. Reservations advised. AE, DC, MC, V. Closed Sun. No lunch Sat., Mon.*

$$$ **Constantia Uitsig.** In a lovely restored farmstead, this comparative new-
★ comer to the Constantia scene has attracted quite a following. Reserve a table on the enclosed veranda for tremendous views of the mountains. The menu is a happy blend of northern Italian and Provençal cuisines. Tomato tart with basil and fontina cheese sings with Mediterranean flavor, as does the excellent homemade pasta. For something more sub-

stantial, try grilled Karoo lamb with Provençal herbs, duck breast grilled with honey and lemon, or Chef Frank Swainston's butter-tender Florentine tripe, braised in tomato and vegetable sauce. His version of the perennially popular tiramisù is also recommended. ✗ *Spaanschemat River Rd., Constantia,* ☎ *021/794–4480. Reservations required. AE, DC, MC, V. No lunch Mon.*

$$$ Emily's Bistro. In a downmarket neighborhood minutes from the city, this unpretentious *boite* serves substantial fare with artistic flair. The small menu highlights innovative dishes with Cape Malay accents, as well as traditional South African cooking. Carrot, leek, and coriander soup is served hot or chilled, and a starter of steamed mussels comes with citrus hollandaise topped with grated cheese. Dishes with local flair include chicken *breyani,* a spiced rice dish layered with onions and lentils, and *kerrie afval,* curried innards with spiced rice. An after-dinner cabaret draws late arrivals for dessert and coffee. ✗ *77 Roodebloem Rd., Woodstock,* ☎ *021/448–2366. Reservations advised for dinner. AE, DC, MC, V. Closed Sun., Mon., and Dec. 25–Jan. No lunch Sat.*

$$$ Fisherman's Cottage. In spite of its name, this long-established restaurant lies several kilometers from the sea in one of the few surviving thatched homes in Plumstead. Country chairs and simple oak tables create a relaxed, cozy atmosphere, enhanced by the personal service of hosts Reinhart and Sigi Kraue. Continental-style dishes are prepared with care. A classic trout tartare combines smoked and fresh salmon trout in herbed yogurt. Fresh linefish is grilled or served in a sauce of Pernod-flavored cream. Desserts are artistic creations—try seasonal fruit with champagne sabayon or a rich mascarpone terrine. ✗ *3 Gray Rd., Plumstead,* ☎ *021/797–6341. Reservations advised. AE, DC, MC, V. BYOB. Closed Sun., Mon., and 1 month in winter. No lunch Sat.*

$$$ Mr. B. This stylish, Chicago-style grill room occupies a large, multilevel space in a Claremont shopping center. A well-trained staff presents an innovative menu emphasizing Italian-American cuisine. Good starters include nuggets of risotto studded with fontina cheese and scallions, and grilled polenta served with Parma ham, cheese, and sun-dried tomato salsa. Garlicky black mushrooms and lemony sautéed shrimp could suffice for a luncheon, and the pasta dishes make carbo-loading a pleasure. Seafood lovers can tuck into Fog City *cioppino,* a San Francisco–style seafood stew. Diners at window-side tables upstairs enjoy good views of Table Mountain. ✗ *Cavendish Sq., Cavendish St., Claremont,* ☎ *021/683–5620. Reservations advised. AE, DC, MC, V. Closed Sun.*

$$$ Parks. This restored Victorian villa in Constantia has been jam-packed since it opened three years ago. The reasons are twofold: The elegant decor is convivial, not intimidating, and Michael Olivier's zesty contemporary cuisine strikes the right chord with local and out-of-town patrons. Starters of Constantia goat cheese terrine, mussels in coconut-turmeric cream, or deep-fried Cajun potato skins with guacamole illustrate the eclectic nature of the menu. Roast duckling with cassis sauce is an Olivier classic, while char-grilled pork fillet is paired with apple and calvados cream and drunken prunes. For dessert, don't pass up a hazelnut shortbread sandwich filled with praline cream on a pool of raspberry coulis. ✗ *114 Constantia Rd., Constantia,* ☎ *021/797–8202. Reservations required. AE, DC, MC, V. Closed Sun. No lunch.*

$$ Africa Cafe. Locals and tourists alike crowd this Observatory restaurant, the country's first to serve indigenous dishes from across the vast continent. Multicolored cloths and stunning hand-glazed crockery brighten the ocher interior of the old terrace house, complementing an equally vibrant cuisine. Fresh fruit cocktails accompany a communal starter tray of snacks from everywhere from Ethiopia to Zambia,

Kenya to Angola; you could easily make a meal of these alone, a tasty melange of patties and dips, puffs, and pastries. The accompanying chili dip is among the best you will taste anywhere. Of the main courses, Malawi chicken macadamia is a favorite; prawns curried in a creamy coconut sauce both titillate and soothe; and vegetarians applaud the Senegalese stuffed papaya. The lunch menu, chalked on a board, offers fewer choices at lower prices. ✕ *213 Lower Main Rd., Observatory,* ☎ *021/479–553. Reservations advised. AE, DC, MC, V. Closed Sun. No lunch Sat.*

$$ Jonkershuis. This establishment offers classic Cape hospitality in a 19th-century building adjoining the gracious manor house at Groot Constantia, the Cape's oldest wine estate. Fresh linefish and roast loin of lamb keep company on the menu with classic *bobotie*—spiced beef mince studded with dried fruit and nut slivers and topped with a savory baked custard—and *smoorsnoek,* a popular Cape fish braised with onion, potato, and chili served with baked sweet potatoes in fresh orange sauce. The traditional chicken pie is made from a recipe handed down through generations of Dutch settlers. If you want a taste of all these dishes, order the unlisted Cape sampler. Jonkershuis also serves hearty breakfasts and light refreshments. ✕ *Groot Constantia Estate, Main Rd., Constantia,* ☎ *021/794–6255. Reservations required in season. AE, DC, MC. No dinner.*

False Bay

$$$ Shrimptons. Tucked away in a hotel on a quiet street off Muizenberg's beachfront, this restaurant appeals to devotees of great seafood, rich sauces, and liberal portions. In her kitchen, owner-chef Hilary Fischoff uses only pristine ingredients, cooks them with care, and presents her creations with artistry. Dishes are based on cream, wine, brandy, and fresh herbs. Look for designer greens with salmon trout, calamari in sweet-and-sour sauce, or grilled black mushrooms on cream cheese topped with smoked salmon as first courses. After that, you'll need a robust appetite to tackle her linefish cooked to order, mixed seafood, or prawn-filled puff pastries. Seafood also dominates the lighter and less-expensive lunch menu. ✕ *19 Alexander Rd., Muizenberg,* ☎ *021/ 788–5225. Reservations advised. AE, DC, MC, V.*

$$ Gaylords. Operating out of a cluttered shop in Muizenberg, Venesh and Nina Ranchod draw diners from all corners of the Cape for tastes of northern India. A platter of assorted appetizers is the ideal way to ease your palate into the fiery flavors: Start with lentil cake squares and aromatic spinach rolls, then proceed to *samoosas* (pastry triangles with spicy fillings) and chili bites, dipped into little pots of scarlet fire or fresh coriander chutney. Goanese curries contain coconut to temper the heat, while Madras-style dishes are simply incendiary, whether you choose fish, seafood, or lamb. Milder dishes include lamb or fish breyani, baked with spiced rice, lentils, and potatoes, or fish korma (a mild curry sauce made with yogurt). ✕ *65 Main Rd., Muizenberg,* ☎ *021/788–5470. Reservations advised. AE, DC, MC, V. Closed Tues. No lunch Mon.*

LODGING

Finding lodging in Cape Town can be an expensive nightmare during high season, December–Easter, when prices rise by as much as 50%. The worst period of all is the South African school holidays, December 15–January 15, when the only hotels with vacancies are probably in Zaire. If you do arrive in Cape Town without a reservation, head for Captour's **Tourist Rendezvous Travel Centre** (*see* Important Addresses and Numbers *in* Cape Town Essentials, *below*), which has a helpful accommodation desk.

Hotels in the city center are a good option if you're here on business or don't want to drive. During the day, the historic city center is a vibrant, exciting place. At night, though, it shuts up tight; night owls may prefer a hotel amid the nonstop action of the redeveloped Waterfront. Hotels in the southern suburbs, especially Constantia, offer unrivaled beauty and tranquillity, and make an ideal base if you're exploring the Winelands and the peninsula. You need a car, though, and should plan on 15–30 minutes to get into town. Atlantic Coast hotels provide the closest thing in Cape Town to a classic beach-holiday atmosphere, in spite of the cold ocean waters.

International flights from the United States and Europe arrive in the morning and return flights depart in the evening. Since most hotels have an 11 AM checkout, you may have to wait for a room if you've just arrived; if you're leaving, you will be hauled kicking and screaming out of your room hours before your flight. Most hotels will try to accommodate you, but they often have no choice in peak season. Some of the larger hotels have residents-only lounges where you can spend the hours awaiting your flight.

The most reliable source of good B&B establishments is the **Portfolio of Places** (☎ 011/880–3414, FAX 011/788–4802) guide to bed and breakfasts. Otherwise, contact **Bed & Breakfast** (17 Talana Rd., Claremont 7700, ☎ 021/61–6543, FAX 021/683–5159). If you don't like tiptoeing around someone's house, or you want to save money, consider taking a fully furnished apartment or holiday flat, especially if you're staying two to three weeks. Among the dependable brokers are **Cape Holiday Homes** (Box 2044, Cape Town 8000, ☎ 021/419–0430) and **Private Places** (Box 489, Milnerton 7435, ☎ 021/52–1200).

For price ranges, *see* Chart 2(A) *in* On the Road with Fodor's.

City Bowl

$$$$ **Cape Sun.** One of the very top hotels in the city center, this 32-story tower dominates the skyline, and is ideally located near the Captour office, St. George's Mall, and the Golden Acre shopping center. The lobby, with its elegant marble floors, paneled ceiling, and green-marble pillars, sets the tone for the hotel. Rooms, done in pale yellows and blues, reflect a Cape Dutch influence: juxtaposed light- and dark-wood paneling and line drawings of Cape Dutch estates and furniture. Guests can opt for a room facing either the sea or Table Mountain. Both views are spectacular, but request a room on a high floor—the sea views from lower rooms are partially obstructed by other buildings. ⊡ *Strand St. (mailing address: Box 4532), Cape Town 8000, ☎ 021/23–8844, FAX 021/23–8875. 350 rooms with bath. 3 restaurants, bar, room service, sauna, exercise room, travel services. AE, DC, MC, V.*

$$$$ **Mount Nelson.** This distinctive pink landmark is the grande dame of
★ Cape Town. Since it opened its doors in 1899 to accommodate passengers of the Union-Castle steamships, it has been the focal point of Cape social life. Its guest book reads like a *Who's Who* of South African history, and it's still *the* place for Cape Town society to hold its functions. Named by both *Tatler* and *Harpers and Queen* magazines as one of the best hotels in the world, it retains an old-fashioned

charm and gentility that other five-star hotels often lack. High tea is still served in the lounge to piano accompaniment; the Grill Room offers a nightly dinner dance; and the staff almost outnumbers the guests. The hotel stands at the top of Government Avenue, but, surrounded by seven acres of manicured gardens, it could just as well be out in the country. For peak season, December–March, it's advisable to book a year in advance. ☎ *76 Orange St., Cape Town 8001,* ☎ *021/23–1000,* ℻. *021/24–7472. 159 rooms with bath. 3 restaurants, bar, 2 pools, tennis, squash. AE, DC, MC, V.*

$$$ **Villa Belmonte.** In a quiet residential neighborhood on the slopes above the city, this small guest house offers privacy and luxury in an attractive Dutch Revival residence. Owners Tabea and Cliff Jacobs have sought to create the feel of an Italian villa through the use of marbling, molded ceilings, and natural wood floors. Wide verandas command superb views of the city, Table Mountain, and Devil's Peak. Rooms, each decorated according to a theme, make effective use of colorful draperies, wicker furniture, and small-pane windows. As punishment for the great views, it's a 20-minute walk to the city center. ☎ *33 Belmont Ave, Oranjezicht 8001,* ☎ *021/462–1576,* ℻ *021/462–1579. 8 rooms with bath. Restaurant, bar, room service, pool. Breakfast included. No children under 13. AE, DC, MC, V.*

$$ **The Capetonian.** In the Foreshore between the Waterfront and the city center, this newly renovated hotel offers a high standard of luxury and elegance—at half the price of the Cape Sun. Floral carpets, wood headboards, African artwork, and draperies in rich autumnal colors give the rooms, which are very large, a warm, inviting feel. Request a room on an upper floor for a good view of the harbor. ☎ *Pier Pl., Heerengracht (mailing address: Box 6856), Roggebaai 8012,* ☎ *021/21– 1150,* ℻ *021/25–2215. 169 rooms with bath. 2 restaurants, bar, room service. AE, DC, MC, V.*

$$ **Holiday Inn Garden Court–Greenmarket Square.** Facing historic Greenmarket Square, this minimum-service hotel can claim one of the best locations in the city, especially if you don't have a car. Rooms are slated for refurbishment, but all have cable TV and air-conditioning. Mountain-facing rooms overlooking the square are very pleasant, but the dawn chorus of vendors setting up their stalls may drive you to distraction. Parking is a major headache in this part of town. ☎ *10 Greenmarket Sq. (mailing address: Box 3775), Cape Town 8000,* ☎ *021/ 23–2040,* ℻ *021/23–3664. 168 rooms with bath. Restaurant, bar. AE, DC, MC, V.*

$$ **Holiday Inn Garden Court–St. George's Mall.** Ideally located at the bottom of St. George's Mall, just seconds from all major public transport and the Captour office, this no-frills hotel offers very competitive rates. Rooms, done in grays and subdued tones, are comfortable and clean. Plump for one of the corner twin rooms—for just R20 more you'll stay in a larger room with huge windows on two sides. The view is still only of the street. ☎ *St. George's Mall (mailing address: Box 5616), Cape Town 8000,* ☎ *021/419–0808,* ℻ *021/419–7010. 136 rooms with bath. Restaurant, bar, room service, indoor pool, sauna, exercise room. AE, DC, MC, V.*

$$ **Mijlof Manor Hotel.** In a residential neighborhood below Signal Hill, this mid-range hotel is built around the original Tamboerskloof farmhouse, which dates back to 1710. With the addition of a modern wing, not much of the old homestead is visible any longer, but the Mijlof remains a comfortable retreat from the city center, 20 minutes away on foot. Cape Dutch–style rooms are large and well equipped, but you can probably do better at the nearby Underberg Guest House. The wood-paneled bar is a popular watering hole. ☎ *5 Military Rd., Tamboer-*

skloof, Cape Town 8001, ☎ *021/26–1476,* ℻ *021/22–2046. 70 rooms with bath. Restaurant, 2 bars, room service, pool, beauty salon. AE, DC, MC, V.*

$$ Townhouse Hotel. Popular with members of Parliament both for its proximity to the government buildings and its easygoing atmosphere, the Townhouse also has extremely competitive rates. Rooms are a bright and countrified with whitewashed, rough brick walls, check curtains, and dried-flower montages. Bathrooms all have separate baths and showers. If you want a view of Table Mountain, request one of the twin-bedded rooms. ⌖ *60 Corporation St. (mailing address: Box 5053), Cape Town 8000,* ☎ *021/45–7050,* ℻ *021/45–3891. 104 rooms with bath. Restaurant, bar, room service, health club. AE, DC, MC, V.*

$$ Underberg Guest House. In a restored Victorian farmhouse in Tam-
★ boerskloof, this lovely guest house caters primarily to businesspeople, who appreciate the privacy and the location, a 20-minute walk from the city center. The rooms are airy and light, thanks to high ceilings and large windows, and possess an elegance seldom found in conventional hotels. Rooms have TVs, minibars, tea- and coffeemakers, and separate bath and shower. ⌖ *Carstens St., Tamboerskloof, Cape Town 8001,* ☎ *021/26–2262,* ℻ *021/24–4059. 9 rooms with bath. Bar, dining room. Breakfast included. No children under 12. AE, DC, MC, V.*

$ Lady Hamilton Hotel. You get good value and an excellent location at this hotel, on a peaceful residential street in Gardens, just 15 minutes on foot from the city center. Rooms are attractive and bright, decorated with blond wood furniture and African-print bedspreads. ⌖ *Union St., Gardens, Cape Town 8001,* ☎ *021/23-3888,* ℻ *021/23–7788. 32 rooms with bath. Restaurant, bar, room service, pool. Breakfast included. AE, DC, MC, V.*

$ Metropole Hotel. Celebrating its 100th birthday in 1996, this basic hotel in the center of town is known for its creaky, old-fashioned charm. The lobby, enlivened by delicate floral wallpaper, centers around a teak-paneled elevator, the second-oldest in Cape Town. Unfortunately, standard rooms are dull and nondescript, but the price *is* right. The Mandarin suites, with rosewood paneling and understated Chinese decor, are far more attractive, but for the extra money you may be better off at the Townhouse Hotel. Street noise may be a problem during the day. ⌖ *38 Long St. (mailing address: Box 3086), Cape Town 8000,* ☎ *021/ 23-6363,* ℻ *021/23-6370. 33 rooms with bath. Restaurant, 3 bars, room service. AE, DC, MC, V.*

Waterfront

$$$$ Victoria & Alfred Hotel. You couldn't find a better location for this upmarket hotel, in a converted warehouse smack in the middle of the Waterfront and surrounded by shops, bars, and restaurants. Rooms are huge, furnished in neo–Cape Dutch style and decorated in muted rust and sea colors. Views from the costlier mountain-facing rooms are spectacular, encompassing not only Table Mountain but the city and docks as well. Waterfront buses leave regularly for the city center, a five-minute ride away. ⌖ *Pierhead (mailing address: Box 50050), Waterfront, Cape Town 8002,* ☎ *021/419–6677,* ℻ *021/419–8955. 68 rooms with bath. Restaurant, bar, room service. AE, DC, MC, V.*

$$ City Lodge. Location is everything at this no-frills chain hotel, a five-minute walk from the Waterfront and 10 minutes from the city center. Rooms are standard, decorated with old ship prints and blond furniture, and all have TVs and tea- and coffeemakers. ⌖ *Corner of Dock and Alfred Rds., Waterfront (mailing address: Box 6025), Rogge-*

baai 8012, ☎ 021/419–9450, FAX 021/419–0460. 164 rooms with bath. Bar, breakfast room, pool. AE, DC, MC, V.

$ **Breakwater Lodge.** You're not going to find another hotel offering these low rates so close to the Waterfront. Next to a 19th-century prison on Portswood Ridge, the Breakwater certainly won't win any awards for charm or coziness. Long, narrow corridors lead to rooms that are tiny and sterile, furnished with the kind of chipboard-and-veneer furniture that you find at do-it-yourself stores. Nevertheless, they are clean and have TVs, phones, and tea- and coffeemakers. Ask for a room with a view of Table Mountain. 🏨 *Portswood Rd., Waterfront, Cape Town 8001, ☎ 021/406–1911, FAX 021/406–1070. 327 rooms, 217 with bath, 110 with shared bath. 2 restaurants, bar. AE, DC, MC, V.*

Atlantic Coast

$$$$ **Bay Hotel.** Of the luxury hotels in and around Cape Town, this beach hotel in Camps Bay is the most relaxed and unpretentious. The three-story structure sits across the road from a white-sand beach, backed by the towering cliffs of the Twelve Apostles. From the raised pool deck, guests look out over a scene of sea and sand, far away from the hurly-burly of Cape Town. Cane furniture, colorful paintings, and attractive peach and sea tones make the rooms light and airy. The quality of service is excellent, with an emphasis on privacy and discretion. Ask for a premier room if you want a sea view. 🏨 *Victoria Rd. (mailing address: Box 32021), Camps Bay 8040, ☎ 021/438–4444, FAX 021/438–4455. 70 rooms with bath. 2 restaurants, bar, room service, pool, billiards. AE, DC, MC, V.*

$$$$ **Ellerman House.** Without a doubt, this is one of the finest (and most
★ expensive) hotels in South Africa. Built in 1912 for shipping magnate Sir John Ellerman, the hotel sits high on a hill in Bantry Bay and enjoys stupendous views out to sea. Broad terraced lawns fronted by elegant balustrades step down the hillside to a sparkling pool. The drawing and living rooms, decorated in Regency style, are elegant yet not forbiddingly formal. Guest rooms benefit from enormous picture windows, high ceilings, and spacious tiled bathrooms. Of particular note is the Africa-theme room, decorated with cane furniture, ostrich-egg lamps, and African sculptures. The hotel accommodates only 14 guests, and a highly trained staff caters to their every whim. In the kitchen, four chefs work to prepare whatever guests request—there are no menus. All drinks except wine and champagne are included in the rates. 🏨 *180 Kloof Rd., Bantry Bay 8060 (mailing address: Box 515, Sea Point 8060), ☎ 021/439–9182, FAX 021/434–7257. 7 rooms with bath. Restaurant, bar, room service, pool, sauna. No children under 18. Breakfast and lunch included. AE, DC, MC, V.*

$$$$ **Place on the Bay.** These luxury self-catering apartments sit right on the beachfront in Camps Bay, within easy walking distance of a host of restaurants and bars. Apartments are tasteful, modern affairs that make extensive use of glass and speckled marble. Many units have good sea views from their balconies. If you really want to have it all, take the magnificent penthouse, which occupies the entire top floor and comes with its own chef, car, chauffeur, and swimming pool. All units are fully serviced. At press time, the owners were considering adding 11 more apartments and a restaurant. 🏨 *Corner of Fairways and Victoria Rds., Camps Bay 8001, ☎ 021/438–7060, FAX 021/438–2692. 21 apartments with bath. Pool. AE, DC, MC, V.*

$$$ **Hout Bay Manor Hotel.** Chapman's Peak provides the backdrop for this charming hotel in Hout Bay, a small fishing village 20 minutes from Cape Town. Built in 1871 in Cape Dutch style, the hotel is popular with older travelers, who appreciate its peace and quiet, broken only by the sound of the courtyard fountain. Public rooms are attractive, with high ceilings and creaking wood floors. Guest rooms use canopy beds, delicate floral fabrics, and claw-foot tubs to create a Victorian feel that doesn't quite match the gray wall-to-wall carpeting. A brick terrace, shaded by oaks and large umbrellas, is an attractive spot for breakfast, drinks, and pub lunches. The beach at Hout Bay and several restaurants are within easy walking distance. ⊞ *Main Rd. (mailing address: Box 27035), Hout Bay, 7872, ☎ 021/790–4730, ☒ 021/790–4952. 11 rooms with bath. Restaurant, bar, room service. Continental breakfast included. AE, DC, MC, V.*

$$$ Peninsula Hotel. Housed in an attractive 11-story building just 100 yards from the ocean, this exclusive Sea Point establishment is ideal for families or groups of friends. Guests can choose from a variety of suites that sleep four to eight people and command incredible views of the sea. The larger suites are the most attractive, full of light and air thanks to picture windows, sliding doors, wide balconies, and white tile floors. The small studio suites, on the other hand, look more like conventional hotel rooms. Each suite has a fully equipped kitchen with microwave. The hotel is a time-share property, so booking over the busy December holiday could be a problem. ⊞ *313 Beach Rd., Sea Point 8001 (mailing address: Box 768, Sea Point 8060), ☎ 021/439–8888, ☒ 021/439–8886. 110 suites with bath. 2 restaurants, bar, room service, 2 pools, sauna, exercise room. AE, DC, MC, V.*

$$ Monkey Valley. This secluded, self-catering resort in Noordhoek is one
★ of the best places on the Peninsula to bring a family. Built on stilts, each of the thatched log cottages lies hidden amid thick vegetation overlooking a nature reserve and the magnificent white sands of Noordhoek Beach. Cottages have two or three bedrooms, fully equipped kitchens, and large balconies. The wood interiors are attractive and rustic, brightened by floral fabrics, country-style furniture, and fireplaces. The resort has its own restaurant, and there is a large grocery store just 5 kilometers (3 miles) away. ⊞ *Mountain Rd. (mailing address: Box 114), Noordhoek 7985, ☎ 021/789–13391, ☒ 021/789–1143. 17 cottages with bath. Restaurant, bar, pool, playground. AE, DC, MC, V.*

Southern Suburbs

$$$$ Cellars–Hohenort Country House Hotel. It's easy to forget the outside
★ world at this idyllic getaway in Constantia. Set in nine acres of gardens on the slopes of Table Mountain, this luxury hotel commands spectacular views across Constantia Valley to False Bay. The 18th-century cellars of the Klaasenbosch wine estate and the Hohenort manor house form the heart of the hotel. Guest rooms are large and elegant, furnished in English-country style with brass beds, flowery valances, and reproduction antiques. Rooms in the manor house feature the best views of the valley. Although the hotel lacks the historical significance of the Alphen (*see below*), it offers a level of luxury and tranquillity that its more famous competitor cannot match. None of the rooms is air-conditioned, however. ⊞ *Hohenort Ave. (mailing address: Box 270), Constantia 7848, ☎ 021/794–2137, ☒ 021/794–2149. 53 rooms with bath. 2 restaurants, 2 bars, room service, 2 pools, tennis court. Breakfast included. No children under 14. AE, DC, MC, V.*

$$$ Alphen Hotel. If you want a taste of gracious Cape living and history,
★ stay at this elegant Constantia hotel. Built in 1752 in Cape Dutch style, this former manor house is now a national monument and one of the Cape's historical treasures. The owners are descendants of the distinguished Cloete family, which has farmed the land around Constantia

since 1657. Cloete paintings and antiques, each with a story to tell, adorn the public rooms. Standard guest rooms, housed in adjoining buildings, are small and don't match the magnificence of the manor house. The hotel has two other drawbacks: no air-conditioning and light traffic noise from the nearby highway. ☎ *Alphen Dr. (mailing address: Box 35), Constantia 7848,* ☎ *021/794–5011,* FAX *021/794–5710. 29 rooms with bath. 2 restaurants, bar, room service, pool. AE, DC, MC, V.*

$$$ Constantia Uitsig. This 200-acre winery has an enviable setting, backed by the magnificent mountains of the Constantiaberg and overlooking the vineyards of Constantia Valley. Rooms, in whitewashed farm cottages set amid manicured lawns and gardens, are comfortable and inviting. Wicker headboards, timber ceilings, and bright floral patterns add a rustic feel. The restaurant in the original farmhouse draws diners from all over the Cape. If you value peace and quiet, this is a great place to stay. ☎ *Spaanschemat River Rd. (mailing address: Box 32), Constantia 7848,* ☎ *021/794–6500,* FAX *021/794–7605. 12 rooms with bath. Restaurant, pool. AE, DC, MC, V.*

$$ Auberge Penrose. Close to the University of Cape Town and the golf courses at Mowbray and Rondebosch, this attractive guest house offers a friendly welcome and attentive service. From the cozy breakfast room, guests enjoy great views of Devil's Peak and the Rhodes Memorial. Rooms are airy and comfortable, with high ceilings, floral draperies, and brass bedsteads. All rooms have telephones, TVs, and minibars. Auberge Penrose sits on a small plot of land close to the road. If you need quiet, you're better off at the Palm House (*see below*). ☎ *9 Rhodes Ave., Cape Town 7700,* ☎ *021/685–7700,* FAX *021/685–7141. 10 rooms with bath. Bar, pool. Breakfast included. AE, DC, MC, V.*

$$ Palm House. Towering palms dominate the manicured lawns of this peaceful guest house in suburban Kenilworth, a 15-minute drive from the city. The house is an enormous, stolid affair, built in the early 1920s by a protegé of Sir Herbert Baker and filled with dark wood paneling, wood staircases, and fireplaces. Guest rooms are large, decorated with bold floral fabrics and reproduction antiques. Rooms upstairs benefit from more air and light than those downstairs. Guests often meet for evening drinks in the drawing room. ☎ *Oxford St., Wynberg 7800,* ☎ *021/761–5009,* FAX *021/761–8776. 9 rooms with bath. Restaurant, bar, pool. Breakfast included. No children under 10. AE, DC, MC, V.*

$$ The Vineyard. Set in pleasant gardens in residential Newlands, this comfortable hotel is built around "Paradise," the 19th-century weekend home of Lady Anne Barnard, and is popular with English tourists. Unfortunately, not much of the old house is evident in the design of the hotel. Rooms are fairly standard, with wall-to-wall carpeting, pale floral bedspreads, and dried-flower arrangements on the walls. Rooms with a view of Table Mountain are considerably more expensive. The hotel is 10 minutes by car from the city, but within walking distance of the Newlands sports arenas and the shops of Cavendish Square. ☎ *Colinton Rd. (mailing address: Box 151), Newlands 7725,* ☎ *021/683– 3044,* FAX *021/683–3365. 124 rooms with bath. 2 restaurants, bar, room service, pool, beauty salon, exercise room. AE, DC, MC, V.*

False Bay

$$ British Hotel. In a stone Victorian building in historic Simon's Town,
★ these self-catering apartments offer the best deal on the peninsula. The four apartments are huge, with fully equipped kitchens, two or three bedrooms, two sitting rooms, and wide Victorian balconies overlook-

ing the harbor. High ceilings, wood floors, and giant windows create a sense of space and elegance. The decor differs from unit to unit but draws much of its inspiration from the turn of the century. Ask for Number Two, a two-bedroom apartment that perfectly balances the old-fashioned and the modern, with claw-foot bathtubs, frosted cane furniture, and sponge-painted walls. ⌕ *St. George's St., Simon's Town (mailing address: 30 Hudson St., Cape Town 8001),* ☎ *021/253–414,* FAX *021/790–4930. 4 apartments with bath. AE, DC, MC, V.*

$ **Lord Nelson Inn.** This hotel sits on the main road in Simon's Town and offers comfortable, no-frills accommodation at a good price. Rooms are small, decorated in country style with pine furniture, muted colors, and wall-to-wall carpeting. If you want a harbor view or a balcony, request a superior room. ⌕ *58 St. George's St., Simon's Town 7995,* ☎ *021/ 786–1368,* FAX *021/786–1009. 10 rooms with bath. 2 restaurants, 2 bars, room service. Breakfast included. AE, DC, MC, V.*

THE ARTS AND NIGHTLIFE

Each month Captour publishes *What's On in the Cape,* probably the best roundup of events in the city, including exhibitions, theater, concerts, and nightlife. The entertainment section of the *Weekly Mail & Guardian* newspaper lists the major cultural events in Cape Town, Johannesburg, and Durban; it's informed, opinionated, and up-to-date. Tickets for almost every cultural and sporting event in the country (including movies) can be purchased at **Computicket** (☎ 021/21–4715), with more than 18 outlets in and around the city. Two of the most convenient outlets are in the Golden Acre on Adderley Street and at the Waterfront. You can also book by phone with Computicket using any major credit card.

The Arts

The **Nico Malan Theatre Centre** (D.F. Malan St., Foreshore 8001, ☎ 021/21–7839), a huge state-subsidized theater complex on the Foreshore, is the home of the Cape Performing Arts Board (CAPAB), the city's main cultural body. CAPAB supports three permanent companies that stage drama, ballet, and opera productions in the Nico's three theaters. Since the election, CAPAB has made a conscious effort to broaden its appeal among non-white South Africans. In addition to such staples as *Evita* and *Crazy for You,* the drama company recently staged some African productions like *Sisters of the Calabash.* CAPAB also stages summer productions of dance, opera, and African jazz at the **Oude Libertas Amphitheatre,** a delightful open-air venue set among vineyards outside Stellenbosch (*see* The Winelands *in* Chapter 5). During the summer, CAPAB produces its own version of Shakespeare in the Park at the **Maynardville Open-Air Theatre** (corner of Church and Wolfe Sts., ☎ 021/77–8591) in Wynberg. Theatergoers often take along a picnic to enjoy on the lawns before the show.

Classical Music
CAPAB also supports a classical orchestra, the **Cape Town Philharmonic Orchestra,** which plays the majority of its concerts at the Nico (*see above*). As part of its program to introduce classical music to the general public, the Philharmonic also stages a series of lunchtime concerts in the foyer of the Nico Malan complex. Far more exciting, though, is the summer program of open-air concerts at the Kirstenbosch National Botanic Gardens. The setting, in the shadow of Table Mountain, is unbeatable.

The Philharmonic's rival is the **Cape Town Symphony Orchestra** (City Hall, Darling St., ☎ 021/462–1250), which plays in the grand old city hall. Since the end of South Africa's isolation, the orchestra has hosted several guest conductors from Europe and the United States. The orchestra's summer program of free concerts at the outdoor AGFA Amphitheatre at the Waterfront is lighthearted and fun.

Film

Ster-Kinekor and Nu Metro screen mainstream American and British movies at cinema complexes all over the city. The Waterfront alone has about 10 cinemas; the closest cinema complex to the center of town is in the Golden Acre on Adderley Street. Check newspaper listings for what's playing.

Imax Cinema (BMW Pavilion, Waterfront, ☎ 021/214–715 or 021/214–743), with its astounding, nearly hemispherical, giant, five-story screen and six-channel wraparound sound (yes, all of that), makes viewers feel as if they're participating in the filmed event. At press time, shows included the *Rolling Stones,* shot during their Steel Wheels/Urban Jungle World Tour; *On the Wing,* a look at the development of aircraft; and *Grand Canyon–The Hidden Secrets.* Show times vary.

The Labia (68 Orange St., Gardens, ☎ 021/24–5927) is an independent art cinema that screens quality mainstream and alternative films, including the works of some of the best European filmmakers. A coffee bar serves snacks.

Theater

The **Baxter Theatre Complex** (Main Rd., Rondebosch, ☎ 021/685–7880) is part of the University of Cape Town and has a reputation for serious drama. Plays by Athol Fugard are often staged here. The complex features a 657-seat theater, a concert hall, a smaller studio, and a restaurant and bar.

Dock Rd. Theatre (Waterfront, ☎ 021/419–7722) stages some of Cape Town's most successful theater productions. The focus is on the works of South African writers, including Pieter-Dirk Uys, Paul Slabolepszy, Jenny Reznick, and Andrew Buckland. Most of the productions have mainstream appeal, but foreigners may not always be familiar with the subject matter.

Nightlife

Since the opening of the Waterfront in 1989, the city's nightlife scene has focused on the revitalized harbor. Sea Point, which had been a center of Cape Town's after-dark scene, has lost much of its business, except for numerous hookers that trawl Main Road. You will always find something to do at the Waterfront, when you consider that you have almost a dozen cinemas, 40 restaurants, and 10 bars from which to choose. The rest of the City Bowl empties out after business hours except for isolated restaurants and bars, and lone couples may not feel safe walking the deserted streets at night. The big exception is the few square blocks centered on the intersection of Long and Strand streets, which have become a cauldron of youth-oriented nightclubs, bars, and restaurants. Even here, exercise caution late at night.

Bars and Pubs

The **Perseverance Tavern** (83 Buitenkant St., Gardens, ☎ 021/461–1981) has a strong claim to be the oldest tavern in the city, dating back to 1836. The facade has been beautifully restored, but you may feel claustrophobic in the small, interconnected rooms. The wood-lined pub at **Mijlof Manor Hotel** (5 Military Rd., ☎ 021/26–1476) in Tamboerskloof is a popular watering hole for the after-work crowd, including politicos. In nearby Gardens, the **Stag's Head** (71 Hope St., Gardens, ☎ 021/454–918) is a rowdy joint that attracts a big crowd of beer-chugging partyers. The **Firkin Brew Pub** (22 Kloof St., ☎ 021/24–4222) is a very civilized inn that brews its own beers; you can sit inside near the brewing vats or outside on the steps. If you're single and want to mingle, slip into something black and head for the trendy **Rick's Café Americain** (196 Loop St., ☎ 021/22–2378).

Down at the Waterfront, the **Sports Bar** (Victoria Wharf, Waterfront, ☎ 021/419–5558) is a huge place with large-screen TVs. The bar gets into the spirit of major foreign sporting events like the Super Bowl and the FA Cup Final—undoubtedly the best place to watch sports in the city. **Quay Four** (Quay 4, ☎ 021/419–2008), also at the Waterfront, is big with the after-work suit-and-tie brigade that clogs the picnic tables on the wooden deck overlooking the harbor. Just outside the entrance to the Waterfront, the **Fireman's Arms** (corner of Buitengracht and Mechau Sts., ☎ 021/419–1513) is a great old bar that dishes up good pizzas cooked in a wood-fired oven. **Heidelberg Tavern** (94 Station Rd., Observatory, ☎ 021/47–1919) is a popular beer hall for students from U.C.T., and often hosts ear-splitting rock bands. During the buildup to free elections, the bar was the target of a terrorist attack. **Dirty Dick's Tavern** (Hout Bay, 021/790–2230), overlooking the harbor at Hout Bay, draws a young crowd relaxing after a hard day at the beach. The **Brunswick Tavern** (17 Bree St., ☎ 021/25–2739) and **Cafe Erte** (265a Main Rd., Sea Point, ☎ 021/434–6624) attract a mainly gay clientele.

Dancing

Nightclubs open and close faster than this book can go to press. Aside from the Waterfront, the area around Loop and Long between Strand and Riebeeck streets is the best place to get a feel for what's going on in town. It doesn't hit its stride until after 11 PM, but you can choose among at least eight clubs and bars. Clubs worth checking out include **The Fringe** (46 Canterbury St., ☎ 021/461–9061), which appeals to the 18- to 25-year-old crowd with its alternative grunge sound; **Havana** (Waterkant St., ☎ 021/419–7041); and the **Moulin Rouge** (Riebeek St., ☎ 021/21–7147). **Oxygen** (Port Rd., ☎ 021/21-5355), near the entrance to the Waterfront, attracts a young, techno crowd. The gay club of the moment is **Club Fusion** (7 Alfred Rd., Green Point, ☎ 021/419–5039).

Jazz

Many of the mainstream jazz clubs in the city also double as restaurants. Cover charges range from R3 to R10. If you're passionate about jazz, get hold of Captour's free brochure *Jazz in the Cape*. Two of the best places to hear jazz are down at the Waterfront. The **Green Dolphin Jazz Restaurant** (Waterfront, ☎ 021/21–7471), a pasta and seafood restaurant, attracts some of the best mainstream musicians in the country as well as a few from overseas. The **Dock Road Cafe** (Waterfront, ☎ 021/419–7722) showcases a lot of young musicians from the University of Cape Town's jazz program. Call ahead to find out what's playing since the café doubles as a cabaret venue. Also worth checking out in town is **Manenberg's Jazz Cafe** (corner of Adderley and Church Sts., ☎ 021/23–8304). **Dizzy's Jazz Cafe** (41 The Drive, Camps Bay, ☎ 021/438–2686) is an intimate club in an old Cape Dutch building in Camps Bay. Come here to listen to small groups that won't completely dominate your dinner or drinks. If you really want to explore the cutting edge of Cape jazz, you have to head to the townships. On Sunday after 4 PM, **Club Ubuntu** in Guguletu (NY1, ☏ 021/419-4732) showcases the best of the township musicians, playing a mix of American and indigenous jazz. To see "jazz" dancing, the Cape's own mix of ballroom and Latin steps, make a beeline for **Baker Street Jazz Club** (corner of Halt Rd. and 28th Ave., Elsies River, ☏ 021/932-3725) on Wednesday, Friday, and Saturday nights. Another great jazz spot is **Riffs Jazz Pub** (39 Wetton Rd., Wetton, ☏ 021/73-2676), a bare-bones joint that features live music from Wednesday through Saturday.

CAPE TOWN ESSENTIALS

Arriving and Departing

By Bus

All intercity buses depart from the Captour office on Adderley Street (*see* Important Addresses and Numbers, *below*). **Greyhound** (1 Adderley St., ☏ 021/418-4312) offers daily overnight service to Johannesburg and Pretoria; the one-way fare is about R300. **Intercape Mainliner** (Captour office, Adderley St., ☏ 021/386-4400) operates a far more extensive network of routes in the Western Cape than Greyhound, with daily service up the West Coast to Springbok (R165), and along the Garden Route to George (R80) and Port Elizabeth (R115); a bus also travels daily to Johannesburg (R270). **Translux Express Bus** (Captour office, Adderley St., ☏ 021/405-3333) offers a similar network of routes at comparable prices.

By Car

Parking in the city center can be a real hassle. So bad is the situation that most hotels charge extra for parking, and even then you're not guaranteed a space. If you don't mind leaving your car in the care of derelict youths, you can usually find parking out on the lots on Buitengracht Street or on the Grand Parade. The Sanlam Golden Acre Parking Garage on Adderley Street offers covered parking.

The main arteries leading out of the city are the N1, which runs to Paarl and, ultimately, Johannesburg; and the N2, which heads out to the Overberg and the Garden Route. The M3 leads to Constantia, Muizenberg, and the small towns of the peninsula; it splits from the N2 just after Groote Schuur Hospital, in the shadow of Devil's Peak.

CAR RENTAL

Most of the large car-rental agencies offer similar rates; expect to pay through the nose if you rent by the day. A Nissan Sentra or Toyota Corolla costs about R100 a day plus a whopping 80¢–R1 per kilometer. If you rent for three days or more, you get 200 kilometers–300 kilometers (124 miles–186 miles) free per day with a daily rate of around R200.

Among the major rental agencies in Cape Town proper are **Avis** (123 Strand St., ☏ 021/24-1177); **Budget Rent-a-Car** (63a Strand St., ☏ 021/23-4290); **Dolphin Car Hire** (345 Main Rd., Sea Point, ☏ 021/439-9696), Europcar's representative in the Cape; and **Imperial Car Rental** (47 Strand St., ☏ 021/23-3300), Hertz's South African subsidiary. You can obtain rates about a third lower at budget agencies like **Alisa Car Rental** (139 Buitengracht St., Cape Town, ☏ 021/22-1515), **Economy Car Hire** (3 Anchor Bay Rd., ☏ 021/434-8304), and **Weelrent** (11

Portswood Rd., Waterfront, ☎ 021/419–7750), but these companies usually offer limited breakdown support.

By Plane

Cape Town International Airport, formerly known as D.F. Malan, lies 22½ kilometers (14 miles) southeast of the city in the Cape Flats. For flight arrival and departure information, call 021/934–0444. International airlines flying into Cape Town include **Air France** (☎ 021/934–8818), **Air Namibia** (☎ 021/934–0757), **British Airways** (☎ 021/25–2970), **KLM** (☎ 021/21–1870), **Lufthansa** (☎ 021/25–1490), **Singapore Airlines** (☎ 021/419–0495), **South African Airways** (☎ 021/25–4610), and **Swissair** (☎ 021/21–4938).

The major domestic carriers serving Cape Town are **Comair** (☎ 021/934–3401), **Phoenix** (☎ 021/418–3306), **South African Airways** (☎ 021/25–4610), and **Sun Air** (☎ 021/934–0918).

The airport is tiny—the domestic and international terminals lie no more than 200 yards apart. In addition to a VAT refund office (*see* Money and Expenses *in* the Gold Guide), it has a Western Cape Tourism Board booth and an accommodation hot line, open daily 7–5, providing information on selected guest houses around the city. Trust Bank exchanges money weekdays 9–3:30 and Saturdays 8:30–10:30; it stays open later for international arrivals and departures.

BETWEEN THE AIRPORT AND CAPE TOWN

Intercape Shuttle (☎ 021/386–4414) operates a minibus service between the city and the airport for R20 per person. Buses drop passengers off at the Tourist Rendezvous Travel Centre in Adderley Street. Buy your tickets at the Intercape Shuttle desk in the domestic arrivals terminal or from the bus driver after hours. Buses depart every half hour.

Taxis are available from the ranks right outside the terminals. Only taxis with special airport licenses are allowed to pick up arriving passengers, and they must use their meter. Expect to pay about R120 for a trip to the center of the city.

Avis (☎ 021/934–0808), **Budget Rent-a-Car** (☎ 021/934–0216), **Dolphin** (☎ 021/934–2265), **Imperial** (☎ 021/934–0213), and **Tempest** (☎ 021/386–2160) all have car-rental offices at the airport (*see also* Arriving and Departing by Car, *above*).

By Train

Cape Town's train station (Adderley St., ☎ 021/405–3871 for intercity train information) lies in the heart of the city, just behind the Tourist Rendezvous Travel Centre. Mainline Passenger Services' *Trans-Karoo* runs daily between Cape Town and Johannesburg; the trip takes about 25 hours and costs R245 in first class. The *Southern Cross* makes the 24-hour trip to Port Elizabeth on Fridays only (R159 in first class); it's a night ride so forget about seeing the splendors of the Garden Route. The luxury *Blue Train* (*see* Rail Travel *in* the Gold Guide) makes the Cape Town–Johannesburg run three times a week in peak season and weekly in the low season; call 021/405–2672 for *Blue Train* information and reservations. *Cape Town Station, Adderley St.,* ☎ *021/405–3871. Reservations office open Mon.–Thurs. 8–4:30, Fri. 8–4, Sat. 8–12. AE, DC, MC, V.*

Getting Around

If you confine yourself to the City Bowl, you won't need a car—in fact, the shortage of parking spaces makes having a car in the city a real nightmare. If you explore the peninsula or the Winelands, though, a rental car becomes your only feasible option, unless you take a guided tour.

By Bus

Apart from the bus to the Table Mountain cableway, the only other bus that visitors are likely to use is the **Waterfront Shuttle.** It runs every 10 minutes between the Waterfront and the Tourist Rendezvous Travel Centre on Adderley Street, with signposted stops along the way. Another shuttle runs through Green Point and along Beach Road to Sea Point every 15–20 minutes. The fare is about R2.

Golden Arrow (☎ 021/461–4365 for route information) operates an extensive network of local buses serving the City Bowl and the outlying suburbs. Generally, service is infrequent and slow. Most buses leave from the Grand Parade, but some (including the buses to the cableway and Hout Bay) leave from a bus stop in front of the OK Bazaars on Adderley Street. An information kiosk at the Grand Parade provides information as well as printed timetables for each bus route. Pay your fare as you enter the bus. The exact fare is preferable (fares vary according to the destination), but the driver will make change if he can. If you travel the same route frequently, consider a clipcard, available at the Grand Parade: The weekly clipcard is good for 10 rides on a designated route within a two-week period; the monthly card allows you 48 trips on a particular route within 37 days. The savings differ from route to route but they're substantial.

By Taxi

Taxis are metered, reasonably priced, and offer an easy, quick way to get around a city where parking is such trouble. Don't expect to see throngs of cabs as in London or New York. You may be lucky enough to hail one on the street, but your best bet is to summon one by phone or head to a major taxi rank—Greenmarket Square, the Tourist Rendezvous Travel Centre, or the top of Adderley Street. **Sea Point Taxis** (☎ 021/434–4444), probably the most reliable of the companies, start the meter at R2.20 and charge R3.70 per kilometer. Other companies are **David's Taxis** (☎ 021/782–2097), **Yellow Taxi Hire** (☎ 082/444–8281), and the more expensive **Marine Taxis** (☎ 021/434–0434). Expect to pay about R15 for a trip from the city center to the Waterfront, and R25 to the hotels in Sea Point.

You will also see **local minibus taxis** tearing around town at high speed, stuffed to capacity with hapless commuters. These buses follow specific routes all over the city and the suburbs, but you can flag them down anywhere along the way. The depot for these taxi buses is on top of the train station. The fare is a very modest R1.

By Train

Cape Metro (☎ 021/405–2991) is Cape Town's commuter line and offers regular service to the southern suburbs and the towns on the False Bay side of the peninsula, including Muizenberg, St. James, Kalk Bay, Fish Hoek, and Simon's Town.

All trains depart from Cape Town Station on Adderley Street. The trip to False Bay takes 45–60 minutes and costs about R7. Cape Metro also serves Paarl, Stellenbosch, and Somerset West in the Winelands (*see* Chapter 5). If you're commuting, consider buying a weekly or monthly pass. The weekly pass gives you a round-trip ticket each day on the same route; the monthly pass allows you to ride as many times as you like, but only on a designated route.

Guided Tours

Orientation

A host of companies offer guided tours of the city, the peninsula, the Winelands, and anywhere else in the Cape you may wish to visit. Among the most reliable operators are **Classic Cape Tours** (☏ 021/782–6026), **Disa Tours** (☏ 021/797–3471, FAX 021/797–7637), **Hylton Ross Tours** (☏ 021/511–1784, FAX 021/511–2401), **Ideal Tours** (☏ 021/468–5415, FAX 021/685–4260), **Mother City Tours** (☏ 021/418–2580, FAX 021/418–2581), **Platinum Tours** (☏ and fax 021/683–1590), **Springbok Atlas** (☏ 021/25–1271), and **Welcome Tours & Safaris** (☏ 021/26–2134, FAX 021/22–1816).

Most of these operators offer the same basic itineraries with only minor variations. Tours are usually in minivans or buses. The city tour usually lasts a half day, and includes stops at the major sights. Full-day peninsula tours, which are sometimes paired with a city tour or a trip up Table Mountain, head down the False Bay side of the peninsula to Cape Point and return via the Atlantic coast.

A cheaper and more casual way to see the sights is with **Topless Tours** (☏ 021/448–2888, FAX 021/448–1836), which runs seven-hour tours of the peninsula (R60) and two-hour tours of the city (R25) aboard topless double-decker buses. On city tours, passengers can hop on and off at designated points and then catch a later bus; in high season, buses leave hourly from the Tourist Rendezvous Travel Centre in Adderley Street (*see* Important Addresses and Numbers, *below*) and the Dock Road Café in the Waterfront.

Boat Tours

Until the middle of this century, most travelers' first glimpse of Cape Town was from the sea—and it's still the best way to get a feel for the city, with its famous mountain as a backdrop. Several companies offer trips into the harbor in a variety of vessels. The tours, all of which leave from the Waterfront, are essentially the same: a one-hour tour of Table Bay (about R30); a 90-minute sunset cruise (R45) with free sparkling wine; and a two- to three-hour cruise out to Robben Island (R70), Nelson Mandela's erstwhile prison home. The weather can be very fickle, so be sure to take a warm jacket and flat shoes. To book a tour phone the motor yacht **Condor** (☏ 021/448–5612); **Le Tigre** (☏ 021/419–7746, FAX 021/25–2459), a 54-foot catamaran; **Sealink** (☏ 021/25–4480, FAX 021/419–7072); **The Spirit of Victoria** (☏ 021/25–4062, FAX 021/461–9733), a 58-foot schooner; or **Waterfront Charters** (☏ 021/25-3804, FAX 021/25–3816).

Drum Beat Charters (☏ 021/438–9208, FAX 021/438–9208) and **Circe** (☏ 021/790–1040) offer one-hour trips (R18) from Hout Bay marina to see the Cape fur seals in their natural habitat on Duiker Island. Unfortunately, you spend only 5–10 minutes with the seals themselves; the rest of the time is spent cruising Hout Bay.

Helicopter Tours

Court Helicopters (Waterfront, ☏ 021/25–2966) and **Civair Helicopters** (Waterfront, ☏ 021/419–5182) offer a variety of tours of the city and surrounding areas, ranging from 20 minutes to several hours. Customized tours can also be arranged.

Robben Island Tours

The boat trips to Robben Island (*see* Boat Tours, *above*) don't actually land on the famous island. If you want to tour the island where Nelson Mandela spent a good chunk of his life, you need to organize a tour through the Department of Corrections, which still administers the island as a prison. Only small groups of visitors are allowed at a time, and it's important that you book well in advance. Write to the commanding officer (Robben Island Jurisdiction, Private Bag, Robben Island 7400) or call 021/411–1006.

Township Tours
For R75, **One City Tours** (☎ 021/387–5351, FAX 021/387–1338) offers interesting and eye-opening tours of the Cape's black townships. Tours are perfectly safe, conducted in minivans, and led by a well-spoken, knowledgeable guide. Visitors are introduced to District Six, a colored neighborhood razed to the ground to satisfy the Group Areas Act, as well as some of the country's most notorious townships and squatter camps, including Crossroads and Khayelitsha. During the tour, you visit the cramped living quarters of a hostel, a spaza shop, and a shebeen (a makeshift bar). The three-hour tour is well worth the time and money, and shows you a side of the country that most white South Africans have never seen.

Walking Tours
Ideal Tours (☎ 021/468–5415, FAX 021/685–4260) conducts a 2½-hour walking tour of Cape Town Monday–Saturday for R50 per person. The tour, which includes a light lunch and all entrance fees, stops at the Castle, the Company's Gardens, the historic buildings in the city center, the Bo-Kaap, and the Houses of Parliament.

Shereen Habib of **Tana-Baru Tours** (☎ 021/24–0719, FAX 021/23–5579) leads two-hour guided walks through the Bo-Kaap, otherwise known as the Malay Quarter. The tour, which costs about R50, winds through the quarter's cobbled streets to the Bo-Kaap Museum, the oldest mosque in the country, and the shrines of various saints. It ends with tea and traditional Malay cakes.

Important Addresses and Numbers

Changing Money
Don't even think about changing money at your hotel. The rates at most hotels are criminal, and the city center is swamped with banks and bureaux de change that give much better rates. After business hours, your best bet is to head to the Waterfront. The Waterfront offices of both **American Express** (Alfred Mall, ☎ 021/21–6021) and **Rennies Travel** (Upper Level, Victoria Wharf, ☎ 021/418–3744) stay open until 7 on weekdays and 5 on weekends.

Consulates
Australian High Commission. *Thibault Sq., BP Centre, 14th Floor,* ☎ *021/419-5425.*

Canadian High Commission. *30 Hout St.,* ☎ *021/23–5240.*

U.K. Consulate. *8 Riebeeck St.,* ☎ *021/25–3670.*

U.S. Consulate. *Broadway Bldg., Heerengracht (bottom of Adderley),* ☎ *021/21–4280.*

Emergencies
Dial 10177 for an **ambulance** and 10111 for the **police.** The police also operate a **Tourist Assistance Unit** (Tulbagh Sq., ☎ 021/418–2853) for foreign visitors who experience trouble or are robbed. The unit provides translators if necessary and will help contact your embassy or consulate.

DOCTORS AND DENTISTS
Doctor and Dental Emergencies (☎ 021/61–3634 or 021/61–2924) is a 24-hour referral service. Otherwise, consult the local telephone directory for names and numbers of doctors and dentists.

HOSPITAL EMERGENCY ROOMS
Groote Schuur Hospital. *Anzio Rd., Observatory,* ☎ *021/404–9111.* ⊙ *24 hrs.*

Red Cross Children's Hospital. *Klipfontein Rd., Rondebosch,* ☎ *021/ 658–5111.* ⊙ *24 hrs.*

Travel Agencies

American Express Travel Service changes money, books trips and airline tickets, and offers a range of services to cardmembers, including holding client mail. *Thibault Sq.,* ☎ *021/419–3085.* ⊙ *Weekdays 8:30–5, Sat. 9–noon.*

Rennies Travel, which represents Thomas Cook in South Africa, has several branches throughout the city but the main office is in the city center on the pedestrian St. George's Mall. In addition to providing the usual services of a travel agent, the office operates a bureau de change (☎ 021/418–1206). *2 St. George's Mall,* ☎ *021/25–2370.* ⊙ *Weekdays 8:30–5, Sat. 9–noon.*

Visitor Information

Captour is the city's official tourist body and by far the most helpful and informative of South Africa's regional promotional offices. Captour's **Tourist Rendezvous Travel Centre** is a huge complex that provides a wealth of information on Cape Town and the Cape, including tours, tour guides, hotels, restaurants, rental cars, shops—you name it. Center staff also assist with inquiries and will make all hotel, tour, and travel bookings. The travel center houses information offices for SATOUR, the Western Cape Tourism Board, the National Parks Board, and Cape Nature Conservation. *Adderley St. (mailing address: Box 1403), Cape Town 8000,* ☎ *021/418–5214,* 𝔽𝔸𝕏 *021/418–5227.* ⊙ *Weekdays 8–7, Sat. 8:30–5, Sun. 9–5.*

The **National Parks Board** office can give you information on all of South Africa's national parks, and accepts reservations for park accommodation and wilderness trails. You can also make reservations here for entry to Kruger National Park. A Parks Board desk at the Tourist Rendezvous Travel Centre offers the same service. *44 Long St.,* ☎ *021/ 22–2810.* ⊙ *Weekdays 8–4:45.*

5 The Western Cape

The wonders of the Western Cape are nearly endless. The jagged mountains, elegant estates, and delicious wines of the Winelands; the pristine, mountain-edged beaches and historic towns of the Overberg; and the glorious wildflowers, old fishing villages, and interior ranges of the West Coast provide some of South Africa's most memorable experiences.

ANCHORED BY CAPE TOWN in the southwest, the Western Cape is South Africa's most delightful province, a sweep of endless mountain ranges, empty beaches, and European history dating back more than 3 centuries. In less than two hours from Cape Town you can reach most of the province's highlights, making the city an ideal regional base.

The historic Winelands, in the city's backyard, produce fine wine amid the exquisite beauty of rocky mountains, serried vines, and elegant Cape Dutch estates. By South African standards, this southwestern region of the Cape is a settled land, with a sense of tradition and continuity lacking in much of the rest of the country. Here, farms have been handed down from one generation to another for centuries, and old-name families like the Cloetes have become part of the fabric of the region.

Even first-time visitors may notice subtle differences between these Cape Afrikaners and their more conservative cousins in the hinterland. For the most part, they are descendants of the landed gentry and educated classes who stayed in the Cape after the British takeover in 1806 and the emancipation of slaves in 1834. Not for them the hard uncertainties of the Great Trek, when ruddy-faced Boer farmers, outraged at British intervention in their lives, loaded their families into ox wagons and set off into the unknown, a rifle in one hand and a Bible in the other.

The genteel atmosphere of the southwestern Cape fades quickly the farther from Cape Town you go. The Overberg, separated from the city by the Hottentots Holland Mountains, presides over the rocky headland of Cape Agulhas, where the Indian and Atlantic oceans meet at the tip of the continent. Unspoiled beaches and coastal mountains are the lure of this remote area. North of Cape Town on the West Coast and Namaqualand, civilization drops away altogether, bar a few lonely fishing villages and mining towns. Each spring, though, the entire region explodes in a spectacular wildflower display that slowly spreads inland to the grassy Hantam Plateau and the Cedarberg mountains.

The wildflowers are just one extraordinary element of a region truly blessed by nature. The Western Cape is famous for its *fynbos* ("feignboss"), the hardy, thin-leaved vegetation that gives much of the province its distinctive look. Fynbos comprises a major part of the Cape floral kingdom, the smallest and richest of the world's six floral kingdoms. More than 8,500 plant species are found in the province, of which 5,000 grow nowhere else on earth. Happily, the region is dotted with nature reserves where you can hike through this profusion of flora, admiring the majesty of the king protea or the shimmering leaves of the silver tree. When the wind blows and mist trails across the mountainsides, the fynbos-covered landscape takes on the look of a Scottish heath.

Not surprisingly, people have taken full advantage of the Cape's natural bonanza. In the Overberg and along the West Coast, rolling wheat fields extend to the horizon, while farther inland jagged mountain ranges hide fertile valleys of apple orchards, orange groves, and vineyards. At sea, hardy fishermen battle icy swells to harvest succulent crayfish (clawless lobsters), delicate perlemoen (a type of abalone), and plump oysters.

For untold centuries, this fertile region supported the Khoikhoi and San, indigenous peoples who lived off the land as pastoralists and hunter-gatherers. With the arrival of European settlers, however, they were

The Western Cape and Namaqualand

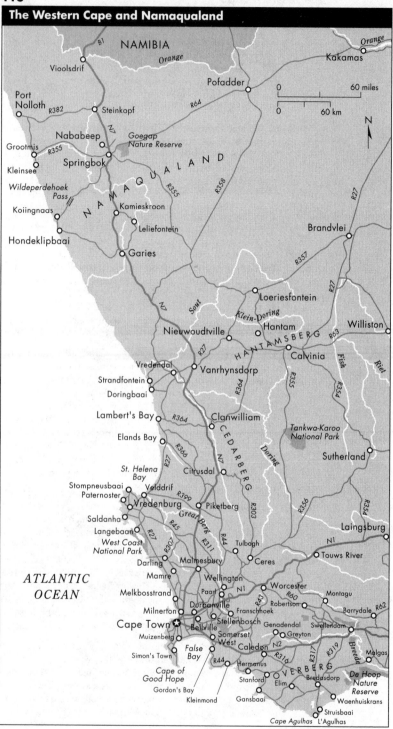

NAMIBIA

Orange

Vioolsdrif

Kakamas

Pofadder

Port Nolloth

R382

Steinkopf

R64

0   60 miles

0   60 km

N

Nababeep

R7

Goegap Nature Reserve

Grootmis

R355

Kleinsee

Springbok

N
A
M
A
Q
U
A
L
A
N
D

R355

R358

R27

Wildeperdehoek Pass

Kamieskroon

Brandvlei

Koiingnaas

Leliefontein

Hondeklipbaai

Garies

N7

Sout

R357

R27

Loeriesfontein

R63

Williston

Klein-Doring

Hantam

Nieuwoudtville

H
A
N
T
A
M
S
B
E
R
G

Calvinia

Fish

Riet

R355

Vredendal

Vanrhynsdorp

R27

R364

Strandfontein

Doringbaai

Tankwa-Karoo National Park

R354

Lambert's Bay

R364

Clanwilliam

C
E
D
A
R
B
E
R
G

Elands Bay

R366

Doring

Sutherland

St. Helena Bay

R27

N7

Citrusdal

Stompneusbaai

Velddrif

R399

R356

R354

Paternoster

Vredenburg

Piketberg

Laingsburg

Saldanha

Great Berg

R303

Langebaan

R27

R45

Tulbagh

N1

West Coast National Park

R207

R311

R44

Ceres

Touws River

Darling

Malmesbury

Mamre

Wellington

Worcester

Montagu

Melkbosstrand

Paarl

N1

R43

R60

Robertson

Barrydale

R62

Milnerton

Durbanville

Franschhoek

Cape Town

Bellville

Stellenbosch

Genadendal

Swellendam

ATLANTIC OCEAN

Muizenberg

Somerset West

Greyton

Malgas

Simon's Town

False Bay

Caledon

N2

R317

R319

Breede

Cape of Good Hope

R44

Hermanus

R31a

O
V
E
R
B
E
R
G

Gordon's Bay

Stanford

Elim

Bredasdorp

De Hoop Nature Reserve

Kleinmond

Gansbaai

Waenhuiskrans

Struisbaai

Cape Agulhas

L'Agulhas

chased off, killed, or enslaved. In the remote recesses of the Cedarberg Mountains and along the West Coast, you can still see the fading rock paintings left by the San, whose few remaining clans have long since retreated into the Kalahari Desert. The population of the Western Cape today is largely "colored," a catchall term to describe South Africans of mixed race and descendants of imported slaves, the San, and the Khoikhoi.

Many visitors spend their entire vacations in the Western Cape after getting their big-game fix in the Eastern Transvaal. Although it's possible to explore Cape Town and the Winelands in three or four days, you need more—a week would suffice—to do the whole area justice. You can get a good sense of the Overberg and the West Coast again on three- or four-day jaunts, but you should set aside an entire week if you plan to tackle the vast distances of Namaqualand, in the Northern Cape. The most practical—and enjoyable—way to explore the region is by rental car.

THE WINELANDS

Individual wine reviews in this chapter were written by Phyllis Hands.

Frank Prial, wine critic for the *New York Times,* recently wrote that he harbored "a nagging suspicion that great wines must be made in spectacular surroundings." If that's true, the French may as well rip up their vines and brew beer, because the Cape Winelands are absolutely stunning. Few places in the world can match the drama of African mountains rising sheer above vine-covered valleys and 200-year-old homesteads snoozing in the shade of giant oaks. It's a place of such enviable beauty that you catch yourself glancing through the local real estate pages.

All of this lies only 45 minutes east of Cape Town in three historic towns and valleys. Founded in 1685, Stellenbosch is a gem; it's also a vibrant university community. Franschhoek, enclosed by towering mountains, is the original home of the Cape's French Huguenots, whose descendants have made a conscious effort to reassert their French heritage. Paarl lies beneath huge granite domes, its main street running 11 kilometers (7 miles) along the Berg River past some of the country's most elegant historical monuments. Throughout the region you will find some of South Africa's best restaurants and hotels.

It's no longer entirely accurate to describe these three valleys as *the* Winelands. Today, they make up only 35% of all the land in the Cape under vine. This wine-growing region is now so vast that you can trek to the fringes of the Karoo Desert in the northeast and still find a grape. There are altogether more than 10 wine routes in the Western Cape, ranging from the Olifants River in the north to the coastal mountains of the Overberg (*see below*). Only in Constantia south of Cape Town (*see* Chapter 4), though, can you find a blend of beauty, history, and sophistication comparable to that of these three valleys.

Each of the valleys has its own wine route where member wineries throw open their estates to the public. They maintain tasting rooms where you can sample their vintages either gratis or for a nominal fee. Happily, no one expects you to be a connoisseur, or even to buy their wines. Just relax and enjoy yourself, and don't hesitate to ask tasting room staff which flavors to expect in what you're drinking. Some wineries have restaurants; at others, you can call ahead to reserve a picnic hamper to enjoy on the estate grounds.

The secret of touring the Winelands is not to hurry. Dally over lunch on a vine-shaded veranda at a 300-year-old estate; enjoy an afternoon nap under a spreading oak; or sip wine while savoring the impossible views. This may not be the Africa of *National Geographic,* but no one's complaining. Nowhere in South Africa is the living more civilized and the culture more self-assured.

The most visible emblem of that culture is Cape Dutch architecture. As you travel from estate to estate, you will see a number of 18th- and 19th-century manor houses that share certain characteristics: thick white-washed walls, thatched roofs curving around elegant gables, and small-pane windows framed by wooden shutters. It's a classic look—a uniquely African look—ideally suited to a land that is hot in summer and cold in winter. The Cape Dutch style developed in the 18th century from traditional long houses, simple, rectangular sheds capped by thatch. As farmers became more prosperous, they added the ornate gables and other features. Several estates, most notably Vergelegen and Boschendal, have opened their manor houses as museums.

Buried for years by sanctions, South African wines are still largely unknown on the international scene. South Africans, however, rarely drink anything else, and Cape reds have recently won a slew of international awards. You must taste Pinotage, South Africa's own varietal, a hybrid of pinot noir and cinsault. For years, the word has been that South African whites would strip the enamel off your teeth. This is no longer the case, and South African whites are pulling down their own awards. If you're coming from abroad, the price of wine—even really good wine—will astonish you. Expect to pay no more than $10 for a first-class bottle.

If you're really serious about wine, arm yourself with *John Platter's Wine Guide,* an annual pocket guide. It's available at most wine shops and bookstores. Keep in mind that many wineries close at lunchtime on Saturday and don't open at all on Sunday.

For more information on shipping wine home, *see* the Gold Guide.

Exploring

The Winelands encompass scores of wineries and estates. This tour profiles 29 of them, chosen for their great wine, their beauty, or their historic significance. It would be a mistake to try to cover them all in less than a week. You have nothing to gain from hightailing it around the Winelands other than a headache. If your interest is more aesthetic and cultural than wine-driven, you would do well to focus on the historic estates of Stellenbosch and Franschhoek, after which you might head south into the Overberg (*see below*). Most of the Paarl wineries on this tour stand out more for the quality of their wine rather than their beauty.

Numbers in the margin correspond to points of interest on the Winelands map.

Somerset West and Stellenbosch

Start in **Somerset West,** a pleasant agricultural town right on the edge of the Winelands, only 30 minutes from Cape Town along the N2. Leave the N2 at the R44/Somerset West exit, and follow the signs to town. You will enter the town on Main Street. Just before you reach the center you'll see the turnoff to Lourensford Road, which runs 3.2 kilometers (2 miles) to **Vergelegen.** The first winery on the tour may well spoil you for the rest. It is one of the most gracious, peaceful, and beau-

★

tiful places in the Cape. Wine-tasting is a major reason to visit here, but you would be mad to leave without touring the grounds.

Vergelegen was established in 1700 by Willem Adriaan van der Stel, who succeeded his father as governor of the Cape. His classic Cape Dutch homestead, with thatch roof and gables, looks like something out of a fairy tale. An octagonal walled garden aflame with flowers surrounds it, and huge camphor trees, planted almost 300 years ago, stand as gnarled sentinels. The homestead is now a museum and is furnished in period style. Other historic buildings include Sir Lionel Phillips's magnificent library (open Mon.–Sat. 11–3) and the old stables, now the reception area and interpretive center. Behind the house, Lady Phillips's Tea Garden serves lunch and tea (*see* Dining, *below*), and the Rose Terrace café looks onto a formal rose garden.

Vergelegen buys a lot of grapes from neighboring farms, since its re-planted vineyards are not yet bearing a full crop. When the vines come of age, expect wine maker Martin Meinert to expand the range of wines. The best of the bunch right now is the Sauvignon Blanc, a crisp, dry white wine with typical fig and gooseberry characteristics. Vergelegen also produces a good Chardonnay. *Lourensford Rd., Somerset West,* ☎ *024/517060,* FAX *024–517559.* ☛ *To estate: R6 adults, R4 children 4–12 and pensioners; tastings free.* ◯ *Daily 9:30–4 (no tastings Sun.). Cellar tours: Mon.–Sat. 10:30, 11:30, and 2:30 (reservations essential).*

❷ Return to the R44 and turn right to reach **Avontuur.** Backed by the impressive mountains of the Helderberg, this winery and racehorse stud look over vine-covered slopes to the distant waters of False Bay and Cape Point. Unlike Vergelegen, this is not an estate around which to plan an entire day. Come here to taste and buy wines in the modern cellars.

The winery produces an adventuresome and tasty range of red and white wines, including Le Blush, a zesty wine with citrus overtones and probably the only pink Chardonnay in the world. This popular wine is fermented in barrels originally used for red wine—it owes its origins to a wine-making accident! Le Chandon, on the other hand, is a serious Chardonnay with a honeyed, citrus nose that shows elegant use of wood. Pay particular attention to Avon Rouge, a nonvintage blend of merlot and cabernet sauvignon. It's a delightful, fruity wine that you can enjoy right away or allow to benefit from two to three years of bottle aging. *Stellenbosch Rd. (R44), Somerset West,* ☎ *024/553–450,* FAX *024/554–600.* ☛ *Tastings free Feb.–Nov., R2 Dec.–Jan.* ◯ *Weekdays 9:30–4:30, Sat. 9–1. No cellar tours.*

❸ The turnoff to **Rust-en-Vrede** lies just over 3 kilometers (2 miles) farther up the R44 on the right (don't follow the accommodation sign to Rust-en-Vrede Guest Farm). Nestled against the base of the Helderberg and shaded by giant oaks, this peaceful winery looks over steep slopes of vines and roses. Owned by former Springbok rugby great Jannie Engelbrecht, it's a comparatively small estate that specializes entirely in red wine—and produces some of the very best in South Africa. Rust-en-Vrede Estate is the flagship wine, a blend of predominantly cabernet sauvignon, shiraz, and just over 10% merlot. It has already won several awards both locally and abroad, but it would do well to mature in the bottle for another 10 years or more. Another interesting wine is the Shiraz, which has an inviting bouquet with the vanillin sweetness that American oak imparts; it will age for 5–8 years. Rust-en-Vrede is one of the few estates that opens its historic winery and beautifully restored Cape Dutch homestead for tours. It also has a short

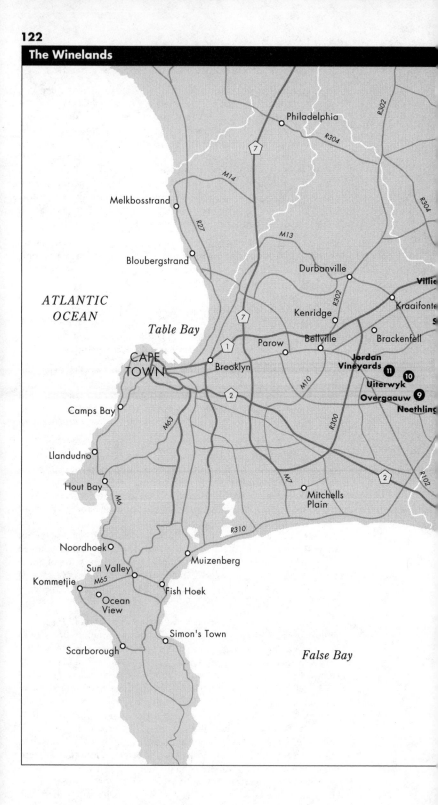

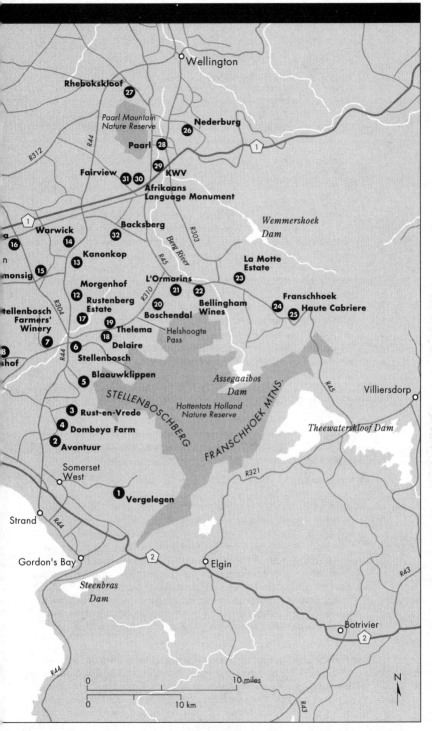

birding trail that meanders through indigenous, riverine forest. *R44, between Stellenbosch and Somerset West,* ☎ *021/881–3881,* FAX *021/881–3000.* ☛ *Tastings free.* ⊙ *Weekdays 8:30–12:30 and 1:30–4:30, Sat. 9–1. Cellar tours on request.*

❹ Next door is **Dombeya Farm,** one of the few places in the Western Cape where visitors can see spinning and hand weaving. The farm makes jerseys, blankets, and wool rugs, all in the bright, feminine patterns that are Dombeya's hallmark. The shop also sells patterns and wool. A garden tearoom serves light lunches and snacks. *Off R44,* ☎ *021/ 881–3746.* ⊙ *Mon.–Sat. 8:30–5.*

Continue another 3.2 kilometers (2 miles) up the R44. Established in
❺ the late 17th century, **Blaauwklippen** sits at the foot of the Stellenboschberg, shaded by oaks. It's a large winery that is well equipped to handle tour buses and will keep even non-oenophiles entertained. From October to April, you can take carriage rides (R2) through the vineyards, and there is also a free museum of old coaches, furniture, and kitchen utensils. If you arrive between noon and 2, consider settling down on the veranda for a Coachman's Lunch of cold meats, cheeses, and pâté. Blaauwklippen produces a good range of both red and white wines. Its Zinfandel is by far the best of the four Zinfandels produced in the Cape, and it has fared extremely well in a competition with American Zinfandels in the United States. The Shiraz and Cabernet Sauvignon are also most commendable. For easy drinking right now, the Red Landau, a blend of cabernet sauvignon and merlot, is good value. A country shop sells a variety of souvenirs, as well as jams, Cape Malay chutneys, and *weinwurst* (a salamilike sausage). *R44 between Stellenbosch and Somerset West,* ☎ *021/880–0133,* FAX *021/880–1250.* ☛ *Tastings R1.70 for booklet of 5 tasting tickets.* ⊙ *Weekdays 9–5, Sat. 9–1. Cellar tours Dec.–Jan. on request; Feb.–Nov., weekdays 11 and 3, Sat. 11.*

From Blaauwklippen, continue north on the R44. Drive through one set of traffic lights and then, at the next set of lights, turn right onto Dorp Street into Stellenbosch.

★ ❻ **Stellenbosch** may be the most delightful town in South Africa. It's small, sophisticated, and beautiful, and you could easily while away a week here and feel all the better for it. The second-oldest town after Cape Town, it actually *feels* old, unlike so many historic towns in South Africa. Wandering the oak-shaded streets, which still have open irrigation furrows, you'll see some of the finest examples of Cape Dutch, Georgian, Victorian, and Regency architecture in the country. The town was founded in 1679 by Simon van der Stel, first governor of the Cape, who recognized the agricultural potential of this fertile valley. Wheat was the major crop grown by the early settlers, but vineyards now blanket the surrounding hills. The town is also home to the University of Stellenbosch, the country's first and most prestigious Afrikaans university.

A brief walking tour of the town starts at the corner of Dorp Street and the R44, where you first enter Stellenbosch. The **Rembrandt van Rijn Art Museum** occupies the historic Libertas Parva manor house, which displays the H shape so typical of Cape Dutch architecture. Built in 1780, the house has hosted some of the biggest names in South African history, including Cecil Rhodes and Barry Herzog. Jan Smuts, who became prime minister and a major player on the world scene after the Great War, was married here. The art museum displays the work of some major South African artists, including Irma Stern, Willie Bester, and sculptor Anton van Wouw. *31 Dorp St.,* ☎ *021/886–4340.* ☛ *Free.* ☉ *Weekdays 9–12:45 and 2–5, Sat. 10–1 and 2–5.*

The **Stellenryk Wine Museum** is housed in the 18th-century wine cellars behind Libertas Parva. The cellar setting is appropriate for the museum's collection of wine-related artifacts, including presses, vats, and an interesting collection of wine vessels ranging from antiquity to the 18th century. *31 Dorp St.,* ☎ *021/887–3480.* ☛ *Free.* ☉ *Weekdays 9–12:45 and 2–5, Sat. 10–1.*

Stroll up oak-lined Dorp Street, Stellenbosch's most historic avenue. Almost the entire street is a national monument, flanked by lovely, restored homes from every period of the town's history. Redolent with tobacco, dried fish, and spices, **Oom Samie Se Winkel** is a Victorian-style general store and one of Stellenbosch's most popular landmarks. In addition to the usual Cape kitsch, Oom Samie's sells some genuine *boere* (farmers') products, including *witblitz* and *mampoer,* the Afrikaner equivalent of moonshine. The shop operates a wine-export business and restaurant, too. *82/84 Dorp St., tel, 021/887–2612.* ☉ *Weekdays 9–6, Sat. 9–5.*

As you continue up Dorp Street, keep an eye out for **La Gratitude** (95 Dorp St.)—the all-seeing eye of God on its gable will be doing the same for you. **Voorgelegen** (176 Dorp St.) and the houses on either side of it form one of the best-preserved Georgian ensembles in town.

When you reach Andringa Street, turn left and then right onto Kerk (Church) Street. On your left is **d'Ouwe Werf,** possibly the country's oldest boarding house (*see* Lodging, *below*), which first took in paying guests as long ago as 1802.

At the corner of Kerk and Ryneveld Streets is the **Stellenbosch Village Museum,** which is well worth a visit. The museum comprises four dwellings scattered within a two-block radius. These houses date from different periods in Stellenbosch's history and have been furnished to reflect changing lifestyles and tastes. The oldest of them is the very basic Schreuderhuis, which dates from 1709. The others date from 1789, 1803, and 1850, respectively. *18 Ryneveld St.,* ☎ *021/887–2902.* ☛ *R4 adults, 50¢ children.* ☉ *Mon.–Sat. 9:30–5, Sun. 2–5.*

Continue down Ryneveld to Plein Street. Turn left and walk to the **Braak,** the grassy town square. Some of Stellenbosch's most historic buildings face the square, which is a national monument. At the southern end is the **Rhenish Church** (Bloem St.), erected by the Missionary Society of Stellenbosch in 1823 as a training school for slaves and coloreds.

St. Mary's Church stands at the far end of the Braak. Built in 1852, it was consecrated by Bishop Robert Gray in 1854 and reflects the growing influence of the English in Stellenbosch. Across Bloem Street from St. Mary's is the **Burgher House,** built in 1797. Today, it houses the offices of Historical Homes in South Africa.

Next to the Burgher House, on an island in Market Street, stands the **V.O.C. Arsenal.** It took 91 years for the Political Council to hammer out the decision that Stellenbosch needed its own magazine. With the hard part behind them, it took just six months in 1777 to complete the structure. *Bloem St., no* ☎. ☛ *R1 adults, children free.* ☉ *Aug.–May, weekdays 9:30–1:30 and 2–5.*

Walk down Market Street past the Tourist Information Bureau (*see* Winelands Essentials, *below*). On your left, facing a large lawn, is the **Rhenish Complex,** one of the most impressive restoration projects ever undertaken in South Africa. The complex consists of the old Cape Dutch Rhenish parsonage (1815); the Leipoldt House, which melds elements of English and Cape architecture; and a two-story building that is typically English.

Continue down Market and turn left on **Herte Street.** The whitewashed cottages along this street were built for freed slaves after the Emancipation Act of 1834. Although they were originally thatched, the houses are still evocative of 19th-century Stellenbosch. From here, follow Herte back to Dorp Street, where the walking tour began.

Around Stellenbosch

From Stellenbosch, wine routes fan out like spokes of a wheel, making excellent day trips if you're staying in town. Several excellent wineries lie nearby off the R310. To reach them, get back in your car, follow Dorp Street across the R44, and turn left at the Shell station.

❼ It's less than a mile to the **Stellenbosch Farmers' Winery** (SFW). Founded by a Kentuckian, William Charles Winshaw, SFW is the largest wholesale wine producer/merchant in South Africa and is responsible for almost 40% of the country's table wine. SFW also produces fortified wines, several brandies, and very good fruit juices and ciders. The SFW flagship is the Zonnebloem range of reds and whites, including among others a good Shiraz (particularly those from the early 1980s) and Blanc de Blanc. The Lanzerac Pinotage was the first of the variety ever made in South Africa (back in 1961), and it's still an excellent wine.

The Farmers' Winery Centre, where tours begin, stands directly opposite the winery above a vineyard of cabernet sauvignon grapes. Here you'll find the wine-tasting center and salesroom. Each summer, concerts ranging from African jazz to opera and ballet are staged at the Oude Libertas Amphitheatre, a delightful open-air venue. For program listings and reservations, contact Computicket or phone 021/808–7473. *Oude Libertas Rd., off R310,* ☎ *021/808–7569,* ℻ *021/886–456.* ☛ *Tastings free.* ⊘ *Weekdays 8:30–5, Sat. 10–12:30. Cellar tours (R6) Mon.–Thurs. 10, 11, and 2:30; Fri. 10 and 11; Sat. 10.*

❽ Continue 3.2 kilometers (2 miles) down the R310 to **Neethlingshof.** A long avenue of pines and oaks leads to this lovely estate, which traces its origins back to 1692. The magnificent 1814 Cape Dutch manor house looks out across formal rose gardens to the Stellenbosch Valley and the Hottentots Holland Mountains. The house is now a first-class restaurant, the Lord Neethling. Lighter meals are served next door at the Palm Terrace. Not surprisingly, Neethlingshof has become a great attraction, so don't be surprised to see tour buses in the parking lot. The tasting room feels very Alpine and gemütlich, and large windows let you see the barrels arrayed in the cellar. The Gewürztraminer is an off-dry, very elegant wine with rose-petal and spice aromas—an excellent accompaniment to Chinese or spicy South African fare. The Weisser Riesling is a good example of the few virtually dry wines made from this grape variety. Neethlingshof also produces an equally good Chardonnay and an excellent Noble Late Harvest sweet dessert wine. Their Pinotage, a good wine with attractive fruitiness and subtle wood tones, will be best after three to five years. *R310,* ☎ *021/883–8988,* ℻ *021/883–8941.* ☛ *Tastings R5.* ⊘ *Weekdays 9–5, weekends 10–4. Cellar tours by appointment.*

Turn right out of Neethlingshof. Just half a kilometer (¼ mile) farther on is the turnoff to three other wineries of note. **Overgaauw** is a small estate that is geared to visitors who are serious about wine. Don't expect grand Cape Dutch manors or majestic panoramas. What you should expect is very fine wine. Overgaauw's wines tend to have restrained elegance and complexity, and they age fantastically. Tria Corda is one of the first Cape Bordeaux–style blends of predominantly cabernet sauvignon with about 20% merlot and 10% cabernet franc. It's a great wine, which will drink well after five years and even better after eight. The Chardonnay, lightly wooded and medium-bodied, should be kept for three to five years to let it develop its full potential. *Stellenbosch Kloof Rd., ☎ 021/881–3815, FAX 021/881–3436. Tastings free. ⊗ Weekdays 9–12:30 and 2–5. No cellar tours.*

Uiterwyk, another 2.5 kilometers (1½ miles) up Stellenbosch Kloof Road, is one of the Cape's most beautiful homesteads. Built in 1791, it's a magnificent example of early Cape Dutch architecture. Unfortunately, the house is not open to the public, although you can walk around the gardens and photograph the exterior. If you're not in the mood for wine, you can also follow one of three bird walks on the estate, which should take between 10 and 30 minutes.

Tastings take place in the modern cellar behind the homestead. The estate produces one of the best Pinotages in the Cape, a robust wine with very good fruit and balance that will age well for 5 to 10 years. The Muller Thurgau is the only wine made from this variety on the local market; it's a pleasant, off-dry wine that's ideal for quaffing. *Stellenbosch Kloof Rd., ☎ 021/881–3711, FAX 021/881–3376. Tastings free. ⊗ Weekdays 9–12:30 and 2–5. Cellar tours Sat. 10.*

Jordan Vineyards lies 2.5 kilometers (1½ miles) farther up the road from Uiterwyk. Although this new winery can't match the historical or architectural splendor of many of the more established estates, it enjoys an enviable setting at the head of Stellenbosch Kloof, flanked by the hills of the Bottelaryberg and overlooking a vision of rolling vineyards and jagged mountains. Gary and Cathy Jordan are a husband-and-wife team who studied at the University of California at Davis and worked at California's Iron Horse Winery. Although they produced their first vintage only in 1992, they have already established their reputation as producers of quality wines. The Sauvignon Blanc is an exciting, lively wine that displays excellent characteristics of gooseberries, figs, and much more. The Jordans also produce a very good Chardonnay and a promising Cabernet Sauvignon. On Saturdays from December to April you can reserve picnic hampers, to enjoy inside or on the lawns at tables with umbrellas. *Stellenbosch Kloof Rd., ☎ 021/881–3441, FAX 021/881-3426. Tastings free. ⊗ Weekdays 10–5, Sat. 9:30–5. Cellar tours by appointment.*

The second important spoke in the Stellenbosch Wine Route runs north from Stellenbosch along the R44. Drive 5 kilometers (3 miles) north on the R44. **Morgenhof** lies in the lee of a steep hill covered with vines and great pine trees. It's a beautiful Cape Dutch estate, with a history stretching back 300 years. In 1993, Morgenhof was acquired by the Huchon-Cointreaus of Cognac, France. They have spared nothing to make this one of the jewels of the Winelands, including a formal French rose garden atop their new underground cellar. With talented Jean Daneel as wine maker, the wines should be equally distinguished. The Merlot/Cabernet Sauvignon is a very fruity, accessible wine with good structure. It can be enjoyed on release or left to mature for a few years. The Sauvignon Blanc, well-balanced and dry, combines tropical fruit and grassiness on the nose that follow through to the finish. The Chardonnay and off-dry Rhine Riesling are also highly recommended. Morgenhof is an excellent place to stop for lunch. From October through April, you can reserve picnic hampers and dine on the lawns under a huge tree. During the rest of the year, the estate serves light lunches of homemade soup, freshly baked bread, cheese, and quiche. Reservations are advisable in summer. *R44, between Paarl and Stellenbosch,* ☎ *021/889–5510,* FAX *021/889–5266.* ☛ *Tastings R2.50.* ☉ *Weekdays 9–4:30, Sat. 10–3; Nov.–Apr., also Sun. 10–3. Cellar tours by appointment.*

⑬ **Kanonkop** lies about 5 kilometers (3 miles) north of Morgenhof along the R44. In the days when ships of the Dutch East India Company used Cape Town as a revictualing station on the way to the East, they would fire a cannon as they entered the harbor to let farmers know they needed supplies. A relay cannon was then fired from a hill on this farm—*Kanonkop* is Afrikaans for Cannon Hill. The beauty of this farm is not in its history or its buildings but in its wine. Since the early 1980s, wine making has been in the hands of legendary Beyers Truter. In 1991, he won the Winemaker of the Year award and the Robert Mondavi Trophy at the London International Wine & Spirit Competition. No one would argue that Kanonkop's Pinotage is the best new-style Pinotage produced in South Africa. It's more wooded than most and shows excellent complexity and fruit; it will age for 8 to 15 years. Paul Sauer is a very good blend of about 80% cabernet sauvignon with the balance made up of equal parts merlot and cabernet franc. *R44, between Paarl and Stellenbosch,* ☎ *021/884–4656,* FAX *021/884–4719.* ☛ *Tastings free.* ☉ *Weekdays 9–5, Sat. 8:30–12:30. No cellar tours.*

⑭ One kilometer (½ mile) farther north is **Warwick.** It's not a member of the Stellenbosch Wine Route, and you should visit this estate only if you're very keen to taste and buy wine—the tasting area is in a tiny cellar room cluttered with wine-making equipment; if possible, make an appointment first. Wine maker Norma Ratcliffe is very traditional in her approach to wine. She spent a couple of vintages in France perfecting her techniques and is now producing first-rate reds. Trilogy is one of the finest blended reds in the Cape, a stylish and complex wine made predominantly from cabernet sauvignon, with about 20% merlot and 10% cabernet franc. The Cabernet Franc is undoubtedly the best wine made from this varietal in the Winelands. The 1992 vintage is a particularly fruity wine—a real standout. *R44, between Paarl and Stellenbosch,* ☎ *021/884–4410,* FAX *021/884–4025.* ☛ *Tastings free, preferably by appointment.* ☉ *Weekdays 8:30–noon and 1:30–4:30, Sat. 9–noon. No cellar tours.*

Two other wineries, interesting for their wine, not their history, lie a few kilometers to the west. Head back down the R44 for about 2 kilo-
⑮ meters (1¼ miles) to reach the turnoff to Kromme Rhee Road. **Simonsig** sits in a sea of vines with tremendous views back toward Stellenbosch and the mountains. Its range of 15 white and red wines covers the whole taste and price spectrum. The Kaapse Vonkel is one of South Africa's best Méthode Cap Classique sparkling wines. Tiara is among the best cabernet blends in the Winelands, and the Pinotage is an excellent example of how well this varietal fares with no wood aging. You can bring your own picnic to enjoy at tables by the small playground. *Kromme Rhee Rd.,* ☎ *021/882–2044,* FAX *021/882–2545.* ☛ *Tastings R4.50.* ☉ *Mon.–Sat. 8:30–5. Cellar tours weekdays 10 and 3, Sat. 10.*

Turn right out of Simonsig and then right again onto the R304 to reach **⑯ Villiera.** This estate is actually part of the Paarl Wine Route, but its location in the open flats near the N1 motorway makes it just as close to Stellenbosch as to Paarl. In just over a decade of wine making, the Grier family has notched up numerous successes—too many to list here. Their Sauvignon Blanc is one of the very best in the Cape, with excellent fruit and balance; it's so popular that one vintage usually sells out before the next becomes available. The Merlot ranks among the top five in the country, with excellent depth of fruit—a great wine. *Corner of R101 and R304,* ☎ *021/882–2002,* FAX *021/882–2314.* ☛ *Tastings free.* ⊙ *Weekdays 8:30–5, Sat. 8:30–1. Cellar tours by appointment.*

It's a straight shot back down the R304 from Villiera to Stellenbosch.

The fourth major spoke in the Stellenbosch Wine Route is the R310 to Franschhoek via remarkably scenic Helshoogte Pass—you'll see signs north of Stellenbosch on the R44.

After a mile, you'll see a small brown sign pointing to the High Rustenberg Hydro. Turn here and drive another mile to the entrance of **⑰ Rustenberg Estate,** on the slopes of the Simonsberg. A narrow lane runs through cattle pastures and groves of oak and birch to the Cape Dutch homestead (1811), a vision of bucolic bliss. Unlike some of the more touristy wineries, Rustenberg feels like a working farm, the complex of Cape Dutch farm buildings smelling like hay and cattle and pressed grapes. The estate is known for red wine, its Rustenberg Cabernet Sauvignon having enjoyed an unblemished record since it was first bottled over 50 years ago. It's a lovely, unblended wine that will age for a decade or two. Try buying five bottles and drinking one every five years. *Off R310, between Stellenbosch and Franschhoek,* ☎ *021/887–3153,* FAX *021/887–8466.* ☛ *Tastings free.* ⊙ *Weekdays 9–12:30 and 2–4:30, Sat. 9–noon. No cellar tours.*

Turn left when you get back to the R310 and begin the winding climb **⑱** up Helshoogte Pass. Perched high above the valley, **Delaire** enjoys one of the most spectacular settings of any winery in the country. Sit on the terrace of the tasting room or restaurant and look past a screen of oaks to the valley below and the majestic crags of the Groot Drakenstein and Simonsberg mountains. It's an ideal place to stop for lunch, or even a short breather. The restaurant (open Tues.–Sat. noon–2) serves light lunches and will provide picnic hampers to visitors who want to follow one of the scenic trails through the estate (Sept. 15–Apr. 15). The tasting room is unpretentious and casual. *R310, between Stellenbosch and Franschhoek,* ☎ *021/885–1756,* FAX *021/885–1270.* ☛ *Tastings R2.30.* ⊙ *Mon.–Sat. 10–5. No cellar tours.*

⑲ Almost opposite Delaire is the entrance to **Thelema.** Situated on the slopes of the Simonsberg, this farm is an excellent example of the exciting developments in the Cape Winelands since the early 1980s. When Gyles and Barbara Webb bought the farm in 1983, there was nothing here but very good soil and old fruit trees. It's a testament to their efforts that the winery and its superb range of wines have been regular prize-winners ever since. Their Sauvignon Blanc is outstanding, one of the five best produced in the Cape. Dry, yet possessed of an amazing fruity complexity and richness, it is often used as a benchmark for South African Sauvignon Blanc. The Cabernet Sauvignon–Merlot blend is also a superb wine—rich, complex, and elegant. The 1992 vintage won Gyles Webb the Diner's Club Winemaker of the Year title in 1994. To cap it all off, the view of the Groot Drakenstein mountains from the tasting room is unforgettable. *R310, between Stellenbosch and Franschhoek,* ☎ *021/885–1924,* 𝖥𝖠𝖷 *021/885–1800.* ☞ *Tastings free.* ☉ *Weekdays 9–5, Sat. 9–1. No cellar tours.*

Franschhoek Valley

From Thelema, the road runs down Helshoogte Pass into the fruit orchards and vines that mark the beginning of the Franschhoek Valley. This is the most isolated and spectacular of the three wine routes, a long valley encircled by towering mountain ranges and fed by a single road. Franschhoek takes its name from its first white settlers, French Huguenots who fled to the Cape to escape Catholic persecution in France. By the early 18th century, 270 of them had settled in the Cape, but their descendants—with names like de Villiers, Malan, and Joubert—now number in the tens of thousands. With their experience in French vineyards, the early Huguenots were instrumental in nurturing a wine-making culture in South Africa. As spectacular as the valley is today, it must have been even more so in the late 17th century when it teemed with game. In calving season, herds of elephants would migrate to the valley via the precipitous Franschhoek Mountains. The last wild elephant in the valley died in the 1930s. Some leopards still survive.

㉑ **Boschendal** lies at the base of Helshoogte Pass. With a history dating back 3 centuries, this lovely estate competes with Groot Constantia as one of the Cape's major attractions—you could easily spend half a day here. Cradled between the Simonsberg and Groot Drakenstein mountains, the farm "Bossendaal" was originally granted to Jean le Long, one of the first French Huguenot settlers in the late 17th century.

Boschendal runs one of the most pleasant wine-tastings in the region: Visitors can sit inside at the Taphuis, a Cape Dutch longhouse and the oldest building on the estate, or outside at wrought-iron tables under a spreading oak. In 1978, Boschendal was the first to pioneer a Cape Blanc de Noir, a pink wine made in a white-wine style from black grapes. The Boschendal Blanc de Noir remains the best-selling wine of this style. If you prefer sparkling wines, try the extremely popular Boschendal Brut, a blend of pinot noir and chardonnay made by the Méthode Cap Classique. From the Taphuis, it's a two-minute drive through vines and fruit trees to the main estate complex, where visitors have three choices for lunch. The excellent Boschendal Restaurant (*see* Dining, *below*) serves a buffet of Cape specialties. Le Café serves light meals at tables arranged under the oaks leading to the manor house. And Le Pique Nique (☉ Nov.–Apr.) provides picnic hampers for visitors to enjoy on the lawns. Calling ahead for the restaurant and the picnic is essential. A gift shop sells wine, locally made rugs, preserves, and other Cape kitsch. *R310, between Franschhoek and Stellenbosch,* ☎ *02211/41030,* 𝖥𝖠𝖷 *02211/41864. Tastings free.* ☉ *Weekdays 8:30–4:30, Sat. 8:30– 12:30. No cellar tours. Vineyard tours weekdays 10:30 and 11:30, Sat. 10:30 (reservations essential).*

㉒ Just after Boschendal the R310 ends at a T junction. Turn right toward Franschhoek and follow the R45 to **L'Ormarins.** Even in a region where superlatives seem to fall short, L'Ormarins stands out as something special. The 1811 manor house, approached through a tunnel of oaks, is spellbinding: a classic Cape Dutch building festooned with flowers and framed by the majestic peaks of the looming Simonsberg and Groot Drakenstein. Although the old house is off-limits to visitors, the huge tasting room next door is modern, even slick. The excellent Optima Reserve is a blend of cabernet sauvignon and merlot, with a trace of cabernet franc. It's a wine of great complexity that will improve in the bottle for 10 to 15 years. If you have an interest in heraldry, take a tour of the old cellars, now used for maturing red wine. A number of the larger casks bear the coat of arms of an original French Huguenot family. *R45,* ☎ *02211/41026,* 📠 *02211/41361.* ☛ *Tastings free.* ⊙ *Weekdays 9–4:30, Sat. 9–12:30. Cellar tours weekdays 10, 11:30, and 3; Sat. 11.*

㉒ Continue east on the R45. **Bellingham Wines** lies deep in the shadows of old oaks, its Cape Dutch manor house almost completely hidden from view. The house is off-limits, but you can stroll unaccompanied through the vineyards, which run up the slope toward the craggy base of the mountains. From December to January, you can also order light luncheon platters to eat under the trees. As far as wine-tasting is concerned, don't expect to waltz in, toss back a couple of glasses, and waltz out again. Bellingham conducts what it calls "informative wine-tastings." Sitting at tables, you will be presented with wine by a winery employee. Each vintage is explained before you sample it.

Bellingham produces both red and white wines. The Sauvignon Blanc is an unwooded dry white wine with good fruit and balance. The Classic is an easy-drinking but elegant blend of cabernet sauvignon, merlot, and cabernet franc. *R45,* ☎ *02211/41011,* 📠 *02211/41712.* ☛ *Tastings R3.* ⊙ *Weekdays 9–5, Sat. 10–12:30. No cellar tours.*

The R45 shares a narrow bridge over the Berg River with the railway line. Less than 2 kilometers (1 mile) beyond the bridge is **La Motte Es-**
㉓ **tate,** owned by a branch of the same Rupert family that owns L'Ormarins. The elegant and rather formal tasting room looks into the cellars through a wall of smoked glass. Visitors sit at a long, marble-topped table and sample five to seven wines. The Shiraz is one of the biggest and boldest that you'll taste of this variety, full of rich flavors; it needs four to eight years to reach its peak. The Millenium is a very good blend of just over 50% cabernet sauvignon with the balance consisting of merlot and a little cabernet franc. This wine needs time to develop, coming into its own in 5 to 10 years. *R45,* ☎ *02212/3119,* 📠 *02212/3446.* ☛ *Tastings R2.60.* ⊙ *Weekdays 9–4:30, Sat. 9–noon. No cellar tours.*

From La Motte the road runs along the valley floor, passing serried rows of vineyards and whitewashed Cape Dutch homes. The village
㉔ of **Franschhoek** lies at the base of the Franschhoek Mountains, which seal off the eastern end of the valley. It's a delightful village, with a pleasant, slow pace that belies the extraordinary number of restaurants, cafés, and small inns in town. It's makes a great stop for lunch or overnight.

The **Huguenot Memorial** (corner of Lambrecht and Huguenot Sts.) stands at the end of the main road through Franschhoek. It was built in 1943 to commemorate the contribution of the Huguenots to South Africa's development. The three arches symbolize the Holy Trinity, the sun and cross form the Huguenots' emblem, and the female figure in front represents Freedom of Conscience.

Next to the memorial is the **Huguenot Memorial Museum.** Its main building is modeled after Thibault's 1791 Saasveld in Cape Town. The museum traces the causes of the Huguenots' flight from France and the life they carved out for themselves in the Cape. Wall displays profile some of the early Huguenot families. Exhibits also focus on other aspects of the region's history: One explains the development of Cape Dutch architecture; another explores the culture and life of the Khoikhoi, also known as Hottentots. *Lambrecht St.,* ☎ *02212/2532.* ☛ *R2 adults, 50¢ children.* ⊙ *Weekdays 9–5, Sat. 9–1 and 2–5, Sun. 2–5.*

One other winery remains on this route. Turn left at the T junction in front of the memorial and follow the R45 as it begins its long climb up Franschhoek Pass. Built on the lower slopes of the Franschhoek Mountains, **Haute Cabriere** is a brand-new complex, the brainchild of Achim von Arnim, one of the Cape's most colorful wine makers. To avoid scarring the mountain, the complex hunkers into the hillside. Inside are a very avant-garde tasting room and restaurant, with a true cellar feel. Von Arnim makes five sparkling wines, four under the Pierre Jourdan label using the Méthode Cap Classique. In 1994, he produced his first vintage of Pinot Noir, a very fruity, mouth-filling wine. It's delicious now but will continue to develop for five years. *R45 to Villiersdorp,* ☎ *02212/2630,* ᐧᐧᐧ *02212/3390.* ☛ *Tastings R5, cellar tours and tastings R10 (by appointment only).* ⊗ *Weekdays 9–5, Sat. 9–1.*

At this point you have two choices. Follow the R45 over the top of Franschhoek Pass and then head south across Viljoens Pass to Grabouw in the Overberg (covered in the next touring section, *below*). Or retrace your steps back down the Franschhoek Valley and continue to Paarl.

North to Paarl

Soon after you pass La Motte on the R45, turn right onto the R303, which runs into North Paarl. Cross under the N1 and continue for a couple of blocks. At the traffic lights, turn right onto Optenhorst Street and follow the signs to Nederburg, on the Paarl Wine Route.

Nederburg is the Cape's most established wine label—no restaurant's wine list would be complete without some of its wine. It's a vast estate, and it is easy to feel overwhelmed by the industrial white buildings. Fortunately, the tasting room is friendly and welcoming, and cellar tours lead visitors through the estate's fine Cape Dutch homestead, built in 1800. You can also reserve picnic hampers to enjoy on the estate's lawns—except during the build-up to the annual Nederburg Auction in March or April. The auction is one of the world's most glamorous wine events, when the very best wine from all over the Cape is sold to the highest bidders—nearly half to overseas buyers. Besides those produced specially for the auction, Nederburg produces about 20 wines under its regular label, covering the spectrum of reds and whites. The estate's Noble Late Harvest is exceptional. For an easy-drinking dry white wine, try Prelude, a successful blend of sauvignon blanc and chardonnay. Paarl Cabernet Sauvignon is a traditional unblended cabernet with subtle wood tones. It ages extremely well for 5 to 10 years. *WR4,* ☎ *02211/623104,* ᐧᐧᐧ *02211/624887.* ☛ *Tastings R5 (glass deposit).* ⊗ *Weekdays 9–5, Nov.–Feb. also open Sat. 9–1. Cellar tours weekdays 10:30 and 2:30 (reservations advised).*

Drive back down Optenhorst and continue straight through the traffic lights. At the next light, turn right onto North Main Street and drive 5 kilometers (3 miles) to **Rhebokskloof.** The winery sits at the head of a shallow valley, backed by hillsides covered with vines and fynbos. It's a lovely place for lunch on a sunny day. The Victorian Restaurant serves à la carte meals and teas on an oak-shaded terrace overlooking the gardens and mountains; in inclement weather meals are served in the Cape Dutch Restaurant, as is a Sunday buffet lunch. Californian John Reagh has been the wine maker here since 1991, producing solid if not yet exciting whites and reds. The Cabernet Sauvignon is a full-bodied wine, with good fruit, cassis, and cedar-box aromas that follow through to the palate. It will develop for four to six years. *WR8,*

☎ 02211/638386, ℻ 02211/638504. ☛ *Tastings R5.* ☉ *Nov.–Apr., daily 9–5; May–Oct., daily 9–4:30. No cellar tours.*

28 Return the way you came and follow Main Street into **Paarl.** The town takes its name from the granite domes of Paarl Mountain, which looms above the town—*paarl* is Afrikaans for "pearl." The first farmers settled here in 1687, two years after the founding of Stellenbosch. The town has its fair share of historic homes and estates, but it lacks the charm of its distinguished neighbor simply because it's so spread out. Main Street, the town's oak-lined thoroughfare, extends some 11 kilometers (7 miles) along the western bank of the Berg River. You can gain a good sense of the town's history on a drive along this lovely street.

Main Street North doglegs to the right at Lady Grey Street before continuing as Main Street South. On your left, the **Paarl Museum** (formerly Oude Pastorie) occupies a gorgeous Cape Dutch home built as a parsonage in 1787. In fact, the building itself is of more interest than the collection, which includes odds and ends donated by local families, including silver, glass, and kitchen utensils. A pleasant café at the side of the museum serves tea and snacks at tables on the museum lawns. *303 Main St.,* ☎ *02211/2–2651.* ☛ *R1 adults, children free.* ☉ *Weekdays 8–5, Sat. 10–4.*

From the Paarl Museum walk about 200 yards along Pastorie Street to the **Afrikaans Language Museum** (Afrikaanse Taal-Museum), in the Gideon Malherbe House. It was from here in 1875 that the Society of True Afrikaners launched their campaign to gain widespread acceptance for Afrikaans, hitherto considered a sort of inferior, kitchen Dutch. The museum will be of limited interest to many visitors, since the displays are entirely in Afrikaans. *Pastorie St.,* ☎ *02211/2–3441.* ☛ *Free.* ☉ *Weekdays 9–1 and 2–5.*

Continue along Main Street past the Paarl Publicity Office (*see* Winelands Essentials, *below*) to **Zeederberg Square,** a grassy park bordered by some excellent examples of Cape Dutch, Georgian, and Victorian homes. A little farther down Main Street on the left is the old **Dutch Reformed Church,** a thatched building dating back to 1805. The cemetery contains the tombstones of the Malherbe family, which was instrumental in the campaign to gain official recognition for Afrikaans.

Continue down Main Street until you see signs leading to KWV Cellars. **KWV** is short for *Ko-operatieve Wijnbouwers Vereniging* (Cooperative Winegrowers' Association), which for nearly 80 years has regulated and controlled the Cape wine industry. KWV sells wine and spirits in over 40 countries and more than 30 U.S. states, and its brandies, sherries, and fortified dessert wines regularly garner gold medals at the International Wine & Spirit Competition in London. It also offers one of the most popular—and most crowded—cellar tours in the Winelands. KWV's cellars are the largest in the world, covering some 55 acres. Among the highlights is the famous Cathedral Cellar, with a barrel-vaulted ceiling and giant vats carved with scenes from the history of Cape wine making. In an adjoining cellar, you can see the five largest vats under one roof in the world. The tour begins with a short audiovisual presentation and ends with a tasting of some of KWV's products. *Kohler St.,* ☎ *02211/73007,* ℻ *02211/63–2079.* ☛ *Cellar tour and tasting R6 (reservations essential). Tours weekdays 9, 11, 2:15, and 3:45; Sat. 10:30, Dec.–Apr. also 11 and 3:45.*

30 Return to Main Street and turn left. A sign on your right points the way to the **Afrikaans Language Monument** (Afrikaanse Taalmonument), set high on a hill overlooking Paarl. Like the Voortrekker Monument in Pretoria, this concrete structure holds a special place in the hearts of Afrikaners, who struggled for years to gain acceptance for their language alongside English. The rising curve of the main pillar is supposed to represent the growth and potential of Afrikaans. When it was erected in 1973, the monument was as much a gesture of political victory as a paean to the Afrikaans language. Ironically, it may become the language's memorial. Under the new South Africa, Afrikaans has become just one of 11 official languages and is gradually losing its dominance. The view from the top of the hill is incredible—a panorama that takes in Table Mountain, False Bay, Paarl Valley, and the various mountain ranges of the Winelands. A short, paved walking trail leads around the hillside past impressive fynbos specimens, particularly proteas. ☞ *Free.* ☉ *Daily 8–5.*

Halfway down the hill from the monument is a turnoff onto a dirt road and a sign for the Paarl Mountain Nature Reserve. The dirt road is **Jan Philips Drive,** which runs 11 kilometers (7 miles) along the mountainside, offering tremendous views over the valley. Along the way, it passes the Mill Water Wildflower Garden and the starting points for myriad trails, including hikes up to the great, granite domes of Paarl Mountain. The dirt road rejoins Main Street at the far end of Paarl.

If you don't take Jan Philips Drive, return to Main Street and turn right. Follow the road (now the R101) under the N1 highway and turn right ③ at the sign to **Fairview.** This is one of the few wineries where visitors might feel comfortable taking their families. Children will get a kick out of seeing peacocks roaming the grounds and goats clambering a spiral staircase into a goat tower. Every afternoon at 4 the goats are milked. Fairview produces a superb line of goat cheeses, all of which you can taste gratis. If you want to put together a picnic for the lawn, a deli counter sells sausages and cold meats to complement the estate's wines and cheeses.

Don't let Fairview's sideshows color your judgment about the wines. Charles Back, a member of the family that sells Backsberg (*see below*), is one of the most successful and innovative wine makers in the Cape, and the estate's wines are excellent and often surprising. Back has produced a Shiraz–Merlot blend, a Shiraz–Gamay, a Crouchen–Chardonnay, a Sauvignon Blanc–Chenin blanc, and an excellent Shiraz Reserve. The Sauvignon Blanc–Semillon (Charles Gerard Reserve) is a highly recommended Bordeaux-style blend—it's a pity there aren't more of them. *WR3, off R101,* ☎ *02211/632450,* 𝔽𝔸𝕏 *02211/632591.* ☞ *Wine and cheese tastings free.* ☉ *Weekdays 8–5:30, Sat. 8–1 (8–5 Dec.–Mar.). Cellar tours by appointment.*

Continue down the R101 to its junction with the R44. Turn left and ③ then left again at the Wine Route sign pointing to **Backsberg,** framed by the mountains of the Simonsberg. For 80 years, this winery has been run by the Back family, well known for producing award-winning wines of good value. An unusual feature of the winery is the self-conducted cellar tour. Visitors follow painted lines around the cellars, pausing to watch video monitors that explain the wine-making process. It's a low-pressure introduction to wine making and an ideal starting point for novices. Backsberg produces a comprehensive range of red and white wines, a Méthode Cap Classique sparkling wine, and a fine brandy made from chenin blanc. Their Chardonnay is consistently one of the best made—a rounded, fruity wine that develops well in the bottle for five or more years. Backsberg is the only producer of a Malbec, full of fruity berry flavors; it won a Veritas Gold award in 1994 and is very easy to

drink. *WR1, between R44 and R45,* ☎ *02211/5141,* ℻ *02211/5144.*
☛ *Tastings and cellar tours free.* ⊙ *Weekdays 8–5:30, Sat. 8–1.*

Sports and the Outdoors

Ballooning
Wineland Ballooning (☎ 02211/63–3192) in Paarl makes 1-hour
flights over the Winelands every morning from mid-October until the
end of April, weather permitting. The balloon holds a maximum of
six people, and the trip costs R750 per person. After the flight, everyone returns to the Grand Roche Hotel for a champagne breakfast.

Golf
Fourteen golf courses lie within a 45-minute drive of the center of the
Winelands, and four are situated within the Winelands themselves. All
accept foreign visitors and most rent clubs. Greens fees for 18 holes
average R40–R80. **Paarl Golf Club** (Wemmershoek Rd., ☎ 02211/
632828), surrounded by mountains, is covered with trees and dotted
with water hazards. **Stellenbosch Golf Club** (Strand Rd., ☎ 021/880–
0244) has long, tree-lined fairways that will pose a problem if you don't
hit the ball straight. **Somerset West Country Club** (Rue de Jacqueline,
☎ 024/852–3625) is an easy course with plenty of leeway for errant
tee-shots. **Erinvale–Somerset West** (Lourensford Rd., ☎ 021/852–
7790) is a Gary Player–designed course nestled beneath the Hottentots Holland Mountains.

Horseback Riding
Several riding outfits offer a range of rides for beginners and experts.
Most lead standard 1- and 2-hour rides, as well as more interesting
trips, including moonlight and sunset rides, wine-tasting trails, and even
overnight camping. In Stellenbosch, contact **Rozendal Riding Trails** (☎
082/650–5794) and **Vineyard Horse Trails** (☎ 021/981–2480). In
Franschhoek, contact **Verdun Stables** (☎ 02212/2635).

Dining

by Myrna
Robins

For a description of South African culinary terms, *see* Pleasures & Pastimes *in* Chapter 1. For price ranges, *see* Chart 1 *in* On the Road with
Fodor's.

Somerset West
$$$ **L'Auberge du Paysan.** Come to this little cottage near Somerset West
for classic French cuisine. Tall upholstered chairs, small brass table
lamps, and snowy linen set the tone for dishes from several Gallic
provinces. Specialties include snails Provençale, seafood casserole,
and roast duck with chestnut sauce, but don't dismiss the excellent
Cape mussel soup and East Coast sole with almonds. For dessert, local
port enhances black cherries wrapped in a pancake flambéed in
brandy. Farm lunches are lighter, alfresco affairs on the little patio.
✗ *Raithby Rd., off R45, between Somerset West and Stellenbosch,*
☎ *024/42–2008. Reservations advised. AE, DC, MC, V. Closed Mon.
and 1 month in winter. No dinner Sun.*
$$ **Lady Phillips Tea Garden.** In summer, you need to reserve a table three
weeks in advance at this idyllic country restaurant on the Vergelegen
estate. A good starter is baked goat cheese with roasted beetroot and
an orange vinaigrette. Main courses range from a generous portion of
quiche and salad to Thai-style green chicken curry and smoked ostrich
fillet with couscous. For dessert, try the pecan tart with honey and laven-
der ice cream. ✗ *Vergelegen Estate, Lourensford Rd., Somerset West,*

☎ *024/517–060. Reservations required Nov.–Apr. AE, DC, MC, V. No dinner.*

Stellenbosch

$$$ **Lord Neethling.** In an 18th-century Cape Dutch manor on the historic Neethlingshof estate, this lovely restaurant overlooks a patchwork of vineyards and the Stellenbosch Mountains. Despite the Cape setting, the Continental menu reflects German tastes. Diners can choose straightforward roasts—both ostrich and beef fillet—or less common dishes like Viennese-style chicken and beef in red-wine sauce served with chiles and *spätzle*. A selection of fruity sorbets makes an agreeable summer dessert, but apple strudel and warm vanilla sauce are more likely to hit the spot on rainy winter days. ✕ *Neethlingshof Estate, R310, Stellenbosch,* ☎ *021/883–8966. Reservations advised. AE, DC, MC, V. No dinner Sun.*

$$ **De Volkskombuis.** Former laborers' dwellings now house the People's Kitchen, on the banks of the Eerste River in Stellenbosch. Bare floorboards, low beamed ceilings, and simple furnishings set the scene for a restaurant devoted to traditional Cape cooking. A good starter is a pâté of smoked *snoek* (a popular Cape fish) or biltong. Main courses include chicken or lamb pie, oxtail, and curried *sosaties* served with *geelrys* (rice with turmeric and raisins). You can always count on finding Malay *bredie* and *bobotie*, too. The Cape country sampler offers smaller portions of four traditional specialties. Help yourself from the dessert trolley to trifle, a slice of brandy tart, or *granadilla* (passionfruit) cheesecake. ✕ *Old Strand Rd., Stellenbosch.* ☎ *021/8887–2121. Reservations required. AE, DC, MC, V. No dinner Sun.*

$ **Vinkel en Koljander.** This casual lunch spot occupies an elegant outbuilding on the 300-year-old Lanzerac estate on the outskirts of Stellenbosch. The menu includes light meals, a few indigenous dishes, and a country table groaning with cheeses, pâtés, salads, breads, and pickles. Among the traditional fare, you'll find pickled cold fish and roasted *boerewors* skewered with onion and tomato and served with polenta. Vegetarians will enjoy a flavorful crepe bake of spinach, mozzarella, black mushrooms, aubergine, and tomato. For dessert, consider iced lemon meringue or pecan and honey tart. ✕ *Lanzerac Hotel, Jonkershoek Rd., Stellenbosch,* ☎ *021/887–1132. Reservations advised. AE, DC, MC, V. No dinner.*

Franschhoek

$$$ **Boschendal Restaurant.** Reserve well in advance for the buffet lunch here at one of the Cape's most beautiful and historic wineries. A wide selection of soups, quiches, and pâtés prefaces a bewildering array of cold and hot main dishes, including pickled fish, roasts, and imaginative salads; traditional Cape dishes are well prepared. End with a sampling of local cheeses and preserves or a classic Cape dessert like Malva pudding. ✕ *R310, between Franschhoek and Stellenbosch,* ☎ *02211/41031. Reservations required. AE, DC, MC, V. Closed 3 wks mid-winter. No dinner.*

$$$ **La Maison de Chamonix.** No expense was spared when this run-down farmstead in Franschhoek was transformed into a winery and upscale restaurant a couple of years ago. Today, it's one of the reasons why Franschhoek enjoys a reputation as the gourmet capital of the Cape. Local smoked salmon trout and oysters, warm or cold, make good preludes to duck breast with honeyed apples or loin of venison with red-wine sauce. Desserts range from light sorbet to a sinful frozen chocolate mousse on citrus sauce. A buffet lunch is served Sunday. ✕ *Uitkyk St., Franschhoek,* ☎ *02212/2393. Reservations required. AE, DC, MC, V. Closed Mon., Aug. No dinner Sun.*

$$$ **Le Quartier Français.** In a 19th-century home in Franschhoek, this restau-
★ rant has garnered impressive local and international awards. On sum-
mer nights glass doors open onto a spotlit garden; in winter, a log fire
burns in the hearth. Chef Emily van Sitters and restaurateur John
Huxter describe their cuisine as Cape Provençal, but it's really too nar-
row a term for their creations. Look for such innovative appetizers as
rounds of smoked marlin and angelfish paired with mousseline of
West Coast mussels and ginger sabayon. For a main course, fresh river
salmon is spiced with cumin and pumpkin seed, accompanied by bean
purée, lemongrass sauce, and roasted squash. Mousse flavored with
rooibos (an indigenous herbal tea) and served with crème brûlée makes
a splendid finale. ✗ *16 Huguenot Rd., Franschhoek,* ☎ *02212/2151.
Reservations required in season. AE, DC, MC, V. No dinner Sun.*

$$ **Le Ballon Rouge.** Diners come all the way from Cape Town to savor
the food at this restaurant in a turn-of-the-century guest house in the
center of Franschhoek. Chef-owner Matthew Gordon brings youthful
inspiration and a devotion to fresh ingredients to his contemporary Cape-
Gallic cuisine. Start with one of his vibrant salads, such as grilled goat
cheese dressed with balsamic or pesto vinaigrette, or Franschhoek
salmon trout. Lamb is a specialty, either garlic-studded roasted leg or
a grilled rack with mustard-herb crust. Desserts are equally appealing,
whether fresh berries accompanied by warm sabayon or French lemon
tart with seasonal fruit coulis. ✗ *12 Reservoir St., Franschhoek,* ☎
02212/2651. Reservations required. AE, DC, MC, V.

$$ **Polfyntjies.** The name means "souvenirs," and this restaurant on the
outskirts of Franschhoek will leave you with lingering memories of Cape
traditional fare. Sitting inside the 19th-century farmhouse or outside,
with pleasant views of vines and forests against a mountain backdrop,
you might choose to begin with sustaining *boontjiesop* (dried bean soup).
For a main course, consider *bobotie* or *bredie*. The two most popular
desserts are Malva pudding and milk tart. ✗ *R45, Franschhoek,* ☎
*0221/23217. Reservations advised. AE, DC, MC, V. Closed Mon. No
dinner Sun.–Thurs.*

Paarl

$$$$ **Bosman's.** Set amid the heady opulence of the Grand Roche Hotel in
★ Paarl, this elegant restaurant ranks as one of the country's finest. It
has won several awards both for its Continental cuisine and its extensive
wine list. The level of service is extraordinary, commensurate with the
finest European restaurants, although some diners may find the attention
a little suffocating. The meal begins with a complimentary *amuse-bouche*.
Pan-fried pigeon in a potato nest and crayfish ravioli are typical starters,
as is fish soup with local mussels. Next, Karoo venison comes topped
with an almond and apple crust, Boland salmon trout is grilled, and
there's usually fresh line fish. Spectacularly presented desserts may in-
clude passion-fruit soufflé with sorbets, or banana spring roll with co-
conut ice cream. ✗ *Grand Roche Hotel, Plantasie St., Paarl,* ☎
02211/63–2727. Reservations advised. AE, DC, MC, V.

$$$ **Rheboksloof.** A Victorian homestead is the setting for four-course prix-
fixe dinners at this Paarl winery. Sit on the terrace on balmy evenings
or under the brass chandeliers inside. Chef Harald Bresselschmidt gives
local ingredients Continental treatment. A typical meal might start with
salmon trout tartare with a buttermilk parfait, continue with curried
crayfish soup, and move on to Namibian *roobibok* (venison) with juniper berry sauce as the main course and cream cheese soufflé with
passion-fruit sauce for dessert. A different estate wine accompanies
each course. Lunch is less formal and features a small à la carte menu
starring such dishes as pan-fried salmon trout on broccoli fondue or

roast duck breast with a litchi and coriander sauce. ✗ *WR8*, ☎ *02211/63–8606. Reservations advised. AE, DC, MC, V. Closed Wed. No dinner Tues.*

$$$ **Roggeland.** For an unforgettable Cape experience, make a beeline for
★ this glorious Cape Dutch manor house on a farm outside Paarl. Chef Topsi Venter, doyenne of the South African culinary scene, is as renowned as a raconteur as she is for her innovative country fare. Her menus change daily, she uses only ingredients grown within a 6-mile radius of the farm, and the kitchen contains neither freezer nor microwave oven. Meals are long, languid rituals, whether it's an al fresco lunch in the garden or a four-course dinner in the 18th-century dining room. An evening might start with baby leeks sparked with fresh ginger and coriander, accompanied by sesame-coated oyster mushrooms. A second course of red radish soup with pink peppercorns may be followed by marinated eye of silverside beef, roasted with pickled green peppers and parsnip chips. Finish with a plum and almond meringue bake. A different wine, included in the price, accompanies each course. ✗ *Roggeland Rd., North Paarl,* ☎ *02211/682–501. Reservations required. AE, DC, MC, V.*

Lodging

The Winelands are sufficiently compact that you can make one hotel your touring base for your entire stay. Stellenbosch and Paarl offer the most flexibility, situated close to dozens of wineries and restaurants, as well as the major highways to Cape Town. Franschhoek is comparatively isolated, which many visitors consider a blessing. Tourist offices (*see* Important Addresses and Numbers *in* Winelands Essentials, *below*) have extensive information on bed-and-breakfasts and self-catering options, many of which are less expensive than hotels and often give you a more personal taste of life in the Winelands.

For price ranges, *see* Chart 2(A) *in* On the Road with Fodor's.

Somerset West

$$$ **Willowbrook Lodge.** Although it doesn't lie in the heart of the traditional Winelands, this lodge makes a terrific base for exploring the entire southwestern Cape, including the peninsula, the Winelands, and the Overberg. The lodge lies hidden among beautiful gardens that extend down to the Lourens River; in the distance, the peaks of the Helderberg are visible. It's a very peaceful place—with no TV in the rooms—and guests enjoy a real sense of privacy. Rooms are large and comfortable, each with its own sliding door opening onto the gardens. ⊞ *Morgenster Ave. (mailing address: Box 1892), Somerset West 7129,* ☎ *024/513–759,* ℻ *024/514–152. 12 rooms with bath. Restaurant, bar, pool. No children under 12. AE, DC, MC, V.*

Stellenbosch

$$$ **Lanzerac Hotel.** For 30 years, this hotel outside Stellenbosch has been a byword in South Africa for luxury. What first strikes you is the sheer beauty of the place: a classic Cape Dutch manor house flanked by the rolling vineyards and mountains of the Jonkershoek Valley. Unfortunately, the house itself has been turned into a private residence and is now off-limits to guests. Nevertheless, the Lanzerac remains a delightful hotel. Guest rooms, in white cottages framing the main house, have a summery Mediterranean feel, thanks to the use of Spanish tile and the creative juxtaposition of rich Cape antiques and bright, colorful fabrics. The overall effect is tasteful and cheery. The hotel is also home to one of the best restaurants in the Winelands, Vinkel en Koljander (*see* Dining, *above*). ⊞ *Jonkershoek Rd., 1 km (½ mi) from Stel-*

lenbosch (mailing address: Box 4, Stellenbosch 7599), ☏ *021/887–1132,* ℻ *021/887–2310. 30 rooms with bath. 2 restaurants, bar, room service, pool. Breakfast included. AE, DC, MC, V.*

$$ **d'Ouwe Werf Country Inn.** Another national monument, this attractive 1802 inn is thought to be the oldest in South Africa. From the street, guests enter the original living room, a beautiful space enlivened by wood floors, a lofty beamed ceiling, and elegant antiques. The hotel is divided into two parts: the old inn with luxury rooms on its Georgian second story and a new wing with more standard rooms. All luxury rooms are furnished with antiques, including four-poster beds, draped sash windows, and bronze bathroom fittings. The standard rooms have reproductions only. A lovely coffee garden in a brick courtyard shaded by trellised vines serves meals and drinks throughout the day. ☏ *30 Church St., Stellenbosch 7600,* ☏ *021/887–1608 or 021/887–4608,* ℻ *021/887–4626. 25 rooms with bath. Restaurant, coffee garden, room service, pool. Breakfast included. AE, DC, MC, V.*

$$ **110 Dorp Street Guest House.** On Stellenbosch's most historic street, this tiny inn occupies an 1811 Georgian home that is also a national monument. Owners Frikkie and Johlene van Deventer go out of their way to make guests feel welcome, whether it's greeting new arrivals with sherry or extending invitations for evening drinks or an impromptu barbecue. The house has beautiful hardwood floors and high ceilings, but otherwise the decor doesn't match the level of service. The rooms, decorated in period style, are comfortable, well-equipped, and large, but they lack polish and style. For the price, though, you can't complain. ☏ *110 Dorp St., Stellenbosch 7600,* ☏ *and* ℻ *021/883–3555. 5 rooms with bath. Breakfast included. MC, V.*

Franschhoek

$$$ **Le Quartier Français.** In the center of Franschhoek, this classy guest house is a Winelands favorite. Separated from the village's main drag by a courtyard bistro and a superb restaurant, the guest house is notable for its sense of privacy and peace. Rooms in two-story whitewashed cottages face onto a pool deck and central garden exploding with flowers. Decor is low-key, with rustic furniture, sponge-painted walls, and small fireplaces. Upstairs rooms have timber beams and mountain views, but they're hot in summer. Rooms have TVs and ceiling fans, but no air-conditioning. ☏ *Corner of Berg and Wilhelmina Sts. (mailing address: Box 237), Franschhoek 7690,* ☏ *02212/2151,* ℻ *02212/3105. 14 rooms with bath. Restaurant, bar, bistro, pool. AE, DC, MC, V.*

$ **Le Ballon Rouge Guest House.** In an old homestead in the center of Franschhoek village, this colonial-style guest house offers good value for money. Rooms open onto a veranda directly fronting the street—ideal for watching the world go by—and are small and feminine, with pretty floral fabrics, brass bedsteads, and country armoires. All have TVs, air-conditioning, and ceiling fans. ☏ *12 Reservoir St. (mailing address: Box 344), Franschhoek 7690,* ☏ *and* ℻ *02212/2651. 7 rooms with bath. Restaurant, room service, pool. Breakfast included. AE, DC, MC, V.*

Paarl

$$$$ **Grande Roche.** A member of the prestigious Relais & Chateaux chain,
★ this establishment can stake a claim as the best hotel in South Africa. In a gorgeous Cape Dutch manor house that dates from the mid-18th century, the hotel sits amid acres of vines beneath Paarl Mountain, overlooking the valley and the Drakenstein Mountains. Rooms (all suites) are housed either in the historical buildings—slave quarters, stables,

and wine cellar—or in attractive, new terrace buildings constructed in traditional Cape Dutch style. Rooms are a tasteful mix of the modern and the old: Reed ceilings and thatch comfortably coexist with heated towel racks and air-conditioning. Despite the hotel's African heritage, the atmosphere is very Continental. The staff, many of whom trained in Europe, outnumber the guests two to one, and offer a level of service extremely rare in South Africa. ☎ *Plantasie St. (mailing address: Box 6038), Paarl 7622,* ☎ *02211/63–2727,* FAX *02211/63–2220. 29 suites with bath. Restaurant, bar, room service, 2 pools, tennis, exercise room. Breakfast included. No children under 10. AE, DC, MC, V.*

$$$$ **Roggeland Country House.** Dating back to 1693, this historic farm is
★ one of the most delightful lodgings in the Winelands. The setting in Dal Josaphat Valley is breathtaking, with stunning views of the craggy Drakenstein Mountains. Guest rooms in restored farm buildings have reed ceilings, country dressers, and mosquito nets (not just for effect). The 1779 manor house, which contains the dining room and lounge, is a masterpiece of Cape Dutch architecture. Don't stay here if you don't like animals: Horses nuzzle you while you take tea on the lawns and a motley collection of dogs roams the estate. Dinner and breakfast in the fine restaurant (*see Dining, above*) are included. ☎ *Roggeland Rd. (mailing address: Box 7210), Northern Paarl 7623,* ☎ *2211/68–2501,* FAX *2211/68–2113. 8 rooms with bath. Restaurant, pool. Breakfast, dinner, and wine included. AE, DC, MC, V.*

$ **Rodeberg Lodge.** Right on Main Street in the heart of Paarl, this homey inn is one of the best examples of Victorian architecture in town. There's nothing flashy about the place—its main attraction is the personal attention of owners Karl and Antoinette Rode. Rooms are simply furnished, with rustic pine furniture, plain bedspreads, and hardwood floors. Downstairs rooms, with their high ceilings and large windows, are a better choice than those upstairs, which feel as if they're in an attic. If you're staying a few days, opt for the self-catering cottage in the pretty gardens at the back of the house. None of the rooms has TV. ☎ *74 Main St. (mailing address: Box 2611), Paarl 7620,* ☎ *02211/633–202,* FAX *02211/633–203. 6 rooms and 1 cottage, all with bath. Continental breakfast included. AE, DC, MC, V.*

Winelands Essentials

Arriving and Departing

BY CAR

From Cape Town it shouldn't take more than 30 minutes to Somerset West, 45 minutes to Stellenbosch and Paarl, and an hour to Franschhoek. If you're heading to Paarl or Franschhoek, it's a straight shot up the N1 before the turnoff onto the R45. To reach Somerset West, take the N2 to the R44/Somerset West turnoff and then follow the signs onto Main Street, the town's main drag. If you continue straight up the R44 instead, you come to Stellenbosch. The quickest way to reach Stellenbosch, however, is to leave the N2 at the Eerste Rivier/Stellenbosch exit and follow the R310 straight into town.

BY TRAIN

Cape Metro trains run from Cape Town to Stellenbosch and Paarl, but locals complain about theft and muggings on the journey. Several trains run during the morning and evening commute, but otherwise you may wait for hours. Trains for the Winelands depart from Platforms 9 and 10 in Cape Town and take about an hour (☎ 021/405–2991 for information).

Getting Around
BY BICYCLE
As long as you stick to the valley floors, you shouldn't have too many problems touring the Winelands on a bike, although summers here are very, very hot. You can rent mountain bikes for R40–R50 a day. In Stellenbosch, contact **Stumble Inn** (☎ 021/887–4049) or **Village Cycles** (☎ 021/883–8593); in Franschhoek, call **Winelands Cycle Tours** (☎ 02212/3195).

BY CAR
Traveling around the Winelands in your own car is a snap. The whole Winelands region is quite small, and it's almost impossible to get lost. To help you even further, most of the wineries, hotels, and major attractions are clearly signposted with large, brown road signs. If you've arrived in the Winelands without a car, call **Avis** (☎ 021/887–0492), **Budget** (☎ 021/883–9103), or **Imperial** (☎ 021/883–8140) in Stellenbosch; in Paarl contact **Avante Car Hire** (272 Main St., ☎ 02211/25869) or **Wine Route Rent-a-Car** (366 Main St., ☎ 02211/28513).

BY TAXI
Roland's Taxis (☎ 021/886–5808) in Stellenbosch will provide a car and driver for up to four people to tour the Winelands for a whole day (9:30–5) for a flat rate of R300–R400. If there are more than two of you, this may work out cheaper than going on a large tour, and you get the added bonus of flexibility. In Paarl, contact **Paarl Radio Taxis** (☎ 02211/2–5671).

Guided Tours
Vineyard Ventures (5 Hanover Rd., Fresnaye, Cape Town 8001, ☎ 021/434–8888) is the best of several companies offering tours of the Winelands. Rita Will and Gillian Stoltzman are knowledgeable and passionate about wine, and will tailor tours to your specific interest. You can also opt for one of their standard one-day tours. All tours feature wine-tastings at top cellars as well as an excellent lunch.

If your interest in wine is limited, you're better off taking a general-interest tour of the Winelands that throws in only a couple of wine-tastings. In the Winelands, contact **Travelmark** (☎ 02211/21994) or **Vintage Cape Tours** (☎ 02211/26092), both based in Paarl. Otherwise, call one of the big Cape Town operators like **Hylton Ross, Ideal Tours,** or **Mother City Tours** (*see* Cape Town Essentials *in* Chapter 4).

SCENIC FLIGHTS
The owner of **Rodeberg Lodge** in Paarl (*see* Lodging, *above*) will take up to three people on scenic flights over the Winelands for R750 an hour. For about R500, **Cape Eco Safaris** (☎ 02211/63–8334) offers 30-minute flights over Paarl and the surrounding area for two to three adults. **Civair** (☎ 021/419–5182) offers 2½-hour helicopter tours of the Winelands and part of the Peninsula for R600 per person, including lunch at a winery.

Important Addresses and Numbers
EMERGENCIES
Dial 10111 for the **police,** 10177 for an **ambulance.**

VISITOR INFORMATION
Franschhoek Vallée Tourisme. *Main Rd., Franschhoek,* ☎ *02212/3603,* FAX *02212/3105.* ☉ *Weekdays 9–5, Sat. 10–4, Sun. 10:30–2.*

Paarl Publicity Office. *216 Main St., Paarl,* ☎ *02211/24842,* FAX *02211/23841.* ☉ *Weekdays 9–5, Sat. 9–1, Sun. 10–1.*

Somerset West Tourist Information Bureau. *11 Victoria St., Somerset West,* ☎ *024/51–4022.* ⊙ *Weekdays 8:30–1 and 2–4:30, Sat. 9–noon.*

Stellenbosch Tourist Bureau. *36 Market St., Stellenbosch,* ☎ *021/883–3584,* FAX *021/883–8017.* ⊙ *Weekdays 8–5:30, Sat. 9–5, Sun. 9:30–3.*

THE OVERBERG

Overberg means "Over the Mountains" in Afrikaans, an apt name for this remote region at the bottom of the continent, separated from the rest of the Cape by mountains. Before 19th-century engineers blasted a route through the Hottentots Holland range, the Overberg developed in comparative isolation. To this day, it possesses a wild emptiness far removed from the settled valleys of the Winelands.

It's a land of immense contrasts, and if you're planning a trip along the Garden Route (*see* Chapter 6), you would be well advised to add the Overberg to your itinerary. The coastal drive from Gordon's Bay to Hermanus is as beautiful as anything in the Cape—an unfolding panorama of deserted beaches, pounding surf, and fractured granite mountains. Once you pass Hermanus and head out onto the windswept plains leading to Cape Agulhas, you have to search harder for the Overberg's riches. Towns are few and far between, the countryside comprising an expanse of wheat fields and sheep pastures. The occasional reward of the drive is a coastline of sublime beauty. Enormous stretches of dunes and unspoiled beaches extend for miles. Unfortunately, no roads parallel the ocean, and you must constantly divert inland before heading to another part of the coast.

Hermanus is the best place in South Africa to watch the annual migration of southern right whales, but you can spot the great creatures all along the coast between July and November, when they sometimes come within 100 feet of shore. Spring is also the best time to see the Overberg's wild flowers, although the region's profusion of coastal and montane fynbos is beautiful year-round.

The upper part of the Overberg, north of the N2 highway, is more like the Winelands, with 18th- and 19th-century towns sheltered in the lee of rocky mountains. Here the draws are apple orchards, inns, and hiking trails that wind through the mountains. The historic towns of Swellendam and Greyton make the most logical touring bases.

Exploring

Towns and sights on this tour are marked on the Western Cape and Namaqualand map.

The following driving tour will take three to four days. For a shorter trip, focus on the splendors of the coastal route from Gordon's Bay to Hermanus, then head north toward the Winelands.

Cape Town to Hermanus

Leave Cape Town via the N2. After Somerset West, take the turnoff to the R44 and **Gordon's Bay,** an attractive resort built on a steep mountain slope overlooking the vast expanse of False Bay. You can often see whales and their calves in False Bay in October and November.

From Gordon's Bay, the road hugs the mountainside, slipping between the craggy peaks of the Hottentots Holland Mountains and the sea far below. The coastal drive between Gordon's Bay and Hermanus is one of the country's best, particularly if you take the time to follow some of the dirt roads leading down to the sea from the highway.

The road passes tiny Rooielsbaai (pronounced roy-els-by) then cuts inland for a few kilometers. A turnoff leads to **Pringle Bay,** a collection of holiday homes sprinkled across the fynbos. The village has little to offer other than a beautiful wide beach (check out the sign warning of quicksand). If you continue through Pringle Bay, the tar road soon gives way to gravel. This road, badly corrugated in patches, runs around the looming pinnacle of **Hangklip** and along a deserted stretch of magnificent beach and dunes to Betty's Bay (*see below*).

If you don't fancy the gravel road, return to the R44 and continue 1.6 kilometers (1 mile) to the turnoff to Stony Point, on the outskirts of Betty's Bay. Follow Porter Drive for 3.2 kilometers (2 miles) until you reach a sign marked MOOI HAWENS and a smaller sign picturing a penguin. Follow the penguin signs to reach a **colony of jackass penguins,** one of only two mainland colonies in southern Africa. The colony lies about 600 yards from the parking area along a rocky coastal path. Along the way, you pass the concrete remains of tank stands, reminders of the days when Betty's Bay was a big whaling station. The jackass penguin is endangered, so the colony has been fenced off as protection against man, dogs, and other predators. This particular colony was once savaged by a leopard.

Return to Porter Drive and turn right to rejoin the R44. Back on the main road, continue another mile to the **Harold Porter National Botanical Garden,** a 440-acre nature reserve in the heart of the coastal fynbos, where the Cape Floral Kingdom is at its richest. The profusion of plants supports 78 species of birds and a wide range of small mammals, including large troops of baboons. You couldn't ask for a more fantastic setting, cradled between the Atlantic and the towering peaks of the 3,000-foot Kogelberg range. Walking trails wind through the reserve and into the mountains via Disa and Leopard's kloofs, which echo with the sound of waterfalls and running streams. Back at the main buildings, a pleasant restaurant serves light meals and teas. *Box 35, Betty's Bay 7141,* ☎ *02823/29311.* ☛ *R2 adults, R1 students and senior citizens.* ☼ *Daily 8–6.*

The small town of **Kleinmond** ("small mouth") lies another 10 kilometers (6 miles) along the coast. The town itself is nothing special—it has a couple of restaurants and guest houses—but it presides over a magnificent stretch of shoreline, backed by the mountains of the Palmietberg. At press time, the **Kleinmond Coastal Nature Reserve,** a 990-acre area of fynbos that extends to the sea, was closed, but the beach and small lagoon that front the reserve are still accessible from the Palmiet Caravan Park. Even more impressive are the 10 kilometers (6 miles) of sandy beach that fringe Sandown Bay, at the eastern edge of town. Much of the beach is nothing more than a sandbar, separating the Atlantic from the huge lagoon formed by the Bot River. Swift currents make bathing risky.

The R44 cuts inland to circumnavigate the Bot River lagoon. Ten kilometers (6 miles) past Kleinmond, the road comes to a junction; turn right onto the R43 toward Hermanus and cross the Bot River.

The R43 swings eastward around the mountains, past the small artists' colony of Onrus. **Onrus Galerie** (Van Blommestein Rd., Onrus, ☎ 0283/62525) has one of the best and most unusual collections of South African paintings, sculpture, glass, ceramics, and jewelry in the Cape. The gallery doubles as a coffee shop, serving freshly brewed coffee and cakes.

Less than 2 kilometers (1 mile) farther is the turnoff to the R320, which leads through the vineyards and orchards of the scenic Hemel-en-Aarde (Heaven on Earth) Valley and over Shaw's Pass to Caledon. **Hamilton Russell Vineyards** lies a short way down this rutted road, in an attractive thatched building overlooking a small dam. This winery produces some of the best wine in South Africa. The Pinot Noir won loud acclaim from Frank Prial of the *New York Times,* and is one of the two best produced in the country. The Chardonnay comes closer to the French style of Chardonnay than any other Cape wine, with lovely fruit and a touch of lemon rind and toast. It will be at its best in 1–2 years. *Off R320,* ☎ *0283/23595.* ☛ *Tastings free.* ☺ *Weekdays 9–5, Sat. 9–1.*

Return to the R43 and drive 3.2 kilometers (2 miles) to Hermanus. On the outskirts of town, keep watch on your left side for a pair of white gateposts set well back from the road, painted with the words ROTARY WAY—if you pass the turnoff to the New Harbour you've gone ★ too far. The **Rotary Way** is a scenic drive that climbs along the spine of the mountains above Hermanus, affording incredible views of the town, Walker Bay, and Hemel-en-Aarde Valley, as well as some of the area's beautiful fynbos. It's a highlight of a trip to the Overberg and you shouldn't miss it. The Rotary Way turns to dirt after a few kilometers and becomes impassable to all but four-wheel-drive vehicles about a mile after that. The entire mountainside is laced with wonderful walking trails, and many of the scenic lookouts have benches if you'd rather sit and soak in the beauty.

Return to the R43 and drive into **Hermanus,** a popular holiday resort and the major coastal town in the Overberg. If you're looking for a base from which to explore the region, Hermanus is your best bet. Restaurants and shops line the streets, and the town retains a pleasant holiday feel—having been spared the worst excesses of developers with more money than taste. The town becomes packed during the Christmas school holidays, though, so head elsewhere if you want solitude.

Just a few kilometers from town, pristine beaches extend as far as the eye can see, and the Kleinriviersberg provides a breathtaking backdrop to the town. Hermanus sits atop a long line of cliffs, which makes it the best place in South Africa to watch the annual whale migration from shore. An 11-kilometer (7-mile) **cliff walk** allows whale-watchers to follow the whales, which often come within 100 feet of the cliffs as they move along the coastline. In addition, a whale-crier, complete with sandwich board and kelp horn, disseminates information on whale sightings.

Originally, Hermanus was a whaling center. The **Old Harbour Museum,** in a small building at the old stone fishing basin, displays some of the horrific harpoons used to lance the giants. There are also exhibits on fishing techniques, local marine life, and angling records. Photographs of old Hermanus and some of its legendary fishermen are also displayed at the PFV Old Harbour Museum Photographic Exhibition, in the white building next to the harbor parking lot. *Old Harbour, Hermanus.* ☛ *R2 adults, R1 children.* ☺ *Mon.–Sat. 9–1 and 2–5.*

On the road east out of town, watch for a small sign to the **Fernkloof Nature Reserve.** This 3,600-acre reserve extends back into the mountains of the Kleinriviersberg and contains more than 1,050 species of montane coastal fynbos, including several species of protea and 48 different types of erica. Walks ranging from 20 minutes to two hours crisscross the reserve and offer great views over the bay. *Fir Ave., Hermanus.* ☎ *0283/21122.* ✏ *Free.* ☾ *Daily sunrise–sunset.*

East from Hermanus

From Hermanus the R43 continues eastward, hugging the strip of land between the mountains and the **Klein River Lagoon.** The lagoon is popular with skiers, boaters, and anglers. You can hire a variety of boats down at Prawn Flats, including motor boats, canoes, and board sailers; expect to pay R20–R40 an hour depending on the type of boat. It's also possible to take a boat up the Klein River into the bird sanctuary to watch the birds roost at sunset. Contact **The Boathouse** (Prawn Flats, off R43, ☎ 0283/770925).

Stanford lies 24 kilometers (15 miles) from Hermanus on the banks of the Klein River. It's a pleasant hamlet, with a decent hotel and some shops, but little else. Turn left at Stanford onto the R326 to Salmonsdam and Riviersonderend. The road runs through rolling sheep country and wheat lands cut by rocky gorges. Along the way is the turnoff to the **Salmonsdam Nature Reserve,** a mountainous area of forests, deep valleys, waterfalls, and fynbos. Continue on the R326 to a four-way junction; turn right onto the R316 and drive through the town of Napier to Bredasdorp.

Bredasdorp is a sleepy agricultural town that has a certain charm—as long as you don't catch it on a Sunday afternoon, when everything's closed and a general air of ennui pervades the brassy, windswept streets.

Housed in a converted church and rectory, the **Bredasdorp Museum** displays an extensive collection of items salvaged from the hundreds of ships that have gone down in the stormy waters of the Cape. In addition to usual cannons and figureheads, the museum displays a surprising array of undamaged household items rescued from the sea, including entire dining room sets, sideboards, china, and phonographs. *Independent St.,* ☎ *02841/41240.* ✏ *R2 adults, R1 children.* ☾ *Mon.–Thurs. 9–4:45, Fri. 9–3:45, Sat. 9–12:45, Sun. 11–12:30.*

From Bredasdorp it's just 37 kilometers (23 miles) through rolling farmland to Cape Agulhas. Although it's the southernmost tip of the African continent, it's less exciting in reality than in concept, so unless reaching the bottom of the continent has some great personal meaning, give it a miss, and skip down to Waenhuiskrans.

On the way to Agulhas you pass through **Struisbaai** (pronounced strayce-bye), a forgettable little town on an unforgettable bay. As far as the eye can see, rolling white dunes enfold turquoise waters polka-dotted with colorful fishing boats. Few places in the world can claim beaches this splendid.

From Struisbaai drive 6½ kilometers (4 miles) through the small settlement of L'Agulhas to the lighthouse that stands sentinel over the Cape. Modeled after the noted Pharos of classical Alexandria, the 1849 Agulhas lighthouse is the second-oldest in South Africa. It's home to the **Agulhas Lighthouse Museum,** which houses an interesting collection of lenses and bulbs, as well as photos and descriptions of famous lighthouses from around the world. You can climb steep stairs and ladders to the top of the lighthouse for a great view over the Cape. Downstairs, a pleasant tearoom dishes up breakfast and light meals. ☎ *02846/56078.* ✏ *R2 adults, R1 children.* ☾ *Tues.–Sat. 9:30–5, Sun. 10–1:30.*

Take the dirt road around the lighthouse and follow the signs to **Cape Agulhas.** A stone marker and flimsy sign mark the southernmost spot on the continent and the point where the Atlantic and Indian Oceans meet. Without the signs, you would never know you were perched at the bottom of Africa. The peninsula is flat, rocky, and undistinguished. It possesses none of the scenic beauty or emphatic finality that makes Cape Point south of Cape Town such a magical place (*see* Chapter 4). At Cape Point, you feel like you're at the end of the earth; at Cape Agulhas, you find yourself wondering where you can get a good cup of tea.

★ Return to Bredasdorp and turn right on the R316 to reach **Waenhuiskrans,** an isolated holiday village set on another of South Africa's most awe-inspiring stretches of coastline. The village is known among English-speaking South Africans as Arniston, after a British ship of that name that was wrecked on the Agulhas reef in 1815. Beautiful beaches, water that assumes Caribbean shades of blue, and mile after mile of towering white dunes attract anglers and holiday-makers alike. Only the frequent southeasters that blow off the sea are likely to put a damper on your enjoyment. For 200 years, a community of Cape Malay fishermen and their families has eked out a living here, setting sail each day in small fishing boats. Today, their village has been named a national monument, and it's a pleasure to wander around the thatched cottages of this still-vibrant community. The village has expanded enormously in the last 10 years, thanks to the construction of a host of holiday homes. Fortunately, much of the new architecture blends effectively with the whitewashed simplicity of the original cottages.

Waenhuiskrans means "wagon-house cliff" in Afrikaans, and the village takes its name from a **vast cave** a mile south of town that is theoretically large enough to house several wagons and their spans of oxen. Signs point the way over the dunes to the cave, which is accessible only at low tide. You need shoes to protect your feet from the sharp rocks, but wear something you don't mind getting wet.

Again, retrace your way to Bredasdorp. This time, take the R319 toward Swellendam. The road runs through mile after mile of rolling farmland, populated by sheep, cattle, and an occasional ostrich. In the far distance loom the mountains of the Langeberg. After 64 kilometers (40 miles), turn right onto the N2 highway. Continue for another 15 kilometers (9 miles) before turning right to the **Bontebok National Park.** Covering just 6,880 acres of coastal fynbos, this is one of the smallest of South Africa's national parks. Don't expect to see big game here— the park contains no elephant, lion, or rhino. What you will see are bontebok, a graceful white-faced antelope nearly exterminated by hunters earlier in the century, as well as red hartebeest, Cape grysbok, steenbok, duiker, and the endangered Cape mountain zebra. Two short walking trails start at the campsite next to the Breede River. *Box 149, Swellendam 6740,* ☎ *0291/42735,* ⊠ *0291/42626.* ☛ *R10 per vehicle.* ☺ *Oct.–Apr. daily 8–7, May–Sept. daily 8–6.*

Return to the junction with the N2 and cross the highway into beau-
★ tiful **Swellendam,** lying in the shadow of the imposing Langeberg mountains. Founded in 1745, it is the third-oldest town in South Africa and many of its historic buildings have been elegantly restored. Even on a casual drive along the main street, you'll see a number of lovely Cape Dutch homes, with their traditional whitewashed walls, gables, and thatched roofs.

★ The centerpiece of the town's historical past is the **Drostdy Museum,** a collection of buildings dating back to the town's earliest days. The Drostdy was built in 1747 by the Dutch East India Company to serve as the residence of the Landdrost, the magistrate who presided over the district. The building is furnished in a style that was common in the mid-19th century. A path leads through the Drostdy kitchen gardens to Mayville, an 1855 middle-class home that blends elements of Cape Dutch and Cape Georgian architecture. Across Swellengrebel Street stand the old jail and the Ambagswerf (closed Sun.), an outdoor exhibit of tools used by the town's blacksmiths, wainwrights, coopers, and tanners. *18 Swellengrebel St.,* ☎ *0291/41138.* ☛ *R3 adults, 50¢ children.* ☉ *Weekdays 9–4:45, weekends and holidays 10–3:45.*

Swellendam's **Dutch Reform Church** is an imposing white edifice, built in 1911 in an eclectic style. The gables are baroque, the windows Gothic, the cupola vaguely eastern, and the steeple a replica of one in Belgium. Surprisingly, all the elements work together wonderfully. Inside is an interesting tiered amphitheater, with banks of curving wood pews facing the pulpit and organ. *Voortrek St.,* ☎ *0291/41917. Services Jan.–Nov. at 10 and 6, Dec. at 9 and 7.*

If you'd like to get your feet on the ground and breathe some clean local air, take a hike in the **Marloth Nature Reserve,** in the Langeberg mountains above town. Five easy walks, ranging from one to four hours, explore some of the mountain gorges. An office at the entrance to the reserve has trail maps and hiking information.

From Swellendam return to the N2 and turn right toward Cape Town. The road sweeps through rich, rolling cropland that extends to the base of the Langeberg mountains. A few kilometers after the town of Riviersonderend (pronounced riff-*ears*-onder-ent), turn right onto the R406, a good gravel road that leads 32 kilometers (20 miles) to the village of **Greyton,** in the lee of the Riviersonderend Mountains. This charming village, filled with white, thatched cottages and quiet lanes, is a popular weekend retreat for Capetonians as well as a permanent home for many retirees. The village offers almost nothing in the way of traditional sights, but it's a great base for walks into the surrounding mountains (*see below*). Even if you don't walk, Greyton is a pleasant place to pause for lunch or tea (*see* Dining and Lodging, *below*).

After Greyton, the R406 becomes paved. Drive 5 kilometers (3 miles) to the turnoff to **Genadendal,** a Moravian Mission station founded in 1737 to educate the Khoikhoi and convert them to Christianity. Walking the streets of this impoverished hamlet today, it's difficult to comprehend the major role this mission played in the early history of South Africa. In the late 18th century it was the second-largest settlement after Cape Town, and its Khoikhoi craftsmen produced the finest silver cutlery and woodwork in the country. Some of the first written works in Afrikaans were printed here, and the colored community greatly influenced the development of Afrikaans as it is heard today. None of this went over well with the white population. By 1909, new legislation prohibited "colored" ownership of land, and in 1926 the Department of Public Education closed the settlement's teacher's training college, arguing that "coloreds" were better employed on neighboring farms. Genadendal began a long slide into obscurity until 1994, when President Nelson Mandela renamed his official residence Genadendal.

In town, you can walk the streets of the settlement and tour the historic buildings facing Church Square. Genadendal is still a mission station, and the German missionaries will often show interested visitors around. Of particular interest is the **Genadendal Mission Museum,** spread through 15 rooms in three buildings. The museum collection, the only one in South Africa to be named a national cultural treasure, includes unique household implements, books, tools, and musical instruments, among them the country's oldest pipe organ. Wall displays examine mission life in the Cape in the 18th and 19th centuries, focusing on the early missionaries' work with the Khoikhoi. Unfortunately, many of the displays are in Afrikaans. *Off R406,* ☎ *02822/8582.* ☛ *R2 adults, R1 children.* ⊙ *Mon.–Thurs. 9–1 and 2–5, Fri. 9–3:30, Sat. 9–noon.*

To head back toward Cape Town, follow the R406 to the N2. After the town of Bot River, the road leaves the wheat fields and climbs into the mountains. It's lovely country, full of rock and pine forest interspersed with orchards. **Sir Lowry's Pass** serves as the gateway to Cape Town and the Winelands, a magnificent breach in the mountains that opens to reveal the curving expanse of False Bay, the long ridge of the peninsula, and, in the distance, Table Mountain.

Off the Beaten Path

About 45 kilometers (32 miles) west of Bredasdorp and accessible only by dirt road, **Elim** is a Moravian mission village founded in 1824. Little has changed in the last hundred years: Simple whitewashed cottages line the few streets, and the settlement's colored residents all belong to the Moravian Church. The whole village has been declared a national monument. The easiest access is via the R317, off the R319 between Cape Agulhas and Bredasdorp.

De Hoop Nature Reserve (☎ 02922/700) is a huge conservation area covering 88,900 acres of isolated coastal terrain as well as a marine reserve extending 5 kilometers (3 miles) out to sea. Massive white-sand dunes, mountains, and rare lowland fynbos are home to eland, bontebok, and Cape mountain zebra, as well as over 250 bird species. Visitors can rent self-catering cottages. Access is via the dirt road between Bredasdorp and Malgas.

Pont Malgas, past De Hoop Nature Reserve on the dirt road from Bredasdorp, is the last hand-drawn car ferry in the country. Two operators use brute strength to pull the ferry across the Breede River. The setting is beautiful, and the ride is unusual. *Fare R6 per vehicle.*

Sports and the Outdoors

Hiking

Walking is one of the major attractions of the Overberg, and almost every town and nature reserve offers a host of trails ranging in length from a few minutes to an entire day. For detailed information about these trails, contact the local visitor information offices (*see* Important Addresses and Numbers *in* Overberg Essentials, *below*).

A fabulous one-day hike is the **Boesmanskloof Trail,** 32 kilometers (20 miles) through the Riviersonderend Mountains from Greyton to the exquisite hamlet of McGregor. McGregor has several charming guest houses and cottages where you can spend the night, but you need to make transport arrangements to get back. Serious hikers should also consider the **Genadendal Hiking Trail,** a two-day hike that wends 24 kilometers (15 miles) through the Riviersonderend Mountains, beginning at the Moravian Mission Church, with one night spent on a farm. Permits are required for both trails. Contact the manager, Vrolijkheid

Nature Conservation Station, Private Bag X614, Robertson 6705 (☎ 02353/621).

Horseback Riding

Greyton Scenic Horse Trails and Riding Centre (82 Main St., Greyton 7233, ☎ 028/254–9009) takes visitors, including novices, on 90-minute rides through the beautiful hills and mountains surrounding Greyton.

Dining and Lodging

For price ranges, *see* Charts 1 and 2(A) *in* On the Road with Fodor's.

Greyton

DINING AND LODGING

$$ **Greyton Lodge.** Built in 1882 as a trading store, this comfortable guest house looks right at home amid the whitewashed Cape homes of historic Greyton. The focal point of the hotel is the tea garden, filled with roses and fruit trees, and dominated by the sheer walls of the Riviersonderend Mountains behind. The standard rooms are small; you're better off taking the pricier deluxe rooms decorated in country style with light floral draperies and brass or antique bedsteads. Only some rooms have phones and none has TV. The lunch menu is inexpensive, and features tried-and-true dishes like ploughman's lunch, steak and chips, salads, and quiche. ⌘ *46 Main St. (mailing address: Box 50), Greyton 7233, ☎ 028/254–9876, ⅁ 028/254–9672. 17 rooms with bath. Restaurant, bar, room service, pool. Breakfast included. AE, DC, MC, V.*

$$ **Post House.** Originally the village post office and now a national monument, this 136-year-old country inn has loads of charm. The rooms, all named after Beatrix Potter characters, face onto a lovely lawn where guests can relax over drinks or tea. The rooms themselves, furnished in Edwardian country style, are dark and in need of redecorating: Rugs are torn, drains back up, and there is a general air of neglect. The inn's new owners face a hard task restoring this country gem to its previous glory, but the potential is enormous. Dinner is a traditional four-course menu that satisfies but rarely shines. ⌘ *Main Rd., Greyton 7233, ☎ 028/254–9995, ⅁ 028/254–9920. 13 rooms with bath. Restaurant, bar, pool. Breakfast included. No children under 12. AE, DC, MC, V.*

Hermanus

DINING

$$ **Burgundy.** This restaurant occupies a fisherman's cottage overlooking the old fishing harbor. Ask for a table on the veranda or the lawn, from where you can savor views of Walker Bay. The menu brings French flair to South African ingredients, with an emphasis on seafood. A good choice is the grilled fresh line fish with champagne beurre blanc, accompanied by a bottle of local wine. Ice-cream crepes are a popular dessert. ✗ *Market Sq., ☎ 0283/22800. Reservations advised. AE, DC, MC, V. Closed Mon. No dinner Sun.*

LODGING

$$ **Marine.** In a sprawling white building on the cliffs overlooking Walker Bay, this elegant hotel is easily the best in Hermanus. The huge sea-facing bed-sitters have excellent views over the bay, and bleached wicker and white tile create a relaxed seaside feel. Public rooms, on the other hand, are formal to a fault, furnished with stiff armchairs, antiques, and heavy drapes—you might feel awkward wandering around in your swimsuit. ☎ *Marine Dr. (mailing address: Box 9), Hermanus 7200, ☎ 0283/701–000, FAX 0283/700–160. 55 rooms with bath. Restaurant, bar, room service, 2 pools, billiards. AE, DC, MC, V.*

$$ **Windsor.** If you come to Hermanus in October or November, stay at this hotel in the heart of town. While it doesn't compare with The Marine (*above*), the hotel's position atop the cliffs makes it the best place to view the annual whale migration. Request one of the second-floor, sea-facing rooms, which have unbeatable views from their huge sliding-glass doors. The hotel itself dates back more than 100 years, and some of the corridors and public rooms look a bit time-worn. ☎ *Marine Dr. (mailing address: Box 3), Hermanus 7200, ☎ and FAX 0283/23– 727. 64 rooms with bath. Restaurant, 2 bars. Breakfast included. AE, DC, MC, V.*

Kleinmond
DINING AND LODGING

$$$ **Beach House on Sandown Bay.** In quiet seaside Kleinmond, this comfortable guest house overlooks a 10-kilometer (6-mile) crescent of beach and a beautiful lagoon. It's another good base for whale-watching in October and November, as well as for walks in the surrounding nature reserves. The hotel itself is attractive and simple. Rooms have white wicker furniture and floral draperies and bedspreads; in sea-facing rooms, sliding doors open onto small balconies with tremendous views of Sandown Bay. The restaurant specializes in seafood, bought fresh in the local harbor. ☎ *Beach Rd. (mailing address: Box 199), Kleinmond 7195, ☎ 02823/3130, FAX 02823/4022. 23 rooms with bath. Restaurant, bar, pool. Breakfast included. AE, DC, MC, V.*

Swellendam
DINING AND LODGING

$$$ **Klippe Rivier Homestead.** Set amid rolling farmland 3.2 kilometers (2 miles) outside Swellendam, this guest house occupies one of the Overberg's most gracious and historic country homes. It was built around 1825 in traditional Cape style, with thick white walls, thatched roof, and a distinctive gable. Guests are housed in enormous rooms in the converted stables. The three downstairs rooms are furnished with antiques in Cape Dutch, Colonial, and Victorian styles. Upstairs, raw wood beams, cane ceilings, and white wicker furniture set the tone for less expensive, country-style rooms. Some public rooms cannot support the sheer volume of antique collectibles, taking on a museumlike quality. Dinner is table d'hôte, prepared with fresh herbs, vegetables, fruit, and cream from surrounding farms. ☎ *On a dirt road off R60 to Ashton (mailing address: Box 483), Swellendam 6740, ☎ 0291/43341, FAX 0291/43337. 6 rooms with bath. Restaurant, saltwater pool. Breakfast included. No children under 10. AE, DC, MC, V.*

Waenhuiskrans (Arniston)
DINING AND LODGING

$$$ **Arniston Hotel.** You could easily spend a week here and still need to
★   be dragged away. The setting, in a tiny fishing village on a crescent of white dunes, has a lot to do with its appeal, but the hotel has also struck a fine balance between elegance and beach-holiday comfort. Rooms have a true beach feel, thanks to the cheery use of turquoise wicker, bold fabrics, and colorful sea prints. Request a room with a sea view, so you can enjoy the ever-changing colors that make this part of the coast so memorable. On request, the hotel takes guests by four-wheel-drive into the dune field for sundowners—not to be missed. A four-

course dinner menu changes daily, but expect plenty of fresh seafood. À la carte lunches on the patio feature light Mediterranean fare. 🗺 *Beach Rd., Waenhuiskrans (mailing address: Box 126, Bredasdorp 7280),* ☎ *02847/59000,* 🖷 *02847/59633. 24 rooms with bath. Restaurant, bar, room service, pool. Breakfast included. No children under 12. AE, DC, MC, V.*

Overberg Essentials

Arriving and Departing

Unless you're on a guided tour, you will need a car to explore the Overberg. Distances are long, towns are few, and public transport is infrequent, if it exists at all.

BY BUS

Intercape Mainliner (☎ 021/386–4400) and **Translux Express Bus** (☎ 021/405–3333) offer regular service from Cape Town along the N2, stopping at Swellendam before continuing on to the Garden Route. Once there, you're stuck unless you arrange for other transport. The ticket agent for both bus lines in Swellendam is **Milestone Tours** (8 Cooper St., Swellendam, ☎ 0291/42137).

BY CAR

Leave Cape Town via the N2 highway. If you're following the above tour, take the R44 turnoff to Gordon's Bay. Otherwise, stay on the N2 over Sir Lowry's Pass to reach Swellendam, 232 kilometers (145 miles) distant.

BY MINIBUS

Mayfly Tours & Transport (☎ 0283/21478) in Hermanus offers a shuttle service between Cape Town and Hermanus and anywhere else in the Overberg. The company also conducts local tours from Hermanus to major sights around the Overberg.

Guided Tours

In addition to the services listed below, all of the large tour operators in Cape Town offer whirlwind tours of the Overberg (*see* Guided Tours *in* Chapter 4).

Cape Country Tours (1 Market St., Greyton 7233, ☎ and 🖷 028/254–9727) leaves from Cape Town on one- and two-day tours of the major attractions of the Overberg.

Tales of Africa Tours (Box 157, Hermanus 7200, ☎ and 🖷 0283/23530) offers half- and one-day minibus tours of the Overberg, leaving from Hermanus. Tours encompass everything from coastal drives to visits to the area's many nature reserves.

Important Addresses and Numbers

EMERGENCIES

Dial 10177 for an **ambulance,** 10111 for the **police.**

VISITOR INFORMATION

Cape Overberg Tourism Association maintains a desk at the Tourist Rendezvous Travel Centre in Cape Town. *Adderley St. (mailing address: Box 1403), Cape Town 8000,* ☎ *021/418–5214,* 🖷 *021/418–5227.* ⊙ *Weekdays 8–7, Sat. 8:30–5, Sun. 9–5.*

Hermanus Publicity Association. *105 Main Rd., Hermanus 7200,* ☎ *0283/22629,* 🖷 *0283/700305.* ⊙ *Weekdays 9–1 and 2–4:30, Sat. 9–4, Sun. 10:30–3.*

Suidpunt Publicity Association has information on Bredasdorp, Elim, Cape Agulhas, Struisbaai, Napier, and Waenhuiskrans. *Dirkie Uys St., Bredasdorp 7280,* ☎ *02841/42584,* ℻ *02841/51019.* ☉ *Weekdays 8:30–4:30, Sat. 9–1.*

Swellendam Publicity Association. *Oefeningshuis, Voortrek St.,* ☎ *0291/42770,* ℻ *0291/42694.* ☉ *Weekdays 9–1 and 2–5, Sat. 9–12:30.*

WEST COAST AND NAMAQUALAND

During much of the year, the West Coast is a featureless expanse of fynbos scrub stretching from Cape Town to Vanrhynsdorp (fan-*rainz*-dorp), 288 kilometers (180 miles) to the north. Lonely fishing villages, home to generations of coloreds, dot a coastline of endless beaches fringing a cold, harsh Atlantic. It's a stark, empty land that you either love or hate. But every spring, the West Coast explodes in a fiesta of wild flowers that transforms the entire region. Even the most hardened urbanites make the pilgrimage to witness this Cinderella miracle, driving up from Cape Town just for the day or basing themselves in coastal towns like Langebaan and Lambert's Bay.

As spring warms to its task, the flower show spreads inland to the Hantam, a high plateau where Afrikaner farmers raise merino sheep and hardscrabble laborers still shear wool by hand. The quality of the morning and evening light—a silky caress of reds, blues, and gold—has long drawn artists, and the delightful farming town of Calvinia is an obvious overnight choice. Spreading south from Calvinia, the high plains of the Hantam collapse into the Cedarberg mountains, one of the great mountain wildernesses of South Africa. Bizarre rock formations hide delicate San (Bushmen) paintings and the last remnants of the enormous cedar forests that once blanketed the region. Hiking here is great, and you can disappear for days at a time into its remote recesses. The historic town of Clanwilliam, lying in the shadow of the Cedarberg, makes a great base for short walks and scenic drives.

Compared to the few days needed to take the West Coast–Cedarberg loop, you'll need to commit twice that to see what may be the greatest floral spectacle on earth—the wild flowers of Namaqualand. This huge semi-desert region extends north from the West Coast to Namibia, hundreds of kilometers from Cape Town. It's a remote, unpopulated area, with few facilities and comforts. In spring, however, it puts on a spectacle that makes the West Coast flowers pale in comparison. Vast fields that seemed barren only a month before blush with blossoms. Purple vygies and Namaqualand daisies brightly splash the hillsides and valleys with color.

Unless it's flower season, think long and hard about venturing this far afield. As in parts of the American west, distances are vast and the landscape brown and sere, and in summer the wind blows as hot as a blast furnace. At these times, Namaqualand has its own stark appeal, burned clean by heat and sun, but it's not a good choice if your holiday is only a couple of weeks long.

It can be difficult to plan a holiday around the flowers in both the West Coast and Namaqualand, since it's impossible to tell exactly when they'll bloom. The season is notoriously fickle, dependent on wind, rain, and sun. The display begins on the coast around July, with cooler mountain areas coming to life as late as August and lasting into October. As you might expect, some years are not nearly as good as others.

Tourist offices in all the towns provide up-to-date—sometimes hourly—information on wildflower action in their areas. Day by day they'll tell you where the flowers are blooming and the best routes to follow. Call them before you head out, or your whole trip may be wasted.

The best time of day to see color is between 11 and 3, but flowers are unlikely to open if the weather is cold and windy. Plants move with the sun, so make an effort to drive with the sun at your back to get the full effect.

Traveling by car is the only way to tour the West Coast and Namaqualand properly. A rental car can easily handle the tours mapped out below, despite the fact that much of the driving is along gravel roads. These roads are all in good condition, but stones can damage the underside of your car, particularly if you drive with a heavy foot. If you venture into Namaqualand, be sure your car is in good condition, carry extra drinking water, and fill up with gas whenever you can—like everything else, service stations are few and far between.

Exploring

Towns and sights on this tour are marked on the Western Cape and Namaqualand map.

West Coast, Hantam, and Cedarberg

A loop around the West Coast, Hantam, and Cedarberg starting from Cape Town will take a minimum of three days. Allow more time if you plan to walk extensively or frolic in fields of flowers.

From Cape Town, take the N1 toward Paarl. After just under 2 kilometers (1 mile), exit left onto the R27 (the sign reads PAARDEN EILAND and MILNERTON) and drive 80 kilometers (50 miles) through fynbos-covered dunes to the junction with the R315. A right turn will bring you to **Darling,** a sleepy village in the heart of wildflower country. In mid-September the village presents an annual Wildflower and Orchid Show (☎ 02241/2422) that's famous throughout the Western Cape. This part of the coast usually flowers about two months after the first rains, and fades out between mid-September and mid-October. Expect to see daisies, bluebells, arum lilies, vygies, and namesias.

Back on the R27, head north 11 kilometers (7 miles) to **West Coast National Park.** Even if you don't spend time here, the road that runs through the park to Langebaan is far more scenic than the R27 and well worth taking. The park is a fabulous mix of lagoon wetlands, pounding surf, and coastal fynbos. For a beautiful detour, follow the rutted dirt track 16 kilometers (10 miles) onto the narrow peninsula that separates the Atlantic from Langebaan Lagoon. On a sunny day, the lagoon assumes a magical color, made all the more impressive by blinding white beaches and the sheer emptiness of the place. Birders will have a field day identifying water birds, and the sandveld flowers are among the best along the West Coast. At the tip of the peninsula's Postberg Nature Reserve, you'll likely catch glimpses of zebra, wildebeest, and bat-eared foxes. *Off the R27,* ☎ *02287/22144.* ☛ *R20 per vehicle Nov. 15–Jan. 7, Easter, and flower season; R10 at other times.* ☼ *Daily 9–5.*

The paved road emerges from the park near **Langebaan.** Turn left out of the park, then right onto Oostewal Street and drive into town. Whereas many of the communities along the West Coast are bleak and uninviting, Langebaan is charming, and it makes a good base for exploring the surrounding area as far north as Rocher Pan Nature Reserve (*see below*). The town sits at the mouth of Langebaan Lagoon, overlooking West Coast National Park and the vast expanse of Saldanha Bay. The beaches are excellent, and the lagoon water is warmer than the ocean—although that's not saying much. There are several restaurants, a yacht club, and even a shop renting sailboards and small boats.

Return to the R27 and continue north. After a few kilometers, turn left onto the R79, which ends at a T junction. From here, you can turn left to Saldanha or right to Vredenburg. **Saldanha** is a large town by West Coast standards but it's of limited interest to tourists. This deepwater port is the terminus for trains carrying iron-ore from the mines of Namaqualand. A huge loading pier dominates the bay and detracts from what would otherwise be a very attractive spot.

Vredenburg is an agricultural center for the surrounding farms and has even less to offer tourists than Saldanha. Shortly after you enter town, turn left on Main Street and follow it out of town. The asphalt gives way to a good-quality gravel road, which runs 16 kilometers (10 miles) through rolling farm country to **Paternoster,** an unspoiled village of white fishermen's cottages perched on a deserted stretch of coastline. The population here is mainly colored, people who for generations have eked out a living harvesting crayfish and other seafood. Despite the overt poverty, the village has a character and sense of identity often lacking in larger towns.

Along the coast just south of Paternoster is the **Columbine Nature Reserve,** a great spot for spring wildflowers, coastal fynbos, and Karoo succulents. Seagulls, cormorants, and sacred ibis are common here. ☎ 02285/718. ☛ R2.50 adults, R1.30 children. ☉ Daily 7–7.

About 1 kilometer (½ mile) outside Paternoster, on the road back to Vredenburg, turn left onto another dirt road and drive to **Stompneusbaai.** Like Paternoster, this is a colored community that relies on the sea for its livelihood. The stench of fish from the local fish-processing factory detracts from the charm of the village's white cottages and their brightly colored roofs. An unimpressive monument just outside of town marks the spot where Vasco da Gama landed in 1497, after a three-month voyage from Europe.

A paved road leads 16 kilometers (10 miles) from Stompneusbaai through St. Helena to a T junction. Turn left onto the R399 and drive 10 kilometers (6 miles) to **Velddrif,** at the mouth of the Berg River. Forming a long estuary as it nears the sea, the Berg is a haven for water birds, including flamingos, pelicans, and the rare blue heron and redshank. Velddrif is a fishing community, and you can still see fishermen hanging bunches of *bokkoms* (fish biltong) to dry in sheds along the estuary.

After the Berg River bridge, turn left on Voortrekker Street, which leads into **Laaiplek,** Velddrif's sister town and the site of the fishing harbor and beach. Turn right on Jameson Street and head out of town. After 11 kilometers (7 miles), the tar road reverts to good-quality gravel.

Twenty-four kilometers (15 miles) from Laaiplek, **Rocher Pan Nature Reserve** (☎ 02625/727) is a small, seasonal pan in the middle of the sandveld that supports a wide variety of birds, including Cape shovelers, African shelducks, and Cape teals. Visitors can sit in bird blinds or follow one of several walking trails.

Continue 32 kilometers (20 miles) to **Elands Bay.** Compared with the barren flats of the sandveld, Elands Bay enjoys an incredible setting, backed by a lagoon fringed with reeds and dotted with flamingos and waterfowl. A line of rocky cliffs runs down one side of the lagoon, ending at Baboon Point and a crayfish-processing factory. Drive out to Baboon Point (the sign says JETTIES) and look back toward the town. Fishing boats ride at anchor on startlingly blue water and, in the distance, a great field of white-sand dunes slopes down to the water's edge. The beach fronting the town is superb and draws crowds of Cape Town surfers on weekends and holidays. Birders, too, flock here to see the 200 species of birds that frequent the lagoon. Several San rock-art sites are also hidden away in the region, but they're almost impossible to find on your own—ask around for guides in Elands Bay or call the Verlorenvlei Country Inn (*see* Dining and Lodging, *below*). Unfortunately, the town itself is completely forgettable, with a characterless hotel and a couple of shops.

Follow the gravel R366 out of town for 4 kilometers (2½ miles), then turn left at the sign to Lambert's Bay. After 13 kilometers (8 miles), turn left again at a T junction. This road passes high above the **Wadrif Salt Pan,** formed by the Langvlei River. After a rain, the pan fills with water and attracts thousands of flamingos and other water birds.

It's another 16 kilometers (10 miles) along empty coastline to **Lambert's Bay.** This isn't some spruced-up version of dock life like Cape Town's Victoria & Alfred Waterfront but a working fishing town—you can smell the fish-processing plants, and the boats in the harbor look like they spend their days battling Atlantic swells. If you don't expect anything cute, the innate charm of the town will seduce you. One of its major attractions is **Bird Island,** accessible along a stone breakwater from the harbor. The island is home to a colony of 14,000 Cape gannets, aggressive seabirds that live packed tightly together, fighting and screaming. The odor and the noise are incredible, but the colony must rate as one of the best bird-watching spectacles in South Africa. If you can see beyond the blur of gannets, you can also sometimes spot jackass penguins and seals.

From Lambert's Bay, take the R364 past the BP station toward Clanwilliam (to which you could proceed directly, *see below,* for a shorter tour). After 5 kilometers (3 miles), turn left onto a dirt road leading to Doringbaai and Vredendal. The wildflowers along the coast usually bloom from mid-July to mid-August, and the ordinarily featureless sandveld explodes with violets, wild tulips, harpuis, and sporrie. After 32 kilometers (20 miles), turn left again to reach **Doringbaai,** perched on a deserted coastline of rocky cliffs. It's a popular holiday retreat for farmers from the Karoo but of little interest to most other travelers. **Strandfontein,** a few kilometers farther north, is another isolated holiday resort, backed by steep hills but ruined by the unsightly brick houses so common in the region. The road becomes tar again at Strandfontein and runs north along the coast. After a few kilometers you descend into the Olifants River valley, an oasis of vineyards, fields, and orchards. Continue into **Vredendal,** a nondescript agricultural center, and then on to Vanrhynsdorp via the R27.

At **Vanrhynsdorp** you have a choice. You can strike north on the N7 into the empty vastness of Namaqualand (*see below*) or cut eastward along the R27 toward the **Hantam,** a high plateau that marks the fringes of the Karoo Desert and the extreme range of the winter rainfall area. The wildflowers usually bloom here in mid-July and last through mid-September. Among the most common are vygies, daisies, katsterte, and pietsnotjies.

To reach the Hantam Plateau, you must first scale the looming wall of the Bokkeveld Escarpment, which rises almost vertically from the flat expanse of the sandveld. The road zigzags up Vanrhyns Pass, providing excellent views back over the Olifants River valley. **Nieuwoudtville,** on the cusp of the escarpment, gets more rain than elsewhere in the Hantam, and its vegetation differs accordingly. The town is famous for its bulbs, including a mass display of more than half a million orange bulbinellas, which are endemic to the area.

Calvinia, 72 kilometers (45 miles) east of Nieuwoudtville, shelters under a looming mesa known as the Hantamsberg. Founded in 1851, it's a lovely farming town, with a relaxed feel and several beautifully restored historic homes. It makes a good base for exploring the **Akkerendam Nature Reserve** north of town. Two hiking trails of one and six hours traverse the slopes of the Hantamsberg and the plateau on top.

The **Calvinia Museum** is one of the best country museums in South Africa. Displays examine the fashions and furnishings that prevailed in this remote corner of South Africa over the past 150 years. Many of the exhibits reflect the town's agricultural focus, especially sheep farming. *44 Church St.,* ☎ *0273/411–043.* ☛ *R1 adults, 50¢ children.* ☉ *Weekdays 8–1 and 2–5, Sat. 8–noon.*

TIME OUT   **Die Hantam Huis,** a lovely 1853 Cape Dutch homestead, is the oldest surviving building in Calvinia. It's now a delightful lunchroom and coffee shop. *Hoop St.,* ☎ *0273/41-1606.*

Drive 37 kilometers (21 miles) back along the R27 toward Nieuwoudtville, then turn left onto the gravel R364 to Clanwilliam. This is a magical 112-kilometer (70-mile) drive, especially in the two to three hours after sunrise or before sunset, when the desert colors take on a glowing richness that is almost mystical. Thirty-two kilometers (20 miles) before Clanwilliam you come to a farm called **Travellers Rest** (☎ 0274/82–2629). A host of San rock paintings lie within a two-hour walk of the farmhouse, but you must get permission before walking out to look for them.

The gravel road descends to Clanwilliam through the beautiful **Cedarberg,** a mountain range known for its San paintings, bizarre rock formations, and, once upon a time, its cedars. Most of the ancient cedars have been cut down, but a few giant specimens still survive in the more remote regions. The Cedarberg is a hiking paradise for Capetonians— a wild, largely unspoiled area where you can disappear from civilization for days at a time. About 172,900 acres of this mountain range have been declared the Cedarberg Wilderness Area, and entry permits are required if you wish to hike or drive into this part of the range. Permits are available from Cape Nature Conservation (Citrusdal District Office, Private Bag X1, Citrusdal 7340, ☎ 022/9212289, FAX 022/9213219); unfortunately, you have to stop in Citrusdal (*see below*) to pick them up.

Clanwilliam serves as the base for hiking trails and drives into the Cedarberg. It's better geared for tourism than Calvinia, and it's equally charming, with tree-shaded streets and several restored 19th-century buildings. The town was founded around 1800 and has blossomed into the center of the rooibos-tea industry. Rooibos is a bush that grows wild in the Cedarberg and forms the foundation of many herbal teas sold worldwide.

Wildflowers hit their peak in Clanwilliam in the second and third weeks in August. One of the best places to see them is the **Ramskop**

Reality check. Call home.

—— *AT&T USADirect® and World Connect®. The fast, easy way to call most anywhere.* ——

Take out AT&T Calling Card or your local calling card.** Lift phone. Dial AT&T Access Number for country you're calling from. Connect to English-speaking operator or voice prompt. Reach the States or over 200 countries. Talk. Say goodbye. Hang up. Resume vacation.

American Samoa	633 2-USA	Korea	009-11	Taiwan*	0080-10288-0
Australia	1800-881-011	Macao ■	0800-111	Thailand♦	0019-991-1111
Cambodia ■	1800-881-001	Malaysia*	800-0011		
China, PRC♦♦♦	10811	Micronesia ■	288		
Cook Islands ■	09-111	New Zealand	000-911		
Fiji ■	004-890-1001	Palau ■	02288		
Guam	018-872	Philippines*	105-11		
Hong Kong	800-1111	Saipan†	235-2872		
India♦	000-117	Singapore	800-0111-111		
Indonesia†	001-801-10	South Africa	0-800-99-0123		
Japan*■	0039-111	Sri Lanka	430-430		

**AT&T
Your True Choice**

**You can also call collect or use most U.S. local calling cards. Countries in bold face permit country-to-country calling in addition to calls to the U.S. World Connect® prices consist of USADirect® rates plus an additional charge based on the country you are calling. Collect calling available to the U.S. only. *Public phones require deposit of coin or phone card. †May not be available from every phone. ♦ Not available from public phones. ♦♦♦Not yet available from all areas. ■ World Connect calls can only be placed to this country. ©1995 AT&T.

For a free wallet sized card of all AT&T Access Numbers, call: 1-800-241-5555.

Wildflower Garden, less than a mile out of town. *Ou Kaapseweg, Clanwilliam,* ☎ *027/482–2133.* ☛ *R6 adults, R2 children.* ☻ *7:30– sunset.*

Return to the N7 and head south to the turnoff to **Algeria.** A scenic dirt road winds into the Cedarberg to this Cape Conservation outpost and campsite, set in an idyllic valley amid towering eucalyptus trees. Algeria is the starting point for several excellent hikes into the Cedarberg. No permit is needed for the short, one-hour hike to a waterfall, or a longer hike to a copse of cedars atop the mountains.

Continue down the N7 to **Citrusdal,** a fruit-growing town in the Olifants River valley surrounded by the peaks of the Cedarberg. From here, it's just 90 minutes back to Cape Town through the **Swartland** (Black Land), which takes its name from the dark renoster bush that grows in the area. Today, the Swartland is a rolling landscape of wheat fields and vineyards. From July until the end of October, you can see plenty of flowers from the highway, including lovely arum lilies. There are a number of commercial protea farms here, too.

Namaqualand

Unless it's flower season, think twice about trekking into this vast desert wilderness. Hotels and restaurants are basic, and the distances are immense. It's 544 kilometers (340 miles) from Cape Town to Springbok, the capital of Namaqualand and a major base for exploring the region's flowers, and a four- to five-hour drive just to reach Kamieskroon, the closest Namaqualand hamlet with a decent hotel. To do the area justice, you need to add three days to a West Coast itinerary or budget a minimum of five days if you're visiting Namaqualand only. Don't come up here looking for traditional tourist sights—aside from the flowers, this is empty, untamed country. The tour below simply maps out some of the most rewarding flower routes.

Namaqualand stretches north from Vanrhynsdorp, a small farming town at the northern limit of the West Coast tour (*see above*). From here it's 144 kilometers (90 miles) along the N7 to **Garies,** a one-horse town cradled amid sun-baked hills. One of the best flower routes runs 100 kilometers (60 miles) from just north of Garies to Hondeklipbaai on the coast. The road winds through rocky hills before descending onto the flat coastal sandveld. Flowers in this region usually bloom at the end of July and early August. If you're lucky, fields along this route will be carpeted with purple vygies, but also look for Namaqualand daisies, aloes, and orchids. Another common plant is the quiver tree, a giant aloe whose bark was used by the San to make quivers for their poison arrows.

Hondeklipbaai itself is a depressing, windblown settlement perched on desolate flats by the sea. It's a diamond-mining area, and huge holes gouged out of the earth mar the terrain. From Hondeklipbaai, take the road toward Kooiingnaas, another diamond-mining settlement, and then northeast to Springbok. The road climbs steeply into the granite mountains to **Wildeperdehoek** (Wild Horses Pass), offering tremendous views back over the coastal plain and the sea. From here, the road winds back and forth through the hills, cresting Messelpad Pass before rejoining the N7 highway 11 kilometers (7 miles) south of Springbok.

Springbok is set in a bowl of rocky hills that form part of the Klipkoppe, a rocky escarpment that stretches from Steinkopf in the north to Bitterfontein in the south. The town owes its existence to the discovery of copper here in 1685. It's a pleasant enough place, especially after the emptiness of the desert, but it offers little more than a chance to fill your gas tank, food, flower information, and a place to spend the night.

Sixteen kilometers (10 miles) outside town is the **Goegap Nature Reserve,** which is transformed each spring into a wildflower mosaic. There are two short walking trails from the information center as well as several longer ones. In season, the reserve conducts daily flower safaris (R20 per person). Goegap is also home to the Hester Malan Wild Flower Garden, which displays an interesting collection of succulents, including the bizarre halfmens (*Pachypodium namaquanum*), consisting of a long, slender trunk topped by a bushel of leaves. *R355 from Springbok,* ☎ *0251/21880,* FAX *0251/81286.* ☛ *R2 adults, R1 children, R5 per vehicle.* ⊙ *Daily 8:30–4:15.*

Another excellent flower drive is a 320-kilometer (200-mile) rectangular route that heads north on the N7 from Springbok to Steinkopf and then west on the paved R382 to Port Nolloth. From there a dirt road leads south through the sandveld to Grootmis, then east along the Buffels River before climbing the Spektakel Pass back to Springbok. If the rains have been good, the route offers some of the best flower viewing in the region. Try to time your return to Springbok to coincide with the sunset, when the entire Spektakel Mountain glows a deep orange-red.

En route, take time from smelling the flowers to walk around **Port Nolloth.** It started life as a copper port, but today it's better known as a fishing and diamond center. Head over to the harbor to check out the diamond-vacuuming boats, with their distinctive hoses trailing astern. Divers use the hoses to vacuum under boulders on the seabed in search of the diamonds that washed into the sea from the Orange River ages ago. It's a highly lucrative endeavor, but not without its dangers—at least one diver has been sucked up the vacuum hose to his death.

Kamieskroon, 72 kilometers (45 miles) south of Springbok on the N7, is another base for exploring Namaqualand in spring. Although the town itself has nothing to recommend it, the Kamieskroon Hotel (*see* Dining and Lodging, *below*) is probably the best source of information on wildflowers in Namaqualand.

The 2,470-acre **Skilpad Wildflower Reserve,** 18 kilometers (11 miles) west of Kamieskroon on the Wolwepoort Road, can usually be counted on for flower displays. *Wolwepoort Rd.,* ☎ *0257/614.* ☛ *R2 per person, R4 per vehicle.* ⊙ *Dawn–dusk.*

An interesting detour from Kamieskroon runs 29 kilometers (18 miles) to **Leliefontein,** an old mission station at the top of the Kamiesberg with spectacular views across the desert to the sea. The wildflowers here bloom much later than those on the coast, often lasting as late as the end of October. Even if there are no flowers, it's a beautiful drive back down the Kamiesberg to Garies, 72 kilometers (45 miles) away.

Rejoin the N7 and drive south back to Vanrhynsdorp and, ultimately, Cape Town.

Dining and Lodging

For price ranges, *see* Charts 1 and 2(A) *in* On the Road with Fodor's.

Elands Bay (West Coast)
DINING AND LODGING

$$$ **Verlorenvlei Country Inn.** Five kilometers (3 miles) from the beaches of Elands Bay, this small guest house sits on the bank of a long estuary, overlooking thick stands of reeds. Bird-watchers descend on the estuary to see more than 200 species of birds, but the area is also rich in San rock art. The inn, in a white building that dates back 150 years, has a rustic, farmlike feeling. Guest rooms are simple, with bare yellow floors, Oregon pine ceilings, and beds shrouded in mosquito nets. Everything is tidy, although the showers can be a bit grungy. The restaurant's three-course dinners present the best and most sophisticated fare on the West Coast, including dishes like mussels wrapped in spinach and crayfish ravioli. Reservations are essential. ⊞ *5 km (3 mi) from Elands Bay on R366 (mailing address: Box 11, Elands Bay 8110),* ☎ *0265/724. 5 rooms with bath. Restaurant, bar, pool. Breakfast included. No children under 15. DC, MC, V.*

Lambert's Bay (West Coast)

DINING

$$ **Muisbosskerm.** For the true flavor of West Coast life, come to this open-
★ air seafood restaurant on the beach south of town. It consists of nothing more than a circular boma (enclosure) of packed *muisbos* (mouse bush), with benches and tables haphazardly arranged in the sandy enclosure. Cooking fires blaze and you watch food being prepared fresh before your eyes: Snoek is smoked in an old drum covered with burlap, bread bakes in a clay oven, and everywhere fish sizzles on grills and in giant pots. Bring your own drink, and prepare to eat as much as you can, using your hands or mussel shells as spoons. Be sure to try some of the Afrikaner specialties like *bokkoms* (dried fish) and *waterblommetjie* (water lily) stew. Unless you have an enormous appetite, don't order the half crayfish (it costs extra). The only drawback is high-season crowding: As many as 150 diners can overwhelm the experience. ✗ *Elands Bay Rd., 5 km (3 mi) south of Lambert's Bay,* ☎ *027/432–1017. Reservations required. V.*

LODGING

$ **Marine Protea.** Next to the harbor in the center of Lambert's Bay, this modern hotel offers conventional comfort but little charm. It's a good overnight choice, though, if you're dining at the nearby Muisbosskerm. Rooms are large, decorated in blue tones, and feature a sitting area with TV and phone. ⊞ *Voortrekker St. (mailing address: Box 249), Lambert's Bay 8130,* ☎ *027/432–1126,* ℻ *027/432–1036. 46 rooms with bath. Restaurant, 2 bars, room service, pool. AE, DC, MC, V.*

Langebaan (West Coast)

DINING AND LODGING

$$ **Farmhouse.** Less than 90 minutes by car from Cape Town, this lovely
★ guest house sits on a hillside overlooking the turquoise waters of Langebaan Lagoon. It's a great base for exploring West Coast National Park and a popular retreat for bird-watchers. The guest house, in a restored farmstead built in the 1860s, features thick white walls, tile floors, and timber beams. The rooms, decorated with rustic pine furniture and bright floral fabrics, have their own fireplaces and views of the lagoon. The hotel's à la carte menu features a good selection of Cape cuisine, prepared fresh and served in the attractive dining room, notable for its Oregon-pine furniture, fireplace, and high ceiling. ⊞ *5 Egret St. (mailing address: Box 160), Langebaan 7357,* ☎ *02287/22062,* ℻ *02287/21980. 10 rooms with bath. Restaurant, bar, pool. Breakfast included. No children under 12. MC, V.*

Calvinia (Hantam)

LODGING

$ **Die Dorphuis.** In a restored Victorian house that is now a national mon-
★ ument, this lovely bed-and-breakfast offers warm Afrikaner hospital-
ity amid elegant period furnishings. Rooms have antique brass bedsteads
and elaborate ceilings, and are hung with photos of old Calvinia. If
you want something completely different, book the slave quarters: The
room, lit only with candles and kerosene lanterns, features a reed floor
and ceiling, and bed covers made from animal skins. ⊞ *Water St. (mailing address: Box 34), Calvinia 8190,* ☎ *0273/411606,* ℻ *0273/41177.
10 rooms with bath. Breakfast included. No credit cards.*

Clanwilliam (Cedarberg)

DINING AND LODGING

$ **Strassberger's Hotel Clanwilliam.** Right on the main street, this friendly,
family-run hotel makes an excellent base for exploring the Cedarberg.
Rooms are large, decorated with rustic cane furniture and plaid country fabrics. Pieter du Toit, a hotel employee, can arrange hikes and tours
into the surrounding mountains. Dinner in the hotel restaurant is a traditional four-course affair that is satisfactory but lacks inspiration. Rein-
holds, the hotel's à la carte restaurant, serves more innovative fare, like
crumbed pork chops with sweet-and-sour sauce. ⊞ *Main Rd. (mailing address: Box 4), Clanwilliam 8135,* ☎ *027/482–1101,* ℻ *027/482–
2678. 17 rooms with bath. 2 restaurants, bar, pool, squash. Breakfast
included. AE, DC, MC, V.*

Kamieskroon (Namaqualand)

DINING AND LODGING

$ **Kamieskroon Hotel.** At first glance, this hotel offers little to distinguish
it from every other one in Namaqualand. The newly renovated rooms
are clean and comfortable, but certainly nothing to write home about.
The reason to come is the hotel's world-renowned series of Namaqualand
photographic workshops (*see* Guided Tours *in* West Coast and Namaqualand Essentials, *below*), which are conducted annually by the
owners. Even if you don't participate in a workshop, you can still benefit from their tremendous knowledge of the area and of how to capture the annual floral miracle on film. They also provide day-to-day
updates on where flowers are blooming. ⊞ *Off N7, Kamieskroon (mailing address: Box 19), Kamieskroon 8241,* ☎ *0257/614,* ℻ *0257/675.
20 rooms with bath. Restaurant, bar. DC, MC, V.*

Port Nolloth (Namaqualand)

LODGING

$ **Bed Rock Lodge.** Across the street from the sea, this weathered old guest
house looks as though it's seen better days. The interior, however, is
delightful, decorated with an eclectic collection of Africana and antiques.
Each room has its own bathroom—not always en suite, however. ⊞
Coast Rd., Port Nolloth, ☎ *0255/8865. 5 rooms with bath. MC, V.*

Springbok (Namaqualand)

DINING AND LODGING

$$$ **Naries Guest House.** Twenty-four kilometers (15 miles) from Spring-
bok along a dirt road, this Cape Dutch–style guest house looks out over
the mountains of the Spektakelberg. The gracious owner makes guests
feel comfortable, and will even lead hikes around the farm. Guest rooms
are large, decorated in bold floral fabrics. Dinner, included in the room
rate, is a four-course feast of robust Afrikaans home-cooking, includ-
ing such dishes as venison stew, pumpkin fritters, and cabbage and beans.
⊞ *24 km (15 mi) west of Springbok on Kleinzee Rd.,* ☎ *0251/22748.
4 rooms with bath. Breakfast and dinner included. MC, V.*

$ Springbok Lodge. Rooms at this lodge in the center of Springbok are clean, cheap, and basic. Most have TVs and kettles for making coffee and tea. The advantage of staying here is the owner, who runs his own information office and is a fount of knowledge about the area. A restaurant serves typical diner food, including English breakfasts and sandwiches. ✆ *37 Voortrekker St. (mailing address: Box 26), Springbok 8240,* ☎ *0251/21321,* FAX *0251/22718. 45 units with bath. Restaurant, tourist office. DC, MC, V.*

West Coast and Namaqualand Essentials

Arriving and Departing

BY BUS

Intercape Mainliner (Captour office, Adderley St., ☎ 021/386–4400) operates daily service up the West Coast to Springbok (R165), stopping at Citrusdal, Clanwilliam, Vanrhynsdorp, Garies, and Kamieskroon.

BY CAR

The best way to travel independently in these areas is by car. The southernmost towns on the West Coast lie within 80 kilometers (50 miles) of Cape Town. Namaqualand is over 320 kilometers (200 miles) away.

Guided Tours

BOAT TOURS

Lambert's Bay Travel and Exploration (Waterfront, Lambert's Bay, ☎ 027/4321715) offers one-hour boat trips (R50) up the coast to see Benguela dolphins, seals, great white sharks, and jackass penguins. Evening trips head up the coast to a quiet bay, where guests feast on crayfish and wine. By advance arrangement, the company also conducts four-wheel-drive expeditions onto the Cedarberg, the Karoo Desert, and Botswana.

ORIENTATION TOURS

Between April and October, Lita Cole of **Namaqualand Guided Tours** (Box 30, Kamieskroon 8241, ☎ 0257/762 after 5 PM, FAX 0257/675) leads one- to three-day hikes into the mountains and sandy plains around Kamieskroon, sleeping in huts, tents, and ruins along the way. For those who don't want to walk, she offers guided driving tours of Namaqualand in your own vehicle.

Rey van Rensburg of **Richtersveld Challenge** (Box 142, Springbok 8240, ☎ 0251/21905, FAX 0251/81460) offers vehicle and hiking tours of Namaqualand, particularly the wild northern area known as the Richtersveld. Rafting down the Orange River can also be arranged.

PHOTOGRAPHIC TOURS

Namaqualand Photographic Workshops (Kamieskroon Hotel, Box 19, Kamieskroon 8241, ☎ 0257/614, FAX 0217/675) are world-famous photographic seminars led by professional photographers Freeman Patterson, Colla Swart, and J.J. van Heerden. Four week-long workshops are held during flower season, consisting of lectures and field trips to photograph the flowers and landscape. Two summer seminars, held outside flower season, include three days of camping.

Important Addresses and Numbers

EMERGENCIES

Dial 10177 for an **ambulance,** 10111 for the **police.**

VISITOR INFORMATION

The **Flowerline** is a central hot line that offers details about where flowers are blooming each day. *Tourist Rendezvous Travel Centre, Adderley St., Cape Town 8001,* ☎ *021/418–3705.* ☉ *June–Oct., daily 8–4.*

Calvinia Tourist Office. *Calvinia Museum, 44 Church St., Calvinia,* ☎ *0273/411–712.* ☉ *Weekdays 8–1 and 2–5, Sat. 8–noon.*

Clanwilliam Tourism Association. *Main Rd., Clanwilliam,* ☎ *027/482–2024,* FAX *027/482–2361.* ☉ *Weekdays in flower season 8:30–4.*

Lambert's Bay Information Office. *Strandveld Museum, D.F. Malan St., Lambert's Bay,* ☎ *027/432–2335,* FAX *027/432–1517.* ☉ *Mon.–Sat. 9–1 and 2–5.*

Springbok. *Old Church, Luckhof St., Springbok,* ☎ *0251/22071,* FAX *0251/21431.* ☉ *Weekdays 7:30–4, variable hrs on weekends in flower season.*

6 Garden Route and Little Karoo

The Garden Route takes its name from the region's riot of vegetation. Here, you'll find some of South Africa's most inspiring scenery: forest-cloaked mountains, myriad rivers, and golden beaches backed by thick bush. You'll also find Plettenberg Bay, South Africa's glitziest beach resort, and Knysna, a town built around an oyster-rich lagoon. The Little Karoo, separated from the coast by a range of mountains, is famous for its turn-of-the-century "feather palaces" and the Cango Caves, one of the world's most impressive networks of underground caverns.

THE 208-KILOMETER (130-MILE) STRETCH of coastline from Mossel Bay to Storms River encompasses some of South Africa's most scenic country. Don't expect the jagged, dramatic beauty of the Western Cape, however. The Garden Route's appeal is softer—a land of lakes and rivers, of green mountains, thick forests, and beaches combed by the Indian Ocean. It's the kind of place where you'll have trouble deciding whether to head to the beach or go on an invigorating hike.

The Garden Route owes its verdant mien to the Outeniqua and Tsitsikamma mountains, forested ranges that shadow the coastline, trapping the moist ocean breezes which then fall as rain. These same mountains are also responsible for robbing the interior of water, creating the semiarid deserts of the Little and Great Karoo. A trip into this sere world of rock and scrub offers a glimpse of what much of South Africa's vast hinterland looks like. The Little Karoo, the narrow strip of land wedged between the Swartberg and Outeniqua ranges, is famous for its ostrich farms, as well as the subterranean splendors of the Cango Caves. Even if all of this leaves you cold, it is still worth the effort to explore some of the spectacular passes that claw through the mountains into the desert interior.

For most travelers, the Garden Route remains very much a "route," a drive of several days from Port Elizabeth to Cape Town, or vice versa, with a flight out of Port Elizabeth to the next destination. Increasingly, though, people are eschewing the standard driving tour in favor of a longer holiday, basing themselves in a central town like Knysna (pronounced "*nize*-nuh") and exploring from there. This certainly has its advantages, not least because almost the entire Garden Route lies less than an hour from this busy town.

In addition, resorts like Plettenberg Bay offer the kind of classic beach vacation you fantasize about during interminable office meetings. The beaches are among the world's best, and you can take your pick of water sports. The ocean may not be as warm as in KwaZulu-Natal, but the quality of the accommodations tends to be far superior.

There's no "best" time to visit the Garden Route, although the water and weather are warmest from December through March. Wildflowers bloom along the Garden Route from July to October, the same time as the annual whale migration along the coast. If money is a major issue, stay away during the peak holiday season (mid-December to mid-March) when hotel prices soar, in some cases nearly doubling.

Until recently, anyone with limited time would have to choose between the Garden Route and the classic African game experience of the Eastern Transvaal. This is no longer the case. The new Shamwari Game Reserve, an hour's drive from Port Elizabeth, has all the hallmarks of becoming a classic for big-game adventure (*see* Chapter 9). It also has the advantage of lying in a malaria-free zone.

EXPLORING

Numbers in the margin correspond to points of interest on the Garden Route map.

 This tour begins in **Mossel Bay,** at the western end of the Garden Route. As a resort town, Mossel Bay can't compete with Knysna or Plettenberg, but it's pleasant nevertheless, built on a hillside over-

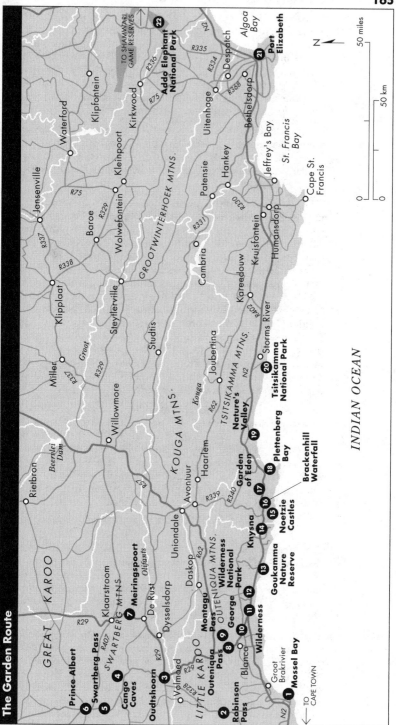

The Garden Route

GREAT KAROO

SWARTBERG MTNS

GROOTWINTERHOEK MTNS.

KOUGA MTNS.

TSITSIKAMMA MTNS.

OUTENIQUA MTNS.

LITTLE KAROO

INDIAN OCEAN

Algoa Bay

Port Elizabeth 21

Despatch

Addo Elephant National Park

TO SHAMWARI GAME RESERVES

22

Uitenhage

Bethelsdorp

Kirkwood

Kleinpoort

Klipfontein

Waterford

Jansenville

Baroe

Wolwefontein

Steytlerville

Klipplaat

Millet

Rietbron

Studtis

Willowmore

Beervlei Dam

Patensie

Hankey

Jeffrey's Bay

St. Francis Bay

Cape St. Francis

Humansdorp

Kareedouw

Kruisfontein

Cambria

Joubertina

Haarlem

Avontuur

Uniondale

Storms River 20

Tsitsikamma National Park

Nature's Valley

Plettenberg Bay 19

Garden of Eden 18

17

Brackenhill Waterfall

16

15 Noetzie Castles

14 Knysna

13

Goukamma Nature Reserve

Wilderness 12

11

George 10

Wilderness National Park

9

Montagu Pass 8

Outeniqua Pass

Robinson Pass 2

Blanco

Groot Brakrivier

Mossel Bay 1

TO CAPE TOWN

De Rust

Dysselsdorp

Daskop

Meiringspoort 7

Klaarstroom

Swartberg Pass 5

Prince Albert 6

Cango Caves 4

Oudtshoorn 3

Volmoed

Rietbron

Konga

Groot

Olifants

N2

R335

R336

R75

R334

R368

R330

R331

R102

R62

R340

R339

R29

R328

R407

R337

R338

R329

R75

R327

0 — 50 miles

0 — 50 km

N

looking the Bay of Mussels and the Outeniqua Mountains. Dolphins—as many as 100 at a time—frequently move through the bay in search of food, and whales swim past during their annual migration (July–October). In addition, boats cruise out to Seal Island, home to a breeding colony of more than 2,000 Cape fur seals (*see* Guided Tours *in* Garden Route Essentials, *below*). The town's main beach, Santos, offers protected bathing and much smaller waves than you will typically find along the Garden Route's coastline.

In 1488, Bartolemeu Dias landed on the site of present-day Mossel Bay after he was blown off course during his search for a route to the East Indies. After that, other Portuguese sailors—including Vasco da Gama—regularly called here to replenish their water supplies from a small spring near the coast.

You can still see this spring and numerous artifacts of this period at the excellent **Bartolomeu Dias Museum Complex.** The complex consists of three museums set amid lawns sloping down to the sea. The Maritime Museum has a full-scale replica of the caravel in which Dias journeyed to the Cape. The Shell Museum may sound hokey, but it's first-rate, with a fine collection of local shells as well as live mollusks and fish in aquariums. The Local History Museum (closed Sunday) traces the history and culture of Mossel Bay itself. Besides the museums, you can see an ancient milkwood tree that served as the first post office in South Africa. In 1500, a Portuguese sailor placed some mail in an old boot and set it under the tree in hopes that another passing ship would deliver it. The tree subsequently became a frequent drop site for letters, and you can still post letters in a mailbox shaped like an old boot. *Corner of Church and Market Sts.,* ☎ *0444/91–1067.* ☛ *Free.* ☼ *Weekdays 9–1 and 2–5, Sat. 10–1, Sun. 2–5.*

Leave Mossel Bay via the R328 and follow the signs to Oudtshoorn in the **Little Karoo.** The Little Karoo is a semiarid region whose landscape differs so radically from the verdant bush of the Garden Route it's difficult to believe they're separated by just a few kilometers. In summer, the Little Karoo can be a blast furnace, while winter nights are bitterly cold. Little Karoo refers to the narrow plain between the Outeniqua and Swartberg mountains, and should not be confused with the Great Karoo, a vast scrub desert that starts on the other side of the Swartberg. The word Karoo derives from the San (Bushman) word for thirst.

② The highlight of the trip between Mossel Bay and Oudtshoorn is **Robinson Pass,** which cuts through the Outeniqua Mountains. Built in 1886 by Sir Thomas Bain, the road climbs through forests of exotic pine and hillsides covered with fynbos. From May through July the proteas bloom, and their magnificent flowers offer a stunning contrast to the fractured rock and deep gorges of these ancient mountains.

③ For more than a century **Oudtshoorn** has been famous for its ostriches. Nowhere else in the world do these huge birds thrive like they do in the Little Karoo. Farmers began raising them in Oudtshoorn around 1870 to satisfy the European demand for feathers to adorn women's hats and dresses. In the years leading up to World War One, ostrich feathers were almost worth their weight in gold, and Oudtshoorn experienced an incredible boom. Many of the beautiful sandstone buildings in town date back to that period, as do the "feather palaces," huge homes built by prosperous feather merchants and buyers. In the evening, after the heat of the day, it's fun to wander the streets to view these old homes. Most are still private but you can visit the sandstone **Town**

House, built in 1909 and furnished in period style. *Corner of High and Loop Sts.,* ☎ 0443/22–7306. ☛ *Free.* ⊙ *Weekdays 9–1 and 2–5.*

The Town House is administered by the **C.P. Nel Museum,** one of the finest country museums in South Africa. Not surprisingly, it focuses on the ostrich and Oudtshoorn's boom period at the beginning of the century. Many of the exhibits are set up like shopfronts, including a chemist's, a bank, and a department store. Others replicate the dining room, bedroom, and music room of a wealthy Oudtshoorn family. A fascinating exhibit traces the history of Oudtshoorn's once-large Jewish community. In the years prior to World War I, Oudtshoorn became known as Little Jerusalem, as nearly the entire feather trade was run by Jewish merchants, many of whom had emigrated to South Africa from Eastern Europe between 1880 and 1910. The exhibit is built around a synagogue that is still in use. *Baron van Reede St.,* ☎ 0443/22–7306. ☛ *Free.* ⊙ *Mon.–Sat. 9–1 and 2–5.*

These days, ostrich farms probably derive as much profit from visiting tourists as they do from the sale of ostrich feathers, meat, and leather. Indeed, the entire town of Oudtshoorn has moved in that direction, offering a host of kitschy attractions that would make Nashville proud.

Three farms compete for the tourist buck, offering almost identical tours. In summer, crowds can be horrendous. **Highgate Ostrich Show Farm** was the first to turn ostrich farming into a major attraction. Knowledgeable guides take you through every step in the production of feathers, ostrich leather, and meat, and explain the bird's extraordinary social and physical characteristics. During the 90-minute tour, you'll get a chance to sit on a penned ostrich and even to ride one around a small enclosure. To cap it all off, three jockeys race the birds up and down a short course. A curio shop sells a variety of ostrich products and kitschy souvenirs. *Off R328 to Mossel Bay,* ☎ 0443/22–7115, FAX 0443/22–7111. ☛ *R15 adults, R8 children.* ⊙ *Daily 8–5. Tours every 15 mins.*

★ ④ From Oudtshoorn, follow the R328 for 32 kilometers (20 miles) to reach the **Cango Caves,** deservedly one of the most popular attractions in the area. The caves are huge and stunningly beautiful, stretching for several kilometers through the mountains. Unfortunately, some of the grandeur is lost when you have to share the experience with as many as 200 people. Indeed, the passage of so many people over the years has turned the rock formations from milky white to red and brown, due to a buildup of iron oxide and acid damage from human breath. The main part of the tour lasts about an hour and passes through three huge chambers notable for their giant stalagmites and stalactites. Some of the guides' commentary is trite, but it's much better and more informative than at Sudwala Caves in the Eastern Transvaal. After the third chamber, you'll have an option to turn back or continue on the "adventure" portion of the tour. Think long and hard about pressing on if you're overweight, very tall, claustrophobic, or have knee or heart problems, because you end up shimmying up narrow chimneys on your belly and wriggling your way through tiny tunnels. It's exhilarating, but the temperature and humidity levels are high, and there's not much oxygen. If you plan to take the second part of the tour, wear shoes with a good tread and old clothes—you'll do a lot of sliding on your bum. *Off R328 between Oudtshoorn and Prince Albert,* ☎ 0443/22–7410. ☛ *R16.50 adults, R8 children.* ⊙ *Daily 9–4. Tours hourly.*

★ ⑤ Drive down the hill from the Cango Caves and turn right onto the R328 toward Prince Albert, on the other side of the mountains. On the way, the road traverses **Swartberg Pass,** one of the scenic highlights of any trip to South Africa. This pass was also built, between 1881 and 1886, by the legendary engineer Sir Thomas Bain, who warned that the road would have to be steep. He wasn't exaggerating. Soon after it begins to climb, the tar gives way to gravel and becomes very narrow. At times, the road barely clings to the mountainside, held in place only by Bain's stone retaining walls. Cresting the pass at 5,230 feet, you look out toward the hot plains of the Great Karoo Desert and the distant mountains of the Nuweveldberg. Of more immediate note is the huge gorge that cuts through the mountains below you, revealing sheer walls of red, red rock. Descending, the road snakes back and forth across the mountain. At every bend, the views seem to get better and better, until you're jinking through narrow cuts in the vertical rock walls.

6 **Prince Albert** is a town time forgot, a classic Karoo town in the shadow of the Swartberg. It has retained some excellent examples of 19th-century architecture, and most of the homes have the corrugated-iron roofs and stoeps so typical of the Karoo. The town offers plenty of small hotels and bed-and-breakfasts, but there's nothing to keep you long except the chance to hike in the mountains or do nothing at all.

7 A good way back to Oudtshoorn is through the **Meiringspoort** via De Rust. The road runs along the bottom of a deep gorge created by the Groot River. It doesn't have the panoramic views of Swartberg Pass, but it's still stunning. The road leapfrogs the river 26 times as it cuts through the red cliffs of the gorge. Halfway through the Meiringspoort is a rest area from which a path leads to a 200-foot waterfall.

8 From Oudtshoorn, take the R29 to George by way of **Outeniqua Pass,** yet another of the stunning passes that cuts through the region's moun-
9 tains. A more historic route leads you over **Montagu Pass,** a narrow gravel road that offers excellent views and some great picnic sites. The road was built in 1843 by Henry Fancourt White, and the old toll house still sits at the bottom of the pass. To get to the head of the pass, turn left onto the R62 at its junction with the R29.

10 **George** is the largest town and de facto capital of the Garden Route, but you won't find much to keep you here. The city lies 11 kilometers (7 miles) from the sea and makes its money from timber rather than tourism. It's a pleasant place, nevertheless, tucked beneath the peaks of the Outeniqua Mountains and graced with plenty of parks and gardens. Named after King George III, the city was laid out in 1811 as a base for logging operations in the surrounding forests.

The **George Museum** has extensive displays on the timber industry of the southern Cape, but it's most interesting for its collection of memorabilia associated with P. W. Botha, who served as prime minister from 1978 to 1989. Botha was the last of the hard-line Nationalist leaders, and the museum takes an unapologetic look at his rule during the country's darkest years. Displays include an AK47 rifle carved from ivory and presented to Botha as a gift by Jonas Savimbi, leader of the Angolan rebel movement UNITA. It's believed that much of UNITA's military campaign was financed by the slaughter of Angola's elephant herds. *Courtenay St.,* ☎ *0441/73–5343.* ☛ *50¢.* ☉ *Weekdays 9–4:30, Sat. 9–12:30.*

A block down York Street from the museum is **St. Mark's Cathedral** (corner of York and Cathedral Sts., no ☎), a tiny Anglican church that gives George its city status. Consecrated in 1850, the stone cathedral is notable for its interesting memorials and large number of stained-glass windows.

Follow Courtenay Street back onto the N2. The road descends steeply to the sea through a heavily forested gorge formed by the Kaaiman's River. Look to your right to see a curved railway bridge spanning the river's mouth. This is one of the most photographed scenes on the Garden Route, especially when the Outeniqua Choo-Tjoe puffs by (*see* Getting Around *in* Garden Route Essentials, *below*). As the road rounds the point, a breathtaking view of mile upon mile of pounding surf and golden beaches unfolds before you.

⓫ This is **Wilderness,** a popular holiday resort for good reason. Backed by thickly forested hills and cliffs, the tiny town presides over a magical stretch of beach between the Kaaiman's and Touw rivers. These rivers constitute the western end of a whole system of beautiful waterways, lakes, and lagoons strung out along the coast, separated from the sea by towering overgrown dunes.

⓬ Much of the area now falls under the control of **Wilderness National Park,** a 6,500-acre reserve that stretches east along the coast for 31 kilometers (19 miles). It's a wetlands paradise and draws birders from all over the country to its two bird hides. Walking trails wend through the park, including the circular 10-kilometer (6-mile) Pied Kingfisher Trail, which covers the best of what Wilderness has to offer: beach, lagoon, marshes, and river. You can rent canoes to explore the lagoon and channels. *Off N2, Wilderness,* ☎ *0441/877–1197.* ☛ *R10 per vehicle.* ☉ *Daily 8–5.*

From Wilderness, the highway runs along a high ridge of vegetated dunes, with occasional glimpses of the ocean on your right and a string of lakes on your left. As beautiful as it is, the view from the road pales in comparison with the scenery down by the beach. Indeed, it would be sheer folly to experience the Garden Route from the highway alone—at the end, you may wonder what all the fuss is about. Instead, take the time to follow some of the small roads (some of them dirt) that lead down to the shore. Road signs mark the turnoffs to beaches that are invari-

⓭ ably spectacular. One of the best is the beach separating the **Goukamma Nature Reserve** from the **Goukamma Marine Nature Reserve.** Backed by steep hills covered with dense bush, it's deserted except for a few fishermen. To get there, turn off the N2 at the Lake Pleasant and Groenvlei exit, drive past the Lake Pleasant Hotel, and follow the dirt road for 3.2 kilometers (2 miles).

⓮ **Knysna** is the most popular destination on the Garden Route. The focus of the town is the beautiful Knysna Lagoon, ringed by forested hills dotted with vacation homes. Towering buttresses of rock, known as the Heads, guard the entrance to the lagoon, funneling the ocean through a narrow channel. The sea approach is so hazardous that Knysna never developed into a major port, like Durban. Today, Knysna is very much a resort town, with a quaint charm lacking in the Garden Route's other major drawing card, Plettenberg Bay (*see below*). Walking is the best way to get around the town center, which is filled with arts-and-crafts shops, galleries, restaurants, and coffeehouses.

Not surprisingly, the town has become popular as a base for exploring the rest of the Garden Route. The only drawback is that the closest beaches lie 20 minutes away by car—if you want a traditional beach holiday, you're probably better off in Plettenberg Bay. Whatever you do, don't leave town without trying some of Knysna's renowned oysters, harvested fresh from the enormous beds in the lagoon.

Besides tourism and oysters, Knysna makes its living from timber. Logging started in the hills in the early 19th century, when settlers harvested the ancient forests of stinkwood and yellowwood. Much of the indigenous forest has now been cleared and replanted with exotic pine and eucalyptus. Habitat loss is largely responsible for the decline of the famous Knysna elephants that still roam wild in the hills above the town. In 1876, as many as 500 elephants lived in the thick forests behind Knysna. Today, only seven remain, and they are seldom seen by anyone except forestry employees. Several walking trails and drives wind through Knysna's forests, many offering tremendous views back over the ocean. Even if you don't see elephants, you're likely to spot the Knysna lourie, a brilliantly plumed forest bird that is a common sight around town. Detailed maps of trails and forestry roads are available from the Knysna Publicity Association (*see* Important Addresses and Numbers *in* Garden Route Essentials, *below*).

You can get a feel for the growth of the town and its industries at the **Knysna Museum,** a complex of minor museums housed in the Old Gaol, a structure that dates back to 1859. The Maritime Museum displays some interesting pictures of old sailing schooners entering the Knysna Heads, as well as trophies from the famous Cape–Rio yacht race. The highlight of the Angling Museum (☛ R2) is a 176-pound coelacanth, a prehistoric fish that was thought to have become extinct 65 million years ago; in 1938, however, a South African fisherman landed a specimen that was very much alive. The Knysna Art Gallery, also in the Old Gaol, is an unattractive exhibition space where local artists display their works. *Corner of Queen and Main Sts.,* ☎ *0445/82–6138.* ☛ *Free.* ☺ *Weekdays 9:30–12:30 and 1:30–4:30, Sat. 9:30–1.*

The most interesting building in the area stands across the lagoon from Knysna, in the exclusive community of Belvidere. **Holy Trinity Church,** built in 1855 of local stone, is a lovely replica of a Norman church of the 11th century. Holy Trinity was erected by Thomas Duthie, a young ensign of the 72nd Highland Regiment who settled in Knysna in 1834. The interior is notable for its beautiful stinkwood and yellowwood timber and stained-glass windows. To reach the church, follow the N2 west out of Knysna and take the Belvidere turnoff just after the bridge. Follow signs from there.

TIME OUT   If you do visit Belvidere, be sure to stop at **Crabs Creek** (Belvidere Rd., ☎ 0445/87–1043), a fun tavern that sits on the bank of the Knysna Lagoon. On a sunny day, you may have to wait for an outside table, but it's worth it—the view across the water to Knysna is better than the food. Fried seafood is the focus—the pint of prawns is very popular—or you can order the usual pub fare.

You can't come to Knysna without making a trip out to the **Heads** at the mouth of the lagoon. These rock sentinels guard the narrow approach to the town and provide great views of both the sea and the lagoon. Only the developed, eastern side of the Heads is accessible by car, via George Rex Drive off the N2. You have two options: to park at the base of the head and follow the walking trails that snake around the rocky cliffs, just feet above the crashing surf; or to drive to the summit, with its panoramic views and easy parking.

Unlike its eastern counterpart, the western side of the Heads is completely unspoiled, part of **Featherbed Nature Reserve,** a private park that has been declared a National Heritage Site. In addition to a bizarre rock arch and a cave once inhabited by the indigenous Khoikhoi, the reserve is home to various small mammals, over 100 species of birds, and 1,000 plant species. It's well worth a visit. To get there, take one of the ferries that departs from the municipal jetty (*see* Guided Tours in Garden Route Essentials, *below*).

Six and a half kilometers (4 miles) east of Knysna along the N2 is the turnoff to Noetzie, a tiny holiday community with a difference. If you thought the presence of a Norman church in Belvidere was odd, then brace yourself for the **Noetzie Castles,** vacation homes built to resemble European castles, crenellations and all. The castles are more a curiosity than anything else—evidence of people with more money than taste. From the parking lot, it's a steep hike down a hill to reach them, but it's worth the trek just to enjoy the magnificent beach.

Brackenhill Waterfall lies 5 kilometers (3 miles) east of the Noetzie turnoff along the N2. A dirt road leads through a plantation of enormous eucalyptus trees to the falls, which plunge into a high-sided gorge overgrown with indigenous forest. Picnic tables make this an attractive spot for lunch or a snack.

If you're not planning on hiking anywhere along the Garden Route, consider a stop at the **Garden of Eden,** a small grove of indigenous trees next to the highway 5 kilometers (3 miles) east of Brackenhill. Despite the traffic noise, the grove gives you a feel for the coastal forests that once blanketed the region. Short walking trails wind past towering Outeniqua yellowwoods, Cape plane trees, and Cape forest ferns. *Off N2, no ☎.* ☛ *R2.* ⊙ *Sunrise–sunset.*

Plettenberg Bay, 32 kilometers (20 miles) east of Knysna, is South Africa's premier beach resort. It attracts large numbers of the BMW crowd from the northern suburbs of Johannesburg—people who dress up for the beach and call each other "doll." Not surprisingly, hotels are expensive, and the place gets packed during school holidays. The town itself, sprawled across the side of a steep hill above the sea, can't compare with charming Knysna, but the beaches and views will astonish you. "Plet," as it is commonly known, presides over a stretch of coastline that has inspired rave reviews since the Portuguese first set eyes on it in 1497. Golden beaches stretch as far as the eye can see, curving round to form what the Portuguese called Bahia Formosa (Beautiful Bay). Three rivers debouch into the sea here, the most spectacular of which—the Keurbooms—backs up to form a large lagoon. Whales and dolphins are frequent visitors to the bay, and are best viewed from the **Robberg Nature Reserve,** a rocky peninsula that juts out into the sea. For swimming, surfing, sailing, fishing, and hiking, you can't do much better than Plet, although the water is still colder than it is around Durban and in northern KwaZulu-Natal (*see* Chapter 7).

From Plet take the N2 east. The road runs across a flat, coastal plain of fynbos, with the forested Tsitsikamma Mountains on your left. Just after the Crags, turn off the N2 onto the R102, a far more interesting and scenic route. The R102 passes through farmland before dropping suddenly to sea level through a steep gorge. It's a great descent, with the road worming back and forth through a tunnel of greenery, impenetrable bush pressing in on either side. At the bottom of the pass, turn right into **Nature's Valley,** a magnificent lagoon hemmed in by bush-cloaked cliffs and hills. Part of the Groot River, the lagoon empties into the sea past a wide, idyllic beach—a popular spot for canoeing and sailboarding. There are toilet and picnic facilities.

From Nature's Valley, the R102 climbs back into the mountains, breasting the Groot River and Bloukrans passes before finally rejoining the N2. It's another 24 kilometers (15 miles) to the turnoff to Tsitsikamma National Park and the mouth of the Storms River.

★ ⓴ **Tsitsikamma National Park** is a narrow belt of coastline extending for 80 kilometers (50 miles) from Oubosstrand to Nature's Valley and beyond. It encompasses some of the most spectacular coastal scenery in the country, including deep gorges, evergreen forests, tidal pools, and long, empty beaches. The best way to see the park is on the five-day Otter Trail, South Africa's most famous hike (*see* Sports and the Outdoors, *below*). A less strenuous highlight is the Storms River mouth, at the midpoint of the park. The river enters the sea through a narrow channel carved between sheer cliffs. Storms River was aptly named: When gale winds blow, as they often do, the sea flies into a pounding fury, hurling spray onto the rocks and whipping spume high up the cliffs. From the visitor center, a .8-kilometer (½-mile) trail descends through the forest (different tree species are all labeled) and over a narrow suspension bridge strung across the river mouth. It's a spectacular walk, a highlight of any trip to the Garden Route. On the other side of the bridge, a steep trail climbs to the top of a bluff overlooking the river and the sea. Other trails, ranging from .8 to 3.2 kilometers (½ to 2 miles), lead either to a cave once inhabited by the Khoikhoi or through the coastal forest. A restaurant with great views of the river and the ocean serves breakfast, lunch, and dinner. *Off N2,* ☏ *04237/607.* ☛ *R5 per vehicle.* ⊙ *Daily 5:30 AM–9:30 PM.*

It's an uneventful 160-kilometer (100-mile) drive from Storms River ㉑ to **Port Elizabeth,** one of South Africa's largest cities and the center of the country's auto industry. When a place bills itself as the "Friendly City," you know it's having a hard time finding a reason for tourists to visit. Indeed, the city has little to hold you long, and most foreign travelers use Port Elizabeth only as an entry or exit point for the Garden Route. The city's beachfront area—its main appeal—is highly developed, both with industrial docklands and kitschy amusement parks. After the splendors of the Garden Route, it can leave a bad taste in your mouth. The old center of the town, however, has some interesting historical buildings, especially around Donkin Reserve and Market Square, with its grand 1858 City Hall.

If you do find yourself in Port Elizabeth for a day, you would be well ㉒ advised to head to **Addo Elephant National Park,** 50 kilometers (31 miles) to the northeast. This small park covers only 35,900 acres, but it's home to a population of over 200 elephants. The Addo bush is very thick, making it harder to find them than you might think. If and when you do come across them, the elephants are likely to be in herds of as many as 50. The park is also home to small populations of buffalo, kudu, black rhino, and red hartebeest. You can explore Addo in your own vehicle during the day or opt for a guided day or night drive with a game ranger (R40 per person). An à la carte restaurant serves all three meals, and the park's rest camp offers accommodation in fully equipped, self-catering cottages. *Access from P.E. via the R335,* ☏ *0464/40–0556. Lodging reservations: Box 787, Pretoria 0001,* ☏ *012/343–1991.* ☛ *R15 per vehicle (free if you stay overnight).* ⊙ *Daily 7–7.*

SPORTS AND THE OUTDOORS

Fishing

In Knysna, **Kelsea Fishing Charters** (☏ 0445/82–5577) offers deep-sea fishing trips in an 8-meter (26-foot) ski boat. The emphasis is on bottom-fishing for reef fish like steenbras, stumpnose, red roman, and cob. Bait and tackle are supplied.

Golf

The two best courses along the Garden Route are in George. Unfortunately, you have to stay at the **Fancourt Hotel and Country Club Estate** (*see* Dining and Lodging, *below*) to play its magnificent 27-hole, Gary Player–designed course. The same policy does not apply, however, at the 18-hole **George Golf Course** (☎ 0441/73–6116). Another worthwhile course is the **Plettenberg Bay Country Club** (☎ 04457/3–2132), situated on a nature reserve in the Piesang Valley.

Hiking and Walking

The Garden Route is one of the most popular hiking regions in the country, and hikers have literally hundreds of trails from which to choose. Tourist offices in all the towns (*see* Important Addresses and Numbers *in* Garden Route Essentials, *below*) have detailed listings and maps of hikes in their area. Some of the more popular trails are listed below.

MOSSEL BAY

The **St. Blaize Trail** is a 13-kilometer (8-mile) hike that starts at the cave below the St. Blaize lighthouse and runs along the coast to Dana Bay. The walk takes about five hours and offers great views of cliffs, ocean, and numerous rocky bays and coves.

PLETTENBERG BAY

The **Robberg Peninsula** is a tremendous spot from which to watch whales and dolphins. Three circular walking trails, ranging in length from 45 minutes to four hours, run along the escarpment and through large areas of fynbos. The vegetation offers little shade, so think twice about venturing out here in mid-summer.

TSITSIKAMMA NATIONAL PARK

Otter Trail is the king of South Africa's hiking trails. It runs along the coast from the mouth of Storms River to Nature's Valley, passing rocky cliffs, beaches, fynbos, rivers, and towering indigenous forest. The trail is only 42 kilometers (25 miles) long, but it's billed as a five-day hike to give you time to swim and just hang out. Accommodation is in overnight huts equipped with sleeping bunks, braais (barbecues), and chemical toilets. You must carry in all food and carry out all trash. Only 12 people are allowed on this popular trail per day, making it vital to book at least a year in advance. *Reserve through National Parks Board, Box 787, Pretoria 0001,* ☎ *012/343–1991,* 🖷 *012/343–0905.*

Horseback Riding

Equitrailing (☎ 04457/9718), 5 kilometers (3 miles) outside Plettenberg, offers various guided horseback rides ranging from 1½ hours to all day, as well as moonlight and champagne rides.

DINING AND LODGING

For price ranges, *see* Charts 1 and 2(B) *in* On the Road with Fodor's.

George

DINING

$$ Copper Pot. Pink walls, candlelit tables, and dark floral drapes set the tone for this elegant restaurant. The specialty is seafood, competently prepared—although many of the dishes could benefit from additional seasoning. An excellent starter is tender calamari sautéed in butter, lemon juice, garlic, and parsley. Other appetizers include spring rolls in phyllo pastry, smoked ostrich, and oysters. For the main course, choose from fish of the day, Mossel Bay sole, or a mild Mauritian curry of mussels, shrimp, calamari, and fish. For more robust fare at lower prices, head next door to The Wine Barrel (☎ 0441/73–4370), the Copper Pot's casual bistro. ✗ *Multi Centre, Meade St.,* ☎ *0441/74–3191. Reservations essential. AE, DC, MC, V. Closed Sun. No lunch Mon., Sat.*

DINING AND LODGING

$$$$ Fancourt Hotel and Country Club Estate. In the shadows of the Outeniqua Mountains, this luxury resort hotel has a country club feel—anyone who doesn't play golf may feel out of place. The showpiece is a 27-hole golf course, open to members and guests only, designed by Gary Player. At the heart of the hotel is an 1860 manor house, now occupied in part by an expensive restaurant. Rooms are located either in the old manor house itself or in white villas scattered around the huge complex. ☎ *Montagu St. (mailing address: Box 2266), George 6530,* ☎ *0441/70–8282,* ℻ *0441/70–7605. 88 units with bath. 4 restaurants, 3 bars, 3 pools, 27-hole golf course, health center. Breakfast included. AE, DC, MC, V.*

LODGING

$$$ Hoogekraal. About 16 kilometers (10 miles) outside George, this historic farm sits on a grassy hill with panoramic views of the Outeniqua Mountains and the Indian Ocean. The farm has been in the same family since the early 18th century, and the lodge is filled with antiques and precious heirlooms. Suites in the original 1760 wing have timber ceilings and antique country armoires and dressers. Other rooms are in a house dating back to 1820. Breakfast is included, and most guests choose to stay for the four-course dinner as well, served at a communal table in the magnificent dining room (*$$$$*, wine included). ☎ *Glentana Rd., off N2 between George and Mossel Bay (mailing address: Box 34, George 6530),* ☎ *0441/79–1277,* ℻ *0441/79–1300. 9 rooms with bath. No children under 5. MC, V.*

Knysna

DINING

$$ La Loerie. Run by a husband-and-wife team, this tiny restaurant serves some of the best fish on the Garden Route. No dinner in Knysna would be complete without fresh oysters from the lagoon. Beyond those, choose among starters like calamari rings, smoked salmon trout, or mussels. For the main course, you can't beat the sole meunière, pan-fried to perfection. If you don't want seafood, consider ostrich fillet in mushrooms or curried lamb. Amarula truffles are a heavenly final touch. ✗ *57 Main St.,* ☎ *0445/2–1616. Reservations essential (phone after 5:30). DC, MC, V. Closed Sun. No lunch Sat.*

$ Pink Umbrella. On a sunny day, this is a great place for an *al fresco* lunch. Chef June David serves only vegetarian and seafood dishes, but her food is good enough to keep even big meat-eaters happy. Her nutty dal topped with sweet chutney sauce is excellent, as is the corn and herb pie. Seafood dishes include a daily special and Mossel Bay sole. For many regulars, the first courses are just a warm-up for the restaurant's desserts, huge concoctions guaranteed to add inches to any waistline. ✗ *14 Kingsway, Leisure Island,* ☎ *0445/2–2409. Reservations essential. MC, V.* ☉ *Daily 9–5.*

$ Knysna Oyster Company. If you love oysters, make a beeline for this
★ tasting tavern, attached to one of the world's largest oyster-farming operations. Diners sit at picnic tables next to the lagoon, with great views of the Heads. Each tasting consists of 6–8 fresh oysters and a basket of brown bread. It's worth ordering a plate of mussels, too, to dunk your bread in the garlic-lemon butter. Chase the oysters with excellent local Mitchells beer—then do it all again. It's easy to spend an entire day like this. ✗ *Long St., Thesens Island,* ☎ *0445/2–2168. No reservations. DC, MC, V.* ☉ *Mon.–Thurs. 8–5, Fri. 8–4, weekends 9–3.*

DINING AND LODGING

$$$$ **Belvidere Manor.** This is one of the most attractive and desirable lodg-
★ ings along the coast. White cottages face each other across a lawn that
slopes down to Knysna Lagoon and a boat jetty. On the other side of
the lagoon, some 6.5 kilometers (4 miles) away, lies Knysna itself. Cottages are airy and bright, with a country feel. Choose from one- and
two-bedroom units, all with dining areas, sitting rooms with fireplaces,
and fully equipped kitchens. The manor house, a lovely 1834 farmstead,
has been converted into a restaurant and guest lounge. In summer,
breakfast is served on a wooden deck looking over the lagoon. Sizable
discounts are offered for long stays. ☎ *Lower Duthie Dr., Belvidere
Estate (mailing address: Box 1195, Knysna 6570),* ☎ *0445/87–1055,*
FAX *0445/87–1059. 33 cottages with bath. Restaurant, room service, pool.
Breakfast included. No children under 10. AE, DC, MC, V.*

LODGING

$$$ **Point Lodge.** This small bed-and-breakfast possesses an enviable site
on a point jutting into Knysna Lagoon. The view from the pool deck
and five of the rooms encompasses bird-rich wetlands, the lagoon, and
the distant Heads. Rooms are decorated in Biggie Best style, South
Africa's equivalent of Laura Ashley—lots of floral and striped fabrics.
In the evening, guests usually meet for drinks in the lounge and bar.
☎ *Off N2 (mailing address: Box 767, Knysna 6570),* ☎ *0445/2–1944,*
FAX *0445/2–3455. 7 rooms with bath. Bar, pool. Breakfast included.
No children under 15. AE, DC, MC, V.*

$$ **Wayside Inn.** This new hotel in the center of Knysna is absolutely charm-
★ ing. The owners have achieved a colonial African feel through the use
of black wrought-iron bedsteads topped with white cotton duvets, pale
yellow walls hung with African art, overhead fans, and wall-to-wall
sisal matting. All rooms have TVs and phones. Continental breakfasts
are served in the rooms on white wicker trays, and picnic hampers are
available for lunch. ☎ *Pledge Sq., 48 Main Rd. (mailing address: Box
2369), Knysna 6570,* ☎ *and* FAX *0445/82–6011. 15 rooms with bath.
Breakfast included. AE, DC, MC, V.*

Mossel Bay

DINING

$$ **Gannet.** Tour-bus crowds occasionally descend on this popular spot,
but don't let that put you off. The emphasis here is solidly on seafood,
whether it's freshly shucked oysters, grilled Mossel Bay sole, or prawn-
tail kebabs. Stick to the simpler grilled dishes—some of the more am-
bitious choices, such as calamari risotto and seafood bisque, miss the
mark. If you don't want seafood, you can order a pizza from the
wood-burning oven. In summer, sit outside on the shaded terrace over-
looking the bay or in the welcoming interior, furnished with an eclec-
tic collection of country antiques. The restaurant also serves full
breakfasts. ✕ *Corner of Market and Church Sts.,* ☎ *0444/91–1885.
Reservations advised. AE, DC, MC, V.*

LODGING

$$ **Old Post Office Tree Guest House.** This pleasant guest house has the
best location of any hotel in Mossel Bay, just meters from the town's
museum complex and overlooking the beach and sea. Guests can relax
at the Blue Oyster Cocktail Bar, a delightful pub and terrace with
panoramic views of Munro's Bay. Despite great views, the rooms have
little to offer. They're dark, with an unfortunate blue-and-yellow decor.
Breakfast is served at the Gannet (*see above*). ☎ *Market St. (mailing
address: Box 349), Mossel Bay 6500,* ☎ *0444/91–3738,* FAX *0444/91–*

3104. *30 rooms with bath. Restaurant, bar, room service, pool. Breakfast included. AE, DC, MC, V.*

Oudtshoorn
DINING AND LODGING

$$$ **Rozenhof Country Lodge.** In a restored Victorian farmhouse looking out at the Swartberg mountains, this lovely guest house is by far your best choice in Oudtshoorn. Antiques and works by South African artists complement the house's yellowwood beams and Spanish-tile floor. Rooms, in white cottages arranged around a central lawn and fountain, are bright and elegant, warmed by old-fashioned brass bedsteads and satinwood furniture. The restaurant serves an excellent five-course dinner, with an emphasis on regional cuisine given a *cordon bleu* twist. Look for such dishes as butternut soup enlivened with cream and nutmeg, phyllo parcels of mackerel, and ostrich paupiettes with port sauce. Nonguests can reserve a table if space allows. ⊞ *264 Baron van Reede St. (mailing address: Box 1190), Oudtshoorn 6620,* ☏ *0443/22–2232,* ℻ *0443/22–3021. 12 rooms with bath. Restaurant, bar, room service, pool. Breakfast included. AE, DC, MC, V.*

Plettenberg Bay
DINING AND LODGING

$$$$ **Hunter's Country House.** Just 10 minutes from town, Hunter's is a so-
★ phisticated lodge that easily outshines the more famous and expensive guest lodges of the Eastern Transvaal. It's one of those places you can't bear to leave. Perhaps it's the overwhelming sense of tranquillity—of pure country silence that can be so difficult to find—or perhaps it's the setting amid gardens that fall away into a valley of indigenous forest. The heart of the lodge is an old farmstead, a lovely thatched building with low beams and large fireplaces. Guest rooms are in individual thatched white cottages, each with its own fireplace and veranda. Victorian antiques grace the rooms, and claw-foot tubs are the centerpiece of many of the gigantic bathrooms. And service is outstanding. Most guests eat at the hotel's excellent table d'hôte restaurant, which brings a French touch to local South African produce. Reservations are essential for nonguests. ⊞ *Off N2, between Plettenberg and Knysna (mailing address: Box 454, Plettenberg Bay 6600,* ☏ *04457/7818,* ℻ *04457/7878. 17 rooms with bath. Restaurant, bar, pool. Breakfast included. No children under 12. AE, DC, MC, V.*

$$$$ **Plettenberg.** High on a rocky point in Plettenberg Bay, this luxury hotel commands unbelievable views of Formosa Bay, the Tsitsikamma Mountains, Keurbooms Lagoon, and miles of magnificent beach. Built around an 1860 manor house, the hotel has two distinct parts: a summery, beachside wing and a more formal winter lounge in the old house. Rooms borrow elements from both aspects of the hotel and the result is bright and refreshing: Sponge-painted yellow walls, bold butterfly-motif fabrics, and original paintings by South African artists. Even if you don't stay here, treat yourself to lunch on the hotel terrace. Diners sit under large fabric umbrellas looking out over a pool that seems to extend right into the incredible views. The lunch menu is small, with a selection of salads and sandwiches as well as a pasta dish and catch of the day. Dinner is a fancier affair, focusing on local meat and seafood. The hotel is a member of the exclusive Relais & Chateaux association. Nonguests must make reservations for dinner. ⊞ *Look Out Rocks (mailing address: Box 719), Plettenberg Bay 6600,* ☏ *04457/3–2030,* ℻ *04457/3–2074. 26 rooms with bath. Restaurant, bar, pool. Breakfast included. No children under 14. AE, DC, MC, V.*

LODGING

$$ Bayview Hotel. In the center of Plettenberg, this comfortable hotel enjoys good views out over Formosa Bay, particularly from the terrace café and bar. Rooms are decorated with rattan furniture and white walls, but the overall effect is rather spartan. Sea-facing rooms on the lower floors suffer from traffic noise; inner rooms are cheaper, cooler, and quieter, but lack that unbeatable view. All rooms have TVs and air-conditioning. The beach is a 10-minute walk away. ☎ *Corner of Main Rd. and Gibb St. (mailing address: Box 1047), Plettenberg Bay 6600, ☎ 04457/3–1961, FAX 04457/3–2059. 35 rooms with bath. Bar, café. Breakfast included. AE, DC, MC, V.*

Port Elizabeth

LODGING

$$ Holiday Inn Garden Court–Kings Beach. Opposite the beach and just five minutes from the airport, this high-rise hotel offers standard rooms, with all the amenities you'd expect from a major hotel chain, including air-conditioning, TVs, and tea- and coffeemakers. Request a sea-facing room on an upper floor—they don't cost any more and the views are great. The Oceanarium and a host of restaurants are within easy walking distance. ☎ *La Roche Dr., Humewood (mailing address: Box 13100, Port Elizabeth 6013, ☎ 041/52–3720, FAX 041/55–5754. 272 rooms with bath. Restaurant, bar, pool. AE, DC, MC, V.*

$ Edward. The rooms look a bit ratty, but for sheer character and history you can't do better than this grand old hotel on Donkin Reserve in the city center. The building dates back to the turn of the century and retains an Edwardian feel—some of the rooms even have four-poster beds. If modern amenities are important to you, though, you're better off at the Holiday Inn. Most rooms at the Edward have neither air-conditioning nor showers (only bathtubs). ☎ *Belmont Terr. (mailing address: Box 319), Port Elizabeth 6001, ☎ 041/56–2056, FAX 041/56–2056. 110 rooms with bath. 2 restaurants, 2 bars, room service. AE, DC, MC, V.*

Sedgefield

DINING AND LODGING

$$$ Lake Pleasant Hotel. This three-star hotel sits on the edge of a beautiful lake in the Goukamma Nature Reserve, and will appeal to anyone who wants to commune with nature. At the heart of the hotel stands a century-old hunting lodge, but today guests can only watch the 200 species of birds that live in the area. All rooms have lake views, the best being the executive suites with large glass doors that open onto lawns spreading down to the water. By contrast, the standard suites feel bland and empty. The hotel is open to nonguests for pub lunches and Sunday lunch buffets, but the table d'hôte dinner is reserved for guests only. ☎ *Off N2 (mailing address: Box 2), Sedgefield 6573, ☎ 04455/3–1313, FAX 04455/3–2040. 25 rooms with bath. Restaurant, bar, pool, boating, fishing. Breakfast included. No children under 6. AE, DC, MC, V.*

Storms River

DINING AND LODGING

$$ Tzitzikama Forest Inn. Motorists don't have a lot of lodging options between Plettenberg Bay and Port Elizabeth. Although this hotel isn't going to win any awards, it's at least clean and comfortable. It's also incredibly peaceful, set in pleasant gardens in the shadow of the Tsitsikamma Mountains. Rooms are in log cabins or alpine-style chalets, all with TVs. Food at the hotel's à la carte restaurant is terrible: Grilled baby chicken is so tough it could fight in the featherweight division, and vegetables are boiled to death. ☎ *Off N2, Storms River 6308,* ☎ *042/541–1711,* ℻ *042/541–1669. 42 rooms with bath. 2 restaurants, 2 bars, pool, tennis. Breakfast included. AE, DC, MC, V.*

$ **Tsitsikamma National Park–Storms River Mouth.** Parks Board lodging seldom gets rave reviews for its charm, but it will be clean and comfortable. An added bonus here is the setting, almost within soaking distance of the pounding surf at the mouth of the Storms River. Choose either a two-bed log cabin or a three-bed oceanette, all with fully equipped kitchens and bathrooms. An à la carte restaurant overlooking the river mouth serves food throughout the day. ☎ *Off N2, near Storms River,* ☎ *04237/607. Reservations: Box 787, Pretoria 0001,* ☎ *012/343–1991,* ℻ *012/343–0905. Restaurant. AE, DC, MC, V.*

Wilderness

DINING AND LODGING

$$$ **Karos Wilderness Hotel.** Set amid attractive lawns and gardens, this huge resort hotel is just minutes from Wilderness Beach and the bird-rich Touws River lagoon. The hotel is especially popular with families who appreciate the wide range of outdoor activities available, including tennis, mini-golf, and swimming. The hotel lacks a beach feel, however, and unless you look outside you could be in any luxury chain hotel anywhere. Rooms are conventional but comfortable, with plenty of blond wood and bold floral fabrics. The hotel's dinner buffet is one of the best you'll find along the coast. ☎ *Off N2 (mailing address: Box 6), Wilderness 6560,* ☎ *0441/9–1110,* ℻ *0441/9–0600. 158 rooms with bath. Restaurant, 2 bars, room service, 3 pools, sauna, 2 tennis courts, bowling green, squash. AE, DC, MC, V.*

LODGING

$ **Wilderness National Park.** Wilderness Restcamp is the larger of two self-catering camps, offering a selection of four-bed log cabins and six-bed cottages. The log cabins, built on stilts, are great. From the veranda you get a lovely view of the reeds and marshes of the Serpentine Channel, and the cabin interior is pleasantly decorated with cane furniture. The cottages, on the other hand, have no appeal, filled with old furniture and grotty carpets. The Ebb and Flow Restcamp, overlooking the river, is much more rustic, consisting of two-bed rondawels (round huts modeled after traditional African dwellings) without their own bathrooms; cooking facilities are limited to a fridge and a hot plate. ☎ *Off N2, Wilderness,* ☎ *0441/877–1197,* ℻ *0441/877–0111. Reservations: Box 787, Pretoria 0001,* ☎ *012/343–1991,* ℻ *012/343– 0905. 10 log cabins, 13 cottages, and 15 rondawels. AE, DC, MC, V.*

GARDEN ROUTE ESSENTIALS

Arriving and Departing

By Bus

Both **Intercape Mainliner** (☎ 021/386–4400) and **Translux Express** (☎ 021/405–3333 in Cape Town, ☎ 041/507–3333 in Port Elizabeth) offer regular service along the Garden Route between Cape Town and Port Elizabeth, stopping at all major destinations; Translux buses also call at Oudtshoorn in the Little Karoo. Intercape offers a package known as the Boarding Pass that allows you to buy a single Cape Town–Port Elizabeth ticket but break your journey anywhere along the Garden Route and catch later buses; it costs R30 more than a regular ticket.

By Car

Mossel Bay, at the western end of the Garden Route, lies 384 kilometers (240 miles) from Cape Town along the N2 highway. A trip up the Garden Route is a logical extension of a driving tour of the Overberg (*see* Chapter 4).

By Plane

If you're coming by plane, it's best to fly into either George, at the western end of the Garden Route, or Port Elizabeth, at the eastern end.

The **George Airport** (☎ 0441/76–9310), 5 kilometers (3 miles) outside of town, is served by **South African Airways** (☎ 0441/76–9000) and **S.A. Express** (☎ 0441/73–8448), the commuter branch of S.A.A.

Port Elizabeth Airport (☎ 041/51–2984) is served by **S.A. Express** (☎ 041/34–4444), **Airlink** (☎ 041/51–2311), and **Phoenix** (☎ 041/507–7363). A taxi from the airport to the city center costs about R25.

By Train

Spoornet's **Southern Cross** (☎ 021/405–3871 in Cape Town, ☎ 041/507–2400 in Port Elizabeth) runs from Cape Town to Port Elizabeth on Friday and returns on Sunday, making stops at George and Oudtshoorn. The journey takes nearly 24 hours, and does not enjoy the same glorious views as the Outeniqua Choo-Tjoe (*see below*).

Getting Around

By Car

Avis (☎ 0441/76–9222), **Budget** (☎ 0441/76–9216), **Dolphin** (☎ 0441/76–9070, and **Imperial** (☎ 0441/76–9218) all have car-rental offices at George Airport.

At Port Elizabeth Airport, you'll find rental desks for **Avis** (☎ 041/51–1306), **Budget** (☎ 041/51–4242), **Dolphin** (☎ 041/51–3890), **Imperial** (☎ 041/51–1268), and **Tempest** (☎ 041/51–1256).

By Train

A highlight of any trip to the Garden Route is a ride aboard the **Outeniqua Choo-Tjoe** (☎ 0441/73–8288 in George, ☎ 0445/2–1361 in Knysna), a vintage steam train that runs between Knysna and George, offering stunning views of some of the Garden Route's most famous scenic landmarks. Two trains run in each direction daily, except on Sunday. The one-way trip takes 2½ hours, and advance reservations are advisable. **Sam's Tours** (☎ 0445/2–3522) offers a minibus shuttle service that handles pick-ups and drop-offs in Knysna and George.

Guided Tours

Boat Tours

KNYSNA

Featherbed Ferries (☎ 0445/81–0590) runs trips to the Featherbed Nature Reserve, on the Western Head of the Knysna Lagoon. Boats leave from the municipal jetty daily at 10 and noon. Once in the reserve, passengers can follow the Bushbuck Trail, a 2.4-kilometer (1½-mile) guided hike through the reserve, and even opt for a fish braai at the reserve's restaurant.

For cruises of Knysna Lagoon, including a trip out to the Heads, contact **John Benn** (☎ 0445/21693) or **Knysna Lagoon Cruises** (☎ 0445/23116). Cruises, which depart from the municipal jetty or the angling club next to the railway station, last about two hours and cost R35 per person. Drinks and light meals are served.

MOSSEL BAY

Romonza (☎ 0444/3101) and the **Infanté dom Henrique** (☎ 0444/950502), two wooden sailing vessels, offer regular one-hour trips to view the seals at Seal Island, as well as sunset cruises and fishing trips. Seal trips leave from the harbor and cost about R20.

WILDERNESS

An excellent way to see Wilderness National Park and its birdlife is aboard the **Kingfisher Ferry** (Freesia Rock, Freesia Rd., ☎ 0441/877–1101), which cruises up the Touw River twice daily. Choose between a four-hour cruise and walk (about R40), which ends at the Touw River Falls, or a simple two-hour cruise (about R25).

Nature Tours

SEDGEFIELD

Goukamma Adventures (☎ 04455/31313) has 3½-hour tours of the Goukamma Nature Reserve in open Land Rovers for a minimum of five people. The tour wends its way amid towering dunes and through coastal fynbos and Knysna Forest. It's particularly popular among birders—more than 250 species have been spotted in the area. Tours depart from the Lake Pleasant Hotel (*see* Dining and Lodging, *above*) and include a short walk on the beach, a picnic lunch, and soft drinks.

Important Addresses and Numbers

Emergencies

Dial 10111 for the **police**, 10177 for an **ambulance.**

Visitor Information

Mossel Bay Marketing Association. *Cnr. Church and Market Sts., Mossel Bay,* ☎ *0444/91–2202.* ☉ *Weekdays 9–5, weekends 10–4.*

Klein Karoo Marketing Association. *Voortrekker St., Oudtshoorn,* ☎ *0443/22–5007.* ☉ *Weekdays 8–5:30, Sat. 8:30–1.*

George Tourism Information. *124 York St., George,* ☎ *0441/877–1101.* ☉ *Weekdays 7:45–4:30, Sat. 9–noon.*

Regional Tourist Information Office. *124 York St., George,* ☎ *0441/73–6355.* ☉ *Weekdays 7:45–4:30.*

Knysna Publicity Association. *40 Main St., Knysna,* ☎ *0445/21610,* FAX *0445/21646.* ☉ *Weekdays 8:30–5, Sat. 9–12:30.*

Plettenberg Bay Business and Publicity Association. *Victoria Cottage, Kloof St., Plettenberg Bay,* ☎ *04457/34065,* FAX *04457/34066.* ☉ *Weekdays 8–5, Sat. 8–1.*

Port Elizabeth Publicity Association. *Donkin Reserve,* ☎ *041/52–1315.* ☉ *Weekdays 8–4:30.*

Wilderness Eco-tourism Association. *Leila's Lane, Wilderness,* ☎ *0441/77–0045.* ☉ *Mon.–Sat. 8:30–5.*

7 Durban and KwaZulu-Natal

Steamy heat, the heady aroma of spices, and a polyglot of English, Indian, and Zulu give bustling Durban a tropical feel. Some of the country's most popular bathing beaches extend north and south of the city; inland you can tour the battlefields where Boer, Briton, and Zulu struggled for control of the country. The Drakensberg mountains are a breathtaking sanctuary of soaring beauty, crisp air, and phenomenal hiking. In the far north, Hluhluwe-Umfolozi and several private reserves offer a big-game experience rivaling that of the Eastern Transvaal.

FOR SOUTH AFRICANS, the comparatively small province of KwaZulu-Natal is one of the premier holiday destinations in the country. Here lie the highest and most beautiful mountains in southern Africa, some of the country's finest game reserves, and a landscape studded with memorials commemorating the great battles between Briton, Boer, and Zulu. The main draw, though, is the subtropical climate and the warm waters of the Indian Ocean. In fact, the entire 480-kilometer (300-mile) coastline from the Wild Coast in the south to the border with Mozambique is essentially one long beach, attracting hordes of bathers, surfers, and anglers.

Durban, South Africa's third-largest city, is the busiest port in Africa. Its chief appeal to tourists is its long strip of high-rise hotels and amusement-park thrills—known as the Golden Mile—fronting its beaches. This area is tacky, unattractive, and phenomenally popular. For those seeking a more tranquil holiday full of sun, sand, and surf, Umhlanga Rocks (pronounced "Um-shlong-a"), an attractive resort town 20 minutes north of Durban, is the ticket.

To find beaches unmarred by commercial development, you need to travel northeast to Zululand. Much of the coastline here is protected, but this means that there are few decent places to rest your head. One notable exception is Rocktail Bay Lodge (*see* Chapter 9), an idyllic getaway in Maputaland, in the far north of the province. With no other buildings for miles, the lodge presides over a landscape of deserted beaches, towering dunes, and virgin bush, making it a highlight of any visit to South Africa.

But you don't have to go all the way to Maputaland to experience the true African wilderness. Just a couple of hours west of Durban are the Drakensberg mountains, offering tremendous hiking amid some of the country's most spectacular, unspoiled scenery. And three hours northeast of Durban, in Zululand, lies a collection of game parks and nature reserves second only to Kruger National Park. One of these, Hluhluwe-Umfolozi Game Reserve, is the jewel in the crown of the Natal Parks Board and the park responsible for bringing the white rhino back from the brink of extinction. It would be a mistake to visit Hluhluwe (pronounced "shoosh-louie") without also exploring the nearby St. Lucia Greater Wetland Park, an enormous estuary where crocodiles, hippos, and sharks all share the same waters (*see* Chapter 9).

Zululand, the region north of the Tugela River, is the traditional home of the Zulu tribe. In the early 19th century, Zulus established themselves under King Shaka as one of the preeminent military powers in the region. At the Battle of Isandlwana, Zulu *impis* (regiments) inflicted one of the most famous defeats on the British army in history, before being ultimately crushed in 1879. A visit to Zululand would be incomplete without learning something of the Zulus' fascinating culture, and a tour of the old battlefields will enthrall history buffs.

Today, Zululand is home to the Inkatha Freedom Party (IFP), the Zulu-based organization that stands in vocal opposition to President Mandela's African National Congress (ANC). Nearly two years after the elections, the Zulu nation continues to exercise enormous influence on national politics, and violent clashes continue to erupt between supporters of the IFP and the ANC.

KwaZulu-Natal's two-part moniker is just one of the many changes introduced since those elections. Previously, the province was known simply as Natal, a name bestowed by explorer Vasco da Gama, who sighted the coastline on Christmas Day, 1497. KwaZulu, "the place of the Zulu," was one of the nominally independent homelands created by the Nationalists (1948–1994) to deprive blacks of their South African citizenship. The two are now one.

During the years of white rule, Natal was seen as a bastion of English-speaking South Africans. Its first white settlers—a party of British officers seeking trade with the Zulu in ivory—established themselves in Port Natal (now Durban) in 1824. The colony of Natal was formally annexed by the British in 1843. Cities like Durban and Pietermaritzburg present strong reminders of the colonial past with their Victorian architecture and public monuments. The province's huge Indian population is another reminder of Britain's imperial legacy. In the 1860s the British brought thousands of Indians to South Africa to work as indentured laborers cutting sugarcane, which grows abundantly on the coastal hills. Today, the Indian population of Durban alone numbers 1 million, and they play a major part in the economic and cultural life of the province.

Warning: Visitors to the northern parts of the province, including Zululand, are advised to take antimalarial drugs.

DURBAN

No city in South Africa feels more African than Durban. Cape Town could be in the Mediterranean, and Johannesburg's endless suburbs could be anywhere in America. Durban alone has the pulse, the look, the complex face of Africa. It may have something to do with the summer heat, a clinging sauna that soaks you with sweat in minutes. Here you don't need to take a township tour to see the emerging new South Africa. Hang out in Farewell Square in the city center and rub shoulders with Zulus, Indians, and whites. Wander into the Indian District or drive along Umgeni Road, and the *real* Africa rises up to meet you in a hundred ways: traditional healers touting animal organs, vegetable and spice vendors crowding the sidewalks, and the incessant hooting of minibus taxis trawling for business. It's by turns colorful, stimulating, and hypnotic.

By no means should you plan an entire holiday around the city, for Durban doesn't offer enough for a long stay. Nevertheless, it's definitely worth a stopover, perhaps between trips to the Drakensberg mountains or the game reserves in the north. Sadly, most visitors' impressions of Durban don't extend beyond the Golden Mile, the beachfront strip of high-rise hotels and carnival rides, where the main indication you're in Africa comes from the piles of souvenirs sold by curio vendors on the promenade.

To get the most from a stay in the city, leave the beachfront behind and explore the areas where Durban's residents live and work. A drive through the lovely neighborhoods of the Berea or a walk through the vibrant markets of the Indian District are infinitely more interesting than the beachfront sideshow. Again, if it's a beach vacation you want, you're better off in Umhlanga Rocks, 20 minutes away to the north.

Durban is a large port city with all the negative baggage that this implies. Don't wander around the Central Business District (CBD) alone at night, and think twice about exploring the city with an expensive

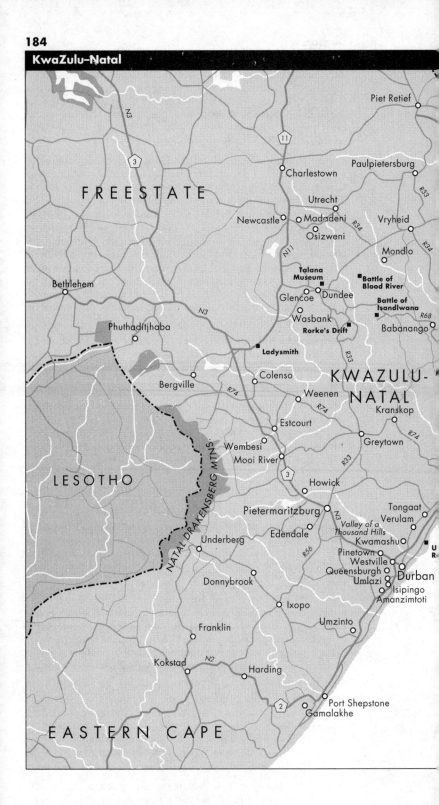

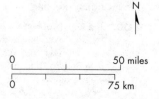

0   50 miles

0   75 km

INDIAN OCEAN

camera slung over your shoulder. Another type of hazard altogether is the school holidays. It's best to avoid Durban and the KwaZulu-Natal coast during summer vacation (mid-December to mid-January), when thousands of "Vaalies," as Transvaal residents are called, descend on the beaches to cavort and carouse en masse.

Exploring

This tour breaks down easily into four parts: the city center around Farewell Square; the Indian District; the Durban beachfront; and outlying attractions. Apart from the outlying districts, all four can be followed on foot, but you may need a taxi or car to get between them.

Numbers in the margin correspond to points of interest on the Durban map.

 The tour starts at the **Tourist Junction** (*see* Important Addresses and Numbers *in* Durban Essentials, *below*), the city's principal tourist information outlet. The office occupies Durban's old railway station, an attractive brick building constructed in 1894 in Flemish Revival style. The "NGR" above the main entrance stands for Natal Government Railways. *160 Pine St., at Soldier's Way,* ☎ *031/304–4934.* ☉ *Weekdays 8–5, weekends 9–2.*

 Cross Pine Street to **St. Paul's Church.** The current church, built in 1909 in Gothic Revival style, stands on the site of a previous church dating back to 1847. From the outside it's not much to look at, but the interior is beautiful. Notice the lovely wood ceiling and the stained-glass chancel windows.

Follow the pedestrian thoroughfare to West Street and cross the street.

Farewell Square stands at the heart of Durban. It's a lovely, shady plaza, bordered by some of the city's most historic buildings. Walkways lined with stately palms and flower beds crisscross the square, leading to monuments honoring Natal's important historic figures. The square stands on the site of the first European encampment in Natal, established by Francis Farewell and Henry Fynn in 1824 as a trading station to purchase ivory from the Zulus. A statue representing Peace honors the Durban volunteers who died during the Boer War (1899–1902); the Cenotaph commemorates the South African dead from the two world wars. The square is at its most pleasant in the morning, before office workers throng it during their lunch break.

Dominating Farewell Square is the imposing **City Hall,** built in 1910 in Edwardian neo-baroque style and looking as if it has been shipped straight from London column by column. The main pediment carries sculptures representing Britannia, Unity, and Patriotism, and allegorical sculptures of the Arts, Music, and Literature adorn the exterior. Ask the guard to allow you inside to look at the huge theater, with its ornate molding and grand parterre boxes.

TIME OUT The **Royal Coffee Shoppe,** in the Royal Hotel, is a popular meeting place for Durban society and pre- and post-theater crowds. Crystal chandeliers, etched glass, and live piano music create a rich atmosphere of old-time Durban. The café serves a selection of coffees, teas, and cakes, as well as quiches, salads, and sandwiches. *Smith St.,* ☎ *031/304–0331.* ☉ *Weekdays 7 AM–11 PM, Sat. 7–noon, Sun. 10–6.*

 Head down the Smith Street side of City Hall to reach the **Durban Natural Science Museum.** Despite its small size, this museum provides an excellent introduction to African wildlife, birds, and insects. It's a

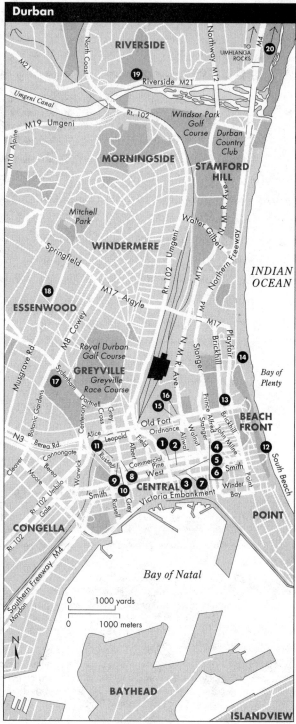

Durban

great place to bring the kids, or to familiarize yourself with the animals before heading up to the game parks in northern KwaZulu-Natal. *City Hall, Smith St.,* ☎ *031/300–6212.* ☛ *Free.* ⊙ *Mon.–Sat. 8:30–5, Sun. 11–5.*

❻ The **Durban Art Gallery,** above the Natural Science Museum, features the work of a number of local and international artists. Recent exhibits have included the FNB Vita Craft Now show, staged to highlight the cultural diversity of handicrafts in South Africa. Exhibits change every few months, so call ahead to find out what's being shown. *City Hall, Smith St.,* ☎ *031/300–6234.* ☛ *Free.* ⊙ *Mon.–Sat. 8:30–5, Sun. 11–5.*

❼ Continue down Smith Street to the **Local History Museum.** At press time, much of this museum was closed for renovations, but it should be fully reopened by 1996. Exhibits focus on Natal's colonial past, including a reconstruction of Henry Fynn's original 1824 wattle-and-daub hut, as well as simulated shopfronts of a turn-of-the-century apothecary and department store. The museum is housed in the old courthouse, built in 1866. During the Zulu War of 1879, when Durban was in danger of attack, the exterior of the building was temporarily provided with loopholes to allow defenders to fire their rifles from inside. *Corner of Smith and Aliwal Sts.,* ☎ *031/300–6241.* ☛ *Free.* ⊙ *Mon.–Sat. 8:30–5, Sun. 11–5.*

★ ❽ From here it's a long trek or short taxi ride to the most interesting part of Durban, the **Indian District,** around the junction of Queen and Grey Streets. Here the streets are thronged with Zulus and Indians, producing an intoxicating mix of Africa and Asia. Narrow doorways lead into fascinating spice shops, and traders touting saris are squeezed in next to traditional herbalists, whose dark stores are hung with wizened claws, animal organs, and roots. Outside on the narrow sidewalks, vendors sell vegetables, hair weaves, and fake Rolexes. Head for Russell Street Extension to see hundreds of Zulu women selling *muti,* traditional medicines concocted from crushed roots, bark, and other natural products. The entire area is popular with pickpockets, so don't carry a lot of money or jewelry, and keep your valuables in a safe place.

❾ The **Jumah Mosque** (corner of Grey and Queen Sts.) dominates the Indian District. Built in 1927 in a style that combines Islamic and colonial features, it's the largest mosque in the Southern Hemisphere. Its colonnaded verandas, gold-domed minaret, and turrets give the surrounding streets much of their character. As long as you take your shoes off, you can go into the mosque through a narrow entrance on Queen Street.

❿ The **Madressa Arcade,** next to the mosque, has a Kiplingesque quality recalling the bazaars of the East. Built in 1927, it's little more than a narrow, winding alley, perfumed by spices and thronged with traders. Here you can buy everything from plastic trinkets to household utensils and Indian music. The arcade has entrances on both Queen and Cathedral streets.

TIME OUT While you're in the Indian District, you should try one of Durban's specialties—the bunny chow. Available from **Patel Vegetarian Refreshment** (Rama Hse., Grey St., ☎ 031/306–1774), a bunny chow consists of a hollowed-out loaf of bread filled with bean curry.

★ ⓫ The most hyped part of the Indian District is the **Victoria Street Market.** Masses of enormous fish and prawns lie tightly packed on beds of ice, and vendors competing for your attention shout their respective prices. In the meat section, goat and sheep heads are stacked into neat piles, while butchers slice and dice every cut of meat imaginable. The noise is deafening. The place pulsates with life, and even if you have no kitchen in which to cook, it's tough to resist joining the fray. In an adjacent building—where all the tour buses pull up—you'll discover a number of curio shops whose proprietors are willing to bargain over wood and stone carvings, beadwork, and basketry. You'll also find a variety of shops selling spices, recordings of African music, and Indian fabrics. The current structures stand on the site of an original, much-loved market, a ramshackle collection of wooden shacks that burned down during the years of Nationalist rule. *Corner of Queen and Russell Sts.,* ☎ *031/306–4021.* ⊙ *Weekdays 6–6, Sat. 6–2, Sun. 10–2.*

If you like Coney Island or Blackpool, you'll probably get a kick out of the **Durban Beachfront.** Nearly 3 kilometers (1½ miles) from the market, it's probably too far for most visitors to walk to. The Golden Mile, as it is known, extends from South Beach, at the base of Durban Point, all the way to North Beach and the Bay of Plenty. The entire shoreline has been developed into an amusement park, with kiddie slides, rickshaw rides, ferris wheels, and even a chairlift that lofts vacationers high above the carnival. South Beach is the focus of much of the tourist schlock; as you head north, it steadily diminishes. Once past the Bay of Plenty, the shoreline is largely empty and undeveloped (*see* Beaches *in* Sports and the Outdoors, *below*).

⑫ For some, the main attraction in South Beach is **Sea World Durban.** Unless you're a fish fanatic, however, consider passing up this small seaside aquarium. It has an interesting collection of tropical fishes, but the tanks holding sharks, sea turtles, and rays are unimpressive. There are daily dolphin and seal shows and shark feedings three times a week. *South Beach,* ☎ *031/37–4079.* ☛ *R20 adults, R12 children.* ⊙ *Daily 9–9. Dolphin and seal shows at 10, 11:30, 2, 3:30, and 5. Fish-feeding daily at 11 and 3. Shark feeding Tues., Thurs., and Sun. at 12:30.*

⑬ Head north along Marine Parade to the **Natal Museum of Military History.** Housed in a huge warehouse on the beachfront, the museum displays a large collection of weapons and military equipment, much of it dating back to World War II. Exhibits from different periods tend to be jumbled together, but military buffs will get a kick out of climbing about on a U.S. Sherman tank, a French Mirage jet fighter plane, and an enormous helicopter. *Corner of Snell Parade and Old Fort Rd.,* ☎ *031/32–6302.* ☛ *R4 adults, R2 children.* ⊙ *Daily 9–5.*

⑭ Continue up the beachfront to **Fitzsimons Snake Park.** The park houses a slithery collection of snakes from around the world, but the accompanying descriptions offer little information about the animals themselves. Live snake demonstrations are held in a small amphitheater daily at 10, 11:30, 1, 2:30, and 3:30. On weekends these shows are followed by a feeding. The park is also home to a few Nile crocodiles, which are fed daily at 2. *Snell Parade,* ☎ *031/37–6456.* ☛ *R10 adults, R5 children.* ⊙ *Daily 9–5.*

You probably need a car to see the remaining attractions on this tour.
⑮ The **Old Fort,** opposite Kingsmead Cricket Ground, is the site of a fortified camp where, in 1842, the 27th Regiment (Inniskilling Fusiliers) survived a Boer siege led by Andries Pretorius. A model of the fort—little more than a *laager* of wagons and trenches—stands inside the park. In 1858, the encampment was transformed into a proper military post, and served until 1897 as headquarters for successive regiments. Today, the Old Fort is a pleasant, overgrown park with a good collection of

cycads. The fort's old magazine has been transformed into a chapel. *Corner of Old Fort Rd. and Old Fort Pl., no ☎. ☛ Free. ⊙ Daily 7–5.*

⑯ Next to the Old Fort is the **Warrior's Gate** and **MOTH Museum.** Built in 1937, the Warrior's Gate is a monument to those who died protecting their country. The MOTH (Memorable Order of Tin Hats) Museum houses an interesting collection of weapons, military equipment, and regimental insignia, most dating from World War II. *Corner of Old Fort Rd. and N.M.R. Ave., ☎ 031/307–3337. ☛ Free. ⊙ Tues., Fri., Sun. 11–3; Sat. 10–noon.*

⑰ The **Durban Botanic Gardens,** opposite the Greyville Racecourse, can't compare with the Kirstenbosch National Botanic Gardens in Cape Town, but they're still a delightful oasis of greenery, interlaced with walking paths, fountains, and bird ponds. The gardens are best known for their orchid house and a collection of rare cycads. *Sydenham Rd., ☎ 031/22–3472, FAX 031/21–7382. ☛ Free. ⊙ Apr. 16–Sept. 15, daily 7:30–5:15; Sept. 16–Apr. 15, daily 7:30–5:45.*

TIME OUT The **Tea Garden** in the Botanic Gardens enjoys a sylvan setting far from the city's hustle and bustle. It's a great place to take the weight off your feet and settle back with a cup of hot tea and cakes. ⊙ *Daily 9:30–4:15.*

★ **⑱** If you visit only one museum in Durban, make it the **Campbell Collections**—they're absolutely superb. Now administered by the University of Natal, the collections include the Killie Campbell Africana Library, the William Campbell Furniture Museum, and the Mashu Museum of Ethnology. The museum is housed in Muckleneuk, a lovely Cape Dutch-inspired home built in 1914 for Sir Marshall Campbell, a wealthy sugar baron, and his family. The house is furnished much as it was when the Campbells lived here, and contains some excellent pieces of Cape furniture as well as an extensive collection of oil paintings by early settlers. The highlight, however, is the Mashu Museum of Ethnology, which displays perhaps the best collection of traditional beadwork in the country, as well as African utensils, weapons, carvings, masks, pottery, and musical instruments. Paintings of African tribesmen by artist Barbara Tyrrell add vitality to the collection. *220 Marriott Rd., at Essenwood Rd., ☎ 031/207–3432. ☛ Free. ⊙ By appointment only.*

⑲ Head north out of Durban on Umgeni Road and cross the river to reach the **Umgeni River Bird Park.** Despite the absence of raptors, it's far bigger and better than the World of Birds near Cape Town. The park is built under high cliffs next to the Umgeni River and features three huge walk-through aviaries, as well as a host of smaller, specialized ones. The variety of birds, both exotic and indigenous, is astonishing; the collection of extravagantly plumaged macaws is particularly outstanding. *Riverside Rd., ☎ 031/83–1733. ☛ R10 adults, R6 children. ⊙ Daily 9–5.*

★ **⑳** Take the M4 (Northern Freeway) out of Durban for 16 kilometers (10 miles) to reach the **Natal Sharks Board,** probably the foremost shark-research institute in the world. Most of the popular bathing beaches in KwaZulu-Natal are protected by shark nets maintained by the institute. Each day, crews on ski boats check the nets and collect any snared sharks. These are then brought back to the institute, dissected, and studied. The Natal Sharks Board offers regular one-hour tours that include a peek into the enormous freezer where shark carcasses are stored, a shark dissection, and a fascinating audiovisual presentation on sharks and shark nets. When you learn the principles on which shark nets work, you may think twice about ever entering the water again. *M12, Umhlanga Rocks,*

☎ *031/561–1001.* ☛ *R8 adults, R4 children. Tours Tues. at 9; Wed. at 9, 11, and 2:30; Thurs. at 9; 1st Sun. of month at 2:30.*

Off the Beaten Path

One of Durban's most spectacular Hindu shrines is the **Shree Ambal-avaanar Alayam Temple** in Umkumbaan, on the outskirts of town. The facade is adorned with brightly painted representations of the Hindu gods, notably Ganesha, Shiva, and Vishnu. The magnificent doors leading to the cella were salvaged from a temple built in 1875 on the banks of the Umbilo River and subsequently destroyed by floods. During an important Hindu festival held around the same time as Easter, unshod fire-walkers cross beds of burning coals. *Bellair Rd., Umkumbaan, no* ☎. *Take M13 (Jan Smuts) from the city; at major fork in road, veer left onto Bellair Rd.*

Shopping

African Art Centre. This nonprofit center acts as a sales outlet for the work of rural artisans. It carries an excellent selection of original African arts and crafts, including Zulu beadwork, ceramics, wood sculptures, and beautifully crafted wire baskets. The store will ship purchases overseas. *8 Guild Hall Arcade,* ☎ *031/304–7915.* ⊙ *Mon.–Thurs. 8:30–5, Fri. 7:30–4, Sat. 8–12:30.*

Africa Art Gallery. Tucked away in a shopping plaza, this small gallery sells an interesting collection of paintings, hand-blown glass, and wood and stone sculpture. This is an excellent place to buy top-quality works by prominent South African artists, both white and black. *5 Granada Centre, Chartwell Dr., Umhlanga Rocks,* ☎ *031/561–2661.* ⊙ *Weekdays 9–5, Sat. 9–1, Sun. 10:30–12:30.*

The most exciting market in the city is the **Victoria Street Market** (*see* Exploring Durban, *above*), where you can buy everything from recordings of African music to curios and curry spices. If you don't want to go all the way to the Indian district for your spices, stop in at the **Spice Emporium** (31 Pine St., ☎ 031/32–6662), near the beachfront. Here you can select from a tantalizing array of fresh spices, as well as hand-mixed curry powders. The shop also sells mixes for creating your own vegetable atchars (Indian relishes), tea masala, and chili bites.

Perhaps the best shopping mall in Durban is **The Workshop** (99 Aliwal St., ☎ 031/304–9894), a slick renovation of the city's cavernous old railway workshops. Here you'll find everything from expensive clothing stores to curio shops, cinemas, and fast-food restaurants. Other major malls in the city are **The Wheel** (55 Gillespie St., ☎ 031/32–4324) and **Musgrave Centre** (Musgrave Rd., Berea, ☎ 031/21–5129). Two giant malls in the suburbs are **The Pavilion** (Jack Martens Dr., Westville, ☎ 031/265–0558) and **La Lucia Mall** (90 William Campbell Dr., ☎ 031/562–8420).

Sports and the Outdoors

Beaches

The sea near Durban, unlike that around the Cape, is comfortably warm year-round: In summer, the water temperature can top 80°F, while in winter 65°F is considered cold. All of KwaZulu-Natal's main beaches are protected by shark nets and staffed with lifeguards. The surf is rough, with a strong undertow, side washes, and rip tides. In order to be able to keep an eye on everybody, lifeguards tend to confine swimmers to fairly narrow stretches of beach. Be on the alert during easterly winds, which tend to bring quantities of Portuguese man-of-wars (bluebottles) and jellyfish inshore.

Though inviting to swimmers and sunbathers, Durban's beaches lack scenic charm. Their long expanse is interrupted every few hundred yards by anti-erosion piers, and the smog overhanging the city makes for an unglamorous backdrop. If you like lots of fun with your sun, though, you won't quibble about these imperfections. The Golden Mile, stretching from South Beach all the way to the Bay of Plenty, is packed with pulsating amusement park rides, water slides, singles bars, and fast-food joints. If you're looking for a less frenetic atmosphere, head for Umhlanga Rocks, to the north. A walk past the Umhlanga Lagoon leads to miles of near-empty beaches backed by virgin bush.

Participant Sports

FISHING

Lynski Charters (☎ 031/561–2031) takes up to six people deep-sea fishing for barracuda, sailfish, sharks, and reef fish. Trips, in a 30-foot Super Cat, cost R250 per person, and include equipment, tackle, bait, and cold drinks. *Gratuity* (☎ 031/84–5736) charges R1500 for up to eight people for a similar trip. In Umhlanga Rocks, **Mike Plotz** (☎ 031/561–3259) launches his small ski boat right off the beach through the waves. His fishing trips cost about R160 per person.

GOLF

As long as you tee off between 7 AM and 9 AM on weekdays, you can play on two of the country's best courses while in town. **Durban Country Club** (W. Gilbert Rd., ☎ 031/23–8282) has hosted more South African Opens than any other course and is regularly rated the best in South Africa. Tees and greens sit atop large sand dunes, and trees add an additional hazard to a course that plays like a links. **Royal Durban Golf Club** (16 Mitchell Crescent, Greyville, ☎ 031/309–1373), situated inside the Greyville race course, offers no protection from the wind and makes hitting the narrow fairways very difficult. Both courses rent clubs. **Roger Manning Golf Shop** (Windsor Park Golf Course, N.M.R. Ave., ☎ 031/23–7354) also rents out clubs for R50–R150 per day.

Spectator Sports

CRICKET

Kingsmead Cricket Ground (2 Kingsmead Close, ☎ 031/32–9703) is home to the Natal provincial team and a frequent venue for international test matches between South Africa and touring teams from abroad.

HORSE RACING

The main season extends from May to August. Meets are usually held Tuesday, Wednesday or Thursday, and every Saturday, and usually consist of nine or ten races. The area's three racecourses take turns holding meets: **Greyville** (Avondale Rd., ☎ 031/309–4545), almost in the city center; **Clairwood Park** (Exit 7 or 8 off Southern Fwy., ☎ 031/42–5332), 11 kilometers (7 miles) out of town; and **Scottsville** (New England Rd. exit off N3, ☎ 0331/45–3405), in Pietermaritzburg. The Durban July at Greyville—probably the country's most famous horse-racing event—is a day when the outrageous fashions worn by female racing fans attract almost as much attention as the horses themselves.

RUGBY

KwaZulu-Natal's team, known as the Banana Boys, plays at **Kings Park Rugby Ground** (West Gilbert Rd., ☎ 031/23–6368). Natal is a strong contender in the annual round-robin Bankfin Currie Cup competition.

SURFING

Surfing commands a fanatical following in Durban, and several international tournaments are staged on the city's beaches or at nearby Umhlanga Rocks. Crowds of more than 10,000 are not unusual for night surfing competitions or the annual Gunston 500 surfing championship event. The most popular surfing beach is probably the Bay of Plenty, on Durban's Golden Mile.

Dining

Critics are often dismissive of Durban's dining scene, claiming that the quality of the city's restaurants leaves much to be desired and that for such a large city the selection is surprisingly limited. Be that as it may, Durban does offer some superb dining, provided you eat to its strengths. Thanks to its huge Indian population, it offers some of the best curry restaurants in the country. Durban's other great strength is its fresh seafood, especially prawns and langoustines, brought down the coast from Mozambique. LM prawns (LM stands for Lourenço Marques, the former Portuguese name for Maputo) are a revered delicacy in South Africa. Served with peri-peri—a spicy Portuguese marinade of chiles, olive oil, garlic, and sometimes tomato—they are a real taste sensation. For a description of South African culinary terms, *see* Pleasures & Pastimes *in* Chapter 1. For price ranges, *see* Chart 1 *in* On the Road with Fodor's.

$$$$ **Colony.** Some of the best food in the city is served in this elegant hideaway in a shabby apartment block near the beachfront. The frequently changing menu—printed to resemble an old newspaper—includes an eclectic choice of dishes with an emphasis on fresh local produce. Start with baked brown mushrooms with garlic butter or beef marrow served on toast with red-wine sauce. For a main course, the roast duck with a fruit-based sauce is magnificent. Another local temptation is warthog pie, served in a deep dish under a light, golden crust. Fresh fruit–flavored sorbet provides a refreshing cap to the meal. ✗ *Oceanic Bldg., 1st Floor, Sol Harris Crescent,* ☎ *031/368–2789. Reservations required. AE, DC, MC, V. Closed Sun. No lunch Sat.*

$$$$ **La Dolce Vita.** For 23 years this Italian restaurant in the CBD has maintained a consistently high standard. In addition to the regular menu, a waiter presents a platter of the day's fresh offerings, which usually features crayfish, langoustines, and tiger prawns so large you'll think twice about swimming in the ocean. On the meat side, veal dishes are highly recommended, as is the tripe braised in a flavorful tomato, garlic, and onion sauce. For an appetizer you might choose fresh asparagus, giant mushrooms sautéed in garlic and butter, or a seafood salad vinaigrette. For dessert, you can't beat crêpes suzette, although the lemon and strawberry sorbet is a superb light alternative. ✗ *Durdoc Centre, 460 Smith St.,* ☎ *031/301–3347. Reservations required. AE, DC, MC, V. Closed Sun. No lunch Sat.*

$$$$ **Royal Grill.** This restaurant in the Royal Hotel offers Durban's most
★ elegant dining experience. The dining room—all that remains of the original Royal—has the grace of an earlier age: Silver and crystal reflect the light from chandeliers, burnished wood glows from decades of polishing, and a pianist or harpist plays unobtrusively in the background. The food is a nouvelle take on classical French cuisine and is usually (but not always) very fine. Spinach ravioli, served with crayfish medallions in a beurre blanc, is superb, as are sautéed shiitake mushrooms with a balsamic vinaigrette. Fillet of rock cod, sautéed in butter, is also excellent. The dessert trolley displays a selection of gâteaux and puddings, most quite heavy on the whipped cream. ✗ *Royal Hotel,*

267 Smith St., ☎ *031/304–0331. Jacket and tie. Reservations advised. AE, DC, MC, V. No dinner Sun.*

$$$$ St. Geran. Owner Robert Mauvis hails from the island of Mauritius, bringing a touch of spice to an otherwise French menu at this elegant restaurant in the CBD. Head straight for calamari in a spicy Creole sauce. For a main course, consider octopus and prawn curry or the excellent *vindaye de poisson,* a mild curry of fresh fish with turmeric and small onions, served alongside black lentils and basmati rice. Grilled lamb and grilled rabbit with garlic and herbs are typical of the meat dishes on offer. Crème brûlée is always popular for dessert, but don't overlook the soufflé au Grand Marnier or flambéed bananas. ✕ *31 Aliwal St.,* ☎ *031/304–7509. Reservations advised. AE, DC, MC, V. Closed Sun. No lunch Sat.*

$$$ Two Moon Junction. This ultra-trendy restaurant in Greyville attracts Durban's cool crowd, as well as a lot of gays. The chalkboard menu is eclectic, but the cuisine tends toward hearty country fare. Starters include mussel chowder and tagliatelle with mushrooms, but you can't do better than the smoked salmon salad. For a main course, choose among lamb shanks, roast duck and lamb, or a Junction burger, two thick beef patties slathered with a tomato salsa. Cajun steak is a good choice, too, served on a green-peppercorn sauce with deep-fried potatoes. If you have room, the dense chocolate cake is excellent. ✕ *Windermere Rd., Greyville,* ☎ *031/303–3078. Reservations advised. AE, DC, MC, V. Closed Sun.*

$$ Baanthai. On the second floor of a converted town house, this Thai restaurant brings a refreshing flavor to Durban's dining scene. Thai chefs, working in an open kitchen, whip up authentic dishes that make heady use of lemongrass, coriander, and *galangal* (a type of ginger). Among the starters, the beef waterfall salad (thinly sliced grilled beef tossed with onions and coriander) is excellent, as are *pad thai* noodles. Other winners are chicken with garlic and pepper and Thai curries made with coconut milk. Brinjal (eggplant) with chiles is a delicious vegetarian option. ✕ *138 Florida Rd.,* ☎ *031/303–4270. Reservations advised. BYOB. AE, DC, MC, V. Closed Sun.*

$$ Christina's. Christina Martin operates South Africa's best cooking school, and her students prepare the meals at this pleasant restaurant on the Berea. The emphasis is on haute cuisine, with great attention paid to presentation and innovation. Not surprisingly, meals are hit-or-miss affairs, but the standards are generally high. The four-course set menu is a very good value. Expect a starter like Thai chicken satay with peanut sauce and atchar, followed by smoked salmon soup. The main course might be stuffed loin of lamb or roast duck with black cherry sauce, followed by a dessert of raspberry soufflé or sticky toffee pudding. Diners can also choose from a selection of à la carte dishes, including sandwiches, linefish, and quiches, which are usually superb. ✕ *130 Florida Rd.,* ☎ *031/303–2522. AE, DC, MC, V. Closed Sun.– Mon. No dinner Sat.–Wed.*

$$ Ulundi. A colonial atmosphere pervades this classy Indian restaurant at the Royal Hotel. Waiters, dressed all in white and wearing turbans, usher you to a table set under palms and cooled by overhead fans. The curries are good, but most dishes are prepared with European taste buds in mind. The eastern snacks (a platter of samoosas, chili bites, and meatballs) lack flavor; you're better off with a starter of *aloo Jeera,* diced potatoes and aubergine in a mild curry sauce served with roti. For a main course, consider the lamb or beef *tharkaree,* a traditional Natal curry—hot and spicy. For a dish with less curry flavor, try the delicate *Ulundi Jhinga,* prawns cooked in a tomato and chutney sauce. One of

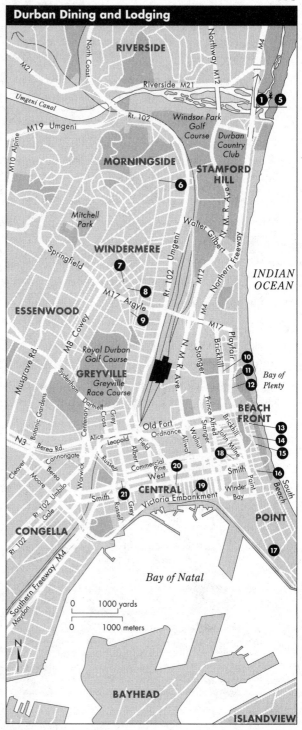

Durban Dining and Lodging

the highlights of a meal here is the complimentary sambals trolley, from which you can select nearly a dozen condiments, including chutney, grated coconut, mango atchar, and bananas in milk. ✕ *Royal Hotel, 267 Smith St.,* ☎ *031/304–0331. Reservations advised. AE, DC, MC, V. Closed Sun.*

$$ Victoria Bar & Restaurant. Adjoining the city's most charismatic and earthy bar, this unpretentious Portuguese restaurant in the docks serves good, no-frills seafood. Red tablecloths and tightly packed tables give it a cozy appeal. Unless you're very hungry, pass on starters: Grilled calamari is tasty but tough; and *chourico* (Portuguese sausage) tastes too much like kielbasa. Excellent main courses are grilled or baked line-fish topped with a tomato and onion sauce, peri-peri chicken, and grilled langoustines. A less expensive alternative to langoustines is prawns à la Victoria, done with garlic and peri-peri. Dessert is limited to ice cream and mousses. ✕ *Corner of Point and Bell Sts.,* ☎ *031/37–4645. Reservations advised. DC, MC, V. Closed Sun.*

$ Loafers Bakery & Coffee Bar. Adjoining an excellent bakery, this coffee shop is a popular hangout for Greyville residents, who stand in line on weekends for a table on the enclosed terrace. It's the kind of place where you can dally over a cappuccino, read the paper, and idle the hours away. Diners can order off the menu or head next door to the bakery to choose from the dozens of tempting cookies, pastries, cakes, and rolls; rich buttery croissants are superb. Or you can have full English breakfasts, toasted sandwiches, pies, and quiches. Several salads are featured on the menu, too, including spinach salad tossed with red apple slices, feta, and tomato, topped with bacon, grated cheese, and garlic croutons. ✕ *514 Windermere Rd.,* ☎ *031/23–2100. AE, DC, MC, V.* ☉ *Daily 7–4.*

$ Pakistani Restaurant. Wander into this tiny Pakistani restaurant near ★ the beachfront, and your first impulse is to flee. Shielded from the street by a green curtain, the restaurant comprises a mere six tables in a bare room. Don't be deterred, for here you'll find some of the best Indian food in the city. The husband-and-wife owners travel to Karachi or Lahore each year just to find new recipes. They buy their meats fresh every day, and their spices, too, are laden with flavor. The painstaking care taken in the kitchen is immediately obvious—the curries are notable for their flavor and subtlety. A real taste sensation is *atchar ghosh,* a slightly sweet curry dish made with boneless chicken and served with roti. Another popular choice is chicken *boti,* cubes of chicken marinated in herbs and spices, then cooked over an open fire. For something lighter, try a *seekh kebab,* skewers of pure ground beef marinated in a green-chile spice and grilled. ✕ *92 West St.,* ☎ *031/32–6883. Reservations advised. No alcohol allowed. MC, V. Closed Mon.*

$ Sea Belle's. The superb curries at this Indian restaurant in La Mercy— a half hour's drive north of the city—draw crowds of Durbanites at lunch. You certainly wouldn't go for the decor, best described as disco industrial (the restaurant doubles as a nightclub). Order the bean curry, not only the cheapest but also the tastiest of the curries on the menu. The prawn curry is excellent, too. Accompanied by rice and rotis, an order of three curries is ample for four persons. ✕ *Sea Belle's Hotel, Beach Rd., La Mercy,* ☎ *0322/91–5551. AE, DC, MC, V.*

Lodging

Apart from the Royal Hotel, all of Durban's main hotels lie along the Golden Mile, Durban's beachfront. Southern Sun, the giant chain that operates Sun and Holiday Inn hotels in South Africa, has a virtual monopoly on Durban accommodation. The plus side of this is that you can be assured of decent facilities and clean rooms; the down side is that few Durban hotels have much character, and prices tend to be fairly standardized. If you want a beach holiday without the amusement-park atmosphere prevailing on the Golden Mile, go on to Umhlanga Rocks, a pleasant, upmarket town a half hour's drive up the coast. The beaches there are excellent, with none of the tackiness and crime that plague Durban's beachfront area. Umhlanga also boasts a host of decent restaurants, cinemas, and shops. For price ranges, *see* Chart 2(A) *in* On the Road with Fodor's.

Durban

$$$$ **The Edward.** One of Durban's oldest hotels, the Edward is currently closed for restoration, but is slated to reopen as a luxury hotel in July, 1996. The current structure, built in 1939 along classic colonial lines, features cut-glass chandeliers, molded ceilings, and subtle art deco touches. The hotel faces directly onto South Beach, just a 10-minute walk from the CBD. ⊡ *Marine Parade (mailing address: Box 105), Durban 4000,* ☎ *031/37–3681,* Ⅸ *031/32–1692. 100 rooms with bath. 3 restaurants, 2 bars, room service, beauty salon. AE, DC, MC, V.*

$$$$ **Royal Hotel.** The city's best hotel and a cherished Durban institution,
★ the Royal stands in the heart of the CBD. The hotel caters mainly to businesspeople, but it's also an excellent option for tourists who don't insist on a beachfront location. It dates back to 1842—the city's infancy— and has frequently hosted visits by British royals. Sadly, the original Royal was replaced in 1978 by a high-rise, and all that remains of the old building is the grand Royal Grill (*see* Dining, *above*). Nevertheless, the hotel maintains some appealing old-fashioned touches. An army of liveried staff provides a level of service rare in South Africa today. Rooms, too, are slightly dated, with two-tone yellowwood furnishings and antique bird prints on the walls. Deluxe-class rooms are larger, featuring separate bath and shower, and spectacular views of Durban harbor (request a room on an upper floor). The hotel's location, right on bustling Farewell Square, is great during the day, but a liability at night, when the CBD shuts down and the streets become unsafe. ⊡ *267 Smith St. (mailing address: Box 1041), Durban 4000,* ☎ *031/304–0331,* Ⅸ *031/304–5055. 272 rooms with bath. 7 restaurants, 5 bars, room service, pool, health club, squash. AE, DC, MC, V.*

$$$ **Holiday Inn Crowne Plaza.** Formerly known as the Elangeni, this is the best hotel on the Durban beachfront, at least until the reopening of the Edward. The 21-story high-rise overlooks North Beach, a two-minute drive from the CBD, and attracts a mix of business, conference, and holiday guests. All rooms have views of the water, but request a room on an upper floor with a full-on ocean view. Rooms are small and narrow, with a beachy, seaside feel at odds with the formality of the marbled lobby and public rooms. ⊡ *63 Snell Parade (mailing address: Box 4094), Durban 4000,* ☎ *031/37–1321,* Ⅸ *031/32–5527. 446 rooms with bath. 3 restaurants, 3 bars, room service, 2 pools, beauty salon. AE, DC, MC, V.*

$$ **Holiday Inn Garden Court–Marine Parade.** If you don't need room service, porters, or a concierge, choose this hotel over the more expensive Crowne Plaza, for the rooms are just as pleasant. You can't beat the location either, midway between South and North beaches, and the CBD is just a 10-minute walk away. Rooms are attractive and modern, with textured wallpaper, bold floral bedspreads, and a small sitting area. All face the sea, but request one on an upper floor. Views from the pool deck on the 30th floor are superb. ⊡ *167 Marine Parade (mailing address: Box 10809), Durban 4056,* ☎ *031/37–3341,*

FAX *031/37–3341. 344 rooms with bath. Restaurant, bar, indoor pool. AE, DC, MC, V.*

$$ Holiday Inn Garden Court–North Beach. Overlooking a relatively quiet stretch of beachfront, this is the most upscale of the Garden Court hotels. It occupies the old five-star Maharani, and while the current hotel is a no-frills affair, some of the Maharani's former elegance shines through in rich wood doors, molded ceilings, and a wood-paneled residents bar. Rooms are large, each with its own sitting area, and decorated in delicate blues and rusts. All have excellent sea views. ⌂ *83/91 Snell Parade (mailing address: Box 10592), Durban 4056,* ☎ *031/32–7361,* FAX *031/37–4058. 270 rooms with bath. Restaurant, breakfast room, bar, pool, beauty salon. AE, DC, MC, V.*

$$ Palace Protea. Facing right onto North Beach, this self-catering hotel is a good option for families; couples can probably do better at one of the nearby Holiday Inns. For groups of up to six, the large deluxe suites are ideal and incredibly cheap. Suites feature fully equipped kitchens, living rooms, two bedrooms, and outstanding sea views. Standard rooms, on the other hand, are small and basic. ⌂ *Corner of Marine Parade and Foster Pl. (mailing address: Box 10539), Durban 4056,* ☎ *031/32–8351,* FAX *031/32–8307. 76 rooms with bath. Restaurant, bar, 2 pools, steam room. AE, DC, MC, V.*

$ Holiday Inn Garden Court–South Beach. This is the cheapest of the Garden Courts on the beachfront, and attracts a lot of budget-minded South African families. Its position, facing the carnival of South Beach and close to the CBD, is ideal if you want to be in the thick of the party action. Rooms are small, with utilitarian furnishings and tiny bathrooms, but the views from the sea-facing rooms are wonderful. ⌂ *73 Marine Parade (mailing address: Box 10199), Durban 4056,* ☎ *031/37–2231,* FAX *031/37–4640. 400 rooms with bath. Restaurant, 2 bars, breakfast room, pool. AE, DC, MC, V.*

Umhlanga Rocks

$$$$ Beverly Hills Sun. In a high-rise building right on the beach, this upmarket hotel is popular with both vacationers and businesspeople. The service is excellent and the facilities are superb. However, if you're the sort of beachgoer who likes to loll about in a bathing suit, you may find this hotel too formal. The public lounge, festooned with huge floral arrangements and yards of gathered drapes, serves a full silver-service tea in the afternoon, and a pianist plays in the evening. Guest rooms are fairly small, but all have terrific sea views, particularly those on the upper floors. The decor makes extensive use of bleached-wood furniture and bold floral fabrics. For a more open, beachy feel, take one of the cabanas, large duplex rooms that open onto a lovely pool deck. ⌂ *Lighthouse Rd. (mailing address: Box 71), Umhlanga Rocks 4320,* ☎ *031/561–2211,* FAX *031/561–3711. 95 rooms with bath. 2 restaurants, 2 bars, room service, pool, beauty salon. Breakfast included. AE, DC, MC, V.*

$$$ Breakers Resort. This resort enjoys an enviable position at the northern tip of Umhlanga, surrounded by the wilds of the Hawaan Forest and overlooking the unspoiled wetlands of Umhlanga Lagoon. Of all the resorts in Umhlanga, this one suffers the least from crowds—amble north along the beach and you will see scarcely another soul and no buildings. The disadvantage is that you probably need a car to get into town, and you can't swim directly in front of the resort because the surf's too dangerous. The building is unattractive, with long, depressing corridors, but the rooms themselves are fine, with fully equipped kitchens and great views of the beach and lagoon. Children pay half price, unless they occupy a sleeper couch, in which case they stay free.

☎ *88 Lagoon Dr. (mailing address; Box 75), Umhlanga Rocks 4320, ☎ 031/561–2271, FAX 031/561–2722. 80 rooms with bath. 2 restaurants, bar, pool, tennis court, playground. Breakfast included. AE, DC, MC, V.*

$$$ **Cabana Beach.** For families wanting a traditional beach holiday, you
★ can't do better than this large resort in Umhlanga. Children under 18 stay free, the bathing beach lies directly in front of the hotel, and there are tons of activities to keep kids happy. Considering its huge size, the Cabana is one of the most attractive hotels on the beach: a whitewashed, Spanish-style structure that steps down to the sea in a series of terraces. The room decor is simple, comfortable, and absolutely appropriate for a beach holiday. Each cabana comes with a fully equipped kitchen, dining/living area, and a veranda with great sea views. Request a tower or beachfront apartment for the most attractive and practical space configuration. ☎ *10 Lagoon Dr. (mailing address: Box 10), Umhlanga Rocks 4320, ☎ 031/561–2371, FAX 031/561–3522. 217 rooms with bath. 3 restaurants, bar, 2 pools, tennis court, health club, squash. Breakfast included. AE, DC, MC, V.*

$$ **Oyster Box.** Facing the ocean and the Umhlanga Rocks lighthouse, this hotel holds a special place in the hearts of older South Africans, many of whom remember when it was just a tearoom set in the midst of thick bush. That was in the 1940s, before the Oyster Box blossomed into a home-away-from-home for Britons traveling to South Africa aboard the old Union-Castle steamships. Today, hemmed in by high-rise hotels, the Oyster Box hides its aging face on 5 acres of lovely gardens. The hotel has lost much of its original appeal as a result of decades of slow decline. What for years could be romantically passed off as faded gentility is now just shabby. But it's still the place to come if you want to catch a glimpse of the old English South Africa: Guests still gather on the veranda for afternoon tea, and a dinner dance is held every Saturday night. The noise of the surf is extremely loud in the sea-facing rooms; take one of the less-expensive garden cottages or wing rooms if you want peace and quiet. ☎ *Lighthouse Rd. (mailing address: Box 22), Umhlanga Rocks 4320, ☎ 031/561–2233, FAX 031/561–4072. 80 rooms with bath. Restaurant, bar, room service, pool, tennis court. Breakfast included. AE, DC, MC, V.*

The Arts and Nightlife

What's on in Durban, a free monthly publication put out by the tourism office, lists a diary of upcoming events. Also, check the entertainment section of the **Natal Mercury,** Durban's principal newspaper. Tickets for shows, movies, concerts, and other events can be obtained through **Computicket** (☎ 031/304–2753), which has outlets throughout the city.

The Arts

The **Playhouse** (Smith St., across from City Hall, ☎ 031/304–3631) stands at the heart of Durban's cultural life. The complex encompasses five performing arts venues, and the Playhouse Company stages productions of music, ballet, drama, opera, and cabaret. The Playhouse is also home to the Natal Philharmonic Orchestra.

Nightlife
BARS AND PUBS

The beachfront area is lined with bars catering to holiday crowds. **Joe Kool's** (137 Lower Marine Parade, ☎ 031/32–9697), a California-style bar and restaurant, packs hordes of young partying singles onto its outdoor terrace. **Cattleman** (139 Lower Marine Parade, ☎ 031/37–0382), a stone's throw down the beach, attracts a slightly older crowd. In the

CBD, **Rick's Cafe Americain** (Smith St., across from City Hall, ☎ 031/304–3297) attracts a sophisticated set, many fresh from a performance at the Playhouse. Perhaps the biggest meet-market in the city is the **Queens Tavern** (16 Stamford Hill Rd., Greyville, ☎ 031/309–4017), a bar-cum-Indian restaurant that is regularly mobbed, particularly on Friday nights. If you're looking for something less frenetic, head to Morningside and the **Keg and Thistle** (Florida Rd., ☎ 031/23–5315), the first in a blossoming chain of pubs across the country, or **Woodcutters** (Windermere Rd., ☎ 031/303–1988). The most charismatic bar in the city is the gritty **Victoria Bar** (Point Rd., ☎ 031/37–4645), down in the docks on Durban Point. Attached to a Portuguese restaurant, it attracts a crowd of weird and wonderful regulars.

NIGHTCLUBS AND LIVE MUSIC

The best places to hear live African music and jazz are **Tekweni Junction** (Umgeni Rd., ☎ 031/309–1282) and the **Moon Hotel** (522 S. Coast Rd., Rossborough, ☎ 031/465–1711). If you want to get down and groove, **Sand Pebbles** (South Beach Ave., ☎ 031/368–2447) is a longstanding beachfront favorite, a multilevel entertainment complex that draws all kinds of people. On Durban Point, **George Cinq** (160 Point Rd., ☎ 031/368–4402) and **330** (330 Point Rd., ☎ 031/37–7172) attract hip crowds of models, glitterati, and wannabes with loud techno music. Over in Morningside, the club of choice among Durban's see-and-be-seen crowd is **Bonkers** (Florida Rd., ☎ 031/303–1146).

Durban Essentials

Arriving and Departing

BY BUS

Greyhound (☎ 031/361–7774) and **Translux Express** (☎ 031/361–8333) offer long-distance bus service to cities all over South Africa. A cheaper company, **Golden Wheels** (☎ 031/29–2894), offers frequent service to Johannesburg only. All intercity buses leave from **New Durban Station,** off N.M.R. Avenue.

BY CAR

Rental Cars. The cheapest rental car costs about R85 per day plus 85¢ per kilometer. Prices fall dramatically if you rent for three days or more and plan to drive long distances. The major rental agencies are **Avis** (Ulundi Pl., City Center, ☎ 031/304–1741), **Berea Car & Bakkie Hire** (Tourist Junction, 160 Pine St., ☎ 031/301–1769), **Dolphin Car Hire** (36 Broad St., ☎ 031/304–7922), **Imperial Car Rental** (34 Aliwal St., ☎ 031/37–3731), and **Tempest Car Hire** (139 Gale St., ☎ 031/307–5211).

BY PLANE

Durban International Airport (☎ 031/42–6111), formerly known as Louis Botha Airport, lies 16 kilometers (10 miles) south of town along the Southern Freeway. **South African Airways** (☎ 031/305–6491) flies direct between Durban and London twice a week. SAA and **British Airways** (☎ 031/305–7118) also offer flights to London via Johannesburg. Domestic airlines serving Durban include SAA, **Comair** (☎ 031/42–6022), **Airlink** (☎ 031/42–2676), and **Phoenix** (☎ 031/306–3066).

Avis (☎ 031/42–3282), **Budget** (☎ 031/42–3809), **Dolphin** (☎ 031/469–0667), **Imperial** (☎ 031/42–0597), and **Tempest** (☎ 031/42–8668) all have car-rental desks in the domestic terminal.

Between the Airport and City Center. The airport company operates a **shuttle bus** from outside the domestic terminal to the City Air Terminal (corner of Smith and Aliwal Sts., ☎ 031/465–5573) in the center of town. Buses run about every hour and the trip takes 20 minutes; the fare is R10 per person. **Airport Shuttle Bus** (☎ 031/708–5676) offers 24-hour minibus service between the airport and any address in Durban. Fares to the city center and beachfront are about R60 for 1–2 people. Taxis aren't much more expensive, about R70.

New Durban Station (N.M.R. Ave., ☎ 031/361–7621) is a huge, ghastly place that is still not finished but already reeks of decay. Interpax's *Trans-Natal* train runs daily between Durban and Johannesburg, stopping at Pietermaritzburg, Estcourt, and Ladysmith. The trip takes 13 hours and costs about R130 one-way.

Getting Around

BY BUS

Durban Transport operates two types of bus service, but you need concern yourself only with the **Mynah buses.** These small buses operate frequently on set routes through the city and along the beachfront, and cost R2 a ride. Bus stops are marked by the symbol of a mynah bird. The main bus depot is Pine Street, between Aliwal and Gardiner. You pay as you board; exact change is not required. Route information is also available at an information office at the corner of Aliwal and Pine Streets (☎ 031/307–3503).

Umhlanga Express Minibus Service (☎ 031/561–2860) operates a weekday minibus service between Durban (across from Tourist Junction) and all the major hotels in Umhlanga Rocks. Buses leave every two hours or so and the trip takes 20 minutes. Saturday service is extremely limited.

BY TAXI

Taxis are metered and expensive. The meter starts at R2.50, and clocks the fare at about R4 a kilometer. Expect to pay about R15 from City Hall to North Beach, and R70 to the airport. The most convenient taxi stands are around City Hall and in front of the beach hotels. Some of the major taxi companies are **Aussie's Radio Taxis** (☎ 031/37–2345), **Bunny Cabs** (☎ 031/32–2914), **Checker Radio Taxis** (☎ 031/21–1133), **Deluxe Radio Taxis** (031/37–1661), and **Morris Radio Taxis** (031/37–2711). **Eagle Radio Taxis** (☎ 031/38–8333) charge about R1 more per kilometer than other companies.

BY TUK TUK

Tuk tuks are three-wheel, open cabs powered by a motorcycle engine. They cruise the beachfront area and are cheaper than taxis for short trips. Negotiate the fare before you set off.

Guided Tours

BOAT TOURS

Sarie Marais Pleasure Cruises (☎ 031/305–4022) and **Isle of Capri** (☎ 031/37–7751) both offer pleasure cruises around Durban Bay. Tours, which last about 90 minutes and cost R20 per person, depart from the jetties next to the Natal Maritime Museum (Victoria Embankment at Aliwal St.).

ORIENTATION TOURS

Strelitzia Tours (☎ 031/86–1904) offers daily minibus tours of Durban for R75. The three-hour tours depart at 9 and touch on all the major historical and scenic points in the city, including the beachfront and harbor, exclusive residential areas like Morningside, the Botanic Gardens, and the Indian District. Other Strelitzia tours include the Valley of a Thousand Hills; Pietermaritzburg and its environs; Zululand; the battlefields; and game reserves like Hluhluwe and St. Lucia.

TOWNSHIP TOURS

Hamba Kahle Tours (☎ 031/7070–1509) takes you to see the other side of South Africa, in the poverty-stricken townships surrounding Durban. Township Fever is a three-hour tour of the northern townships, including stops in Kwa-Mashu, Bhambayi, and the Ghandi Museum in Phoenix. Get to Grips is a four-hour tour that takes you into hostels and squatter camps, and includes dancing, dinner, and drinks. Shebeen Crawling is a pub crawl through several township bars; the tour includes dinner and drinks.

WALKING TOURS

Durban Unlimited (Tourist Junction, 160 Pine St., ☎ 031/304–4934) offers a series of city walking tours during the week for R20 per person. Tours depart from the Tourist Junction weekdays at 9:45 and return at 12:30. The Oriental Walkabout explores the Indian District, including Victoria Market and several mosques. The Historical Walkabout covers the major historical monuments in the city, while the Feel of Durban Walkabout explores some of the city's military past, including the Old Fort, Warrior's Gate, and the original armory.

Important Addresses and Numbers

CONSULATES

United Kingdom. *320 Smith St., City Center,* ☎ *031/305–2929.*

United States. *Durban Bay House, 333 Smith St., City Center,* ☎ *031/ 304–4737.*

EMERGENCIES

Dial 10177 for an **ambulance,** 10111 for the **police,** and 031/309–3333 for the **fire brigade.**

HOSPITALS

Addington Hospital (Erskine Terr., South Beach, ☎ 031/32–2111) operates a 24-hour emergency ward.

LATE-NIGHT PHARMACIES

Daynite Pharmacy (corner of West St. and Point Rd., ☎ 031/368–3666) is open daily until 10:30.

TRAVEL AGENCIES

Rennies is the South African representative of Thomas Cook, and also operates a foreign-exchange desk. *320 West St., at Smith St.,* ☎ *031/ 305–3800.* ⊙ *Weekdays 8:30–4:30, Sat. 8:30–noon.*

American Express offers a full range of client services (no client mail pick-up on Saturday). The Amex foreign-exchange bureau (350 Smith St., ☎ 031/301–5562) is in a separate office, just 200 yards away. *2 Durban Club Pl., off Smith St.,* ☎ *031/301–5541.* ⊙ *Weekdays 8–5, Sat. 8:30–noon.*

VISITOR INFORMATION

The **Tourist Junction,** in the restored old station building, houses a number of tourist-oriented companies and services, where you can find information on almost everything that's happening in Durban and KwaZulu-Natal. Among the companies represented are Durban Unlimited, the city's tourism authority; an accommodation service; an intercity train reservations office; a Natal Parks Board booking desk; regional KwaZulu-Natal tourist offices; and various bus and transport companies. *160 Pine St.,* ☎ *031/304–4934.* ⊙ *Weekdays 8–5, weekends 9–2.*

Umhlanga Publicity Association. *Chartwell Dr., off Lighthouse Rd., Umhlanga Rocks,* ☎ *031/561–4257.* ⏱ *Weekdays 8:30–4:30, Sat. 9–12:30.*

EXCURSIONS FROM DURBAN

Pietermaritzburg

Numbers in the margin correspond to points of interest on the Pietermaritzburg map.

Pietermaritzburg lies in a bowl of hills in the Natal Midlands, 80 kilometers (50 miles) inland from Durban. The city is the current co-capital of KwaZulu-Natal along with Ulundi in Zululand. It's a pleasant town, with wide, tree-lined streets and a temperate climate that escapes the worst of the coastal heat and humidity. Its redbrick colonial architecture offers tangible reminders of Natal's and South Africa's British past; dozens of late-19th-century buildings line the streets in the center of town. It's worth visiting just to see this slice of Victorian England.

For a city so closely associated with the British presence in South Africa, Pietermaritzburg's pedigree is strictly Afrikaans. The town was first settled in 1838 by Voortrekkers escaping British rule in the Cape. The city takes its name from Pieter Mauritz Retief, commonly known as Piet Retief, the famous Voortrekker leader who was murdered by the Zulu king, Dingane.

❶ The starting point for a tour of Pietermaritzburg is the **Pietermaritzburg Publicity Association,** which distributes detailed pamphlets and maps of the town. The office is housed in a classic redbrick building erected in 1884 to house the Borough Police. In those days, the bell tower used to signal a curfew for blacks at 9 each night. *177 Commercial Rd.,* ☎ *0331/45–1348.* ⏱ *Weekdays 8:30–4:30, Sat. 8:30–12:30.*

❷ Across the street from the Publicity Association is the **Tatham Art Gallery,** housed in the old Supreme Court. Completed in 1871, it's yet another of Pietermaritzburg's fine redbrick colonial structures. The museum is first-rate, with a solid collection of 19th-century English and French paintings. Of keenest interest, though, is the South African Collection, which displays works by contemporary black and white artists, including linocuts and such traditional crafts as beadwork, baskets, and tribal ear plugs. The museum also presents a program of changing exhibits. *Commercial St., across from Publicity Assoc.,* ☎ *0331/42–1804.* ☛ *Free.* ⏱ *Tues.–Sun. 10–6.*

❸ The **Supreme Court Gardens** lie next to the art gallery and serve as the city's memorial park. Several monuments commemorate those who died in wars that raged in this country and abroad: the Zulu War of 1879, the Boer War (1899–1902), and World War I. The monuments all have a very English feel, emphasized by the legends on the commemorative stones extolling Queen, Country, and Empire.

❹ Across Commercial Street from the gardens stands the imposing **City Hall** (corner of Church and Commercial Sts.), the largest all-brick structure in the Southern Hemisphere. Built in 1900, it's a classic Victorian edifice, notable for its stained-glass windows, soaring clock tower, and ornate gables and domes.

❺ Head down Church Street from City Hall to reach the **Voortrekker Museum.** The museum occupies the Church of the Vow, an immensely important monument in the eyes of many Afrikaners. After the murder

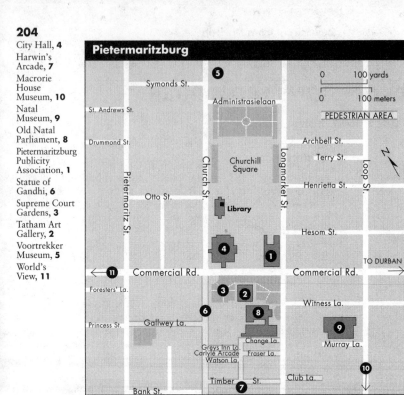

of Voortrekker leader Piet Retief in 1838, the Voortrekkers sought revenge on the Zulus and their king, Dingane. A Boer commando under the leadership of Andries Pretorius vowed to build a church if God granted them victory. The result was the Battle of Blood River (*see* Zululand and the Battlefields, *below*), in which 3,000 Zulus died and the Boers managed to emerge without a single casualty. Constructed in 1841 in typical Cape Dutch style, the church now houses a variety of Voortrekker artifacts, including an old wagon, flintlock rifles, and Piet Retief's prayer book. Next door, the thatched home of Andries Pretorius is also open to the public. *Church St., ☎ 0331/94–6834. ☞ Free. ☉ Weekdays 9–4, Sat. 8–noon.*

Head back up Church Street, cross Commercial Avenue, and stroll up the Maritzburg Mall, a quasi-pedestrian thoroughfare lined with some superb examples of Victorian architecture. Fronting the Colonial Building is a **statue of Gandhi.** The statue marks the centenary of the day in 1893 when Gandhi, an Indian who had come to South Africa as a lawyer, was thrown off a train at Pietermaritzburg station because he was riding in a whites-only carriage. He later insisted that "My active nonviolence began from that date."

Turn left down Greys Inn Lane to reach what many consider to be Pietermaritzburg's biggest attraction, a warren of charming pedestrian lanes and alleys lined with shops, cafés, and small businesses. Of particular interest is **Harwin's Arcade,** which extends between Timber Street and Theatre Lane through an Edwardian building constructed in Renaissance Revival style. A skylight runs the entire length of the two-story arcade, which houses a bookstore and other small shops.

From the arcade head down Theatre Lane to Longmarket Street and turn left. The street runs past the **Old Natal Parliament** (corner of Longmarket and Commercial Sts.), which once housed the twin-chamber colonial parliament. A statue of Queen Victoria stands in front of the redbrick building, which was erected in 1889.

❾ Turn right on Commercial Street and then right again on Loop Street to reach the **Natal Museum.** One of five national museums in the country, this museum contains a little of everything: A natural science hall features displays of dinosaurs, African animals, sea life, and Natal birds; a history section recreates an 1880s Pietermaritzburg street complete with a settler's cottage, shops, a pharmacy, and a smithy; the exhibition on sub-Saharan cultures is by far the most interesting, highlighting religious, ceremonial, military, and household artifacts from across the continent. Several San (Bushman) rock paintings are on display, too. *237 Loop St.,* ☎ *0331/45–1404.* ☛ *R2 adults, 50¢ children.* ☉ *Mon.– Sat. 9–4:30, Sun. 2–5.*

❿ You need a car to reach the **Macrorie House Museum,** a lovely residence with a corrugated-iron roof and ornate ironwork typical of old Pietermaritzburg. Bishop Macrorie lived in the house from 1870 to 1892, and it's been furnished to reflect that period. *Corner of Loop and Pine Sts.,* ☎ *0331/94–2161.* ☛ *R2 adults, R1 children.* ☉ *Tues.–Thurs. 9– 1, Sun. 11–4.*

⑪ For a good view of Pietermaritzburg, head back down Loop Street and turn left on Commercial Road. After a while, Commercial becomes Old Howick Road. Follow the signs to **World's View,** a spectacular outlook commanding panoramic views of the city and miles of surrounding countryside. The viewpoint lies on the route used by the Voortrekkers on their long migration from the Cape in the 19th century. A large diagram traces their route, and labels the major landscape features.

Dining

$ Green Door. This trendy little restaurant occupies an ancient building tucked away at the end of a narrow alley. Alternative rock music provides an interesting counterpoint to creaky wood floors and slate walls. The menu features a variety of soups, salads, pies, and sandwiches. The pita sandwich with hummus is very good, but contains enough garlic to clear a room. Guests can also sit outside on a small veranda. ✗ *Club La.,* ☎ *0331/94–4764. MC, V. Closed Sun. No dinner Mon., Tues.*

$ Tatham Coffee Shop. On the second floor of the Tatham Art Gallery, this pleasant café serves a wonderful selection of teas and coffees, as well as light meals and desserts. Among the heartier dishes are cottage pie, chicken curry, quiche, and lasagna. If the weather's fine, sit outside on the narrow veranda overlooking Commercial Road. ✗ *Commercial Rd., across from Publicity Assoc.,* ☎ *0331/42–8327. No credit cards.* ☉ *Tues.–Sun. 10–5:30.*

Arriving and Departing

By Bus. Greyhound (☎ 031/361–7774) and **Translux** (031/361–7461) buses stop at the Pietermaritzburg Publicity Association on their runs between Johannesburg and Durban.

By Car. The easiest way to reach Pietermaritzburg from Durban is along the N3, a direct 80-kilometer (50-mile) run. Far more interesting and scenic, however, is the route that follows Old Main Road (R103) through the Valley of a Thousand Hills (*see below*) and rejoins the N3 east of Pietermaritzburg.

By Train. Interpax trains (☎ 031/361–7652) between Johannesburg and Durban stop daily in Pietermaritzburg.

Valley of a Thousand Hills

Only 45 kilometers (28 miles) inland from Durban, the Valley of a Thousand Hills makes a beautiful half-day excursion from the city. The name is an apt description of this area of plunging gorges and bush-covered hills. The Old Main Road (M103) from Durban to Pietermaritzburg runs along the crest of the hills, offering some tremendous views. This is the route taken by runners during the annual Comrades Marathon, South Africa's most famous road race. Each year, thousands of masochistic participants sign up for the 80-kilometer (50-mile) event, which is run "uphill" to Pietermaritzburg one year and "downhill" to Durban the next. It may be wiser, however, to come in a car instead. In fact, for generations, Durbanites have driven up to the Valley of a Thousand Hills on weekends for lunch or tea. In addition to several tearooms and small restaurants, the route is dotted with craft shops, farm stalls, and even a hokey safari park. To get here, follow the M13 out of Durban. Stay on this road through the suburbs of Kloof and Gillitts until you see the turnoff to Old Main Road (R103) and the Valley of a Thousand Hills.

Dining

$$ **Mal Bre's Dining Room and Coffee Shop.** This is one of those places
★ you come back to again and again. The restaurant couldn't be better situated—in an old trading store with breathtaking views over the Valley of a Thousand Hills. Diners may choose between a formal dining room inside and a casual coffee shop that offers outdoor seating on the lawn. No reservations are accepted in the coffee shop, so try to arrive early for lunch to avoid a wait that can run to an hour or more. (Even so, it's almost worth it: The view from the tables on the lawn is heavenly.) Standard dishes are Greek lamb pie in a delicate phyllo pastry, quiche, and a sublime sandwich made with sun-dried tomatoes, parmesan, olive oil, salami, and salad greens. ✗ *Raven's Croft, Old Main Rd., Drummond,* ☏ *0325/3–4598. Reservations essential for dining room. AE, DC, MC, V. Dining room: No dinner Sun.–Tues., no lunch weekdays. Coffee shop:* ◷ *Tues.–Sun. 9:30–4, Fri.–Sat. 6–10. Closed Mon.*

THE DRAKENSBERG

The Afrikaners call them the Drakensberg, the Dragon Mountains. To Zulus, they are *uKhalamba*—the Barrier of Spears. Both are apt designations for this wall of rock that rises from the Natal grasslands, forming a natural fortress protecting the mountain kingdom of Lesotho. The Drakensberg is the highest range in southern Africa and possesses some of the most spectacular scenery in the country. It's a hiker's dream, and you could easily pass several days here just soaking up the awesome views.

The blue-tinted mountains seem to stain the landscape, cooling the "champagne air"—as the natives refer to the heady, sparkling breezes that blow around the precipices and pinnacles. The mountains, with names like Giant's Castle, Cathedral Peak, and the Sentinel, seem to have a special atmosphere, as well as unique topography. It's no surprise that South African–born J.R.R. Tolkien—legendary author of the cult classic *Lord of the Rings*—was inspired by the fantastic shapes of the Drakensberg massif when he created the phantasmagorical settings of his Middle Earth.

The Drakensberg is not a typical mountain range—it's actually an escarpment separating a high interior plateau from the coastal lowlands of Natal. It's a continuation of the same escarpment that divides the Transvaal highveld from the hot malarial zones of the lowveld (*see* Chapter 3). However, the Natal Drakensberg, or Berg as it is commonly known, is far wilder and more spectacular than its Transvaal counterpart. Many of the peaks—some of which top 10,000 feet—are the source of sparkling streams and mighty rivers that have carved out myriad valleys and dramatic gorges. You can hike for days and not meet a soul, and the mountains retain an untamed majesty missing in the commercially forested peaks of the Eastern Transvaal.

On the other hand, accommodations in the Natal Drakensberg can't hope to compete with the chi-chi lodges of the Eastern Transvaal. The Berg resorts are family-oriented establishments, by and large, that emphasize the outdoors. Most offer a comprehensive round of sporting activities, including daily guided hikes, horseback rides, tennis, lawn bowls, even golf. A long hike through the Berg leaves you too tired to care whether your hotel leaves a mint on your pillow.

Besides hiking and drinking in the sheer beauty of the mountains, the other great attraction of the Berg is the San (Bushman) paintings. The San are a hunter-gatherer people that once roamed the entire country. More than 5,000 of their paintings are sprinkled in scores of caves and on rock overhangs throughout the Berg—probably the finest collection of rock paintings in the country. They tell the stories of bygone hunts, dances, and battles, and touch on the almost mystical relationship of the San with the animals they hunted. With the arrival of the Nguni peoples from the north and white settlers from the southwest, the San were driven out of their traditional hunting lands, and they retreated into the remote fastnesses of the Drakensberg and the Kalahari Desert. San attacks in Natal in the late-19th century occasioned harsh punitive raids by white settlers, and by 1880 the last San had disappeared from the Berg. Today, only a few clans remain in the very heart of the Kalahari Desert.

The best times to visit the Berg are spring (September–October) and autumn (March–April). Summer sees the Berg at its greenest and the weather at its warmest, but vicious afternoon thunderstorms, which can put a severe damper on long hikes, are an almost daily occurrence. In winter, the mountains lose their lush overcoat and turn brown and sere. Winter days in the valleys, where most of the resorts are located, are usually sunny and pleasant, with only occasional cold snaps (don't be put off by alarmist reports of frigid weather). Nights are chilly, however, and you should pack plenty of warm clothing if you plan to hike high up into the mountains or camp overnight. Snow is common at higher elevations. Hikers heading above the 10,000-foot level are advised to sign the mountain register at the nearest Natal Parks Board office in case of emergency.

Exploring

Numbers in the margin correspond to points of interest on the Drakensberg map.

The Natal Drakensberg is not conducive to traditional touring. The nature of the attractions and the limited road system make a connect-the-dots tour impractical and unrewarding. Check into a resort for two or three days instead and use it as a base for hiking and exploring the immediate area.

❶ **Giant's Castle Game Reserve,** an 85,500-acre reserve in the Central Berg region, encompasses rolling grasslands as well as some of the highest peaks in the Drakensberg. A host of trails, ranging in length from two hours to overnight, start at the main visitor center. The most popular tourist attraction is the Main Caves, which have the finest collection of San paintings in the Drakensberg. More than 500 paintings, some now barely discernible, adorn the faces of two huge rock overhangs just a 30-minute walk from the camp. Many of the paintings depict eland hunts, for the huge antelope holds a special religious significance for the San. Guided tours (R5 per person) of the caves are conducted 9–3 daily, on the hour. Another fascinating attraction is the Lammergeyer Hide, set high on a cliff, where bird-watchers can observe the endangered lammergeyer, or bearded vulture. On weekend mornings between May and September, rangers put out meat and bones for these birds below the hide. Besides giving birders a close-up view of the vultures, the feeding program is intended to draw the birds away from nearby farmland, where they might feed on poisoned carcasses. Afrikaner farmers erroneously believe that the birds kill their young livestock, hence the name *lammergeyer,* "lamb-killer." The hide accommodates a maximum of six people (R25 per person), and reservations are essential (Hide Bookings, Giant's Castle Game Reserve, Private Bag X7055, Estcourt 3310, ☎ 0363/2–4616). A ranger drives you up to the blind at 7:30 AM, and you're on your own for the walk back. *Mooi River toll plaza exit off N3 or Central Berg/Giant's Castle exit near Estcourt,* ☎ *0363/2–4718.* ☛ *R5.* ☉ *Oct.–Mar. daily 5–7, Apr.–Sept. daily 6–6.*

❷ **Injasuti,** 20 miles down a dirt road off the Central Berg/Loskop Road, is a collection of huts (*see* Dining and Lodging, *below*) set in the northern section of the Giant's Castle Game Reserve. A number of spectacular hikes start from here, including a guided 3-mile walk (R5) up the Injasuti Valley to Battle Cave, which holds one of the most fascinating collections of San paintings in the country. Some 750 paintings cover the rock walls of the cave, but it's the subject matter that is most enthralling: One vignette clearly depicts two Bushman clans at war with one another. Tours of Battle Cave leave daily from the camp office at 8:30, and reservations are essential. *Private Bag X7010, Estcourt 3310,* ☎ *036/488–1050.* ☛ *R5.* ☉ *Oct.–Mar. daily 5–7, Apr.–Sept. daily 6–6.*

The R600, accessible from the N3 via Winterton, leads to many of the resorts and attractions of the Central Berg. Twenty-seven kilometers ❸ (17 miles) down the R600 from Winterton is the turnoff to the **Ardmore Ceramic Art Studio.** Started on a farm by artist Fée Berning in 1985, the studio is now home to nearly 40 Zulu and Sotho artists, each pursuing their own artistic visions in clay. Their ceramics have won national and international awards and are displayed in galleries around the world. The work is colorful and very African, with zebras and giraffes serving as handles on teapots, bowls, and platters. You can watch artists at work or just browse through the collection, housed in a converted farm shed. The studio ships purchases overseas. *D275, off R600, Central Berg,* ☎ *036/468–1314.* ☉ *Daily 9–4:30.*

★ ❹ A few kilometers farther down the R600 is the turnoff to the **Drakensberg Boys' Choir School** (Off R600, ☎ 036/468–1012, FAX 036/468–1709). Mentioned in the same breath as the Vienna and Harlem boys' choirs, this is one of the most famous choirs in the world. It performs in the school's auditorium on Wednesdays at 3:30 and sometimes on Saturdays. Performances run the musical gamut from the classics to

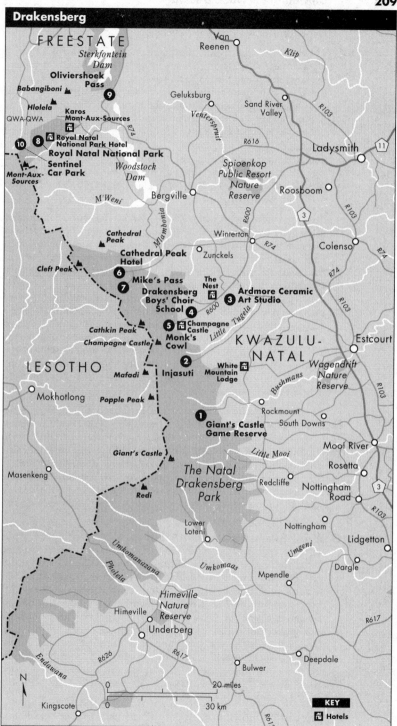

FREESTATE

Sterkfontein Dam

Van Reenen

Klip

R103

Oliviershoek Pass ⑨

Babangiboni

Geluksburg

Sand River Valley

Ventersprit

R616

Hlolela

QWA-QWA

Karos Mont-Aux-Sources

R74

Ladysmith ⑪

Royal Natal National Park Hotel

⑧ **Royal Natal National Park**

⑩ **Sentinel Car Park**

Mont-Aux-Sources

Woodstock Dam

M'Weni

Bergville

Mlambonia

Spioenkop Public Resort Nature Reserve

R600

Roosboom

Winterton

R74

Colenso

R103

R74

Cathedral Peak

Zunckels

Cathedral Peak Hotel

Cleft Peak ⑥

⑦ **Mike's Pass**

Drakensberg Boys' Choir School ④

The Nest

③ **Ardmore Ceramic Art Studio**

R600

Little Tugela

Cathkin Peak

⑤ **Champagne Castle**

Monk's Cowl

Champagne Castle

KWAZULU-NATAL

Wagendrift Nature Reserve

Estcourt

Mafadi

② **Injasuti**

White Mountain Lodge

Bushmans

LESOTHO

Popple Peak

Mokhotlong

① **Giant's Castle Game Reserve**

Rockmount

South Downs

R103

Mooi River

Little Mooi

Rosetta

Masenkeng

Giant's Castle

The Natal Drakensberg Park

Redcliffe

Nottingham Road ③

R103

Redi

Lower Loteni

Nottingham

Lidgetton

Umkomanazana

Umkomaas

Umgeni

Mpendle

Dargle

Pholela

Himeville Nature Reserve

Himeville

Underberg

R617

Endawana

R26

R617

Bulwer

Deepdale

N

0   20 miles

0   30 km

Kingscote

KEY

🏨 Hotels

ethnic songs. Tickets cost R20 and reservations are essential. There are no performances during school holidays.

⑤ The R600 runs directly into the mountains, ending at **Monk's Cowl,** a Natal Parks Board station and the gateway to several amazing day and overnight hikes into the High Drakensberg. Among the highlights is a one-hour walk to Sterkspruit Falls, the largest waterfall in the area, and a 3½-hour walk to the top of the Little Berg. On this walk you pass the Sphinx—a formation that looks like the famous Egyptian monument—and Breakfast Falls before joining the contour trail for panoramic views of Champagne Castle, Cathkin Peak, Dragon's Back, and Sterkhorn. Hikers who wish to camp out in the mountains must sign the mountain register and pay R6 per person per night. *Private Bag X2, Winterton 3340,* ☎ *036/468–1103.* ☛ *R5.* ☉ *Oct.–Mar. daily 5–7, Apr.–Sept. daily 6–6.*

⑥ Another tremendous base for hikes—and drives—into the mountains is the **Cathedral Peak Hotel** (*see* Dining and Lodging, *below*), accessible from Winterton or via dirt roads off the R600. Although the Natal Parks Board levies R5 per person to enter the area, the hotel acts as the de facto center for hikers heading into the surrounding mountains. It publishes an excellent hiking booklet that describes all the trails, indicating their length and level of difficulty. A scale model of the area in the hotel lobby gives hikers a sense of the lay of the land before they set off. Cathedral Peak (9,900 feet) is the easiest of the major peaks to scale. Anyone who is fit and accustomed to long hikes can make the 12-mile round-trip journey from the hotel to the summit; only the last portion is difficult. Budget 9–10 hours to get up and down, allowing plenty of time to drink in the view from the top—surely one of the highlights of a stay in the region.

⑦ About 4 kilometers (2½ miles) before the Cathedral Peak Hotel is the turnoff to **Mike's Pass,** a winding forestry road that leads to the top of the Little Berg. A four-wheel-drive vehicle is recommended, but in clear, dry weather a regular car can make it up with little difficulty. This road ends at a parking area that offers one of the finest views of the main rock face of the Drakensberg you can get without donning hiking boots. For additional views, wander along some of the forestry roads that run along the top of the Little Berg. ☛ *R5 per person and R10 per vehicle.*

⑧ Access to **Royal Natal National Park** is via the R74, north of Bergville. The park contains some of the most stunning mountain scenery in the Drakensberg. The highlight is the Amphitheatre, a sheer rock wall measuring an unbelievable 5 kilometers (3 miles) across and more than 1,500 feet high. Another showstopper is the Tugela River, which flows off Mont-aux-Sources (10,836 feet) and plunges nearly 3,000 feet over the plateau in a series of five spectacular falls. The park's most popular and scenic walk winds up the Tugela Gorge, a six-hour hike that crosses the river several times and passes through a tunnel before emerging into the Amphitheatre. Hikers often turn back at the first fording of the river; but persevere, for the scenery gets better and better. *North Berg Rd., off R74,* ☎ *036/438–6303.* ☛ *R5.* ☉ *Oct.–Mar. daily 5–7, Apr.–Sept. daily 6–6.*

⑨ Just past the turnoff to Royal Natal National Park, the northbound R74 begins a twisty ascent up the **Oliviershoek Pass** (6,912 feet), offering tremendous views back over the plains and hills. If these views don't satiate you, continue on the R74 past the Sterkfontein Dam until the road ends at a T junction. Turn left onto the R712 and head into Qwa Qwa, also known as Phuthaditjhaba. Follow signs to the Witsieshoek Mountain Resort. Just before the resort, the road splits and continues for about 13 kilometers (8 miles) to the **Sentinal Car Park** (8,580 feet), where you can follow a path some 150 yards to the very edge of the Drakensberg escarpment. The views from here are breathtaking—the entire Royal Natal National Park lies below you, and you can see all the way to Estcourt. The car park is also the starting point for a strenuous hike to the top of Mont-aux-Sources. From the car park, it's an easy drive back down the R712 to Harrismith and the N3 highway to Johannesburg and Durban.

Sports and the Outdoors

Horseback Riding

All resorts offer horseback rides through the mountains for everyone from beginners to experts. Most of these rides last two–three hours. **Rugged Glen** (☎ 036/438–6303) in Royal Natal National Park, and **Hillside** (☎ 0363/244350), a campsite in the Giant's Castle Game Reserve, also conduct morning and afternoon guided rides through their respective parks. No experience is necessary, and rides cost R20 per hour. Hillside also offers more adventurous two- and three-day pony trails that take riders through some of the most breathtaking scenery in the Drakensberg. Riders sleep in caves or huts in the mountains, and the Natal Parks Board provides everything you need except food. Bookings for these rides, which cost about R200 per day, must be made with the reservations officer (Natal Parks Board, Box 662, Pietermaritzburg 3200, ☎ 0331/47–1981).

Dining and Lodging

Restaurants are few in the mountains, so most resort rates include dinner and breakfast. Don't expect gourmet grub out here: The emphasis is on down-home South African cooking, including lots of roasts and boiled vegetables. Most resorts serve either a four- or five-course set menu or a buffet. Either way, the quality of the food tends to be mediocre. For price ranges, see Charts 1 and 2(A) in On the Road with Fodor's.

$$$ Karos Mont-Aux-Sources. Although this hotel is more than 8 kilometers (5 miles) from the hiking trails of Royal Natal National Park, it more than compensates with its views—stunning panoramas of the Drakensberg that take in the Amphitheatre, the Eastern Buttress, and miles of the escarpment. They are the hotel's greatest asset, so be sure to request a front-facing room. The rooms themselves are no great shakes, being reminiscent of chain hotels around the world. Likewise, the public rooms lack warmth, seeming more suited to the hotel's mid-week conference business. Breakfast and dinner are served buffet-style, with extensive selections ranging from roasts to vegetarian curries. ⌨ *Northern Berg Rd. off R74 (mailing address: Private Bag X1670, Bergville 3350),* ☎ *and* FAX *036/438–6230. 73 rooms with bath. Restaurant, bar, room service, 2 pools, miniature golf, tennis court, horseback riding, squash, volleyball. Breakfast and dinner included. AE, DC, MC, V.*

$$ ★ Cathedral Peak Hotel. Few hotels in South Africa can rival the exquisite setting of this large resort, high above the Ulamboza River and ringed by towering peaks. Hiking trails start right from the hotel and wend their way through a dozen mountains and valleys. No buildings obscure the incredible views, and you won't be running into guests from other hotels since there are none. Opt for a luxury room—they cost just a few rand more and are far more pleasant than the standard rooms or thatched bungalows. French doors open onto private verandas overlooking the gardens or the mountains, and pine furnishings give the rooms a pleasant, rustic feel. Besides its tremendous location, the hotel's other big advantages are a nine-hole golf course and daily helicopter sightseeing trips. The major drawback is the food, which can paralyze your taste buds with boredom—insipid roasts and cream-covered cakes and parfaits. ☎ *Cathedral Peak Rd. from Winterton (mailing address: P.O. Winterton 3340), ☎ and* FAX *036/488–1888. 90 rooms with bath. Restaurant, 2 bars, room service, pool, 9-hole golf course, tennis court, croquet, exercise room, horseback riding, squash. Breakfast and dinner included. AE, DC, MC, V.*

$$ **Champagne Castle.** Along with Cathedral Peak, this old family-style hotel enjoys one of the best settings of any of the Berg resorts. It lies right in the mountains, with magnificent views down Champagne Valley to the towering Champagne Castle and Cathkin Peak. A host of hiking trails begin practically on the hotel's doorstep, and the trailheads at Monk's Cowl lie just minutes away. There's nothing remotely fancy about the hotel itself, but it's a peaceful haven where genteel traditions linger—gentlemen are still required to wear ties to dinner. Rooms, in thatched *rondawels* and bungalows scattered through the pleasant gardens, are unexceptional but comfortable. Meals are served buffet-style, with an emphasis on traditional South African roasts and vegetables. Unfortunately, the food's very ordinary, far below the standards set by the Nest (*see below*). ☎ *R600, Central Berg (mailing address: Private Bag X8, Winterton 3340), ☎ 036/468–1063,* FAX *036/468–1306. 45 rooms with bath. Restaurant, 2 bars, pool, putting green, tennis court, horseback riding, volleyball. Breakfast, lunch, and dinner included. AE, DC, MC, V.*

$$ **The Nest.** Most of the guests at this well-run resort seem content to park themselves on the sun-drenched lawns, soak in the dazzling mountain views, and await the next round of tea, drinks, or meals. Few manage to muster the energy to drive the 8 kilometers (5 miles) to the trailheads at Monk's Cowl. The hotel, built by Italian POWs, is one of the most attractive and appealing of the Berg resorts. Rooms are very pleasant, with pine ceilings, simple cane furniture, heated towel racks, and under-floor heating (there are no TVs). Be sure to request a mountain-facing room. All meals are table d'hôte, with an emphasis on traditional South African cuisine, including home-cooked specialties like roasts, oxtail, and cottage pie. The quality of the food is much higher than at any of the other Berg resorts. ☎ *R600, Central Berg (mailing address: Private Bag X14, Winterton 3340), ☎ 036/468– 1068,* FAX *036/468–1390. 53 rooms with bath. Restaurant, bar, pool, tennis court, croquet, horseback riding, mountain bikes, playground. Breakfast, lunch, and dinner included. AE, DC, MC, V.*

$$ **Royal Natal National Park Hotel.** The "Royal" in this hotel's name refers to the visit of King George VI in 1947, and the place retains an old-fashioned colonial charm. Situated within the boundaries of Royal Natal National Park, it's an ideal stopover for hikers and walkers— fall out of bed and you're likely to find yourself at the start of a trail. Indeed, the hotel's setting is magnificent, encircled as it is by mountains including the towering cliffs of the Amphitheatre and the Eastern Buttress. For some reason, though, the hotel was designed with an almost obsessive desire to shield its guests from the surrounding beauty—neither the public areas nor the rooms have views worth mentioning. Thankfully, the hotel gardens provide a lovely substitute. Rooms are clean and simple, with white walls and light floral patterns; no TV. ☎ *Northern Berg Rd., off R74 (mailing address: Private Bag 4, Mont-aux-Sources 3353), ☎ 036/438–6200,* FAX *036/438–6101. 64* *rooms with bath. Restaurant, bar, pool, horseback riding, tennis court. Breakfast and dinner included. AE, DC, MC, V.*

$ **White Mountain Lodge.** This lodge has one major attraction: It's the only fully catered hotel close to the spectacular San paintings and hikes of Giant's Castle Game Reserve. For all that, it offers very basic accommodation, either in thatched bungalows or in trailer homes. The bungalows are utilitarian and threadbare, with thin industrial carpet, thatch festooned with spider webs, and bare-bones furniture. Kitchenettes are a standard feature, but there are no TVs or phones. Meals are served in a restored 140-year-old mill. Expect the usual South African fare, done in uninspiring fashion—tasteless *bobotie*, gray roast pork, and thin tomato soup. 🕾 *Giant's Castle Rd. from Estcourt (mailing address: Box 609, Estcourt 3310),* ☎ *0363/2–4437. 28 rooms with bath. Restaurant, bar, pool, horseback riding, volleyball, boating, fishing. AE, DC, MC, V.*

Self-Catering Lodging

$ **Giant's Castle.** This camp offers comfortable but basic accommodation in Giant's Castle Game Reserve. Hidden away in a beautiful valley close to the sheer face of the High Drakensberg, it is an ideal base for viewing the San paintings in the Main Caves and bearded vultures from the Lammergeyer Hide (*see* Exploring the Drakensberg, *above*). Accommodations are either in bungalows, which share communal kitchens, or in self-contained cottages. You must provide your own food, which is then cooked by camp staff. A store in the main office sells staples like milk, bread, charcoal, and packs of meat. Giant's Castle also manages three mountain huts, situated at the 7,260-foot level and a 4- to 5-hour walk from the main camp. The huts are rudimentary, furnished only with bunk beds and mattresses. Hikers must provide all their own cooking facilities, food, and bedding. 🕾 *Reserve through Natal Parks Board, Box 1750, Pietermaritzburg 3200,* ☎ *0331/47–1981,* 🖷 *0331/47–1980. 13 bungalows and 4 cottages with bath, 3 mountain huts. AE, DC, MC, V.*

$ **Injasuti.** In the northern section of the Giant's Castle Game Reserve, this camp lies at the head of the Injasuti Valley, with great views of Cathkin Peak, Monk's Cowl, and Champagne Castle. The camp operates much like the one at Giant's Castle, except that you do your own cooking and washing. Cabins sleep up to six people and all feature kitchens and a dining room/living room. Electricity is available only from 5:30 until 10 each night. Injasuti also manages three caves in the mountains where hikers can sleep overnight. The caves feature only basic toilet facilities and hikers must bring everything else with them, including bedding and food. Reservations for caves must be made through the camp manager (Private Bag X7010, Estcourt 3310, ☎ 036/488–1050). 🕾 *Reserve through Natal Parks Board Reservations, Box 1750, Pietermaritzburg 3200,* ☎ *0331/47–1981,* 🖷 *0331/47–1980. 17 cabins with bath, 3 caves. AE, DC, MC, V.*

$ **Tendele Hutted Camp.** Smack in the middle of Royal Natal National Park, this camp makes a great base for long hikes into the mountains. Accommodations are in a variety of bungalows, cottages, and chalets, each with excellent views of the sheer rock face of the Amphitheatre. You must bring all your own food, although you can purchase staples and frozen meat at the main visitor center and at the Royal Natal National Park Hotel. In the bungalows and cottages, all food is prepared by the camp staff, but the chalets are self-catering. If you don't fancy providing for yourself, you can always walk to the hotel for your meals, although you should make reservations first. 🕾 *Natal Parks Board Reservations, Box 1750, Pietermaritzburg 3200,* ☎ *0331/47–1981,*

FAX *0331/47–1980. 28 bungalows, chalets, and cottages, all with bath. AE, DC, MC, V.*

Drakensberg Essentials

Arriving and Departing

The main resort area of the Drakensberg lies 380 kilometers (250 miles) from Johannesburg and 240 kilometers (150 miles) from Durban—an almost direct shot along the N3 motorway. A car is not strictly necessary for a trip to the Berg, although it is certainly a convenience. On request, most resorts will pick up guests at the **Greyhound** (☎ 011/333–2130 or 031/361–7774) or **Translux** (☎ 031/361–7461) terminals in Estcourt (Municipal Library, Victoria St.), Ladysmith (Ted's Service Station), or Swinburne (Montrose Service Area). Buses from both lines stop at these towns as least once a day on their runs between Durban and Johannesburg. Once at the resort—particularly those situated right in the mountains—most guests are content to hike or enjoy the hotel facilities. If you do want to see some of the surrounding area, you can usually arrange for guided tours and transport.

Guided Tours

Mount Aire (Box 229, Winterton 3340, ☎ 036/468–1141), near the main resorts in the Central Berg, offers 20-minute scenic flights over the mountains. For two or three passengers, expect to pay about R120 per person.

Important Addresses and Numbers

VISITOR INFORMATION

Drakensberg Publicity Association. *Tatham St., Bergville,* ☎ *036/448–1557.* ☉ *Weekdays 9–4.*

ZULULAND AND THE BATTLEFIELDS

Zululand stretches north from the Tugela River all the way to the border of Mozambique. It's a region of rolling grasslands, gorgeous beaches, and classic African bush. It has also seen more than its share of bloodshed and death. Modern South Africa was forged in the fiery crucible of Zululand and northern Natal. Here, Boers battled Zulus, Zulus battled British, and British battled Boers. The most interesting historical sites, however, involve the battles against the Zulus. Names like Isandlwana, Rorke's Drift, and Blood River have taken their place in the roll of legendary military encounters.

Indeed, no African tribe has captured the Western imagination quite like the Zulus. A host of books and movies have explored their warrior culture and extolled their martial valor. Until the early 19th century, the Zulus were a small, unheralded group, part of the Nguni peoples who migrated to southern Africa from the north. King Shaka (1787–1828), the illegitimate son of a Zulu chief, changed all that. Prior to Shaka, warfare among the Nguni had been a desultory affair in which small bands of warriors would hurl spears at one another from a distance and then retire. Shaka introduced the short stabbing spear (*assegai*), teaching his warriors to close with the enemy in hand-to-hand combat. He also developed the famous chest-and-horns formation, a cattle analogy for a classic maneuver in which you outflank and encircle your enemy. In less than a decade, Shaka created a military machine unrivaled in black Africa. By the time of his assassination in 1828, Shaka had destroyed 300 tribes and extended Zulu power for 800 kilometers (500 miles) through the north, south, and west.

Fifty years after Shaka's death, the British still considered the Zulus a major threat to their planned federation of white states in South Africa. The British solution, in 1879, was to instigate a war to destroy the Zulu kingdom. They employed a similar tactic 20 years later to bring the Boer republics to heel and the rich goldfields of the Witwatersrand into their own hands.

The best way to tour the battlefields is with an expert guide who can bring the history to life (*see* Guided Tours *in* Zululand and the Battlefields Essentials, *below*). Unless you've done extensive research or have a vivid imagination, you may find it difficult to conjure up the furious events of a century ago. Many of the battle sites are little more than open grassland, graced with the occasional memorial stone. If you're not a history buff, it's better to head straight to the game reserves and natural wonders of northern Zululand (*see* Chapter 9).

Exploring

Towns and sights on this tour appear on the KwaZulu-Natal map.

Head north up the coast from Durban on the N2. Today, Zululand starts on the other side of the Tugela River. In Shaka's day, the Zulu empire was much larger, encompassing much of present-day KwaZulu-Natal. Shaka himself had his military kraal at Dukuza, the site of present-day **Stanger,** on the north coast. The KwaZulu Monuments Council (☎ 0358/79–1854) is currently erecting an interpretive center in Stanger that will focus on the Shaka period, as well as dispense information on sites in the area.

Leave the N2 at Gingindlovu and follow the R68 toward Eshowe. Eshowe is a pleasant town, high up in the hills and with great views of the Dhlinza Forest and fields of sugarcane. It is the site of **Fort Nongqayi,** which houses the **Zululand Historical Museum.** The fort was built in 1883 and served as the headquarters of the Nongqai Police, a black police contingent under British command. Museum displays trace the role of the fort in the Bambata Rebellion of 1906, when Chief Bambata took up arms to protest a £1 poll tax on every African male. A particularly interesting exhibit deals with John Dunn (1834–95), the son of settler parents, who was fluent in Zulu, Afrikaans, and English. He became Chief Cetshwayo's political adviser in 1856 and was given the status of a Zulu chief. Dunn observed Zulu customs and laws, going so far as to marry 49 Zulu wives, by whom he had 117 children. Periodically, the descendants of John Dunn stage reunions. *Nongqai Rd., Eshowe,* ☎ *0354/4–1141,* ℻ *0354/7–4733.* ☛ *Free.* ☉ *Daily 9–4.*

Return to the R68 and continue toward Melmoth. After 13 kilometers (8 miles) you reach the turnoff to **Shakaland,** a living museum of Zulu culture and one of the most popular tourist stops in the region. Originally the movie set for *Shaka Zulu*, Shakaland consists of a traditional Zulu kraal, with thatched beehive huts arranged in a circle around a central cattle enclosure. The emphasis here is on Zulu culture as it existed under King Shaka in the 19th century. You can watch Zulus, dressed in animal skins or beaded aprons, engaged in everyday tasks: making beer, forging spears, and crafting beadwork. Opt for a three-hour day tour or spend the night (*see* Dining and Lodging, *below*). A Zulu cultural advisor leads you through the kraal, explaining the significance of the layout and the roles played by men and women in traditional Zulu society. A highlight of the visit is a half-hour dance performance, featuring a variety of Zulu and other traditional dances. The whole setup is touristy and some critics have labeled it a Zulu Disneyland, but you learn a great deal about Zulu culture nevertheless. A buffet lunch of Zulu specialties and Western food is included in the tour. *Off R68, 13 km (8 mi) north of Eshowe,* ☎ *03546/912,* ☒ *03546/824.* ☛ *R85 (includes lunch). Daily tours at 11 and 12:30.*

Return to the R68 and turn left. After a few kilometers you come to the tiny settlement of Nkwalini. Turn right onto the R34 toward Empangeni to reach the **Jabulani Rehabilitation Centre.** Run by the Natal Cripples' Care Association, the center is home to more than 100 Zulus with disabilities, many of whom have been victims of polio. The residents learn a variety of crafts, from beadwork to spear- and shield-making, and much of their work is used and sold at tourist centers like Shakaland. The center has its own crafts outlet, prices here are often much lower than at the major curio shops, and you can watch the artisans at work. A small museum houses some antique spears and knobkerries (wooden fighting sticks). *R34, between Nkwalini and Empangeni,* ☎ *0351/92–8144.* ☛ *Free.* ☉ *Daily 8–5.*

Return to the R68 and turn right. The road snakes up and over the beautiful **Nkwalini Pass,** offering knockout views of valleys and hills dotted with Zulu kraals. Stay on the R34 through the town of Melmoth and then continue for another 32 kilometers (20 miles) to the turnoff to the R66 and **Ulundi.** Ulundi is currently the joint capital—with Pietermaritzberg—of KwaZulu-Natal. Except for a huge legislative complex, however, it's an empty, ghastly place, full of blowing trash and ramshackle buildings.

A mile before you reach Ulundi you'll see the turnoff to the **Battle of Ulundi Memorial** (Cetshwayo Hwy., no ☎). A stone temple with a silver dome marks the site of the battle on the sun-baked uplands surrounding Ulundi. The Battle of Ulundi marked the culmination of the Zulu War of 1879. Lord Chelmsford, smarting from his defeat at Isandlwana (*see below*), personally led the march on Ulundi and King Cetshwayo's royal kraal, Ondini. Cetshwayo, already disheartened by heavy losses at Kambula and Gingindlovu, sent messengers to the British seeking peace. In reply, Chelmsford demanded the disbandment of the Zulu regiment system and the surrender of the royal cattle herd. For the Zulu, to whom cattle represent the very thread of the social fabric, such terms were unacceptable.

On July 4, 1879, a British force of 5,317 crossed the White Mfolozi River, marched onto the open plain near Ondini, and formed an infantry square. Mounted troops then harassed the 15,000-strong Zulu force into making an undisciplined attack. None of the Zulu warriors got within 30 yards of the British square before being cut down by rifle and artillery fire. Within 45 minutes, the Zulus were in flight and the British 17th Lancers and a flying column gave pursuit, spearing the fleeing Zulus from horseback. The Zulu dead numbered 1,500. British losses amounted to a mere 13.

The British burned Ondini to the ground, and King Cetshwayo fled into the Ngome Forest. He was captured two months later and exiled to Cape Town and, finally, to England. Although he was restored to the throne as a puppet in 1883, the Zulu empire had been shattered.

Continue down the dirt road to the **KwaZulu Cultural Museum–Ondini,** the original site of King Cetshwayo's royal kraal. Ondini was modeled after Dingane's kraal at Mgungundlovu (*see below*). At the time of its destruction in 1879, the kraal consisted of 1,500 huts and was home to some 5,000 people. Today, only the royal enclosure has been restored, but a stroll among the deserted beehive huts gives you a feel for the kraal's size and scope. An interesting site museum at the entrance traces the history of the Zulu kings and displays the silver mug and bible presented to King Cetshwayo by Queen Victoria in 1882. The Cultural Museum, in a separate building, is excellent and well worth a visit. It houses a superb collection of beadwork from various tribes, plus detailed exhibits on Zulu life, including some of the changes in Zulu customs in modern times. *Cetshwayo Hwy., ☎ 0358/79–1854.* ☛ *R3.* ☺ *Weekdays 8–4, weekends 9–4.*

Retrace your route back down the R66 and turn right onto the R34 toward Vryheid. The turnoff to **Mgungundlovu** and the **Grave of Piet Retief** lies just a few miles farther on. Mgungundlovu was the site of Dingane's royal kraal and home to his 500 wives. Dingane (ruled 1828–1840) was Shaka's younger brother; he killed Shaka in 1828 to seize power for himself. During Dingane's rule, the Zulu came under increasing pressure from white settlers moving into the area. In 1837, Piet Retief and a party of Voortrekkers petitioned Dingane for land. The king agreed on condition that Retief retrieve some Zulu cattle stolen by a rival chief. Retief duly recovered the cattle and returned to Mgungundlovu with nearly 100 men. Dingane welcomed the Voortrekkers into the royal kraal, instructing them to leave their guns and horses outside. Once they were inside, Dingane shouted "Kill the wizards!" and 8 to 10 warriors seized each of the unarmed men. The Voortrekkers were dragged to Execution Hill and murdered. A monument now stands on the hill where Piet Retief and his men are buried. Retaliation from the Voortrekkers was slow in coming but ultimately terrible. At the Battle of Blood River (*see below*), in December 1838, Dingane's army was completely destroyed. Dingane burned Mgungundlovu to the ground and fled to the north. He met his end in 1840 at the hands of another brother, Mpande, who succeeded him as king. Today, the beehive huts of the royal enclosure have been reconstructed on their original foundations and a guide leads short tours of the kraal. A site museum has also just opened, but as yet it contains little of interest. *R34, ☎ 03545/2254.* ☛ *Free.* ☺ *Daily 8–5.*

Continue up the R34 for 6.4 kilometers (4 miles) and then turn left onto a good-quality dirt road, to Babanango. This road runs 32 kilometers (20 miles) through some of the most beautiful countryside in Zululand, with seemingly endless views over rolling grasslands. The dirt road ends at the tarred R68. Turn right and drive less than a mile into the pleasant hamlet of **Babanango.**

TIME OUT Stan's Pub (16 Justice St., ☎ 0358/35-0029) in the six-room Babanango Hotel, is one of the country's most famous watering holes. It's a tiny place crammed full of bric-a-brac, pictures of naked women, rude bar sayings, and uniforms used in the filming of *Zulu Dawn*. The owner, Stan, is a genial fellow, a former Royal Marine who served in Burma during World War II. The pub serves light lunches, including good pies with curry gravy and fries. It's worth a stop if you don't mind the bare-bums-and-boobs decor.

From Babanango, follow the R68 for 30 miles to the turnoff to Isandlwana. The **Battle of Isandlwana,** on January 22, 1879, was a major defeat for the British army. Coming as it did at the very beginning of the Zulu War, the defeat sent shudders of apprehension through the corridors of Whitehall and ultimately cost Lord Chelmsford his command. Chelmsford was in personal charge of one of three invasion columns that were supposed to sweep into Zululand and converge on Cetshwayo's capital at Ulundi. On January 20, Chelmsford crossed the

Buffalo River into Zululand, leaving behind a small force at Rorke's Drift to guard the column's supplies. He encamped at Isandlwana. Two days later, believing there was no danger of attack, he led a large portion of his troops on a mission in support of another commander, leaving the camp woefully unprepared to defend itself. Unknown to Chelmsford, the heart of the Zulu army—20,000 men—had taken up a position just 5 kilometers (3 miles) away. Despite their obvious advantage, the Zulus stayed their attack, persuaded by a *sangoma* (diviner) that the moment was not propitious. When a British patrol stumbled on the hidden army, however, it rose up and charged. Using Shaka's classic chest-and-horns formation, the Zulus swept toward the British positions arrayed beneath the distinctive peak of Isandlwana. The battle hung in the balance until the Zulus' left horn outflanked the British. The fighting continued for two hours before the British fled the field, with the Zulus in triumphant pursuit. About 1,000 Zulus perished in the attack, as did 1,329 British troops, including 52 officers. A further 300–400 British soldiers fled by various routes back toward Rorke's Drift and Natal. Today, the battlefield is dotted with whitewashed stone cairns and memorials marking the resting places of fallen soldiers. Even now, as you stand on the hillside overlooking the vast plain, the thought of 20,000 warriors rushing forward with their short stabbing spears is enough to make you shudder. The visitor center houses a small museum of mementos and artifacts. *Off R68, no ☎. ☛ R3. ☉ Daily 8–4.*

★ Turn left when you get back to the R68, and continue for 35 kilometers (22 miles) to the turnoff to **Rorke's Drift.** This is by far the best of the Zulu War battlefields to see without a guide. An excellent museum and orientation center superbly retell the story of the battle, with electronic diagrams, battle sounds, and dioramas. From the British perspective, this was the most glorious battle of the Zulu War, the more so since it took place just hours after the disaster at Isandlwana. The British force at Rorke's Drift consisted of just 141 men, of whom 35 were ailing. They occupied a Swedish mission church and house, which had been converted into a storehouse and hospital. The Zulu forces numbered some 3,000–4,000 men, comprised of the reserve regiments from Isandlwana. When a survivor from Isandlwana sounded the warning at 3:15 PM, the tiny British force hastily erected a stockade of flour bags and biscuit boxes around the mission. The Zulus attacked 75 minutes later and the fighting raged for 12 hours before the Zulus faltered. When the smoke cleared, 500 Zulus and 17 Britons lay dead. More Victoria Crosses, 11 in all, were won at Rorke's Drift than at any other battle in British history. The staunch resilience of the British defenders has been immortalized in the classic movie *Zulu. Rorke's Drift Rd., off R68, ☎ 03425/627. ☛ Free. ☉ Daily 8–5.*

Rorke's Drift is still a mission station, run by the Evangelical Lutheran Church. The **Rorke's Drift ELC Art and Craft Centre** at the mission sells super pottery, hand-woven rugs, and linocuts, all created by mission artists. *Rorke's Drift Rd., off R68, no ☎. ☉ Weekdays 8–4:30, weekends 10–3.*

Retrace your steps to the R68 and turn left. After 24 kilometers (15 miles), the road intersects with the R33. Turn right and drive 21 kilometers (13 miles) to the turnoff to the site of the **Battle of Blood River,** one of the most important events in the history of South Africa. This battle, fought between the Boers and the Zulus in 1838, predates the Anglo-Zulu War by over 40 years. After the murder of Piet Retief and his men at Mgungundlovu in February 1838 (*see above*), Dingane dispatched Zulu impis to kill all the white settlers in Natal. The Voortrekkers bore the brunt of the Zulu assault. For the next 10 months, their future hung in the balance: Entire settlements were wiped out and a Boer commando was smashed at the Battle of Italeni. By November, a new commando of 464 men and 64 wagons under Andries Pretorius had moved out to challenge the Zulus. On Sunday, November 9, the Boers took a vow that should God grant them victory they would forever remember that day as a sabbath and build a church in commemoration. They repeated the vow every night for the next five weeks. On December 16, an enormous Zulu force attacked the Boers, who had circled their wagons in a strategic position backed by the Blood River and a deep *donga,* or gully. Armed with only spears, the Zulus were no match for the Boer riflemen. At the end of the battle, 3,000 Zulus lay dead, but not a single Boer had fallen. The immediate effect of the victory was to open Natal to white settlement, but the long-term effects were far more dramatic. The intensely religious Voortrekkers saw their great victory as a confirmation of their role as God's chosen people. This deeply held conviction lay at the spiritual heart of the apartheid system that surfaced over a century later, in 1948. Indeed, when you see the monument, there's no mistaking the gravity and importance that the Nationalist Government ascribed to its erection. The laager of 64 wagons has been reconstructed in exacting detail, made from a mix of cast steel and bronze that is expected to last at least 200 years. It's a truly haunting monument, made even more poignant by its position on empty grasslands that seem to stretch for eternity. *Off R33, between Dundee and Vryheid,* ☎ *03424/695.* ☛ *R1.* ☉ *Daily 7–5.*

Retrace your route down the R33 and enter Dundee, a small coal-mining town. The first-rate **Talana Museum,** on the outskirts of Dundee, encompasses nine separate buildings and is well worth a visit. Fascinating exhibits trace the history of the area from the early San hunter-gatherers to the rise of the Zulu nation, the extermination of the cannibal tribes of the Biggarsberg, and finally the vicious battles of the Boer War (1899–1902). The museum itself stands on the site of the Battle of Talana (October 10, 1899), the opening battle in the Boer War. Two of the museum buildings were used by the British as dressing stations during the battle, which was won by the British. *2 km (1 mi) outside Dundee on R33 to Vryheid,* ☎ *0341/2–2654.* ☛ *R2 adults, R1 children.* ☉ *Weekdays 8–4, weekends 10–4.*

TIME OUT The **Miners Rest Tea Shop,** in a delightfully restored miner's cottage on the grounds of the Talana Museum, serves refreshments as well as more substantial dishes like peri-peri chicken livers or spinach, feta, and chicken pie in phyllo pastry. The food is good, and the atmosphere most welcoming. *Talana Museum,* ☎ *0341/2–1704.* ☉ *Tues.–Sun. 9:30–4.*

From Dundee, take the R602 toward **Ladysmith.** The town became famous around the world during the Boer War, when it outlasted a Boer siege of 118 days. Nearly 20,000 people were caught in the town when the Boers attacked on November 2, 1899. During the next four months, there was little fighting around Ladysmith itself—the Boers seemed content to shell the town with their Long Tom siege guns—but the town's food supply steadily dwindled. By the end of the siege, the desperate residents were slaughtering half-starved horses to supplement their diets, and 28 people died each day of sickness and malnutrition.

Much of the early part of the war revolved around British attempts to raise the siege. The incompetence of the British general, Sir Redvers

Buller, became apparent during repeated attempts to smash the Boer lines, resulting in heavy British losses at Spioenkop, Vaalkrans, and Colenso. Finally, sheer weight of numbers saw the British defeat the Boers in the epic 10-day Battle of Tugela Heights, and raise the siege of Ladysmith on February 28, 1900.

The **Ladysmith Siege Museum** brings the period of the siege skillfully to life, with the use of electronic mapping, artifacts from the period, and black-and-white photos. The museum can arrange guided tours, but it also sells two self-guiding pamphlets: the "Siege Town Walkabout" and the "Siege Town Drive-about." *Murchison St., next to Town Hall,* ☎ *0361/2–2231.* ☛ *50¢.* ☼ *Weekdays 8–12:30 and 1:30–4, Sat. 8–noon.*

Next to the Siege Museum, directly in front of Town Hall, stands a replica of a **Long Tom,** the 6-inch Creusot gun used by the Boers during the siege. Also in front of Town Hall are two howitzers used by the British and christened Castor and Pollux.

Dining and Lodging

For price ranges, *see* Charts 1 and 2(A) *in* On the Road with Fodor's.

Babanango

LODGING

$$$ Babanango Valley Lodge. This tiny guest lodge lies at the end of a rutted, 15-kilometer (9-mile) dirt road on a 5,000-acre cattle farm. Obviously, it's not the sort of place where you constantly pop in and out, but that's okay—you probably won't want to leave anyway. The lodge sits at the head of a steep valley, far from any other buildings and with tremendous views of acacia-studded grasslands and hills. John and Meryn Turner, the charming young hosts, go out of their way to make guests feel at home. John being a registered guide (*see* Important Addresses and Numbers *in* Zululand and the Battlefields Essentials, *below*), many people stay at the lodge as part of his battlefields tour. Rooms are decorated with rustic armoires and dressers, white fluffy duvets, and frilly lamp shades—simple, comfortable country stuff. The four-course table d'hôte dinner focuses on traditional South African fare, including fresh farm produce. ☒ *15 km (9 mi) off R68, near Babanango (mailing address: Box 10, Babanango 3850),* ☎ *and* FAX *0358/35–0062. 4 rooms with bath. Pool. Breakfast and dinner included. MC, V.*

Eshowe

DINING AND LODGING

$$$ Shakaland. Shakaland is best known as a living museum of traditional Zulu culture (*see* Exploring Zululand and the Battlefields, *above*), but it's also possible to stay overnight at the complex, an experience that is far more rewarding than the three-hour daytime tour. Overnight guests see a more extensive program of cultural events than day visitors (the program begins at 4 PM and concludes at 11 AM the next day), and get to experience a night in a quasi-traditional Zulu dwelling. The rooms here are among the most attractive and luxurious of all the African-inspired accommodations in the country: Enormous beehive thatch huts supported by rope-wrapped struts are decorated with African bedspreads, reed matting, and interesting African art that create an appealing ethnic elegance. Modern bathrooms are attached to all but three huts. All meals are included in the price, and feature a selection of Western-style dishes as well as some Zulu specialties. ☒ *Off R68, 13 km (8 mi) north of Eshowe (mailing address: Box 103, Eshowe 3815),* ☎ *03546/912,*

FAX *03546/824. 40 rooms, 37 with bath. Restaurant, bar, pool, shop. Breakfast, dinner, and cultural tour included. AE, DC, MC, V.*

Ladysmith

DINING AND LODGING

$ **Royal Hotel.** This three-star hotel will suffice if you find yourself in Ladysmith at the end of the day. It's a typical South African country hotel that has seen more glorious days. Expect small, run-down rooms and ancient furniture, although TVs and air-conditioning are standard features. The hotel was built in 1880, just 19 years before the town was attacked by the Boers during the Boer War. During the siege, a shell from a Long Tom gun exploded on the hotel veranda, killing a doctor. The hotel offers several dining options, from a family-style Italian restaurant to expensive Continental cuisine in Swainsons. ⚐ *140 Murchison St., Ladysmith 3370, ☎ and* FAX *0361/2–2176. 71 rooms with bath. 3 restaurants, 3 bars, room service. Breakfast included. AE, DC, MC, V.*

Melmoth

LODGING

$$$ **Simunye Pioneer Settlement.** If Shakaland is too commercial for your
★ tastes, consider this small settlement tucked away in a remote valley of Zululand. Like Shakaland, Simunye attempts to introduce you to traditional Zulu culture, but the emphasis here extends to contemporary Zulu lifestyles, too. You'll reach the camp on horseback or oxwagon, and the one-hour ride into the valley is one of the highlights of a visit. During a stay, you'll watch Zulu dancing and visit a working kraal, complete with traditional beehive huts, and learn about Zulu culture and meet the kraal's residents. You can opt to sleep overnight in one of the beehive huts; otherwise, stay in the more luxurious main camp, built into the side of a hill overlooking the Mfule River. Rooms, built of stone and thatch, are a classy mix of Zulu and pioneer cultures. There's no electricity—light is provided by candles and hurricane lanterns. Unfortunately, the stone bathrooms were designed more for their aesthetic value than any practical purposes: Awkward steps lead to a hand-filled stone bath, and just getting in and out requires balance and agility. For this reason alone, Simunye would be difficult for the elderly or anyone with disabilities. Most people stay only one night, but try to book for two days over a weekend and arrange to attend a wedding or coming-out ceremony in a neighboring village. These ceremonies are purely local affairs, and you won't experience a more authentic celebration of rural Zulu culture. ⚐ *D256, off the R34, 6.4 km (4 mi) south of Melmoth (mailing address: Box 103, Eshowe 3815), ☎ 03546/912,* FAX *03546/824. 6 rooms with bath. Breakfast, lunch, and dinner included. AE, MC, V.*

Rorke's Drift

LODGING

$$$$ **Fugitives' Drift Lodge.** Set on a 4,000-acre game farm, this attractive lodge is a Zulu battlefields favorite. It lies just a couple of miles from the site of the famous engagement at Rorke's Drift and overlooks the drift where survivors of the British defeat at Isandlwana fled across the Buffalo River. Even more important, the owner is Dave Rattray, the best battlefield guide in the country (*see* Guided Tours *in* Zululand and the Battlefields Essentials, *below*). From its position high above the river, the lodge presides over a panorama of classic Zululand—thorn trees, savannah, and, in the distance, the distinctive peak of Isandlwana. Rooms, in individual cottages that open onto lovely lawns and gardens, feature fireplaces, antique dressers, and wicker furniture. The focal point of the lodge is the lounge and dining room, a stone-floored hall

decorated with old rifles, British regimental flags, Zulu spears, and antique military prints. All meals are included in the price, and guests eat together at a communal table. The lodge has no electricity. ⌂ *On Rorke's Drift Rd. (mailing address: P.O. Rorke's Drift 3016),* ☎ *03425/843,* FAX *0341/2–3319. 6 chalets with bath. Dining room, bar. Breakfast, lunch, and dinner included. DC, MC, V.*

Zululand and the Battlefields Essentials

Getting Around
Unless you're on a tour, it's almost impossible to see this part of the country without your own car. Your best bet is to rent a car in Durban, and perhaps combine a trip to the battlefields with a self-drive tour of KwaZulu-Natal's game reserves. Roads are in excellent condition, although some of the access roads to the battlefields are of gravel.

Guided Tours
The visitor information offices in Dundee and Ladysmith (*see below*) have lists of registered battlefield guides. At Talana Museum in Dundee you can also rent or buy cassette tapes describing the events at Rorke's Drift and Isandlwana.

Of all the battlefields guides in the region, **David Rattray** (☎ 0341/2–3319) is widely considered to be the finest. His accounts of the action at Rorke's Drift, Isandlwana, and Fugitives' Drift sometimes move listeners to tears. Many combine one of David's tours with a stay at his lodge, just a couple of miles from Rorke's Drift (*see* Dining and Lodging, *above*). David is slowly losing his voice, so part of the tour now consists of David's taped narrative. Tours cost R110 per person.

Other reputable guides to the Zulu battlefields are **Evan Jones** (☎ 0341/22618), **John Turner** (☎ and FAX 0358/35–0062), and **Foy Vermaak** (☎ 03425/925). If you're more interested in the battles of the Boer War, contact **Pam McFadden** (☎ 0341/22654) or **Maureen Richards** (☎ 0361/22231).

Visitor Information
Eshowe Information Centre. *Main St.,* ☎ *0354/4–1141, ext. 155.* ☉ *Weekdays 7:30–4.*

Ladysmith Information Bureau. *Town Hall, Murchison St.,* ☎ *0361/2–2992.* ☉ *Weekdays 8–12:30 and 1:30–4, Sat. 8–noon.*

Talana Museum. *R33, 3 km (2 mi) outside Dundee,* ☎ *0341/2–2654,* FAX *0341/2–2376.* ☉ *Weekdays 8–4, Sat. 10–4, Sun. noon–4.*

8 Victoria Falls

Straddling the border between Zimbabwe and Zambia, Victoria Falls deserve their reputation as one of the natural wonders of the world. Equally impressive is the setting, a living reminder of Livingstone's wild Africa: Elephants browse on islands upstream, lions pose as golf-course hazards, and monkeys frolic on hotel lawns. The small settlement of Victoria Falls has blossomed into a full-fledged adventure center, with the experiences of outrageous white-water rafting, the highest bungee-jumping in the world, canoeing on the Zambezi, and game drives nearly on your doorstep.

VICTORIA FALLS, WHICH PLUNGE 300 FEET into a gorge permanently hidden by a veil of roaring spray, span the entire 2-kilometer (1-mile) width of the Zambezi River. In the Kololo language, they're known as Mosi-Oa-Tunya—"the Smoke that Thunders." On a clear day, their white spray is visible from 50 miles away, a writhing mist rising above the woodland savannah like the smoke from a bush fire. To call the falls the Eighth Wonder of the World does little to suggest the blockbuster drama, the majesty, and the exquisite beauty of this quintessentially African sight.

Picture a Niagara Falls twice as tall and twice as wide and you still will not be prepared for the spectacle of Victoria Falls. Here, elephants come to bathe in the river, crocodiles patrol the deep pools, and hippos feed on upstream islands. At any moment you expect Humphrey Bogart and Katharine Hepburn to chug into view on the *African Queen*. Despite the growing influx of tourists, nothing can destroy the overwhelming sense that Africa—Livingstone's Africa—lies all around you.

Dr. David Livingstone was, of course, one of the 19th century's most intrepid explorers, one whose missionary zeal took him deep into the impenetrable country known as "darkest Africa." Local tribesmen, who had come to trust the missionary-explorer, told him about Mosi-Oa-Tunya during his 1855 expedition to establish a trading route to the east coast. On November 16 of that year, he reached present-day Livingstone Island, just above the falls, by dugout canoe. His uncharacteristically emotional diary entry for the day reads "scenes so lovely must have been gazed on by angels in their flight." He confesses that he even carved his name on a tree by the falls, the only time he ever indulged in that touristic vice. Livingstone was the first European to see the falls, and in the grand tradition of colonial exploration, dutifully named them after Queen Victoria.

Victoria Falls lie in the southeastern corner of Zimbabwe, a part of the country that is still mostly wild. They're like a violent hiccup in the 3,200-kilometer (2,000-mile) course of the Zambezi from its source in the northern Lunda highlands to the Indian Ocean in the east. The river serves as the border between Zambia and Zimbabwe, with each country competing for tourist dollars. Most visitors opt to stay on the Zimbabwean side, in the town of Victoria Falls, crossing over to visit the Zambian side for a highly recommended side trip.

In the late 1940s, when the town served as a refueling stop for Imperial Airways' seaplane route between South Africa and Britain, pilots referred to the small settlement as "jungle junction." Today, Victoria Falls is a burgeoning town totally given over to the pursuit of tourist business, yet there is still a whiff of the old jungle junction. Unlike the parks in South Africa, national parks here are unfenced, and elephants could parade down the town's main street if they felt so inclined. As it is, they usually don't cross the belt of woodland that encircles the town—venture into this bush fringe at your own risk—leaving the cultivated hotel lawns to troops of baboons and monkeys.

Victoria Falls has much more to offer than just a view of the falls. Some of southern Africa's greatest game parks lie within easy driving distance of the town. It is also a center for adventure sports, whether it's bungee-jumping, microlighting (motorized hang gliding), or white-water rafting down the Zambezi, in certain months one of the most thrilling one-day trips in the world. You could easily spend five days in the area and not exhaust all the sporting possibilities.

To see the falls at their most spectacular, go during the April–June high-water peak, when more than 2 million gallons of water roar down every second. The weather during these months tends to be sunny and pleasant. In September–October, when it is very hot, the water level is at its lowest and large sections of the falls dry up, although white-water rafting is then at its best. November–March is the rainy season, when the climate turns muggy and even hotter, and malaria-carrying mosquitos pose their greatest threat. Regardless of what time of year you visit, you must take antimalarial drugs.

EXPLORING

Numbers in the margin correspond to points of interest on the Victoria Falls map.

The town of Victoria Falls is tiny and easily explored on foot. Most of the shops and safari operators are clustered around the intersection of Park Way and Livingstone Way. Head down Livingstone Way and

❶ turn left before the Post Office to reach the **Falls Craft Village.** The "village" consists of lifesize model homes typical of five different Zimbabwean tribes, as well as a San (Bushman) dwelling. A pamphlet and on-site guides explain the living arrangements, various crafts, and the uses of different tools. If you've an hour to spare, it's probably worthwhile. At the back of the village you can watch artisans carving the stone and wood sculptures that are sold in the adjoining shop. For Z$10 you can have a *N'ganga* or witch doctor throw the bones to tell your fortune. *Stand 206, Sopers Crescent,* ☎ *13/4309.* ☛ *Z$25 adults, Z$12 children.* ☉ *Daily 8:30–1, 2–5.*

Several touristy curio and craft shops lie just beyond the Falls Craft Village. Here you can buy everything from an 8-foot-tall wooden giraffe to soapstone carvings and brightly colored Zimbabwean batiks. For a true African market experience, however, walk into either of the large white buildings on the left. Inside, seated on the floor and on carved wooden stools, dozens of local women sell crocheted tablecloths, woven baskets, carvings, and charms. The women bargain hard, but they are more than willing to trade their wares for the shoes on your feet, the T-shirts off your back, and other articles of clothing.

If you're concerned about how to get a near-lifesize giraffe or a 50-pound carving back home, there's an international shipping agent sandwiched between the curio shops.

❷ Return to Livingstone Way, cross the street, and head down Mallet Drive to the **Victoria Falls Hotel** (*see* Dining and Lodging, *below*). Much of the town's history revolves around this monument to colonial nostalgia. It was built in 1904 by the railway company, which had extended the line to the falls earlier that same year. The original hotel, built right next to the railway line, was a simple wood and corrugated-iron structure that accommodated only 20 guests. It wasn't nearly large enough, and many early guests had to remain on the train to sleep and only take their meals in the hotel. In 1920, the hotel instituted its famous trolley service, a narrow-gauge railway that carried guests between the hotel and the falls. No engines were used; gravity was enough to carry the guests down, but it took two men to push each trolley back up. The service was discontinued in 1957, but one of these early trolleys is on view in the central courtyard of the hotel.

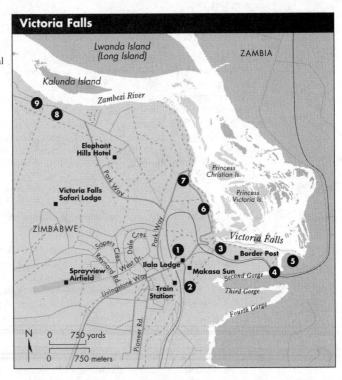

Victoria Falls

TIME OUT A respite on the terrace of the **Victoria Falls Hotel** (Mallet Dr., ☎
13/4751) remains one of the highlights of a visit to the Falls. Under the
shade of a giant Zimbabwe mahogany tree, guests can take in the view
over the Zambezi River gorge, the Victoria Falls bridge, and a rising cur-
tain of spray from the Falls. It's an ideal place to sip a drink or have
some tea before continuing to the Falls themselves.

A walking trail leads from the bottom of the hotel gardens to the falls.
It's a ten-minute walk through virgin bush. A second, 30-minute trail
descends steeply into the gorge to the river itself.

★ ❸ **Victoria Falls National Park** is *the* attraction in Zimbabwe, and for good
reason. You should plan to spend at least two hours soaking in its splendors. If you visit the Falls during the high-water peak in April–June,
you'll do well to carry a raincoat or umbrella (you can rent them at the
entrance), and to protect your camera in a waterproof bag, because
the spray from the falls creates a permanent downpour. Indeed, during high water the spray is so dense that it obscures much of the view
from the Zimbabwe side and you should make an effort to see the falls
from the Zambian side as well (*see below*). The constant drizzle has
created a unique rain forest that extends in a narrow band along the
edge of the falls. A trail running through this dripping green world is
overgrown with African ebony, Cape fig, Natal mahogany, wild date
palms, ferns, and flame lilies. Side trails lead to viewpoints overlooking the falls. The most spectacular is Danger Point, a slippery rock out-
cropping that overlooks the narrow gorge through which the Zambezi
River funnels out of the Falls. In low-water months (September–November), most of the water goes over the Falls through the Devil's Cataract,
a narrow passage separated from the main expanse of the Falls by
Cataract Island. A statue of David Livingstone stands on a terrace next

to one of the Devil's Cataract viewpoints. During the full moon, the park stays open late so you can see the lunar rainbow formed by the spray—one of the most beautiful sights in Africa. ☞ *Z$20 adults, Z$5 children.* ☉ *Daily 6–6, later during full moon.*

④ Exit from the National Park and turn left to reach the **Victoria Falls Bridge,** a graceful structure that spans the gorge formed by the Zambezi River, 360 feet below. Built in 1905, it's a living monument to Cecil Rhodes's dream of completing a Cape-to-Cairo rail line. It would have been far easier and less expensive to build the bridge upstream from the Falls, but Rhodes was captivated by the romance of a railway bridge passing over this natural wonder. Miraculously, only two people were killed during construction of the bridge. Today, steam-powered trains continue to chug across the span, their billowing black smoke in stark contrast to the ever-present veil of mist created by the pounding cataracts. To get onto the bridge, you first have to pass through Zimbabwean immigration and customs controls. Depending on crowds, the simple procedure can take from five minutes to a half hour. The border posts are open daily 6–6. From the bridge, you get a knockout view of the Boiling Pot—a churning cauldron of water—as well as a section of the falls. An added bonus is watching lunatics hurling themselves off the bridge in the sport's highest bungee-jump (*see* Participant Sports, *below*).

It's about a one-mile walk to the Zambian border post from Zimbabwe. Zambian taxis will carry you there if it's too hot or you don't feel up to the trek. Zambian immigration charges US$10, or its equivalent, for an entry permit. Check the cost of a permit in rand, as it's sometimes cheaper than paying in dollars.

★ **⑤** The Zambian equivalent of Zimbabwe's Victoria Falls National Park is **Mosi-Oa-Tunya National Park,** whose entrance lies just beyond the immigration control area. During high water (April–June), the Zambian side of the falls provides a far more spectacular vantage point than the Zimbabwean one, for the simple reason that the view is less obscured by spray. Regardless of the time of year, it would be a mistake not to arrange to see the falls from the Zambian side as well. The most impressive views are from the trail leading to the Knife's Edge and Eastern Cataract. The trail runs through dense rain forest, with side paths leading to several viewpoints overlooking the Eastern Cataract. This section of the falls dries up when the water is low, leaving an eerie stone face; in high water, when it's a thundering torrent, be prepared to get completely doused with spray. After a few hundred yards, the trail takes you across a narrow bridge over a gorge to a high, thin outcrop—the Knife's Edge—with unrivaled views of the Victoria Falls Bridge and Danger Point. If you don't fancy getting soaked, you can still get a panoramic view of the falls from a spot near the curio market. *Livingstone Rd., no* ☏. ☞ *Free.* ☉ *Daily 6–6.*

⑥ Back on the Zimbabwean side, an interesting drive, walk, or bike ride is **Zambezi Drive,** a 4-kilometer (2½-mile) loop road that turns off Livingstone Way just before the entrance to Victoria Falls National Park (as you come from town). The road passes through pristine bush, so it's not uncommon to encounter elephants and other animals as they head down to the river. Keep a sharp lookout if you're not in a vehicle; remember, you venture there at your own risk. Even more scenic than the tarred loop road is a walking path that runs for several miles along the river; to reach the beginning of the path, follow Zambezi Drive almost to the river's edge; the fence of Victoria Falls National Park will be on your right.

❼ Midway along Zambezi Drive stands the **Big Tree,** a giant baobab said to be 1,500 years old. The tree measures 80 feet in circumference and about the same in height. Early pioneers on their way north into Zambia used to camp under its massive branches. The baobab is known as the upside-down tree for obvious reasons, and several African legends offer explanations for the phenomenon. According to Khoisan (Bushman) lore, in the beginning of time the Creator handed each of the animals a tree to plant. The hyena was the last in line, and when his turn came all the beautiful trees had already been given to other animals. In fact, the only tree left was an almost leafless specimen as fat as it was tall. The hyena was so angry with God for giving him such an ugly tree that he deliberately planted it upside down.

From the Big Tree, Zambezi Drive heads back south and joins Park Way. Turn left and continue less than 1 kilometer (½ mile) to return to town. If you turn right on Park Way and continue for 6.4 kilometers ❽ (4 miles), you come to **Zambezi Nature Sanctuary,** a grandiose name for a run-of-the-mill tourist trap. It's a small zoo with several wild cats in cages and a crocodile farm displaying hundreds of Nile crocodiles. Feeding time for these prehistoric-looking beasts is 11 AM. *Park Way,* ☎ *13/4567.* ☛ *Z$25 adults, Z$10 children.* ☉ *Daily 8–4:30.*

❾ Another hundred meters farther up the road is the entrance to **Zambezi National Park,** a 138,000-acre strip of land that runs alongside the Zambezi River. Game-viewing here is generally good, particularly in the dry season (September–October), when various species converge on the river to drink and bathe. A few of the park roads are negotiable in a standard rental car, but a four-wheel-drive vehicle is recommended. Accommodations in the park range from self-catering lodges that sleep six (about Z$250) to rustic fishing and bush camps (about Z$160) where you must provide everything except the toilet and shower. Reservations must be made through the Central Booking Office (Box 8151, Causeway, Harare, Zimbabwe, ☎ 4/70–6077). *Park Way, no ☎.* ☛ *Z$20 adults, Z$10 children per day.*

SPORTS AND THE OUTDOORS

Bungee-Jumping

If the idea of white-water rafting doesn't start your pulse throbbing, take heart: You can always bungee-jump off the Victoria Falls bridge, a 366-foot freefall that is the highest in the world. As you plunge toward what seems certain death in the Zambezi River below, a video and photo company will catch the whole thrilling escapade on film to sell to you—or your survivors. The folks who run this masochistic operation are from **African Extreme,** an offshoot of Kiwi Extreme, the company that pioneered commercial jumping. A jump costs US$90, and all participants must sign a waiver form. Book through Shearwater Safaris or head out to the registration office at the Zambian end of the bridge. Jumps take place Tuesday–Sunday, 8–12:45. The bridge lies in the no-man's-land between Zimbabwe and Zambia. Jumpers should request a gate pass from Zimbabwe immigration; you may want to bring along your passport as well.

Canoeing

Canoeing on the Zambezi River above the falls is a relaxing, fun alternative (or supplement) to white-water rafting. The river here is wide and sluggish, winding through islands of vegetation, splitting into myriad channels, and then suddenly debouching into broad stretches of open water. Occasionally, small rapids—nothing to worry about—propel you through narrows. Along the way, you are likely to spot crocodiles, hippos, and elephants. The one-hour game drive through Zambezi National Park to reach the launching point for the canoes is an added bonus. Most trips provide a bush breakfast before you start, a brief coffee or tea break, and a slap-up lunch on an island in the river. You can select either a half- or full-day trip, or even longer expeditions lasting two to three days, with nights at primitive tented camps along the river. Previous experience and a high degree of physical fitness are not required. Expect to pay about US$60 for a half day, and US$80 for a full day. The main operators are **Kandahar Safaris** (Soper's Arcade, ☎ 13/4502), **Safari Par Excellence** (Shop 4, Pumula Centre, ☎ 13/4424, FAX 13/4510), and **Zambezi Canoe Company** (Shop 14, Soper's Arcade, ☎ 13/2058).

Golf

Elephant Hills Golf Course (Park Way, ☎ 13/4793, ext. 1742 for caddy master, ext. 1893 for pro shop), 6.4 kilometers (4 miles) out of town, is a full 18-hole course laid out in a bulge formed by the Zambezi River. The course is fairly flat, with manicured fairways wending through woodland savannah. Although the course is fenced, you will probably have to share the fairways with warthogs, baboons, waterbuck, and impala. It might pay to hit the ball straight—last year, a pride of lions was sighted lounging in the rough. Eighteen holes cost Z$125, nine holes are Z$75. Rental clubs are available.

Horseback Riding

Safari Par Excellence (Shop 4, Pumula Centre, ☎ 13/4424, FAX 13/4510) conducts horseback game-viewing safaris for experienced riders that range anywhere from 2½ hours to one, two, or three days. Novice riders can go out for 1½ hours, but they will not be allowed close to animals such as elephants and lions. Expect to pay about US$40 for a short ride and US$100 for a full day.

White-Water Rafting

The Zambezi offers the best one-day white-water rafting in the world, and a trip down the river is one of the highlights of a stay in Africa. Rafting takes place in the deep gorges extending more than 24 kilometers (15 miles) from the base of the falls. In peak season, the majority of the 23-odd rapids along the river are classified as Grade 4 or 5, Grade 5 being the most difficult rapids commercially runnable. Despite this, you don't need prior rafting experience and shouldn't let inexperience deter you. Prime season is mid-August to mid-December, with the best rafting usually in September–October, when the water is at its lowest and the rapids at their most spectacular. In January–February and June–July, high water resulting from the rainy season softens many of the rapids but creates dangerous currents and whirlpools; during these months some operators offer only half-day trips. In April and May, the water is usually too high to permit rafting at all.

You can choose between oar boats and paddle boats. In an oar boat, your job is simply to hang on and use your body weight to help keep the boat upright; a professional oarsman does the rest. On a paddle boat, you are given a paddle and expected to use it, since the boat is likely to flip in rapids if it loses steering momentum. As it's much easier to fall out of a paddle boat, first-timers and older rafters should probably opt for an oar boat. All rafters wear helmets and life jackets, and each trip is preceded by a safety talk and practice sessions in calm water. The sport is not without danger and the river has claimed a few lives and caused a number of injuries; rafters are therefore required to sign an indemnity form. Probably the most difficult part of the whole trip, though, is the horrendously steep trek into and out of the gorge—it's an almost sheer 750-foot climb. For this phase, it's best to be physically fit; if you're going to have a heart attack, it'll be here.

The major operator on the river is **Shearwater Adventures** (Soper's Arcade, Park Way, ☎ 13/4471, FAX 13/4341), an outfit capable of putting 26 boats in the water on a single day. **Sobek** (309 Park Way, Victoria Falls, ☎ 13/2069), an American company, was the first to start commercial rafting down the Zambezi, back in 1981. It has an excellent safety record and a reputation for having the best guides on the river. Sobek operates from the Zambian side of the river, which allows them to launch their boats at the Boiling Pot, right next to the falls. Because of this, they run the river from Rapid No. 1, whereas the Zimbabwe operators can only put their boats in the water above Rapid No. 4. **Safari Par Excellence** (Shop 4, Pumula Centre, ☎ 13/4424, FAX 13/4510) is the only company that offers a choice of rafting from Zambia or Zimbabwe. The fourth major operator, **Frontiers White Water Rafting** (Shop 1, Park Way, ☎ 113/5800, FAX 011/4417), is based on the Zimbabwe side of the river. Costs are the same regardless of which company you use: Half-day rafting costs about US$75, a full-day run about US$90. Lunch and drinks are included. Most of these companies also offer extended three-, five-, and seven-day rafting trips.

DINING AND LODGING

Foreigners have to settle their hotel bills in foreign currency, either with cash, credit cards, or traveler's checks. Hotel rooms in Victoria Falls are expensive, and the high prices are often unjustified. It's not necessary to stay close to the falls and the town: You'll probably only visit the falls once, and the town itself has little to offer. Furthermore, the outlying hotels tend to offer better value and facilities, and they all operate free shuttles to and from town.

Victoria Falls is a culinary wasteland. In town you'll find a couple of nondescript pizza joints, a steak house, and a Wimpy's, but otherwise you're reliant on hotel restaurant fare. Several of the hotels offer a nightly barbecue accompanied by marimba music. If you're looking for something a little different, try the Boma Restaurant at the Victoria Falls Safari Lodge (*see below*), where guests sit in a traditional African enclosure around a fire and sample various game meats; traditional dancers perform twice nightly. It costs about Z$90 per person.

CATEGORY	COST*
$$$$	over $250
$$$	$200–$250
$$	$150–$200
$	under $150

All prices are in U.S. dollars and refer to a standard double room, including tax.

$$$$ **Victoria Falls Hotel.** For many years, this hotel *was* Victoria Falls. Built in 1904, only months after the railway reached the falls, the hotel stood for decades as a colonial outpost in the African wilds, attracting some of the continent's most colorful characters as well as the occasional visiting royal. Today, the hotel offers visitors—many of them elderly—a

reprise of the days when gin-and-tonic was taken as the cure for malaria and Britain was considered home. The hotel still holds a nightly dinner-dance (jacket and tie suggested). Wide corridors hung with brass chandeliers are decorated with black-and-white photos of bygone days. However, the image of colonial Africa cannot withstand the constant influx of tour groups. You now have to be a real old-timer or highly imaginative to conjure up the colonial past. The hotel's famed service and aura of luxury are history, too. The suites are still elegant, but the regular rooms are faded and drab, burdened with brown floral bedspreads and simple beige curtains. What has not changed are the hotel's superb setting and gardens. The garden terrace, beneath a towering Zimbabwe mahogany, overlooks the Zambezi bridge and the whirling spray from the falls. Light meals and drinks are served here during the day, and at night there's a barbecue. A pleasant walking trail leads down through the bush to the falls, ten minutes away. ⌕ *Mallet Dr. (mailing address: Box 10), Victoria Falls, Zimbabwe,* ☎ *13/4751,* FAX *13/4586. 141 rooms with bath. 2 restaurants, 2 bars, room service, pool, hair salon, tennis, playground. Breakfast included. AE, DC, MC, V.*

$$$ **Victoria Falls Safari Lodge.** This is by far the best hotel in Victoria Falls
★ and it costs *less* than the Victoria Falls Hotel. A little more than 6 kilometers (4 miles) outside town, the hotel sits on a hilltop overlooking the Zambezi River and miles of bush in Zambezi National Park. A water hole below the lodge attracts herds of game, including buffalo and elephant. The lodge itself is magnificent, drawing its inspiration from the colorful Ndebele culture. Soaring thatch roofs, huge wooden beams, and reed ceilings envelop the visitor in a luxurious African atmosphere. The sides of the lodge are completely open to admit cooling breezes (there's no air-conditioning). In the rooms you can fold back the glass and wood screens leading to your private veranda if you want to sleep *al fresco*—just remember to put your mosquito net down. Geometric Ndebele designs add bursts of color to painted chairs, beams, cushions, and woven rugs. All rooms have scenic views, but request one overlooking the water hole. A courtesy bus shuttles guests to and from Victoria Falls. ⌕ *Off Park Way, 6 km (4 mi) from Victoria Falls (mailing address: Box 29, Victoria Falls, Zimbabwe),* ☎ *13/3202,* FAX *13/3205. 72 rooms with bath. 2 restaurants, 2 bars, room service, 2 pools, travel services. Breakfast included. AE, MC, V.*

$$ **Elephant Hills Hotel.** Also 6.4 kilometers (4 miles) from town, this large hotel sits high on a hill above the Zambezi. It's a resort and conference hotel, but don't let that drive you away. The service, rooms, and facilities are far superior to those of the more expensive Victoria Falls Hotel. The extensive use of thatch and avant-garde African sculpture, masks, and batiks helps to minimize the hotel's size and business emphasis. Rooms, too, have an understated African flair: Rough gray walls are the neutral background for wicker furniture, modern African art, and Ndebele rugs. All rooms feature air-conditioning, overhead fans, and cable TV. Request a front-facing room—for a few dollars more you get memorable views of the Zambezi River, miles of virgin bush, and clouds of spray from the distant falls. From the open-air Mapopoma bar and Kasibi restaurant, guests have a similar knockout view. A shuttle bus runs hourly to town. ⌕ *Park Way, 6 km (4 mi) from Victoria Falls (mailing address: Box 300, Victoria Falls, Zimbabwe),* ☎ *13/4793,* FAX *13/4655. 276 rooms with bath. 3 restaurants, 3 bars, room service, pool, hair salon, golf, tennis, squash, exercise room, casino, business services. Breakfast included. AE, DC, MC, V.*

$$ **Ilala Lodge.** Often overlooked in the stampede to stay in Victoria
★ Falls's mediocre large hotels, this small hotel is a gem. It lies right near the center of town, opposite the Makasa Sun and just ten minutes from

the falls on foot. Thatched roofs give the lodge a pleasant, African feel. The dining room, with its curving thatched shelter, raw beams, and outdoor seating, is particularly attractive. Rooms feature African paintings, woven wall hangings, delicately caned chairs, and tables and dressers made from old railway sleepers. French doors open onto a narrow strip of lawn backed by thick bush. Unlike most of the other hotels, Ilala Lodge has no fence around it, so at night it's not uncommon to find elephants browsing outside your window or buck grazing on the lawn. None of the rooms has air-conditioning, but they do feature overhead fans, cable TV, and separate bath and shower. ☎ *411 Livingstone Way (mailing address: Box 18), Victoria Falls, Zimbabwe, ☎ 13/4737, ℻ 13/4417. 16 rooms with bath. Restaurant, 3 bars, room service, pool, nightclub. Breakfast included. DC, MC, V.*

NIGHTLIFE

Casinos
The **Makasa Sun Casino** (Livingstone Way, ☎ 13/4275) attracts a hard-eyed crowd of locals as well as the blue-rinse brigade, all furiously feeding the slot machines throughout the day and into the night. You can also play blackjack and roulette. The **Elephant Hills Casino** (Park Way, ☎ 13/4793) is more upmarket and operates only in the evenings, from 8 until late. Games include blackjack, roulette, Zambezi poker, and punto banco, as well as a wide variety of Vegas-style slot machines. No one under 18 is admitted.

Pubs and Nightclubs
Explorers (Soper's Arcade, Park Way, ☎ 13/4298) is the big watering hole in town for young locals and disheveled overland tourists traveling on the big commercial trucks. It's dark, crowded, and rowdy. Z$5 cover charge. **Downtime**, in the Ilala Lodge (Livingstone Way, ☎ 13/4737), is the town's only nightclub. Ilala Lodge also operates a large, open-air bar where the most of the rafting companies replay the day's videos of the white-water action and display photos shot along the river.

Traditional Dancing
The Victoria Falls Hotel stages a nightly **Africa Spectacular,** a one-hour display of costumed Makishi, Shangaan, and other tribal performers dancing to the beat of a half dozen drummers. Spectators sit around a roaring fire in a traditional *boma,* or reed enclosure. The show is worth seeing just for the fantastic costumes and masks of the Makishi dancers and stilt-walkers. You can purchase masks, drums, dolls, and other crafts from two craft shops adjoining the boma. *Victoria Falls Hotel, Mallet Dr., ☎ 13/4751. ☛ Z$40. Shows daily at 7.*

Falls Craft Village is a less atmospheric spot to see traditional dancing *Stand 206, Soper's Crescent, ☎ 13/4309. ☛ Z$60. Shows daily at 6:30.*

VICTORIA FALLS ESSENTIALS

Zimbabwe Formalities

Money Matters
You must settle your Zimbabwean hotel bills in foreign currency, either with cash, credit cards, or traveler's checks, and if you are leaving by air pay an airport departure tax of US$20 (*see* Coming and Going, *below*).

Zimbabwe's unit of currency is the Zimbabwe dollar (Z$), broken into 100 cents. At press time, US$1 bought Z$8.3. It's not absolutely necessary to change money into Zimbabwe dollars, since everyone from taxi drivers to curio vendors accepts foreign currency (the same applies on the Zambian side of the falls). And the prices for most Victoria Falls activities are usually quoted in U.S. dollars. If you want Zimbabwe dollars for tips and small purchases, you can get decent rates at **Zimbank, Barclays,** and **Standard Chartered,** all of which have branches next to one another on Livingstone Way. Bank hours are Monday–Tuesday and Thursday–Friday 8–3, Wednesday 8–1, and Saturday 8–11:30. A Zimbank airport branch keeps sporadic hours.

Passports and Visas

Citizens of the United States, Australia, New Zealand, and E.U. countries do not require visas to enter Zimbabwe. South Africans still require a visa, but these are now free. Zambian visas are required of citizens of all non-Commonwealth countries; the Zambian authorities issue visas at the border for US$10 or the equivalent.

Telephones

The Zimbabwe phone system is not nearly as good as South Africa's, but if you don't get through, keep trying. The country code for Zimbabwe is 263, and the area code for Victoria Falls is 13.

Arriving and Departing

By Plane

Victoria Falls Airport (☎ 13/4250) lies 22 kilometers (14 miles) south of town. **South African Airways** offers direct flights between Johannesburg and Victoria Falls on Tuesday, Saturday, and Sunday. **Air Zimbabwe** (☎ 13/4316 in Victoria Falls) flies direct between Johannesburg and Victoria Falls on Monday and Thursday. Otherwise, you can fly through Harare and catch a connecting flight on to Victoria Falls. If you have to spend the night in Harare, the best hotel in town is **Meikles** (corner of Jason Moyo and Third Sts., Harare, ☎ 4/795655), in downtown Harare. Cheaper options are the various three- and four-star **Cresta** hotels (☎ 011/787–9500 in South Africa for reservations).

BETWEEN THE AIRPORT AND TOWN

Most hotels send free shuttle buses to meet incoming Air Zimbabwe and South African Airways flights and provide free airport transfers for departing guests. An **Air Zimbabwe** bus also meets incoming South African Airways and Air Zimbabwe flights to take passengers to the airport in good time for departures. The bus stops at the Rainbow Hotel, the Makasa Sun, Victoria Falls Hotel, and the Sprayview Hotel. Tickets cost Z$30. Taxis between town and the airport cost about Z$90.

DEPARTURE TAX

All foreigners leaving by air must pay a US$20 departure tax, or the equivalent. If you don't have exact change, Zimbank on Livingstone Way (*see* Money Matters, *above*) sells departure stamps, and you may pay in Zimbabwe dollars providing you can produce a Zimbabwean receipt for your foreign-exchange transaction. Zimbank also operates an agency at the airport, but its hours change frequently.

By Train

South Africa's most luxurious trains, the *Blue Train* and **Rovos Rail** (*see* the Gold Guide), periodically run north from Pretoria to Zimbabwe, calling at Bulawayo and Victoria Falls on the two-night journey. Rovos Rail usually makes the trip twice a month, the *Blue Train* only once.

Getting Around

By Bicycle

Biking is a great way to get around town or over to Zambia. With a mountain bike you can also explore some of the roads and trails that wind through the bush around Victoria Falls. Remember, though, that there is no fence between you and the wildlife, so proceed at your own risk. **Bush Trackers** (Stand 258A, Adam Standers Dr., ☎ 2024), next to the Falls Traditional Village, rents out mountain bikes for about Z$15 an hour. You'll need to leave your passport details and a Z$100 deposit.

By Bus

Most of the outlying hotels operate shuttle buses that run hourly to town. Zimbabwe Sun runs an hourly shuttle bus connecting the Victoria Falls Hotel, the Makasa Sun, and Elephant Hills, 6.4 kilometers (4 miles) out of town; the bus also stops at the falls.

By Car

Most of the attractions in town are within walking distance or just a short taxi ride away. As a result, it's probably not worth renting a car. You can take rental cars on some roads in the nearby national parks, but to explore these parks properly you really need a four-wheel-drive vehicle. An even better option is to go game-viewing in an open Land Rover with a local safari operator (*see below*). **Avis** (corner of Livingstone Way and Mallet Dr., ☎ 13/4532) no longer has a desk at the airport, but if you have a confirmed reservation they will deliver the vehicle to the airport. **Hertz** (Bata Bldg., Park Way, ☎ 13/4267, FAX 13/4225) has desks in town and at the airport (☎ 13/432522). Each company offers different rate packages, but for a midsize car like a Nissan Sunny or Opel Kadett, expect to pay about Z$300 per day plus Z$3 per kilometer; if you rent for more than five days, it will cost about Z$600 a day with 250 free kilometers each day.

By Taxi

Taxis are a cheap and convenient way to get around town. Hotels can summon them quickly or you can find them at the falls. Taxis are metered, but expect to pay about Z$6 from town to the falls, and Z$15 from town to Elephant Hills. If you're heading to Zambia, Zambian taxis will pick you up at the Zimbabwean border post, drive you the 1.6 kilometers (1 mile) to the Zambian control post, and from there continue into Livingstone.

Guided Tours

Victoria Falls is practically sinking under the weight of all the safari operators that have sprung up in the last few years. Most offer a few special tours of their own design, but survive by selling the same trips as everyone else. You can book your rafting, bungee-jumping, scenic flights, and game drives at almost all of the safari companies listed below. The major operators in Victoria Falls are **Dabula Safaris** (309 Park Way, ☎ 13/4453), **Safari Par Excellence** (Shop 4, Pumula Centre, Park Way, ☎ 13/4424, FAX 13/4510), **Shearwater Adventures** (Soper's Arcade, ☎ 13/4471, FAX 13/4341), **Touch the Wild** (Victoria Falls Hotel, Mallet Dr., ☎ 13/4694), **United Touring Company** (**UTC**; Zimbank Bldg., Livingstone Way, ☎ 13/4267), and **Zambezi Wilderness Safaris** (Ilala Lodge, Livingstone Way, ☎ 13/4637, FAX 13/4417).

Boat Trips

A host of operators offer boat cruises on the Zambezi River above the falls, usually in large, twin-deck boats or in smaller pontoon boats. During these trips, you're likely to see hippos, crocodiles, and often elephants. The most popular trip is a two-hour sundowner cruise (Z$100), essentially a booze cruise that gives guests a great view of the sunset from the water. Breakfast, lunch, and bird-watching cruises are also available. Most boat trips depart from the jetties near the A'Zambezi Hotel, about 8 kilometers (5 miles) north of town. Major operators include **Dabula Safaris, Mosi Oa Tunya Cruises** (299 Rumsey Rd., ☎ 13/4780, ℻ 13/4780), **Shearwater Adventures** (Soper's Arcade, ☎ 13/4471, ℻ 13/4341), **UTC,** and **Zambezi Wilderness Safaris.** Perhaps the least expensive of them all is **Kalambeza Safaris** (Park Way, ☎ 13/4480, ℻ 13/4644). If you're looking for a less touristy version of a booze cruise, consider the Wine Route offered by **Zambezi Canoe Company** (*see* Canoeing, *above*), a three-hour sunset canoe trip featuring sundowners.

Game Drives

Some of Africa's best game parks lie within a couple of hours' drive of Victoria Falls, including Zambezi National Park, Hwange, and Chobe in Botswana. Game drives are usually conducted in open four-wheel-drive vehicles and led by a licensed guide.

ZAMBEZI NATIONAL PARK

Dabula Safaris, UTC, and **Zambezi Wilderness Safaris** all offer half-day (US$25 per person) and full-day (US$50) game drives through Zambezi National Park. The full-day excursion includes lunch, sometimes on a boat on the Zambezi River. **Victoria Falls Safari Lodge** (*see* Dining and Lodging, *above*) offers five-hour night drives in open vehicles with spotlights. Night drives offer the chance to see nocturnal animals like bushbabies, spring hares, and, if you're lucky, lions and leopards on the prowl. The trip costs about Z$300 and includes drinks and a light dinner.

HWANGE NATIONAL PARK

UTC and **Touch the Wild** conduct full-day game drives to Hwange National Park, about 80 kilometers (50 miles) from Victoria Falls. You leave Victoria Falls at 5:30 AM and return at 7 PM. The full-day trip, including lunch and snacks, costs about US$80. UTC also offers two-night excursions to the park.

CHOBE NATIONAL PARK

UTC currently operates two-night trips to Botswana's Chobe National Park, an area famed for its elephant population. You stay at the lodges of your choice, and view game from both an open vehicle and a river boat. At press time, **Safari Par Excellence** was planning one-day game drives to Chobe.

Game Walks

Walking is a great way to see the bush. Although you see fewer animals while walking than from a vehicle, you get a better feel for the region's ecology, learn about the medicinal uses of trees and plants, and also how to recognize animal spoor. **Dabula Safaris** and **Backpackers Africa** (book through Safari Par Excellence or ☎ 13/4510) both offer half- and full-day walking safaris in Zambezi National Park. Walks are led by an armed guide. Half-day walks include drinks and cost about US$40; full-day trips (about US$100) also include lunch.

Microlight Flights

Batoka Sky (book through Shearwater Adventures) takes passengers over the falls in two-person microlight aircraft, essentially motorized hang gliders. You sit in an open-air cockpit behind the pilot, protected only by a crash helmet. The flight over the falls (about US$80) lasts 15 minutes, but you can also take a 30-minute flight that heads upriver from the falls in search of game. Make no mistake, this is a more dangerous way to see the falls than in a helicopter or fixed-wing plane—it's also probably the most exciting. Batoka Sky operates out of Zambia. The company meets interested clients on the Victoria Falls bridge at 7 AM and 8:30 AM and in the afternoon at 3 and 4:15; you need to clear Zimbabwe immigration first. Budget about three hours from pick-up to drop-off.

Orientation Tours

Touch the Wild and **UTC** conduct 90-minute guided tours of the falls (US$10), although there's no earthly reason why you can't visit the falls on your own. Another UTC tour (US$12) combines a visit to the falls with a trip to the Traditional Craft Village and the Big Tree. You can easily do this on your own, too.

Touch the Wild offers a Meet the People tour, on which tourists travel to communal tribal lands near Victoria Falls to talk to Ndebele villagers and visit a school. The tour lasts two hours and costs about US$25.

Dabula Safaris offers a four-hour Zambian tour (US$60) that gives you a view of the falls from the Zambian side and stops at the Livingstone Museum and various curio shops. **UTC** also offers half- and full-day Zambian tours.

Scenic Flights

Flying over the falls in a plane or helicopter is an exhilarating experience. Helicopter flights tend to be briefer and more expensive, but they offer better views—and photo opportunities—than planes do. **Southern Cross Aviation** (Elephant Hills Hotel, ☎ 13/4618, ℻ 13/4609) has 25-minute plane flights over the falls and some Zambezi River gorges for about US$40; a 40-minute flight (US$60) also includes game-spotting over Zambezi National Park. Similar flights in a helicopter last 12 (US$60) or 30 minutes (US$100). **United Air** (☎ 113/4530 or 113/4220) has 12-minute helicopter (US$60) and 15-minute plane (US$40) flights over the falls, and 30-minute flights that combine a trip over the falls with game-spotting nearby.

If you're looking for something a little different, consider **Seaplane Safaris Africa** (book through Safari Par Excellence), which takes up to five passengers on 20-minute flights over the falls in a seaplane. The plane takes off from the Zambezi River, 3 kilometers (2 miles) upstream from the falls. Flights cost about US$50 per person.

Important Addresses and Numbers

At press time, **Victoria Falls Publicity Association** staff wasn't much help—instead, seek advice from the many safari companies in town. *412 Park Way,* ☎ *4202.* ۞ *Weekdays 8–12:30 and 2–4, Sat. 8–noon.*

9 Big Game Adventures

Nowhere on the continent do wild animals enjoy better protection than in South Africa, and nowhere do you have a better chance of seeing Africa's big game—elephant, black and white rhino, lion, buffalo, cheetah, and leopard. The experience of tracking game in a Land Rover or of taking a wilderness trail with an armed ranger will fill you with awe for the elemental magic of the African bush.

MENTION AFRICA AND MOST OF US conjure up visions of wildlife—lions roaring in the gathering dusk, antelope skittering across the savannah, a leopard silhouetted by the setting sun. The images never fail to fascinate and draw us in, and once you experience them in the flesh you're hooked. The look, the feel—the dusty smell—of the African bush seep into your soul, and long after you've gone you find yourself missing it with an almost physical longing. The wildlife experience in South Africa rivals the very best on the continent, and a trip to the bush should be a major part of your vacation.

Do everyone a favor, though, and pass up the impulse to rush out and buy khakis and a pith helmet. The classic safari is dead. Hemingway and the great white hunters took it to their graves, along with thousands upon thousands of equally dead animals. The closest you'll come to a real safari today is if you spend an ungodly sum of money to trek into the wastes of Selous National Park in Tanzania to nail some unfortunate lion.

Indeed, too many wildlife documentaries have conditioned foreign visitors into thinking that Africa is overrun with animals, and they half expect to be greeted by a lion in the airport's arrival hall. The truth is far less romantic—and much safer—especially in South Africa, where fences or rivers enclose all major reserves. The rest of the country is farmland, towns, and suburbs.

South Africa has 12 national parks and a host of provincial reserves, but only a few contain all the indigenous species that once roamed the veld in vast herds. The crown jewel of South Africa's reserves is Kruger National Park, the second-largest game reserve in Africa. It's a magnificent tract of pristine wilderness that is home to an astonishing number of animals. Like all of South Africa's parks, it's completely open to the public, and you can tour and view game from the comfort of your own car. Good roads, plentiful and cheap accommodations, and excellent facilities are what differentiate South African parks from their East African counterparts.

The other, much more expensive option is to stay in a lodge on a private game reserve. If you can afford it, don't miss out, because these exclusive lodges offer a wildlife experience without parallel. You could spend a month bumping fenders with tourist minibuses in East Africa and never get as close to game as in these lodges. Bouncing over dirt tracks in an open Land Rover, you *know* you're in Africa. These luxury lodges give you a taste of the bush and the experience of living out in the wilds. Sure, you get comfortable beds, flush toilets, running water, hot showers—even air-conditioning—but the bush lies right outside your door, and nothing stops an elephant from joining you for dinner.

Talk to travel agents about private lodges and sooner or later they will start babbling about the Big Five. This was originally a hunting term referring to those animals that posed the greatest risk to hunters on foot—elephant, black rhino, leopard, lion, and buffalo—yet it has now become the single most important criteria used in evaluating a lodge or reserve. While the Big Five label may have helped engender tourist interest in African wildlife, it can also demean the entire bush experience, turning it into a treasure hunt. You will be amazed how many visitors ignore a gorgeous animal that doesn't "rank" in the Big Five, or lose interest in a species once they've checked it off their list. After you've spent a few days in the bush, you will also recognize the idiocy of racing around in search of five animals when there are another 150 equally fascinating species all around you. It's up to you to tell your ranger exactly what kind of game experience you want.

It's no coincidence that old game-watching hands find their thrills in the smaller, rarer animals—and in birds. South Africans are maniacal bird-watchers for very good reason: It's one of the best birding regions in the world. More than 500 species of birds have been recorded in Kruger alone, and their beauty and diversity are extraordinary. Don't overlook them just because they're small and harmless—your trip will be poorer for it.

Whether you're searching for elephant or the arrow-marked babbler, a sturdy pair of binoculars is essential, as is a camera. Use a happy-snappy instamatic only if you want pictures of you and your companions out in the bush; forget about it if you want good wildlife shots. Ideally, you should use a 35-millimeter camera with at least a 300-millimeter lens and a sand bag to act as a rest, since you can't set up a regular tripod on a vehicle. The best all-purpose film is ASA100, but ASA400 is great for action photography, like a cheetah hunt. Light readings in the African glare can be tricky, so be sure to bracket your shots. No matter what camera or film you use, you're bound to take an embarrassing number of bum shots—animals caught fleeing—so it pays to shoot bucketloads of film.

And just because you're going to Africa, don't think you can pack light cottons and nothing else. If you're heading to a private lodge, be sure to take a warm jacket, even in mid-summer (December–March), since it can get mighty cold on an exposed Land Rover at 8 PM. All lodges provide blankets on their vehicles, but that's often not enough. In winter, consider bringing along an industrial heater, too, because the early morning air could freeze the balls off a brass monkey.

No two people can agree on the "best" time to visit the bush. Summer (December—March) is hellishly hot, with afternoon rain a good possibility, but the bush is green, the animals sleek and glossy, and the birdlife prolific. Unfortunately, it's the worst time of year to spot game. All of the foliage makes finding game harder, and animals tend to disperse over a wide area since they are no longer reliant on water holes and rivers. Winter, on the other hand, is a superb time for game-viewing, since trees are bare and animals congregate around the few remaining water sources. Because the weather's cooler, you may also see lions and leopards hunting by day. Most lodges drop their rates dramatically during winter months, often lopping as much as 30%–40% off their peak season prices. The drawback to a winter visit is the cold, and the fact that the bush looks dead and the animals thin and out of condition.

A happy compromise may be the shoulder seasons. In October and November the weather is pleasant, the trees have blossoms, and migrant birds are arriving—even better, the antelope herds begin to drop their young. In April, the temperature is also fine, many of the migrant birds are still around, and the annual rutting season has begun, when males compete for the right to mate with females.

Whatever the time of year, take precautions against malaria. The disease is no joking matter, and it claims its share of victims in South Africa every year. Summer is the height of malaria season, when the annual rains provide plentiful breeding grounds for mosquitos. With a couple of notable exceptions, every reserve and lodge in this chapter lies in a malarial zone, and it's imperative that you take prophylactics. At press time, Lariam (Mefloquine) was the preferred drug, but it has possible side effects. See your doctor at least a month before you depart.

NATIONAL PARKS AND GAME RESERVES

If you picture yourself bouncing across the golden plains of Africa in an old Land Rover in pursuit of big game, South Africa's national parks will disappoint you. They bear less resemblance to the Serengeti than to American national parks: They are superbly managed, frequently overcrowded, and a little too civilized. You could tour Kruger National Park in a Porsche if you so desired. Many of the park roads are paved, and rangers even set up speed traps to nail overzealous game-watchers (take your car off-road and the dung will really hit the fan). Signposts throughout the park direct visitors to everything from scenic outlooks to picnic sites and rest areas selling soft drinks and snacks.

It's no wonder, then, that foreign visitors sometimes act like they're in a giant petting zoo. In recent years, an Asian tourist was eaten when he left his car to hug some cuddly lions, and a European's rental car was turned into Swiss cheese when he drove too close to an elephant and her calf. South Africa's game reserves may impose a veneer of domesticity on the wilderness, but underneath it's the same raw, violent Africa you see on National Geographic specials.

The national parks look the way they do for good reason: They are the country's natural heritage, set up for the use and enjoyment of its citizens, which until recently meant whites only. For white South African families, a trip to a game reserve is an annual rite, as certain as death and taxes. We're talking load up the station wagon, smack the kids into the back, and drive, baby, drive. On December weekends, Kruger's rest camps look like they're on fire because of all the barbecue smoke. One reason for this popularity is their affordability: A couple probably won't pay more than R250 per night to stay in a rest camp.

Until recently, foreign tourists comprised an insignificant minority of visitors to the national parks, and if they didn't like what they found they could just lump it. That attitude is changing, but South Africa's game parks are still not geared to foreign tourists and their needs. Accommodation in the park rest camps is cheap, comfortable, and numbingly institutional. In Kruger, the National Parks Board symbol—the head of a kudu bull—is plastered over everything from your towel to the sheets to the bathroom walls. All the camps are fenced against the animals, and some have better facilities than small towns: gas stations, mechanics, grocery stores, laundromats, cafeterias, restaurants—even a car wash. And the restaurants' food tends to be mediocre. Not surprisingly, many foreign tourists shy away from the rest camps in favor of luxury hotels on the park fringes.

It would be the biggest mistake of your trip, though, to write off the public parks. Few people can afford to stay in the exclusive private lodges more than a few days, and the game reserves offer visitors a chance to explore some of Africa's richest and most beautiful country at a fraction of the cost, especially if you drive yourself. Armed with a good field guide to wildlife, you can learn an enormous amount about African game from the driver's seat of a rental car.

It does take time to develop your ability to find motionless game in thick bush. On the first day, you're less likely to spot an animal than to run it over. All those fancy stripes and tawny colors really do work.

Slowly, though, you learn to recognize the small clues that give away an animal in the bush: the flick of a tail, the toss of a horn, even fresh dung. To see any of this, you have to drive *slowly*, 10–15 miles per hour. Fight the urge to pin back your ears and tear around a park at 30 mph hoping to find something big. The only way to spot game at that speed is if it's standing in the road or if you come upon a scrum of cars already at a sighting. But remember that being the 10th car at a game-sighting is less exciting than finding the animal yourself. Not only do the other cars detract from the experience, but you feel like a scavenger—a sort of voyeuristic vulture.

The best time to find game is in the early morning and early evening, when the animals are most active. During the heat of the day most of the game retreats into thick bush to find shade. So should you. Rest camp gates open around 5 AM in summer, and you should hit the road soon after that.

An indispensable aid is a good park map, showing not only the roads but also the location of water holes, different ecozones, and the types of animals you can expect to find in each. It's no good driving around open grassland searching for black rhino when the lumbering browsers are miles away in a woodland region. You can buy these maps when you enter a park or at rest camp shops, and it would be a foolish economy to pass them up. Kruger's map is particularly outstanding.

When planning your day's game drive, plot your route around as many water holes and rivers as possible. Except during the height of the summer rains, most game must come to permanent water sources to drink. In winter, when the land is at its most parched, a tour of water holes is bound to reap rewards. Even better, take a picnic lunch along and park at the same water hole for several hours. Not only will you see plenty of animals, but you'll find yourself slipping into the drama of the bush. Has that kudu seen the huge crocodile? What's making the impala nervous? What's sitting on my car?

The parks covered below are the only ones in the country that have the Big Five.

Kruger National Park

Larger than Israel or Wales, Kruger National Park encompasses some of the most stunning and diverse terrain on the continent, from crocodile-infested rivers to rocky mountains and thick thornscrub. And roaming this classic slice of Africa are animals in numbers large enough to make a conservationist squeal: 2,000 lions, 7,500 elephants, and 27,000 buffalo, to list but a few. With credentials like these, it's no surprise that Kruger offers the country's best and most fulfilling game experience.

Kruger lies in the hot, malarial fug of the lowveld, a subtropical section of the Eastern and Northern Transvaal that abuts Mozambique. The park cuts a swath 80 kilometers (50 miles) wide and 320 kilometers (200 miles) long from Zimbabwe and the Limpopo River in the north to the Crocodile River in the south. Along the way, it crosses 14 different ecozones, each supporting a great variety of plants, birds, and animals.

The southern and central sections of the park are where you will see the most game. Riverine forests, thorny thickets, and large grassy plains studded with knobthorn and marula trees are typical of this region and make ideal habitats for a variety of animals, including black

Kruger National Park

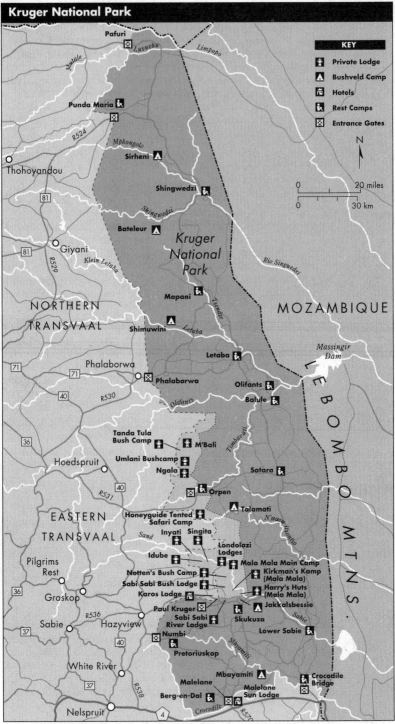

KEY

🚹 Private Lodge
🔺 Bushveld Camp
🏨 Hotels
🚻 Rest Camps
⊠ Entrance Gates

N

0   20 miles
0   30 km

Pafuri

Luvuvhu   Limpopo

Mutale

Punda Maria

R524

Mphongolo

Sirheni

Thohoyandou

Shingwedzi

Shingwedzi

R81

Bateleur

Kruger National Park

MOZAMBIQUE

Rio Singwedzi

R81

Giyani

Klein Letaba

R529

NORTHERN TRANSVAAL

Mopani

Tsendze

Massingir Dam

Shimuwini

Letaba

R71

Phalaborwa

R71

Letaba

R40

R530

Phalaborwa

Olifants

Olifants

Balule

L E B O M B O

Tanda Tula Bush Camp

M'Bali

Timbavati

R36

Umlani Bushcamp

Hoedspruit

Ngala

Satara

R40

R531

Orpen

Talamati

N'waswitshaka

EASTERN TRANSVAAL

Honeyguide Tented Safari Camp

Inyati   Singita

Sand

Pilgrims Rest

Londolozi Lodges

Idube

Mala Mala Main Camp

M T N S.

R36

Notten's Bush Camp

Kirkman's Kamp (Mala Mala)

Graskop

Sabi Sabi Bush Lodge

Harry's Huts (Mala Mala)

Karos Lodge

Paul Kruger

Jackalsbessie

Sabie

R536

Sabi Sabi River Lodge

Skukuza

R37

Hazyview

Numbi

Sabie

White River

Pretoriuskop

Lower Sabie

R37

Mbayamiti

R538

Malelane

Crocodile Bridge

Berg-en-Dal

Malelane Sun Lodge

Nelspruit

Crocodile

4

R570

and white rhino (once on the verge of extinction), leopard, and giraffe. The most consistently rewarding drive in the park is along the road paralleling the Sabie River from Skukuza to Lower Sabie.

As you head north to Olifants and Letaba, you enter major elephant country, although you're likely to spot any number of other animals as well, including lion and cheetah. North of Letaba, however, the landscape becomes a monotonous blur of mopane, nutrient-poor land that supports only stunted mopane trees, which even the animals avoid. Some species, most notably tsessebe and roan antelope, thrive up here nevertheless. If you have a week in Kruger, it's worth driving north to check it out. With less than that, you should stick to the southern and central sections of the park.

Summer in Kruger can be stinking hot—temperatures of 100°F are common—and many northern European visitors become simpering puddles of discontent. If you feel the heat, come at another time or stay in the cool uplands of the Transvaal Drakensberg (*see* Chapter 3) and visit Kruger just for game drives. Whatever you do, *avoid the park during school vacations*. In the July and Christmas holidays, Kruger looks more like summer camp than a game reserve. Reservations are hard to obtain (book a year in advance), and hour-long traffic jams at game-sightings are not uncommon.

Park Activities

See Kruger Essentials, *below,* for information about reservations and fees.

Bush Drives
First-time visitors sometimes feel a little lost driving themselves through the park: They don't know what to look for, and they can't identify the animals they do find. An affordable solution is to hire a game ranger to show you the park and its animals. The rest camps at Berg-en-Dal, Letaba, and Skukuza all offer ranger-led bush drives in open-air Land Rovers (minimum of two people). Not only can rangers explain the finer points of what you're seeing, but they can also take you into areas off-limits to the public. They may even take you on short walks through the bush, something else you can't do on your own. A half-day trip costs R75 per person, not much more than hiring a car for a day. A full-day excursion is R150. Book drives at least a week in advance.

Night Drives
★ Even if you tour the park by yourself during the day, be sure to go on a ranger-led night drive, when the park is closed to regular visitors. Passengers sit in large, open-air vehicles, and use powerful spotlights to pick out animals, including a number of nocturnal creatures you would never otherwise see, including bushbabies, servals, civets, and, if you're really lucky, aardvarks. Night is also the time when hyenas, lions, and leopards hunt. The major rest camps offer these drives, with the notable exception of Lower Sabie and Olifants. The three- to four-hour trip leaves the rest camps half an hour before the gates close. Night drives cost about R50 per person (children are half-price), and again it's advisable to reserve a few days in advance.

Wilderness Trails
★ Spend a few days hiking through the wilds of Africa and you'll probably never be satisfied driving around a game reserve again. On foot, you gain an affinity for the animals and the bush that's impossible in the confines of a car. Kruger has seven wilderness trails, each of which can accommodate eight people. Led by an armed ranger, you'll spend the day walking through the bush, returning each day to the same trail

camp. These trails are not get-fit hikes but slow meanders, the point being to learn about your surroundings: the medicinal purposes of trees, the role of dung beetles in the ecology, even how to recognize animals by their spoor. In general, you can't get as close to animals on foot as you can in a vehicle. You *will* see animals, though, and many hikers can recount face-to-face encounters with everything from rhino to elephant and lion. It's a heart-pumping thrill you won't soon forget. Hikes last three nights and two days (starting on Sundays and Wednesdays), and you should be prepared to walk as much as 12 miles a day. No one under 12 or over 60 is allowed. Hikers sleep in rustic, two-bed huts and share a reed-wall bathroom with flush toilets and showers. Meals are simple bush fare, including stews and barbecues; you must provide your own booze and soft drinks. These trails are incredibly popular—try to reserve at least 13 months in advance. The cost is R850 per person per day.

Bushman Trail. Situated in the southwestern corner of the park, this trail takes its name from the San rock paintings and sites found in the area. The trail camp lies in a secluded valley dominated by granite hills and cliffs. Game sightings frequently include white rhino, elephant, and buffalo. Check in at Berg-en-Dal.

Metsimetsi Trail. The permanent water of the nearby N'waswitsontso River makes this one of the best trails for winter game-viewing. Midway between Skukuza and Satara, the trail camp hunkers in the lee of a mountain in an area of gorges, cliffs, and rolling savannah. Check in at Skukuza.

Napi Trail. Sightings of white rhino are common on this trail, which runs through mixed bushveld between Pretoriuskop and Skukuza. Other frequent sightings include black rhino, cheetah, leopard, elephant, and wild dog. The trail camp hides in dense riverine forest at the confluence of the Napi and Mbyamiti rivers. Check in at Pretoriuskop.

Nyalaland Trail. They don't come much remoter than this trail camp, in pristine wilderness in the far north of the park. Bird-watching is the big thrill in this land of huge baobabs and fever trees. The camp lies on the bank of the Madzaringwe Spruit, near the Luvuvhu River. You're almost sure to see hippo, crocodiles, nyala, and elephant. Check in at Punda Maria.

Olifants Trail. East of Olifants rest camp, this trail camp commands a great view of the Olifants River and affords regular sightings of elephant, lion, buffalo, and hippo. The landscape varies from riverine forest to the rocky foothills of the Lebombo Mountains. Check in at Olifants.

Sweni Trail. East of Satara, this trail camp overlooks the Sweni Spruit and savannah dotted with marula and knobthorn trees. The area attracts large herds of zebra, wildebeest, and buffalo—with their attendant predators, lion and spotted hyena. Check in at Satara.

Wolhuter Trail. If you want to come face-to-face with a white rhino, choose this trail midway between Berg-en-Dal and Pretoriuskop. The undulating bushveld, interspersed with rocky *kopjes* (hills), is ideal habitat for these tremendous prehistoric beasts, but you're also likely to see elephant, buffalo, and lion. Check in at Berg-en-Dal.

Lodging

Unless you stay in a hotel outside Kruger, you are dependent on park-administered rest camps. Accommodation at these camps is usually in free-standing chalets or thatched *rondawels,* round huts modeled after traditional African dwellings. All rooms have air-conditioning, fridges, and *braais* (barbecues), and most come with kitchenettes and en suite bathrooms. You may as well face up to the fact that you're going to miss an episode or two of *ER*—there's no TV in the park, and to call a friend for the latest scoop you'll have to use the public phones near the main buildings. It's necessary to book a year in advance if you want a room during peak seasons (December–January and July). Reservations must be made directly with the National Parks Board (Box 787, Pretoria 0001, ☎ 012/343–1991, ℻ 0121/343–0905).

All of the major rest camps operate restaurants and cafeterias. Less-popular camps in the north have à la carte restaurants that serve pretty decent fare, including game steaks. Restaurants in the other camps all offer set-menu meals. Without exception, the food bears the over-cooked, under-seasoned imprimatur of a government institution—a wildebeest on the hoof looks good next to this stuff. Dinner is a tra-ditional four-course affair of soup, fish, a roast of some kind, and dessert, served buffet-style. Lunch is similar but mercifully smaller. To add in-sult to gastric injury, prices are high: about R30 for lunch and R35 for dinner. A marginally better option is to order something from the cafe-teria, which serves up reasonably priced burgers, hot dogs, curry, bacon and egg, and a variety of toasted sandwiches.

With choices like these, it's not surprising the majority of South African visitors cook their own food. Indeed, braaiing is a time-honored tra-dition in Kruger, as intrinsic to a park visit as a barbecue is to Amer-icans on the Fourth of July. Even the rest areas dotted through the park have free gas grills for visitors who wish to cook their breakfast after an early morning game drive. If you are going to do your own cook-ing, try to reserve a rondawel equipped not only with a kitchenette but also a full complement of kitchen utensils.

Almost every rest camp has a shop offering a limited selection of gro-ceries, charcoal, curios, and books. Don't waltz into these places look-ing for a sprig of mint for your Thai beef salad. They sell only the bare essentials, including canned foods, milk, bread, a selection of frozen meats, and beer and wine. If you do find fresh vegetables, they're likely to be potatoes and onions. Consider buying a cooler and stock-ing up at a grocery store outside the park instead.

Rest Camps

For a couple staying in an en suite rondawel expect to pay R260 per night. Costs increase for additional beds. Tent accomodations start at R35 per night.

Balule. On the bank of the Olifants River, this rustic camp differs rad-ically from the others and will appeal to those who want to experi-ence the true feel of the bush. There are no shops or restaurants, and there's no electricity—only lanterns. Accommodation is in basic, three-bed huts with no windows (vents only) and shared bathroom facili-ties. Cooking is done in a communal kitchen. Visitors must check in at Olifants (*see below*), 11 kilometers (7 miles) away. *No facilities.*

Berg-en-Dal. Built in 1984, this rest camp lies at the southern tip of the park, in a basin surrounded by rocky hills. Berg-en-Dal is known for its white rhino, leopard, and wild dog, but it lacks the tremendous game density of some of the camps farther north. A small dam runs by one side of the perimeter fence, offering good game-viewing, including a close look at cruising crocodiles. Unfortunately, Berg-en-Dal itself is hideous, by far the ugliest rest camp in Kruger. Instead of the tasteful thatched rondawels used so effectively elsewhere, it is built of institutional brick. Even the thatched roofs can't leaven the depressing, bureaucratic feel. Berg-en-Dal has two types of accommodation: Three-bed chalets and family cottages that sleep six in two bedrooms. All huts come with fully equipped kitchens, including pots, pans, and cutlery. The units with the best views of the surrounding bush are numbers 26 (family cottage), 25, 27, and 30–39. *Restaurant, cafeteria, shop, gas station, laundromat, pool, bush drives, night drives.*

Crocodile Bridge. In the southeastern corner of the park, this small rest camp doubles as an entrance gate and makes a convenient stopover for visitors who arrive too late to reach another camp. The Crocodile River provides the scenic backdrop for the camp, which lies in an area of open savannah broken by marula and knobthorn trees. The road leading from the camp to Lower Sabie is well known for its sightings of general game as well as buffalo, rhino, cheetah, and lion. A hippo pool lies just 5 kilometers (3 miles) away. Accommodations are in two- or three-bed huts with fully equipped kitchenettes and en-suite bathrooms. *Shop, gas station, laundromat.*

Letaba. Overlooking the frequently dry Letaba River, this lovely camp sits in the middle of elephant country in the central section of the park. Excellent game-viewing sites in the area are the Engelhardt and Mingerhout dams. The camp itself has a real bush feel: All the huts are thatched, and the grounds are overgrown with apple leaf trees, acacias, mopane, and lala palms. The restaurant and snack bar, with attractive outdoor seating, look out over the broad, sandy river bed. Even if you aren't staying at Letaba, stop in for the superb exhibit on elephants at the Environmental Education Centre. The display examines the social and physical characteristics of the huge animals, from their development in the womb to their death from starvation due to tooth loss. Letaba is also home to a collection of the greatest tusks found in the park. Accommodations are in large cottages and two-, three-, and four-bed rondawels, some without bathrooms and kitchenettes. Cooking utensils are not provided. Unfortunately, dense local foliage means that few rooms have views. Units C17–C30 and D32–D37 offer the best outlooks. Attractive alternatives are the large, East African–style safari tents furnished with four beds, tables and chairs, a fridge, and a fan. The campground, on the fence perimeter, offers lots of shade. *Restaurant, cafeteria, shop, A.A. car-repair workshop, gas station, laundromat, bush drives, night drives.*

Lower Sabie. This is one of the most popular camps in Kruger for good reason: It commands tremendous views over a broad sweep of the Sabie River, and sits in one of the best game-viewing areas of the park (along with Skukuza and Satara). The camp is well known for white rhino, lion, and cheetah, and elephant and buffalo frequently come down to the river to drink. The vegetation around the camp consists mainly of grassland savannah interspersed with marula trees and knobthorn, and there are plenty of watering holes within a few minutes' drive. Lower Sabie is small compared with minitowns like Skukuza, and you get a pretty good feel for the surrounding bush. Accommodations are in five-bed cottages and one-, two-, three-, and five-bed huts, some of which lack kitchens and bathrooms. Cooking utensils are also not provided. The huts with the best views of the river are numbers 3–24 and 73–96. *Restaurant, cafeteria, shop, gas station, laundromat.*

Mopani. Built in the lee of a rocky *kopje* overlooking a dam, this huge settlement is the newest and most attractive of Kruger's rest camps. The dam and the camp are an oasis for both animals and people amid the numbing monotony of the mopane shrubveld in the northern section of the park. You will probably see more game from the rest camp than you will in hours of sweaty driving through the surrounding country. Constructed of rough stone, wood, and thatch, the camp merges well into the thick vegetation. Shaded wood walkways connect the public areas, which all overlook the dam—the view from the open-air bar is outstanding. The restaurant is à la carte (you must reserve before 6) and the food far superior to the buffet-style swill served at other rest camps. The cottages, too, are better equipped and much larger than their counterparts elsewhere in Kruger. Units with kitchenettes come with a full complement of crockery, cutlery, and cooking utensils, and six-bed family cottages are nothing less than fully furnished houses. Among the two-bed huts with views of Pioneer Dam are numbers 4, 7, 9–12, 47, 49, 51–52, 54, 101, and 102. The family cottages with the best views are numbers 5, 43, 45, 48, and 53. *Restaurant, cafeteria, bar, shop, pool, gas station, laundromat, night drives.*

Olifants. In the central section of the park, Olifants has the best setting of all the Kruger camps. It sits high atop cliffs on a rocky ridge, with panoramic views over the distant hills and the Olifants River below. A lovely terrace, sheltered by thatch, allows visitors to sit for hours with a pair of binoculars and pick out the animals below. Lions often make kills in the river valley, and elephant, buffalo, giraffe, kudu, and other game come down to drink and bathe. If you have to give up your first-born to secure one of the thatched rondawels overlooking the valley (numbers 1–12), do so. It's worth reserving these rondawels for at least two nights (book a year in advance) so you can hang out on the veranda and watch Africa unfold below—you won't be disappointed. Olifants offers a lot more than a good view, however. It's a charming old camp, graced with wonderful indigenous trees like sycamores and knobbly figs, mopane, and sausage trees. Accommodations are in two- and three-bed thatched rondawels, some with fully equipped kitchens. The camp has two drawbacks: no night drives and no swimming pool. *Restaurant, cafeteria, shop, laundromat, gas station.*

Orpen. Little needs to be said about this tiny rest camp, which lies just yards from Orpen Gate, in the central section of the park. The only reason to stay here is if you arrive at the gate too late to make it to another camp before the roads are closed. None of the two-bedroom units has a bathroom or cooking facilities. The rooms, arranged in a rough semicircle around a large lawn, look out toward the perimeter fence, about 50 yards away. *Shop, gas station.*

Pretoriuskop. This large rest camp, conveniently close to the Numbi Gate in the southwest corner of the park, makes a good overnight stop for new arrivals. The landscape here consists of rocky kopjes and steep ridges that provide an ideal habitat for mountain reedbuck and klipspringers. The area's sourveld vegetation also attracts browsers like giraffe and kudu, as well as white rhino, lion, and wild dog. At press time, the camp was being renovated and had a bleak, unappealing feel. Like several other Kruger camps, Pretoriuskop is laid out so guests see less of the surrounding bush than of their neighbors grilling boerewors and chops. Accommodations are in typical thatched rondawels and cottages, some of which lack bathrooms and kitchens. The campground enjoys some shade, but sites lack privacy. *Restaurant, cafeteria, shop, laundromat, pool, gas station, night drives.*

Punda Maria. Few foreign tourists make it to this camp in the far northern end of the park, near Zimbabwe. This is a shame, for in many ways it offers the best bush experience of any of the major rest camps. It's a small enclave, with whitewashed, thatched cottages arranged in terraces on a hill. The camp lies in the sandveld, a botanically rich area notable for its unique plant life and birds. An interesting nature trail winds through the settlement. Two-bed huts all come with en suite bathrooms, and many have fully equipped kitchenettes. *Restaurant, shop, gas station.*

Satara. Second in size only to Skukuza, this camp sits in the middle of the hot plains between Olifants and Lower Sabie, in the central section of Kruger. The knobthorn veld surrounding the camp provides the best grazing in the park and attracts large concentrations of game, which in turn attract plenty of lion. Just standing at the perimeter fence, you often see giraffe, zebra, waterbuck, and other antelope. Keep an eye out, too, for rare sable, black rhino, and eland. Despite its size, Satara has far more appeal than Skukuza, possibly because it offers more privacy—the huts aren't all piled on top of one another, and possibly because of the tremendous birdlife that flies in from the bush. The restaurant and snack bar are very pleasant, with shady seating overlooking the lawns and the bush beyond. Accommodations are in large cottages and two- or three-bed thatched rondawels, some with kitchenettes (no cooking utensils). The rondawels, arranged in large circles, face inward onto a central, parklike space. The only huts with good views of the bush are numbers G161–G179. The best of the lot is G167, close to the fence. Campsites are secluded, with an excellent view of the bush, although none of the sites enjoys much shade. *Restaurant, cafeteria, shop, laundromat, A.A. repair workshop, gas station, night drives.*

Shingwedzi. This camp lies in the northern section of the park, amid the blistering plains of mopane shrubveld. The camp benefits enormously from the riverine growth associated with the Shingwedzi River and Kanniedood Dam. As a result, you will probably find more game right around the camp than anywhere else in the region. Among the species that thrive in the harsh mopane environment are elephant, roan antelope, Sharpe's grysbok, and tsessebe. The use of thatch and unworked tree trunks as roof supports gives the camp a rugged, pioneer feel. Both the restaurant (à la carte) and outdoor cafeteria have views over the Shingwedzi River. Accommodations are of two types, A and B. Choose A. These whitewashed units have steeply pitched thatch roofs that accommodate an additional two-bed loft; some also have fully equipped kitchenettes. The B units, painted a dull beige, are built of brick and roofed with unsightly tile; only one has a bathroom and none has a kitchenette. It's anyone's guess why all of the huts face each other across a mopane grove, ignoring the lovely views of the bush beyond the perimeter fence. The campground is large but barren, with almost no shade. *Restaurant, cafeteria, shop, gas station, pool, laundromat, night drives.*

Skukuza. This is by far the largest camp in Kruger, and serves as the park's headquarters. It's large enough to pass for a small town, and as a result it has completely lost all bush feel. At times you wonder if you're in a game reserve at all. Skukuza is popular for good reason, though. It's easily accessible by both air and road, and it lies in a region of thorn thicket that supports a high density of game, including lion, cheetah, and hyena. The camp itself sits on a bank of the crocodile-infested Sabie River, with good views of thick reeds and grazing waterbuck. A museum and education center offer an interesting look at the history and ecology of the park. Accommodations are in two- or three-bed rondawels and four-bed cottages. Some rondawels lack kitchens, but all have fridges. The rondawels with the best riverfront views are numbers 88–92. Guests also have the option of staying in permanent tents of the sort used on luxury East African safaris. Sited on a concrete platform, each tent comes with two or four beds, a cupboard, fridge, and fan. *2 restaurants, cafeteria, grocery, library, A.A. repair workshop, gas station, police, bank, post office, car rental, bush drives, night drives.*

Bushveld Camps

If you're prepared to cook for yourself, Kruger's bushveld camps are infinitely more attractive than the major rest camps. They're small and intimate—you can't get lost the way you can at Skukuza—and access is restricted to residents only. As a result, you experience more of the bush and less of fellow tourists. These camps do not have restaurants, gas pumps, or grocery stores, but all huts have fully equipped kitchens. The only drawback is that most of the cottages are intended for four or more people. Because of the four bed minimum requirement, bush camps start at R475 per night.

Bateleur. Hidden in the northern reaches of the park, this is one of the most remote and untrammeled destinations in Kruger. Shaded by tall trees, the camp overlooks the dry watercourse of the Mashokwe Spruit. A raised platform provides an excellent vantage point from which to view game coming to drink from rainy-season pools, and two nearby dams draw a variety of animals. The camp accommodates a total of 34 people in seven family cottages. Each thatched cottage has two bathrooms, a fully equipped kitchenette, and veranda. *Bush drives, night drives.*

Jakkalsbessie. You couldn't ask for a better game-viewing location, along the Sabie River near Skukuza. The game density here is among the highest in southern Africa. The only drawback is the noise from aircraft landing at Skukuza airport. Eight family cottages can house a maximum of 32 visitors. Each of the thatched cottages features two bedrooms, two bathrooms, a fully equipped kitchen, and a veranda. An added bonus is the camp's proximity to the big grocery store at Skukuza. *No facilities.*

Mbyamiti. Close to the park gate at Crocodile Bridge, this large camp overlooks the normally dry sands of the Mbyamiti River. The vegetation consists of mixed combretum woodland, which attracts healthy populations of kudu, impala, and elephant, as well as lion and black and white rhino. The camp consists of 15 thatched cottages, which can accommodate 70 people. All cottages have large verandas and fully equipped kitchens. *Night drives.*

Shimuwini. Bird-lovers descend in droves on this isolated camp, set on a lovely dam on the Letaba River. Towering jackalberry and sycamore figs offer welcome shade, as well as refuge to a host of local and migratory birds. Away from the river, the riverine forest quickly gives way to mopane-bushwillow woodland, not typically known for supporting large amounts of game. Even so, roan and sable move through the area, and in the peak of summer elephants arrive to browse on the mopane. The camp can house 71 guests in two- and three-bedroom cottages, all with verandas and kitchens. *Bush drives, night drives.*

Sirheni. Another major bird-watching camp, Sirheni sits on the edge of Sirheni Dam, in the far north of the park. A rewarding drive for birders and game-spotters alike runs along the Mphongolo River, but the area can't rival the game density of the Sabie and Crocodile river basins farther south. A maximum of 80 guests can stay in the camp's one- and two-bedroom cottages, all with their own verandas and fully equipped kitchens. *Bush drives, night drives.*

Talamati. On the banks of the normally dry N'waswitsontso River in Kruger's central section, this tranquil camp offers one of the best game-viewing experiences in the park. Grassy plains and mixed woodlands provide an ideal habitat for herds of impala, zebra, and wildebeest, as well as lion, cheetah, and elephant. Two hides (blinds) give guests a chance to watch birds and game from the camp itself. The camp can house 80 people in four- and six-bed cottages, all fully equipped. *Bush drives, night drives.*

Near Kruger National Park

For price ranges, *see* Chart 2(A) *in* On the Road with Fodor's.

$$$$ **Karos Lodge.** Like Malelane Lodge, this attractive hotel next to the Paul
★ Kruger Gate offers visitors a luxury alternative to the bare-bones accommodation of Kruger's rest camps. The hotel has two major advantages over its main competitor: Guests have quick access to the
south-central portion of the park, where game-viewing is best; and the
hotel *feels* likes it's in the wilds of Africa, whereas Malelane Lodge could
be anywhere. Dinner is served in a traditional *boma,* a traditional reed
enclosure around a blazing campfire; rangers lead guided walks through
the surrounding bush; and guests can even sleep overnight in a tree house.
The rooms are connected by a raised wood walkway that passes
through thick indigenous forest. Rooms have Spanish-tile floors and
standard hotel furniture, as well as air-conditioning, cable TVs, and
minibars. ⌧ *R536, next to Paul Kruger Gate (mailing address: Box
888, Hazyview 1242),* ☎ *01311/6–5671,* ⛶ *01311/6–5676. 96 doubles with bath. 2 restaurants, 4 bars, room service, pool, tennis. Breakfast included. AE, DC, MC, V.*

$$$$ **Malelane Sun Lodge.** This pleasant hotel offers a level of luxury that
cannot be matched by rest camps inside the park. If you're prepared
to pay the entrance fee to Kruger Park every day, you can have the best
of Kruger and a comfortable base, too. The hotel sits just yards from
the park's Malelane Gate, overlooking the Crocodile River. The focal
point is a creatively sculpted swimming pool, edged with manicured
lawns and served by a thatched bar area. Rooms, done in subtle greens
and lit by faux miners' lanterns, are more attractive than those at
Karos (*see below*), but the hotel lacks the bush feel that Karos captures so well. Its main advantage is its proximity to Swaziland and the
casino there. ⌧ *Off N4 toward Malelane Gate (mailing address: Box
392, Malelane 1320),* ☎ *01313/3–0331,* ⛶ *01313/3–0145. 102
rooms with bath. Restaurant, 2 bars, room service, pool, 9-hole golf
course, tennis, squash. Breakfast included. AE, DC, MC, V.*

Kruger Essentials

Arriving and Departing

For information about bus, train, and plane transport to Nelspruit,
50 kilometers (31 miles) from Kruger's Numbi Gate and 64 kilometers (40 miles) from Malelane Gate, *see* Eastern Transvaal Essentials
in Chapter 3.

BY CAR

From Johannesburg, drive north on the N1 to Pretoria and then head
east on the N4 to Nelspruit, where you can choose which of the park's
entrances to use. The Malelane and Numbi gates, closest to Nelspruit,
are about four hours from Johannesburg.

BY PLANE

Two airlines fly into the park or to nearby airports. **Comair** (☎
01311/6–5644) offers two flights daily between Johannesburg and
Skukuza, the park headquarters and the largest rest camp in the park.
All passengers landing at Skukuza must pay an R50 entrance fee to
the park. **S.A. Airlink** (☎ 01524/8–5823) sends at least one flight a
day from Johannesburg to Phalaborwa, a mining town on the edge of
the park's central section.

Getting Around

Avis (☎ 01311/6–5651) is the only car-rental agency with an office at Skukuza, inside the park. If you have five or more people in your group, consider hiring a minibus. Not only do you get your own window, but you also sit much higher than in a regular car—a big plus when you're searching for game hidden in dense bush. Avis also has a rental desk at Phalaborwa airport (☎ 01524/5169).

Depending on the month, rest camp gates close between 5:30 and 6:30 at night and open again between 4:30 and 6:30 in the morning. The driver of any vehicle caught on the roads between these hours is liable to a fine or prosecution.

Reservations and Fees

Admission to the park is R20 per vehicle, plus R20 for each day-visitor (children are R10). If you're staying overnight or longer, you pay the vehicle fee plus a one-time fee of R10 per person (R7.50 for children). Reservations for all accommodations, bush drives, and wilderness trails must be made through the **National Parks Board** (Box 787, Pretoria 0001, ☎ 012/343–1991, FAX 012/343–0905).

Safari Operators

Comair (☎ 011/921–0209) is the biggest safari company in Kruger. Visitors can choose from a variety of tour packages ranging from quickie overnight jaunts to five-day extravaganzas that also take in the scenic splendors of the Eastern Transvaal Escarpment (*see* Chapter 3). Visitors fly into Skukuza on one of Comair's regularly scheduled flights, tour the park in minibuses, and sleep in rest camps, usually Skukuza. Tour leaders are knowledgeable about the park's ecosystems, and usually know where to find animals you would probably miss on your own. Other operators offering minibus tours of Kruger Park are **Mfafa** (Box 3334, Nelspruit 1200, ☎ and FAX 01317/6–8398), **Springbok Atlas** (Box 10902, Johannesburg 2000, ☎ 011/493–3780, FAX 011/493–3770), and **Welcome Tours** (Box 997, Johannesburg 2000, ☎ 011/442–8905, FAX 011/442–8865).

Hluhluwe–Umfolozi Game Reserve

Hluhluwe–Umfolozi ("shoosh-louie uhm-fuh-low-zee") lies in Zululand, 264 kilometers (165 miles) up the north coast from Durban. In an area of just 906 square kilometers (350 square miles), Hluhluwe delivers the Big Five, all the plains game, as well as species like nyala and red duiker that are rare in other parts of the country. Equally important, it boasts one of the most biologically diverse habitats on the planet, a unique mix of forest, woodland, savannah, and grassland. You will find about 1,250 different species of plants and trees here—more than in some entire countries.

The park is administered by the highly regarded Natal Parks Board, the wildlife arm of KwaZulu-Natal province. Thanks to its conservation efforts, the park can take credit for saving the white rhino from extinction. So successful was the park at increasing white rhino numbers that in 1960 it established its now-famous Rhino Capture Unit to relocate rhinos to other reserves in Africa. The park is now trying to do for the black rhino what it did for its white cousins. Poaching has decimated Africa's black rhino population from 14,000 a decade ago to a saddening 2,250. Twenty percent of Africa's remaining black rhinos live in this reserve, and you won't get a better chance than this of seeing them in the wild.

Until 1989, the reserve consisted of two separate parks, Hluhluwe in the north and Umfolozi in the south, separated by a fenced corridor. Although a road (R618) still runs through this corridor, the fences have been removed and the parks now operates as a single entity. Hluhluwe and the corridor are the most scenic areas of the park, notable for their bush-covered hills and knockout views, while Umfolozi is better known for its broad plains.

Compared with Kruger, Hluhluwe–Umfolozi is tiny—less than six percent of Kruger's size—but such comparisons can be misleading. You can spend days driving around this park and still not see everything, or feel like you're going in circles. Probably the biggest advantage Hluhluwe has over Kruger is that game-viewing is good all year round, whereas Kruger has seasonal peaks and valleys. Another bonus is its proximity to Mkuzi Game Reserve and the spectacular coastal reserves of Greater St. Lucia Wetland Park (*see* Excursions from Hluhluwe–Umfolozi, *below*). The park is also close enough to Durban to make it a worthwhile one- or two-day excursion.

Hluhluwe–Umfolozi Game Reserve is marked on the northeast corner of the KwaZulu-Natal map in Chapter 7.

Park Activities

See Hluhluwe–Umfolozi Essentials, *below,* for information about reservations and fees.

Bush Walks

Armed rangers lead groups of eight on two- to three-hour bush walks departing from Hilltop Camp. You rarely see much game on these walks, but you do learn a great deal about the area's ecology and how to recognize the signs of the bush, including animal spoor. Walks leave daily at 5:30 AM and 3:30 PM (6 and 3 in winter), and cost about R18; reserve a few days in advance at Hilltop Camp reception.

Game Drives

A great way to see the park is on game drives led by rangers. These drives (about R40 per person) hold several advantages over driving yourself around the park: You sit high up in an open-air vehicle, with a good view and the wind in your face; a ranger explains the finer points of animal behavior and ecology; and your guide has a good idea where to find animals like leopard, cheetah, and lion. Game drives leave daily (except Sunday) at 5:30 AM in summer, 6:30 AM in winter. The park also offers three-hour night drives, during which you search for nocturnal animals with powerful spotlights. These three-hour drives depart at 7, and you should make advance reservations at the Hilltop reception desk.

Wilderness Trails

The park's wilderness trails are every bit as popular as Kruger's, but they tend to be tougher and more rustic. Led by an armed ranger, you must be able to walk 10 miles a day for a period of three days and four nights. All equipment, food, and baggage are carried by donkeys. The first and last nights are spent at Mndindini, a permanent tented camp. The other two are spent under canvas in the bush. While in the bush, hikers bathe in the Mfolozi River or have a hot bucket shower; toilet facilities consist of a spade and toilet-paper roll. Trails, open March–November, are limited to eight people, and should be reserved a year in advance. Expect to pay about R800 per person.

If that sounds too easy, you can always opt for the **Umfolozi Primitive Trail.** On this trek hikers carry all their own kit and sleep out under the stars. A campfire burns all night to scare off animals, and each participant is expected to sit a 90-minute watch. A ranger acts as guide.

A more genteel wilderness experience is **Weekend Trails,** based out of the tented Dengezi Wilderness Camp, where you're guaranteed a bed and some creature comforts. The idea behind these trails is to instill in the participants an appreciation for the beauty of the untamed bush. The weekend begins on Friday at 2:30 and ends on Sunday at 3. Participation is limited to eight people, and costs about R450 per person.

Lodging

Like Kruger, Hluhluwe–Umfolozi offers a range of accommodations in government-run rest camps, with an emphasis on self-catering (only Hilltop has a restaurant). Unfortunately, most foreign visitors can't avail themselves of the park's secluded bush lodges and camps, as each of them must be reserved en bloc, and the smallest accommodates at least eight people.

Hilltop Camp. It may be a government-run camp, but this newly renovated lodge in the Hluhluwe half of the park has plenty of fans. Perched on the crest of a hill, it commands panoramic views over the park, the Hlaza and Nkwakwa hills, and Zululand. Thatch and ocher-colored walls give it an appropriately African feel. Scattered across the crown of the hill, self-contained chalets have high thatched ceilings, rattan furniture, and small verandas. If you plan to eat all your meals in the restaurant, forgo the more expensive chalets with fully equipped kitchens. If you're on a tight budget, opt for a basic rondawel with two beds, a basin, and a fridge; toilet facilities are communal. *Natal Parks Board, Box 1750, Pietermaritzburg 3200, ☎ 0331/ 47–1981,* ℻ *0331/47–1980. Restaurant, bar, shop, gas station. AE, DC, MC, V.*

Near Hluhluwe–Umfolozi

For price ranges, *see* Chart 2(A) *in* On the Road with Fodor's.

$$$$ **Zululand Tree Lodge.** Eight miles from the park, this classy lodge lies
★ in a forest of fever trees on the 3,700-acre Ubizane Game Reserve, a small park stocked with white rhino and plains game. It's by far the most luxurious accommodation in the area, and makes a great base from which to explore Hluhluwe, Mkuzi, and St. Lucia. Built of thatch and wood, the open-sided lodge sits on stilts overlooking the Mzinene River. Rooms are in separate cottages, also on stilts, along the riverbank. The rooms themselves are small, but among the most tastefully decorated you will find: Mosquito nets cover old-fashioned iron bedsteads made up with fluffy white duvets, and African-print cushions, wicker, and reed matting add a real *Out of Africa* feel. If you want the experience of sleeping *al fresco,* fold back the huge wood shutters dividing the bedroom from the open deck. Game rangers lead bush walks and game drives through the small reserve. ☎ *Hluhluwe Rd. (mailing address: Box 116, Hluhluwe 3960), ☎ 035/562–1020,* ℻ *035/562–1032. 20 rooms with bath. Restaurant, bar, pool. Breakfast, dinner, and game drives included. AE, DC, MC, V.*

Excursions from Hluhluwe–Umfolozi

Mkuzi Game Reserve. Thirty miles north of Hluhluwe–Umfolozi, this 88,900-acre reserve lies in the shadow of the Ubombo Mountains, between the Mkuze and Msunduze Rivers. The park is famous for its birds and rhinos. More than 400 bird species have been spotted here, including myriad waterfowl drawn to the park's shallow pans in summer. Several blinds, particularly those overlooking Nsumo Pan, offer superb views. Along with Hluhluwe, Mkuzi is probably the best place in Africa to see rhino in the wild. With an area only a fraction of the size of Kruger, the park supports a population of some 70 black and 120 white rhino. You won't find any lion, buffalo, or elephant, but the low-lying thornveld supports healthy populations of general game, including zebra, giraffe, kudu, and nyala. The park also features a spectacular forest of towering sycamore figs. *Follow N2 north from Hluhluwe for 37 kilometers (23 miles) and follow signs,* ☎ *0331/47–1961 for general information.* ☛ *R15 per vehicle, R5 per person.* ☉ *Daily 6–6.*

Greater St. Lucia Wetland Park. This huge park is one of the most important coastal and wetland areas in the world. The focal point is Lake St. Lucia, a broad, 95,545-acre lake dotted with islands and populated by hundreds of crocodiles and hippos. Bird-watchers rave about the avian life, too—at times, the lake is pink with flamingos. The Natal Parks Board offers guided trips up the estuary aboard the *Santa Lucia,* an 80-seat motor launch that makes the 90-minute voyage three times daily (reservations are essential). The Parks Board maintains an office and self-catering camp in the little fishing village of St. Lucia, near the mouth of the estuary. The village is also the access point to the thin strip of land that runs up the coast between Lake St. Lucia and the Indian Ocean, with some of the country's best beaches as well as the highest vegetated dunes in the world. The area is also a magnet for beer-swilling fishermen with more horsepower than sense and real cowboy mentalities. *24 km (15 mi) east of the Mtubatuba exit of the N2. Mailing address: Natal Parks Board, Private Bag X01, St. Lucia Estuary 3936,* ☎ *035/590–1340,* 🖷 *035/590–1343. Boat tours R25 adults, R12.50 children. Tours daily at 8, 10:30, and 2:30.*

Hluhluwe–Umfolozi Essentials

Arriving and Departing

BY CAR
From Durban, drive north on the N2 highway to Mtubatuba, then cut west on the R618 to Mambeni Gate; otherwise, continue up the N2 to the Hluhluwe exit and follow the signs to the park and Memorial Gate. The whole trip takes about three hours.

BY PLANE
Two carriers fly into the park or a nearby airport. **S.A. Airlink** (☎ 011/394–2430) operates one flight daily between Johannesburg and Hluhluwe. Otherwise, you must rely on frequent **Comair** (☎ 0351/4–1361) service into Richards Bay, about 60 miles south of Hluhluwe–Umfolozi. **Avis** (☎ 0351/98–6555) and **Imperial** (☎ 0351/4–1414) have car-rental offices at the Richards Bay airport.

Reservations and Fees
Admission to the park costs R15 per vehicle plus an additional R5 per person. The park is open October–March from 5 AM to 7 PM and April–September 6–6. Reservations for all accommodations and wilderness trails must be made through the **Natal Parks Board** (Box 1750, Pietermaritzburg 3200, ☎ 0331/47–1981, 🖷 0331/47–1980).

Safari Operators
Zululand Safaris (Box 79, Hluhluwe 3960, ☎ 035/562–0144, 🖷 035/562–0205) is by far the largest tour operator in Zululand and offers a full range of half- and full-day game drives in Hluhluwe–Um-

folozi, as well as night drives and bush walks. The company also leads game drives into the nearby Mkuzi Game Reserve, and guided tours to the bird-rich wetlands and beaches of St. Lucia (*see above*).

Pilanesberg National Park

Abutting Sun City, the 150,000-acre Pilanesberg National Park rises from the arid parchment of the North West Province. Like Tanzania's Ngorongoro Conservation Area, Pilanesberg is centered around the caldera of an extinct volcano dating back some 100 million years. It lacks the drama and mind-numbing scale of Ngorongoro, but it's lovely nonetheless—rings of concentric mountains converge on a central lake filled with crocodiles and hippos. Open grassland, rocky crags, and densely forested gorges provide ideal habitats for a wide range of plains and woodland game, including the rare brown hyena, sable, and gemsbok.

With the introduction of lion in 1993, Pilanesberg National Park can now boast the Big Five. The lions are just the latest scene in a modern-day remake of that biblical hit Noah's Ark. Since 1979, more than 6,000 animals have been relocated to the park, including some elephants that spent most of their lives in the United States. Today, it's hard to believe that the park, itself reclaimed from farmland, was ever anything but wild. The lion and elephant populations are still low for an area this size, but the park should reach its full carrying capacity within five years.

Most tourists combine a trip to the Pilanesberg with a visit to Sun City next door. Safari companies based in Sun City can show you the park on game drives, but many people opt to drive themselves. As beautiful as the park is, however, it's no substitute for a trip to the Eastern Transvaal and Kruger National Park. Its major pluses are its proximity to Sun City and Johannesburg, just 90 minutes away—and the fact that it's malaria-free.

Lodging

Unless you stay at Manyane, the park's government-run rest camp, be prepared to drop a lot of cash to stay in game lodges that fail to deliver an authentic bush experience. The major exception is Tshukudu (*see* Private Game Reserves and Lodges, *below*), a luxury safari lodge that offers an Eastern Transvaal-style game experience. Many visitors to the Pilanesberg stay in Sun City, visiting the park only on game drives.

For price ranges, *see* Chart 2(A) *in* On the Road with Fodor's.

$$$$ **Bakubung.** Abutting the national park, this lodge sits at the head of a long valley with terrific views of pristine bushveld. The lodge takes its name, meaning "People of the Hippo," from a hippo pool that forms the lodge's central attraction, and it's not unusual to have hippos grazing 100 feet from the terrace restaurant. Despite this, the lodge never really succeeds in creating a bush feel, perhaps because it's such a big convention and family destination. The lodge's brick buildings also feel vaguely institutional. Nevertheless, the guest rooms, particularly the executive studios, are very pleasant, thanks to light pine furniture, colorful African bedspreads, and super views of the valley. Ask for an upstairs room if you want a thatch ceiling. The lodge conducts game drives (at extra cost) in open-air vehicles, and guests can accompany rangers on guided walks. A free shuttle bus runs every 1–2 hours to Sun City, 10 kilometers (6 miles) away. ⌘ *Pilanesberg Nat. Park (mailing address: Box 294, Sun City 0316),* ☎ *01465/2–*

1861, ℻ 01465/2–1621. 76 rooms, 50 chalets, all with bath. Restaurant, bar, café, pool, tennis, game drives. Breakfast and dinner included. AE, DC, MC, V.

$$$$ **Kwa Maritane.** You won't hear too many complaints about this lodge's setting, in a bowl of rocky hills on the edge of the national park. Unfortunately, the hotel fails to take advantage of its greatest asset: Many of the hotel buildings look inward onto swimming pools and lawns. And, as at Bakubung, the bustle of convention goers and children tends to drown out the mesmerizing sound of the bush. The big exception is the resort's terrific blind, overlooking a water hole and connected to the lodge via a tunnel. Guest rooms, with high thatched ceilings and large glass doors that open onto a veranda, are comfortable, if generic. Prints of African game offer some reminder of the lodge's setting, but the overall effect is too little too late. Guests can pay to go on day or night game drives in open-air vehicles, or on guided walks with an armed ranger. A free shuttle runs regularly to Sun City. ⚏ *Pilanesberg Nat. Park (mailing address: Box 39, Sun City 0316),* ☎ *01465/2–1820, ℻ 01465/2–1147. 155 rooms with bath. Restaurant, bar, 2 pools, animal blind, tennis, minigolf, sauna, game drives. Breakfast and dinner included. AE, DC, MC, V.*

$ **Manyane.** The cheapest lodging in the Sun City area, the park's main rest camp lies in thinly wooded savannah east of the Pilanesberg's volcanic ridges. Modeled after Kruger's modern rest camps, Manyane is short on charm but long on functional efficiency and cleanliness. Thatch roofing helps soften the harsh lines of bare tile floors and ugly brick. Guests can choose either a two-, four-, or six-bed chalet, all with fully equipped kitchens and bathrooms. An à la carte restaurant is open for all three meals. ⚏ *Pilanesberg Nat. Park,* ☎ *01465/5–6135. Reservations: Box 937, Lonehill 2062,* ☎ *011/465–5423, ℻ 011/465–1228. 60 chalets with bath. Restaurant, bar, pool, minigolf, playground. AE, DC, MC, V.*

Pilanesberg Essentials

Arriving and Departing

For information about getting to and from the park, *see* Sun City *in* Chapter 2.

Guided Tours

Pilanesberg Safaris (☎ 01465/5–6135) conducts 2½-hour game drives in open-air vehicles. Game drives leave early in the morning, in the afternoon, and at night, when rangers illuminate nocturnal animals with a powerful spotlight. Rangers are in radio contact with other vehicles in the field, allowing them to coordinate the search for game. The company also offers 3½-hour bush walks, led by an armed ranger who focuses on the small details of the bush, ranging from the medicinal uses of various trees to the identification of animal spoor. If you prefer to see the big picture, go up in a hot-air balloon (☎ 01465/2–1561); a four-hour flight costs about R900 per person. The company operates from Sun City and the park's Manyane rest camp.

Reservations and Fees

Entry to the park costs R13 for adults, R7 for children. The park gates are open September–March 5:30–7 and April–August 6–6:30. Direct all inquiries to Pilanesberg National Park (Box 6651, Rustenburg 0300, ☎ 01465/5–6135).

PRIVATE GAME RESERVES AND LODGES

You never forget your first kill. Mine was at night with three other tourists. We were trailing a pride of 13 lions padding single-file through thick bush. We battled to keep up in an open Land Rover, picking our way around rocks and flattening scrub that blocked our advance. Murderous thorns scraped the side of the vehicle, forcing us to duck again and again. Ahead, another Land Rover's spotlight caught the reflected glow of impala eyes and the rangers immediately doused their lights to avoid blinding the jittery antelope. We edged forward in the weak moonlight, tracing the outline of the lead lioness as she slunk closer and closer to the herd. When she charged, we all heard the thump of contact, the cry of a panicked impala, then silence. The arrival of the rest of the pride set off a free-for-all of slashing claws, snarling, and ripping flesh. The impala was devoured in seconds. It was cruel, it was thrilling—it was Africa. And it's the kind of experience that only a private lodge can offer.

No lodge can *guarantee* you a kill, but nowhere are your chances of seeing one better. And if you don't witness this elemental spectacle, you will come within spitting distance of more animals than you imagined possible: hyenas in a den, an elephant herd, even a leopard with her cubs. Most lodges will show you the Big Five in three days or less.

These game lodges are not zoos or a Disney Africa. Most reviewed here are either in a national park or abutting one with no fence in between. You can get close to the animals only because, after many years of exposure, they no longer see the game vehicles as a threat. That doesn't mean they don't sometimes object to your presence: An elephant charge will clear out more than your sinuses.

The quality of the game-viewing is obviously the major attraction of a private game lodge, but the appeal goes far beyond that. These lodges also sell exclusivity, and many of them go out of their way to unite shameless luxury and bush living—the sense that you really are living in the African wilds. Camps are all unfenced, so animals (including lion and elephant) can and do wander through the camp. Thatch roofs, mosquito nets, and mounted trophies add to the ambience, although more and more lodges are now opting for luxury East African safari tents to provide that extra bush touch. Dinners are served in an open-air boma. On game drives, the ranger will stop at a scenic viewpoint so you can enjoy a gin-and-tonic with the sunset. If you stay more than two days, most lodges will also serve a bush braai, a full barbecue spread out in the veld, with hurricane lanterns hanging in the thorn trees, a crackling fire, and the sounds of Africa all around you. Under a full moon, it's incredibly romantic.

Make no mistake, you pay for all this pampering. Expect to spend anywhere from US$500 to US$1200 per night per couple. All meals and game drives are included (although for that kind of money they should probably throw in a buffalo as well). A visit to one of these lodges will be your single biggest expense on a trip to southern Africa. If you can afford it, a three-night stay is ideal, but two nights are usually sufficient to see the big game.

The time you spend at a private lodge is tightly structured. With some exceptions, the lodges offer almost identical programs of events. An early morning game drive is followed by breakfast and a short bush walk. After lunch, many people sleep or swim until tea before heading out for the evening or nighttime game drive. Dinner is usually served around 9.

During the four-hour game drives, you'll sit on tiered benches in open, four-wheel-drive vehicles. Depending on the lodge, the vehicle will seat anywhere from six to 10 guests. The rear bench has the best view, but it's tough to hear the ranger from the back, and you spend a lot of time ducking thorn branches. You're better off on the first bench where you can talk easily with the ranger.

On game drives, rangers stay in contact with one another via radio. If one finds a rhino, for example, he relays its location to the others so they can bring their guests to have a look. It's a double-edged sword. The more vehicles you have in the field, the more game everyone is likely to see. At the same time, too many vehicles create a rush-hour effect that can destroy the whole atmosphere—and the environment. In choosing a game lodge, remember to check how much land a lodge can traverse and how many vehicles they use.

For better or worse, the quality of your bush experience depends most heavily on your game ranger. He is your host for your entire stay: taking you on game drives, often eating meals with you, and taking responsibility for both finding the animals and explaining their habits and behavior. A good ranger will have you lauding the glories of Africa; a bad one just makes the bill look bigger.

The vast majority of rangers are white and male. Many have degrees in wildlife management, but they are just as often hired for their looks and charm. The image of the great white hunter with a deep tan and khaki uniform is still a major crowd-pleaser. Unfortunately, some of them believe in their own press. Being driven around the bush by a pair of testicles with a rifle gets old very quickly, so don't hesitate to request another ranger. Thankfully, most rangers are personable, knowledgeable, and devoted to conservation. The turnover rate is so high, however, that it's impossible in this book to recommend a particular ranger at a specific lodge. The best you can do is select a lodge that has a proven ranger-training program.

At the end of your stay, you are expected to tip both the ranger and the tracker, who monitors the animal spoor from a seat mounted on the front of the vehicle. These trackers are invariably blacks who grew up in the area and know the bush intimately. Some of them become rangers, but few speak English well enough to communicate the extraordinary wealth of their knowledge. Tipping guidelines vary from lodge to lodge, but plan to give about R25 per person per day to the ranger and not much less to the tracker; an additional tip of R100 for the general staff would be sufficient for a couple staying two days.

All lodges organize transport if requested. Most have their own airstrips carved out of the bush and fly guests in on chartered aircraft at extra cost. Otherwise, they will arrange to pick you up at the nearest airport. If you're driving yourself, the lodge will send you detailed instructions, since many dirt back roads don't appear on maps and lack names.

CATEGORY	COST*
$$$$	over R1600
$$$	R1200–R1600
$$	R800–R1200
$	under R800

All prices are per person sharing a double room, including all meals, bush walks, and game drives.

In the Eastern Transvaal

The Eastern Transvaal is the heart of South Africa's big-game country, where you'll find the country's most famous private lodges and some of the best wildlife-viewing in the world. All lodges reviewed below lie in game reserves adjoining the immense Kruger National Park (*see above*). In the last couple of years, most of the veterinary fences separating Kruger from these reserves have been dismantled, allowing game to roam freely back and forth.

The most famous and exclusive of these parks is the **Sabi Sand Game Reserve.** Collectively owned and managed, the 153,000-acre reserve is home to dozens of private lodges, including Mala Mala and Londolozi. The Sabi Sand fully deserves its exalted reputation, boasting perhaps the highest game density of any private reserve in southern Africa. North of the Sabi Sand lies the 59,000-acre **Manyeleti Game Reserve.** During the apartheid era, this park was reserved for blacks, who were not allowed into the country's major national reserves. It remains a public park today, although a couple of lodges have won private concessions. The **Timbavati Game Reserve,** also collectively owned and managed, lies north of the Manyeleti. The 185,000-acre Timbavati is renowned for its rare white lions, the product of a recessive gene that surfaces occasionally. Game-viewing is good up here, but it can't rival Sabi Sand, largely owing to a wide belt of mopane shrubveld, an unproductive habitat that supports little besides elephants, roan antelope, and tsessebe. Generally speaking, the Timbavati has plenty of lions and more elephant breeding herds than Sabi Sand, but it lacks a large rhino population.

All lodges will arrange pickups from the airports at Skukuza, Nelspruit, or Phalaborwa. For information about arriving in the Eastern Transvaal, *see* Kruger National Park, *above,* or Chapter 3.

Lodges covered below are marked on the Kruger National Park map.

Honeyguide Tented Safari Camp

$ This tented camp offers the best value of all the Eastern Transvaal lodges, especially if you participate in one of their highly regarded foot safaris. The lodge lies in the 59,280-acre Manyeleti Game Reserve adjoining Kruger National Park. A fence still separates the two reserves, but it's slated to come down by May 1996. Honeyguide was one of the first lodges to use the luxury East African–style safari tents that have since become so popular. But to call these comfortable canvas homes tents is really an insult, because they offer everything a more conventional room does while giving guests the true feel of camping in the wild. Each tent is large enough to accommodate two beds, a cupboard, clothing shelves, and battery-operated lights. An en suite bathroom, accessed through the back zip of the tent, affords complete privacy, as well as hot showers. A shaded wood deck extends from the front of the tent and overlooks a dry riverbed and thick riverine forest. Despite its economy price tag, the camp offers some true luxury touches: tea or coffee served in your tent at dawn, and a fully stocked bar on each vehicle for sundowners.

Game Experience: The Manyeleti Game Reserve is a public park but it's amazingly underused, and you will see very few other vehicles. The park's grassy plains and mixed woodland attract good herds of general game and their attendant predators. Honeyguide's competent rangers have all completed training courses or worked in other lodges. You can either opt for traditional game-viewing in open-air vehicles or book a three- or four-day foot safari, during which you track animals on foot accompanied by a ranger. You'd probably see fewer animals than from a vehicle, but come back with a much better feel for the bush. On these trips, you spend only the last night at Honeyguide, the other one or two being at a rustic bush camp with no running water. Honeyguide has exclusive rights over 12,300 acres, but its two vehicles can traverse almost the entire reserve. *Box 786064, Sandton 2146, ☎ 011/483–2734, FAX 011/728–3767. 16 guests. Bar, pool, airstrip. AE, MC, V.*

Idube

$$ Tucked away in the Sabi Sand Game Reserve, this small lodge sits in a grassy clearing overlooking a dry stream and a water hole. Idube prides itself on its personal attention and relaxed atmosphere, and it gets a lot of repeat business as a result. Guests eat together at long tables, and the informal atmosphere generated by the staff makes this potentially awkward experience easy and fun. The public rooms make effective use of thatch, wood, and African art to create a bush ambience. The guest rooms, however, are a disappointment, built of institutional brick with tile roofs and floors. They're very large, though, and huge sliding doors give guests a good view of the surrounding bush.

Game Experience: Idube offers visitors probably the most affordable chance of seeing the Big Five. Nearly 70% of guests who stay 2–3 nights go away with memories of elephant, lion, leopard, buffalo, and rhino. The reason is simple: The lodge is part of a consortium of six adjoining lodges that pool their land and cooperate via radio in finding the big game. During a game drive, as many as 14 vehicles might be combing 24,700 acres, and it's almost inevitable that they will find the animals. Of the six lodges, though, Idube's rangers probably put the least emphasis on the Big Five, preferring to give guests quality sightings of a couple of these animals rather than showing just the tail end of all five. *Box 2617, Northcliff 2115, ☎ 011/888–3713, FAX 011/888–2181. 18 guests. Bar, pool, airstrip. No children under 12. AE, DC, MC, V.*

Inyati

$$$ Set on a hillside in Sabi Sand, this lovely lodge presides over a broad sweep of lawns running down to the Sand River and a hippo pool. Life here unfolds on the thatched veranda, where guests use binoculars to scan the bush-covered hills for lion and other game. A wooden viewing deck, set under large trees by the river, offers an even better vantage point from which to see animals coming to drink.

Inyati delivers the animals and much, much more. The service is among the best of all the lodges, a welcome mix of professionalism and friendliness. A glass of champagne might materialize after a game drive, or a bottle of sherry may accompany sautéed mushrooms at lunch. The food at Inyati is excellent, head and shoulders above that at comparably priced lodges. Surprisingly, the guest rooms are nothing fancy: Simple thatched cottages with rustic log furniture and Africa-inspired materials and curios. They all have air-conditioning, and rooms 1–3 and 6–9 have good river views.

Game Experience: Inyati is part of the same consortium of six lodges as Idube and Ulusaba, and can rely on the eyes of rangers in as many as 14 vehicles to find animals. The lodge puts more emphasis on the Big Five than Idube, and guests will probably find these animals within two days. Most of the rangers here are black and extremely knowledgeable about the bush. George, the senior ranger, is one of the finest in Sabi Sand. The lodge also offers trips on the Sand River on a large floating pontoon powered by a silent bass motor. *Box 38838, Booysens 2016,* ☎ *011/493–0755,* 𝕱𝕬𝕏 *011/493–0837. 23 guests. Bar, pool, blind, gym, airstrip. No children under 12. AE, DC, MC, V.*

Londolozi

In the heart of Sabi Sand Game Reserve, Londolozi offers a better bush experience than its more famous and expensive neighbor, Mala Mala. The service is outstanding, and the quality of the accommodations and food superior. Londolozi is part of the Conservation Corporation, one of the most highly regarded wildlife companies on the continent. All waste is recycled or composted, none of the rooms uses air-conditioning, and rangers show enormous respect for the land. Londolozi comprises three camps, all within a few hundred yards of each other on a bank of the Sand River.

$$$$ **Bush Camp.** A step down from Tree Camp, this lodge employs many of the same decorative devices as its upscale neighbor but lacks its charm. The stone and thatch structure lies in a forest of ebony and boerbean and commands impressive views of the river. Dark beams, wicker furniture, and African art set the tone for the main lounge, which opens onto a broad deck supported on stilts above the riverbank. Rooms, in stone cottages hidden in the forest, differ little from those at Tree Camp. *16 guests. Bar, pool, airstrip.*

$$$$ **Tree Camp.** Shaded by thick riverine forest, this magnificent lodge is
★ Londolozi's top-of-the-line camp. The lodge is built into the riverbank, and makes clever use of the natural rock and indigenous forest. The main living area consists of a huge, thatched A-frame with a wooden deck on stilts jutting out over the river. Guest rooms, in thatched chalets, are an exquisite blend of modern luxury and *Out of Africa* chic: Track lighting captures the glow of burnished Rhodesian teak; mosquito nets drape languidly over snow-white beds; and old railway sleepers, skillfully crafted into furniture and window frames, add to the rich textures of the room. From the wraparound deck, you look out onto a world of cool green forest. *8 guests. Bar, pool, airstrip.*

$$$ **Main Camp.** The largest of the three camps, Main Camp accommodates 24 guests in chalets or less-expensive rondawels. The lodge is an enormous, thatched A-frame that extends out onto a broad wood deck above the riverbank. Fireplaces, comfy armchairs, and bookcases filled with wildlife literature give the room a warm, lived-in feel. Rising from below the deck, an enormous jackalberry tree provides cooling shade. Guests can choose between modern chalets or rondawels that date back more than 20 years. Chalet rooms are smaller than in the satellite camps, but they are lovely nonetheless. Sliding glass doors lead onto a private deck overlooking the forest and river. Inside, rosewood chests and headboards, mosquito nets, and hessian mats work their bush magic. The very basic rondawels are only worth considering if money is a major consideration. Small and with no view, they possess none of the charm of the large chalets. *24 guests. Bar, pool, airstrip.*

Game Experience: Londolozi's rangers make a major effort to find the Big Five, but they do a good job of showing guests other animals, too. The lodge is particularly famous for its leopards, and was the first to habituate these shy animals to the presence of vehicles. Although rangers don't require formal qualifications, they undergo a rigorous two- to three-month training program and can explain animal behavior in layman's terms. They stay with sightings longer than those of most lodges, and will position their Land Rover so guests can take the best possible photos. The game density in this part of the reserve is excellent, thanks in no small part to the 12 miles of Sand River that meander through the property. Londolozi puts a maximum of nine vehicles into the field, a tiny number when you consider they have traversing rights over 37,000 acres. *Box 1211, Sunninghill Park 2157, ☎ 011/803–8421, FAX 011/803–1810. AE, DC, MC, V.*

Mala Mala

Mala Mala enjoys a reputation as the best safari lodge in Africa. Its name carries a real cachet in jet-set circles, and international celebrities, politicians, and industry tycoons flock here. It's also the most expensive lodge in the country and intends to stay that way, catering to a clientele that equates stratospheric prices with quality. Without question, Mala Mala does offer a superb experience, but after many years the competition has caught up. Today, Mala Mala's guest rooms can't hold a candle to the glorious mix of bush and luxury offered by Londolozi's Tree Camp or Singita, and its food is no better than that of a half-dozen other lodges in the Eastern Transvaal. What Mala Mala does do better than anyone else is game drives. You *will* see the animals here up close, and game drives are invariably a delight. Mala Mala's rangers are legendary—strapping young men with BS degrees who mix charm with a comprehensive knowledge of the bush and its animals. Your ranger is more than your guide to the game—he is your host and valet, hovering by your elbow to fetch you drinks, pool towels, whatever. He may eat his meals with you, and it almost comes as a surprise when he doesn't follow you into the bedroom at the end of the day. Some visitors may find the constant attention irritating. Mala Mala operates three camps, ranging from the ultra-expensive Main Camp to the budget Harry's Huts.

$$$$ **Main Camp.** For first-time visitors to Africa, this large camp overlooking the Sand River offers a very gentle introduction to the bush. The magnificently appointed guest rooms, in a mix of rondawels and larger suites, could be in any luxury hotel in the world. Each room has two bathrooms to make it easier for couples to prepare for early morning game drives, and such amenities as hair dryers, air-conditioning, and telephones. Beige wall-to-wall carpeting adds to its generic hotel feel. Fortunately, the main public area is steeped in African lore. Drawing on the camp's history as a hunting lodge, the lounge displays a host of animal skins and heads, old hunting spears, and antique rifles. Massive elephant tusks frame a huge fireplace, and African sculptures and reference books dot the tables. *50 guests. Bar, pool, airstrip.*

$$$ **Kirkman's Kamp.** This lodge is an absolute delight, with far more
★   charm—at a much lower price—than Main Camp. At its core stands a 1920s farmstead, a relic of the days when this area was a cattle ranch. With its corrugated-iron roof and deep verandas, it has a strong colonial feel that will appeal to Britons and those who've watched *Out of Africa* more than twice. The theme of the camp is Harry Kirkman, the manager of the cattle farm and one of the first game rangers at Kruger National Park. The main room, with high wood ceilings and creaking overhead fans, is lined with trophy heads, old maps of the Transvaal, sepia photos of Kirkman's hunting experiences, and antique rifles. It all spirits you back to another age, and the atmosphere is magical. The farmstead and guest rooms overlook a broad sweep of lawn leading down to the Sand River. The rooms, constructed in recent years, continue the colonial theme, with claw-foot tubs in the bathrooms, white

wood-slat ceilings, old photos, and French doors opening onto a small veranda. *20 guests. Bar, pool, airstrip.*

$$ **Harry's Huts.** This is Mala Mala's budget lodge, competitively priced with most of the other lodges in Sabi Sand. The huge advantage of staying here is that you get the unbeatable Mala Mala game experience at a fraction of the cost of Main Camp, which explains why it's almost always full. Tucked away in thick riverine forest, the lodge faces the Sand River across a lawn dominated by a huge marula topped by a strangler fig. But it isn't going to win any aesthetic awards. The rectangular cottages, painted in geometric Ndebele style, are roofed with a wavy composite material more often found on prefabricated huts and hideous '60s architecture. The rooms are small, rustic, and very simple. The main public areas are also plain, furnished in wicker. Lunch and breakfast are served on the veranda overlooking the river; dinner is in the boma. *16 guests. Bar, pool, airstrip.*

Game Experience: Mala Mala started the whole frenzy about the Big Five, and it still places a huge emphasis on delivering buffalo, leopard, lion, elephant, and rhino. They even give out Big Five certificates—something of a formality since the vast majority of guests see the Big Five within two days. Thankfully, the rangers don't make you feel like you're taking an animal inventory, and they stop for as long as you like at other animals, too. Mala Mala has been operating for 30 years as a photo safari lodge, and much of the game is now completely habituated to the presence of the lodge's Land Rovers, allowing them extremely close. The biggest advantage Mala Mala has over its competition, however, is its size: 54,300 acres, a full third of the Sabi Sand Game Reserve, including a 20-mile boundary with the Kruger National Park. A maximum of 16 vehicles traverse the land at any one time. Another major bonus is the lodge's 33 miles of river frontage, which attracts animals to the sweet grasses that grow on the banks. The dense riverine forest is an ideal habitat for leopards and birds. *Box 2575, Randburg 2125, ☎ 011/789–2677, ℻ 011/886–4382. AE, DC, MC, V.*

M'Bali

$$$ This beautiful tented camp lies at the northern tip of the Timbavati Game Reserve. Built on a hillside overlooking a dam, it enjoys the best view of any tented camp—elephants come to bathe below the lodge daily in winter, and on a clear day you can see all the way to the Transvaal Escarpment. Sand pathways run down the hillside to the guest tents, on raised wood platforms supported by stilts. Dismiss the image of some pokey little tent in a campsite. These are huge, intended to re-create the spirit of the old East African hunting safaris. Mosquito nets shroud the beds, and each tent is equipped with bedside tables, a closet, and electric lights. An A-frame thatch shelter shields the tent from the sun and rain. The only drawback is the location of the bathroom, underneath the wood deck and reached by way of very steep stairs. At night, after the electricity is turned off, these stairs become treacherous. Elderly visitors should ask to stay in the lodge's single stone cottage instead.

Game Experience: Rhino are thin on the ground in this part of the Timbavati, so it's unlikely you will find all of the Big Five. However, most guests do see elephant and lion, and frequently buffalo. M'Bali places a stronger emphasis on walking and the bush experience than do most lodges, and they encourage guests to do a long walk instead of a game drive at least once during their stay. In winter, guests encounter elephant almost every day on these walks. The rangers are all highly qualified and knowledgeable about the animals and the area's ecosystem. On game drives, the lodge puts a maximum of two vehicles into the field, but rangers coordinate game-sightings with three vehicles from a sister lodge, Motswari. They have traversing rights over an enormous area of 34,600 acres. *Box 67865, Bryanston 2021, ☎ 011/463–1990, FAX 011/463–1992. 18 guests. Bar, pool, airstrip. AE, DC, MC, V.*

Ngala

$$$ This exclusive lodge lies in mopane shrubveld in the Timbavati Game Reserve. Part of the Conservation Corporation, Ngala offers the same level of professionalism and service as Londolozi (*see above*). The main lodge has a Mediterranean style and sophistication that are refreshing after the hunting-lodge decor espoused by so many lodges. Track lighting and dark-slate flooring and tables provide an elegant counterpoint to high thatched ceilings and African art. A massive, double-sided fireplace dominates the lodge, opening on one side onto a lounge filled with comfy sofas and chairs and on the other a dining room. Dinner at Ngala is more formal than at most lodges, served in a reed-enclosed boma or in a tree-filled courtyard lit by lanterns; crystal glasses and silver place settings enhance the sophisticated atmosphere. Guest cottages, set in mopane shrubveld with no views, contain two rooms, each with its own thatched veranda. Rooms make extensive use of hemp carpeting, thatch, and dark beams to create an appealing warmth.

Game Experience: Ngala's rangers are first-class: entertaining, well-informed, and attentive to guests' needs. Unless you specifically tell them you want to concentrate on birds or trees, they do focus on the Big Five. And with eight vehicles traversing an enormous territory of 35,800 acres, you'll have a good chance of seeing them. In general, the Timbavati sees bigger herds of elephant and buffalo than the Sabi Sand, but it's not as good for leopard, rhino, and cheetah. Ngala's main advantage over Sabi Sand is its proximity to four major ecozones—mopane shrubveld, marula combretum, acacia scrub, and riverine forest—that provide habitats for a wide range of animals. Unfortunately, Ngala sits at the northern end of the property in the mopane belt, which is unproductive and barren for much of the year. To reach the other ecozones, you must drive 30 minutes through the mopane and then 30 minutes back, shortening your game-viewing by an hour. For the same reason, bush walks from camp are less interesting than those offered in Sabi Sand. *Box 1211, Sunninghill Park 2157, ☎ 011/803–8241, FAX 011/803–1810. 42 guests. Bar, pool, airstrip. AE, DC, MC, V.*

Notten's Bush Camp

$
★ You probably won't see the Big Five at this delightful little camp, but you may have the bush experience of your life. Sandwiched between Mala Mala, Londolozi, and Sabi Sabi, Notten's family-run operation is the antithesis of the animal treasure hunts conducted by its more famous neighbors. Owners Gilly and Bambi Notten personally tend to their guests, and a stay at their camp is like visiting good friends who happen to live in the bush. It's a measure of their success that 70% of their guests are return visitors. The lodge sleeps 10 people in simple cottages lit only by paraffin lamps and candles. At night, flickering torches line the walkways and a hurricane lantern on your veranda guides you back to your room.

After the evening game drive, guests meet for drinks in the boma and then dine together under the stars. The atmosphere is more like that of a dinner party than a commercial lodge, and Gilly Notten regales her guests with hilarious tales about life in the bush. Breakfast and tea are served in an open-sided shelter overlooking a grassy plain and a pan where animals come to drink. A lounge area is furnished with comfy chairs, bookshelves filled with wildlife literature, and a fridge where guests help themselves to drinks. The bush camp operates an honor bar—just help yourself and settle your account when you leave (you're welcome to bring your own booze, too). For weekends and major holidays, you need to make reservations about 6 months in advance; at other times, two months is usually sufficient.

Game Experience: Notten's has traversal rights over 4,900 acres but only one Land Rover, so the chances of finding the Big Five are slim. When you do find leopard, lion, or rhino, though, you don't have to share the sighting with a horde of other vehicles. A wise strategy for first-time visitors is to get your big-game fix at a large lodge and then come here to unwind and get a feel for the bush. The ranger is informative and fun, and Joe, the tracker, is one of the best in Sabi Sand. On morning bush walks, he offers a wealth of information about everything from trees to insects and birds. *Box 622 Hazyview 1242, ☎ and FAX 01311/6–5105. 10 guests. Honor bar, pool. No children under 10. No credit cards.*

Sabi Sabi

At the southern end of Sabi Sand Game Reserve, Sabi Sabi is often mentioned in the same breath with Mala Mala and Londolozi. It shouldn't be. More than at any other lodge, you feel like just another guest—one of thousands that are shunted in and out annually. The lodge packs more than 100 guests into its two camps, and doesn't have enough land to support the 20 vehicles needed to accommodate them. The sense that you're staying in a big hotel is not helped by the attitudes of the staff and management: Waiters drop continual hints about tips; and you must sign a chit or pay cash for every drink, whereas most lodges simply add the cost to your final bill. Considering that you're here to focus on nature and animals, these continual reminders of money are out of place.

$$$$ **Bush Lodge.** This large lodge overlooks a water hole and a dry river course. The reception area leads back through attractive open courtyards to a thatched, open-sided dining area, an airy bar, and a lounge where residents can watch nature videos. Public rooms are tastefully decorated with African art and artifacts, animal skulls, and African prints. A viewing deck offers magnificent views of game at the water hole, as does the pool. Chalets, all thatched, are connected by walkways that wend through manicured lawns and beneath enormous shade trees. Standard chalets are a bit pokey and dark, and can't compare with the accommodations at comparably priced lodges. The thatched suites, on the other hand, are lovely, decorated with wicker and pretty African-print bedspreads and upholstery. Each suite has a deck overlooking the dry river course, as well as air-conditioning. Suites 20 and 21 have the best views of the water hole. *54 guests. Bar, pool, airstrip.*

$$$$ **River Lodge.** Shaded by giant jackalberry trees, this attractive lodge is smaller and more relaxed than Bush Lodge. It's popular among birders, who spend hours peering into the thick riverine forest that surrounds the camp. The lodge looks onto a dry riverbed, beyond which lies the perennial Sabie River. Guest rooms are spread out along the river. Otherwise, amenities are very similar to those at Bush Lodge. *48 guests. Bar, pool, airstrip.*

Game Experience: Sabi Sabi puts 20 vehicles onto 12,300 acres, an area one fourth the size of Mala Mala. This translates into plentiful game sightings but also much greater environmental damage and a high volume of traffic around major sightings. Sabi Sabi markets the Big Five experience heavily, and with so many vehicles in the field it's almost certain that guests will see these animals in two or three days. Indeed, rangers may deliberately space out the sightings over the course of your stay to maintain a level of suspense. Sabi Sabi's major advantage over its competitors is its 6 miles of Sabie River frontage. The Sabie is the only river in Sabi Sand with year-round water, and it supports a greater diversity of animal life than any river in southern Africa. Sweet grasses and dense riverine forest attract large numbers of general game, as well as birds, hippo, leopard, and crocodiles. *Box 52665, Saxonwold 2132, ☎ 011/483–3939, ℻ 011/483–3799. AE, DC, MC, V.*

Singita

$$$
★ This is undoubtedly the most luxurious lodge in Sabi Sand Game Reserve. In its decor, atmosphere, and modus operandi, it bears a striking resemblance to Londolozi, probably because the same Conservation Corporation manages and promotes the property. For unfettered extravagance, though, Singita leaves Londolozi far behind. Overlooking the Sand River, the lodge's eight guest cottages are each bigger than a small house, featuring double-sided fireplaces, separate living rooms, enormous verandas—even an outside shower in case your inner Tarzan feels confined in the cavernous one in the bathroom. Mosquito nets, railway-sleeper furniture, masks, beads, and animal skulls round out the African decor. Singita also has air-conditioning, unlike Londolozi.

The main lodge consists of a giant, thatched A-frame and a large deck raised on stilts overlooking the river. An enormous fireplace, topped by a stuffed buffalo head, dominates the room, and zebra skins, skulls, and trophy horns complete the safari theme. At dinner, fine glass and china foster a colonial formality that works surprisingly well.

Game Experience: Singita offers an almost identical game-viewing experience to Londolozi (*above*), since its rangers are trained by Conservation Corporation and its two Land Rovers traverse the same 37,000 acres. The rangers from both lodges relay game-sightings to one another via radio. *Box 1211, Sunninghill Park 2157, ☎ 011/803–8241, ℻ 011/803–1810. 16 guests. Bar, pool, airstrip. AE, DC, MC, V.*

Tanda Tula Bush Camp

$$
★ This luxury tented camp in the Timbavati brings you closer to the bush than almost any other lodge. When lions roar nearby, the noise sounds like it's coming from under the bed. The reason is simple: Guests sleep in East African safari–style tents with huge window flaps that roll up, leaving you staring at the bush largely through mosquito netting. The effect is magical and much more rewarding than sleeping in a conventional room. Of the three tented camps in the Eastern Transvaal, Tanda Tula is by far the most luxurious. Its eight tents, all with en suite bathrooms and their own wood decks, overlook the dry bed of the Nhlaralumi River. Each tent is beautifully decorated with wicker chairs, bedspreads made from colorful African materials, and elegant side tables, a cupboard, and dresser. An oscillating fan and electric lights add a convenient modern touch. A large, open-sided thatched shelter serves

as the main lounge, where breakfast and lunch are served. Of particular note are Tanda Tula's bush braais, held in the dry bed of the Nhlaralumi River with the moon reflecting off the bright sand.

Game Experience: Tanda Tula does not place a strong emphasis on the Big Five, and you're unlikely to see all these animals in a two- or three-day stay. The camp operates only two vehicles on an area of 14,800 acres, but two vehicles from other lodges sometimes provide additional help finding game. This part of the Eastern Transvaal is known for its elephant, lion, and wild dog, but rhino are scarce. Tanda Tula's game rangers are well trained and extremely attentive to the desires of their guests. *Box 151, Hoedspruit 1380, ☎ and ℻ fax 01528/3–2435. Reservations: Box 32, Constantia 7848, Western Cape, ☎ 021/794–6500, ℻ 021/794–7605. 16 guests. Bar, pool. No children under 12. AE, DC, MC, V.*

Ulusaba Rocklodge

$$$ Perched atop a rocky hill in Sabi Sand Game Reserve, this magnificent aerie has all the makings of the finest game lodge on the continent. The lodge is literally built into the side of a cliff, 800 feet above a water hole and the bushveld plains. The road leading up to the lodge is so steep that guests must be driven up in four-wheel-drive vehicles, and the view from the top is mind-blowing. A maze of stone walkways and steps gives the lodge a fortresslike feel, and log railings are all that prevent guests from doing a swan dive over the cliffs. In the inky blackness of an African night, Ulusaba seems to hover over the veld like a spacecraft.

Travel writers could spout platitudes about this lodge forever, but the truth remains that Ulusaba has been a disaster in recent years. A long period of heavy-handed management fostered a poisonous atmosphere marked by rapid staff turnover and an underlying current of surliness. At press time, though, the lodge had been sold and a new owner is giving Ulusaba a makeover. It's worth doing some follow-up research since this lodge is potentially so fabulous. If you can, opt for one of the new rooms, some of the finest accommodation you will find in a game lodge. Huge windows offer panoramic views of the bush, while high thatch ceilings, white stucco walls, and natural wicker create a light, airy effect. The older rooms, on the other hand, are small, very ordinary, and lack air-conditioning. Considering the magnificence of the view, the windows are surprisingly small as well.

Game Experience: Ulusaba belongs to the same consortium of six game lodges as Inyati and Idube (*see above*), so the quality of its game viewing is superb and guests are likely to see the Big Five in 2–3 days. With the lodge under new management, it's impossible to gauge the quality of the rangers, but it can only improve. *Box 239, Lonehill 2062, ☎ 011/465–6646, ℻ 011/465–2825. 22 guests. Bar, pool, airstrip. AE, DC, MC, V.*

Umlani Bushcamp

$ Snoozing under enormous shade trees in the Timbavati, this superb bush camp offers visitors a very different experience from the other lodges. The focus here is on a bush experience, as opposed to the search for big game, and accommodations are accordingly rustic. Guests sleep in huts made from reeds and thatch, and the door is a simple reed curtain. The bed—you do get one—is protected by a mosquito net, but you'll have to brave the creepy-crawlies to reach the open-air bathroom, a communal affair shielded by reeds. Kerosene lanterns add to the bush feel. It's not everyone's cup of tea, but you really feel like you're out in the African wilds, and the atmosphere is fun and relaxed.

Game Experience: Umlani places a strong emphasis on bush walks, and an armed ranger usually leads guests on a two- to three-hour walk each morning. Animals run from humans who are on foot, so don't expect to get up close and personal with an elephant. However, the thrill of seeing big game while on foot, even from 50 yards away, more than compensates—plus you learn a tremendous amount about bushveld ecology. In the evening, a ranger takes guests on a conventional game drive. Umlani's sole vehicle has traversal rights over 24,700 acres and cooperates with Tanda Tula and another lodge in the search for game. Nevertheless, you would be lucky to see all of the Big Five during a stay. *Box 26350, Arcadia, Pretoria 0007,* ☎ *012/329–3765,* 🅵🅰🅇 *012/329–6441. 10 guests. Bar, pool. AE, DC, MC, V.*

In KwaZulu-Natal

KwaZulu-Natal's best private lodges lie in northern Zululand and Maputaland, a remote region close to Mozambique. With one exception, the lodges reviewed here do not offer the Big Five. However, they are sufficiently close to one another and Hluhluwe–Umfolozi Game Reserve to allow you to put together a bush experience that delivers the Big Five and a great deal more, including superb bird-watching and an unrivaled beach paradise. Malaria does pose a problem, however, and summers are hot, hot, hot.

For information about arriving and departing, contact the individual lodges listed *below; see also* Hluhluwe–Umfolozi Game Reserve, *above.*

Lodges covered below are marked on the northeast corner of KwaZulu-Natal map in Chapter 7.

Ndumo Wilderness Camp

$ This bush camp lies in Ndumo Game Reserve in Maputaland, a remote northern region of KwaZulu-Natal, near the Mozambique border. The 24,700-acre park does not have the Big Five, and visitors wanting to see big game should head elsewhere. What makes Ndumo famous is its birds. Along with Mkuzi (*see* National Parks and Game Reserves, *above*), the park is probably the premier bird-watching locale in the country. Over 400 species of birds—60% of all the birds in South Africa—have been spotted here, including the gorgeous purple-crested lourie, the green coucal, and the elusive trogon. Myriad waterfowl also flock to the reserve's Nyamiti and Banzi pans, and summer migrants take up residence from October until April.

Ndumo Wilderness Camp is a small tented lodge raised on stilts in a fig forest abutting Banzi Pan. Wooden walkways connect the camp's luxurious East African safari–style tents, each with its own bathroom and veranda overlooking the pan. The pan is home to scores of crocodiles, and the stillness of the night is often shattered by the sound of their splashes or the panicked screams of a doomed bush pig. The main lodge is an open-sided thatch shelter with broad decks extending over the water. Armed with a pair of binoculars, you could sit here for hours and never get bored.

Game Experience: Ndumo has no lion or elephant, but it supports a healthy population of black and white rhino, rare suni antelope, and red duiker, as well as the usual plains animals. And even though it may not have the Big Five, it is one of the most beautiful reserves in the country. Forests of yellow fever trees are mirrored in glassy lakes, and giant sycamore figs provide shelter for crowned eagles and owls. Crocodiles numbering in the hundreds bask on the grassy banks, while hippos honk and blow in deep pools. In addition to the usual game drives, rangers often take guests on extended bush walks. The best time to visit is October, when migrant birds return and antelope start bearing their young. *Box 651171, Benmore 2010,* ☎ *011/884–1458,* FAX *011/883–6255. 16 guests. Bar, pool. AE, DC, MC, V.*

Phinda Resource Reserve

Only five years old, this Conservation Corporation reserve has already taken its place among the great game experiences of South Africa. Phinda (pin-duh) is Zulu for "return," referring to the restoration of 42,000 acres of former farmland in northern Zululand to bushveld. While the quality of Phinda's game-viewing doesn't yet equal that of the established lodges of the Eastern Transvaal, it may well be superior in another five years. The reserve is remarkable not only for its seven different ecosystems, but also for its novel approach to the entire bush experience. In addition to the usual combination of game drives and bush walks, Phinda offers a medley of adventures from flight-seeing to beach safaris that take advantage of the reserve's incredible location near Greater St. Lucia Wetland Park and rhino-rich Mkuzi Game Reserve.

$$ ★ **Forest Lodge.** Hidden in one of the last remaining sand forests in the world, this fabulous lodge overlooks a small water hole where nyalas, warthog, and baboons frequently come to drink. The lodge is a real departure from the traditional thatched structures so common in South Africa. It's very modern, with a vaguely Japanese feel thanks to glass-panel walls, light woods, and a deliberately spare, clean look. The effect is stylish and very elegant, softened by modern African art and sculpture. Guest suites use the same architectural concepts as the lodge, where walls have become windows, and rely on the dense forest (or curtains) for their privacy. As a result, guests feel very close to their surroundings, and it's possible to lie in bed or shower while watching delicate nyalas grazing just feet away. This lodge is a winner. *32 guests. Bar, pool, airstrip.*

$$ **Nyala Lodge.** This attractive thatched lodge sits on a rocky hill overlooking miles of bushveld plains and the Ubombo Mountains. Wide verandas lead into the lounge and bar, graced with high ceilings, dark beams, and cool tile floors. In winter, guests can snuggle into cushioned wicker chairs next to a blazing log fire. Brick pathways wind down the hillside from the lodge to elegant split-level suites with mosquito nets, thatched roofs, and large decks overlooking the reserve. African baskets, beadwork, and grass matting beautifully complement the bush atmosphere. *40 guests. Bar, pool, airstrip.*

Game Experience: With the recent addition of buffalo, Phinda can now deliver the Big Five, although perhaps not as consistently as its competition in the Eastern Transvaal. It more than compensates, however, with its sheer diversity of habitats, ranging from savannah and mountain woodland to broad-leaved woodland, sand forest, palm veld, wetland, and riverine forest. The bird life here is extraordinary, too. Phinda's other trump is its adventure trips, including boat or canoe trips down the Mzinene River for a close-up look at crocodiles, hippos, and birds; walking safaris with an armed ranger in Mkuzi Game Reserve, where guests track aggressive black rhino on foot; big-game fishing or scuba-diving off the deserted Maputaland coast; sightseeing flights over Phinda and the highest vegetated dunes in the world; and Maputaland beach safaris, a combination of flight-seeing, four-wheel beach driving, and snorkeling. Depending on whether you choose Phinda's resort or safari plan, these trips may or may not be included in the general rate. *Box 1211, Sunninghill Park 2157,* ☎ *011/803–8421,* ℻ *011/803–1810. AE, DC, MC, V.*

Rocktail Bay Lodge

$
★   If Robinson Crusoe had washed ashore on the pristine coastline of Maputaland, he wouldn't have found anybody to call Friday—and he certainly wouldn't have cared what day of the week it was. It's that empty and that magnificent. No other buildings lie within 10 miles of Rocktail Bay Lodge, tucked away in Maputaland Coastal Reserve, a narrow strip of wilderness that stretches from St. Lucia all the way to Mozambique. If you love untouched beaches, fishing, snorkeling, and walking, coming here will be one of the highlights of a visit to South Africa. Rocktail Bay is not a game lodge—the only animals you're likely to see are loggerhead and leatherback turtles. It is included in this chapter because it lies far from any other major tourist destination and operates much like a game lodge. In fact, unless you have a four-wheel-drive vehicle, the lodge must collect you for the final 11-kilometer (7-mile) journey along deep sand tracks carved through coastal dune forest.

The lodge lies in a swale formed by enormous dunes fronting the ocean. Walkways tunnel through the dune forest to a golden beach that sweeps in a gentle arc to Black Rock, several miles to the north. There are no lifeguards or shark nets, but the swimming and snorkeling are fabulous. The lodge consists of 10 simple A-frame chalets raised on wood platforms above the forest floor. Wood and thatch create a rustic ambience, complemented by solar lighting and basic furnishings. A large veranda and adjoining thatched bar provide the backdrop for alfresco meals under a giant Natal mahogany tree. These are interrupted only by Gremlin, a tame thick-tailed bushbaby with a sweet tooth.

From a weather standpoint, the best times to come are probably spring (September–October) and autumn (March–May). In summer, the temperature regularly soars past 100°F, and swimming during winter is a brisk proposition. August is the windiest month.

Game Experience: Rocktail Bay *does not offer traditional game-viewing,* although many guests combine a visit here with a trip to Phinda (*see above*), about 95 kilometers (60 miles) to the south. Besides glorious beaches, its major attraction is the annual arrival of giant loggerhead and leatherback turtles to lay their eggs. The beaches here are one of the few known laying areas of these endangered animals, and the season extends from the end of October through February. During these months, rangers lead after-dinner walks down the beach to look for turtles, and guests can expect to cover as much as 16 kilometers (10 miles) in a night. Other activities include great surf fishing (tackle provided), snorkeling, and long beach walks. Rangers also lead excursions to see hippo pools, the rich birdlife of Lake Sibaya, and Kosi Bay, where the local Tembe people catch fish using an age-old method of basket-netting. For many people, though, a trip to Rocktail Bay is a chance to kick back and just soak in the atmosphere of an unspoiled coastal wilderness. *Box 651171, Benmore 2010,* ☎ *011/884–1458,* ℻ *011/883–6255. 20 guests. Bar, pool. AE, DC, MC, V.*

In Pilanesberg National Park

Pilanesberg National Park lies 176 kilometers (110 miles) northwest of Johannesburg, adjacent to Sun City. For more information on the park, including advice on arriving and departing from Sun City, *see* National Parks and Game Reserves, *above, and* Chapter 2.

Tshukudu Game Lodge

$$ Few private lodges can match the beauty of this tiny luxury lodge inside Pilanesberg. Built into the side of a steep, rocky hill, Tshukudu overlooks open grassland and a large water hole where elephants come to bathe. If you watch long enough, you'll probably see most of the Big Five from your veranda. Winding stone stairways lead up the hill to lovely thatched chalets decorated with wicker furniture, bold African materials, and black-slate floors. Fireplaces, minibars, and mosquito nets are standard, and sunken bathtubs command spectacular views of the water hole. It's a long 132-step climb to the main lodge on the summit, making this an impractical choice for the elderly or those with disabilities. The lodge will leave you breathless for other reasons, too: The extensive use of stone and thatch creates a natural look that blends beautifully into the rocky hillside. At night, guests can use a spotlight to illuminate game at the water hole below.

Game Experience: Tshukudu lies in the middle of the 135,850-acre Pilanesberg National Park, and as a result must share the park roads with other visitors. The biggest drawback, though, is a park regulation banning off-road driving, which means rangers can't follow animals into the bush. Under these circumstances, you're unlikely to see a hunt or a kill. Your chances of seeing the Big Five will be virtually guaranteed, however, if the proposed plan to radio-collar animals is adopted. By just following the signal, rangers will be able to track down any animal they choose. So, sure, you'd get to see all the game, but who cares? Gone would be the adventure and suspense of tracking, and you might as well go to a zoo. *Box 294, Sun City 0319,* ☎ *01465/2–1861,* ℻ *01465/2–1621. 12 guests. Bar, pool. No children under 16. AE, DC, MC, V.*

In the Garden Route Vicinity

When it comes to game-viewing, the great advantage that the Cape has over the Eastern Transvaal is the absence of malaria. For information on reaching Port Elizabeth, the major city in the Garden Route area, *see* Chapter 6.

Shamwari Game Reserves

An hour's drive from Port Elizabeth, Shamwari is the only major game lodge in the Cape, and it is ideally situated for tourists traveling the Garden Route (*see* Chapter 6). It's a comparatively new reserve and as yet doesn't offer the full Big Five experience. It has plentiful general game, however, as well as leopard, buffalo, elephant, and rhino. Don't come here expecting the classic safari lodge experience of East Africa or the Eastern Transvaal—you'll be sorely disappointed. Shamwari's showpiece lodge, an Edwardian mansion, would look right at home in the English countryside, and the reserve's mixed vegetation is about as far from thorn-tree savannah as you can get. Still, the setting is absolutely magnificent: Rolling mountains stretch as far as the eye can see, riven by forested valleys, gorges, and rivers.

Guests can choose from among four lodges, including a couple of inexpensive self-catering options.

Shamwari is marked on the South Africa map at the front of this book.

$$ Long Lee Manor. As long as you don't expect roaring campfires and bush living, this pink Edwardian mansion will knock your socks off. Tastefully restored, the manor looks past manicured lawns, fountains, and white balustrades to grassy plains dotted with game. The interior is a rich spectacle of wood paneling, graceful staircases, and original art. Request one of the original en suite bedrooms upstairs, decorated with antique dressers and armoires, four-poster beds, and delicate floral fabrics. Standard rooms in an adjoining wing employ sisal matting, mosquito nets, and painted country wardrobes to create a welcoming, old-fashioned feel. Unlike those of most lodges in South Africa, all rooms have TVs and phones. Long Lee's only drawback is its location, on the very edge of the reserve with a plain view of neighboring farms and buildings. *23 guests. Bar, pool, tennis, gym, steam room, airstrip.*

$$ Shamwari Lodge. With its thatch roof, safari decor, and white guest cottages, this pleasant lodge comes closest to the kind of accommodations offered by private game reserves in the Eastern Transvaal. Hidden in the cleft of a steep valley, the lodge faces in on a circle of lawns and a swimming pool. Low wood beams, animal paintings, and a mounted buffalo head set the tone of the main lounge, while the five luxury guest rooms have wall-to-wall carpeting, under-floor heating, and private patios. *10 guests. Bar, pool, steam room, airstrip.*

$ Carn Ingly. Although this restored pioneer cottage also dates back to 1860, it feels more modern than Highfield and lacks the time-worn charm of that structure. Situated in the heart of the reserve, it operates on the same block-reservation, self-catering plan, including use of a four-wheel-drive vehicle and ranger (extra cost). Mounted eland heads adorn the walls and a giant fireplace dominates a living room furnished with art-deco sofas. *6 guests. Pool.*

$ Highfield. Don't be surprised to find rhinos grazing on the lawns of this charming farmhouse dating back to 1860. Overlooking a bush-cloaked valley, the old house now operates as a self-catering lodge and must be booked *en bloc* (six guests maximum). The interior is decorated in period style, with lovely antique dressers, old-fashioned bedsteads, and timber floors and ceilings. The cottage has a fully equipped kitchen and is serviced daily. Guests also have a ranger and four-wheel-drive vehicle at their disposal, although game drives do cost extra. Even so, this is one of the best deals in the country. *6 guests. Pool.*

Game Experience: Shamwari is a work in progress. Much of the reserve has only recently been reclaimed from farmland, and the game-restocking program is still underway. Shamwari's lions are kept in a separate enclosure and probably won't be released into the reserve for another 5–6 years. The elephant numbers, too, are very low, and rangers rely on radio transmitters to locate them. Even so, the lodge is well worth a visit and has all the hallmarks of becoming a great game reserve. The park marks the convergence of five different biomes: semiarid Karoo scrub, eastern grassland, savannah, thick coastal bushveld, and fynbos, a hardy heath that predominates in the Cape. This diversity of habitat translates into a wide diversity of animals, including species such as blesbok and springbok that you won't find in the Eastern Transvaal, as well as 300 species of birds. Shamwari also has good populations of black and white rhino, and general game like zebra, wildebeest, and giraffe. No more than 10 vehicles at a time traverse the reserve's 19,760 acres. *Box 7814, Newton Park 6055,* ☎ *042/851–1196,* FAX *042/851–1224. No children under 12 without prior arrangement. AE, DC, MC, V.*

INDEX

NOTES

Fodor's Travel Publications

Available at bookstores everywhere, or call 1–800–533–6478, 24 hours a day.

Gold Guides

U.S.

Alaska

Arizona

Boston

California

Cape Cod, Martha's Vineyard, Nantucket

The Carolinas & the Georgia Coast

Chicago

Colorado

Florida

Hawaii

Las Vegas, Reno, Tahoe

Los Angeles

Maine, Vermont, New Hampshire

Maui

Miami & the Keys

New England

New Orleans

New York City

Pacific North Coast

Philadelphia & the Pennsylvania Dutch Country

The Rockies

San Diego

San Francisco

Santa Fe, Taos, Albuquerque

Seattle & Vancouver

The South

U.S. & British Virgin Islands

USA

Virginia & Maryland

Waikiki

Washington, D.C.

Foreign

Australia & New Zealand

Austria

The Bahamas

Bermuda

Budapest

Canada

Cancún, Cozumel, Yucatán Peninsula

Caribbean

China

Costa Rica, Belize, Guatemala

Cuba

The Czech Republic & Slovakia

Eastern Europe

Egypt

Europe

Florence, Tuscany & Umbria

France

Germany

Great Britain

Greece

Hong Kong

India

Ireland

Israel

Italy

Japan

Kenya & Tanzania

Korea

London

Madrid & Barcelona

Mexico

Montréal & Québec City

Moscow, St. Petersburg, Kiev

The Netherlands, Belgium & Luxembourg

New Zealand

Norway

Nova Scotia, New Brunswick, Prince Edward Island

Paris

Portugal

Provence & the Riviera

Scandinavia

Scotland

Singapore

South Africa

South America

Southeast Asia

Spain

Sweden

Switzerland

Thailand

Tokyo

Toronto

Turkey

Vienna & the Danube

Fodor's Special-Interest Guides

Branson

Caribbean Ports of Call

The Complete Guide to America's National Parks

Condé Nast Traveler Caribbean Resort and Cruise Ship Finder

Cruises and Ports of Call

Fodor's London Companion

France by Train

Halliday's New England Food Explorer

Healthy Escapes

Italy by Train

Kodak Guide to Shooting Great Travel Pictures

Shadow Traffic's New York Shortcuts and Traffic Tips

Sunday in New York

Sunday in San Francisco

Walt Disney World, Universal Studios and Orlando

Walt Disney World for Adults

Where Should We Take the Kids? California

Where Should We Take the Kids? Family Adventures

Where Should We Take the Kids? Northeast

Special Series

Affordables
Caribbean
Europe
Florida
France
Germany
Great Britain
Italy
London
Paris

Fodor's Bed & Breakfasts and Country Inns
America's Best B&Bs
California's Best B&Bs
Canada's Great Country Inns
Cottages, B&Bs and Country Inns of England and Wales
The Mid-Atlantic's Best B&Bs
New England's Best B&Bs
The Pacific Northwest's Best B&Bs
The South's Best B&Bs
The Southwest's Best B&Bs
The Upper Great Lakes' Best B&Bs

The Berkeley Guides
California
Central America
Eastern Europe
Europe
France
Germany & Austria
Great Britain & Ireland
Italy
London
Mexico
Pacific Northwest & Alaska
Paris
San Francisco

Compass American Guides
Arizona
Canada
Chicago
Colorado
Hawaii
Idaho
Hollywood
Las Vegas
Maine
Manhattan
Montana
New Mexico
New Orleans
Oregon
San Francisco
Santa Fe
South Carolina
South Dakota
Southwest
Texas
Utah
Virginia
Washington
Wine Country
Wisconsin
Wyoming

Fodor's Citypacks
Atlanta
Hong Kong
London
New York City
Paris
Rome
San Francisco
Washington, D.C.

Fodor's Español
California
Caribe Occidental
Caribe Oriental
Gran Bretaña
Londres
Mexico

Nueva York
Paris

Fodor's Exploring Guides
Australia
Boston & New England
Britain
California
Caribbean
China
Egypt
Florence & Tuscany
Florida
France
Germany
Ireland
Israel
Italy
Japan
London
Mexico
Moscow & St. Petersburg
New York City
Paris
Prague
Provence
Rome
San Francisco
Scotland
Singapore & Malaysia
Spain
Thailand
Turkey
Venice

Fodor's Flashmaps
Boston
New York
San Francisco
Washington, D.C.

Fodor's Pocket Guides
Acapulco
Atlanta
Barbados

Jamaica
London
New York City
Paris
Prague
Puerto Rico
Rome
San Francisco
Washington, D.C.

Rivages Guides
Bed and Breakfasts of Character and Charm in France
Hotels and Country Inns of Character and Charm in France
Hotels and Country Inns of Character and Charm in Italy

Short Escapes
Country Getaways in Britain
Country Getaways in France
Country Getaways in New England
Country Getaways Near New York City

Fodor's Sports
Golf Digest's Best Places to Play
Skiing USA
USA Today The Complete Four Sport Stadium Guide

Fodor's Vacation Planners
Great American Learning Vacations
Great American Sports & Adventure Vacations
Great American Vacations
National Parks and Seashores of the East
National Parks of the West